816.9003
Si4L   v.4   64313

THE SIMMS LETTERS

WILLIAM GILMORE SIMMS

"I should not care a straw, *if I had the means to put myself on record.* Secure of this, my fame might be left without fear to the guardianship of posterity. And it is posterity alone which judges."

(From a cameo brooch given by Simms to Mrs. Simms in 1859 and now in the possession of Mary C. Simms Oliphant)

The Letters
of
William Gilmore Simms

Collected and Edited

by

MARY C. SIMMS OLIPHANT

ALFRED TAYLOR ODELL

T. C. DUNCAN EAVES

Introduction by DONALD DAVIDSON

Biographical Sketch by ALEXANDER S. SALLEY

VIDEO VOLANS

In five volumes

VOLUME IV—1858–1866

Edited by

MARY C. SIMMS OLIPHANT

T. C. DUNCAN EAVES

UNIVERSITY OF SOUTH CAROLINA PRESS
COLUMBIA
1955

PREFACE

In editing Volume IV of *The Letters of William Gilmore Simms* we have used the same method adopted by us in editing Volumes II and III and discussed in detail in the "Preface" to Volume II. In the footnotes to the letters in this volume a reference to "introductory sketch" is, as in the case of those in the two preceding volumes, to the short biographies included in "Simms' Circle" and "The Family Circle," pages xc-cl of Volume I of the *Letters*.

Again we want to express our appreciation for the aid and encouragement we have received from the University of South Carolina, the University of Arkansas, Furman University, the University South Caroliniana Society, the South Caroliniana Library, and the University of South Carolina Press. We also want to thank our friends and relatives mentioned in the prefaces to previous volumes for the help they have given us in the preparation of this one. Especially are we indebted to Mr. Alexander S. Salley, Professor Hyder E. Rollins, Professor Ben D. Kimpel, Mrs. John S. Reynolds, Mrs. Edwin O'Kelly, Miss Georgia H. Clark, Miss Delia Mattison, Miss Geraldine Beard, and Mrs. Lilla M. Hawes.

We particularly want to thank Mrs. Lawson Sandford, of Yonkers, New York, who, since this volume was set in type, has kindly turned over to us the papers of James Lawson and his family. We are, therefore, here able to give a more nearly complete factual account of the Lawsons than has hitherto been possible and to correct some errors made in annotations in earlier volumes. James Lawson, the son of Christina Thomson and John Lawson, of Glasgow, was married to Mary Eliza Donaldson (October 18, 1816—January 28, 1886), the daughter of Mary Baker (July 21, 1786—June 7, 1839) and Robert Donaldson (December 17, 1781—January 19, 1850), on December 17, 1835. Their children were Christina (March 2, 1837—May 4, 1928), Mary (January 14, 1839—January 15, 1893), Catherine Forrest ("Kate") (October 15, 1840—February 24, 1866), James

(August 5, 1842—September 9, 1912), William Gilmore Simms (October 4, 1849—March 5, 1860), Cornelia Bockee ("Nellie") (July 14, 1857—September 14, 1934), and Flora Donaldson (February 9, 1859—September 19, 1860). All died unmarried except Mary, who on October 26, 1865, was married to Thomas Sarjeant Sandford (March 3, 1838—January 28, 1892), a lawyer, who was secretary to the Steamship Conferences, New York City. The Cornelia whose death Simms mentions in his letter to Lawson of March 3, 1836, was Cornelia Donaldson (April 23, 1813—February 17, 1836), Mrs. Lawson's sister. Caroline Donaldson (August 14, 1808—April 2, 1884), Mrs. Lawson's other sister, formed part of the Lawson household until her death. Letters to Lawson from his sister Janet Lawson (b. April 29, 1807) written during 1854 show that Lawson's sister whom Simms mentions in his letter to Lawson of August 2, 1854, as "shortly expected" in New York City was Elizabeth Lawson (b. December 10, 1818), who later that year came from her home in Gourock, Scotland, to visit her brother and his family. In note 34, February 13, 1854, we identify the Donaldson of the firm of Bockee and Donaldson as Mrs. Lawson's father, Robert Donaldson. Since he died in 1850, the Robert Donaldson who was a member of the firm in 1854 was doubtless his only son (June 23, 1811—December 9, 1889). In letters to Lawson of August 11, 1845, and April 15, 1850, Simms speaks of Lawson's cousin Alexander Thompson: Simms should have spelled his name *Thomson*. In note 154, August 8, 1846, and note 208, October 14, 1850, we incorrectly give Catherine Forrest Lawson's name as Catherine Sinclair Lawson. The biographical sketches of James Lawson in the Duyckincks' *Cyclopædia,* the *Dictionary of American Biography,* and elsewhere give the date of his birth as November 9, 1799, and we too have given 1799 as the year of his birth in our sketch of him in Volume I of the *Letters,* page cxviii. The Lawson family Bible, however, gives November 9, 1798, as the date of his birth. The Bible records the marriage of Christina Thomson and John Lawson on October 13, 1797, and the births of the following children: James on November 9, 1798; Helen on April 9, 1800; John (d. April 23, 1802) on December 15, 1801; Janet (d. January 1, 1804) on May 6, 1803; John (d. January 2, 1806) on December 12, 1804; Janet on April 29, 1807; Alexander (d. September 26, 1810) on June 30, 1809; Alexander Thomson (d. February 7, 1814) on May 28,

1811; Christina (d. April 3, 1813) on April 30, 1812; John on January 18, 1814; Christina on January 18, 1816; and Elizabeth on December 10, 1818. Since it is unlikely that the date of birth of each of the first five children would be incorrectly recorded, as would have to be the case if James Lawson were born in 1799, the year of his birth was probably 1798. A letter from Simms to Lawson dated November 15, 1868 (to be included in Volume V of the *Letters*), shows, however, that Simms (and possibly the Lawsons) *thought* that Lawson was born in 1799. He died on March 24, 1880.

Mary C. Simms Oliphant

T. C. Duncan Eaves

December 5, 1954

CONTENTS

ILLUSTRATIONS

DEPOSITORIES OR OWNERS OF MANUSCRIPTS

ASS	Mr. Alexander S. Salley, Columbia, South Carolina
BPL	Boston Public Library
BU	Brown University
C	Columbia University
C:F	Ferris Collection, Columbia University
CLS	Charleston Library Society
CWB	Mr. Clifton Waller Barrett, New York City
D	Duke University
HEH	Henry E. Huntington Library
JSB	Mr. John S. Billings, Beech Island, South Carolina, and New York City
JW	Miss Julia Walpole, Birmingham, Alabama
KSHS	Kansas State Historical Society
LC:H	The Papers of James H. Hammond, Library of Congress
LC:S	William Gilmore Simms Collection, Library of Congress
MHS	Massachusetts Historical Society
MK	Miss Mary Kollock, Darlington, South Carolina
NCU:M	William Porcher Miles Papers, Southern Historical Collection, University of North Carolina
NYHS	New-York Historical Society
NYPL:A	A. W. Anthony Collection, New York Public Library
NYPL:BG	Bryant-Godwin Collection, New York Public Library
NYPL:D	Duyckinck Collection, New York Public Library
NYPL:S	William Gilmore Simms Collection, New York Public Library
NYSL	New York State Library
P	Princeton University
PFL	Free Library of Philadelphia, Ridgeway Branch
PHS	Historical Society of Pennsylvania

PI	Peabody Institute
SCHC	South Carolina Historical Commission
SCL	South Caroliniana Library, University of South Carolina
SCL:CCS	Charles Carroll Simms Collection, South Caroliniana Library, University of South Carolina
SRB	Mrs. Sam Rice Baker, Montgomery, Alabama
THS	Tennessee Historical Society
VSL	Virginia State Library
VU	University of Virginia
Y	Yale University

LIST OF LETTERS

In the following list of letters for this volume of the letters of William Gilmore Simms the address as Simms wrote it follows the name of the addressee. Under the name of the addressee is the postmark, followed by the price of sending the letter. If no address is given, the cover has not survived; if no postmark is given, the cover lacks one. Depositories or owners of the manuscripts of Simms' letters are indicated in the last column. If we have not located the original of a letter, that space is left blank and the source of our text is given in a footnote to that letter.

1858

No.	Date	Addressee	Owner or Depository
857.	January 9	JOSEPH HENRY	SCL
858.	January 9	PETER FORCE	CWB
859.	January 15	GEORGE BANCROFT	MHS
860.	January 25	MARY LAWSON	SCL
861.	January 25	WILLIAM PORCHER MILES	NCU:M
862.	January 25	MARCUS CLAUDIUS MARCELLUS HAMMOND	SCL
863.	January 25	JOSEPH S. CARELS | Lebanon, | Tennessee. *Postmark:* Midway | Jan 26 | [*Three-cents stamp*]	SCL
864.	January 26	GEORGE BANCROFT	MHS
865.	January 28	JAMES HENRY HAMMOND	LC:H
866.	February?	WILLIAM PORCHER MILES	NCU:M
867.	February 8	WILLIAM PORCHER MILES	NCU:M
868.	February 22	JAMES HENRY HAMMOND	LC:H
869.	March 1	JOHN REUBEN THOMPSON	NYPL:A
870.	March 21	WILLIAM PORCHER MILES	NCU:M
871.	March 27	HARRY HAMMOND	LC:H
872.	March 27	JAMES HENRY HAMMOND	LC:H
873.	March 27	WILLIAM PORCHER MILES	NCU:M
874.	April 12	JAMES HENRY HAMMOND	LC:H
875.	April 12	JAMES HENRY HAMMOND	LC:H
876.	April 12	WILLIAM PORCHER MILES	NCU:M
877.	May 8	JAMES HENRY HAMMOND	LC:H
878.	May 9	JAMES HENRY HAMMOND	LC:H
879.	May 15	JAMES HENRY HAMMOND	LC:H
880.	May 21	JAMES HENRY HAMMOND	LC:H
881.	June 2	JAMES HENRY HAMMOND	LC:H
882.	June 10	JAMES HENRY HAMMOND	LC:H
883.	June 11	JAMES HENRY HAMMOND	LC:H

No.	Date	Addressee	Owner or Depository
884.	June 18	JAMES THOMAS FIELDS	SCL
885.	June 26	JAMES HENRY HAMMOND	LC:H
886.	July 2	GEORGE PAYNE RAINSFORD JAMES	SCL
887.	July 10	MARY LAWSON	SCL
888.	July 10	JAMES HENRY HAMMOND	LC:H
889.	July 16	JAMES HENRY HAMMOND	LC:H
890.	July 19	ISRAEL KEECH TEFFT	SCL
891.	August 1	JAMES HENRY HAMMOND	LC:H
892.	August 1	JAMES HENRY HAMMOND	LC:H
893.	August 2	JAMES HENRY HAMMOND	LC:H
894.	August 2	MARY LAWSON	SCL
895.	August 7	JAMES HENRY HAMMOND	LC:H
896.	August 19	GEORGE BANCROFT	MHS
897.	September 24	JAMES HENRY HAMMOND	LC:H
898.	October 12	JAMES HENRY HAMMOND	LC:H
899.	October 16	JAMES HENRY HAMMOND	LC:H
900.	October 16	HENRY BARTON DAWSON	NYSL
901.	November 2	WILLIAM PORCHER MILES | Charleston. | Boy.	NCU:M
902.	November 22	JAMES HENRY HAMMOND	LC:H
903.	December 15	ISRAEL KEECH TEFFT	SCL

1859

No.	Date	Addressee	Owner or Depository
904.	January 10	JAMES HENRY HAMMOND	LC:H
905.	January 14	EVERT AUGUSTUS DUYCKINCK	NYPL:D
906.	January 19	HENRY BARTON DAWSON	NYHS
907.	January 20	ALEXANDER DALLAS BACHE	HEH
908.	January 28	MARY LAWSON	SCL
909.	January 29	EVERT AUGUSTUS DUYCKINCK	NYPL:D
910.	January 29	JOHN ESTEN COOKE	KSHS
911.	January 31	CHARLES EDWARD BENNETT	SCL
912.	February 3	WILLIAM PORCHER MILES	NCU:M
913.	February 3	ISRAEL KEECH TEFFT	SCL
914.	February 14	AUGUSTUS OLIVER ANDREWS	
915.	February 21	JAMES LAWSON	SCL
916.	February 21	HENRY BARTON DAWSON	P
917.	February 28	MARY LAWSON	SCL
918.	March 1	JAMES DUNWOODY BROWNSON DE BOW	D
919.	March 2	JAMES HENRY HAMMOND	LC:H
920.	March 15	HENRY BARTON DAWSON	NYHS
921.	March 18	EVERT AUGUSTUS DUYCKINCK | (Clinton Place) | New York *Postmark:* Midy S C | Mch 19 | [*Three-cents stamp*]	NYPL:D
922.	April 3	WILLIAM HAWKINS FERRIS | New York	C:F
923.	April 9	JAMES HENRY HAMMOND	LC:H

No.	Date	Addressee	Owner or Depository
924.	April 11	JAMES HENRY HAMMOND	LC:H
925.	April 15	JAMES GARDNER	
926.	April 22	EVERT AUGUSTUS DUYCKINCK	NYPL:D
927.	April 23	HENRY BARTON DAWSON	CWB
928.	April 23	R. P. COLLINS	ASS
929.	May 15	GAMALIEL LYMAN DWIGHT | Providence, | Rhode Island. *Postmark:* Midway S C | May 15 | [*Three-cents stamp*]	BU
930.	May 23	JAMES HENRY HAMMOND	LC:H
931.	May 23	WILLIAM HAWKINS FERRIS	C:F
932.	May 25	JAMES GARDNER	
933.	June 13	ARMISTEAD BURT	D
934.	June 14	WILLIAM HAWKINS FERRIS	C:F
935.	June 30	HENRY BARTON DAWSON	NYPL:S
936.	July 1	W. L. LINCOLN	SCL
937.	July 8	HENRY BARTON DAWSON	NYHS
938.	July 9	WILLIAM HAWKINS FERRIS	C:F
939.	July 24	JOHN D. LEGARÉ	ASS
940.	July 26	MARY LAWSON	SCL
941.	July 26	JOHN ESTEN COOKE | Richmond, | Virginia. *Postmark:* Charl [*Remainder of postmark lost with removal of stamp*]	LC:S
942.	July 26	HENRY BARTON DAWSON	NYHS
943.	August 11	JAMES HENRY HAMMOND	LC:H
944.	August 23	HENRY BARTON DAWSON	NYHS
945.	August 24	JAMES HENRY HAMMOND	LC:H
946.	September 4	WILLIAM HAWKINS FERRIS	C:F
947.	September 18	MARCUS CLAUDIUS MARCELLUS HAMMOND	LC:H
948.	September 18	JAMES HENRY HAMMOND	LC:H
949.	September?	ORVILLE JAMES VICTOR	CWB
950.	November 15	MARY LAWSON	SCL
951.	November 26	WILLIAM PORCHER MILES	NCU:M
952.	December 7	JOHN ESTEN COOKE	KSHS
953.	December 16	RETURN JONATHAN MEIGS, JR.	THS

1860

954.	1860?	WHEELER, WILSON AND COMPANY	
955.	January 2	JAMES GARDNER	
956.	January 18	WILLIAM PORCHER MILES	NCU:M
957.	January 20	WILLIAM PORCHER MILES	NCU:M
958.	January 20	JOHN S. CUNNINGHAM	
959.	January 20	JOHN ESTEN COOKE	NYSL
960.	January 26	WILLIAM PORCHER MILES	NCU:M
961.	February 5	WILLIAM PORCHER MILES	NCU:M

No.	Date	Addressee	Owner or Depository
962.	February 8	ED. C. CHAPMAN	CWB
963.	February 21	JOSEPH HENRY | Smithsonian Institution. | Washington | D. C. | To Introduce | Mr. Lawson.	SCL
964.	February 24	JAMES LAWSON	SCL
965.	February 25	JAMES LAWSON	SCL
966.	February 26	WILLIAM PORCHER MILES	NCU:M
967.	February 27	WILLIAM PORCHER MILES	NCU:M
968.	February 28	JAMES LAWSON	SCL
969.	March 3	JAMES LAWSON	SCL
970.	March 5	WILLIAM PORCHER MILES	NCU:M
971.	March 11	JAMES LAWSON	SCL
972.	March 21	JAMES LAWSON	SCL
973.	March 22	HENRY BARTON DAWSON	NYHS
974.	April 9	WILLIAM PORCHER MILES	NCU:M
975.	April 9	JAMES LAWSON	SCL
976.	April 14	JOHN ESTEN COOKE	SCL
977.	April 26	THOMAS PENNANT BARTON	BPL
978. c.	April 28	JAMES LAWSON	SCL
979.	May 10	WILLIAM PORCHER MILES	NCU:M
980.	May 21	WILLIAM PORCHER MILES	NCU:M
981.	May 28	EVERT AUGUSTUS DUYCKINCK	NYPL:D
982.	June 11	JOHN REUBEN THOMPSON	VU
983.	June 12	WILLIAM PORCHER MILES	NCU:M
984.	July 2	WILLIAM PORCHER MILES	NCU:M
985.	July 15	WILLIAM PORCHER MILES	NCU:M
986.	August 1	JAMES DUNWOODY BROWNSON DE BOW	D
987.	August 31	WILLIAM PORCHER MILES	NCU:M
988.	September 1	BENSON JOHN LOSSING	SCL
989.	September 15	JAMES LAWSON	SCL
990.	September 17	ISRAEL KEECH TEFFT	SCL
991.	September 25	JAMES LAWSON	SCL
992.	September 26	ANDREW M. ROSS	C
993.	September 28	WILLIAM PORCHER MILES	NCU:M
994.	October 9	JAMES HENRY HAMMOND	LC:H
995.	October 16	JAMES LAWSON	SCL
996.	October 20	JAMES LAWSON	SCL
997.	October 21	JAMES LAWSON	SCL
998.	October 22	JAMES LAWSON	SCL
999.	October 24	JAMES LAWSON	SCL
1000. c.	November 4	JAMES LAWSON	SCL
1001.	November 4	WILLIAM PORCHER MILES	NCU:M
1002.	November 5	JAMES LAWSON	SCL
1003.	November 6	JAMES LAWSON	SCL
1004. c.	November 10	JAMES LAWSON	SCL
1005.	November 12	WILLIAM PORCHER MILES	NCU:M

| | | | Owner or |
No.	Date	Addressee	Depository
1006.	November 13	JAMES LAWSON	SCL
1007.	November 14	WILLIAM SIMS REYNOLDS	JW
1008.	November 20	JAMES LAWSON	SCL
1009.	November 20	JOHN JACOB BOCKEE	
1010.	November 20	SIMON GRATZ	PHS
1011. *c.*November 21		JAMES LAWSON	SCL
1012. *c.*November 22		JAMES LAWSON	SCL
1013. *c.*November 23		JAMES LAWSON	SCL
1014.	November 23	WILLIAM HAWKINS FERRIS	C:F
1015.	November?	WILLIAM PORCHER MILES	NCU:M
1016.	November?	WILLIAM PORCHER MILES	NCU:M
1017.	November 30	JAMES LAWSON	SCL
1018.	December 5	WILLIAM PORCHER MILES	NCU:M
1019.	December 5	JAMES LAWSON	SCL
1020.	December 5	JAMES HENRY HAMMOND	LC:H
1021.	December 5	JAMES LAWSON	SCL
1022.	December 10	ORVILLE JAMES VICTOR	CWB
1023.	December 12	JOHN JACOB BOCKEE	
1024.	December 12	ARTHUR PERONNEAU HAYNE | Charleston | S. C. | To introduce | Mr. B. J. Lossing	SCL
1025.	December 13	WILLIAM LAVAL | Charleston | So. Caro. | To introduce | Mr B. J. Lossing	SCL
1026.	December 13	JAMES LAWSON | (Lawson & Walker) | Wall Street, | New-York	SCL
		Postmark: Midway S C | Decr 15 | Wm Porcher Miles | M. C.	
1027.	December 17	EVERT AUGUSTUS DUYCKINCK | (Clinton Place) | New York	NYPL:D
		Postmark: Midway S C | Dec 18/60 | [*Three-cents stamp*]	
1028.	December 18	JAMES LAWSON	SCL
1029.	December 19	JAMES LAWSON	SCL
1030.	December 27	WILLIAM PORCHER MILES	NCU:M
1031.	December 31	JAMES LAWSON	SCL
1032.	December 31	WILLIAM PORCHER MILES | Charleston, | South Carolina.	NCU:M
		Postmark: Midway S C | Jan 1st/61 | [*Three-cents stamp*]	

1861

1033.	January 1	ISRAEL KEECH TEFFT	C
1034.	January 12	WILLIAM PORCHER MILES	NCU:M
1035.	January 13	WILLIAM PORCHER MILES	NCU:M
1036.	January 15	DAVID FLAVEL JAMISON	SCL
1037.	February 19	JAMES LAWSON	SCL
1038.	February 20	WILLIAM PORCHER MILES	NCU:M
1039.	February 22	WILLIAM PORCHER MILES	NCU:M

No.	Date	Addressee	Owner or Depository
1040.	February 24	WILLIAM PORCHER MILES	NCU:M
1041.	March 2	WILLIAM PORCHER MILES	NCU:M
1042.	March 3	JAMES LAWSON	SCL
1043.	March 3	WADDY THOMPSON	SCHC
1044.	March 3	BENJAMIN FRANKLIN PERRY	SRB
1045.	March 7	WILLIAM PORCHER MILES	NCU:M
1046.	March 12	WILLIAM PORCHER MILES	NCU:M
1047.	March 15	EVERT AUGUSTUS DUYCKINCK	NYPL:D
1048.	March 17	JAMES LAWSON	SCL
1049.	April 2	WILLIAM PORCHER MILES	NCU:M
1050.	c.April 15	MARGARET MAXWELL MARTIN	
1051.	April 17	WILLIAM PORCHER MILES	NCU:M
1052.	May 8	JAMES LAWSON	SCL
1053.	May 11	WILLIAM PORCHER MILES	NCU:M
1054.	June 8	WILLIAM PORCHER MILES	NCU:M
1055.	June 14	JAMES HENRY HAMMOND	LC:H
1056.	July 4	JAMES LAWSON	SCL
1057.	August?	ALFRED PROCTOR ALDRICH	NYHS
1058.	August 20	JAMES LAWSON	SCL
1059.	August 20	BENSON JOHN LOSSING	SCL
1060.	August 23	FRANCIS PEYRE PORCHER	SCL
1061.	November 7	WILLIAM GILMORE SIMMS, JR.	SCL
1062.	November 9	MARCUS CLAUDIUS MARCELLUS HAMMOND	SCL
1063.	November 18	JAMES HENRY HAMMOND	LC:H
1064.	December 2	JAMES HENRY HAMMOND	LC:H
1065.	December 22	WILLIAM PORCHER MILES	NCU:M

1862

No.	Date	Addressee	Owner or Depository
1066.	January?	JOHN REUBEN THOMPSON	VU
1067.	January 15	WILLIAM PORCHER MILES	NCU:M
1068.	January 31	WILLIAM PORCHER MILES	NCU:M
1069.	c.March 27	RICHARD YEADON	
1070.	April 10	WILLIAM PORCHER MILES	NCU:M
1071.	April 10	JAMES HENRY HAMMOND	LC:H
1072.	June 17	RICHARD YEADON	
1073.	June 27	JOHN DICKSON BRUNS, WILLIAM GREGG, JAMES HENRY HAMMOND, and OTHERS	
1074.	September 20	THE EDITORS OF THE *SOUTHERN ILLUSTRATED NEWS*	
1075.	October 28	JAMES HENRY HAMMOND	LC:H
1076.	December 4	JAMES HENRY HAMMOND	Augusta,	Georgia *Postmark:* Midway S C	Dec 4	LC:H
1077.	December?	MARGARET MAXWELL MARTIN	

1863

No.	Date	Addressee	Owner or Depository
1078.	January 10	JOHN REUBEN THOMPSON	Richmond,	Virginia.	VU
		Postmark: Midway S C	Jay 12	[*Two five-cents stamps*]	
1079.	March 27	CORNELIUS KOLLOCK	MK
1080.	April 14	FRANCIS PEYRE PORCHER	SCL
1081.	April?	THE EDITOR OF THE *MAGNOLIA WEEKLY*	
1082.	June 22	PAUL HAMILTON HAYNE	D
1083.	July 4	PAUL HAMILTON HAYNE	D
1084.	July	MARCUS CLAUDIUS MARCELLUS HAMMOND	D
1085.	July 17	JOHN REUBEN THOMPSON	VU
1086.	July 29	PAUL HAMILTON HAYNE	D
1087.	September 23	PAUL HAMILTON HAYNE	D
1088.	October 15	JOHN REUBEN THOMPSON	VU
1089.	October 20	FRANCIS PEYRE PORCHER	SCL

1864

No.	Date	Addressee	Owner or Depository
1090.	February 1	JAMES RYDER RANDALL	SCL
1091. *c.*February 15	MARCUS CLAUDIUS MARCELLUS HAMMOND	D
1092.	February 23	JACOB KEITH SASS	
1093.	March 28	EDWARD ROACH	SCL:CCS
1094.	April 15	EDWARD ROACH	SCL:CCS
1095.	April 28	EDWARD ROACH	SCL:CCS
1096.	May 3	EDWARD ROACH	SCL:CCS
1097.	May 8	PAUL HAMILTON HAYNE	SCL
1098.	May 15	JOHN REUBEN THOMPSON	VU
1099.	May 15	MARCUS CLAUDIUS MARCELLUS HAMMOND	D
1100.	June 2	ANNA AUGUSTA SINGLETON SIMMS ROACH	SCL:CCS
1101. *c.*June 20	ANNA AUGUSTA SINGLETON SIMMS ROACH	CLS
1102.	July 28	JAMES HENRY HAMMOND	LC:H
1103. *c.*August 1	PAUL HAMILTON HAYNE	D
1104.	August 20	PAUL HAMILTON HAYNE	NYHS
1105.	September 19	PAUL HAMILTON HAYNE	Greenville C. H.	South Carolina	SCL
		Postmark: Midway S C	Sept 20	
1106.	October	MARCUS CLAUDIUS MARCELLUS HAMMOND	D
1107.	November 8	WILLIAM GILMORE SIMMS, JR.	SCL:CCS

No.	Date	Addressee	Owner or Depository
1141.	December 5	JAMES LAWSON	SCL
1142.	December 19	EVERT AUGUSTUS DUYCKINCK | 20 Clinton Place | New York.	NYPL:D
		Postmark: Charleston S. C. | Dec 20 | [*Three-cents stamp*]	
1143.	December?	EVERT AUGUSTUS DUYCKINCK	NYPL:D

1866

No.	Date	Addressee	Owner or Depository
1144.	January 2	WILLIAM HAWKINS FERRIS	C:F
1145.	January 8	EVERT AUGUSTUS DUYCKINCK | 20 Clinton Place, | New York.	NYPL:D
		Postmark: Charleston S. C. | Jan 8 | [*Three-cents stamp*]	
1146.	January 16	ROBERT MACOY AND DANIEL SICKELS	SCL
1147.	February 10	EVERT AUGUSTUS DUYCKINCK	NYPL:D
1148.	February 19	JOHN A. MCALLISTER	PFL
1149.	February 20	EVERT AUGUSTUS DUYCKINCK	NYPL:D
1150.	March 5	EVERT AUGUSTUS DUYCKINCK	NYPL:D
1151.	March 5	WILLIAM HAWKINS FERRIS	C:F
1152.	March 5	JAMES LAWSON | Lawson & Walker, | Wall Street | New York.	SCL
		Postmark: Charleston S. C. | Mar 6 | [*Two three-cents stamps*]	
1153.	March 21	EVERT AUGUSTUS DUYCKINCK | 20 Clinton Place | 8th. Street | N. Y. | To introduce | Dr. Bruns.	NYPL:D
1154.	March 24	WILLIAM HAWKINS FERRIS	C:F
1155.	April 3	WILLIAM BLAKE TRASK | Historiographer N. Eng. | Historic-Geneal. Society | 13 Bromfield Street | Boston, | Mass.	NYPL:S
		Postmark: Charleston S. C. | Apr 3 | [*Stamp removed*]	
1156.	April 5	EVERT AUGUSTUS DUYCKINCK	NYPL:D
1157.	April 11	JOHN PENDLETON KENNEDY	PI
1158.	April 13	WILLIAM HAWKINS FERRIS	C:F
1159.	April 14	JAMES LAWSON	SCL
1160.	April 14	EVERT AUGUSTUS DUYCKINCK	NYPL:D
1161.	April 14	JOHN ESTEN COOKE | Millwood | Near Winchester, | Virginia.	LC:S
		Postmark: Charleston S. C. | Apr 16 | [*Stamp removed*]	
1162.	April 27	ANDREW H. H. DAWSON	SCL
1163.	April 27	JAMES LAWSON	SCL

No.	Date	Addressee	Owner or Depository
1164.	May 4	JOHN ESTEN COOKE	Millwood,	Near Winchester,	Virginia. *Postmark:* Charleston S. C.	MY 5	[*Stamp removed*]	VSL
1165.	May 15	JOHN PENDLETON KENNEDY	PI
1166.	May 25	JAMES LAWSON	SCL
1167.	May 25	WILLIAM HAWKINS FERRIS	C:F
1168.	May 28	WILLIAM HAWKINS FERRIS	C:F
1169.	June 1	WILLIAM HAWKINS FERRIS	C:F
1170.	June 8	WILLIAM GILMORE SIMMS, JR.	SCL
1171.	June 12	ANNA AUGUSTA SINGLETON SIMMS ROACH	SCL:CCS
1172.	June 12	WILLIAM GILMORE SIMMS, JR.	SCL
1173.	June 24	WILLIAM GILMORE SIMMS, JR.	SCL
1174.	June 24	JOHN PENDLETON KENNEDY	PI
1175.	June 24	JAMES LAWRENCE ORR	SCHC
1176.	July 1	EVERT AUGUSTUS DUYCKINCK	NYPL:D
1177.	July 7	EVERT AUGUSTUS DUYCKINCK	NYPL:D
1178.	July 7	ANNA AUGUSTA SINGLETON SIMMS ROACH	SCL:CCS
1179.	July 11	EVERT AUGUSTUS DUYCKINCK	NYPL:D
1180.	July 12	WILLIAM GILMORE SIMMS, JR.	SCL
1181.	July 25	EDWARD ROACH	SCL:CCS
1182.	July 28	EVERT AUGUSTUS DUYCKINCK	NYPL:D
1183. *c.*August 1		FLETCHER HARPER?	NYPL:S
1184.	August 2	WILLIAM HAWKINS FERRIS	C:F
1185.	August 3	EVERT AUGUSTUS DUYCKINCK	20 Clinton Place,	New York. *Postmark:* Yonkers N. Y.	Aug 3	[*Three-cents stamp*]	NYPL:D
1186.	August 3	EVERT AUGUSTUS DUYCKINCK	NYPL:D
1187.	August 3	ANNA AUGUSTA SINGLETON SIMMS ROACH	SCL:CCS
1188.	August 7	WILLIAM HAWKINS FERRIS	C:F
1189.	August 9	WILLIAM HAWKINS FERRIS	C:F
1190.	August 15	EVERT AUGUSTUS DUYCKINCK	NYPL:D
1191.	September 1	EDWARD ROACH	SCL:CCS
1192.	September 2	ANNA AUGUSTA SINGLETON SIMMS ROACH	SCL
1193.	September 15	ANNA AUGUSTA SINGLETON SIMMS ROACH	SCL:CCS
1194.	September 18	ANNA AUGUSTA SINGLETON SIMMS ROACH	SCL:CCS
1195.	September 18	SIMMS' CHILDREN	SCL
1196.	September 18	WILLIAM HAWKINS FERRIS	U. S. Treasury	Wall Street	N. Y.	C:F

ABBREVIATIONS AND SHORT TITLES

Godey's   *Godey's Lady's Book and Magazine*

Graham's   *Graham's Illustrated Magazine of Literature, Romance, Art, and Fashion*

O. R.   *The War of the Rebellion: A Compilation of the Official Records of the Union and Confederate Armies,* 4 series (Washington: Government Printing Office, 1880-1901)

S. L. M.   *Southern Literary Messenger: Devoted to Literature, Science, and Art*

S. Q. R.   *Southern Quarterly Review*

THE LETTERS

of

WILLIAM GILMORE SIMMS

1858-1866

1858

857: To Joseph Henry [1]

Woodlands, S. C.
Jany 9. 1858.

Professor Jos. Henry.
Smithsonian Institution.

My dear Professor.

Pray let this note bring you to the acquaintance of my friend, General Hammond, now of the Senate in place of Butler.[2] You will find him a just and enlightened man, upon whom, I think, you may confidently rely, as a Gentleman & Statesman. Pray make his acquaintance in my name. He has with him his wife and daughter. The former, a most amiable & pious lady, whom I could wish your wife to know. And, please say to your daughter, Mary, that Kate Hammond (about her own age) is a favorite of mine, and may well become a favorite of hers.[3] Will you try & bring your folks to an intimate knowledge of my friends? God bless you all.

Yours Ever truly

W. Gilmore Simms

---

[1] Henry (1797-1878), a native of New York State, was a prominent physicist, known for his work on the electromagnet. He was the first secretary and director of the Smithsonian Institution and was largely responsible for formulating its policies. In reviewing the *Annual Report . . . of the Smithsonian Institution . . . 1858* (1859) in the Charleston *Mercury* of Jan. 19, 1859, Simms writes: "Professor Henry, with all who know him, is regarded as one of the purest of men; a modest, circumspect and considerate gentleman, and a profound and devoted seeker after the undeveloped truths of science."

[2] Andrew Pickens Butler (see note 18, March 15, 1843) died on May 25, 1857. In Nov., 1857, James Henry Hammond (see introductory sketch) was elected to his seat in the United States Senate. See note 69, Aug. 23, 1857, and note 87, Dec. 12, 1857.

[3] For Catherine E. FitzSimons Hammond (Mrs. J. H.), see note 227. Nov. 24, 1852. For Hammond's daughter Katherine, see note 22, Jan. 23, 1857. Mrs. Henry was the former Harriet L. Alexander, of Schenectady, N. Y., Henry's first cousin, whom he had married in May, 1830.

[3]

858: To Peter Force [4]

Woodlands, S. C.
Jany 9. 1858.

Peter Force, Esq.

My dear Mr. Force.

Will you oblige me by making the acquaintance, as soon as convenient, of General Hammond, the Senator from S. C. in place of Butler. He is an old & long tried friend of mine, & you will find him one of great intellectual resources and energy of conduct. I particularly wish him to become acquainted with your Library & general collection. He is by nature & education one who will sympathize with your tastes & pursuits; one who will contribute, all that he can, in his public capacity, to promote the interest of Science, Letters & the Arts. With best wishes, my dear Mr. Force, believe me to be very truly Yours &c

W. Gilmore Simms

P. S. Oblige me by using my name in making Genl. H's acquaintance.

859: To George Bancroft [5]

Woodlands, Midway P. O.
So. Caro. Jany. 15. 1858

Hon. Geo. Bancroft.

My dear Mr. Bancroft.

What do *you* think of the monstrous impertinences of this book of Mr. Hamilton, by which Geo. Washington whittles down into Alex. Hamilton? [6] How far are you prepared to admit the claim of an Aide de Camp, or Secretary, who writes under dictation, to be the real author of the letter — the conciever of all its ideas,

---

[4] See note 310, Oct. 12, 1845.

[5] At this time George Bancroft (1800-1891), the historian, was living in New York City.

[6] Simms later reviewed Volume I of John Church Hamilton's *History of the Republic of the United States of America, as Traced in the Writings of Alexander Hamilton and of His Contemporaries,* 7 vols. (New York: D. Appleton & Company, 1857-1864), in an article entitled "Hamilton versus Washington," Charleston *Mercury,* Jan. 25, 1858 (see letter to Bancroft of Jan. 26, 1858). Hamilton (1792-1882) was the son of Alexander Hamilton (1757-1804), the statesman.

— the first augmentor of its arguments. Were it not that the world is so topsy turvy at the present moment, and that it is the misfortune in our country, that nothing shall be recognized as permanent, I should regard this claim of Mr. H. for his ancestor, as simply that of a lunatic, from a diseased sanity, in the case of a little brain. But, really, such is the ignorance of the press, — such the impudence of criticism in general, that we are forced to argue the case even with the madman, and the chance is, that, in degree with the extravagance of the claim, will be the liberality of the verdict. In the rage for novelty, it may be that the *smartness* of a Hamilton, will be found much more valuable & worthy than the *wisdom* of a Washington; for the difference between the two is precisely this, between smartness & wisdom. That admirably balanced capacity which was the distinguishing feature of Washington's mind, was a thing of weight not of show; while Hamilton's mind was decidedly *conventional;* grasping the *known* in political philosophy very well & acutely, but incapable of that application of it, to the necessities of the time, which made the great secret of Washington's capacity. Hamilton knew very well what men had written — what was in books — but Washington knew what America needed at the time, and what was the distinguishing feature of the American *man & mind.* Look at Washingtons letters before & after his connection with Hamilton & you find them quite equal in thought & argument — nay in style & grammar, to any thing that was done *for* him, during his association with H. or any of his aides. But all of W's aides wrote for him. He wanted them for this one purpose. What he wanted of them was the capacity to clothe his ideas in clear English. H. was fluent, but not more so than Laurens,[7] & not, by any means so direct & manly. The beauty of it is, that the present Historian not only makes H. the soul of Washington but the soul of the country. Every thing originates with him. Even Morris [8] cannot be allowed the rascally credit of inventing a U. S. Bank. And he would take (in spite of A. H.'s own letter[ )], the credit from J. Laurens, of concieving the idea of arming the Southern Negroes. Is the man a mere fool, or is he gloriously mad, or as gloriously fuddled! Do give me some clue to the

---

[7] John Laurens (1754-1782), son of Henry Laurens, was a lieutenant colonel during the American Revolution and at one time an aide on Washington's staff.

[8] Robert Morris (1734-1806), minister of finance (1781-1784), who was instrumental in establishing the Bank of North America (1782).

mystery. I could smile at the chapter of noble genealogy at the opening of his volume; but the impertinences of the rest are too atrocious for laughter. It will certainly be a case to create alarm, to such as you, who use an amanuensis, to be taught that your secretary who puts down what you tell him, and is only asked to do so, in tolerable English & in readable chirography, is the father & mother of your thoughts & inventions. Pardon me this hasty scribblement, which I send as first written & without perusal. I have simply written out the first gushings of an impatient overflow — not of bile, but of astonishment.

Yours truly

W. Gilmore Simms

860: To Mary Lawson [9]

Woodlands, S. C.
Jany 25. 1858.

My dear Mary.

While you are revelling in Balls and Parties, I am here drudging in clearing lands, drainage, sawing lumber, hauling, logrolling & burning woods. I have burned more than 10,000 cords this winter, of oak, pine, hickory, ash, maple, bay, poplar, &c. which, your father will tell you, would, in the N. Y. market, be worth some $40,000. In our Charleston market, it would have brought that money. I have cleared some 50 acres of heavily timbered land, and am still busy getting it ready for a crop of corn & cotton. Meanwhile, I have had my wife & all my young children, suffering with an epidemical catarrh;[10] I have had 15 negroes down with it, at the same time, have lost one little negro, & have had an old one at the point of death. We are all now improving. So, while you have been enjoying yourself with balls & parties, my experience has been of the sort I am telling you. Such is life, my child. Congratulate yourself that your lot has been cast in pleasant places; that you have no cares, the single one excepted of prepar-

[9] Mary (b. 1839) was the daughter of Mary Eliza Donaldson and James Lawson (see introductory sketch of the Lawsons). In 1865 she married Thomas Sarjeant Sandford (see note 111, Sept. 9, 1865).

[10] Simms' children alive at this time were Anna Augusta Singleton (1827-1898), William Gilmore, Jr. (1843-1912), Mary Lawson (1846-1908), Chevillette Eliza (1848-1914), Sydney Roach (1851-1858), Beverley Hammond (1854-1858), and Govan Singleton (1856-1891).

ing Mary Lawson to shine for a large party of a winter's evening. But riches take wings, Mary, dear; so carry yourself with modesty, do not take airs, and remember that the sword of Damocles hangs over every sleeping beauty. That excellent old drudge, your father, cannot be working for you always, so avoid extravagance, which will only, by compelling his extra labours, shorten his days. Though sore with toil, with a great deal of work on hand, poor in pocket, & somewhat in spirit, owing $5000, and with a sick family, we cherish hope. We have $70,000 capital & I trust to make it yield me $5000 a year, as soon as I am fairly started. God willing, we shall get fairly on our legs in a year or two. Gilmore is at the Military Academy, Augusta on a visit to Savannah, your namesake, Mary Lawson at Beaufort, and the rest of us here.[11] On the 15th. Feby. my wife & self will remove to the city on a proposed sojourn of 6 or 8 weeks.[12] My domestic condition is such that I have had to say to my friends in Congress, I can take no appointment.[13] It is impossible to leave home in present circumstances. Think of my disappointment. I give up a dream of 30 years, and do so without repining. Let this make you content to forego for a season, the realization of your dreams. — We are to have a visit from Ad. Richards & his new wife.[14] I thank you for your report of her. But you do not say whether she is beautiful or not. What an omission. Nor do you say any thing of Bockee, or Forrest. I see by the papers that the latter has been ill at Cincinnati. What's the matter with him, and when is he to enact Timon?[15] Write me soon, my dear girl, & tell me all the news.

---

[11] Gilmore was a cadet at the King's Mountain Military School, Yorkville (now York), S. C. (see note 180, Sept. 15, 1855); Augusta was visiting the Israel Keech Teffts (see introductory sketch); and Mary Lawson was visiting the William Fullers (see note 72, Aug. 23, 1856) at Pocotaligo, Beaufort District, S. C.

[12] Chevillette Simms always went to Charleston for her *accouchements*. Harriet Myddleton Simms was born on March 14.

[13] See James H. Hammond's letters to Simms of Dec. 19 and Dec. 30, 1857 (originals in the Hammond Papers, Library of Congress). We have not located Simms' letter to Hammond written between these dates in which he says he cannot accept any appointment. See also Simms' letter to Harry Hammond of March 27, 1858.

[14] Thomas Addison Richards (see introductory sketch of the Richards family) had recently married Mary Anthony, of Providence, R. I. See letter to Mary Lawson of Oct. 27, 1857.

[15] For John Jacob Bockee and Edwin Forrest, see introductory sketches. In 1856 Forrest was stricken with a combination of gout and inflammatory rheumatism and retired from the stage for almost five years (see Montrose J. Moses, *The Fabulous Forrest* [Boston: Little, Brown, and Company, 1929], p. 305). Simms' adaptation of *Timon of Athens* was never performed (see letter to Lawson of Oct. 21, 1852, and following letters to Lawson).

We all rejoice to hear that you are all well & so happy. Tell that Old Curmudgeon, your father, that I long to hear from him. My love to your Queen Mother, to all & to yourself.

Yours devotedly

W. G. S.

861 : To William Porcher Miles [16]

Woodlands, S. C. Jany. 25. [1858] [17]

Hon. W. P. Miles.

My dear Miles.

I pity the straits to which you are reduced. How could you, at your time of life, and with your present labors upon you,[18] undertake such a profitless toil as a company oration. And how can I help you? Wm. Washington was a brave dashing legionary colonel, who was always ready to fight. But he was a heavy personage, brilliant only in the field; a man of brawn & muscle, weighing some 230 pounds nett, but with as little of the spiritual in him as any man in the service. He was brave, powerful — had the ardency of the soldier, and would make a good picture at the head of a charge of cavalry. And, *voila tout!* You might begin by drawing a sketch of the melancholy condition to which South Carolina was reduced, after the fall of her chief city, and the defeat of Gates.[19] Our armies scattered to the winds, our Partisans skulking in swamp & forest, the Loyalists raging over the face of the country, like flame in the autumn grass of the prairies, while the British covered every salient position with mailed warriors & castellated fortresses. We were without men, money, or the weapons of war. It was then that Washington came to our

[16] See introductory sketch of the Miles brothers.

[17] Dated by Simms' discussion of Miles' forthcoming oration at the dedication of a monument to Col. William Washington (1752-1810) at Magnolia Cemetery, Charleston, by the Washington Light Infantry. The ceremony was in progress on May 5, 1858, when the platform fell during the recital of an ode by Dr. Samuel Henry Dickson (see introductory sketch) and two children were killed and a third injured. Because of this accident and a high wind, Miles' address and Dickson's ode were postponed until the night of May 7, when they were delivered at Hibernian Hall. See the Charleston *Mercury* of May 6 and 8. Miles' oration is printed in full in the latter issue.

[18] Miles was a member of Congress from March 4, 1857, until his resignation in Dec., 1860.

[19] Charles Town was surrendered to the British on May 12, 1780. Gen. Horatio Gates (*c.* 1728/29-1806) was defeated at Camden on Aug. 16, 1780.

relief—took upon himself a legionary corps, of cavalry, like that of Pulaski,[20] and you may follow his progress, with that of Greene, Morgan, Pickens, Marion Sumter [21] & others, to all the fields in which he fought, to the closing battle at Eutaw, where, doing better than Lee [22] and a good many more, he fell gallantly, wounded & a prisoner in the hands of the enemy. My novel of Eutaw relates something of this matter, using, for the purpose of refuting certain errors, the report of Moore, the Poet, of these events, in connection with the Life of Lord Ed. Fitzgerald. To this work I refer you. The chapters which relate to Eutaw will afford you some hints of the Battle. I must refer you to my History also.[23] By following the historical facts, you will have an opportunity of describing & declaiming, *a la Hedley,* [24] using the superlatives of the language to their utter exhaustion. You may safely dilate on the courageous valour of your hero, his promptness, celerity, audacity—not deficient in prudence, but not suffering it to enfeeble his performances. He was at the Cowpens, at Hobkirk's, I think, captured Rugely, & by a ruse de guerre which you may use freely;[25] his command, at the beginning of the war, in 1780, was surprised by Tarleton [26] & dispersed, and the reproach of this surprise has incorrectly lain at his door. Relieve him of that, for he was not at the time present or in command. It was Huger,[27] I think, who suffered the surprise. After the battle of Eutaw he pretty much disappears from the scene, except as a citizen. He became a married man & planter, was I think in the Legislature, & lived & died in the respect of his fellow citizens, maintaining his popularity to the last. If now, in addition to this, you will use Garden's Anecdotes of the Rev. one or both volumes contain something—the first, I think,

---

[20] Gen. Casimir Pulaski (*c.* 1748-1779).

[21] Gens. Nathanael Greene (1742-1786), Daniel Morgan (1736-1802), Andrew Pickens (1739-1817), Francis Marion (*c.* 1732-1795), and Thomas Sumter (1734-1832).

[22] Henry ("Light Horse Harry") Lee (1756-1818) was a lientenant colonel at the Battle of Eutaw (1781).

[23] See Thomas Moore, *The Life and Death of Lord Edward Fitzgerald* (2nd ed.; London: Longman, Rees, Orme, Brown, & Green, 1831), I, 23-26; *Eutaw* (New York: Redfield, 1856), pp. 509-525; and *The History of South Carolina* (Charleston: S. Babcock & Co., 1840), pp. 262-267.

[24] An allusion to Joel Tyler Headley (see introductory sketch).

[25] The battles of Cowpens, Hobkirk's Hill, and Rugeley's Mill were all fought in 1781. At Rugeley's Mill Washington tricked Col. Rowland Rugeley and 110 men into surrendering by bringing up a pine log hewn to look like a cannon and mounted on wheels.

[26] Gen. Sir Banastre Tarleton (1754-1833).

[27] Gen. Isaac Huger (1742/43-1797).

an oration of Garden on the same subject. This may help you greatly. The 2 vols are different series. Consult both. The first published is an octavo, the second a duodecimo.[28] Both, I fancy, may be found in the Library of Congress. If not, call upon my old friend, Peter Force; use my name in making his acquaintance. He will be glad to welcome you. His library is his Lion. He will be proud to show it to you, and I have no doubt he has both of these volumes. My own library is at the moment hardly available to my use. I have it stored away mostly in outhouses,[29] while I am repairing its old abode. By dilating upon the distressed condition of Carolina, describing the approach to her assistance of gallant cavaliers from Maryland & Virginia, showing Washington conspicuous among them, painting the battles where he fought, just as if he were the Ajax in each, say Cowpens, Hobkirk, Eutaw, &c. and winding up with the graceful finish of his warlike career in the full enjoyment of civic honours, you may eke out an half hour's discourse without difficulty. But see Garden by all means. I do not know that I can suggest any thing further. Washington took large part in several of the industrial projects of S. C. in the Legislature—one of which was the connection of the Ashley with the Edisto, by Canal — a measure which is just as important to Charleston now as then.[30] — If you think of any one point upon which I can make a suggestion, I will gladly come to your help. But just now I find I can get nothing out of my own brains by any sort of cudgelling. I am torn to pieces by cares & anxieties; have the whole plantation — in dilapidated condition — thrust suddenly upon me. Am poor, in debt; and my publisher [31] has temporarily suspended, & books are (temporarily I trust) no longer saleable. Add to this, we have a dozen negroes sick with an epidemical catarrh; my children just recovering from it; my wife severely sick & for a week confined to her bed from the same cause; and I am clearing

---

[28] Alexander Garden, *Anecdotes of the American Revolution* [*Revolutionary War in America*], 2 Series (Charleston: Printed by A. E. Miller, 1822-1828). "General William Washington" appears in the First Series, pp. 68-75.

[29] These were twelve small brick storehouses built in a semicircle at the rear of the main house. Two are still standing, and the foundations of the others can be traced.

[30] Washington was a member of the South Carolina House of Representatives during 1789-1792 and of the South Carolina Senate during 1792-1804. The proposed Edisto-Ashley Canal was discussed in the South Carolina legislature for a great many years.

[31] Justus Starr Redfield. See note 29, May 15, 1853.

swamp land, which is very tough, rolling logs, burning piles, ditching & draining. Is it wonderful that I cannot coerce thought to performance, or even call up memory to do the ordinary duties of the page & messenger of learning. Beyond my occasional contributions to the Mercury & occasional revision of old verses of my boyhood, I am really doing nothing with my pen, except in response to such a call as you have made, and I have them daily, and answer them all, I suspect, just as feebly as I have done to yours.[32] — I am glad that you have found Hammond what you thought him. Do not attach undue importance to the blunt directness of his tone and manner. This is not only a mental characteristic, but it is somewhat due to his country training & associations. You will find him an honest man. Speak to him freely & mince no matters with him. Suggest your doubts. He is at once a bold & cautious man. And, you will be surprised to hear it — for this is not the common opinion — his chief deficiency is self-esteem. I have told him this. [33] He needs sympathy & encouragement. Tell him frankly when you approve & be moderate of your censure. — Thanks for the information you give me. Flibustiering is the moral necessity of all of Anglo Norman breed. It is the necessity of all progressive races. The proceedings of Paulding were brutally insolent, and deserve the severest censure. It was at once an outrage on the liberties of the citizen and the sovereign rights of another State. I am sorry that Walker is not a hero! He is then only a Walker. He should be a *charger* to be a hero.[34]

God bless you, my dear fellow and send you on safely, strengthening your position at every step you take. Mormonism is, perhaps, one of those subjects which will try the national capacity for tension,[35] and Kansas should be the field upon which the South should concentrate all its strength for a final issue.[36] But

---

[32] Simms wrote most of the literary notices published in the Charleston *Mercury* during this period. He also occasionally acted as "correspondent" from Barnwell and elsewhere.

[33] See letter to James H. Hammond of Aug. 18, 1852.

[34] At this time the well-known affair of the arrest (on Dec. 8, 1857) by Commodore Hiram Paulding (1797-1878) of William Walker (1824-1860), the adventurer, and about one hundred and fifty filibusters who had landed at Gregtown, Nicaragua, was being discussed at length in the United States Congress.

[35] See note 97, Dec. 28, 1857.

[36] The Territory of Kansas had applied for admission into the Union under the Lecompton Constitution, which guaranteed the protection of slave property already in Kansas regardless of the ultimate decision on the slavery clause.

I talk importunely to a professional Legislator. Do not forget to send me every pamphlet & document you can lay hands on.

Yours Ever truly

W. Gilmore Simms

862: To Marcus Claudius Marcellus Hammond [37]

Woodlands, Jan. 25. [1858] [38]

Dear Major.

Thanks for your attention to the Bank business. You shall have your money in due season.[39] Thanks also for the enclosure. What do you say to giving it a place in De Bow's Review. If you say so, I will send it to him, or to Russell's Mag.[40] after

---

The admission of Kansas was hotly debated in Congress (see following letters); but though the bill for admission met the approval of Buchanan and was passed by the Senate, it was defeated in the House.

[37] See introductory sketch of the Hammonds.

[38] Dated by Simms' reference to the meeting of James H. Hammond and William Porcher Miles (see letter to Miles of Jan. 25). The MS. of this letter is in bad condition, water-stained and frayed at the edges. One word and parts of others are missing.

[39] We are unable to explain this transaction.

[40] The first issue of *Russell's Magazine* (Charleston) is dated April, 1857. Paul Hamilton Hayne (see introductory sketch) and William Buchanan Carlisle were the editors, the firm of Russell and Jones (John Russell and James C. Jones) the publisher. Russell (see introductory sketch) became an associate editor after the second number, and with the number for Dec., 1858, George C. Hurlbut joined the staff. The last issue is dated March, 1860. Most of the contributions to *Russell's* are unsigned, but John Russell's own copy (now in the New York Public Library) identifies the following poems as Simms': "The Soul," I (July, 1857), 337; "Ballad. If Not Ready," "Original Sonnet. Addressed to America," and "Ballad. The Sleeping Child," II (Dec., 1857), 211, 228, 264; "The Life March," II (Feb., 1858), 446-449; "The Hero Worker," "The Fruitless Life," "'Come Back Soon,'" "The Water Oak," "Heroes and Hero Worship," "Palms of Florida," "Love and Hate.—Impromptu," "Flowers. Lily, Kalmia and Azalæa," "The Papaya," "The Saracenia," "Creepers," and "Winged Seeds," III (April, 1858), 8-10, 15, 20, 29, 35, 47, 59, 69, 76; "Vines," "The Cypress," "The New Moon," "The Snow Drop," "The Love-Babe Beauty" (three sonnets), "The Chimney Cricket," "Palmetto Royal," and "Forest Lunch," III (May, 1858), 129, 137, 142, 150-154, 164, 168; "Cane Swamp. Hibiscus," "Spanish Curlews," "Odoriforous Shrubs," "The Oak," "Sonnets" ("The Tear and Smile," "Infant Teaching," and "The Bliss in Tears"), "Indians Spearing Salmon," "'Oh! Mingle Not,'" "Ballad" ("How long wilt thou delay to bring . . ."), "White Lily," and "Wood Pelican," III (June, 1858), 206, 213, 222, 252, 262, 267, 270; "Why the Tyrant?" (two sonnets), "Speech of Sorrow," "Hope," "To My Friend, with My Portrait" (three sonnets), "The Thunder Storm," "Care," "The Poet," and "Dionea Muscipula," III (July, 1858), 298, 304, 334, 337, 353, 367; "Arcadia," "Fan-Leaf Palmetto," "Power in Aim," "Sonnets. The Child Sleeping in Its Mother's Arms" ("Life-Omens," "How We Err," "Mistaken Omens," "Life in Growth," and one untitled), III (Sept., 1858), 507, 530, 535, 536-537; "'Volans Video,'" and "A Cuban Areyto," IV (Oct., 1858), 17-21, 51; "Lamia—The Beautiful Sin," IV (Nov., 1858), 167-

taking out what I want.[41] But it would be better to have it copied — you can get your daughter [42] to do that before sending it, so that, if the M.S. were lost, the material would remain. Thanks also for the honor of having my name linked with that of your progeny. You had better take another wing of it & even though you add a prefix, still Gilmore S. would be apt to stick to the urchin & is besides not wanting in euphony.[43]—I got yesterday a letter from Aldrich [44] appointing a meeting with you at his house. But the letter only reached me the day of the propose[d] meeting. It was, accordingly, physi[cally] impossible to come. But even had it reached me in season, the visit was impossible. My wife has been for ten days, & still is, very ill in bed with a severe catarrhal affection which seems to be neuralgic also. All of my children have been down with it, & are bettering. We have had four or five little negroes suffering in the same way, & have lost one. We have 12 or 15 negroes also down, and one so sick that her death was momently expected. There has been quite an epidemic among us, & I have kept my post; would have been sick also but I have not had time for it. And my daughter [45] is in Savannah, and my wife could not be left alone. There, you have a chapter of my cares, & not half. With no means, no money, my

---

170; "Hayne: A Dirge," IV (Dec., 1858), 247-248; "To a Young Girl," V (Aug., 1859), 407-409; "Fragment. Finale of the Dandy-Lion," "The Finale of the Flirt," "Soul-Music," and "Fragment. Virtue," VI (Oct., 1859), 56, 72, 82; and "The Exile.—A Ballad," VI (Dec., 1859), 205-206. Simms also contributed the following articles to *Russell's*: "Southern Poetry.—Caldwell," III (April, 1858), 36-47; "Literary Prospects of the South," III (June, 1858), 193-206; "Marion—The Carolina Partisan" (two numbers), IV (Oct. and Nov., 1858), 1-16, 113-128; and "Reminiscences of the Revolution," VI (Oct., 1859), 59-72. *Russell's* also contains an epigrammatic statement by Simms, "The Ideal in Art," III (April, 1858), 59, and Chap. xxxvii of *The Cassique of Kiawah,* IV (Feb., 1859), 443-455.

Russell's contains a long review of Simms' *The Life of Nathanael Greene* entitled "Nathaniel [*sic*] Greene" (identified by Russell as by William John Grayson), III (Sept., 1858), 481-496, and two long articles entitled "The Miscellaneous Poems of Wm. Gilmore Simms" and "The Dramatic Poems of Wm. Gilmore Simms" (identified by Russell as by Paul Hamilton Hayne), both printed under the general heading of "The Poets, and Poetry of the South," II (Nov. and Dec., 1857), 152-160, 240-259. Other notices of Simms' works and remarks about him printed in *Russell's* are noted elsewhere in this edition of Simms' *Letters*.

[41] Probably the unsigned "Memoir—Col. M. C. Hammond, of S. C.," published in *De Bow's Review,* XXIV (April, 1858), 338-346.

[42] Probably Katharine. See note 166, Dec. 21, 1856.

[43] Gilmore Simms Hammond was born on Dec. 11, 1858. He died on Feb. 28, 1892.

[44] Alfred Proctor Aldrich. See introductory sketch.

[45] Augusta. See letter to Mary Lawson of Jan. 25.

publisher [46] on his [ba]ck, no books selling, a dilapidated [esta]te to rescue from ruin, new lands to be [ope]ned, negroes reformed, who have almost [been] allowed to do what they pleased, you will readily concieve that my hands, head & heart have been full to bursting. I will write you hereafter; write to Hamburg now, at random. Meanwhile report progress & show how you get on. I will visit you at Athens as soon as I can.[47] I am ill at ease. Want time, & a *little* money; but can get on, if time be allowed me. I see what can be done, & God help me, will do it. Wrote to the General — sent him letters. But have not heard from him since he left home.[48] Miles writes me that he dined with him — likes him, as he was prepared to do.[49] Pray make my best regards to Madame H.[50] She is a sensible wife to bring you boys. Thank her for me, for the honour done me. I shall send the youngster a present some day. Meanwhile, God bles[s] & keep you all prosperously.

> Yours Ever truly
>
> W. Gilmore Simm[s]

863: To Joseph S. Carels [51]

> Woodlands, S. C.
>
> Jany 25. 1858.

Jos. S. Carels, Esq.

My dear Sir:

No ingenuous young stranger is ever intrusive in his approach to me. It is such only that I always welcome. I comply cheerfully with your request; happy to feel, that my young countrymen, of the South, are anxious to make themselves familiar with art &

---

[46] Justus Starr Redfield.

[47] The Charleston *Mercury* of March 6, 1858, reprints from the Edgefield *Advertiser* (n. d.) an account of M. C. M. Hammond's removal from Edgefield District, S. C., to Athens, Ga. Hamburg, in Edgefield District, was where Hammond got his mail prior to his removal to Athens.

[48] We have not located this letter from Simms to James H. Hammond. Apparently the latest letter Simms had received from him is that dated Dec. 30 (cited note 86, Dec. 12, 1857).

[49] See Simms' remarks to William Porcher Miles in his letter of Jan. 25.

[50] The former Harriet Pamela Davies. See note 68, April 23, 1849.

[51] The cover of this letter gives Carels' address as Lebanon, Tenn. We have been unable to discover any information about him.

letters. It is an ambition that needs encouragement. We have too little of it — too little ambition of any kind.

Yours Kindlily, &c.

W. Gilmore Simms.

864: To GEORGE BANCROFT [52]

Woodlands, Midway P. O.

Hon. Geo. Bancroft.   So. Caro. Jany. 26. 1858.

My dear Mr. Bancroft.

Your letter (for which please recieve my thanks) confirms all my own impressions touching Mr. J. C. Hamilton's volume. I beg to refer you to a hasty editorial article which I published on the subject in the columns of the Charleston Mercury (Jany. 25).[53] You will see it in any of your reading rooms. Be so good as to look at it, & tell me whether I am not quite right in my estimates of all the parties. I infer that you will think so; for I feel sure that no men of honest judgment, who are at all familiar with our revolutionary characters can differ materially. I am glad that so far as you have written, your opinion jumps with my own. Had I waited a little longer I could have discussed sundry other points which I have left unconsidered.

Very truly Yours &c.

W. Gilmore Simms

865: To JAMES HENRY HAMMOND [54]

Woodlands, Jany. 28, 1858.

My dear Hammond.

The question is not so much whether you will be better able than your predecessors to do, or recover any thing for the

---

[52] On the back of this letter Bancroft wrote: "W. G. Simms Ansd. May 21/58." We have not located Bancroft's letter.

[53] For Simms' opinion of Volume I of John Church Hamilton's *History of the Republic of the United States of America, as Traced in the Writings of Alexander Hamilton and of His Contemporaries,* see letter to Bancroft of Jan. 15, 1858. Simms' article in the *Mercury* is entitled "Hamilton versus Washington."

[54] This letter is in reply to Hammond's of Jan. 20, asking advice as to his future conduct in the United States Senate. Simms herein quotes or paraphrases several passages from Hammond's letter. Hammond again wrote Simms on Feb. 7 in reply to this letter of Jan. 28 and another which we have not located. The originals of Hammond's letters are in the Hammond Papers, Library of Congress.

South; — whether you will succeed in organizing her representatives for more efficient action; for a hope in short, whether you will aggrandize her by gains of territory, or strengthen her by increase of representation & states; — but, whether you shall maintain her *status,* that of your State, & your own. Not one of your friends, or fondest admirers, ever expected that, with all your powers, you could bring about any immediate results of advantage. These will depend pretty much on the chapter of accidents; which will continually afford opportunities; of which, a brave, quick, intelligent mind, will take due advantage. In the conflict between South & North, the great object with us, is the extrication of the former from the folds of the latter. If we could get our Southern representatives up to your standards & mine, the game would be an easy one; for we are stronger in the sinews of war, really; in fighting men & wealth, than our enemies. And this final issue — for it will come — will depend upon the merest caprices — casualties — a bloody fight in the house — possibly flibustierism — possibly Mormonism — possibly the moving off, at a tangent, of some remote state, like California; which, with a grand port on the Pacific, looking to the East, will assuredly, as soon as she can set up for herself, — having her own shipping, — and when she finds she can get no more money from the Confederacy, — will most certainly form herself into an independent Republic, sweeping Oregon & all Mexico in the west along with her. The dissolution of the Union will, I say, be the result of casualties & events which are not within the pale of mere calculation; and, as I have long been satisfied, no revolution can be effected, among any people, of the cautious, calculating nature of the Anglo-Norman, or Anglo-American race, until the usurpation shall invade the household, & be brought home to every man's door, in a sense of [per]sonal [55] danger, or pecuniary loss & privation. I had my doubts, accordingly, from the beginning, in regard to the adoption of Kanzas & her *pro slavery* constitution [56] as a test. I should fear any test for an *agricultural* people, short of the actual usurpation, or invasion of their immediate possessions. We are to look to the nature of an agricultural population, whose habitual conflict being only with God & the Seasons, reduces them to a sort of habitual fatalism. *'Che sara, sara!'* — they are apt to cry.

---

[55] The MS. is torn.
[56] The Lecompton Constitution.

This is due not to the fact that they are agriculturists, but to the fact that, sparsely settled, as agriculture requires, they are not accustomed to that constant attrition of rival minds & interests which sharpens the wits, & makes daring & eager the enterprises of all commercial people. I take for granted, therefore, that our people will do nothing, recognize no test, whether of patriotism or honour, so long as the issue is a remote one, or seemingly so. The usurpation must be brought home to them in some way, personal & pecunious. The *argumentum ad crumenam* is the most effectual; though a bloody conflict in the House, would necessarily precipitate the event, as teaching both sides that they can no longer meet in council in safety. But, my dear H., the very *fatalism* which is the moral of an agricultural people, & which makes them accept shame & loss, rather than disturb an existing condition, will make them just as ready to follow a brave great leader recklessly & eagerly, if he dashes out audaciously in a daring track. They obey their impulses. Flibustierism in politics, a *coup d'etat,* will rouse them up to intensity; and there will be a charm in the outbreak, like that which enthusiasm feels in the trumpet call to battle. This was the History of our share in the Revolution. It *was* forced upon the North, by absolute home trespasses of the British. With us, the populace were carried off their feet by the audacity of their leaders. They dashed ahead, talked big, beat the drum of defiance, and satisfied the people, that the game was really in their hands. And, it is my conviction that Mr. Calhoun, [57] with his intensity, his one ideadness, his resources of intellect, if he had had the personal courage of Henry Clay would have carried the South — the whole South with him. He had ardor & intensity, but not the capacity for self-sacrifice. I have had an admirable description of the scene which took place in the Whig Caucus, after the election of Harrison, when the measure was contemplated of calling an Extra Session; a measure which helped to break down the Whig party. At this Caucus, every member was pledged beforehand, two excepted, to *oppose* the measure, as it was justly feared. But Clay had made it his hobby for the time. He entered the assembly, passed down its lines, speaking as he went, in triumphant manner, with bold fearless eloquence, breast open, and, at length, confronting Webster, he seemed to concentrate the whole weight of what he had to

---

[57] John Caldwell Calhoun. See introductory sketch.

say upon him. And so powerful was his eloquence, so keen his shafts, so personal their aim, that Webster actually crouched under him, and slid down in his seat, so that his head was almost on a level with his belly. And Clay triumphed. There were but *two,* after he was done, who voted in opposition to the measure.[58] And Clay had pretty much the sort of associates to deal with that you have. And they were just as inferior to him, as yours are to you. I know well the sort of materials with which you have to deal, and knowing them as we both do, and knowing you as I do; knowing of what you are capable, and what are your resources, if you would not suffer the demon of self distrust to enfeeble you, I am satisfied that in your policy you should yield nothing to the feebleness which surrounds you & cannot support you. You should stand firm as Atlas, though you stand alone. Were I simply to counsel with reference to the merest selfish policy, such should be my counsel. But the same counsel applies to the necessities of the country, as well as your own dignity & heroism. It is *our* policy to maintain the attitude of defiance, and though beaten & defeated today, we shall not be dishonored; we shall have surrendered no principle, which, however small the profitable result, conceded, would be dishonour. And even those who are not fire eaters here, are just as tenacious of the ancient position of S. C., as those who are; & desire to maintain appearances, though they may be too cowardly to encounter issues. "You say the South (in Congress) is utterly disorganized, & you fear demoralized." I know that. I knew it long ago. And what could you expect? Weak men in power, can neither be brave, nor honest. But what of that? You call a council of war, and all your officers shrink back from the proposition of battle. What then? You *know,* in general issues, that battle is life. Shall *you* shrink? Shall you reduce yourself to the level of these underlings whom you despise? No! You give battle. You may be defeated. But your sense of what is right sustains you; and the very instincts of the cowards sustain you! And your country will sustain you, even though they share the apprehensions of the cowardly. Take the responsibility as old Jackson [59] did! I grant you that these people all regard you as a rival; but all ordinary men, in the moment of battle, submit to a rival, whom they fear,

---

[58] We have been unable to discover any account of this caucus other than Simms'.

[59] Andrew Jackson.

& whom they hate, perhaps, but whose courage & wisdom brings them safety; extricates them from meshes from which they cannot extricate themselves. But, if you go into battle with this s'pirit, you can not be defeated. Public opinion is growing with you. Even at the North, large masses only wait to escape the issue, and any pretext will serve their purpose. If we are firm, yet not exacting, they will recede. Public opinion, at the North, is beginning to see that slavery is their profit! At the South, the recent money crisis has opened the eyes of thousands, to the superior securities of the South, over the treacherous plausibilities of Northern capital & enterprise. If Cotton were brought down to 5 cents, as I told Rhett & Colcock, before our last issue on that subject — secession would be easy, not of S. C. only, but of all the South.[60] Recently, the fact that, while cotton was 17 cents in the Liverpool market, it had sunk, in Charleston & Savannah, to 12, did a wonderful deal towards refining the vulgar mind, among ourselves, to our arguments in behalf of the independence of the South. Even G. Britain begins — see the 'Times' — to recognize the virtues of African labour, in cotton raising,[61] & I am inclined to think that G. B. & France will both lose in the course of the next 5 years, all feeling of hostility to our institutions. In politics, if you cannot gain the victory, you have only to gain *time*. Time is every thing. As the French Cardinal [62] said — 'Time & myself against the world!' Now, I say, try for an organization of the Southern members. I conscientiously believe that their people is *everywhere in advance of them all*. The fact is, you live in a world of convention simply, when you are in Washington. There is no moral in society. The place lives wholly by Congress. Ordinary men are immediately subsidized by the habitual & familiar modes of speech & thinking — in other words by party *claquers*. There is no virtue as there is no enthusiasm. You cannot make any sensation *there*, by any eloquence or argument; by any originality or force; by any thing short of brute violence, or some monstrous excess; for there is no reverence for superiority — no sense of superiority, no impulse to admiration; and it is the policy of the underlings that this should be so, and they readily attach themselves to party, not merely to derive their

---

[60] Robert Barnwell Rhett (see introductory sketch of the Rhetts) and William Ferguson Colcock (see note 227, Nov. 17, 1846) were ardent secessionists.
[61] Simms is doubtless referring to the London *Times,* though we have not located the article which he has in mind.
[62] Jules Mazarin (1602-1661).

own support and strength from it, but to subdue & keep down individuality. It is this which prevents your organization of the Southern members. So long as they can keep from being read out of the books of the Democratic Party, so long will they (as they suppose) have a plea with the people. But the D. Party is now in fact a Southern Party; the success of the Republicans will render it wholly so; & so destroy it; for it will then be in a hopeless minority, & then will be the time, and not before, when any man shall be able to form a Southern organization on proper sectional grounds. But there is no reason that the attempt at Southern organization should not be made, at every season, if only to maintain a respectable cohort which shall constitute the nucleus for future organization. To this, rather than to any efficient action in the Congress itself, would I have you address your efforts. Nor must you submit to defeat. You will be disappointed repeatedly. But you must persevere, in reference to the importance of the object, & in order to take advantage of the vicissitudes in politics. I must, of course, leave your processes to yourself, as I know personally but little of the material in which you have to work. I had supposed that Jefferson Davis [63] would be your most trustworthy person. Hunter [64] is a graceful phlegmatic, having good abilities & a classical mind, but too sluggish of temperament for any audacity. Gen. Quitman [65] struck me as an old granny, with an enormous deal of vanity. I should count nothing upon him, though his vanity might be used freely, in making him efficient in conducting a charge, carrying an outpost, or making a feint or sortie. Of all these men, so far as I have seen them personally, or followed their tracks in Congress (either House) I regard you as the only one having the proper resources for generalship; always provided you have your purpose fixed, and do not vacillate through any premature despair of achieving the result. If you despond, you will do nothing. And you must beware of a mistake which Mr. Calhoun made, and Mr. Rhett, — that of attempting to do too much; to absorb in yourself the minor duties, ambitious of all the apparent power.

---

[63] Jefferson Davis (1808-1893), later president of the Confederate States, was a member of Congress (1845-1846) and United States senator from Mississippi (1847-1851, 1857-1861).

[64] Robert Mercer Taliaferro Hunter (1809-1887) was a member of Congress (1837-1843, 1845-1847) and United States senator from Virginia (1847-1861).

[65] John Anthony Quitman (1799-1858) was a member of Congress from Mississippi (1855-1858).

The greatest secret in effecting an organization, will be to find something for every body to do; within the compass of his abilities, and calculated, in some degree, to put him responsibly before the people. In this you really enable them to attain that which most of them desire: some guaranty to themselves & to the public, that they are not out of place. You thus serve their vanity, and, at the same time, do for them what few can do for themselves,—put them in situations which will exercise their endowments, no matter what their degree. It will be difficult for *you* to do this, or rather to forbear doing yourself. You will be apt to mar, by meddling with them *in details,* — even as you were wont to do with Harry and Spann.[66] Your own mind has one remarkable trait, which is very rarely to be seen in our public men. While you possess a large power of generalization, you are also a person of singularly nice detail; and your fondness for details sometimes interferes with your boldness as a generalizer. You cannot well use the magnifier & the microscope together; and your dignity as a general officer, is sometimes forfeited by your attention to the petty subjects which you should always trust to your Lieutenants. Upon this dignity, especially, you will need to insist carefully, if you would lead successfully. That quality of the soul & character asserts itself, in the first instance, by its grasp of the general truth, necessity & modus operandi. It wills — commands — counsels — exhorts, and does this regally. What you speak should be delivered as Law; not as if addressing those around you, but as if soliloquizing. You must not be too familiar, or you will become cheap. A quiet reserved manner, will save you from some of those sharp abruptnesses [67] with which you sometimes mortify the vanity of other people. And if you will grasp the wholeness of your own position — the designs of the North — the best interests of the South which are in jeopardy; the still vaster interests which it has for development — its own honor — the honour of its representatives; — you can take such a tone, in addressing your Caucus, as will not only force them to recognize your power, but will be calculated to compel them to take position along with you, or suffer shamefully by the contrast between you, in the estimation of posterity. By all means, use all efforts, in effecting an organization. *Divide et impera!* is the game of the North; and our poor devils of the

---

[66] Hammond's sons. See note 7, Jan. 30, 1851, and note 181, Dec. 30, 1856.
[67] Simms wrote *abruptness.*

South (such men for example as Douglas) fancy they can win the favour of the North by a treachery which loses them all their capital in the South.[68] Had he studied history, or did he see any thing except through the medium of a blinding ambition, he would see that no man of the South has ever reached the Presidency who could not carry the South with him. It is this capital, held certainly in hand, which can alone secure the aid of a Northern cohort, sufficient to give a Southern nominee the election. Douglas goes over to the Republicans without a single regiment. So far he occupies the ground. But only with *them*. But they will ask, after a while, what capital he brings with him; and they will probably content themselves with sucking the orange, and flinging away the skin. If elected to the Presidency, he will be so by a strictly sectional vote, and one which will declare to the South, in tones of thunder — "Delenda est Carthago!" It will be the fiat of doom to the Slave States, or a trumpet note to drive them into Independence. These things might be shown to all your ambitious associates. No one of them stands any chance who is not identified with the South, or who shall seriously forfeit its confidence. And, just at this moment, when I hold slavery to be strengthening itself, East & West, in Europe & Northern America, — strengthening itself by its own sheer capacity of production, & by the power which it asserts over Commerce & Manufactures equally, — it would be perfectly suicidal, to say, or do any thing, which should argue a diminution of confidence in ourselves, or in the moral of slavery. I would not have *you* present to Congress the ultimatum of Kanzas or Disunion. I would have you say that such would be your counsel to the South — nay, you need not say that even — but that, it will be for your constituents to determine what they will do in the event of the rejection of Kanzas because of a Slave Constitution. You are there with limited powers. You are not authorized to answer for your people, in their future actions. You will not withhold your counsel, & that will be, to peril any extreme rather than submit to Dishonour. And you have said, that the

---

[68] Stephen Arnold Douglas (1813-1861), unsuccessful candidate for the nomination for president by the Democratic Party in 1852 and 1856 and unsuccessful candidate for president on the Democratic ticket in 1860, was a member of Congress (1843-1847) and United States senator from Illinois (1847-1861). In the Senate on Dec. 8, 1857, he had denounced the Lecompton Constitution, and on Dec. 9 he had delivered a speech giving the reasons for his denunciation (see *Congressional Globe,* 35 Cong., 1 Sess., pp. 5, 14-18).

rejection of Kanzas, because of her Slave Constitution, will be a dishonour. And we are agreed on the subject. It will not only be dishonour, but doom! You might add that our enemies have driven us to the wall. That neither you, for yourself, nor the South, desire, for the development of our Institutions, any more territory—that the 850,000 square miles which we now possess, would content us, *if rendered secure against assault.* That Kanzas, as an element of value to the South, is of no moment; but that it rises into importance, of the most vital sort, when her recognition depends wholly upon the exclusion & denunciation of an Institution, which is inextricably wrapt up in the property, safety, prosperity & absolute existence of the South! Secure us against these assaults, and the South, limited in her slave population, incapable of any increase, but by the slow processes of nature, would care for no addition to her territory; that she is no propagandist of her Institution. Louisiana was not purchased with any view to slavery, but as a natural outlet to the West; and all the acquisition that has been made for the South is Texas; — while the North is grasping territory on every hand. It is the North, that, by declaring deadly hostility to slavery, has forced upon the Slave States the necessity of endeavouring (being still pacific as all agricultural regions are) of warding off the danger thru constitutional processes, rather than disturb the integrity of the Union. Driven from this mode of defense, you force upon the South the necessity of breaking with you forever. — And this meets some of your difficulties and enables you to reconcile the attitudes of one who represents a special section, and yet, who acknowledges the virtue which may exist in all. So far as outer pressure is concerned, the South wishes to maintain the Union; but if the internal pressure is such, from her Sister States, you compel her to choose between all the perils of Independence & Union. — You say that you propose to declare that you vote with Indifference for the Le Compton Constitution. You *cannot* vote with indifference upon a subject which, you admit, involves the honour, if not the safety of the South. It does not matter what value you put upon Kansas. It does not matter how erring were your predecessors in making a test of its *pro-slavery* conditions, from which your people shrink. The fact is patent, that it is made so, and you must battle with reference to the recognition of this question. You cannot repudiate the test. As an individual this might be done. But you represent a region that, whether wisely or unwisely, has made the question. If needs be, you might say this, in connection with your own disclaimer; but be sure to add, that Kansas, *per se,* is nothing to us, as we seek no propagandism. It is only because of the inveterate hostility of the North to what is equally our right & necessity, that Kansas rises into any importance whatever. — You say that "you are not in favour of any further extension of slave territory — that our 850,000 sq. miles are enough for us; &c." But you will be answered. "So, perhaps, it might, as we have no means of adding to our slave labour save by natural increase; but who shall say that the slave trade will not be reopened? And who shall secure us in continued possession of our 850,000 sq. miles?["] In this question lies the true reason why we contend for Kanzas. Not because it is so much territory; but because it is one of the outposts in a conflict, which, this lost, brings the enemy upon our established territory. It is the Redan to our Malakoff.[69] No one dreams that the hostile parties will be content with simply abridging our progress. It is not to cut our wings that they strive, but to cut our throat. They do not conceal their purpose that our utter destruction is determined upon. They have certainly played an open game with us, & distinctly avow themselves deadlily determined upon the utter annihilation of slavery so soon as they can secure the power under the Constitution. And it is in order to the acquisition of this power, & not any desire for the mere increase of territory that they seek Kanzas. But, aside from Kanzas, the retention of our present area is an impossible thing. The property of slavery is to seek new lands as the old become unprofitable; for negro slavery rarely improves exhausted lands, except under remarkable management. It is too slovenly a labor. Accordingly, it will pass out from Virginia, North Carolina & Kentucky, and these States, under any circumstances, will be lost to that Institution within 20 years:—would have been lost before this, but for the provocation to state, social & personal pride, which the abolition warfare had roused to anger. It is evident that we shall require new territory to supply the place of the old. All Mexico would be civilized by negro slavery naturally, in the course of the next hundred years, were it suffered to take the natural course of things. Slavery would linger in S. C. during

---

[69] Malakoff was the name given the chief fortification of Sevastopol during the Crimean War. It was a great stone tower and was flanked by fortifications called the Redan and the Little Redan.

that time; but, in all probability, all the upper country & a great part of the middle would share the condition of N. C. & Virginia. At all events S. C. would become a frontier. Would Texas be left us? No! Already the enemy is preparing to compass possession of 3/4 of that region, & calculates upon 2 at least, or more, free states out of it. Thus, with Virginia & N. C. & Kentucky lost, a large part of Texas &c. what becomes of our area of 850,000 sq. miles? When we are not allowed to substitute the new for the old territory? What remains to us will be "like the scorpion girt by fire." The Slave States will die inch by inch, upward, like the tail of a snake! But, even suppose us left in possession of this 850,000 miles, with all our soil & coast & climate, rivers & staples, resources of every sort, how shall we be better able to develope them than now, so long as we remain in a confederacy which is hostile, & denies us the exercise of independent action of every kind? I am willing to agree that if we were segregated from the North, & isolated like Cuba, with our present advantages, we could, as you say, rule the world through our resources; but the present connection saps us of the fruits of these resources, as fast as they accumulate; and keeps us in a continued sense of insecurity with regard to the capital. I do not believe that Kanzas would be of any real relief, or help, or strength; but, in the absence of that courage, conduct, concentration &c. on the part of our people, which keeps them from taking the bull by the horns, in the case of Kanzas, the only mode left us, is to secure increase of territory in order to [gain] more political weight in Congress. You will say, 'but this is idle, as the North makes 3 states to our 1.' I am agreed hereto; but recur back to the original position; — the question has been made for us, & Kanzas is the stake which is to decide our dishonor & the *status* of slavery; and it is the moral of the issue, & not its profit, which demands that we fight for it to the last. We must make no concessions. It will not do to stop effort, & cry out 'the grapes are sour.' This course will be at once regarded by friends & foes, as a cowardice & a base yielding of the struggle through the working of some shameful motive. — To tell our people that we ought to be content with 850,000 sq miles, when our enemy, after a long fight, says you shall have no more, will be construed to be a backing down, a backing out, &, in addition to the hiss & scorn which will follow it, will be the renewal of aggression, in search of what remains. All that you say touching the policy of the South in the develop-

ment of her resources will be simply didactical — proper enough,
at home, and discoursing before an agricultural or commercial
society, or on some set occasion. But it advances you not a step,
& would be out of place, if spoken in your place in Congress.
You might say discursively — 'were we separated from *you,*
850,000 sq. m. would suffice us, & we should then develope such
resources as would rule you & the world' — but, to be dwelt
upon, or made use of as an exhortation to the South, when she is
engaged in what we hold to be a life & death issue, it would be
offensive in her ears. To declare our content with our present
area is just what Black Republicanism requires you to do. ["]We
are content,["] says a portion — the most moderate of that
party — ["]to let you live as Slave States, you who are already
such; but you are not to grow; you shall not increase;" — and
the point of honour with us lies in our courage to resist this insolence, and triumph by conquest over the impudent menace.
You declare your unwillingness to acquire territory at all, North
or South; and so do I; and I wish Kanzas & California & Oregon,
&c, had been at the bottom of the sea, before we got them, or
somewhere beyond our reach forever. But, how idle this talk with
the fact staring us in the face perpetually, that the people of this
country have no appetite superior to this greed after land? We
have already got the territory & are now to dispose of it; and we
shall be getting more daily, & will have to dispose of that also;
and it is clear that, unless our disruption, as a Confederacy, shall
soon happen, we shall extend our possessions over every country
that lies in our hemisphere & within our grasp. We may wish it
otherwise; may bitterly regret the fate that is so suicidally prosperous; but it is idle to do so, except musingly, as one murmurs
over a sorrow in his armchair by the evening fire. It has nothing
to do with the necessity that presses. Neither our complaints,
nor our arguments, will tend to arrest this Norman appetite for
the possession of domain; and if, in your speech, you refer to the
subject of regret at all, it should only be *en passant.* How shall
we dispose of it, when we get it? How get our share of it? How
manage, as that it shall not be used for our injury? These are
the questions. Having done your best with the members of the
South, to organize them, & bring them up to the first issue —
Kanzas, as a Slave State, or the South as an Independent power,
capable, as you justly phrase it, of ruling the Union within the
Union, and coercing the world without: — we will suppose you

fail in bringing them to this point; and in all probability you will fail; for inferior men will distrust their people, just in degree as they distrust themselves. — Supposing then that you fail. You are then to *show,* in your speech, that you *have* failed. You have to show that *you* have striven against this failure. You have to show why an agricultural people, the best material for armies in the world, is slow always to any resistance until the pressure actually inconveniences them. You are to show, however, that this is due, not to timidity, but to the natural training of agriculture — the reasons being suggested in preceding pages. You can illustrate from the History of the Laconians, in comparison with the Athenians; the one purely agricultural, the other commercial. You may show that the constant aggressions of the Athenians finally so roused the Lacedæmonians, that they subdued & crushed Athens forever. And the aggressions were very much of the same sort with those of the North upon the South. It is curious for example, that the Athenians overran the Megarid & conquered the Megareans, for *seducing* & *harbouring their fugitive slaves,* and for *appropriating to themselves the common territory;* while the commercial aggressions of the Athenians, in turn, upon the agricultural states, and the continued exaction & appropriation by Athens, of the subsidies raised by the agricultural states for their defense against the Persians (our Tariff engendered by the necessities occasioned by the War with Britain of 1815) drove the Lacedæmonians to the necessity of arming against & destroying Athens. The events of the world, in all nations, come round periodically. You say to the North you are even thus driving the South to the wall. We really want no increase of territory; but if ours, we must not be dishonored by a denial of our right. We would live in peace with you with our 850,000 sq. miles, & be satisfied; but if you will not suffer us to live in peace, we shall quit you. We have submitted to a great deal of aggression. We shall no doubt submit to much more, as is evident in this issue. But you will one day go too far. The cup will be too full after a while. The last feather breaks the camel's back; and the Agricultural States, goaded by insult, stung by sarcasm, drained of their resources, robbed of their possessions, denied their rights, and their very safety threatened, will turn upon you, and grown relentless from persecution, will take terrible revenge & rend you. And in all this, there will be no *hifalutin.* These *are facts.* The morals & temperament of a people are among the highest class facts. Their pride, their sentiment, their passion, all are facts. The mere number of sq. m. that we have, is among their *material facts,* but the *moral facts* possess a terrible power, and enter necessarily into every argument which would grasp the influences operating upon national destinies & actions. Look to *all* the facts. This is what I would have you do. Do not be one of the first to enter upon the discussion. Let it advance, considerably, before you break ground. Cogitate, meanwhile, over the daily changing phases of the discussion. Single out your man for the action. Fasten upon him. But, meanwhile, be chary of your speech without doors. Do not suffer your purposes to be suspected. Hold yourself in reserve. I do not wish you to make a fire eating speech. On the contrary, I would have you singularly calm, temperate in all things, but firm & manly, with a gravity & dignity commensurate with the serious situation of the South & of the whole country. If you deal in any thing didactical, an elaborate survey of the Union, as a whole, in former days and at present, might be made. Exhibit its wonderful prosperity, *as a result of its wholeness.* Show to what power & prosperity, far beyond the capacity of Imagination of number to concieve, it must still rise, could its people only resolve to be just & temperate. Show that the North, which boasts perpetually of its prosperity, *owes every thing to the Confederacy!* Show that she perils all of this, when she drives the South to the wall! That she will do this, & rouse the South to extremity, in spite of the natural supineness of every agricultural region! Warn them that there is no secret, now in possession of men, calculated to give us immunity beyond that which was possessed by all past empires. That we are treading in their foot steps, imitating their brutal greed, by which all ancient nations forfeited their charters of liberty & prosperity. That all the old confederacies, Greece, Rome, the Italian, the Swiss, were all broken up (and I think even the Jews, & in all probability the Assyrian & Egyptian), in consequence of the trespasses of the larger provinces upon the small; usually great cities (centralism) involving the commercial population. These always drove the rustic population into rebellion & secession, because of their perpetual aggressions, usurpations & excessive taxation. That the same result will be reached among ourselves; that, whatever charm once lay in the idea of Union, is rapidly dying out every where; that the idea of the Union, as a necessity for safety, could only be held valid under a foreign or external pressure, which is now no longer felt to be a danger. Of this sort of material for generalization & home application, there is abundance. And, in speaking, if you speak more in sorrow than in anger; forbear all abuse—do not seek to carry the war into the enemies country; only in defense of your own; and speak of the Union, as of a something sacred, which you would sacredly preserve, as long as it ensures justice, peace and protection to your people; but not an hour longer! But beware how you treat lightly a cause of quarrel — an issue — which, whether they are cowardly or not, has inflamed your people to such a degree — and ought to inflame them — that the masses every where, & even states — see Alabama for example — declare the wrong to be such, if committed, as to justify & demand disunion! [70] Analyse all that you indicate, as your probable topic, and you find it to resolve itself into a frank and almost cordial concession to the North of what it demands; — that you shall have none of the national acquisition of territory; that slavery, however it may grow — however the policy of other states may change in its favour, so as to lead to a reopening of the slave trade — shall always be circumscribed within a domain, a large part of which, as we all see, it cannot retain. You demand & exact no securities for what you *have,* and you know that the aggression upon this will be continued & increased in due degree with the increase of power on the part of our assailants. What you say about our development of what we have, & the wondrous growth to power, to which due exertion will bring us, will be denounced as mere declamation, a perfect mockery, which will utterly fail to mollify, after the concession you will have made. My notion is that you should have but one creed, — i.e. *"I know but the South, & the South in danger!"* This was the instinct of Calhoun — of Butler; — and had they but possessed real intrepidity of heart, they would have succeeded in organizing the South. But neither of them had policy, or courage — of the right kind. Calhoun, in his love of power, sought to absorb all the working in himself. Rhett was equally unwise. Butler's vanity kept him only & always a mere talker & a table companion. Maintain their *one* instinct — which kept

---

[70] In Jan., 1858, the General Assembly of Alabama provided for a state convention to be held in the event that Kansas should apply for admission to the Union under the Lecompton Constitution and be refused by Congress (see Clarence Phillips Denman, *The Secession Movement in Alabama* [Montgomery: Alabama State Department of Archives and History, 1933], p. 75n). The Charleston *Mercury* of Jan. 23 reprints the resolutions from the Montgomery *Mail* of Jan. 15 and carries an editorial on them.

them always strong at home — and couple it with a policy which teaches that you can only organize, by properly *using your associates;* by letting them do every thing that they can *in the public eye;* giving them opportunities for exhibition; while you prime, load & fire them off, without letting even themselves, see that it is your finger that works the trigger. How far does a Georgia platform go? You have seen this of Alabama, within a few days. Content yourself *with any thing* upon which you may join *issue* with the *Republican Party.* This will identify you at once with the Democratic & the extreme South. Accept Kanzas as a test — accept any test; the true issue being that which will soonest bring about such a crisis as will force the South into position. If you speak contemptuously of the Kanzas issue, and repudiate it as a test, you offend, & drive from you, every public man of your own side, who has been seeking to make it so. I would have you forbear every thing of this sort; would have you single out such a man as Douglas, and without declaring any policy at all, fasten upon him, upon his course & arguments, and, assuming the grounds previously taken by the South, in respect to Kanzas, as settled & patent for use, continue the fight with all your vigour, as if the outpost were the central battery. It will be time enough, hereafter, when you have established yourself as a fighting leader, to indicate a change of policy for your people. Such a change, when the issue is actually pending, will be as fatal as if you sought to alter your line of battle with the enemy at the *pas de charge.* Here, where I am, knowing little of the details of the field, I can, of course, only deal in generalities. But I know our people, and their necessities; & think I know *you,* & your resources. I have great faith in them, and your fame is very precious to me. I have too often stood pledged for it, not to feel very anxious that you should acquit yourself admirably, as I well know that you can, in your present situation. Do not distrust yourself, but give yourself time. Rather exercise, all you can, in colloquial debate, in which I hold you to be very strong, than engage too soon in any elaborated, or declaratory speech. You will have sufficient time & opportunity for this. You are now in one of the proudest positions in the country, and, as I have thought, & said, privately, the *highest place* may be yours, if you will only exercise a calm & dignified policy. Discriminate in what you say between the Black Republicans & the North. Assume — and in a measure it is true — that a faction of Destructives has temporarily got possession of

power in the North — a faction which neither represents the
intellect, nor the wealth, nor the commerce, nor the manufactures
of the North; which, in fact, represents nothing but the restless
impulse of reckless masses, which are daily undergoing expansion
by the influx of a foreign *personnel*. Speak with regard to the
Union with due respect and regret. Speak of it as some thing
which, if possible, you would preserve. Mr Rhett spoke of it
only as of that which he would exultingly destroy at every
hazard.[71] But show that the preservation of the Union can only
be made sure, with the due recognition of all the rights & securities of the South. And in this connection you can urge the fact
that the South does not seek, & has not sought, the propagation
of her institutions; would be quite content with them as they are;
but, driven to extremity, will accept of any issues which can be
made to relieve her from an intolerable, unscrupulous, relentless
persecution, that must, unresisted, become a destructive tyranny!
Whether the Union is preserved or not, you can make yourself
the first man in it, if maintained; & the first man in the South,
in the event of dissolution! But to do this, you must maintain your
own & the attitude of the State. Contrive, if the Kansas issue
be repudiated, that the blame shall rest on other shoulders than
your own. Mark, too, that Douglas and Wise [72] are both bidding
for the Presidency by this very ostentatious repudiation. Douglas
despairs of his hope in the South; & for good reasons. Wise, by
the way, is a madman, with just enough of small political cunning
to decieve himself, as to the impression he may make upon the
North. They will suck the one dry, and scorn the other! Both
of them know that the South should have the next President.
But the North will repudiate this idea, if they feel that they have
the power to elect their man independently of the South. The
rational portion of the North will be willing — nay, prefer — to
take a Southern man of dignity, ability & character, and they can
only succeed through the Democratic party. This party will
require (being in great part Southern) one who is recognized by
the South as a proper representative — they will not dare put
forth a nominee who has broken bonds, or is under suspicion.
But they will require also that, tho' true to the South, he shall
be temperate, dignified, not easily warped from side to side;

---

[71] Robert Barnwell Rhett was a member of Congress during 1837-1849 and
United States senator during 1850-1852.
[72] Henry Alexander Wise (1806-1876) was a member of Congress (1833-
1844), minister to Brazil (1844-1847), and governor of Virginia (1856-1860).

having no rash indirection, and one, too, whom the temperate portion of the North will be content with. And this temperate portion will not expect such a nominee to yield one jot of his sectionality. They will respect a man the more for his fidelity to his section. They would have been content even to take Mr. Calhoun, but that the office-seekers well knew who were his favorites, and the great majority could entertain no hopes of favour at his hands. This is one of the secret motives of party in choosing a nominee whose antecedents leave them in doubt of his predilections. A new man is always preferred for this reason especially! — I have thus, my dear H. written you a long, desultory & I fear, a dull letter. It has been written under indisposition, anxiety & trouble. My wife has been for the last ten days very ill with a catarrh, which, I fear, has been coupled with neuralgia. She still suffers tho' something better. Intense pains of face, crushing pains of the head, have nearly driven her distracted. I have had my children sick, &, but that I have no time for it, I should probably have been sick myself. I am able to do nothing logical, & have just written as I felt. But I have thought every night since I got your letter, & still my conclusions are the same. You will give me credit for feeling very anxious about you, if I am not able to give you any succour. If any thing occurs to me, I will write again. I would write more now, but I feel that I could scarcely say any thing which will, not before this, have passed through your own mind. Heaven send you a safe & glorious deliverance, & it will, if you will be but true to yourself & not suffer your self-distrust to baffle your Genius.[73]

Yours Ever faithfully

W. G. S.

---

[73] In his reply of Feb. 7 Hammond writes : "I thank you for your long letter. I read it carefully & shall read it again. We differ in nothing except your estimate of me. I have not opened my mouth in the Senate, but I have made forty senatorial speeches—to myself—there—along the streets, here in my study. Your letter strikes pretty much through the series. There are some things in it—that about Athens & Sparta, for instance, which I don't believe & never heard of before—that were not in my speeches, & which I shall bring in on digestion, if I ever acquire Senatorial legs." On March 4 Hammond delivered a speech in favor of the admission of Kansas under the Lecompton Constitution (see Simms' letter to him of March 27).

866: To WILLIAM PORCHER MILES

[February? 1858] [74]

My dear Miles.

I can well understand your difficulties touching Kanzas as a subject. You must not ask what your friends or the public may expect at your hands; only what is proper at your hands. Do not rush into any debate, either with the desire of answering any such expectation, or of merely figuring on the floor. Does it need that you should speak? Can you do any good by it — effect any result; is any thing left unsaid, or said improperly, on the part of the South, and by other men, which you should supply, or which needs revision? Put these questions to yourself on all the occasions. Your best course will be to break ground first in the *colloquial* debate. This is, indeed, the true field always, except on very extraordinary occasions. — I will write more hereafter. — I cover to your care a packet which you will oblige me by having put into DeBow's hands.[75] If you have any postage to pay (which I suppose not) do not hesitate to tell me. In haste — and trouble, (but still truly yours —)

W. Gilmore Simms

867: To WILLIAM PORCHER MILES

Woodlands, S. C. Feb. 8. [1858] [76]

My dear Miles.

It is fortunate for you that the occasion which invites your oratory is of a sort which is easily satisfied. It is the worst objection to such performances that they *never do sufficiently task the intellect & soul* of the speaker. It is the very facility with which you may answer expectation that defeats the possibility of effort. You have only to deal in superb commonplaces, vague

---

[74] Simms' remarks about Kansas and his advice to Miles "to break ground first in the *colloquial* debate" indicate that this letter was written prior to his letter of Feb. 8.

[75] Perhaps the MS. of "Memoir—Col. M. C. Hammond, of S. C." (see note 41, Jan. 25, 1858).

[76] William Peterfield Trent in *William Gilmore Simms* (Boston and New York: Houghton, Mifflin and Company, 1892), pp. 249-250, refers to this letter, which he misdates 1860. The correct year is established by Simms' references to Miles' forthcoming oration on William Washington (see letter to Miles of Jan. 25) and to the Kansas question (see letter to Hammond of Jan. 28). On the back of this letter Miles wrote: "Ansd. Feb. 24th." Trent's biography of Simms is hereafter cited as "Trent."

misty generalities, and your audience is satisfied. Mark you, I
do not say that *you* are satisfied, or that the wise are satisfied,
or Thought satisfied, or Art satisfied. No! No! But that those are
satisfied who never had any expectations. Seymour would better
serve these people, a thousand times, than either you or I! [77] Get
through it, *mon ami,* as well as you can, and resolve never to
accept another appointment which does not involve the great occasion & the necessity for such argument as shall task equally
your thought & soul! In respect to your present situation, & its
exhausting effects, — which exhaust without employing, and enfeeble without compensating, — I think I warned you already in
repeated conversations. You will find it even more soul-sapping
than what is called society in Charleston. But, keep your soul clear
& calm; in respect to the political issues of South & North, you
have only to obey your *Instincts,* applying them to the several
cases as they arise. Briefly, the antagonism of North & South
is vital, & the natural growth equally of society & interests. You
cannot well err in identifying yourself without reserve with your
section. In respect to the exactions of the social world *there,* you
have only to resolve to set aside so many hours, in every 24, for
your own purposes of self-reflection & study, & never suffer
yourself to be invaded during that period. Aim at acquiring
expertness in colloquial debate rather than by elaborate set efforts.
We have, as a political & social body, survived all that sort of
thing; and require now, rather sharp gladiatorial or partisan
practise, than regular seiges and blockades. In other words, you
are in the field, with cavalry & a flying camp. But I cannot easily
counsel you where I am. I can only fling out some general hint,
which may be valueless, as inapplicable to your conditions. Cultivate Hammond. He will need the help of *honest* & *fearless*
Lieutenants. Even morally, he is a far superior man to 19 in
20 of the politicians you will meet, & he will be faithful to his
pledges & his past. In regard to Kansas, if the Southern members
will present one front, firm & united, the North will yield. But
do not suffer them to mouth & sputter. Better calm resolve, no
debate, no dispute. Let them but say 'we leave en masse if Kansas
be rejected — go home to our Constituents & say that farther
representation in Congress is useless & dishonoring.['] If pre-

---

[77] While campaigning for Buchanan, Horatio Seymour (1810-1886), governor
of New York during 1852-1854, had delivered in Springfield, Mass., on July 4,
1856, a speech denouncing abolition, prohibition, and nativism. Doubtless Simms
is here alluding to that speech.

pared for that, with one voice, you may do any thing. Don't forget to send me ample supplies of garden seeds of every sort. I need a good deal myself & have undertaken to supply some ladies

Yours truly

W. Gilmore Simms.

868: To James Henry Hammond

Charleston, Feb 22. [1858] [78]

My dear Hammond.

I write hurriedly to say that I am now in Charleston, where I shall be in all probability, for the next six weeks, having come down to await my wife's accouchement which approaches.[79] Your letter, after a long interval, has reached me here. I shall write you in a day or two more fully and on one or two points upon which I wish you to be prepared. I am not content that you should be merely a partisan or sectional politician when it is in your power to be a philosophical one. Meanwhile, give your servant a ten dollar Bill, and a slip of paper on which you write — 'A copy of Grote's History of Greece, — Harper's Edition.' It is, I think, in 12 vols. at 75 per vol. Send to the book shop of Frank Taylor.[80] Take Grote and read carefully all the parts — about the 8th. vol. relating to the causes of the Pelopponnesian War. My own copy is in the country, so that I cannot refer you to book & chapter. But read it to yourself, in secret. When you get leisure to think at home get the English Edition of Grote. It is one of the very great books of the age — perhaps the only really great philosophical Histy ever written by an Englishman. It is a book for your library. But *ad int.* the Harper Edit. will suffice.[81] In a day or two I will write you more fully. At this moment, I am troubled, weary, anxious, and altogether unfit for any thing. My drafts upon my publisher [82] have been returned protested — my wife nears her accouchement — my eldest son is down with measles at York-

---

[78] This letter is a reply to Hammond's dated Feb. 7, 1858 (cited note 54, Jan. 28, 1858). Hammond again wrote Simms on March 5 and March 24. The originals are in the Hammond Papers, Library of Congress.

[79] Harriet Myddleton Simms was born on March 14.

[80] 402 Pennsylvania Avenue. See the Washington *Directory* for this year.

[81] See Hammond's comments in his letter of Feb. 7, quoted in note 73, Jan. 28, 1858. George Grote's *A History of Greece* . . . , 12 vols. (London: J. Murray, 1846-1856), was republished by Harper and Brothers in 1856.

[82] Justus Starr Redfield.

ville [83] — my money runs short — books don't sell just now, in comparison with Bread, Beef, Beer & Brandy, and my head is in a chaotic condition. I have not seen Heart since the reciept of your letter.[84] — In respect to Documents, send me any thing. I collect, bind, put away, & have a good library of American things. If you can pick up any Docs. of the Senate, of last year, send them; for Butler, sick & absent, sent me nothing the last six months of his public service, except exhortations to defend South Carolina, & give him help to do so.[85] Keitt [86] sends me spasmodically; Miles more regularly, but only of the House Documents. — *Do not omit any thing* & address me for the present here. I got the quarto which you refer to, & thank you.[87] — My daughter [88] acknowledges garden seeds from you sent to the plantation. I would like a similar supply sent here. I have a lot here 220 by 192 which I am desirous, while here, of getting prepared & planted for the summer.— In a day or two, nothing happening, look to hear from me. In meanwhile, keep cool, bide your time, load heavily, & make every shot tell. Choose your man. Your cause is that of the South. *The natural antagonisms of the sections* will render the conflict inevitable spite of amnesty & compromise. Sooner or later this issue will be made. The question is one of time only, & this depends upon the degree of provocation. For your part, be as *reserved* as possible till the time comes for striking. Do not make yourself too cheap or talk too freely. These rascal politicians are great pick tooths. *Trust none.* Use all! Keep your head cool. Few drinks. No suppers. Keep home with your wife. And prepare your batteries as much in private as possible. — If you can pick up the four octavos of George Finlay, upon Byzantium, Trebizond, & Mediæval Greece — there is none but

---

[83] Gilmore was a cadet at the King's Mountain Military School.

[84] For John Heart's proposal to buy the Rhetts' share of the Charleston *Mercury,* turn it into an organ for Hammond, and make Simms the editor, see letter to Hammond of March 27, 1858.

[85] See Simms' remarks in his letter to James H. Hammond of Sept. 7, 1856.

[86] Lawrence Massillon Keitt (see note 162, July 11, 1850). The present Keitt family in South Carolina say that Keitt's first name should be spelled *Lawrence,* though Mrs. Keitt's visiting card in the William Porcher Miles Papers, Southern Historical Collection, University of North Carolina, has it *Laurence.*

[87] In a postscript to his letter of Feb. 7 (cited note 54, Jan. 28, 1858) Hammond writes: "Do you want any Docs. I dont send. Let me know. Did you get 1st vol. Japan?" The "1st vol. Japan" is Francis L. Hawks' compilation, *Narrative of the Expedition of an American Squadron to the China Seas and Japan, Performed in the Years 1852, 1853 and 1854, under the Command of Commodore M. C. Perry, United States Navy, by Order of the Government of the United States* . . . (Washington: A. O. P. Nicholson, Printer, 1856).

[88] Augusta.

an English Edition — buy them.[89] They will afford you fine
illustrative material. They exhibit a fine view of the operations of
Centralism in the destruction of states. But be cool & patient.
There is no hurry. Let the enemy expend as much of his ammunition as possible.

Yours in Haste

W. Gilmore Simms

869: To JOHN REUBEN THOMPSON [90]

Charleston, March 1. [1858] [91]

My dear Thompson.

I congratulate [you] on the real beauty of your inauguration
Poem. It is exceedingly happy. I have seen your March number,
but not recieved it. Do send me two copies *here*. Send me also
copies of the proceedings when put forth in separate publication.
— I cover to you another collection of "Areytos." [92] You must let
me know frankly when I trespass — when they become tedious.
I contribute them only with the notion that they will help you
to fill out *respectably* certain pages — knowing well how difficult

---

[89] W. Blackwood and Sons, Edinburgh and London, published Finlay's *History of the Byzantine and Greek Empires, from DCCXVI to MCCCCLIII*, 2
vols. (1855) ; *The History of Greece, from Its Conquest by the Crusaders to
Its Conquest by the Turks, and of the Empire of Trebizond: 1204-1461* (1851) ;
and *The History of Greece under Othoman and Venetian Domination* (1856).
The same firm also published Finlay's *Greece under the Romans . . .* (1844).

[90] See introductory sketch.

[91] Dated by Simms' reference to Thompson's "Inauguration of the Equestrian
Statue of Washington. Richmond, Virginia, 22 February 1858. Opening Ode,"
S. L. M., XXVI (March, 1858), 161-166. In the Charleston *Mercury* of March
13 Simms praises Thompson's "Ode" in a review of the March issue of the
Messenger.

[92] During 1857 Simms published the following poems (signed "Adrian Beau-
fain") in the *Southern Literary Messenger:* "Ballad. Ah! Hearts That Late,"
"The Wanderer's Star," "Southern Areyto" ("Oh! the days, Oh! the nights
. . . "), and "Song. If from My Heart, I Tear Thee," XXIV (Feb.), 149-151;
"Areytos; or Songs of the South," consisting of "Beside the Sea," "Shall All
Then Be Forgotten," "Oh, the South," "Now, When the Spring Is Over," "Ask
Me Not Whither," and "Eva," XXV (Dec.), 464-468. Possibly several of the
unsigned poems in the *Messenger* for this year are also by Simms. During 1858
he published the following poems in the *Messenger:* "Christmas Ballads. Altered
or Imitated from the Old English" (unsigned), consisting of "The Lorde
Chrystmasse," "In Excelsis Gloria," and "Mary Moder," XXVI (Jan.), 72-74
(the first two of these had earlier been published in "Maise in Milk") ;
"Areytos; or, Songs of the South" (signed "Adrian Beaufain"), consisting of
"My Muse, 'Tis Time for Moving," "Song Be Ours," "Eyes, Eyes, Ye Have
Led Me to Ruin," "River Serenade," "Death, but Never Dishonour," "I Have

this task is on occasion. Write me here, where I am awaiting very anxiously a family event.[93]

Yours Ever truly

W. Gilmore Simms

J. R. T.

870: To WILLIAM PORCHER MILES

Charleston 21. March. [1858] [94]

My dear Miles.

Your speech is a good one, in spite of the subject. But that was one to leave you little opportunity. The truth is that whether the Retiring Board could *give* reasons or not, they *had,* or might have had good reasons for Cashiering one half at least of those whom they proposed to shelve.[95] Don't waste yourself any farther upon the subject. When you speak again, let it be with reference

---

Had Dreams," "To-morrow We Part," and "Low Sleeps the Bard," XXVI (Feb.), 92-98; "Martyrdom of the Patriots. Italy 1830" (signed "Carador"), XXVI (March), 184-187, earlier published as "Lines in Memory of the Italian Patriots . . . " in *Roberts' Semi-Monthly Magazine* (see note 56, April 8, 1841) ; "Areytos; or Songs of the South" (unsigned), consisting of "Well, If That Dream of Bliss," "Oh! Had I But the Power," "My Hope Is in the Yellow Leaf," "Coo-coo! Te Weet Tu Whu!," "Song of Seventy-Six," "The Serenader Implores His Mistress to Come Forth," "I Seek to Sing of Glory," "Ask Me No More for Song," "Were I a Bird," and "Ah! Look Not Thus Unkindly," XXVI (April), 245-251; "Areytos; or, Songs of the South" (signed "Adrian Beaufain"), consisting of "Quiet Is on the Earth," "Render Thy Tribute to Beauty," "Destined to Sever," "The Mournful God of Florid's Cape," "And Yet, This Lonely Realm Is Free," "Forget Not the Trophy," " 'Twas a Vision [of] Fair Ladye," "Go, Thou Faithless One," "Love on to the Last," and "This Flower It Blooms 'Mid a Ruin," XXVII (July), 19-25; "Areytos; or Songs of the South" (signed "Adrian Beaufain"), consisting of "The Amulet," "While the Silent Night," "Woodland Vespers," "Serenader Implores His Mistress to Awaken," "The Serenader Bids His Lady 'Good Night,' " "Be It Folly or Frenzy," "Friends Are Nigh," "What, after Long Season," "Fare Thee Well, Sweet River!," "Oh! Linger We Not," "Ballad.—'The Sigh That Says,' " and "No! Never, Though Loved Be the Voice," XXVII (Sept.), 191-199. Possibly he was also the author of one or two of the unsigned poems published in the *Messenger* during 1858.

Simms' "Southern Poets and Poetry," an article published in the Charleston *Mercury* of Dec. 10, 1857, is reprinted in the *Messenger,* XXVI (Feb., 1858), 157-158.

[93] Harriet Myddleton Simms was born on March 14.

[94] Part of this letter is quoted (somewhat inaccurately) by Trent, p. 250, who misdates it 1860. The correct year is established by Simms' references to Miles' and Hunter's speeches (see notes 95, 96, and 97, below).

[95] On March 2 Miles spoke in favor of a resolution "that the President be requested to communicate to the Senate the records of proceedings of the several naval courts of inquiry, organized under the act of Congress approved January 16, 1857, to amend an act entitled 'An act to promote the efficiency of the Navy.' " The resolution was passed by the House on March 4. See *Congressional Globe,* 35 Cong., 1 Sess., pp. 932, 956.

to the broadest issues between North & South. Take a survey of the whole field. Review our losses by the connexion; the Northern gains. Kanzas was always a humbug — a mere tub thrown to the South. Missouri, itself, is only nominally a Slave State, tho' with a considerable interest in slaves.[96] Mr. Hunter's speech is a tame, timid, compromising one, though well written.[97] It will not do for the time. We want thunderbolts, not gossamer for the combat. — This, of course, is all *inter nos*. If you can get me some good tomato & guinea squash seed at the Pat office, do so, & forward to me *here*.

Yours ever truly

W. Gilmore Simms

871: To HARRY HAMMOND

Charleston, March 27. [1858] [98]

My dear Harry Hammond.

I have been kept so anxious, in the midst of a series of family afflictions & annoyances,[99] that, though I recieved your very tasteful present ten days ago, I have scarcely been able to examine it.[100] Believe me to be very grateful for this token of your re-membrance. I only regret that Fate denied me the privilege of being your companion in Europe.[101] I might have helped your poetical associations in Greece & Italy, & you could have helped me in studies which I have but too long & unwisely neglected. But it is possible that we may yet visit the Classic regions together, though I shall then be too old, except for the sympathetic survey of tombs & trophies of the Past; while you are *riant* in the imagi-

---

[96] Miles' speech in favor of the admission of Kansas under the Lecompton Constitution, delivered in the United States House of Representatives on March 31 (see letter to Miles of April 12), is largely concerned with "the broadest issues between North and South."

[97] On March 12 Robert Mercer Taliaferro Hunter delivered a speech in the United States Senate in favor of the admission of Kansas under the Lecompton Constitution. See *Congressional Globe,* 35 Cong., 1 Sess., pp. 1093-1098.

[98] Dated by Simms' remarks about James H. Hammond's "debut in Washington." See note 107, below.

[99] Nash Roach, Simms' father-in-law (see introductory sketch of the Simms family circle) died on Feb. 28; the family tombstone at Woodlands says that he was sixty-six. Harriet Myddleton Simms was born on March 14.

[100] Doubtless the unknown collection later invaded by insects to which Simms refers in his letter to M. C. M. Hammond of Sept. 18, 1859.

[101] Harry returned from Europe in Oct., 1857. See James H. Hammond's letter to Simms of Oct. 28, quoted in note 85, Nov. 10, 1857.

nations which describe a vast & wondrous Future. Still, we should refresh each other by wandering together. Let *me* hope for it, at all events. At present, the realization of this dream is scarcely possible. It is very doubtful, whether *a purely literary man of the South,* could ever find so much favour with any administration as to get such an appointment as would be desirable. And just at this juncture I could accept none but such, if any. Besides, I have so neglected my French & Italian that it is pretty hard work for me to read a page understandingly without a dictionary, & to speak either would be impossible, — and I am too old to go to school again. Yet the former language is perhaps absolutely necessary to a diplomat, except in England. But for this, I might strain a point & accept a chargés station on the Continent, — say Naples or Turin. And then, perhaps, you would accompany me as Secy. of Legation — no, attaché — for they do not allow to a chargé a Secy. of Legation. But, in truth, I have banished the idea from my mind. Should an appointment ever be tendered me, it will be a surprise. I cannot seek one. I have so counselled your father who wrote me earnestly on the subject.[102] Of course, should I go to Europe, I should over all things desire to make my writings better known to the people of the Continent. Some of them have been translated & among literary men, I am not utterly unknown.[103] But a Southern writer has no such machinery as they wield in Boston, N. York & Philadelphia, proffering their writers upon foreign notice, & I have been content to address myself usually to a purely Southern public. — You thank me for my opinion of your letters, to Papa & Mama. The opinion was unforced. Your letters surprised me. The style was so good & clear — the thought so prompt — the studies made so generally lucid & marked by grasp. You are copious in language & should cultivate it. You are not too copious, — for though Thought is sometimes forgotten in a too facile utterance, yet without facile utterance Thought itself is unmalleable. Practice. I persuaded your

---

[102] See James H. Hammond's letters to Simms of Dec. 19 and Dec. 30, 1857 (originals in the Hammond Papers, Library of Congress). We have not located Simms' letter to Hammond written between these dates and concerned with such an appointment.

[103] During 1846-1854 German translations were published of *The Wigwam and the Cabin, The Yemassee, Katharine Walton, Marie De Berniere, The Sword and the Distaff, Richard Hurdis, Guy Rivers, Border Beagles,* and *The Partisan.* A German translation of *The Cassique of Kiawah* was published in 1861. See Trent, pp. 341-342, and A. S. Salley, *Catalogue of the Salley Collection of the Works of Wm. Gilmore Simms* (Columbia, S. C.: The State Company, 1943), pp. 30, 69, 79-80, 88, 102-103.

father to let me put your letters into a magazine. I revised them here & there; there was not much of this to do; but some of the sentences were clogged & cumbrous & the members needed a little transposition. You have seen, no doubt, where I took the liberty of an old soldier, & revised your discipline.[104] I am glad to see that you continue to write. I wish you would prepare for Russell's a paper on vine growing which your father read me, & which needs but little — always supposing you correct in your statistics — to make an excellent & useful essay.[105] — You are at Redclyffe? It is possible that I may wish to visit Augusta sometime this spring or summer. I have a book to write the scene of which is in that precinct. In the event of my going thither, I would pay you a visit, & should write to you beforehand.[106] — Your father has made a good debut in Washington. His speech tells.[107] I may say to *you,* that, knowing his powers & resources, it is not enough *for me.* But he had been so long out of the field that time is necessary to work himself free in the harness. And when I say that his speech is not enough for me, do not suppose me as indicating any thing but the higher standard which I impose upon him, beyond that of most persons. *He* understands me. The speech is eminently able — & true. He grapples the bull by the horns; but I hold it to be only the entering wedge. He will do far better yet. Write me, my dear boy, and believe me

Your friend

W. Gilmore Simms

P. S.

Regards to Spann.

---

[104] Harry's letters were published as "European Correspondence" in *Russell's Magazine.* See note 73, Aug. 23, 1857.

[105] This paper was published as three unsigned articles entitled "Notes on Wine and Vine Culture in France," *Russell's Magazine,* III (June, July, and Sept., 1858), 207-213, 338-345, 501-507.

[106] Simms visited James H. Hammond at Redcliffe (see note 160, Dec. 21, 1856) in late July, arriving on or around July 23. Though he later says he has discarded his plan to write a novel having an Augusta, Ga., setting (see letters to James H. Hammond of July 16 and Aug. 1, 1858), the novel was eventually written and published as "Joscelyn" (see note 282, Nov. 4, 1866).

[107] His speech in the United States Senate on the admission of Kansas. See note 113, March 27, 1858.

872: To James Henry Hammond

Charleston, March 27. [1858] [108]

My dear Hammond.

I have your last letter. When I spoke of making a sensation *in Washington,* I meant only *at Washington,* and among your contemporaries. It was of them that I chiefly spoke. Life in the political field renders men intensely selfish in general, small men jealous, & pretentious persons vain as well as jealous & selfish. That you could make a sensation through the country, I did not doubt, *if you were true to yourself;* and I had my objects, which, no doubt, you have already divined, in the long & earnest, tho' perhaps tedious letter that I sent you.[109] But do not make the mistake of supposing that men defeat their own advancing when they make themselves *felt &* feared. The great body of mankind are exceedingly curlike, and the stroke of the whip, which rouses the noble nature to fury, only compels the masses to lick the hand that scourges. Enough on this head. — I have seen Farrar & Hart.[110] The former is your warm & sturdy supporter. I fancy he

---

[108] Dated by Simms' discussion of the Charleston *Mercury* (see note 110, below). Hammond wrote Simms on March 24, but evidently Simms had not received that letter when this one was written. The letter to which Simms refers in his opening sentence is one which we have not located and which Hammond also mentions in his letter of March 24: "I wrote to you only a day or two ago. . . . " Hammond's reply to this letter of March 27 is dated April 3. The originals are in the Hammond Papers, Library of Congress.

[109] See letter of Jan. 28, 1858.

[110] Probably in January of this year John Heart, co-editor and co-proprietor of the Charleston *Mercury* (see note 133, Aug. 29, 1848), wanted a group of his friends to purchase the shares of the *Mercury* owned by Robert Barnwell Rhett and Robert Barnwell Rhett, Jr. (see introductory sketch of the Rhetts). The *Mercury,* which was at this time heavily in debt, would then become an organ for Hammond, who opposed the violent secessionist views of the Rhetts. Heart's plan also called for Simms to be made editor of the newspaper. Simms forwarded to Hammond a letter he had received from Heart (we have not located Heart's letter or Simms' cover) and Hammond wrote to Simms on Feb. 7 (letter cited note 54, Jan. 28, 1858): "I return you Hearts letter. What, *exactly,* does he want me to do? . . . I want no special organ for myself. I would not have one in particular if I were a Pres. or Emperor. I know well the trouble, embarrassment & disadvantages of mouth pieces, other than one's own mouth. But from old association I would not like to see the Mercury go down. . . . The Rhetts have played the devil with it. But the Rhetts may be in position shortly again. I think the chances are that we shall split the Union on this Kansas matter. . . . A few weeks then you see may bring the Rhetts up. Better wait for that. Yet in the mean time I will give reasonable aid & comfort to the Mercury & Heart, whom I never saw, but have heard is my friend & was so when I lacked friends—such can never be forgotten. As for you the Mercury & all that is beneath you. Don't touch it *responsibly.* My dear fellow, consider yourself, as we *now* consider Milton & Shakespeare. Confide implicitly in the glory you *have achieved* & which will be accorded to

will do Hart's business for him effectually. At least, he will so arrange the machinery that it will be done. The Rhetts are to be bought out by $12,000. But, *inter nos,* there is a heavy debt & mortgage on the Mercury, much more, I fancy, than it would sell for. On seeing the statement, I broached to Hart the propriety of suffering foreclosure of mortgage, & buying the property in open market. It certainly would not bring half the price of the mortgage. But he fears, & probably with reason, that such public sale would affect the prestige of the paper. It will certainly take a long time, & very favorable auspices, to get it into good paying condition. It has been badly managed & edited in a still worse manner. Farrar has been very urgent with me to take hold of it. In a letter from Miles, he intimates the same thing.[111] But this is impossible. I am too old to resume the labours of a daily press, & a political one too; & have besides too much that requires my constant devotion. Now, if you could happen upon the right man, & you are in the way of doing so, it may be well to seize upon him. I have been doing a good deal for the Mercury during the last three years, and have been content with an occasional box of cigars & a demijohn of wine, by way of quid. It is certain that this quid must grow into a very decided consideration to make me continue

you in another age, & don't dabble in any thing unworthy of it in such a way that it shall appear *upon the record."* Simms doubtless communicated some of these views to Heart, and Heart again wrote to Simms, who forwarded his letter to Hammond (we have not located Heart's letter or Simms' cover). In returning Heart's letter, Hammond wrote to Simms on March 24: "I . . . now only drop a line in returning Heart's letter. I wrote to Farrar urging him to assist Heart in his views. If the Mercury was free of the Rhetts & well conducted it would be the most influential paper in the South. I concur in most things with the Rhetts except that at bottom I prefer—at least to *try* the Union—after the Free States have the ascendancy, for if they will have sense enough to drop all this Abolitionism as I rather think they will, & refrain from Sectionalism, we can yet rule the country—I think. It is clear here that but a few care a copper about negroes. They want *power* & *spoils* & have taken this way to get them. But they can't keep them. The South is & ever will be henceforth nearly united & we can always divide the North & govern it essentially. But to keep the South to-gether & the North at bay we must let no aggression pass unnoticed or unresisted. Yet there is no necessity for croaking, for denouncing, for keeping our voices always strained to the highest key & using no language but vituperation as the Rhetts do, & can't help doing."

Samuel S. Farrar, a native of Virginia, came to Charleston in 1826 and was employed by the house of Fleming, Ross and Co. In 1832 he founded a wholesale grocery business, which the Charleston *Directory* for 1859 lists as S. S. Farrar, Bros. and Co., at the corner of East Bay and Cumberland streets. His partners in the firm were his brothers, Charles D. and John C. Farrar, and Stephen Owens. He died on April 27, 1861, and his obituary appears in the Charleston *Mercury* of April 29.

Simms frequently misspells Heart's name. See following letters.

[111] Doubtless William Porcher Miles' letter of Feb. 24, which we have not located. See note 76, Feb. 8, 1858.

doing even so much as I have done.[112] — In respect to your speech, you have every reason to be satisfied.[113] There is scarcely any difference of opinion in the State. Your friends are all satisfied. As regards the Edgefield paper, I fancy that its tone & temper will hurt nobody so much as the Editor. I suppose you can readily conjecture the influence under which he writes.[114] — I met Henry Gourdin [115] a few days ago. He has been cold towards you hitherto. Why, I know not unless because of some Columbia influence. He is now enthusiastic, as far as his temperament can be so, in your favour. He speaks of you as the proper leader of the State, & worthy to wear the mantle of Calhoun. In fact, I have found my eulogies cold & tame in comparison with most that I

---

[112] In his reply of April 3 Hammond writes: "From the expose of the Mercury I think with you that the mortgage should be foreclosed & the property sold. Something of prestige might be lost for a time—but not $40,000 worth. It is too much to expect any sensible man to give $10,000 or $12,000 for *liabilities* amounting to $56,000 & assets worth at most $25,000. I would not do it or ask any friend to do it. Let the paper be sold. Heart can buy it— clear of debt for $20,000. That will be $5,000 for prestige, for a New Mercury can be set up for $15,000 with New Type &c. &c.

"Now for an Editor I concur that besides your other business & your inclinations it is a position below your reputation, unless like [William Cullen] Bryant you had been at it always. But how would Col. E. B. Bryan do? Ask Heart & others, & let me say *he can be got.* How would Godard Bailey do? He is now here in an office of $1800, & Miles & Keitt say he is vastly improved & would do *well.*" For Simms' further discussion of the *Mercury* (eventually purchased by the Rhetts), see letter to Hammond of April 12, 1858.

Edward Benjamin Bryan, of St. John's, Colleton District, S. C., was graduated from the United States Military Academy and after his retirement from the army served in the South Carolina House and Senate. He was a contributor to the *Southern Quarterly Review* during Simms' editorship. He died on April 28, 1861, at the age of thirty-five (see the Charleston *Mercury* of April 29, 1861). In 1858 Godard Bailey, a native of Charleston and former bank officer in that city, was employed as a clerk in the Department of the Interior (see the Washington *Directory* for that year).

[113] Hammond's speech in favor of the admission of Kansas under the Lecompton Constitution was delivered on March 4 (see the *Congressional Globe,* 35 Cong., 1 Sess., pp. 959-962, and *Appendix to the Congressional Globe,* 35 Cong., 1 Sess., pp. 68-71). It was printed as a pamphlet (Washington: Printed by L. Towers, 1858) and is included in *Selections from the Letters and Speeches of the Hon. James H. Hammond, of South Carolina* (New York: John F. Trow & Co., Printers, 1866), pp. 301-322. The speech was enthusiastically praised in Southern newspapers, and a few Northern ones gave it their approval, though in general the North was resentful (see Elizabeth Merritt, *James Henry Hammond* [Baltimore: The Johns Hopkins Press, 1923], pp. 118-119).

[114] The Edgefield *Advertiser* of March 17 says of Hammond's speech: "It is a performance of uncommon merit, both as to matter and manner, and our readers will find themselves well repaid for the slight trouble of reading it. Although its facts are not new, they are yet for the most part true and forcible . . . and the effort as a whole, although perhaps injudiciously timed, is worthy of its author's antecedents. . . . " We are unable to identify the editor of the *Advertiser* at this time; the masthead of the newspaper gives the proprietors as A. Simkins, D. R. Durisoe and Elijah Keese.

[115] See note 8, Jan. 30, 1851.

heard. For while I was willing to say you had done well & ably, I yet knew what you could do, & how much better & abler you could be, with a little more familiarity with the scene. I could have wished especially that you had carried out your matter to a more elaborately wrought conclusion. Your finish was an abrupt one, leaving still a good deal to be said. Of course, I knew what you were likely to say, in such a scene, at such a time, & on such subjects. It is enough for me that you struck the right chord *for the South*. The first great lesson is to teach our people their strength & resources, & in what they consist. If we can break down the tariff to a nominal thing, we can get direct trade, not before, & direct trade for the South is the first great essential of independence, next to the formation of our own opinion. I will do what I can for the Mercury, but cannot do much unless at great self-sacrifice — or rather the sacrifice of objects which ought to be of paramount consideration with me. I am poor as a church mouse, & need all my time & energies in placing our domestic affairs in paying condition. But of these matters when next we meet. — There is a matter upon which you can enable me to do an old neighbor a kindness. Capt. Thos. Paine, U. S. N. is one of those whom the *retiring* Board sought to shelve. He has challenged investigation & is quite able to do it. He is sober, honest, gentlemanly, has never disobeyed orders, & never been charged with offense. The Secretary [116] has answered him that there is nothing against him. He has petitioned the President [117] & Miles has charge of the process and is in full cognizance of all the facts. Do consult him, & see the President. I can assure you confidently of the truth of all that is here said. He has been mutilated in battle; one leg being supplied with wooden extensions (War of 1812) and his only offence is, perhaps, that he has lost his best teeth in the service. He is an old man, but vigorous. There is something base in a Gov. which tries to get rid of this class of officers on miserable pretences. If they are to be shelved, let it be by operation of law, & such as has no *ex post facto* operation. Let them understand, when entering the service, what they have to expect. Otherwise, let them be cashiered, upon trial, for vicious practice or incompetence. To fling them aside after they have done a life-long duty, and when their emoluments have accus-

---

[116] Isaac Toucey (1792-1869), of Connecticut, was secretary of the navy at this time.

[117] James Buchanan.

tomed them to a certain mode of life, is eminently cruel. To keep
them in suspense in respect to their fate is quite as bad. This man
has nothing but old age against him. He was never a brilliant
man, but he fought like a Trojan. Do serve me, & see the President, and do what you can for the old sea dog. He believes that
you can do every thing; has been to me this evening, & I promised him cheerfully to write & entreat you. See Miles, who will
put you in possession of all the facts in the case.[118] — There: you
have a long scribble. May it prove in some degree satisfactory.
If it is not, pray suppose my capacity not equal to my will. In
truth, I doubt if my faculties are not failing me. I cudgel my
brains in vain for adequate thought for any occasion. My best
regards to your wife & Kate. God bless & strengthen you for
your work.

Yours Ever truly

W. Gilmore Simms.

J. H. H.

873: To William Porcher Miles

Charleston March 27. [1858] [119]

My dear Miles.

Do not trouble yourself about the seeds. When I mentioned
the Guinea Squash, & Tomato, I wished to improve upon what
we had, thinking that the Dept. dealt only in choice varieties, &
recieved them from abroad.[120] — I have just written to Hammond
to beg him to cooperate with you in reference to the case of Capt.
Paine, who is a worthy man whose only offence is that he has
been suffered to lose his teeth in the service, and to acquire a
habit of life from his previous emoluments, which it will not be
easy for him to abandon at near 70. In respect to the Mercury,
I have been conferring with some of Hammonds friends & with
Hart. Any change of proprietorship would no doubt benefit the
paper. It needs new auspices & better editorship. But I would

---

[118] Capt. Samuel G. Kelly, of the Division of Naval History, Department
of the Navy, writes us that Capt. Paine, a native of Rhode Island, who spent
most of his service in the navy in and around Charleston, was placed on the
reserve list on Sept. 13, 1855, and that his status had not been changed at the
time of his death on Nov. 9, 1859.

[119] Dated by Simms' reference to his letter to Hammond of the same date.
The MS. of this letter is badly water-stained.

[120] See letter of March 21.

not have Hammond to own a dollar in it. The establishment scarcely pays expences now, & is heavily in debt. The Bank of the State alone holds a mortgage upon it of $17,000, & Rhett demands $12,000 for his share, while there are other floating debts which will probably bring it up to $40,000. Of course, all this is confidential. The amount absolutely necessary to be raised will be that of Rhett. The paper then can keep up its current progress by its current reciepts. I counselled Hart to suffer its foreclosure of mortgage & buy it at public sale, when, I have no doubt, he could get it at half the money. But he objects, that some of the prestige of the paper would be forfeited by the exposure. Perhaps so. In respect to myself, I feel too old, too weary, & have too many domestic & personal cares, to say nothing of the interests of my profession, to involve myself more deeply in its conduct than I have been doing. In fact, I shall have to lessen my labours upon it, as the only equivalent I have ever got has been my cigars & an occasional demijohn of strong waters. It is scarcely possible that I should take any decided part in the conduct of the Mercury. To edit it well, will require not only great ability but unwearied devotion to the one duty. It has been very badly conducted for ten years. All the papers of Charleston lack industry even when not utterly wanting in talent. Shall I, at fifty, now descend to the drudgery of a daily press? No, *mon ami*, it is impossible. I am growing worthless. My brains no longer obey my will. I feel that power is passing from me. — The debate on the Kanzas question in the house, will probably provoke you into speech.[121] Wait the occasion & be prepared for, but do not *seek* it. You will find adequate ideas *if you let yourself alone.* Your temperament will force you into the field, & *if you will forget yourself* — forget that any body hears or looks to you, you will do credit to yourself & argument. Be bold! bold! bold! We are simply planting the dragon's teeth, & must not be mortified because such seed do not instantly bear fruit. Grasp your subject fully. What is that? Not Kanzas. The d——d region, as I told Butler long ago, could never be a slave state. Missouri itself is only nominally so and only because [*two or three words illegible*] the cotton & sugar growing regions. The others are only partially Slave States, kept in position by prestige & pride rather than by interest. Let your arguments show to the tropical states,

---

[121] Miles spoke on March 31. See letter to him of April 12.

if I may so call them. The course of Hunter, Crittenden [122] &
others, is not the result of their Know Nothing proclivities. It is
due wholly to their situation, which, as they say in Mississippi,
is a State of Betweenity. They will go with us if we separate,
because of our merchants & manufacturers, & finally seek to kill
the goose that lays them the Golden Eggs, just as the North
seeks now, because of the arrogance of wealth — that arrogance
that goes before fall. But, I must stop. I am wearied with the pen.
I have just scrawled a long letter to Hammond. He is true. I
could wish to be with you both just now for a season. But, I
am greatly troubled — embarrassed in domestic & pecuniary efforts, with hardly thought enough to determine heads or tails on
the toss of a copper. God bless you, my dear fellow, & help
you. Keep you calm. Be cool, bold, prompt. You *feel* the right,
& this is the best secret of eloquence, if you can only forget yourself.

Yours truly &c

W. Gilmore Simms.

874: To James Henry Hammond [123]

Charleston. April 12. 1858

My dear Hammond.

I can only write you a hurried letter as I am busied in preparations to take my wife up to the plantation tomorrow. She is
feeble & needs change of air. I have my hands full just now of a
variety of toils, some of which are complicated. I had a long interview with Hart two days ago, & went with him over the affairs of the Mercury.[124] There is a debt, as far as I could learn,
of near $40,000 apart from the $12,000 that Rhett requires for
his share. Hart asked $10,000 for his. It is understood that Hart
or Rhett is to buy out the other. I exhorted H. to sell, and not
to buy. The R's can't buy. If they do, they are ruined. H. really
keeps up the paper. It is his constant application & pressing ex-

---

[122] John Jordan Crittenden (1787-1863), United States senator from Kentucky (1817-1819, 1835-1841, 1842-1848, 1855-1861) and member of Congress
(1861-1863), was a strong Unionist.

[123] This letter is a reply to Hammond's dated April 3. Hammond's answer
is dated May 3. The originals are in the Hammond Papers, Library of
Congress.

[124] For Simms' and Hammond's earlier discussion about the Charleston
Mercury, see letter of March 27, 1858.

ertions that get the patronage, the advertising custom, & the
discounts in Bank. And he does all the office work. Old Rhett
writes an occasional article, always on the one text;[125] Young
Rhett's work upon the paper might be done by an ordinary man in
20 minutes per diem. If R. became sole proprietor he would lose
all patronage, get no business, no Bank favours; and to maintain
the paper for one year out of his own pocket would ruin him. If he
buys, the establishment will be in market in 12 months & under
foreclosure of mortgage, & in that event it could be bought for
$10,000 or less, — scarcely more. I urged all these things upon
H. and he agreed. At his request I called to see Farrar; but he
not being in, I communicated the affair confidentially to his
brother, who was already aware of the interest that Sam had
taken in the matter.[126] Heart is satisfied to follow my advice. Between ourselves, the sooner he gets out of the concern the better.
A new paper could be started with no encumbrances. But of
this, hereafter. We discussed the subject of the Editorship. But
he asserts that neither Bryan nor Bailey would answer, and I
am inclined to agree with him.[127] The former rides the hobby of
the African Slave trade, and talked of Adams as his backer. You
will probably be sought as an ally of A. for the Senate. Do not
commit yourself in any way. He is not the man to make any
sacrifices for you. He did not. You owe him nothing. He wrote
to me that you stood no chance of election unless you went to
Columbia. He was cool decidedly &, I fancy something more
than indifferent.[128] Bailey will never be worth any thing. He is a
desultory man, who, as an Editor would do nothing. In his necessity alone, has he buckled down to an office which leaves him
no discretion. Besides, the Editorship of the Mercury would never
yield *him* $1800, since it would require that there should be an
assistant. Bryan has been to see Heart, & the latter says, came

---

[125] Secession.

[126] Samuel S. Farrar had two brothers, Charles and John. See note 110,
March 27, 1858.

[127] In his letter to Simms of April 3 Hammond had suggested Edward
Benjamin Bryan or Godard Bailey as possible editors of the *Mercury* (see
Hammond's remarks, quoted in note 112, March 27, 1858).

[128] In his message to the legislature of Nov. 24, 1856, James Hopkins Adams
(1812-1861), governor of South Carolina during 1854-1856, had recommended
the revival of foreign trade in slaves (see *House Journal,* pp. 34-37, and *Senate
Journal,* pp. 10-13). In 1858 he was an isolationist and was strongly supported
by a faction in that group during the senatorial election which took place in
late 1858, when James Chesnut, Jr. (see introductory sketch), was elected.
See Harold S. Schultz, *Nationalism and Sectionalism in South Carolina 1852-
1860* (Durham, N. C.: Duke University Press, 1950), pp. 171, 176n.

to him *drunk*. Of course, he would not employ him. I suggested to H. the name of Elwood Fisher, whom I do not personally know. He says that E. F. would do, but for the fact that his manners are bad; that he is pragmatical, disputatious, & would consume his time in ostentatious habits, — carriage & pair, — & in controversies at the street corners in which his rugged, dogmatical temper would only make enemies for the establishment.[129] Truly, the getting of the right sort of man, as Editor, is not the least difficult thing in the way of such a paper.[130] I am to leave town as I said tomorrow, to be absent probably two weeks. If in that space of time you write me, address me at Midway. What you say touching myself in connection with a certain office, is simply a proof of your friendly judgment.[131] In our country I am regarded simply as a Poet & Novelist, & even in these capacities they know not exactly where to rank me. But they are all satisfied that such persons have no practical virtues, & as for statesmanship, they would as soon think of making a statesman out of whipt syllabub as out of a Poet of any degree, good, bad, or indifferent. In this state of our public opinion, I long since gave up the idea of being any thing in the Body Politic. I am too old now for the necessary training, and this in connection with the fact that nothing can come of the suggestion, is sufficient for us, whatever my convictions, or yours in my favour, to keep us from any exposure of them. — I have written all this nervously and hurriedly. Something, — perhaps the season — makes me unwellish — feverish, with singular lassitude & self abandon. I have a great deal of work on hand, & try to do it; but I labor languidly & I fear inefficiently. Write

---

[129] Fisher (1808-1862), a native of Lynchburg, Va., who lived in Cincinnati, Ohio, during the 1840's, was an attorney and the author of *Lecture on the North and the South, Delivered before the Young Men's Mercantile Library Association, of Cincinnati, Ohio, January 16, 1849* (Charleston: Printed by A. J. Burke, 1849), which Hammond had reviewed in the *Southern Quarterly Review* (see letter to Tucker of April 5, 1849). At the time of his death Fisher was living in Atlanta, Ga. (see *S. L. M.*, XXXIV [Sept. and Oct., 1862], 585).

[130] In June the Rhetts took over the *Mercury*. Robert Barnwell Rhett, Jr., became the editor and undertook to give the paper a somewhat more moderate tone than that employed previously. See Laura A. White, *Robert Barnwell Rhett: Father of Secession* (New York: The Century Co., [1931]), pp. 145-146.

[131] In his letter of April 3 Hammond writes: "See here Simms (*inter nos*) various sets are trying to use my name & influence in So Ca for selfish purposes & especially to send me a colleague here. I mean to steer clear of all that. I will have no hand in it. If I could name a colleague if I *must* name one, I mean to name *you*. I would not turn on my heel for choice among the rest. But I would stay my time out here with you for a co-adjutor & I think you are the *very man.*"

to me at Midway if you can. Your letters are grateful. I have some troubles & doubts, which I will not inflict upon you in a letter. When you get a good opportunity — do not *force* one, by any means, — speak one more speech this Session, if only to confirm & deepen the impression of your first speech. Follow out the train of thought & argument in that — it is the right vein — the country as an entirety & in its true relations. A third speech might enable you to rise to a figure of vision, the boldest flight of rhetoric in which you could take a prophetic survey of the probable future. But that third speech would keep for another Session.[132] Here, all's right with you. Keep your ground, & say little. Be circumspect in your correspondence. There are those who have been heard to say that they *counselled your speech*. Regards to Mrs. H.

Yours Ever truly

Simms

875: To James Henry Hammond

Charleston April 12, 1858

My dear Hammond.

I had just closed one letter to you, when I remembered a matter about which my interest with you, and yours with the President has been already invoked. I allude to the affair of Capt. Thos. Paine, of the Navy, about which I wrote you some ten days ago.[133] Miles is acquainted with all the particulars & with the object of his application. The old man is in trouble. His son has recently failed in business & has involved him, according to the belief here, in a loss of some 12 or 15000 dollars, perhaps the extent of all his savings for his old age. He has been to see me several times, and his distress must excuse his importunity. If you can do any thing with President or department, it will be perhaps quite as much an act of justice as charity, for the old man is faultless. He has demanded trial & investigation, and is told that there are no charges against him. He is a sober man, has

---

[132] In his reply of May 3 Hammond writes: "You say I must speak again. There will be no proper occasion again this Session to discuss fully the Relations of North & South, or for much speaking on any subject." He did, however, deliver a short speech on British aggression (see Simms' letter to him of June 10, 1858).

[133] See letter of March 27.

never once been charged with offence or disobedience; and the case is one in which the President may properly interfere. Do see what can be done, as promptly as possible, & let me know.

Yours Ever truly

Simms

876: To William Porcher Miles

Charleston, 12 April [1858][134]

My dear Miles.

I have just time to say that I thank you for your letter, and promise to read your speech, when I recieve it, with the interest of a friend & the scrutiny of a critic.[135] I have no doubt that you have done yourself credit. Only, in speaking, do not attempt fine writing. Remember, you are to be a debater in Congress, not an orator. Beware, at all times, of being essayical. Be as direct and earnest as possible. You only need time & practice. You have the necessary resources for argument, & you have the energy of a vigorous manhood. Do not distrust yourself; and do not take too much pains with yourself. Let yourself as much alone as possible. Lose yourself always in your subject, and Be Bold! Bold! Bold! as was written on all the chamber doors in the Enchanted Castle of Spenser — over all but *one,* upon which was written — Be not *too* bold![136] — I propose to go tomorrow to the plantation for two weeks. If, meanwhile, your speech be published, address me copies both at Charleston, & at Midway P. Offices. Let me beg you to do me another favour. I have a fair friend & young kinswoman recently married, in whose behalf I solicited from Keitt—she is one of his Constituents — supplies of seeds for the vegetable & flower gardens. With his usual carelessness he has neglected to send any. Will you supply her? If you can, send her all that you can, for both gardens. She is particularly fond of flowers. Address her, "Mrs. Dr. William Fuller.
     Pocotaligo, P. O.
     South Carolina."

---

[134] On the back of this letter Miles wrote: "Ansd.—Ap. 22nd/58."

[135] On March 31 Miles delivered in the House of Representatives a speech in favor of the admission of Kansas under the Lecompton Constitution. See *Appendix to the Congressional Globe,* 35 Cong., 1 Sess., pp. 285-289.

[136] *Faerie Queene,* Book III, Canto xi, Stanza 54. This quotation appears to have been one of Simms' favorites (see letter to Tucker of May 30, 1850).

The sooner you execute this commission the better. Night before last, I spent 3 hours with J. W. M. [137] He was well, as usual; so were all the family. God bless you, mon ami, & endow you for your duties with the necessary wisdom & courage.

Yours Ever truly

W. Gilmore Simms.

P. S. I note what you say touching the Mercury & the Editor. But, find, upon inquiry, that the persons named for the latter duties, will *not* do. There are sufficient reasons shown, but of this hereafter.[138]

877: To James Henry Hammond

Woodlands, May 8. 1858.

My dear Hammond.

I see by the papers that your Colleague, Judge Evans, has succumbed to Fate, and left his place vacant. It will be supplied, temporarily, I presume, by the Governor's appointment, and who that will be will be a difficult question; as he is, though a Gentleman, a man of kinks & biases, finicking and likely to be led into the appointment of some outré favorite. *Nous verrons.* My object in writing you thus promptly, is to beg that you will take no part in the nomination of a successor. It would only do you harm to do so; and any inclination towards myself, such as you manifested in a previous letter, would be quite useless.[139] Even were it otherwise, your participation in the affair, would only make you many enemies. Better evade the subject wholly, which you can easily do, excusing yourself on the score of delicacy & propriety. Left to themselves, your friends will probably rally on Chestnut;[140] & he will be your best ally, in the quarter from whence he comes, & where your friends need a proper point d'appui. He will neutralize, at home, the hostile influences of

---

[137] James Warley Miles. See introductory sketch of the Miles brothers.

[138] Miles, like Hammond, probably suggested Edward Benjamin Bryan and Godard Bailey. See note 112, March 27, 1858, and letter to Hammond of April 12, 1858.

[139] Josiah James Evans (see note 245, Dec. 15, 1852) died on May 6. Governor Robert Francis Withers Allston (see note 312, Nov. 30, 1847) appointed Arthur Peronneau Hayne as his successor (see letter to Hammond of May 15, 1858). In his letter to Simms of April 3 Hammond had expressed a desire to support Simms for the Senate (see note 131, April 12, 1858).

[140] James Chesnut, Jr. Simms frequently misspells his name.

Sumter, and Columbia,[141] especially if supported by your friends. Many of them concieve themselves in some degree indebted to him, for timely withdrawal from the late Canvas, enabling you to ride in without effort & on so triumphant a majority. Let them requite the obligation, if they think it one, and thus do you a real service, in giving you a really clever colleague, who, I think will under the circumstances, naturally attach himself to your cohort. I am speaking honestly, my dear Hammond, for whatever my political ambition might have been, it is very fairly burnt out; & whatever my vanity may be, I am still satisfied to feed it, in my own obscure fashion, as a simple bookworm. I may believe, as you do, that I could very worthily fill the vacated seat; at least quite as well as any whom we *now* can send. But, satisfied that the notion of success would be idle, and burdened as I am with so large a family, & so many home cares, I am resigned to this Fate which would seem to have denied a field to all my more youthful aspirations. It is probable that the friends of Orr [142] will now bring him forward. Let the contest be between Chesnut & himself, and do you wink neither on the one nor the other. You can afford to let the game be played out without your intervention & it is your policy that it should. I write without any knowledge of the public tendencies at home. It is probable that through Keitt, Boyce [143] &c you will be better informed in Washington than I am here. I hope so. Of course, you will be governed by circumstances, & I only speak so far as the game appears to me. Meanwhile, take no one man in Washington into your fullest confidence. I would sooner have you trust Miles than any body there. He is above all trickery. But better commit yourself on this subject to none. Let your hands be free of all participation in a struggle, in which, elect whom they will *now,* the party can really be only *mediocre.* Preserve your ascendancy by your forbearance. — My Cotton is very promising. All up & some with four leaves; the Corn also full of promise. I plant 270 acres Cotton & 300 of Corn; and if things continue as they promise, **I** shall be able to wipe off all scores of my old father in law. I am

---

[141] Simms is here referring to the Hamptons, of Columbia, and the Mannings, of the High Hills of Santee, near Sumter, both opponents of Hammond.

[142] James Lawrence Orr. See introductory sketch.

[143] William Waters Boyce (1818-1890), a native of Charleston, was admitted to the bar in 1839 and practiced law in Winnsboro, S. C. He was a member of Congress from March 4, 1853, until his resignation on Dec. 21, 1860. He was a member of the Confederate Congress, and in 1866 moved to Washington, D. C., where he practiced law until his retirement a few years before his death.

here alone, my family all in the city. I shall be here all the month; and be up at intervals throughout the summer. I am resolved to devote myself to the recovery of lost ground, & to make the interest a paying one, if this be possible. Present me gratefully to Mrs. H. & Kate. What's Paul [144] doing. Don't let him hang about Washington. I wrote Harry some time ago, acknowledging a nice little present he sent me.[145] I heard of him afterwards on a brief visit to the city; but he has not answered me yet.

God bless you, my friend, and make you wise.

Yours faithfully

W. Gilmore Simms

878: To JAMES HENRY HAMMOND

Woodlands. May 9. [1858] [146]

My dear Hammond.

Since writing you yesterday, a packet from the city brings me your letter of the 3d. I have noted its contents, & see that your brother members are even more incompetent than I thought them.[147] I do not see how you could have done otherwise than you

---

[144] Hammond's son. See note 87, Oct. 4, 1853.

[145] See letter to Harry Hammond of March 27, 1858.

[146] This letter is in reply to Hammond's dated May 3, 1858 (cited note 123, April 12, 1858).

[147] In his letter of May 3 Hammond writes: "You have heard before now that the Con. Rep. has been adopted by both Houses & Kansas admitted with Lecompton so far as Congress can admit her. I send you the Globe with the principal speeches. Read To[o]mbs & Sewards or the marked passages. The South here unanimously concur that there was no concession, no compromise, & the North says with one breath there was & in the next that there was not. It was funny to see them squirming. I objected & still do to the bungling & improper phraseology of the Bill. There was no occasion to refer to admission or rejection, as *we had decided that,* & the question was a very different, though it involved it—a thing that could not have been avoided in any event save by giving Kansas *all* she asked. I had the bill essentially modified before it was reported for it provided that the votes should read 'for proposition & *admission*' or 'against proposition & admission' which was very distinctly voting for or against admission in direct form; & if instead of leaving Hunter & Stephens to make my objections I had gone myself to Green & English they would have erased every objectionable word as I ascertained when too late. They had not been informed of my other objections. This must not be put in the papers however. I was sorry Quitman & Bonham went off. They have gained no reputation for sense or Statesmanship by it." The men Hammond here mentions are as follows: Robert Toombs (1810-1885), senator from Georgia; William Henry Seward (1801-1872), senator from New York; Robert Mercer Taliaferro Hunter (1809-1887), senator from Virginia; Alexander Hamilton Stephens (1812-1883), representative from Georgia; James Stephen Green (1817-1870), senator from Missouri; William Hayden English (1822-

did, in the Kansas question. The course of Bonham was *ad cap-
tandum.*[148] He would out-herod herod. That is all. I take for
granted that it did not much matter how any of the Southern
members voted. The Kanzas imbroglio is only made worse in
Congress; and I had from the first, as I told Butler, come to the
conclusion that K. could never be a free state, & that the delusion
of making it such, would only work to the diversion of our attention from other & more serious matters; as I assume it was
meant to do. For the present the thing is ended, & the country
has so much gain to congratulate herself upon, as it takes for the
time, the matter out of the hands of Congress, where, it is quite
impossible that the South should gain anything substantial now.
— When I said — you should speak again,[149] it was only with
regard to the probable opportunity & necessity. Your policy is no
doubt judicious; and, holding yourself in reserve, and gaining
foothold, you will no doubt be able to strike more to the purpose
whenever you shall deem it necessary to square off to an antagonist. Still, though no doubt very well to disarm, when you can,
a jealous rivalry, by a judicious forbearance, I would not have
you suffer a single good opportunity to escape you, of putting in
a facer. Your *rôle* was the right one, that of eschewing, with contempt, all the small politics of parties, and generalizing only with
regard to the grand interests of the federation. Nor do I counsel
set speeches; but a vigilant watch over the debate, when the
speakers are the best men, will enable you to put in effectually in
the colloquial way, or in that semi colloquial way in which, I
fancy you would particularly excel. It may be possible, for you,
before the Session closes, to double up certain of the assailants
of your speech, and confirm fully the impression which it made.
Not that this is necessary, but that I like a politician to rivet his
nails as well as drive them. My chief reason for desiring [150] you
to take the field again, was personal. I confess myself anxious
that you should make yourself felt, silencing every thing like cavil
or doubt. — In respect to the crop, I am of opinion that the frost
did far less injury than was believed. I think it likely, nay certain, that all your cotton, which was up on the high dry lands,

---

1896), representative from Indiana; John Anthony Quitman (1799-1858), representative from Mississippi; and Milledge Luke Bonham (1813-1890), representative from South Carolina.

[148] For Bonham's remarks in the House of Representatives on April 29 and
30, see *Congressional Globe,* 35 Cong., 1 Sess., pp. 1887ff.

[149] See Simms' first letter to Hammond of April 12.

[150] Simms wrote *desire.*

escaped without hurt. It has been so in all places that I have seen. It is so with me. The frost only struck to the roots with the cotton in swamp, bottom or wet lands. Some of my neighbours, who had planted their swamp lands first — very foolishly — were compelled to plough up & replant; but in all other descriptions of land, there was no harm done, except in small occasional spots, more or less damp & wet. The peaches are unhurt; the plums, &c. In the gardens the green peas slightly; the snap beans; but not mortally. The corn is nipt only, & not killed. This is true, as far as I can hear throughout the district, & I take for granted that your lands have fared no worse than ours. Once more, God bless you.

Yours truly

W. G. S.

P. S. I have recieved some documents from you & Miles, and noticed them Editorially in the Mercury.[151] — By the way, did you get my Letter touching Captain Paine, and will you be able to do any thing for the old man.[152] He comes to me when in town, with a very sad & wistful visage. When you can report any thing decisive, do let me hear.

879: To James Henry Hammond

Woodlands, S. C. 15 May. [1858] [153]

My dear Hammond.

You have a colleague, *pro tem.* and *such* a colleague![154] You remember the conjecture which I expressed recently in regard to the appointment as probably to be made by the Govr., drawing my conclusion from what I know of the *petit* & *finicking* na-

---

[151] In an article on the "Patent Office Report," Charleston *Mercury* of May 1, Simms writes: "We must acknowledge, generally, the sundry favors we owe to our Senator, Gen. Hammond, and our immediate Representative, the Hon. Mr. Miles, in the various speeches of members, and publications of Government which, from time to time, we have had at their hands. . . ."

[152] See letters of March 27 and April 12 (second).

[153] Hammond's reply to this letter is dated May 21, 1858. The original is in the Hammond Papers, Library of Congress.

[154] Arthur Peronneau Hayne (1790-1867), brother of Robert Young Hayne, was appointed by Governor Robert Francis Withers Allston to fill the vacancy in the United States Senate caused by the death of Josiah James Evans (see letter to James H. Hammond of May 8). Hayne served from May 11 to Dec. 2, 1858.

ture of the latter.[155] Could ever the event more completely justify
the conjecture. I cannot resist the impulse of submitting to you the
enclosed which I have just recieved from young Paul Hayne, the
nephew of the new Senator.[156] He pours out his indignation with
a natural burst of feeling which will please, perhaps, while it
amuses you. Of course, I need not say to you that it would never
do for any body besides ourselves to see or hear of this enclosure;
so laugh over it, and send it back to me quietly. I send it rather
to show that there were others, it would seem — & to my great
surprise — even in Charleston, to think with yourself in respect
to this position, in connection with my name. Let me add that if
I had been asked, I should have predicted Allston's exact course
in the matter — could almost have spotted his man.[157] But I am
headachy. God bless you.

Yours Ever

W. Gilmore Simms

880: To James Henry Hammond

Charleston, 21 May. [1858] [158]

dear Hammond.

Enclosed I cover you a letter which I recieved when at the
plantation. You will see, from a portion of the contents, why I
send it to you. Return it to me when you have read.[159] I only
wish you to be possessed of what is public opinion here. I presume you know enough of your new colleague to know exactly
how to treat him. Of course, with the most distinguished but

---

[155] See letter of May 8.

[156] We have not located this letter from Paul Hamilton Hayne (see introductory sketch). His father, Paul Hamilton Hayne, Sr. (1803-1831), was a
younger brother of Arthur Peronneau Hayne.

[157] In his reply of May 21 Hammond writes: "Col. Hayne took his seat
yesterday. . . . I would have asked Allston to appoint you but I was sure he
would have appointed any body rather than one recommended by me. How
would you like to come on at least for the next Session? . . . I think it would
be a good thing for *you*, to spend one winter here & let it be seen what you
can do. If no political advancement followed, it would be pleasant & useful to
you in many ways, & afford agreeable reminiscences. If you will encourage
your friends I think you can be elected as from what I understand Allston
appointed Hayne under the understanding that he did not desire to come back.
Doubtless Allston would like it himself."

[158] Dated by Simms' discussion of Governor Robert Francis Withers Allston's
appointment of Arthur Peronneau Hayne to the United States Senate. See
letter to Hammond of May 15.

[159] We have not located this letter.

formal courtesy. He is a wonderful peacock, very absurd & silly, but a gentleman, — excruciatingly nice; honorable & courteous; but it will be well so to carry yourself as to leave no one in doubt that there is no intellectual intercourse between you. I feel shocked at the idea that, any how, his *niaiseries* will, in some degree, fasten upon his colleagues & the State that sends him. I intimated that Allston would send you some *outré* monster,[160] & never was prediction more completely verified. When I left the country on Monday last, my crop, & the crops generally were doing well. But we were beginning to want rain. But night before last, we had fine showers here, & last night another. I presume that these have extended to the interior. They looked as if they were pretty general. If so, I have no doubt that you are doing as well in your section as we in ours. And our fields have rarely looked more promising. I had cotton with six leaves, & we were beginning to thin out.

God bless you.
Yours faithfully

W. Gilmore Simms.

J. H. H.

881: To James Henry Hammond [161]

Woodlands, S. C.

June 2. 1858.

My dear Hammond.

Do not, I pray you, say a single word about the Senate.[162] It will not suit me at all, even if there were any prospect of my election; which there is not. I feel that it is quite too late in life to commence a new vocation, & one of such exacting responsibilities & onerous duties. I can well concieve how willing you are to escape from it. But you must hold on yet awhile. It better suits you than me; and you better suit it. Your mind has been kept in training for it, & you had the advantage of an early novitiate. The case is far otherwise with me. My ideas now revolve in a

---

[160] See letter of May 8.

[161] This letter is a reply to Hammond's of May 21. Hammond's reply to this letter and those of June 10 and June 11 is dated June 20. The originals are in the Hammond Papers, Library of Congress.

[162] See Hammond's remarks in his letter of May 21, quoted in note 157, May 15, 1858.

narrow, almost a domestic circle, & my mind is almost fettered
to one province of art & exercise, so exclusively as to forbid that
I should enter *con amore* upon another, and unless one goes lovingly to public duties, they will be irksome, and he will not do
himself honour. If I went to the Senate, I should be trying to do
something; and I should have a great deal more to learn, than
I could learn with ease; and I am totally out of practise as a
debater and public speaker. I should be expected to take the floor,
& should myself desire to do so; but to prepare for this, as I
should, would cost me more anxious labour than I am willing,
at my latter days, to encounter. I am losing all ambition & will
be content now to slide gently through the rest of my life, as one
goes down a placid river, shaded by foliage, with a gentle breeze,
to be lost finally in the great ocean. Do not, therefore, I pray you,
do any thing to make me thought of in the capacity of a Senator.
Ten years ago, I should have been very proud of the field, but
I have lost my impulse to exertion, & the distinction enters my
ear only as a drowsy purring of a fat tabby on the hearth rug. It
is pleasantly murmurous, I grant you, but if it means that I must
waken, burnish & buckle on armour, & take the spear in hand,
in God's name, let us have none of it. — And yet, I confess, it
was pleasant to learn that when it was reported in Charleston
that I had recieved the appointment, the language of the people
was unqualified approval. Disgust followed when H. recieved
the appointment. Allston told Richardson [163] who congratulated
him on my appointment, that he could not appoint me, though
he had thought of me, because he *could not see & have a conference* with me. What about? To ask, no doubt, if I would be
a Candidate. He, it is reported, is desirous of the place. Had he
made me any such suggestion, I would have treated it as an indignity! What right has a Governor, appointing a fit man to a
public office, as we are to assume he does, make it a condition
that he shall not serve in the office for which he is fitted & shall
not seek it. I will seize on an early opportunity to expose the impudence & the absurdity of this sort of requisition, which is one
quite familiar, I believe, among our Governors. [164] — You are

---

[163] Probably Francis DeLiesseline Richardson, Charleston lawyer, who had
been a member of the State legislature during 1848-1849. Richardson was the
brother of Maynard Davis Richardson, one of Simms' earliest friends (see letters
to Lawson of Oct. 25, 1832, and Jan. 19, 1833).

[164] We have not located any such exposé by Simms.

to have a dinner in Barnwell, & I will try & get to it.[165] But I am very busy. Corn & Cotton both looking well here, but beginning to suffer from drought. Address me at Charleston, as I shall go down next Monday.[166] My best regards to Mrs. H. & Kate.

God bless you.

W. G. S.

J. H. H.

882: To James Henry Hammond [167]

Charleston, June 10. 1858.

My dear Hammond.

Your last brief speech, I have read with a great deal of pleasure, and though evidently effortless, it is here spoken of everywhere with great favour.[168] It is a seasonable *caveat* well administered & at the right moment. I write now hurriedly, having only just got to town, to say that the occasion is one which you can use very admirably, though you may not fully concur with my notions of all that may be said, & that I would say. In the first place, I regard all these reported outrages of the British Cruisers as the grossest exaggerations of a matter which, however we may object to it, need not be rendered more heinous than it is. These Yankee Captains love to lie in respect to John Bull, especially when they can show or report some bullying & swagger of their own. You will note that sundry of them had made quite a heroic report of their own bluster. How far a foreign & maritime power, may be justified in the right of visit & search, is a point by no means settled. The right of visit of course implies the right of search; otherwise it would be an absurdity. As a great maritime power ourselves, it may be well & wise to pause long before we insist that it should not be asserted & maintained as a right. It is only the feeble power that insists upon exemption from it. A second question must decide

---

165 This dinner was given on Oct. 29, at which time Hammond delivered a speech. See letter to him of Nov. 22, 1858.

166 June 7.

167 Hammond's reply to this letter and those of June 2 and June 11 is dated June 20. The original is in the Hammond Papers, Library of Congress.

168 On May 31 Hammond delivered a short speech on the resolutions submitted by the Committee on Foreign Relations concerning British aggression in the Gulf of Mexico. See *Congressional Globe*, 35 Cong., 1 Sess., pp. 2529-2530.

upon its *degrees* in times of peace & war. Certainly, one of our revenue cutters would be justified in pursuing out of our own waters, & capturing upon the high seas, even in time of peace, a Contrabandista, evidently seeking to smuggle forbidden goods. Of course she exercises this right of capture with responsibilities. And her justification will only be found for her nation, in the fact of her being able to prove her case. We should legislate with reference to our idea of what *should* be the law of nations on the subject. But this is to argue the matter in a national point of view. To discuss the present supposed aggressions upon our commerce, suggests some considerations which are peculiar to the Southern States. Are we to give a sanction to any war in behalf of Yankee commerce, with that very nation which furnishes almost the exclusive market for our staples? Are we to help to strengthen the hands of that section which now seeks to destroy all our securities, and this too against a nation which, by reason of their manufactures & our productions, constitutes our natural ally, offensive & defensive? The true source of British antipathy to this country as an entirety is wholly due to the antagonistic interests of the Northern States as maritime & manufacturing; and slavery in the U. S. is only assailed by G. B. in consequence of her desire to relieve herself of any dependence upon a country — regarded as a whole — in which she finds her most formidable commercial rival. Are we with open eyes to surrender all our present interests, and all our future securities, by suffering ourselves to be plunged into a war with our best customer, in behalf of our most bitter assailant. Is not the moment an auspicious one to say to the North, — 'Before we strike a blow, or suffer one to be struck, we must take new guarantees for the future; we must establish our securities anew, & on a more certain basis. No more taxes paid by the South for the maintenance of Northern commerce; no more troops from the South, for fighting those battles from which you carry off all the spoils; no more strengthening by our blood or treasure of that section which only needs more strength, to destroy ourselves; and which boldly threatens our destruction at the very moment when she consumes our treasures & exhausts our strength, in the aggrandizement of her own states & cities.['] The terms between North & South are no longer of such social sympathy as to make it a matter of course that we shall recognize the claims of the section only when blows are to be expected, but at all other periods are denied to know either its favour or protection. The argument is one which needs to be addressed equally to the South & North. It will be one which will encourage the former with an increased knowledge of its resources for the maintenance of the sectional status in or out of the Confederacy; and we only need the general knowledge of this capacity diffused among our people, to realize our Independence. It is our ignorance that makes us cowards. The North has taught us that we have none of the national securities; how should we sacrifice ourselves for national sympathies which are not suffered [to] [169] exist? These texts afford ample materi[al][170] for another *caveat*. One might say, we have shown ourselves solicitous of nationality. We proved it in the Revolution; proved it in the war of 1812; proved it by great concessions & enormous sacrifices, of blood, treasure & annual subscription & assessment; and yet are denied the national securities, the national respect & sympathies; the protection of the national Ægis; every thing that should make a nation precious to our love, or valuable to our interest. We will make no more sacrifices of any sort, unless we be made secure of the national advantages — unless our securities are rendered firm, by such guarantees as the Statesmen of the South in their assembled wisdom (make this point especially in behalf of your vain puplings & talking potatoes) shall demand. If with this *caveat* you declare war, or provoke conflict with that power which constitutes the chief & almost sole market of the South, expect no help from us. We shall fold our arms & look on, struggle as you may; & strike no blow against our enemy, unless he actually assails our coasts. And we will let him know this. You yourselves have taught us this lesson by your own fruitful example. And you have forced upon us the necessity of its adoption by your incessant wrongs done to us, & your perpetual assaults upon our pride, our peace, our institutions & interests. — There is yet another matter. It is a warning to the democratic party, South & North, — especially of the South. It is the game of the Democratic Party to plunge us into foreign war. This is its only hope to maintain its effective organization. It is only by bringing the whole country under a sense of external & hostile pressure, that it can rally to any purpose, and temporarily put down the Black Republicanism of

---

[169] The MS. is torn.
[170] The MS. is torn.

the North. But virtually, out of the South, the Democratic Party is a dead thing. Shall this Party then of the South, be suffered for its own selfish maintenance, to plunge the country into a war which, while it lasts, must be fatal to Southern Agriculture. Cannot this danger be made clear, if not to themselves, at least to the people of the South. I am disposed to think that now is the time to effect an extrication of the people of the South from their demagogues. — But enough. I have written this hasty scrawl, in order that if you choose you may not lose a good opportunity of delivering a more formidable blow than any yet. I am not well. Suffering from headache. God bless you.

W. Gilmore Simms

P. S. I am just back from the Plantation. We are suffering from drought. No rain on the Edisto for six weeks. The more advanced corn will come to nothing unless we get rain within the week. It is shooting. My cotton is excellent & promises well. I had plenty of forms two weeks & more ago, & some of my cotton was two feet high & branching finely. While I write, we have fine rains in the city, & the clouds are stretched away in the North & West, which, if they spread far enough will walk the Edisto. Folks here are more disgusted than ever with that foolish old man, your colleague.[171] I met Allston yesterday, & complimented him upon the growing dimensions of his abdomen. I could not help, a moment after, feeling that a sarcasm, at the expense of his brains, had been implied in the special recognition of his guts!

883: To James Henry Hammond [172]

Charleston 11. June 1858

My dear Hammond.

A few more words on the subject of my preceding letter. The aggressions of the British cruisers, whether small or large, are all strictly due to the hostile feelings of the North to the South. They declared the Slave Trade Piracy; they made a league with the British to put it down, & a tacit league with all the powers of Europe to put down the states where slavery was still maintained. They have legitimated, for these objects, the assumptions

---

171 Arthur Peronneau Hayne. See preceding letters.
172 Hammond's reply to this letter and those of June 2 and June 10 is dated June 20. The original is in the Hammond Papers, Library of Congress.

of the British cruisers; since a fleet for the object of putting down the slave trade, justifies not merely the right of search & visitation, but the right to sink the vessel which is suspected; and men of war, are rarely nice discriminators in respecting of rights & duties. If we had not entered into the entangling alliance with G. B. for keeping up a fleet on the African coast against the slave trade, & thus sanctioned their like watch on the Cuban coast, where the slaves are expected to be delivered, we should have no cause of quarrel or complaint now, with respect to these alleged assaults upon our shipping. I am not unwilling that we should so add to our national marine as to make it commensurate to the stake we have in commerce; but, as a preliminary, I should require, on the part of the South, that our vessels of war be recalled from their watch upon the African coast, to the defence of our shipping on our own. This I should insist upon, as a preliminary, along with the utter withdrawal from the treaty which requires us to keep up a fleet for the purpose of this watch; — a measure which tacitly declares the South to be engaged in an infamous employment, in the very working of their slaves; for, if the *trade* in slaves be piracy, the *retention* of the *same people in slavery,* is crime! It seems to me that you might very well say, — 'I am for maintaining the honour of the nation, if you will give us the securities of a nation; but I warn you that the time approaches when we shall, *ex necessitate,* be forced to declare that, recognizing you only as an enemy, quite as hostile to our section as G. B — nay, more so, — it will become the duty of self preservation to look to our own securities, at every hazard, & necessarily first, by withholding from you all support in *any war,* which, while it endangers our possessions, destroys our commerce, paralyses our agriculture, and must fall most heavily upon *us* as the exporting region of *world-staples* of the greatest magnitude; — never realizes for us either the profits or the pride of the nation; and only increases *your* power to the increase of *our* danger. We have none of the national securities. You make no wars for our benefit; — you surrender our slaves to the enemy — ban our institutions; — your flag shelters not our property, and we know the nation only as the antagonist, who, under the guise of a confederacy, deliberately prepares us for the sacrifice. You must give us the national securities if you would have us accord you our support or sympathies in any future wars.' These considerations ought to be made known, even while you vote for an increase of navy, — nay, because of your vote. The time must come when we can consent to no increase & it is well that they should have our premonitions. We accord something to a *present* emergency, & especially as we would loathe taking the Northern States by surprise! But they must have their warning. And, even while we accord the appropriations, essential to the safety & honour of the nation *now,* it is equally essential, for our own securities, that we declare there must be an end of this; that we no longer feel that we have a common cause; and are made too painfully conscious that the strengthening of the arms of the confederacy, is substantially the strengthening of a despotism which shows itself too incessantly hostile to ourselves, to make it any satisfaction to us to exhibit any sympathies, in a conflict with that foreign power with which our interests especially would bring us into alliance. By nicely discriminating this argument, you might make a very noble one, — and one which would tell emphatically upon both South & North. I have written very hurriedly, *but am sure of the thoughts — the truth, justice & propriety of it all.* I am quite too unwell to express them as they should be expressed; but, if you concur with me, & have the opportunity afforded you, you can bring them out with trumpet accompaniments.

[*Close of letter missing.*]

884: To James Thomas Fields [173]

Charleston, S. C. June 18. 1858.
J. T. Fields, Esq.

My dear Fields.

I thank you for your prompt frank letter. I shall look for that dainty little volume with eagerness. I had a glimpse of it in Paul Hayne's hands and saw sundry things that were quite new to me.[174] Your letter encourages me to say to you that I have not recieved & would like to recieve all the clever books of Mrs. Jameson especially in 'blue & gold' — the poems of Mr. Saxe, Bowrings Matins, and the Poems of Motherwell. I know them all &

---

[173] See note 16, *c.* Jan. 18, 1854.
[174] Fields' *A Few Verses for a Few Friends* (Cambridge: Printed at the Riverside Press, [1858]), printed for private distribution, is reviewed by Simms in the Charleston *Mercury* of July 17, 1858.

can speak of them with a grateful pen.[175] I am thinking of a
new collection of 'Southern Passages', & 'Areytos', & should
greatly like an edition in blue & gold. When the poetical epoch
comes round again, and the public feels a return of its periodical
furore in behalf of verse, advise me of your readiness to avail
yourself of the spasm.[176] It is just possible that I may get North
this summer; but I am deep in cotton, & troubled with all sorts
of plantation reforms. I have nearly 300 acres in cotton, and
anxiously looking east & west, north & south, to see whence the
wind will blow. God forgive you.

Yours faithfully

W. Gilmore Simms.

885: To James Henry Hammond [177]

Charleston. June 26. 1858.

My dear Hammond.

By this time, I trust you are once more restored in safety to
Redclyffe, and in the full enjoyment of a long term of ease &
recreation.[178] You have, so far as I can see and hear, endured
the fatigues of the Session much better than you had anticipated;
that you would have still more bravely gone through it, I have
no question, could you have sufficiently subdued your desires of
the flesh. A man with your insubordinate stomach has no right
to an appetite at all. Now, you insist on appetites which are
totally inconsistent with your rights. These, in such matters, depend wholly on your capacity to enjoy. With the stomach of an
ostrich, you might urge some reasonable claim to eat everything
you lay eyes on; but as you are, always growling over the in-

---

[175] The firm of Ticknor and Fields, Boston, was the American publisher of
various works by Mrs. Anna Brownell Jameson (1794-1860). The firm also
issued editions of John Godfrey Saxe's *Poems,* Sir John Bowring's *Matins and
Vespers,* and William Motherwell's *Poetical Works.* Simms reviews Saxe's
Poems in the Charleston *Mercury* of July 17. In the *Mercury* of July 19 he
reviews a number of Ticknor and Fields' publications, including works by Long-
fellow, Leigh Hunt, Mrs. Jameson, and Bowring.

[176] This collection was printed as *Simms's Poems Areytos or Songs and
Ballads of the South with Other Poems* (Charleston: Russell and Jones, 1860).

[177] This letter is a reply to Hammond's of June 20. Hammond's answer
is dated July 3. The originals are in the Hammond Papers, Library of Congress.

[178] In his letter of June 20 Hammond writes from Washington: "I owe you
several letters & knowing your engagements to be equal to mine — arduous as I
deem mine to be—I simply acknowledge infirmity. . . . Tomorrow I leave & hope
to reach Redcliffe on Wednesday [June 23]."

firmities of your stomach, it is mere insolence & presumption to
spread yourself out for the creature comforts in any region, especially such a one as Washington. But a wilful man must needs
have his way, and that you have done so well, in other respects,
makes us indulgent to your shortcomings & *over*comings in this.
But were you only wise enough to forget that you have a stomach at all, and surrender the whole control to your brain, I
have no doubt you would become a better worker, — so, a better
liver, and so a happier man. In regard to your official career, you
have no reason to doubt or be dissatisfied.[179] You have silenced
your enemies and rejoiced your friends. There is but one opinion as to your course and your performances. You have fully
proved your capacity and resource to be equal to the exigencies
of State. You have spoken sparingly, and this was quite proper
to you as a new member; but when you have spoken, it has always been with force, propriety, and the dignity which becomes
a Senator. The part taken by you in the colloquial debate on the
addition to the Navy satisfies me that I was quite right in suggesting [180] this particular province to you as especially favourable
to the development of your peculiar resources.[181] You have done
quite enough this Session to produce the happiest effects throughout the State, and your popularity is now such that no man, no
set of men, can venture to oppose you. You are able now to prescribe terms to the politicians. As I heard yesterday said in conversation, you have only to declare yourself & make whom you
please your associates in power. In fact, with a people such as
ours, they can only be satisfied with the assurance that they have
a man in power whose genius & prudence may be relied on, to
maintain, not so much their securities, as their pride. Having such
a one, they care little or nothing for the rest. This was one of
the secrets of their veneration for Mr. Calhoun. They can sleep
at ease, satisfied of one man at the helm of State. You will beware how you assert this power; it is one thing to be conscious
of the possession; quite another to be constantly exercising it.
If you will take my counsel you will in no wise interfere in the
election of your colleague. *It is not possible for you to get a colleague out of the ranks of those who are desirous of the office,*

---

[179] In his letter of June 20 Hammond writes: "Write me & tell me *frankly*
how far & in what particulars I have fallen short of public expectation & your
own—*no blinking.*"

[180] Simms wrote *suggestion.*

[181] See *Congressional Globe,* 35 Cong., 1 Sess., pp. 2735ff.

who will not secretly regard you as too overshadowing for his self-esteem. Even as at Washington, we have too many illustrious obscures, whose only claim is based upon vanity & presumption. Such people are never magnanimous, & have no sympathies. They think of fame & reputation as the Tuscans are said to do of fever, that there is only a certain small quantity in the world, & that what is caught by one man is so much lost to another. In other words, when men build their pretensions upon an inordinate appetite, without any stomach (you see where I get this figure) they hate the appetite that, quite as good as their own, is blessed with corresponding digestion. Having no specific endowment, only a general craving, they are naturally envious & jealous of him, who with or without the craving, possesses the endowment in eminent degree. Such is your relation to most of the pretenders in the State. And that they should be thus envious & faithless as envious, is matter of law, and a due result of their necessity. It is a natural instinct that makes incompetents loathe superiority. By keeping aloof from this struggle, you provoke the hostility of none of these parties, and they will tear each other fast enough. Let them feed upon each other.[182] I have done recently what is unusual with me, broached here the subject of a public dinner to you, in recognition of the wisdom of your course, and in expression of our full approval. It is well entertained — enthusiastically even — by all to whom I have spoken. The question is whether the affair shall take place this Summer, or to be left over till November, when you will be preparing to resume your seat in Congress. This latter suggestion meets with favor, especially as so many of your commercial admirers are gone northward, or will be going, during the hot weather. You are a favorite here of the people, the business classes; but no favorite with a large proportion of the legal profession, who are also the Legislators, and who belong to the aspiring order of whom I spoke on the previous page. Were your name, before the people, you could beat any citizen here out of sight; yet, I

---

182 In his reply of July 3 Hammond writes: "All that you recommend me to do in these regards has my hearty concurrence. I had resolved on it already. I have suggested you as Senator for Evans term, if that & the long one is divided. Beyond that I have refused to make up my own mind as to a Colleague lest I might let it be known. My own Son, who may be an elector, I will not attempt to influence. Nor do I wish to intrude on State politics at all." Hammond's son Spann did become an elector upon his election to the South Carolina House of Representatives in the fall of 1858 (see note 215, July 10, 1858).

believe there were but 3 or 4 of the delegates from these parishes who did not vote against you. When I broached the subject of the dinner, there were some who immediately began to talk of heading the list with certain names. You are aware that it is usual here to initiate every movement under the auspices of a certain clique. A Lecturer, or orator, or mountebank, foreign count, or foreign fiddler, — all require to be introduced by Mess'rs Petigru, King, Dixon, Pringle, *et id omne genus.* I protested at once against any resort whatsoever to these men, and said that if they were appealed to, I should withhold my name. That neither Gen. Hammond nor myself needed any sanction from these or any other persons, nor their introduction to the people of S. C. any where, and that, in the case of these and certain other gentlemen who were usually referred to, there were good reasons for supposing that they were rather Hammond's enemies than friends, and I wished such a dinner as should exhibit no Judas kissing at the table. I wished no poison in the wine of tribute. That if it were needed that any name be used to invoke the people of Charleston to do you honour, mine was ready; and if I made the call singly, with my own name only, to the friends & admirers of Gen. H., who approved of his course, & were desirous of doing honour to his intents & public services, I was quite satisfied that the one name would bring together every *honest* admirer and we desired no other. We certainly wished to see in no conspicuous place at the board, those men who had been hostile to the last moment, & who if they showed any other temper now, would do so meanly, and with a sneaking and scoundrelly policy.[183] — The result of these expressions has been to open a new view among the parties thus addressed, by which we may succeed in lifting the people into self consciousness as well as strength, at the expense of the *cliques.* For that matter, & to this end, the appointment of Hayne

---

[183] In his reply of July 3 Hammond writes: "As to the dinner in Charleston let it subside. I shall have one here on the 22nd & another at Barnwell some time. There is no occasion for either. I should be glad to escape these & I beg there will be no more or I shall be ashamed to go back to Washington. Petigru is my enemy. King I despise. Dickson & Pringle I think friendly to me. But your advice is good, to conciliate all as far as decent." For James Louis Petigru and Samuel Henry Dickson, see introductory sketches; for William Alston Pringle, see note 134, Dec. 8, 1856. Mitchell King (1783-1862) was a distinguished Charleston lawyer, who twice held the position of recorder and judge of the city court. He was a member of the board of trustees of the College of Charleston for a great many years and twice acted as president of the College.

by Allston, is answering a very admirable purpose. The appointment disgusted every body, *in limine,* and the conduct of the foolish old man not merely confirmed public anticipation, but so exceeded the worst, that a general revulsion of the public stomach, has been the consequence, and the disgust is warmed into indignation.[184] This has led, necessarily, to a somewhat keen resolve that no more simulacra shall be suffered to rise to power. Throughout the State the feeling is the same, and it is to be hoped that even Governors will be chosen now with some regard to the interests & dignity of the State. My own opinion is that Hayne was the *nominee* of Petigru. I jumped to the conclusion, the moment I heard of the appointment, & said to several friends, 'that appointment comes from St. Michael's Alley.'[185] Since this, the *on dit* goes to confirm it. I will give you my reasons, when we meet, for entertaining this opinion. No matter what the source, the event is beneficial locally. Hayne was the creature of a clique which has always been allied with your enemies; and who, for reasons already given, would always be inimical to men of real ability & independence. And all my reflections go to confirm me in the conviction that you have need only to maintain a certain prudent forbearance & temperance in discourse & society. Do not make free with affairs. Be circumspect as well in conversation as in correspondence. We are both but too apt to be over-communicative, and too much familiarity is our equal & unwise characteristic. In my case, while I know my fault, there has been no policy to render it necessary that I should seek to amend. In yours, the necessity for prudence is more urgent than ever. But you are only required to forbear — to make no active demonstration for or against any body — to use your power, — and you have it now — with the greatest moderation, — and moderation is the first great essential of wisdom. The era, in your case, should be one of good feelings. You are *rectus in curia,* at last — keep so, by reticence. It will be sufficient if you let out at Washington, or at home, only on great occasions, when you are expected to speak. I repeat, my dear H., that there are no two opinions in respect to your public course; you have the ear of the people; it needs only a wise & gentle demeanour now to win their

---

[184] See Simms' earlier remarks about Governor Allston's appointment of Arthur Peronneau Hayne to the United States Senate in letters to Hammond of May 15, May 21, and June 2, 1858.

[185] Petigru's law office was at 8 St. Michael's Alley.

affections. But, let your freedoms & familiarities, be tempered by
a slight increase of reserve in all communications with the crowd.
I will illustrate this caution when we meet. And now, about that
meeting: It will be in my power to pay you a visit in July,
should your family be in condition to recieve a guest, & should
you be at home. I will give you a few days, & wish especially to
spend at least one day or two in Augusta, in order to get from
the Sandhills, a bird's eye view of the city & the environs, with
somebody at my elbow to point out & describe localities. Judge
Starnes [186] invited me last year. Ascertain if he is accessible this
summer, & whether July would suit him, & let me know promptly. Should he not prove available, do contrive it that I shall be afforded a few hours shelter in the Sandhills, with somebody to
show me all the points, & name them, &c. A few hours would
suffice with some intelligent man, and you, perhaps, could accompany me for the purpose.[187] — Keitt is here, preparing for his
Oration on the 28th.[188] He read it to me last night in order to
get my verbal corrections. It is flowery & flimsy, but portions of
it will probably tell upon a popular audience. This *entre nous*.
He is a good fellow, loose & uncertain, with a vagrant fancy;
who means no harm; but, his vanity & want of purpose, will
probably founder his batteau in *smooth* waters. I have a kindly
feeling for him; but fear that he is not saveable. He will hardly
suffer himself to improve, or pass a single inch higher in political
or social stature. I am in pretty good physical condition; but my
wife recuperates slowly, and we have one of our children teething, so that I propose going to the island for a week or two.[189]
Tell your wife that little Beverley Hammond [190] is one of the
noblest looking fellows, of the Saxon type, that the city can show.
My son Gilmore has just got back from Yorkville,[191] a tall fellow, nearly my height, though but 15. We are suffering from

---

[186] Ebenezer Starnes. See note 51, May 6, 1857.

[187] Simms was planning to write a romance with an Augusta, Ga., setting and
wanted to familiarize himself with the region. Though he later writes that he
has discarded his plan, the romance was eventually written and published as
"Joscelyn" (see note 282, Nov. 4, 1866). He visited Hammond the latter part
of July and remained for about a week. See letters to Hammond of July 10 and
Aug. 1 and to Tefft of July 19.

[188] On June 28 Lawrence Massillon Keitt delivered an oration at the laying
of the cornerstone of the Calhoun Monument on the Citadel Academy green,
Charleston. See the Charleston *Mercury* of June 29.

[189] Chevillette Simms took Govan to Sullivan's Island. See letter to Mary
Lawson of July 10.

[190] Simms' son.

[191] Gilmore was a cadet at the King's Mountain Military School.

drought, & I am quite anxious. Cotton doing well. I have 270 acres planted against Mr. Roach's 150 — and with the same force. I begin to see where all the error has been. Next year, (D. V.) my 270 shall be 400 acres, & with the same force, with the increase of mule power only. God be with you.

W. Gilmore Simms

886: To GEORGE PAYNE RAINSFORD JAMES [192]

Charleston, S. C. July 2. 1858

Hon. G. P. R. James.

My dear James.

It is a long time since we have had any converse together. The fault is yours, since I hold you my debtor for a couple of scribbles, long time ago, to which you have vouchsafed no response.[193] None, at least, has ever reached me. I write now to remind you of your *lachesse,* and to enclose the printed scrap, from the *Mercury* of this city, which you will find within, and dedicated to your last publication. It is from my pen, though it appears editorially. It is not, of course, designed as a criticism; — only an acknowledgement; and, I trust, that it will satisfy you that I keep you in grateful recollection, & your writings in equally grateful appreciation. I rejoice to think that this volume inaugurates a new and uniform edition.[194] Is it so? Am I mistaken in assuming that the *vignette* is from the pencil of that clever son of your friend Myers, of whom something was told me, when last in Richmond, in respect to his large promise in art.[195] I rejoice to find that you can still work, & with your wonted vigour. Let me hear from you soon, and please report grateful progress. Present me with affectionate respect to your wife, & the fair Florence, and say to

---

[192] See introductory sketch. In 1852 James was appointed British consul at Norfolk, Va. In 1858 he was living in Richmond, and in Sept., 1858, he left Virginia to become British consul general at Venice.

[193] We have not located any letter to James but this one of July 2.

[194] Simms reviews *Lord Montagu's Page: An Historical Romance of the Seventeenth Century* (Philadelphia: Childs & Peterson, 1858) in the *Mercury* of July 3.

[195] This edition of *Lord Montagu's Page* contains a portrait of James and an illustrative vignette. The vignette was drawn by William Barksdale Myers, Richmond painter and illustrator, who died in 1873 at the age of thirty-two. His father was Gustavus Adolphus Myers (1801-1869), a prominent Richmond lawyer and patron of the arts.

your son that he is not forgotten though not of the tender-gender.[196]

Yours Ever truly

W. Gilmore Simms

887: To Mary Lawson

Charleston, July 10. 1858.

My dear Mary.

It gives me great pleasure to hear from you at last, and this time I answer you promptly. That I have not hitherto done so, you must ascribe to the variety of cares, toils, anxieties and changes of position which are almost inseparable from my life at present. One week I am at the plantation; the next in town; and sometimes, as for the last ten days, I am running to & fro between the city and Sullivan's island, whither my wife has gone in order to recruit one of our children who suffers from teething. Did I tell you in a previous letter that she had added the twelfth to her [197] list, in a fine little girl whom we call Hattie (Harriett) Myddleton. With the exception of Govan and my wife herself, we are all pretty well. Gilmore is now on the island with his mother. He is almost as tall as I am, very stalwart; a good swimmer, good shot, good horseman; and is at the head of his section in the Military Academy,[198] his class containing 52. He is backward, however, in many of those respects which your father & myself deem essential; but his docility and moral are excellent. In these respects, he is a model boy. I rejoice to hear so well of Jimmy. I shall always congratulate him and myself upon the counsel I gave your father, to send him from home and

---

[196] In 1828 James married Frances Thomas (1800-1891), daughter of Honoratus Leigh Thomas (1769-1846), a London physician. The Jameses' daughter, Florence Frances (1834-1894), later became a well-known lecturer on literature and its allied subjects and in 1870 married John Williams. The Jameses had three sons alive in 1858, George Walter (1832-1887), Courtenay Hunter (1836-1864), and Charles Leigh (1846-1911). George was living in Wisconsin and Courtenay, a lawyer, who had accompanied Walker on his filibustering expedition into Nicaragua (see note 34, Jan. 25, 1858), appears to have been living in Central America; Charles, therefore, is probably the son here mentioned by Simms.

[197] Simms first wrote *my*, then struck through the word and wrote **her** above it.

[198] The King's Mountain Military School.

throw him among stout and emulous boys.[199] To be brought up
among girls entirely, is a dangerous thing for boys. They either
degrade him to a milksop, or make him a petty despot. Where he
is, he will probably acquire *manhood,* which is the greatest of
human virtues. I am no less rejoiced to find that Willy Gilly [200]
is developing so finely. Give him a gun, or a horse; teach him
boxing; any thing but pamper him into a popinjay. Don't give
him finger rings, or breast pins, or watches; and let him wear the
plainest clothes; if you would have him what he should be. You
say nothing of Mama, or Christie or Kate,[201] and very little
of Papa; all of whom, I trust, are doing well. You will present
me to all of them most affectionately. It is possible, indeed, that
I shall visit you at Budd's Lake.[202] I think it likely that I shall
visit N. Y. early in August. I have much business with my publisher, who has urged me to take up my abode with him.[203] I
have promised to do so; but propose to run up & spend a few
days with you. All this will depend upon affairs at home. You
are aware that I have it upon me to restore a dilapidated but
very valuable estate. I have been doing a good deal towards it;
and might have hoped to extricate it this year; but the seasons
are adverse; we have had a two months drouth which will cut
short my corn crop. I have 330 acres of corn, and 270 of cotton,
to say nothing of rice, peas & potatoes; so that, you see, I have
a great deal which waits upon the seasons. If you would grow to
be a wise woman you would try to understand all these things.
When I see you, I will give you some lessons. Let me assure you,
I really wish to pay you a visit & will contrive it if I can. But
when you reflect upon the number of my children, the toils of
my profession, the burden of the plantation, you will see how
difficult it is for me to say any thing positively in advance.
I have not only these anxieties upon me, but my friends are
doing all they can, in my despite, to send me to the Senate of

---

[199] This advice was not given James Lawson in any letter known by us to
survive. We have been unable to identify the school which James Lawson, Jr.
(b. 1842), attended.

[200] William Gilmore Simms Lawson (1848-1860).

[201] Lawson's daughters Christina (b. 1837) and Catherine Forrest (1840-
1866).

[202] The Lawsons lived at 144 West Twelfth Street, New York City, but had
a summer home at Budd's Lake, New Jersey.

[203] Justus Starr Redfield lived at 31 Sands Street, Brooklyn. His business
address was 34 Beekman Street, New York City. See the Brooklyn and New
York City directories for this period.

the U. S.[204] I have implored & argued against it, but they are still urgent. I shall escape the honour if I can. Among my items, by the way, I must not omit to mention, that Augusta has been some time engaged to one of my wife's cousins, Edward Roach, a very excellent young man, who depends for his resources upon his own exertions; but he is one of the most moral, prudent & industrious young men, who will give her the best securities of happiness. The affair will probably take place in October, or thereabouts.[205] I think now, my dear Mary, that I have fully emptied all my little budget. You will empty what you please of it, upon your household. It is enough, at closing, to say that God keeps me above water; that if not rich, I am not starving; and that my hope is strong, if life be spared me, to leave my children a permanent household, and a firm support. I am not sick, though not quite well, and only want respite. I have a great deal of work before me from which I do not shrink, if health & strength be spared me. Add to this, I rejoice in the health & happiness of my friends, and of yourself & yours in particular. Write me soon, and your letter will probably anticipate my departure for N. Y. Love & a kiss to Mama, Christie, Kate, & the masculine members. God bless you.

Your friend

W. G. S.

888: To JAMES HENRY HAMMOND [206]

My dear Hammond.

Charleston So. Ca. July 10. 1858

I have just got your letter. I repeat — you are perfectly successful thus far.[207] You have done enough to satisfy friends & foes

---

[204] In the Charleston *Mercury* of July 2 "Up Country" nominates Simms for the Senate as "one in every way worthy of this high trust, and to whom, having been for so long a time guilty of neglect, the State should now offer this well-merited tribute, and call to her service one, modest in wisdom, but brave in principle and bold in the defence of her honor." Simms is again nominated in the Charleston *Courier* of Oct. 19, and this latter nomination is highly praised by "Marion" in the *Courier* of Oct. 23. See also Simms' letter to Hammond of June 2 and note 283, Nov. 2, 1858.

[205] Augusta's wedding date was postponed until Dec. 29 because of the deaths of Sydney Roach and Beverley Hammond Simms (see Simms' letters written during the latter part of this year). Edward Roach was the son of Nash Roach's half-brother Edward (see note 225, July 19, 1858).

[206] This letter is a reply to Hammond's of July 3, which is an answer to Simms' of June 26. The next letter from Hammond to Simms which we have located is dated Aug. 13. The originals are in the Hammond Papers, Library of Congress.

[207] See letter of June 26.

equally that you are adequate to the position, and to the representation of the State, and the exigencies of the times. What you have said has been well said, — forcible, to the point, and in maintenance of the position of the State. That you have spoken infrequently is naturally ascribed to the fact that your position is a novel one — that you have had a great deal of headway to recover — that it was necessary that you should *feel* your way, in an unfamiliar situation, and it would have been mere rashness and presumption to have attempted continual debate when the issues were not necessarily provocative, and when, on subordinate affairs & matters of detail, there were so many who could deliver themselves quite as well, and even better than yourself, — simply because of their longer practice & better familiarity with the scene of performance. I was anxious that you should engage twice or thrice in debate, simply that you might unfold yourself in general views, and simply as the main body of your constituents can only judge of the performances of their Senators from the part they take upon the floor. They know but little of the work in Committee, in Caucus or Council, and the labor of research & report making. It will be quite time to attempt Leadership in debate, when you have reached your third session. You only require time to recover your political tone, and to feel at perfect ease in your saddle. Your great deficiency, as I told you long ago, was that of self-esteem.[208] You distrust yourself in consequence of the very elevation of your own standards. But there is a process for overcoming this embarrassing influence, which too frequently keeps you from utterance, where, were you to speak your thought, you would establish your principle. This process is simply so to analyze the constituents of your body (the Senate or House) and find their measure of performance. Once in possession of the several standards, of mind & moral, under which they work, and you measure their feat.[209] It is then an involuntary process which makes you compare with theirs your own standards of thought & judgment. The rest is easy. But we will talk all this over when I see you. At this moment, I cannot well say at what time I can come up. The last of this month probably. I have my wife & one of my children sick on the island.[210] I am kept between town & island, with divided family. I shall have

---

[208] See letter of Aug. 18, 1852.
[209] Simms wrote *feet*.
[210] Chevillette Simms had taken Govan, sick with teething, to Sullivan's Island. See letter to Mary Lawson of July 10.

to go north in August; to see about my publications & publisher.[211]
He succumbed, I think I told you, to the crisis of last autumn,
and I know not yet the extent of my losses. My dfts were returned unhonored. My father in laws illness & death, my wife's
confinement & extreme sickness,[212] compelled me to give up all
my Lecturing engagements & invitations, and cut off some $1200
from my poor little income. The debt of the plantation is about
$5000, and a great deal of this was in petty sums which I have
been compelled to meet or evade. You may judge of my straits
for the last ten months. I am literally living from hand to mouth.
But I have just had an offer from a publisher of $3000 for one
years writings — incessant of course, — in weekly instalments
of matter, to the tune of 3 or four or five chapters per week, &
weekly pay.[213] I shall accept it though I drop in the harness.
This, of course, even if there were no other reasons, would forbid
my thinking of the Senate. Do you have nothing to do with that
project & it will die out. There are scores of Richmond's in the
field [214] — such as they are; and your only cause for anxiety will
be the one doubt whether you may not get for colleague some
concieted pretentious talking potato who will be perpetually on
the floor & striving to make capital at your expense. You will
not need to fear from the result, but the consciousness of such
a game will be annoying. — I will write you a week before hand
to advise you of my coming, & get you to have your carriage at
Augusta. Best regards to your wife, Kate & the boys. I hear
generally that Spann will be elected.[215] Tell him not to make himself cheap.

Yours truly

W. Gilmore Simms.

---

[211] Justus Starr Redfield.

[212] Nash Roach died on Feb. 28; Harriet Myddleton Simms was born on
March 14.

[213] We have not identified the New York publisher of a weekly who made
this offer, which Simms eventually turned down. For Simms' further remarks
about it, see letters to James H. Hammond of July 16, 1858; to Mary Lawson
of Aug. 2, 1858; and to De Bow of March 1, 1859.

[214] See *Richard III*, V, iv, 2.

[215] Spann Hammond was elected to the South Carolina House of Representatives and served during 1858-1859.

889: To James Henry Hammond

Charleston. 16 July. 1858.

My dear Hammond.

It will be impossible for me to be with you by the 22d. so as to be present at the Beach Island Dinner. This failure will be of no moment to you, but I could have wished it otherwise, for sundry reasons. Be cautious of your speech. Say nothing of yourself. Be gentle & forbearing. And confine yourself as much as possible to *national* generalities. It might be well to indicate some sectional clues as to the future, especially anent this matter of war. I cannot resist the conviction that the Dem. Leaders will force it upon Buchanan by the 3d. year of his administration, if not the 2d.; even tho', deferring toadyishly to Britain, he may reluct. It is not only our policy (the South) to escape war, but it is our policy to make a war the rock upon which to split the sides of both Dem. & Black Republicans. The sooner the South can force a sectional issue, & without seeming to do so — leaving it to the B. R., the better for our battle. They will utterly crush the N. Democrats at next election, tho', I fancy, Seward & not Fremont will be the man. *He* will carry Pennsylvania, &, with proper exertions, N. Jersey.[216] So mote it be! We shall never be able to rally the Southern leaders, on right grounds, till the fate of the Dem. Party organization shall take from them all hope. But I need not bore you with this talk. You will, no doubt, see for yourself. Only, say nothing of *yourself*. Take the high position of a Senator, regarding only the grand issues which affect the nation. And do not dwell upon them. Throw out suggestions, and leave the details to others.[217] If you will send for me to the R. R. depôt at Augusta on Friday next, the *23d.* inst. I shall endeavour to be with you. My daughter Augusta will probably accompany me on a week's visit to Mrs. H. — a week or less. — I am greatly occupied. I expect to go to N. Y. as soon as I return from Redclyffe. While with you, I must take that bird's eye view of the precinct of Augusta. On my way up, I visit our

---

[216] William Henry Seward (1801-1872), United States senator from New York (1849-1861), was one of the most prominent aspirants for the Republican nomination for president in 1860. John Charles Frémont (1813-1890) had been the Republican nominee for president in 1856.

[217] For a discussion of Hammond's speech at the dinner held in his honor at Beech Island, S. C., on July 22, see Merritt, *James Henry Hammond,* pp. 122-124. See also Simms' letter to Hammond of Aug. 1 and Hammond's letter to Simms of Aug. 13 (original in the Hammond Papers, Library of Congress).

plantation, where things begin to look better. We have had good showers after two months drouth. I have no more to say. Except — speak fearlessly as to your own people. You have the general ear now — they wish for nothing better *now,* than to be suffered to approve. Use your capital prudently, and with due modesty. Above all, my dear fellow, drink nothing. That good foolish fellow Keitt, it is reported here currently, got drunk after or during his oration, & was with difficulty carried from the stand & into the Citadel.[218] Say nothing of it, for if it gets abroad it will greatly hurt him with his Constituents, & there are two or three *mauvaises sujets,* who are eager and anxious to get into his place, and find him tripping. — I am not well. My wife & young child[219] are something better, and will leave the island tomorrow. I have offers from N. Y. for an engagement of 3 years at $3000 per ann. for exclusive scribbling, and it waits only a few words to close the contract.[220] I shall make my will before beginning the work; for, I fancy, it will be my death warrant. But, what can be done, and what import? Are you not also becoming heartily tired of the drudgeries which men call life? I want to see you on many accounts, not the least of which is Spiritualism. Did you confer with any medium while at Washington? Why did you not run to N. Y. Why not go with me for a few weeks after leaving Redclyffe. I shall only be gone 2 or 3 weeks.

Yours & God Bless you

Simms.

P. S. The morning train leaves here, after the 20th. at 5½. This, I suppose, will bring us to Augusta at 12. M. or thereabouts. I shall go to our plantation on *Thursday next,* the 22d., and the next day, 23d. take again the morning train. So that my daughter & self will have only *day* travelling to Redclyffe. Will you look to it? — And let your wife & Kate know.

---

[218] See note 188, June 26, 1858.

[219] Govan. See letter to Mary Lawson of July 10.

[220] For this offer, later turned down by Simms, see letters to Hammond of July 10, 1858; to Mary Lawson of Aug. 2, 1858; and to De Bow of March 1, 1859.

890: To Israel Keech Tefft

Charleston, So Caro. July 19. [1858][221]

My dear Tefft.

Your note of 18th. June covered a letter from Mr. Charles H. Denison who designs a collection of his brother's writings, and another of the biographies & genealogies of the Denison family. I suppose he has written to you on both subjects.[222] I have just made out to answer him, my time having been greatly, though desultorily taken up, for the last month, going to & fro, & with the cares of a sick family. I have been proposing & hoping to visit you for a long time past, in order to [have] a consultation with you touching the best material for an Historical Romance the scene of which should be in and about Savannah. Nothing but more pressing calls upon my time has prevented me carrying out this intention. But you may find me with you when you least expect it, &, warned of my object, I trust, that you will scratch the heads of your most antique Reminiscents, and see what you can get out of them which shall help my purpose.[223] — Augusta has, of course, written to advise you & Mama[224] of her engagement with Edward Roach. He is a most excellent and amiable young man who will no doubt make her a devoted husband. He is a cousin of my wife, with all his connections unexceptionable, his own character above reproach. He has no resources but in his own industry, and, with good sound sense, lacks all brilliancy. But he has youth, health, good family, good morals, industry & nice feeling. Altogether, she could not have done better for the security of her future happiness. Both families approve. They will reside in this City, where he is engaged clerking it upon a moderate salary. He will require to live with his mother & sisters; a common property — good dwelling house, & their own servants — enabling them to live with a degree of comfort, which, separate, neither of the parties could command. The mother is the widow of the treasurer of Charleston, he & his father having held the office, without reproach, for more than a quarter of a century & in spite of all the caprices of politics

---

[221] Dated by Simms' discussion of Augusta's engagement to Edward Roach. See preceding and following letters.

[222] We have not identified the Denisons.

[223] Simms appears not to have written a novel with a Savannah setting.

[224] Mrs. Tefft, the former Penelope Waite. See note 233, Dec. 26, 1851.

& party.[225] In a few days, Augusta will probably run up with us to Augusta where we shall spend a week with the Hammond family.[226] I go to take the *coup d'œil* of that precinct, with regard to a Revolutionary novel. You will readily concieve that with town house to provide, eight children to watch, train, educate, *nurse,* a plantation to manage, perpetual contracts with publishers to meet — a horridly large correspondence forced upon me daily, and rarely upon any of my proper concerns — my hands are perpetually full of toils & my head of cares & anxieties. In the midst of these, certain of my misjudging friends, are busied urging me to accept the nomination for the Senate of the U. S.[227] I entreat escape, as a matter of course; cannot afford it; cannot neglect my domestic duties, plantation & professional interests, which I should most certainly would have to do, if I desired to acquit myself honorably in such a situation. Besides, my dear old friend, *it comes too late.* It might have suited me ten years ago to have become a politician. I had, indeed, somewhat trained myself for the business of Statesmanship. But the time went by when I might have used my political capital profitably for myself & country. The high places were conferred upon Jacks & Jills, Demagogues & What Nots; and with a sigh, I long since abandoned all aspirations of the sort, & tried my best to forget all the Statesmanship I had ever studied. To commence a new vocation and such a vocation at 52 is not the business of a wise man. I am too rusty; and — which is more, I have learned to value *Life's Candle,* as of much more importance than *Life's Game* — would rather not see the one too rapidly *burn* out, in seeing the other unprofitably *played* out. So, I eschew politics & the Senate if I can, and with God's blessing shall probably escape the threatening danger, though my very good friends, somewhat misjudging me, are disposed to regard my objections as those which are common to the modest young politician who craves most keenly while denying most vociferously — or as those of the damsel, reported by Byron, who "Swearing she would ne'er con-

---

[225] Edward Roach (1837-1901) was the son of Edward and the grandson of William Roach. Edward's mother was Esther Ann Conyers Roach (1805-1865). He had two brothers, William and B. Manley, and three sisters, Julia V. (who, in 1875, married Judge Pleasant Green Wood, of Selma, Ala.), Claudia (who died unmarried), and Clara (who also died unmarried). The Charleston directories for this period give Edward's and his mother's address as 11 Society Street. He is listed simply as "clerk."

[226] Simms and Augusta planned to arrive at Redcliffe on July 23. See letter to Hammond of July 16.

[227] See letter to Mary Lawson of July 10.

sent, consented." [228] But, enough. God forgive us all, my dear
Tefft & his blessing upon you, Mama, and even that wicked
young widow, the fair Sarah,[229] on whom you will please bestow
my most considerate regards. Love to Mama.

Yours Ever truly.

W. Gilmore Simms.

891: To JAMES HENRY HAMMOND

Charlesto[n, August 1, 1858] [230]

My dear Hammond.

We reached the city in safety, & found Dr. Stoney [231] duly in
awaiting at the depôt, to whom we surrendered the fair Kate,
who was to proceed instanter to the Island Steamer.[232] I take for
granted that she got there in safety. Augusta did some shopping
for her, and sent down to her yesterday. We may hear of her
tomorrow. As far as I can learn — and I made due inquiries of
various sources, the city is quite healthy. There is no yellow
fever in town, and no sickness. On that score, therefore, for the
present at least, you & Mrs. H. may make yourselves easy. —
There has been an attack on me in one of the Augusta papers,
based on the report that I was taking notes in order to [write]
a story of Georgia. This attack charges me with having done the
"greatest injury to Georgia", and grounds this charge upon some
clerical error which it alleges me to have made touching the
course of the Savannah river; I having said, in some geographical
notice, that it ran to *Charleston!* — Could you concieve of such
stupid malignity. It has a fling at S. C. calls Georgia the *'Union
State'*, and there are other ridiculous & malignant innuendoes.

---

228 "And [Julia] whispering 'I will ne'er consent'—consented." See *Don Juan,*
Canto I, Stanza cxvii, line 8.
229 Sarah Tefft, widow of Tefft's son William Pitt. See note 129, July 8,
1854.
230 The upper right corner of the MS. has been torn off, and the date and
several other words of the text are missing. The year is established by Simms'
discussion of Hammond's speech delivered at a dinner in his honor at Beech
Island, S. C., on July 22, 1858. We have dated the letter Aug. 1 (a Sunday)
because Simms refers to "yesterday (Saturday)" and obviously has only recently
arrived in Charleston from Redcliffe, where he had gone probably on July 23
for a week's visit (see letter to Hammond of July 16).
231 Probably C. F. Stoney, a druggist of the firm of Stoney and Wiltberger
(J. R. Wiltberger), 245 King Street, Charleston. His residence was at 24 Hasel
Street. See the Charleston directories for this period.
232 The steamer for Sullivan's Island.

There is no doing any thing with or for this people! And my mistake, if I did make it, was made 20 years ago, in a little geography of S. C.[233] Now, if this is to be the sort of treatment which I am to anticipate, I will write no book about Georgia. I can plant my story any where else. I can really get nothing by laying the scene in that State, and the invention would be wholly mine. Her history affords little *per se*. Here, at the very outset, an attempt is made to create a prejudice against me & my book, with no sort of pretext, and evidently for a malignant purpose only. What could I expect from the continued presence of such a spirit of [malignancy], but that every thing which I wrote would be cavilled & carped at; and unless I made all the Georgia parties heroes and demigods, and made invidious, or odious comparisons in respect to all of S. C. stock, I should be denounced as a reviler & slanderer. In all probability this attack, which appears as a communication in a paper called the Despatch, is from the pen of some Yankee shopkeeper, who thus revenges my attacks upon the North, by seeking to awaken the jealousies of Georgia against me & S. C.[234] I have mislaid the paper or I should send it to you.[235] The long & short of it is briefly, I shall forego the Georgia subject altogether. I feel that I should work in fear & trembling, not daring to say a syllable, even where fortified by history, which should fail to paint Georgia as superior, at least, to S. C. I should certainly expect no favour, and might as reasonably calculate upon no justice! I'll have none of them.[236] — Yesterday (Saturday) I went into the city, saw several people, and among them the Editor of the Mercury.[237] As I expected, your speech has greatly ruffled the ultras. Rhett says that numerous applications have been made him, for space in his columns to reply; that the 7th Cong. District [238] is in arms; says that the cry is that you are for submission; and that the expression of your opinions will operate against the Alabama Disunionists. I

---

[233] We can find no such error in Simms' *The Geography of South Carolina* . . . (Charleston: Babcock & Co., 1843).

[234] For the furore caused by Simms' lectures delivered in the North during the fall of 1856, see his letters written during the latter part of that year.

[235] We have been unable to locate a file for this period of the Augusta *Evening Dispatch,* a daily published during 1857-1861.

[236] Simms did not "forego the Georgia subject": "Joscelyn" was eventually finished in 1866 and published serially in the *Old Guard.* See note 282, Nov. 4, 1866.

[237] Robert Barnwell Rhett, Jr.

[238] In 1858 South Carolina did not have a 7th Congressional District.

told him that you were quite able to defend yourself; that you
were not fully or correctly reported; that you were misunderstood
in many things; that your qualifications of phrase & opinion did
not seem to be taken into account; that you were not less willing
to go out of the Confederacy now than before; and you would
cheerfully do so, and so perhaps would most of the Members
from the Cotton States, if their several peoples had not expressly
told them, they should do no such t[hin]g[; that since]
coerced [?] to maintain the South in the Union, you were for
carrying on the war constitutionally until the people themselves
were ripe for revolution; that meanwhile you exhorted them (in
S. C.) to keep to their arms, to relax no vigilance; to maintain
their advanced position until their sisters, some at least, should
march up & form upon them; that S. C. being thus in the advance, & ready for a charge, could do nothing more than maintain her attitude. That to carry on the war now, constitutionally,
we must wait for some aggression; that agitation without aim
or even pretext, was rather proof of weakness than of strength
or purpose. That in all probability we should have cause before
very long, in the utter overthrow of the Dem. Party, and in the
usurpation of the Govt. by the Blk Repub. That you held now,
as ever, that this was disunion *per se.* But that, even then, the
question was whether we should act, before the usurping party
should declare itself by offensive enactments. That it might be
they would content themselves with the spoils of office, as the
Whigs had hitherto done, &c. That, perhaps, nothing would so
soon tend to their overthrow; but that any how, you were prepared to keep S. C. in line & ready for action among the first,
whenever public sentiment could be prepared for the issue. That
there must be good subject for issue. Kanzas was not now, &
never had been a proper issue. Kanzas was disposed of. There
was not at present any proper pretext. But there were causes of
apprehension. For these we ought to be ready. For these you were
ready — now, or at any time hereafter. But that you were not
willing to be perpetually in a pother, tearing the passions to
pieces, with no enemy before you, and no overt provocation to
the war. In telling him this, I gave him to understand that you
had much other matter in reserve. That you ha[d already gone]
far beyond the usual stretch of [*several words missing*] politicians; but that your trump cards were only to be played, when

it was proper to put out your strength; that there was material in your hands, which could only be properly used in Congress; & that in a domestic speech among your constituents, you would be unwise to expose your argument fully, lest your political enemies might avail themselves of it. I told him that you considered the reports of your speech to be very inadequate, & in some respects positively unjust. That some of the *expositions* of it, only proved that you had not been fully understood, &c. And that you would prepare yourself fully & clearly for your speech in Barnwell.[239] He said that Montgomery's report came to him in a most wretched manner — that he had to rewrite it, as well as he could, judging as frequently by the context as by any thing else; & gathering some hints from your letter.[240] He adverted to Cunningham's exposé, as mollifying some matter.[241] But said (& this *inter nos*) that it was Cunningham's game to separate you from the Mercury, and secure for his own paper whatever support might accrue from your appropriation exclusively by himself. This, you will see, is a point which requires you to be cautious. I reproached Rhett with not having gone up himself. He now regrets not having done so. Would have done so if he had thought that Montgomery would prove so incompetent. He says the Columbia Carolinian has already denounced him for not denouncing you, &c.[242] But enough. You have your cues, and are prepared for their use. Do not answer in the newspapers. Keep yourself in reserve for the speech, and let the speech cover all your assailants. Many of these, no doubt, will be of the Tobin order, & I think it likely he will be among them, as I am told

---

[239] Hammond spoke at Barnwell Court House on Oct. 29. See Simms' letter to him of Nov. 22, 1858.

[240] The *Mercury* of July 27 carries a three-column account of the dinner in honor of Hammond and of Hammond's speech signed "L. M. M." and dated "Hamburg, July 22." Montgomery (whom we are unable to identify) reports that Hammond's position is that the South would be better out of the Union, but that she is not likely to dissolve the Union except in the face of some great issue such as the tariff or slavery; that the South should unite and watch and stand firm; and that the South should not expand the institution of slavery by reopening the slave trade. For another account of the dinner, see the *Mercury* of July 24, which quotes from the Augusta *Constitutionalist* of July 23. Hammond's speech was not published.

[241] At this time John Cunningham (see note 217, Oct. 30, 1846) was editor of the Charleston *Evening News,* of which we have been unable to locate a file for this period.

[242] We have been unable to locate a file of the *South Carolinian* for this period.

that he has decided to come out against Keitt.[243] Best regards to
Mrs. H. and God bless you both.

Yours Ever

Simms

892: To James Henry Hammond

Charleston, Augt. 1. [1858] [244]

dear Hammond.

After I had sealed my letter to you, I laid hands on the within
notice which I prepared for the Mercury. You will note that I
there touch upon that matter of the Patent office which formed
the subject of one of my suggestions to you in a late conversation.[245]

I forgot to say that Yeadon's full endorsement of your speech
was one of the serious causes of complaint among the Secessionists.[246] I took for granted that such would be the case. — Talk
as little of the matter as possible, but prepare yourself carefully.[247]
There is no difficulty in your argument if you will elaborate it.
You may ask the people for special instructions by way of getting
from your opponents a *modus operandi*. To quarrel with you on
a mere matter of opinion as to what is the appearance of the
weather, is one of those points upon which you might possibly
amuse yourself & your hearers profitably. If you would only say,
as I do, that I desire to be rid of bad company, and would cheerfully secede for that reason, alone, could I influence the Cotton
States, it might be well.

Yours Ever

W. G. S.

---

[243] John Etienne Tobin (1821-1868), of Barnwell District, was a lawyer,
admitted to the bar at Columbia in 1843. He served twice in the state legislature, but gradually withdrew from the law, gave up politics, and devoted his
time to his plantation, near Blackville. During the Confederate War he was a
brigadier general of the South Carolina Militia. We are unable to find any
record of his opposing Lawrence Massillon Keitt for the United States House of
Representatives.

[244] Dated by Simms' reference to his preceding letter to Hammond of the
same date.

[245] In the Charleston *Mercury* of May 1, 1858, Simms proposes for "the
Government . . . to have somebody—a well salaried officer, having nothing else
to do than simply to sift the Patent Office; select, and illustrate, and publish the
few inventions which have some uses, and tumble all the rest into the Potomac."

[246] Richard Yeadon (see introductory sketch) reports on the Beech Island
dinner and Hammond's speech in a letter written from Kalmia (near Aiken,
S. C.) and dated July 24, published in the Charleston *Courier* of July 27.

[247] For the speech to be delivered at Barnwell Court House on Oct. 29.

893 : To James Henry Hammond

Cha[rleston,] Au[g. 2, 1858] [248]

dear Hammond.

The people of S. C. have, in the most emphatic manner de-clared that, in any action with regard to the Nat. Gov. we are to wait the cooperation of our Sister States. Who are our Sister States? Not the South, but the Cotton States. It is assumed that we are far in advance of these. This may be true or not; but, at all events, with the assumption, it is left to us, simply, for the present, & until the people otherwise decide, we are to keep line, dress, mark time, and be in readiness for the signal to advance. What is expected, meanwhile, of a representative. He is to keep the head of the outpost, report progress, see that all's well, and fight whatever battle can be fought, *in* the Union, even if not *for* the Union. It is not for the Union that we fight; but for ourselves, in a condition which our people have decided, we are not yet to be permitted to change. This, I take it, is your attitude.[249] Meanwhile, you are not simply to beat your drum & blow your trumpet all the while, — nor at all, unless there be such decided evidence of the enemy's advance, as should prompt you to report their progress to your people. Do they advance, in carrying the elections for the Black Republicans? The Whigs, who were Black Rep. under another name, carried the offices pro tem. & made no advance. Recently the B. R. were defeated by the D. P.[250] But the D. P. were defeated in respect to Kanzas. Was Kanzas likely to be carried at any time by the South, with Missouri only nominally a slave state, and with the South, lacking population, unable to colonize new territory? This is a question soon discussed. This was another of our false issues; beginning in delusion & ending in defeat. There is nothing, at this moment, which would serve as a pretext for new agitation, & we should only waste our strength, beginning agitati[on withou]t

---

[248] The upper right corner of the MS. is torn off, and the date and several other words of the text are missing. On the back of the MS. is written "W. G. Simms 1858 2 Aug," the "2 Aug" in a handwriting different from the other and neither in Simms'. The year is certainly correct (see Simms' references to Hammond's forthcoming Barnwell speech, delivered on Oct. 29), and the month is likewise correct (see Simms' remark that he leaves for "New York next Saturday"—in his letter to Hammond of Aug. 7 he writes that he is leaving that afternoon) ; the day is probable.

[249] Simms is here attempting to summarize or clarify Hammond's position.
[250] The Democratic Party.

aim or object. The question arises. Will the B. R. succeed in
carrying the Presidency, & obtaining such an ascendency at the
next Election, as will enable them to change the Constitution. The
next question is — Is the Election of a B. R. President, cause, *per
se,* of Secession? That is a question for your people to decide.
How will you recommend? That is your difficulty. You may say
the mere Election, and carrying the offices, does not involve necessarily the adoption of measures which shall either hurt or dishonour us. Shall we wait or not for the measures themselves,
and try the adm. by its measures. Were we less antagonistic this
would be prudent counsel. It is for you to consider whether this
counsel, however, will be consistent with the previous avowals,
resolves & declarations of the South & of S. C. in particular. It
is a point of honour to inquire in what degree the mere triumph
tends to degrade us, and leave doubtful our securities. It is
enough, perhaps, where the antagonism is so decided, that the
South is at the mercy of a party, sectionally hostile, and though
they may forbear today, there is still a continual doubt & apprehension lest they assail tomorrow — throw us off guard by temporary forbearance, demoralize accordingly, & swoop down upon
us in a moment of drowse & despondency. Consider all these things
in reference to your Barnwell speech, & shape it accordingly.
I myself, with all the guarantees possible from the North, would
go out of the Union with 2 or 3 of the Cotton States, on the
simple ground that our relations are unprofitable, that our bargain is a bad one, that the tariff is sucking our substance, and
that sooner or later, we shall be required to succumb, from mere
exhaustion. You have hopes, however, that the triumphs of B.
R. are merely temporary, that there is a revolu[tion brewing in
their opinio]n on the subject of slavery; that [Eng., F]rance &
other European nations are receding from their former notions
and beginning to approve, & that these influences will be sufficient to reform public opinion at the North. This may be so.
Still, it might be better to give it as a faint hope, which should
prevent us from being precipitate in action, rather than as a security upon which we should so rely as to relax our vigilance. I
wish you to examine these points carefully; especially as it is
thought that to give any more decided & emphatic an opinion
would tend to discourage other sisters of the Cotton States, who
are gradually forging their way up to our advanced position. So
far as I have gathered from you, I do not see that you mean more

or less than I have stated. I do not understand you as relaxing any jot of vigilance or suspicion, or that you have changed any opinion as to our rights & duties that you have ever entertained. All that you mean is that S. C. having resolved for the present to remain in the Union, in waiting on her Southern Sisters, you are for avoiding all mere mouthing—all unnecessary agitation— especially at a time when there is no real issue before the country; your people simply lying on their arms, in readiness as ever, to take advantage of any opening in the game, and prepared for the cooperation with such states as shall march up to her side. Am I not right in this? If so, make it clear in your speech. We both see farther, it is true, and see many things which few persons conjecture; but sufficient for the day is the evil thereof. These may wait. Our children will have their own battles to fight, and it will be part of our duty to prepare them to do so, with as good heart, or better, than [any of us have] shown. — But at all events, write out y[our Ba]rnwell speech. You are here evidently & greatly misunderstood, & you deserve it. You have been too careless of public opinion. The Mercury is anxious to support you, & will, I doubt not, do so thoroughly if you make yourself clear by your own report. — I go (D. V.) to New York next Saturday,[251] having some important business negotiations on hand. Hope to be back in three weeks. Best regards to Mrs. H. & a kiss for Bettina.[252] I shall try to see Kate sometime this week. God bless you.

Yours ever &c.

W. Gilmore Simms

J. H. H.

894: To Mary Lawson

Charleston, August 2. 1858.

My dear Mary.

I have just got back to the city after a weeks absence on the Savannah river, and find your kind letter awaiting me. I hasten to say that it is not a matter of choice but business, which will carry me to N. Y. while you are absent from it. I am about to arrange for the publication of certain new novels, *serially,* in a

---

[251] Aug. 7. See letter to Hammond of that date.

[252] Hammond's daughter Elizabeth, usually called "Betty." See note 193, Oct. 17, 1849.

N. Y. weekly paper. The negotiations have so far advanced as to require my presence *now,* and before any thing farther can be done.[253] I propose, therefore, to sail from Charleston in the Steamer of Saturday next, the 7th. inst. and (D. V.) expect to reach N. Y. on Monday Night, or Tuesday Morning early. I shall accept Mr. Redfield's invitation to lodge with him while you are absent. He lives at Brooklyn.[254] I shall as soon after I arrive as possible, seek out your father in Wall Street, and take a trip with him to Budd's Lake whenever he first goes after my arrival, and where I hope to spend a few merrie days with you.[255] This is all I can do, for I shall be required to return to Charleston in two weeks.[256] I will bring on the Daguerreotypes. Our house is full of country cousins just now & in an uproar with the children. Love to all, and God's blessing upon you.

Your friend as Ever

W. Gilmore Simms

895: To James Henry Hammond

Charleston, 7 Aug. 1858.

Dear Hammond.

I proceed (D. V.) to N. Y. in the Steamer of this afternoon. Should you write me, during the next two weeks, address me "Care of J. S. Redfield, Publisher, New York." Kate spent the morning of yesterday with us, but would not stay to dinner, though we had provided a shoulder of the finest mutton! She was for a party that evening, Dessaussure's, on the Island.[257] She is looking well. Thus far, though terribly hot, the town is reported as continuing healthy. The island is certainly so. I saw Farrar yesterday, who goes with me, by the way, this afternoon.[258] He

---

[253] Simms turned down this offer of $3,000 annually (see letters to Hammond of July 10, 1858, and to De Bow of March 1, 1859). We are unable to identify the New York weekly which made the offer.

[254] 31 Sands Street. See note 203, July 1858.

[255] Lawson's business address was 62 Wall Street. His family was spending the summer at Budd's Lake, N. J. (see letter to Mary Lawson of July 10, 1858).

[256] Simms returned to Charleston on Aug. 24. See letter to Bancroft of Aug. 19.

[257] We have not identified the particular family of DeSaussures that was spending the summer at Sullivan's Island.

[258] The Charleston *Courier* of Aug. 9 lists Simms and Samuel S. Farrar as among the passengers on the *Nashville,* which cleared Charleston Harbor on Aug. 7.

says — "Tell H. to let them hear him only from the Senate House." And I say so too. After the Barnwell dinner, accept no more invitations. Your assailants in the Mercury are evidently one-idead people. One of them is undoubtedly Spratt, whose Hobby of the African slave trade, you treated so irreverently. The other is probably Bryan. This latter, however, is mere conjecture.[259] By no means answer any of these assailants. They are noisy in proportion to their smallness of number. The more numerous & influential are no doubt with you, even to the extent of your speech as reported. But do not let that persuade you to extremes of language or opinion. Modify, when you can, those sentiments which go to backing the old hobbies off of the wharf. Best regards to Madame & a kiss for Bet. God bless you with the adequate wisdom.

Yours faithfully

W. Gilmore Simms.

P. S. I have not one of those quartos of which you asked me. Send a sett.[260]

896: To George Bancroft

144 Twelfth St.

New York.

[August 19, 1858][261]

My dear Mr. Bancroft.

I penned the enclosed notice of your volume for the Editorial columns of the Charleston Mercury, just before I left home. Since reaching this place, the paper has published it. I trust you will find in it a proof of my desire to be pleased & gratified, & that

---

The Charleston *Mercury* of Aug. 2 carries two letters attacking Hammond's Beech Island speech. One, dated Charleston, July 29, is signed "South"; the other, undated, is signed "A Leaguer of the South." The *Mercury* of Aug. 3 carries a second letter from "South," dated Charleston, Aug. 2.

For Leonidas W. Spratt, see note 156, June 9, 1851; for Edward Benjamin Bryan, see note 112, March 27, 1858.

260 This set of books, which we are unable to identify, was doubtless mentioned by Hammond during Simms' recent visit to Redcliffe. Probably it was a set of government publications.

261 On the back of this letter Bancroft wrote: "W. G. Simms Aug 19/58." Bancroft, whose home was in New York City, probably received the letter on the same day that Simms wrote it.

I have been so.[262] I should be glad to call & see you, but I have been exceedingly absorbed ever since my arrival, and my return home will take place so soon that it is scarcely possible that I should find the time to look you up. I sail for Charleston (D. V.) on Saturday next.[263] With the hope that you will wear out this hot summer, without impairing your own energies & health, I am

Very truly Yours, &c

W. Gilmore Simms.

897: To James Henry Hammond

Charleston, Sep. 24. [1858][264]

Oh! dear Hammond, weep for me! I am crushed to earth. I have buried in one grave, within twelve hours of each other, my two brave beautiful boys, Sydney, & your little namesake, Beverley Hammond, two as noble little fellows as ever lived. It was a dreadful struggle of 12 days with one, & nine with the other.[265] It is a terrible stroke of fate, leaving us almost desolate. I feel heart broken, hope crushed, and altogether wretched. I can write no more. God's blessing upon you & yours. Weep for me

[262] Simms reviews Volume VII of Bancroft's *A History of the United States* . . . (Boston: Little, Brown and Company, 1858) in the *Mercury* of Aug. 10. In his review he praises Bancroft for both his research and his style and writes at length of his own ideas of the proper aims of the historian.

[263] Aug. 21. Simms returned to Charleston on Aug. 24 on the *Marion* (see the Charleston *Courier* of Aug. 25).

[264] Hammond's reply to this letter is dated Sept. 29, 1858. Hammond had also written to Simms on Aug. 13, Sept. 14, and Sept. 21. The originals are in the Hammond Papers, Library of Congress.

[265] In a letter not located by us Simms had earlier written Hammond of the illness of his two sons (see Hammond's letter to Simms of Sept. 21). William Porcher Miles writes in a letter to Hammond dated Sept. 23 (original in the Hammond Papers, Library of Congress): "At the request of Mr. Simms I write to inform you of the death of two of his little boys. The elder, Sydney, died yesterday morning and the younger, Beverley Hammond, your little namesake, last night. The disease was Yellow Fever of a very persistent and inveterate type. One was sick twelve, and the other, nine days. They received every possible care and attention in the way both of medical attendance and unceasing nursing and watching—but it was all in vain. Poor Simms is of course sorely distressed for his heart was wrapt up in these little boys and the sudden gap in the family circle will long be felt by them all. These children were peculiarly interesting and every one who was thrown with them became attached to them." The funeral service for Beverley Hammond was held at St. Paul's Church, Charleston, at 10:00 A.M., Sept. 23 (see the Charleston *Courier* and *Mercury* of that date). Neither the *Courier* nor the *Mercury* carries an account of the death of Sydney.

& mine, dear friend, for I know that your sensibilities are keen enough to feel for the great agonies of mine.[266]

Yours ever faithfully even now.

W. Gilmore Simms

J. H. H.

898: To James Henry Hammond

Charleston, 12 Oct. [1858][267]

dear Hammond.

I have not been able to write — can hardly write now. I have a fourth child taken down with fever, and for the last three days all my tortures have been renewed. My little girl, Chevillette, ten years old, was taken before day light on Sunday. She is this morning better, and we have reason to think & hope that the attack is a slight one, that milder form of the disease which is manageable.[268] But we dare not exult. The disease is terribly treacherous. Unless some sudden & unexpected change takes place, there is no danger. But in half an hour after one of my poor boys was said by the Physicians to be doing well, he was seized with convulsions. This was your little namesake. So, at one time, both boys were said to be doing well. Yet! — I am not well myself; have been taking medicine. Am now better. But you may well conjecture in what condition. I have two more children who are liable,[269] & cannot leave the city lest the disease should break out elswhere. I am a bear chain'd to the stake. Go, fearlessly, to the Barnwell dinner, & correct the vulgar report of your speech.[270]

---

[266] In his reply of Sept. 29 Hammond writes: "I do weep with my dear Simms & for you in this crowning calamity of your life. It would be vain to attempt to offer consolation. It cannot be doubted that God has so smitten you for some good & wise purpose, but time & time only can reconcile you to the blow. I have often wished to see those boys, especially the one who bore my name. It grieves me that I never did. But we shall all meet I trust in a better world than this. Do be careful of your own health. God help you to bear up."

[267] This letter is a reply to Hammond's dated Oct. 9, 1858 (original in the Hammond Papers, Library of Congress).

[268] Apparently Mary Lawson also contracted yellow fever about this time. See letter to Hammond of Oct. 16.

[269] Govan and Hattie.

[270] Hammond spoke at Barnwell Court House on Oct. 29. See Simms' letter to him of Nov. 22.

Your own good sense will tell you how. For my part, I have no brain now to counsel. But God be with you.

Your friend

W. Gilmore Simms

899: To James Henry Hammond

Charleston, Oct. 16. [1858][271]

My dear Hammond.

My little girl Chevillette is convalescent, now out of all danger. Her attack, thank God, has been of very mild type. She & her older sister Mary Lawson had yellow fever in 1854 and to this it is probably owing that they now escape.[272] The disease in the city is abating, but every now & then we hear of it suddenly pouncing down upon some unsuspecting victim, and I cannot forget that I have two other younger children who are still liable. Judge then of the continual terrors that haunt my thoughts, and will continue to haunt me, until, after a frost, we shall be able to escape this horrid city. God give you the necessary strength, health & wisdom to do yourself justice at Barnwell. *Be true to yourself & your own mind & conscience,* and send all other considerations to the devil! — I rejoice to see that Spann and Aldrich are elected.[273] Wife & daughter send regards to Mrs. H.[,] Kate & Bet. May God keep & bless you all.

Yours sadly but faithfully

Simms

---

[271] Hammond's reply to this letter is dated Oct. 26, 1858 (original in the Hammond Papers, Library of Congress).

[272] Simms' son Gilmore also had yellow fever at that time. See letter to Duyckinck of Nov. 9, 1854.

[273] Spann Hammond served in the South Carolina House of Representatives during 1858-1859, Alfred Proctor Aldrich (see introductory sketch) during 1858-1865.

900: To HENRY BARTON DAWSON [274]

Charleston, Oct. 16. 1858

Henry B. Dawson, Esq.

dear Sir:

I am in reciept of your letter, & the proof sheets of your work
embodying the affair of Fort Sullivan & others.[275] I regret that
I can only hastily glance at these proofs. A terrible domestic
calamity which has recently swept over my house, and has torn
from me two of its most precious inmates,[276] leaves me almost
wholly incapable of thought or study of any sort, & I can only
say hurriedly, and without seeking to verify any thing, that your
account of Fort Sullivan appears to be generally correct, though
you do not seem to be aware that Clinton did endeavor to cross
the Breach from Long to Sullivan, made two attempts in vessels,
& was so terribly handled by the rifles of Thompson that he
abandoned the attempt. You do not seem to have been in possession of Drayton's Memoirs which contain the best authorities
for this affair. Perhaps, if you will procure my history of S. C.
which you may do out of Mr. Bancroft's library, your revision
might be made complete from that source.[277] — I would counsel
you to modify greatly the harsh language which you employ
touching the N. C. Regulators.[278] They were a far superior class

---

[274] Dawson (1821-1889), editor and historian, was born in England and came
to New York City in 1834. He was the author of a number of works on
American history, and during 1866-1875 he edited the *Historical Magazine*
(New York), to which Simms was a contributor.

[275] These were proof sheets of at least Chapters IX and X of Volume I
("The Battle of Moore's Creek Bridge" and "The Attack on Sullivan's Island")
of *Battles of the United States, by Sea and Land: Embracing Those of the
Revolutionary and Indian Wars, the War of 1812, and the Mexican War; with
Important Official Documents*, 2 vols. (New York: Johnson, Fry, and Company, [1858-1859?]), issued in numbers of 32 pages each and priced at twenty-
five cents a number (see Simms' review of the first 16 numbers of the work in
the Charleston *Mercury* of June 27, 1859).

[276] See preceding letters.

[277] Dawson did not follow Simms' suggestions and alter his account of Sir
Henry Clinton's action against Col. William Thomson (see *Battles*, I, 137-138).
Nor does his chapter contain references to either John Drayton's *Memoirs of the
American Revolution . . .* , 2 vols. (Charleston: Printed by A. E. Miller, 1821),
or Simms' *The History of South Carolina* (Charleston: S. Babcock & Co.,
1840).

[278] Dawson writes (p. 128): "In the early days of the Revolution, there
existed a body of ignorant and disorderly men, on the frontiers of North
Carolina, who styled themselves Regulators. With all the recklessness and
ignorance usually found among the pioneers, these men assumed to 'regulate'
the affairs of those around them, setting all government at defiance, and
endeavoring to control or stop the administration of justice throughout the new

of people to most of the Loyalists. There are several N. C. writings which would set you right on this score: but see Dr. Hawks,[279] and a few words from him will enable you to put yourself right.

Very respectfully Yr obt Servt &c

W. Gilmore Simms.

901: To WILLIAM PORCHER MILES

Tuesday MG. 12. M.

[November 2, 1858][280]

dear Miles.

You see I am not off yet. But I am all prepared for a start this day at 2½. God bless you and all of yours. My love to James.[281] Of course you have read Hammond's speech, & I trust, like it.[282] It is a very manly, frank, comprehensive speech, & ought to do good. Let me hear from you at the Plantation, and if possible see you. Do look in upon my little family, *en passant,* and beg James to do likewise. I leave them with fear & trembling, knowing not what I may not have to hear, & they to bear. I need not say to you & James, that no living men will be more grateful as visitors to my household than you both. — I enclose you a scrap from a Rochester paper which has been sent me by some unknown friend, possibly the Editor himself. You will see by that, that the impression of my Northern Lectures, and of the Lecturer, was not unfavorable in a city where I had more than 1000 hearers; and where, under considerable excitement, I made a sharp extempore speech, of very nearly the tenor of Hammond's Senate

settlements of the West." In a footnote to this passage, however, he remarks: "There is no doubt that these *'Regulators'* originally represented a people contending for their rights against the oppressions of the government. This object, however, was abandoned after the battle of Alamance; and the subsequent engagements of this body to fight the battles of the Crown show that other parties were engaged in it."

279 Francis Lister Hawks (1798-1866), born at New Bern, N. C., was a Protestant Episcopal clergyman, lawyer, and historian. In the 1850's he was rector of the Church of the Mediator, New York City.

280 On the back of this letter Miles wrote: "ansd. Nov. 4th/58." Nov. 2 fell on Tuesday.

281 James Warley Miles.

282 James H. Hammond's speech delivered at Barnwell on Oct. 29. See letter to Hammond of Nov. 22.

Speech, in addition to my Lecture, in which, you may be sure, I did not mince matters.[283]

Yours Ever lovingly

W. Gilmore Simms

Hon. W. P. Miles.

P. S. I send the medical pamphlet for Dr. Miles.[284]

902: To JAMES HENRY HAMMOND

Woodlands, S. C. Nov. 22 [1858][285]

My dear Hammond.

This is the first day that I have touched pen & paper for the last three weeks. I have been toiling to get the house to rights; had to lay new floors, & have had no room to sleep in; to turn or write in; could not get at books, pen, ink, paper, or any thing. I have been quite an invalid besides; headachy, almost feverish; dreadfully constipated for several days after coming up, and so debilitated that I had energy for nothing. I came up, leaving my family, though counselled that I should incur some risk in bring-

---

[283] The Rochester *Union and Advertiser* of Oct. 26, 1858, contains the following paragraph about Simms: "The Legislature of South Carolina will elect at its next session a successor to Judge [Josiah James] Evans for the unexpired term, and also for the succeeding regular term. The Charleston Courier [of Oct. 19] says public sentiment points strongly to W. Gilmore Simms, LL.D., who a few winters since received such shabby treatment from the fanatical press and people of northern cities while on a lecturing tour. Rochester, we believe, formed the exception. Here Mr. Simms was treated with due respect and courtesy, a fact which he handsomely acknowledged before his departure. Certainly South Carolina's interests would be safe in the hands of Mr. Simms, than whom she has no more loyal son or able champion." The editor of the *Union and Advertiser* was Isaac Butts (1816-1874). Butts was the editor of the Rochester *Daily Advertiser* during 1845-1848 and 1849-1851. In 1852 he purchased a half interest in the Rochester *Daily Union*, which was merged with the *Daily Advertiser* in 1857 to form the *Union and Advertiser*, Butts serving as editor of both until 1864. His paper had praised and defended Simms at the time of his Northern lecture tour (see note 123, Nov. 12, 1856, and note 127, Nov. 21, 1856). Hammond's "Senate Speech" is that on the admission of Kansas, delivered on March 4, 1858 (see note 113, March 27, 1858).

[284] Francis Turquand Miles (1827-1903), brother of William Porcher Miles, was graduated from the College of Charleston and the Medical College of the State of South Carolina, at Charleston, where he devoted himself to the study of anatomy and physiology and where he later taught anatomy. During the Confederate War he served first as a private, then as a surgeon. After the War he taught at the Medical College of the State of South Carolina; Washington College, at Baltimore; and the University of Maryland.

[285] This letter is a reply to Hammond's of Oct. 26, Nov. 3 and 4 (a double letter), and Nov. 5. Hammond again wrote Simms on Nov. 28. The originals are in the Hammond Papers, Library of Congress.

ing the fever with me. It is thought wonderful that I should have escaped. But thus far, God has shielded me. Since I left town, my fourth son [286] was taken, though with the disease in a very mild form. My wife kept the fact from me till he recovered. I have thus had five children with this horrid pestilence in less than two months, & two negroes. We doctored the negroes ourselves, & they recovered, and two of the children had the fever in 1854.[287] What you say, of the absurd superstition which carries us annually to town, to incur these terrors & dangers, when we have a plantation that is quite healthy, is sorrowfully true; but I have been for twenty years, trying to persuade my family to abandon Charleston, have proposed a dozen places, but all in vain. I had to contend with a habit that had matured into a superstition. I have now resolved to build myself a rude summer house, in a spot of pinelands, on the plantation itself. Poverty alone prevents me from making a settlement in a more imposing & attractive region. I have read and meditated your speech a very great deal.[288] It is a very noble & masterly performance, immeasurably superior to most of the things that you have done, and simply because it was done under a coercive strain, which, in spite of your ailments of body, brought all your mind to bear upon it. It will, it ought & will, give you a national reputation. It is as profound, comprehensive & thoughtful, as any speech delivered for 20 years in Congress. It places you fairly within the ranks occupied by Clay, Calhoun & Webster. It is the speech of a statesman, such a speech, my dear Hammond — you will suffer me the egotism — as I alone, of all your friends, well knew that you were capable of making. I have long since been satisfied that your mind only wanted the adequate field, *and the adequate provocation,* to assert its perfect mastery, over all the contemporary politicians. I knew what you could do, when, a year ago, I counselled you to strike at *Douglas.*[289] Perhaps, Seward, would have been your better mark, but Douglas was more certainly the popular idol. I do not say all this to please, but to provoke you. I believe, the field open,

---

[286] Govan.

[287] Chevillette and Mary Lawson. See letter to Duyckinck of Nov. 9, 1854.

[288] Hammond spoke at Barnwell Court House on Oct. 29. His speech, in which he advises South Carolina to remain in the Union as a matter of policy unless pushed to the wall by the abolitionists, was printed by Walker, Evans and Co., Charleston, in 1858. It is included in *Selections from the Letters and Speeches of the Hon. James H. Hammond, of South Carolina,* pp. 323-357.

[289] See letter of Jan. 28, 1858.

& your true position reached, *your health* will improve. But you are not to mind health. You have made an *entree*. This speech secures *that*. And now, keep in position. In minor respects, the speech is secure from criticism. It is admirably well written. It is almost faultless in point of style. It is worthy of McDuffie [290] in his best day, and there are points in which it resembles him. You lack his vehemency, but you have something more than his *tenacity*. The speech, as an English composition, is perfectly classical. I do not see more than one or two places, where I would have you change a word, or amend a period. It is national, without surrendering any substantiality of your section. The seceders & altruists have long since been reduced to mere vituperation & declamation, empty & violent resolutions from which they have been compelled to beg or bluster their way out. You have found the popular mind in a certain condition & have accepted the facts of that condition in order to make your argument. You are thus grounded in what is, rightly speaking, the popular instinct in the South. That instinct is based upon certain relations, *which the North has the power to change à plaisir*. Here your distinction lies. Now, that you have deprived a certain class of our politicians of their favorite hobbies, you will of course offend *them*. You must look for that. You require a man to dismount from his favorite donkey & go henceforth on foot. That is an offense to make him angry. But do not care for this. It is a nobler & a surer play, henceforth, to teach. We have found a people wanting in qualities to bring them up to those issues which are probably inevitable; and we must wait upon the people, with a modest patience, and wait upon events. If the North drives us to the wall, — then! And what will constitute a driving to the wall? This you indicate. And this leads us to the only point upon which *we* have a difference. It is the difference *of opinion as to the facts in the case,* and not any difference of principle. Is our position so assured as you deem it. Are our securities thus good. Will the North no more trespass, offensively & injuriously. I do not concur with you on your hope, nor altogether as to the facts — might do so, if we had to contend with fanaticism alone — but fanaticism has never been our danger. It was cold-blooded selfish policy, of selfish politicians & interested sections. But even here, you have an argument upon which you fall back. Perhaps I am wrong.

---

[290] George McDuffie. See introductory sketch.

Well, what then? You are prepared. I counsel preparation, watch, vigilance & indicate the dangers. Sufficient for the day is the evil thereof. Let us wait upon it, especially as you yourselves, my people, have deliberately resolved to wait. When the events arrive, which our ultra patriots fear, are we the worse off, because we have kept ourselves cool & made no bluster. Enough. You have made a great & noble speech which will make you a national reputation & not hurt you here except with a small minority. God bless you. Write me. I am more wretched than you.

W. G. S.

903: To Israel Keech Tefft

Woodlands, S. C.

Decr. 15. 1858.

My dear Tefft.

Our child is to be married on the 29th. The terrible afflictions in our family, this autumn, render it impossible that the wedding should be other than a private one! [291] She will have no company. But you & Mama [292] have claims beyond all others. You have shown for her a parental regard, which has been as sweet to me as to her! And I could wish you both to be present. Come then, my friends, and we will sadly commune together, as becomes those to whom this world is gradually changing its lines, for the darker, the graver, the more profound, solemn & mysterious! We will give you a quiet room; and meet once more, in grateful reünion, though neither of us have any good reasons to be glad! If we are submissive it is, perhaps, all that the good God will expect from creatures so feeble, so frail, so constantly faltering, and *who have had such losses!* [293] You & Mama will come as guests of my wife & self, to spend the Christmas Holidays simply. Augusta has just gone to the city to make her preparations. God bless you, dear friends. God bless you!

Yours Ever

W. Gilmore Simms

---

[291] Augusta's marriage to Edward Roach had originally been planned for October (see letter to Mary Lawson of July 10, 1858), but was postponed because of the deaths of Sydney Roach and Beverley Hammond and the illnesses of Chevillette, Mary Lawson, and Govan (see preceding letters).

[292] Mrs. Tefft, the former Penelope Waite.

[293] All of Tefft's children had died. See note 141, Dec. 17, 1853.

1859

Woodlands, Jany. 10. 1859.

My dear Hammond.

The main fact in your last letter by no means surprises me.[2] On the contrary, it is one which I somewhat confidently anticipated. You will remember, just after your election as Senator, my telling you to accept, to go, and realize your destiny, and, in so many words, indicated the high position to which I held it probable that you would be called.[3] I do not claim to have said this from inspiration. I did not regard the conviction as needing prophetic suggestion. It was based upon what I knew of your endowments, which, in a certain contingency which is at least possible even now, might almost be held certain to secure you the support of a large portion of the country. And all that was required of you was to let yourself alone — simply to do the business before you — to let your mind out — working freely and fearlessly according to your knowledge and opinions, and abide the result. The danger is that you will not let your mind alone —

---

[1] This letter is a reply to Hammond's of Jan. 1, written from Washington. Shortly after his arrival there Hammond had written Simms on Dec. 15: "I am very sorry it did not turn out as you *apprehended* it might & that you are not here with me. When I left Columbia it was understood Chesnut did not wish to come on this Session & I was surprised at his election. I have not heard a word from him & it is not a little unpleasant to have to say so ten times a day; as well as to represent So Ca virtually *alone* so long as I have done. I do wish you were here." The originals are in the Hammond Papers, Library of Congress.

[2] In his letter of Jan. 1 Hammond writes: "My Barnwell Speech has secured to me the ear of [the] whole country, & imposed upon it the belief that I am [an] honest, disinterested, & fearless man, not without a fair share of talent. The thinking & patriotic men want just such a man for the next Presidency & if they can find him are disposed to rally & unite in his support. Of this I have abundant proof & with *the man*, their success would be certain. You don't know the overtures I receive daily from almost all quarters. If I had the *physique* of Orr or Douglass [*sic*], I would set up for it. But as it is, I would as soon think of scaling the walls of heaven."

[3] We have not located this letter, also mentioned by Simms in his letter to Hammond of Dec. 12, 1857.

that your skulking body will be full of its suggestions, and you
have been so long in the habit of exercising your fancies upon
your physical fears, and ailments, — crotchets of disease and what
not; that you will continue this habit so as to become cowardly,
in contemplation of the toils and cares which such a station will
necessarily involve. Once for all, let me entreat you to let yourself alone — do not bother yourself about your body at all. It will
be quite time enough to think about that when you fall down in
the harness, like an overloaded wagon horse, and require to be
picked up & carried to the Commons. Your physique is really
good enow, and in much better state than you have given it credit
for. It is your mind, restive, properly speaking inadequately employed, that has generated all your physical infirmities. To that
you owe your dyspepsia mostly — that and Florida cigars. And
to that you owe your piles. I believe that you will always be
healthier while at your post in Washington than doing nothing
in Carolina, but worrying yourself about plantation details, & the
errantries of idle boys. Now, in this matter, for Heaven's sake
suffer yourself to be — quiet. Suffer your destiny to work out
all its issues, without any introspective impediment offered by
yourself. I do not ask you to *do* any thing, in respect to the nomination or the result. Rather leave others to do. Do not engage in
any talk on the subject which you can possibly avoid, especially
with earwigs & talking potatoes. You will have enough of them
always about you, where you are, and but few persons in whom
you can really trust. The subject is not one for mere company
or conversation, and the more you can escape speech upon it, the
better. When forced to speak every thing like levity should be
avoided — all reference to party, and every reference to your own
condition. The simple speech of Wm. Lowndes will suit you
exactly. "It is an affair which should neither be sought nor
avoided." [4] You are briefly no candidate for any thing. You are
in the attitude of the Roman at his domestic plough handle, and
only when actually summoned away from that to the chair of
State do you believe that you must go. This is not only the true
position for a Southern Gentleman, but accords, I fancy, equally

---

[4] When notified in Dec., 1821, that the South Carolina legislature had nominated him for president of the United States, William Lowndes (1782-1822),
at that time a member of Congress from South Carolina, replied with these
words. See Mrs. St. Julien Ravenel, *Life and Times of William Lowndes of
South Carolina* (Boston and New York: Houghton, Mifflin and Company,
1901), pp. 223-231.

with your situation & real sentiment. Of course, you will suffer
yourself to engage in no such speculations with any body as to
the game to be played either by your friends or others, for that
would be to endanger your reputation (now your best capital any
how) for stern, simple integrity & elevation of character, &
patriotism of thought & purpose. To talk commonly, or even
casually about the election at all, will be to risk being brought
into making calculations &c. and you will endanger every thing
by it. — And now, the question occurs — what is the real prospect, as seen through the cloud, — if any body can see through
it. That you should be *nominated* will depend wholly upon the
fate of the Democratic Party. It is only from the ranks of this
party, and the conservative allies which it finds from the ranks
of the old national parties, Whig, Federal or what not, — that
you could expect a call. But the Democratics will die hard. That
they are dying is sufficiently apparent. Nothing can save them
but a foreign war, or some grand acquisition of territory, and
even this will hardly save them, since the Black Republicans are
sufficiently reckless to seize upon the same capital. Of course, it
will be the true policy of the South to oppose every movement of
whatever sort that promises much excitement of the public mind.
You will oppose every measure calculated to disturb the peace,
or needlessly agitate. The Democrats would have died out in
Polk's time but for the Texas, & Oregon agitation, & but for the
War with Mexico. They cannot survive a quiet progress of events
for five years at any time. Nor can the Republicans! Now, what
is the value of their material for the purposes of agitation at the
North; for unless the people there are getting tired of being in
hot water, I need not say, the next President will no doubt be
elected wholly by a section. Unless there be very great reaction
at the North there can be no chance for the formation of any
third party much less one which will be likely to have any weight
in the balance. There must be such a dying out of the Democrats
on one hand, and such a weariness & fear, if not disgust of the
Republicans on the other, as to afford the adequate hope & material for the organization of a truly *national* party — using the
word which, hitherto, we have ignored in the South, but which
we should perhaps regard as legitimate so long as we are in the
Union. Not that I care that we should keep in it. That the Republicans will kill off the Democrats in the North I have no ques-

tion; that they will finally perish themselves in the progress of events, & by a new division of parties at home, is also clear to me. But how long are they to take in dying out? My notion is that the Black Republicans have by no means reached the length of their tether; and my doubt is whether they will reach it until they have fairly got possession of the Government. This will be too late for any thing, or calculation based upon present conditions. A Conservative Party, by the way, is usually too timid, as too conscientious, perhaps, to effect any thing in a time of revolution. It does not concieve the policy of fighting fire with fire. It wakes up too late, organizes too slowly, and fights only after saying a long prayer. And it is half beaten before its battle begins. Another reason why *you* should do nothing, and *talk* nothing, is the small reliance to be placed upon such a party, until *the affairs of the country shall become really desperate.* The really working & business world, when urged by despair, will always conquer. And one thing rather favors the organization of this party now. It is that the trade of the country has *not* recovered from the revulsion of 1856! This is *felt* and, no doubt, this feeling works to a considerable extent in the Northern mind. Some thing may be made of it. But the Democrats, as I said, will die hard, & will hold on to the last. It is only when no longer able to lift a leg, and when the meanest puppy of the opposition may lift its leg over it with impunity that it will be content to give up the Ghost. In fact, it is far less a Democratic party than is the *Republican* (at the North) and in truth, if not in name, its vulgar capital has been taken from it. The Northern (quasi) allies of the Democratic Party, proper, are really the best educated & most aristocratic people of New England, their social position driving the common people from their party. — You see that Douglas & Orr are preparing for a fierce struggle, as Pres. & V. P. in the organization of a *National Democratic* Party, and there will be no doubt a new programme, with the introduction of some popular elements. *Nous verrons.* They will thus endeavour to infuse new blood into the old veins, and make double bids for North & South, mostly, no doubt, in the shape of proposed territorial acquisitions, Cuba for the South, and (*quien sabe?*) Canada for the North, — or any thing you please which will inaugurate a grand excitement. Whatever happens in regard to these parties, & whatever the policies they contemplate — your policy is to eschew them all —

to avoid speech of all, and let the politicians find you too much absorbed in business to engage in politics, and too much absorbed in drink & dinner & good fellowship to be disturbed by business. But take no ground, personally, except the negative one of Lowndes which involves also the positive. "Such an affair is not to be sought — it involves too terrible a responsibility, especially *now!* — Such an office, with all its terrible responsibility, even now, is not to be declined, by any true son of the soil, who loves his country & is prepared to die, or live for her, as she pleases." But remember what Norman Maurice says —

> "You may make me, Sirs,
> A Senator, but not a Candidate." [5]

And here is all. If the matter becomes very urgent, you should be at the pains to say to *Northern* men, — "Gentlemen, I fear you misunderstand me. At all events, I must not suffer you to do so. My policy, were I in power, should certainly be national and conservative. But it should also be Southern, for I regard the South as the essential fountain of national salvation. I am a Southron, — *a capite ad calcem.*["] Just be a man — be yourself. Stop your lugubrious dilations touching your physical infirmities. You are good for fifty years yet — in Washington. Submit to Fate, if she requires it, without murmuring. But, do nothing yourself directly or indirectly, either to promote or prevent. Let yourself alone, and let the blind weights of Destiny work on as they will in the curtained spheres where the Lottery of Life is carried on.

Enough. I have given you a long, and I fear, a tiresome epistle. But the subject is one, on your account, which provokes me. It is not easy for me to write now. My mind & body are both in wretched condition. I do not know well what is the matter with me. My brain no longer works. I am doing little at the desk. Have a great dread of exertion. Suffer from doubts, fears, depressions. Little things bother me. I am sad & spiritless, yet irritable. My affairs do not prosper. My friends (yourself excepted) seem to have deserted me. I get no letters save from Charleston Duns. My crop though doubling those of my predecessor,[6] and exceeding this year that of the last, is yet only half a crop, far short of my expectations. If, by the way, (& this

---

[5] III, iii.

[6] During 1859 Simms usually speaks of Nash Roach as "my predecessor."

Entre Nous) if you should hear suddenly by telegraph, that the Collectorship, or Post Office Department of Charleston, was *par accident,* vacated, then, if you can, get me the office. Either will do. If I must drudge on to the end of the chapter, I will try to do as little as I can, and secure the highest amount of compensation for my drudgery. I see nothing else. I will not attempt to turn anyone from office — Heaven forbid — but the thing is possible that the incumbent of one or other of these offices may withdraw, in some way, and leave a comfortable fauteuil vacant. Now, the field once vacated, there would be scores of Candidates in a jiffy at Washington. I wish you, therefore, to be prepared to anticipate them all, for either of these offices — I see no other.[7] As for going abroad with young children & negro nurses, that is impossible. — Present me, with affectionate New Years Wishes to Mrs. H. & Kate. Say to them that my daughter Augusta has gone to her new home in Charleston, — leaving our poor old household drearier than ever. My eldest boy goes off, tonight, after a brief furlough, to Yorkville.[8] You know not, my friend, how vacant every thing is here, here, in my heart as in my household. I am terribly bruised, sick, sad & very weary of a lifelong struggle, drawing water in a sieve, working against the bans of Destiny. God be with you in mercy.

Yours Ever

Simms

905 : To Evert Augustus Duyckinck [9]

Woodlands, Jany. 14. 1859.

My dear Duyckinck.

In the utter chaos of my thoughts, my heart and mind, for the last three months, I really do not remember whether I answered your kind and genial letter.[10] I should think I did so, from my habitual promptitude to answer friend or foe; but I fail to fix one fact in my memory which might satisfy me that I did. Lest I should not have done so, I prefer to write you now, and perhaps again. Not that I have any thing to say, for my mind seems to have grown barren, and the events of my life re-

---

[7] Simms did not receive either appointment.
[8] Gilmore was a cadet at the King's Mountain Military School.
[9] See introductory sketch.
[10] Doubtless this letter, which we have not located, was a letter of condolence on the deaths of Sydney Roach and Beverley Hammond Simms.

cently have been all singularly & exclusively domestic; but just
to assure you that your letter was very grateful to me, and that
I do not forget your kindness, & would not forfeit your friendship. I have passed through some bitter ordeals, of late, but have
reached, I trust, a degree of resignation, which enables me to
look back upon the trial without bitterness and to the future with
hope and confidence in God. Still, I am not well, either in mind
or body, and though toiling daily in a thousand ways which require thought and produce weariness, I yet feel a degree of lassitude & weariness, which results in a mournful state of depression
that I cannot wholly shake off. I apprehend from it finally, a
severe sickness which shall purge and purify the system — if
it does not sink under it; even as we see, in the natural world,
a prolonged term of heaviness in the atmosphere, cleansed by
storm and convulsion. It is possible that something of my present
state of mind is due to a considerable change in my mental habit.
The duties of the plantation have been such as to tear me away
from the desk, very much against my will; and my mind chafes
with its own creations & conceptions, which my hands refuse to
shape out in definite & intelligible form. I greatly grieve at this;
for my heart is in my profession; but the pecuniary interest at
stake is a very large one, and my family, though thinned by its
recent mournful losses, is yet one sufficiently numerous to render
necessary all my provisions for the morrow. I am now clearing
lands for the next crop, and hope to get some 70 to 100 acres
additional, in readiness for culture this spring. I have not been
as successful as I anticipated; though I have doubled the crops
of my worthy Predecessor. There is a small debt on the plantation, which a single successful season would extinguish, and
after that I should have tolerably plain, and perhaps gratefully
fair sailing. And if energy, will, cheerful courage, & I trust, a
constantly growing knowledge of my new duties, can achieve success, I flatter myself with the belief that I shall secure it. Meanwhile, however, I am doing nothing in my own vocation. I have
literally written nothing for months, except hurried critiques for
the newspapers, and a few mournful ballads.[11] My novel,[12] which
Redfield has in press is not quite finished, but a week or ten days

---

[11] Simms was reviewing books for the Charleston *Mercury*. One of these
"mournful ballads" is "Midnight Chaunt in Autumn" (see letter to Hayne of
May 8, 1864).

[12] *The Cassique of Kiawah.* See following letters and note 137, May 23, 1859.

will probably suffice for that. And more than one fondly cherished plan has been working in my brain, imploring utterance for a long season past. It is one of my most earnest prayers to be permitted to resume my labours in my own fields. But I stifle the thirst as I may, and content myself, as well as I can, with the faint echoes of performance from other pens, which reach me through the din of magazines & newspapers. An occasional letter from yourself is frequently craved, with reference to this appetite. Pray, my friend, let me hear from you, and soon, and at length, & frequently. I feel very sad & dreary; am very lonesome in my woods, and a voice, at once of letters and friendship, would be a great solace. Present me gratefully to your wife, & George, & the Pantons,[13] and believe me

Ever faithfully Yours &c

W. Gilmore Simms.

906: To Henry Barton Dawson

Woodlands (Midway P. O.)

Henry B. Dawson, Esq.   S. C. Jany. 19. 1859.

My dear Sir:

Your letter of Nov. 5. advises me that I shall, from time to time, recieve the several parts of your work, as it is serially issued;[14] and you request my suggestions as you proceed. I did not write to you in answer immediately, but resolved to wait the reciept of the numbers, in order that my reply should have its value in its comments upon them. But as none of them have as yet reached me, I think it only proper to advise you of the fact, lest they should have been forgotten by your publisher,[15] or possibly, taken a wrong direction. I need not say to you that, if in their examination I see occasion to suggest alteration or correction, I shall very cheerfully indicate the propriety or necessity of doing so.

Your obt Servt. &c

W. Gilmore Simms

---

[13] Margaret Wolfe Panton Duyckinck (see note 64, Feb. 16, 1850), George Long Duyckinck (see note 215, June 6, 1845), and Henry and John Albert Panton (see note 66, Feb. 16, 1850).

[14] *Battles of the United States.* See letter to Dawson of Oct. 16, 1858.

[15] Johnson, Fry, and Company.

907: To Alexander Dallas Bache [16]

(Woodlands, S. C.)
Midway P. O. Jan. 20. [1859] [17]

Professor A. D. Bache.

My dear Professor.

Let me congratulate you, honestly & heartily, on the handsome compliment paid to you in Europe.[18] No man more fully deserved it! Had it been an American compliment, I had distrusted it! I am doubtful of all tributes of American origin! I am afraid we are a nation of rascals! In our general ignorance, & universal presumption, we must be cheaters or cheated! But a tribute like this, such an acknowledgement, is above question; and when felt to be due, as, in this instance, it is by some thousands like myself, we clap hands, & congratulate ourselves that there is some salt, — some saving grace left, in the world! Once more, I congratulate you. Pardon this rude scrawl, but I am very sick, and sad, & am the chief in a house of mourning

Your friend & servt.

W. Gilmore Simms.

908: To Mary Lawson

Woodlands, Midway P. O.
So Caro: Jany. 28. 1859.

My dear Mary.

How could you suppose that I should ever leave your letters for any length of time unanswered, unless under very trying & absolute embarrassments? Be sure that if you wrote me, your letter never reached its point of destination. In truth, I have been murmuring somewhat at your protracted silence, which I

---

[16] Bache (1806-1867), the physicist, was at various times president of Girard College, a professor at the University of Pennsylvania, superintendent of the United States Coast Survey, regent of the Smithsonian Institution, and president of the National Academy of Sciences. He was a member of the leading scientific societies and academies of America and of Europe.

[17] Dated by Simms' reference to his being "the chief in a house of mourning"—an allusion to the deaths of Sydney Roach and Beverley Hammond Simms (see preceding letters).

[18] We are unable to identify conclusively the "compliment" Simms here has in mind. It may be Sardinia's awarding him a gold medal, which the Charleston *Mercury* of Feb. 23, 1859, reports he has been authorized to accept.

ascribed to the Holidays, and seeing visitors, and making calls, & having parties, and altogether being very happy for the Season, in spite of the claims of absent friends. I rejoice & am grateful that I hear at last, and hear so good an account of the health and happiness of all you dear ones, and of the pleasant employments — which seem so grateful — of my fair Correspondent in particular. — To answer you, *seriatim,* and briefly as becoming — we are — all that are left of us — as well physically as usual. There is some sickness still at our hearts which it will take some time to heal. The large gaps made previously in my circle, have been widened by the departure of Augusta, who was married on the 28th. of December,[19] and left us early in January for the city where she now resides. Yet you ask after her marriage, and speak of it as a mere rumour. Now, it is some weeks since a package was sent your father, by the Steamer, covering cakes & cards, for your family, Duyckinck's, and the Richards's of N. Y. & Providence.[20] A letter was sent to your father, at the same time, apprising him of the fact. You could not suppose *we* should ever forget you. Nay, had not the marriage been very private, as a matter of course — only the two families being present,[21] I should certainly have invited you & your sisters, if no more. Augusta has married a young man of great worth & integrity, who has to depend upon his industry & virtue for his success. But these are sterling qualities with him. He is modest, temperate — gentle — devoted & shy — not brilliant, but of excellent good sense & judgment, and does not pretend to more than he knows. Her chances of peace & happiness I hold to be particularly good. — I congratulate your parents on the happy celebration of their 23d. Anniversary of Marriage. In two years they may celebrate the Silver Wedding of the Germans. May they both live, consciously, and with sensibilities all keen, — to celebrate the Golden Wedding. I send a kiss through your velvet lips from my bearded ones, to your mother, and you may hug

---

[19] In his letter to Tefft of Dec. 15, 1858, Simms says that Augusta is to be married on Dec. 29, and Augusta's descendants say that she was married on Dec. 29.

[20] In 1855 William Carey Richards (see introductory sketch of the Richards family) removed from New York City to Providence, R. I., where he became associate pastor of the First Baptist Church. From 1855 to 1862 he was associate pastor of the Brown Street Baptist Church in Providence. Thomas Addison Richards remained in New York City.

[21] The Israel Keech Teffts were also present at Augusta's marriage to Edward Roach. See letters to Tefft of Dec. 15, 1858, and Feb. 3, 1859.

your father, in a brotherly manner on my account, if not your own. So you are to be a Numismatologist. Well, if I pick up any thing rare, I will send it you. But the chances are not much in my way. I am busy clearing lands, making compost, cutting ditches, making fences, building houses, giving physic, killing hogs, rearing cabbages, speculating on fertilizers, trying experiments in lime, salt, guano, &c! Hear! And I am very sad withal, my dear Mary. The head working while the eyes water & the heart bleeds. I could wind myself in sackcloth & roll in ashes. I have not shaved for months, and look like a griesly bear fresh from the Rocky Mountains. — Present me gratefully to the Richards's, and when next you see the Armitage's, affectionately to them.[22] I owe them nothing but kindness. Your report of your little Nellie [23] persuades me to tell you of our Hattie, & little Govan. They are both large fine children, fat & rosy. But I tremble now to brag about my children, lest I rouse the Fate that hangs over my dwelling to a renewal of her wrath! May God spare us, my dear Mary, in the dear ones whom we love. My wife sends her regards. Our boy Gilmore is again at Yorkville,[24] after his Christmas vacation. He is growing a very tall & stout fellow, will probably overtop his father by several inches, is modest & industrious—was at the head of his section of sixty five, and has a first rate report from his commandant. He shoots rides, runs & wrestles with any of his mates, & is full of what the British call 'pluck'. Will hold his own promptly, and suffers no insult, or indignity; yet, withal, is as docile to proper authority as I would have him. Say to your father that, though not yet as successful as I anticipated as a planter, I have more than doubled the crops of my predecessor, during the last six years of his life. I owe some money, however, and am needy; but with time, and God's favour, my own energies & application will, I trust, enable me to work through triumphantly. Time is what I want.

Yours, my dear Mary, most affectionately

W. Gilmore Simms

---

[22] The Benjamin Armitages became friends of Simms during the early 1830's. Lawson lived at their home before his marriage, and Simms also stayed there during his visits to New York City at that time. For Simms' earlier references to the Armitages, see letters to Lawson of Jan. 27, 1836, and April 19, 1847.

[23] Cornelia (b. 1857). See letter to Lawson of July 25, 1857.

[24] At the King's Mountain Military School.

909: To Evert Augustus Duyckinck

Woodlands, Jany 29. [1859] [25]

My dear Duyckinck.

I have your letter, & the copies of the Century. If you can send me the nos. of this work I shall be pleased to have it. But, just now, I can afford to subscribe to nothing. I may send a trifle for its pages as *quid*. Suffer me to suggest that the standards of the work are quite too high for the vulgar, and they constitute so large a portion of our paying population that they need to be considered. The work is a shade too essayical. The essays need condensation. [26] I see that Dr. Francis has published a volume of reminiscences.[27] Can you get me a copy? I should like one under the old man's hand, and feel a little touched that he has not thought proper to send me one. *Mais!* — I am doing just nothing in Literature. The plantation cares distract me. And my heart is still very sore, and my head craves rest. I shall soon finish my romance of the Cassique,[28] & then! Ah, then! My daughter (eldest) was married last month, & has left me for Charleston. This makes another sad gap in my household. I feel the vacancy, & the voices of solitude & silence make me shudder. My boys! My boys! — Ah! my friend, we who live so much in our children, how it lacerates all the fibers of life when they are torn from us. You have felt it all! But I — I have buried 7 children, and at every burial, how many strings of earth were severed. I have a larger family in heaven than on earth! Should I not long to rejoin them? But I will not muse on this. I note that you too have threatening aspects over your house. God avert them! [29] I seldom or never hear from Lawson. My correspondent of the family is

[25] Dated by Simms' references to Augusta's marriage to Edward Roach and to the deaths of his sons Sydney Roach and Beverley Hammond. See preceding letters.

[26] The *Century a National Newspaper of Politics, Commerce, Finance, Economy, Literature, Science and Art* (New York), a weekly edited and published by Thomas McElrath (see note 93, March 18, 1859), ran from Dec. 25, 1858, through 1861. The *Century* aimed at keeping an impersonal tone and the editors of its various departments are not given and only a few poems and articles carry signatures. Duyckinck appears, however, to have been the literary editor.

[27] John Wakefield Francis, *Old New York; or, Reminiscences of the Past Sixty Years. Being an Enlarged and Revised Edition of the Anniversary Discourse Delivered before the New York Historical Society, (November 17, 1857,)* (New York: Charles Roe, 1858). For Francis, see introductory sketch.

[28] *The Cassique of Kiawah.*

[29] Frances Cooper Panton, daughter of Henry H. Panton and sister of Mrs. Duyckinck, died on March 24, 1859. See letter to Duyckinck of April 22, 1859.

Mary, who sends me, on the average, a monthly letter, and a pleasant one. His hobby is an innocent one. But it is a hobby. My life — all life — is too serious for indulgence in these things. Do not you fall into them; though you may do so with more safety than most people. Yet, you might be engaged in better things. Your familiarity with English Literature will enable you to do a great deal of good through the Century, for a class of people, who will never get the good things of literature save through some such medium. Make my respects to your wife, my regards to your brother, my remembrances to Panton & Darley.[30] Write me as often as you can, for the voices of friends are specially sweet to me just now, and I am

Yours

W. Gilmore Simms

P. S. I recognized your hand, here & there, in the Century— graceful and easy as ever, merry.[31]

910: To John Esten Cooke

Woodlands. (Midway P. O.)
So. Caro. Jany 29. 1859.

My dear Mr. Cooke.

I thank you for your long and very grateful letter. You write, however, as if you had not heard of my great afflictions. My dear young friend, you are a bachelor, I believe. You do not know what it is to have dear children, and to lose them. Two of mine, — two most noble boys — gentle, loving, ingenuous, of noble faces, — genuine Saxon, — keen, quick, ardent tempers — were stricken down by yellow fever, last autumn, — dying within a few hours of each other, and I have suffered, as I never suffered before. In some respects I shall never get over it. I am getting too old not to feel acutely, & long, such losses. I have buried seven children out of thirteen. An eighth, my eldest

---

[30] Margaret Wolfe Panton Duyckinck, George Long Duyckinck, probably Henry Panton, and Felix Octavius Carr Darley (see note 6, Jan. 19, 1849).

[31] In "Periodical Publications," Charleston *Mercury,* Feb. 22, 1859, Simms writes of the *Century:* "It is a well-filled weekly, the standards of which are decidedly higher than the ordinary periodical average. Its selections are well made, and it has a strong array of American contributors, among whom we recognize some 'fine Roman hands.'" None of Duyckinck's contributions to the periodical are signed.

daughter, was married the other day, & has left me for her husbands residence in Charleston. And a dreadful vacancy prevails throughout my house. I miss so many precious voices that my heart sinks perpetually, and my eyes fill, as the sudden silence rushes on my senses. My mind seems sluggish, and refuses to work with its accustomed impulse. My novel (Cassique of Kiawah — a Colonial Story of S. C. 1664.) is yet unfinished, though nearly all stereotyped. The business of the plantation devolved wholly upon me last year, and I have to restore & repair a neglected & half-dilapidated establishment. There is also some debt & I have no money, and though making better crops than my predecessor, it needs extraordinary energies & exertions, and some good fortune, to enable me to put things *rectus in curia.* I do not despair, but I am harrassed & wearied; long for rest; long to get back to the quiet atmosphere of the Muses, and weave my inventions, and make a more grateful world of my own, here in a corner to myself, where I shall hear no din of the multitude, and be vexed by no vulgar cares of society. What with clearing lands, cutting ditches, burning woods, building fences & houses, making compost; fattening hogs; and doing a thousand things such as appertain to a large Southern plantation, you may readily concieve the little that I have been able to do in letters. I am only consoled for my own incapacity by a knowledge of the present condition of the literary market. Even were I prepared to publish, it would be almost throwing away a book to throw it into market now. That my poor old labors should have afforded to you & yours so much satisfaction, is a great satisfaction to me. It is still more grateful to meet a brother author who is so magnanimous as to declare himself so frankly & affectionately. It is seldom that we find such noble liberality in the guild. G. P. R. James, by the way, in his letters & in his conversation, was always warmly generous. I really believe he has said & written to me in terms of higher compliment than all our authors put together, yourself perhaps excepted & in this letter especially. Kennedy has complimented me warmly; Bryant as warmly as belonged to his temperament; Herbert (who committed suicide) wrote the most eulogistic reviews of the Yemassee, and some other of my writings (except one review of Leggett) which have ever been printed;[32] though I must not forget the singularly high

---

[32] For these reviews by Henry William Herbert and William Leggett (see introductory sketches), see letter to Griswold of Dec. 6, 1846.

eulogium of Albany Fonblanque, in the London Examiner, of one of my novellettes.[33] But I am gliding into egotism. I designed simply to express the pride which I felt, in having such testimonials from such men — men above petty jealousies, who were competent to judge, & had themselves been successful workers in the great literary Common. I shall certainly feel anxious to peruse your paper & shall look for it. I take for granted it will appear in the Messenger.[34] Did you know, by the way, that my 'Atalantis' had been honored by a complimentary notice from Tom Campbell in the London Metropolitan, 25 years ago or more?[35] James (G. P. R.) proposed to me that we should write a work together; but the distance between us was too great & my labors at the time too oppressive; but I have often thought of one of your Virginia subjects, as one to be handled successfully from a novel point of view. I mean the Old French War & Braddock's Defeat. I urged it upon Kennedy, & he told me he had once felt a [*one word illegible*] towards it.[36] Now, I have a plan for such a work which will strike you when you hear of it as one of equal susceptibilities & novelty; but I must reserve the detail for our next meeting. Perhaps you will be pleased to pay me a visit this spring; and see our rude home at Woodlands; where you will find a welcome if nothing more. Excuse this bald scribble, but my mind is too jaded for any thing better. Once more, thanks for your genial epistle. God keep you.

Your friend

W. Gilmore Simms

P. S. I read "Only a Woman's Hair" with a great deal of pleasure, but without detecting the author, nor did I know it was

---

[33] In 1841 Albany Fonblanque (1793-1872), editor and proprietor of the London *Examiner*, published in the *Examiner* a highly favorable review of Simms' "Grayling; or, 'Murder Will Out.'" See note 1, Jan. 29, 1842.

[34] Cooke published a highly complimentary unsigned article on Simms' Revolutionary romances in *S. L. M.*, XXVIII (May, 1859), 355-370, entitled "William Gilmore Simms." Cooke begins by remarking: "We regard the republication, in their present handsome and convenient form, of Mr. Simms' Revolutionary romances, as something very nearly amounting to a national benefit." He concludes his estimate of Simms thus: "Mr. Simms occupies a position in the eyes of the Southern people which is most enviable. The chivalric gentleman—the accomplished scholar—the untiring defender of the South, and all its rights and interests—he is everywhere recognized as one of our most worthy citizens, and distinguished ornaments." The Charleston *Mercury* of May 25, 1859, carries an abridgment of Cooke's article.

[35] See note 268, Dec. 6, 1846.

[36] See letters to Kennedy of Feb. 16 and May 12, 1851.

yours except from a paragraph by Duyckinck, in the Century, a few days ago.[37]

911: To CHARLES EDWARD BENNETT [38]

Woodlands, Midway P. O.
So. Caro. Jany. 31. 1859.

Mr. Charles Edw. Bennett.

My dear young friend.

It gives me pleasure to comply with the modestly expressed wishes of all young persons, and when their requests convey compliment, it seems to an author a sort of pledge from posterity. I send you my autograph, accordingly, without scruple, though I must take leave to counsel you that autograph-seeking is but a poor occupation, for a youth having energies & talents.[39] It will do for the *blazé,* who can do nothing more himself. Take my advice, and find out, as soon as you can, what you are specially good for, and do it — and nothing else! Seek to achieve nobly & earnestly, yourself, that your own manhood shall not belie [40] the promise of your boyhood.

Your friend

W. Gilmore Simms

912: To WILLIAM PORCHER MILES [41]

Woodlands. Feb. 3. 1859.

My dear Miles.

You are right, no doubt, in all you say; but — do you remember what the Seminole chief said to the Missionary? "Your words are very good, & very true, but — after all, the pain is still here — here in the temples." And do you not see that if Grief is a messenger of God, she must give pain, or she cannot perform her mission. Now, mark you, I simply tell my friend of my pain,

---

[37] "Only a Woman's Hair," an unsigned short story, was published in *Harper's New Monthly Magazine,* XVIII (Jan., 1859), 195-202. It is identified as Cooke's in a review of *Harper's* in the *Century* for Dec. 25, 1858.

[38] Not identified.

[39] Simms first wrote *with a youth have energies & talents,* then struck through *with* and inserted *for,* but failed to correct *have.*

[40] Simms wrote *believe,* an obvious slip of the pen.

[41] Part of this letter is printed in Trent, p. 248.

not expecting him to give relief. But it is a relief to have some
dear friend to whom we can show our sores with confidence,
even as we find a pleasure, looking at a lovely landscape, to have
some sympathizing being near us to whom we can say — "How
beautiful!" — It is the error of friends to suppose that they
are expected to give comfort. They are only expected to give
sympathy. He who gives us tear for tear, is the loving Christian
friend. Failing to give comfort, knowing that we have no art of
healing in grievous cases, we are apt to grow impatient of the
sufferer, and to say with the Irish General — "D——n you. —
Do you suppose there is no one kilt but yourself.["] Let us
talk no more of this. I am, my dear Miles, just about as strong
& just about as weak, as most ordinary mortals. No more — no
less! Perhaps, if I had only great griefs to contend with, —
griefs from God — I should bear up more nobly. But, unfortunately, I have others, & petty ones, and I am not capable of a
conflict with the flies & gnats, and musquitos. I get out of temper; and naturally exaggerate the evils for which I have no adequate weapon. You speak of Fame! My ear is getting very cold
to it; & even where I still have any yearnings, I am like to be
mortified. Have you seen the dead set made at my reputation as
an author by the Black Republicans, under the lead of the Tribune?[42] They would tear from me the fruits of thirty years of
labour. Now, scorning them, and all contemporary criticism as I
do, I should not care a straw, *if I had the means to put myself
on record*. Secure of this, my fame might be left without fear to
the guardianship of posterity. And it is posterity alone which
judges. — But, again I stop, for all this is wretched egotism. —
Don't touch Cuba. She is the bait which the Democratic Party

---

[42] Charles Anderson Dana (1819-1897) omitted Simms and some other
Southern poets from *The Household Book of Poetry* (New York: D. Appleton
and Company, 1859). He was attacked for so doing in various reviews of the
anthology (see, for example, *S. L. M.*, XXVII [Oct., 1858], 313-314). Dana's
omissions were defended in an editorial in the New York *Tribune* of Nov. 20,
1858, ascribed to Dana by *S. L. M.*, XXVII (Dec., 1858), 470-472, and by
Russell's Magazine, IV (Jan., 1859), 348-353. In a letter "to a literary gentleman" of South Carolina, published and discussed in *Russell's*, IV (March,
1859), 546-550, Dana, a member of the editorial staff of the *Tribune* at that
time, writes (p. 547): ". . . I had nothing to do with it, and never heard
of it or saw it, till I read it in the paper after its publication. Its style of
remark is not one I could have used; for I quite agree with my critic in regarding Mr. Simms as one of the most distinguished ornaments of American
literature; although, after no casual study of his writings, I still remain of
the opinion that his reputation will always rest upon his prose works rather
than his poems."

holds out to the South. Beware how you enter this field. The Democratic Party has but one chance left for life, that of involving us in foreign war. It is a mere delusion to suppose that our chances of getting Cuba are less, if separate, than as a whole. *If separate, we control the whole commerce — all the shipping of the North! It is better to be separate before we take Cuba.* Take it now, and we have a burning brand we shall never extinguish. It is the only process for bolstering up the Dem. Party, and while that Party lives the South can never be secure. — But, I forget, my dear Miles, I am too spasmodic now for a politician. I have hurts & cares, which keep me from thought. Make the most you can of this scribble, for there is truth in it. I see a thousand miles ahead in this matter. God bless you.

Yours Ever

Simms.

913: To Israel Keech Tefft

Woodlands, S. C. Feb. 3. 1859.

My dear Tefft.

Have you got an autograph of Robt. Southey? If not, I can supply you with one. I have one at the bottom of the title page of a copy of Hennepin, [43] which was bought out of Southey's Library. It is genuine, & though in small characters, very legible & clear. If you desire it, let me know. — You have put me into a sad pother. A letter of yours, to Augusta, she was imprudent enough to send here. It spoke of your own, & Mama's *mortification,* at taking us by surprise in your visit. Now, my dear old fellow, you did *not* take us by surprise, except in this, that we had *not* recieved your letter advising of your coming. Had we done that, my wife would have been apprized of it. The real mischief was in the mails. But, even though surprised, could you suppose that we had no welcome for you? Did *I* not write you that, though Augusta could not, *I* should invite you.[44] Do let Mama write to my wife & set her at ease. She is in grievous tribulation.

---

[43] Probably Louis Hennepin's *A New Discovery of a Vast Country in America* . . ., originally published in French and first translated into English in 1698.

[44] See letter to Tefft of Dec. 15, 1858, an invitation to him and Mrs. Tefft to attend the marriage of Augusta to Edward Roach.

Love to Mama, and the young widow. [45] For yourself, health & good spirits, and another visit from the fair Bremer,[46] until you have a brimmer!

Yours Ever

W. Gilmore Simms.

914: To AUGUSTUS OLIVER ANDREWS [47]

Woodlands, S. C., February 14, 1859.

A. O. Andrews, Esq., President Chamber of Commerce of Charleston:

My Dear Sir:

I should find great pleasure in complying with your wishes, so gratefully expressed, to dine with the members of your "Chamber" on the return of their anniversary for this year; but circumstances deny me this privilege, and I can only express the regret which I feel in being compelled to hold myself aloof from a *re-union* which promises so much good fellowship with the "solid men" of my native city.

I should have been pleased to be present for other reasons than those which affect my own simple gratification. Were I with you, and on such an occasion, I should certainly seize the opportunity to present to your view my speculations on a subject of permanent importance to the welfare of your city — a subject which has engaged my thoughts, at intervals, for more than twenty years, and in which I have learned to differ, in vital respects, from most persons—I mean the local climate; the causes of epidemics in the low latitudes, and the possible remedies and preventives. This subject, and the establishment of *direct communication with Europe,* through your own shipping, constitute, to my mind, the most important subjects for the earnest consideration of your "Chamber."

---

[45] Sarah Tefft, widow of Tefft's son William Pitt. See note 129, July 8, 1854.

[46] Fredrika Bremer (see note 178, Sept. 11, 1850) visited Tefft in May, 1850 (see her *The Homes of the New World; Impressions of America,* tr. Mary Howitt [New York: Harper & Brothers, 1853], I, 339-357). For her description of Tefft, see note 69, March 4, 1852.

[47] We have not located the original of this letter, printed in the Charleston *Mercury* of Feb. 18, 1859. Andrews (1817-1880) was a merchant living at 29 Hasel Street, Charleston (see the city directories for this period). He later operated a brokerage concern and around 1879 became president of the Home Insurance Company. He was elected president of the Charleston Chamber of Commerce in 1859 and served for twelve consecutive terms.

It would be easier to deliver my views on the former topic *orally,* than to elaborate them on paper — since my professional and domestic duties find me enough to do — and properly to report my conclusions on so vexed a subject — one so intimate and which has divided the public and professional mind for two hundred years, would task a whole year's labor of the pen, and require a very copious octavo.

But I may, even in the brief compass of a letter, suggest certain clues of thought and study which may give the necessary provocation to other minds; and, as a word *"to the wise"* is usually sufficient for *them,* it is possible that what I may say, even in these brief limits, may be of some service to others in the consideration of this topic.

1. First, then, I deny that marsh, swamp, filth or decaying vegetation, are at all *essential* to the *generation* of disease in your city. I deny that *miasma* is absolutely essential to *malaria.* We have the marsh, filth, swamp, hard labor and poverty and squalid habitations always, every year, but cholera and yellow fever only occasionally. Vegetation does not begin to decay, but is most beautiful and fresh when our pestilences are most furious. I admit that exhalations from swamp, morass and filth may—nay, must — increase the malignity of the epidemic, but assert that they cannot *generate* it by themselves, and independantly of that condition of the atmosphere, which is essential in its production, that all these are perfectly harmless.

2. I contend that a certain condition of atmosphere, arising from a continued prevalence of certain winds, which are in their character feeble, and not adequate to maintain the atmospheric equilibrium, &c., keep the atmosphere in that degree of agitation which is necessary to its purity, is the *first* essential condition, and this condition implies a certain degree of fixation or stagnation in the atmosphere in which the air currents do not run at all, or if they do — pursuing only one course — into a *cul de sac.*

3. I hold that this fixation, or comparative stagnation in the atmosphere, must first be produced before it can be impregnated with *miasma.* So long as the winds blow with *riancy* to and fro, with frequent changes from one point of the compass to the other, the exhalations from the earth cannot be localized, but must be dispersed infinitely through a thousand miles of space.

4. I hold, however, that when the air is thus comparatively stagnant, it *needs* no impregnation from any foreign source to

become *malaria;* it is then *per se malaria,* being like the blood and water — nay, more subtle than either as a fluid — capable of purification only by progress and its own circulation.

5. I hold that in the general notion of the impregnation of the atmosphere by *miasma,* as the essentiality of *malaria,* we have been diverted from our true necessity, which must contemplate *ventilation* as much more important even than cleanliness. We *must* drink the air, though we may find a substitute for bad water; and every introduction of the stagnant atmosphere acts directly upon the lungs, and upon the circulation, and diseases all. And here I might stop, satisfied with indicating my general notion as to the source of the epidemic, but that I deem it proper to add, that if these premises be true and well grounded, *any climate may be rendered healthier,* if not absolutely healthy, by *mechanical agency.* Let me add, that I have no doubt that in the course of the next fifty years cities will be kept thoroughly ventilated by steam, and that every sleeping room will be kept pure by a pleasant agitation of the atmosphere, maintained in free and equal circulation by the employment of a simple piece of furniture, with fans,[48] and worked by clock machinery — ropes, weights and pulleys.[49]

But I am at the bottom of my sheet. I am sorry that my space and time do not allow me to dwell longer upon a subject which, properly developed, would require a volume. Were I able to prepare this volume, my first care would be to meet and anticipate every *exceptional* case — the usual mode of argumentation adopted by all *routine* disputers, and all who are in permanent possession of an ancient hobby. I persuade myself that I am prepared to do this, but the labor is immense, experiments costly, my time greatly absorbed, and my means very limited. If what I have said shall suggest a single clue to any active and independent mind, not fettered by a pet theory, I will be quite satisfied. You will smile, perhaps, when I add to this, that, probably, in about one hundred years, cities will not only be ventilated by steam, but lighted by balloons. The time is hardly arrived yet for either. The public mind has to *unlearn* a thousand *old* things before it can fairly grapple with a single new truth.

---

[48] The *Mercury* prints *vans.*

[49] Simms writes similarly in his letter to Edwin Troxell Freedley of Dec. 26, 1857.

I add a brief toast, which, if you please, may be offered during your festivities.

I am, dear sir, with distinguished consideration,

Your ob't servant,

W. Gilmore Simms.

"Independence of thinking, courage in truth, the first grand necessities of all moral progress."

915: To JAMES LAWSON

Woodlands. Feb. 21. [1859]⁵⁰

My dear Lawson.

God's peace & blessing upon you and your household. I congratulate you that your wife is *not past bearing;* & that she has borne you another scion, to form another link of love around your heart. The birth of the child is news to me. But I was aware, some time ago, from a friendly correspondent, that her advent might be soon expected. I congratulate Lyde, on being such an excellent mother in Israel. A woman never recieves a soul at all until she loves, never a soul to be saved until she has children, never a soul with wings until she has many of them. With seven children, you both may be regarded as people having a chance for salvation. To secure this, see that you rear these young ones as you should, to honour their parents, love & reverence God, love their neighbour, and, in process of time, rear as numerous a flock as their parents. These serve to soothe our declining years, and plant *immortelles* above our graves. I have had *thirteen.* Of these but six remain. I have buried *seven.* You, my friend, have thus far been spared. You have never known what it is to have the heart strings torn & lacerated, wrench by wrench, pang by pang, as one after another of your dear ones has been torn from you by the inexorable fates. May you never have such an experience as mine. Frequent agonies of this sort keep me in constant dread of new ones, and my prayer to God daily is that he will suffer those he has left me to live & mature, for our comfort & his glory. Do not forget, my friend, to remember God.

---

⁵⁰ Dated by Simms' reference to Lawson's seven children (Christina, Mary, Kate, James, William Gilmore Simms, Nellie, and Flora, the baby) and to his own six (Augusta, Gilmore, Mary Lawson, Chevillette, Govan, and Hattie).

Do not forget *him* in the possession of his gifts. He punishes forgetfulness almost the same as ingratitude. It is, in such a case, ingratitude. If you do not, of your own free will & grateful heart, remember him, by prayer, humility & righteous doing, he will compel your memory in agonies & tears. May he spare you these, dear friend, and may you give him no cause to do otherwise. Once more, God bless you & yours. — I am, as ever busy — clearing land, digging ditches, making & hauling out & scattering manure, preparing to plant. We begin planting on the fourth of March (corn) [.] April 1. we begin planting cotton. These constitute our main crops; to these add, rye, rice, potatoes, groundnuts, &c. and you have the objects of our cultivation. I have cleared 60 acres new land this year. I shall manure 300. I have doubled the crops of my predecessor, yet failed to reach my standard. With God's help, I hope to realize good results in a year or two; but every thing was in a state of dilapidation. I ought to make 150 bales cotton. If I do that in the next 2 years, I shall be *rectus in curia.* Love to Lyde, the girls & boys. In a few days I shall write Mary.

God bless & be with you.

W. Gilmore Simms

916: To Henry Barton Dawson

Woodlands (Midway P. O.) S. C.
Feb. 21. 1859.

My dear Sir:

About the small actions to which you refer, it is exceedingly difficult to provide details. They are so scattered, that I find it impossible, without great research, to say any thing about them. If you could lay hands upon the several numbers of the Magnolia Magazine (see Mr. Evert A. Duyckinck) or, if not, procure a copy of Johnson's Reminiscenses, you would certainly chance upon some of them. As Editor of the Magnolia, I published several accounts, from several hands, upon which you might rely. Dr. Johnson copied several of these into his volume.[51] My own time

---

[51] "Revolutionary Incidents" by various contributors, among them Benjamin Franklin Perry and Andrew Pickens Butler (see letter to Perry of May 26, 1843), were published in the *Magnolia*, N. S., I (July, Aug., and Sept., 1842), 40-43, 99-102, 173-176; N. S., II (Jan., Feb., May, and June, 1843), 30-40, 109-111, 326-330, 380-383. Dr. Joseph Johnson (see note 17, March 15, 1843) reprinted several of these in *Traditions and Reminiscences Chiefly of the American Revolution in the South* . . . (Charleston, S. C.: Walker and James, 1851), pp. 422-444.

is so terribly occupied just now, that I am incapable of any asides. Mills [52] may give you some clues. See also McCall's Georgia [53] — When Georgia was overrun by the British a few hundred of her militia joined Pickens [54] & other S. C. captains, & were engaged in the battles of S. C. in the up country. This affords to McCall, a pretext for including them in his Histy. of Georgia. One vol. of R. Izard's Corresp., as you are aware, has been published. But if in asking if S. C. would feel any interest in the publication of the residue, you mean to ask, if any patronage is expected here, I must think not. My own labours of this class have been so uphill, & so little encouraged here, that I see nothing to hope.[55] Russell & Jones have *not* recieved, nor have I, any of your numbers.[56] I was in Charleston a week ago, & asked after them in vain. Write to I. K. Tefft, Savannah: Say I indicated him to you, & it is probable he may furnish you many clues with regard to that State.

Yours truly

W. Gilmore Simms

Henry B. Dawson, Esq.

917: To Mary Lawson

Woodlands. Feb. 28. 1859.

My dear Mary.

Yours & your father's letters were recieved at the same time. I answered his instantly in order to express my congratulations upon the recent & important, as well as grateful event in your family, & to send my affectionate remembrances especially to your mother.[57] A press of labour on my hands compelled me to defer

---

[52] Robert Mills, *Statistics of South Carolina, Including a View of Its Natural, Civil, and Military History, General and Particular* (Charleston, S. C.: Hurlbut and Lloyd, 1826).

[53] Hugh McCall, *The History of Georgia, Containing Brief Sketches of the Most Remarkable Events up to the Present Day*, 2 vols. (Savannah: Seymour & Williams, 1811-1816).

[54] Gen. Andrew Pickens (1739-1817).

[55] Volume I of the *Correspondence of Mr. Ralph Izard, of South Carolina, from the Year 1774 to 1804; with a Short Memoir* was published by C. S. Francis and Co., New York, in 1844. The memoir of Izard (1741/2-1804), Revolutionary patriot, diplomat, and United States senator, was written by Anne Izard Deas. Dawson did not publish a second volume.

[56] Of *Battles of the United States*. See letters to Dawson of Oct. 16, 1858, and Jan. 19, 1859.

[57] See letter to Lawson of Feb. 21, congratulating him on the birth of his daughter Flora.

writing to you until now, and now that I do write, I am still compelled to use all possible despatch. My table is crowded with letters to be answered. Rarely do I send fewer than two or three letters to the P. O. daily, and once or twice every week, I send a dozen. It appears, in spite of all my efforts to cut down this burden, that it rather increases than diminishes. What with my literary, business & special plantation correspondence, my social & friendly is frequently compelled to wait an occasional day of general jail delivery, when I square accounts with a dozen friends, some of whom are very fair young ladies like yourself. I have no doubt that the P. O. frequently recieves much more than it renders up. I *know* the fact to be so not unfrequently in my own case. My daughter writes me wonderingly, that you should not have recieved her cake. A package, I presume of goodly bulk, was specially made up to your father's address, including samples for the two Richards, Duyckinck, &c.[58] This package was put on board the Steamer by her brother-in-law, in person, who is of the firm here, which is the Charleston Agency of the Boat.[59] Can it have been recieved by that James Lawson who made the speech & sang the song at the Burns Celebration?[60] Perhaps! My daughter is very comfortably settled in Charleston with her husband's family, where she has a couple of rooms, a parlour & piazza. Her husband is a young man who depends chiefly on his own exertions & his income is at present small. The family owns the house they live in and have their own servants, & some small funded capital. There are three brothers, all in mercantile life, and all of high character, of acknowledged purity & integrity of character. Augusta & her husband have grown up from child-

---

[58] See letter to Mary Lawson of Jan. 28, 1859, in which he earlier discusses this package for the Lawsons, the Thomas Addison Richardses, the William Carey Richardses, and the Evert Augustus Duyckincks.

[59] William Roach was a member of the firm of Henry Missroon and Co., at the corner of East Bay and Adger's Wharf. The firm operated two steam-packets between Charleston and New York City, the *Marion* and the *Southerner*. See the advertisement of the firm in the Charleston *Directory* for 1859.

[60] On Jan. 25, 1859, the Burns Club of the City of New York held a festival at Astor House in celebration of the centennial birthday of Robert Burns. On the previous evening it had sponsored an oration given by Henry Ward Beecher. At the festival William Cullen Bryant acted as honorary chairman. An account of the proceedings was edited by Joseph Cunningham, president of the Club, and published as *The Centennial Birth-Day of Robert Burns as Celebrated by the Burns Club of the City of New York Tuesday, January, 25th. 1859* (New York: Lang & Laing, 1860). No James Lawson is mentioned as having spoken or sung. Other celebrations in honor of Burns were given in 1859 in New York City, Brooklyn, and elsewhere, and possibly Simms has in mind one of these.

hood together, and know each other well. He is a modest young man, of moderate intelligence, simplicity of character & good sense, without show or pretension. In morals, temper, character, & all those things which guarantee happiness, he is a man in a thousand; and these guarantees are to me much more important than brilliancy of intellect, or wealth.[61] — I trust that you will remember me gratefully to the Armitages whenever you encounter them. I owe them nothing but kindness during those young days when I had the happiness to know them first. And convey, if you please like remembrances to the Bacon's.[62] I certainly am glad to hear of the reconciliation between Ellet & his wife before his death. If now she will be only reconciled to *herself,* it would be another good step towards reconciliation with duty, prayer, and a simpler plan of existence, which she specially needs.[63] I congratulate you on the Sewing Machine. You will find it a great acquisition. As for the complication of it, don't fear that. Why, *my* Mary Lawson works on it daily here, for her own amusement. My wife & eldest daughter [64] learned the use of it in a single week, & they have done an immense deal of work upon it. But you are right in concieving that your mind will need its exercises as well as your fingers. You should acquire a habit of reading, & thinking together. Go through a course of reading, and study as you read. Make yourself well acquainted with the Poets especially. And why should you not acquire the Continental languages, Italian & Spanish. Why not the German. Half a dozen young Ladies might get up an evening class, three times a week, at their several houses, and under a good tutor, would in one summer learn to read freely either of the two former; perhaps speak them; and in one year would surely go pretty deep in a knowledge of the German. But for my labours, and my incessant practise in English, I should be a good German, French, Spanish & Ital.

---

[61] For Edward Roach's family, see note 225, July 19, 1858.

[62] If the Bacons, like the Armitages (see note 22, Jan. 28, 1859), were friends of Simms' youth, they doubtless were the Francis Bacons. Francis Bacon is first listed in the New York City directories in 1834-1835, and he is the only one of the Bacons listed then who is still listed in 1858. In 1834-1835 he is described as a merchant at 46 Exchange Place, in 1858 as a dealer in pianos at 135 Grand Avenue and 149 Baxter Street with a residence at 22 Union Place.

[63] Elizabeth Fries Lummis Ellet says in an undated letter written to the Robert Balmannos shortly before William Henry Ellet's death (original in the New York Public Library) : "Alas, my dear Friends—there is no hope of my husband's life. He is fast sinking. The physicians say there is no hope. I am busy with him day & night. I read prayers & the Bible to him." For the Ellets, see introductory sketch; for the Balmannos, see note 116, May 28, 1852.

[64] Augusta.

scholar. Alas for me, I have now pretty much forgotten all that I ever knew; for, where the language is one not daily spoken in our ears, it must be daily made familiar to our eyes. — Alas! farther! My thought now is of the crops, of cotton, corn, potatoes, peas, poultry, cows & calves, hogs & sheep, goats & oxen; of ditching, fencing, ploughing, planting; and poetry & art, & letters, & language, are fast giving way to mere material things. I have a book nearly finished now, & which I hope to finish soon, which has been lingering & languishing in my hands for more than a year.[65] My griefs & miseries of the last year made me almost oblivious of what I have written, & in resuming my task I had to summon fancy against her will, & sometimes felt the necessity of writing sportively, with a head aching, a heart full almost to bursting, & eyes dropping great tears upon the paper even as I wrote. Ah! My dear Mary, you know not how I have been crushed since I saw you last. But enough. I must not vex your young spirit with the sorrows and disappointments of a broken one. We are living here in comparative seclusion, seeing nobody if we can help it unless branches of the family, and drudging on in the daily routine of duties in which we have little heart. Since Augusta's marriage we have had no company & have invited none. I hear that Mr. & Mrs. Sherwood [66] have reached Charleston; but we shall not invite them here. We cannot entertain them. My wife is still very much depressed, & unequal to the charge of company; and I have neither time nor spirit for it. Let me hear from you, my dear child, whenever you can spare time & think of me. And tell me all the details of your own & the domestic progress. Report the children severally, and see that you look up Wordsworth and read the poem "We are Seven." Gilmore is still at the Academy [67] & is well reported. *Here,* we are now but four, Mary L.; Chevillette E.; Govan S.; and Hattie M. (My boys! My boys!) What are left are well. Hattie is thought to be a beauty. May you all see her — see all, — some day. My warm & affectionate love to your mother, & a kiss; a *masculine* one, remember; kisses for Christie & Katie; blessings upon the boys and all, and a friend's & fatherly kiss, dear Mary, for yourself. God keep you all in the hollow of *his* Hand!

Yours Ever faithfully

W. Gilmore Simms.

---

[65] *The Cassique of Kiawah.*
[66] Mr. and Mrs. William K. Sherwood. See note 15, June 26, 1837.
[67] The King's Mountain Military School.

918: To James Dunwoody Brownson De Bow [68]

Woodlands, March 1. [1859][69]

My dear Professor.

Your offer, though quite complimentary does not tempt me. I have long since gone far beyond that limit. When I now write for a periodical, the *argumentum ad crumenam,* must be much more weighty. I have just rejected an arrangement which promised $3000 per annum.[70] To persuade me to a monthly paper for ten months, *the amount must be such as to move me to give up every thing else;* for in no other way could I do justice to myself or the periodical. I find it no wisdom to attempt more. Such a labour, having due respect to the reputation of the writer, requires the concentration of all his faculties, much previous design, and the nicest art in preparation. I am glad to think that you are doing well. You see, I take for granted, my occasional notices of you in the Mercury.[71] Touching the notice of your family, I will try to remember the source & to look it up in my library.[72] I really do not know of any writers now among us except Hayne, Timrod, Fred Porcher, Grayson and Hurlbut.[73] These all contribute to Russell, but might be procured to contribute to you occasionally. Try Meek [74] of Alabama (Mobile) [.] I shall always be pleased to hear from you, and of your prosperity.

Yours very truly

W. Gilmore Simms

P. S. You ask if I have any duplicates of your Review. It is possible I have, but if so, they are at my town residence. Have you

68 See note 42, Feb. 17, 1852.

69 Simms' reference to *Russell's Magazine* (see note 40, Jan. 25, 1858) dates this letter as 1858 or 1859. His remark that he has "had a great deal of grief and trouble in the last 12 months" is almost certainly a reference to the deaths of Sydney Roach and Beverley Hammond Simms. We have, therefore, dated it 1859.

70 Doubtless the proposed arrangement with the New York weekly discussed in letters to Hammond of July 10 and July 16, 1858, and to Mary Lawson of Aug. 2, 1858.

71 Simms' most recent notice of *De Bow's Review* is in the issue of Feb. 22.

72 We have not located this notice.

73 Paul Hamilton Hayne (see introductory sketch), Henry Timrod (see introductory sketch), Frederick Adolphus Porcher (see note 213, c. Nov. 1, 1849), William John Grayson (see introductory sketch), and George C. Hurlbut. Hurlbut, one of the editors of *Russell's Magazine,* was a frequent contributor of both prose and poetry to that magazine.

74 Alexander Beaufort Meek. See introductory sketch.

forgotten that I gave to your brother,[75] years ago, more than 60 numbers, on his promise to provide me with some vols. that were wanting. Yet he never did so. Nevertheless, should I find on my visiting Charleston, that I have now any duplicates, I will advise you & they shall be at your call. — I have had a great deal of grief and trouble in the last 12 months, and have still much toil & trouble before me; this contributes to make me unwilling to incur any new labours, or to make engagements, unless with urgent motives, and a very valuable consideration. I have a large family, a growing one, and I never know what it is to have a dollar to spare.

919: To JAMES HENRY HAMMOND

Woodlands, March 2. [1859][76]

My dear Hammond.

I have been so busied, so worried, so depressed in mood and condition, that I have had neither time nor heart to write to anybody, & my brains have been so addled that I have seemed to myself to lack all capacity for thought. But I have neither forgotten you, nor been unobservant of those things which might concern you. I recently ran down to the city for a week, and suggested a good many things to young Rhett, of the Mercury,[77] who really appears to be anxious to favour you, as far as he can consistently with those influences which have always controlled the Mercury. I take for granted that you have detected in the wishy washy strain, the author of the long series of papers addressed to you in that paper.[78] They come from Columbia, and

---

[75] Benjamin Franklin De Bow, born in 1821 or 1822, was associated with his brother as managing editor of *De Bow's Review* for about twenty years. Before the Confederate War he lived in Charleston, New Orleans, and Washington; during the War, in Charleston and Columbia; and afterwards in New York City and Elizabeth, N. J. He died in 1867.

[76] This letter is a reply to Hammond's dated Washington, Feb. 26, 1859, in which he writes: "It is so long since I have received a letter from you. I feel lost when I don't hear from you. What is the matter? Are you sick? Are you in trouble? Are you too full of work? It is not my vocation to write. I abhor it for myself, but respect it in you, for it is yours. Do let me hear from you & about you. There is nothing here worth mentioning. Sham, sham, & sham again in *all* things." Hammond again wrote Simms on March 13. The originals are in the Hammond Papers, Library of Congress.

[77] Robert Barnwell Rhett, Jr., editor of the Charleston *Mercury*.

[78] A series of nine articles signed "Plain Truth" and concerned with Hammond's speeches at Beech Island and Barnwell (see note 240, Aug. 1, 1858, and note 288, Nov. 22, 1858) was published in the *Mercury* of Jan. 12, Jan. 14, Jan. 21, Jan. 24, Jan. 28, Feb. 1, Feb. 10, Feb. 21, and Feb. 25, 1859. We are unable to identify the author.

much of their offensive parts was stricken out by Rhett. They attempted to bully him from Columbia, but he defied them. Their turgid declamation, wordiness & windiness, have done you no harm at home. On the contrary, as they express but one idea, and that almost an offensive commonplace here, they bore the reader rather than impress him. I doubt, indeed, if anybody reads them, unless a few ancient ravens. I told Rhett that you had done more towards commanding the great body of our people to a confidence in their own powers of combativeness & resistance than had ever been done before, by the very temperate character of your argument, which, without violence or threat, made resistance a feasible thing, and showed when it would be a proper resort. — That, though you might have *let down,* the ancient extremists, you had raised up midway between the great body of the people, not only of S. C. but the whole South, by studiously forbearing to startle them by any *extremism*. That even such men as Yeadon had accepted your alternatives & pledged themselves to the final issue whenever these alternatives should be reached. That this never could be effected, with the great body of the people, until the extremists had been let down. That there was no harm in letting them down, since they had nothing themselves to counsel, and indicated nothing for performance; had, in fact, given up the game; and only quarrelled with you & all others who showed that in their hands & through their policy nothing had yet been done, or could be done. That the avoidance of all violence now, which you counselled, was not inconsistent with their absolute practical acquiescence in the condition of things; and that briefly, you had lifted the popular mind immensely to a conviction that they had the power of resistance, which could not but be successful in the assertion of their rights whenever a genuine practical issue should be made. That even if your course had rebuked the extremists, it had by no means discouraged the idea of resistance; but had rather commended it to the *reason* of the great multitude, and yourself as one who could most rationally embody and enforce it. I counselled him that the Democratic party, as such, was doomed, unless they could plunge us into foreign war, on some plausible pretext, or without pretext, and by bringing on us external pressure, defeat temporarily the Republicans, only by the coercion of a national exigency operating upon the masses & upon the Northern communities. I gave him a variety of texts besides, on which he will probably dilate. I have seen with pleasure the ticket for Prest. & V. Pres. in the Savannah papers. It is a very strong one. Choate is not only a singularly able man, but a truly national & I believe virtuous one. He belongs to the conservative and Gentlemanly classes of New England.[79] But I fear that the Democratic Party, though too feeble for success, will not feel how feeble it is, and will struggle on as a party to the defeat of any new organization. The only hope by which to defeat the Republicans, must be found in the organization of a new party drawn from the best portions of all others; all those who would save the Confederacy, and, which is pretty much the same thing, bring back the government to a sense of honesty, propriety and economy, if not patriotism. But, even if the elements of such a party should be sufficiently numerous, the difficulty would still be great in the way of seasonable organization. It requires an immense deal of labour & skill, & great length of time, to mature such an organization so as to give it good working capacity. The executive mind is a very rare one in all countries, and even when found in this, it has to wage a lifelong conflict with vanity & pretention, which in this country, are rendered terribly active & insolent by the very nature of our institutions. Let me know what you have touching these matters where you are. I would counsel you especially, my dear H. not to be too cheap; socially: a little more reserve in society than you have at home, and a little more caution in speech; bringing out others & encouraging others, while silent, or only soliciting yourself, would be only prudent. Your life — when on the shelf — like mine, has been too much *abandon;* i.e. we have discoursed *ad libitum,* from a sense of absolute freedom from all responsibility. It is not so with you now. You must no longer permit yourself this *abandon,* until you get home once more to those circles in which you can feel quite secure. And there are very few, anywhere, in which you can be safe. Do not, by any means, suffer yourself to be persuaded to visit Philadelphia or New York. Hurry home, and when you get home, contrive to write a letter to some friend, solely upon some one or more agricultural (purely agricultural) subject, in which you should show yourself especially concerned. I could wish you to

---

[79] The Savannah *Republican* of Feb. 26 nominates Hammond for president and Rufus Choate (1799-1859), a member of Congress (1831-1834) and United States senator from Massachusetts (1841-1845), for vice-president. The reactions of the Augusta *Constitutionalist* (for Hammond but silent on Choate) and of the Savannah *Morning News* (against both Hammond and Choate) are discussed in the *Republican* of Feb. 28 and March 1.

take the vine for example. If you have forgotten your Italian, get
Harry to translate for you, the celebrated poem of Redi,[80] *'Bacco
in Toscana'* — *ditirambo;* or go into one of the Bookstores in
Washington or Balto. or Richmond, and procure one of the new
editions, *in blue & gold* (of Ticknor & Fields) containing the
poetical works of Leigh Hunt, who has made an admirable translation of it from Redi.[81] You may remember my telling you of
Redi, expressing a wish to translate his 'Bacco in Tuscany,' and
to add to it a fellow poem on the grapes of the South, bringing
in all our peculiar sectional names, as Scuppernong, Catawba,
&c. as Redi has done those of Tuscany — indicating the peculiar
character & excellence of the several varieties. Now, a letter to
any friend, as if in reply to his inquiries, beginning in a playful
vein, congratulating yourself on the escape to your fields in Spring,
your contemplation of your vinery, your renewal of your reading
of the Bacco, & of your remembrances of Toscana; mention the
varieties of Tuscany, as reported by Redi, and insist upon those
of the South. And, by the way, so far back as 1684 no less than
five original varieties of the grape of Carolina were sent to Great
Britain! And pronounced so fine as to prompt a prediction then
in favour of the future cultivation of the vine here, in competition with France & Italy. Make an array of all the local names
that you can hit, name those which are nameless, & for these
names look to the nomenclature of the Red men; there should be
the Isundiga (the name of the Savannah river[)] — the Uchee,
your Silver bluff region; the Isacana (Satilla) Edisto, Evelano,
&c. &c. Blend in your letter, with a certain amount of playfulness,
a certain large amount of enthusiasm in the subject, & write it
carefully, as well as playfully; well and gracefully, without allowing the *labor limæ* to be suspected — the *ars celare artem* being
as requisite to this production, as to any work deliberately designed of art. I would have you, in brief, occasionally before the
country, yet studiously keep you from any political attitude. I
should have them see you as vinedresser, forgetting, in the
pleasure of your fields, & gratefully forgetting the uneasy Seat
of State; the hot stifling atmosphere of politics; the stresses of
faction; the poor vanities of debate; in short that little world of
little things that confounds fame with mere notoriety, and achieve-

---

[80] Francesco Redi (1626-1698).

[81] Ticknor and Fields, Boston, published a two-volume edition of Hunt's
Poems in 1857.

ment, with a petty & perpetual skipping across the stage. When you have thought over this, I think you will see much more in my suggestion than will strike any common mind. *State* usually lifts a man out of human sympathy. Whenever you can put a man of State, in position to appeal *indirectly* to the popular humanity, you create a certain degree of sympathy in his behalf, which softens their sentiment of reverence into love; this done, and it is easy to awaken enthusiasm. D. Webster's letter to his overseer, his farmer, had it been published ten years before it was, would have done as much towards making common people love him, as his great speeches ever did toward compelling their reverence.[82] But, you will understand me. Should you concieve of this matter as I do, and prepare this letter, then send it to me *for revision.* Do not suppose I am so presumptuous as to assume in this more than a capacity, as somewhat practised in Art, to detect whatever might be, in any degree, in conflict with the seeming *motor* of the letter. There may be a single word, here or there, which might be inharmonious. It might be necessary to omit or to supply some single sentence. And all this you will suffer me to do; the letter, however, to be returned to you for your final judgment. It might be well, indeed, that you should address the letter *to me,* as if in reply to inquiries of mine; and my pursuits might legitimate a reference to Redi's poem, and you might refer further to my suggestion of an adjunct poem insisting upon our native grapes, &c. But I have said enow.[83] — Here is letter enough, a' God's name. You reproach me for not writing; yet when I do write I send a treatise. Several have I sent you this Session of similar length, & in return I get such a billet (in dimensions) as you would despatch to a young Damsel as a Valentine.

God spare & help you.

Simms

P. S. I address this to you at Washington where I suppose you will be kept some weeks, and where I trust you will oppose all grants of all extraordinary powers to the President; where you will insist upon knowing for what are all these warlike preparations. The notion, no doubt is, that we should be in readiness,

---

[82] A number of letters from Webster to his overseer, Charles Porter Wright, are included in Fletcher Webster's edition of *The Private Correspondence of Daniel Webster,* 2 vols. (Boston: Little, Brown and Company, 1857).

[83] We have found no evidence to indicate that Hammond wrote such a letter.

just so soon as the grand imbroglio takes place in Europe, &
England, Italy, Austria, France & Russia, are again by the ears;
and they will all probably be very soon — to take advantage of
their snarls, and dart with all our talons upon Cuba. But, the
truth is, we will burn our fingers any how by the acquisition of
Cuba; we shall actually, by absorbing her, deprive her of every
chance of acquiring the slaves necessary for her culture. We
should ruin her & not help ourselves. Properly taught, the acquisition of Cuba is a great abolition or Black Republican
Policy, — if that party were capable of a great policy.

920: To HENRY BARTON DAWSON

Woodlands, March 15. [1859] [84]

My dear Sir:

I think it likely that Russell & Jones (Charleston) may be
able to procure for you, from private hands, a copy of my Hist.
of S. C. But *I know* that Mr. Bancroft has, or had, a copy in
his Library. Since writing to you last, it has occurred to me that
Mrs. Ellett's *Domestic* Hist. of the Revolution, and her Women
of the Revolution,[85] will afford you some of the very details which
you desire, in respect to the *minor* battles occurring in the South.
The former work will, I am sure. Scribner was the publisher. Do
not overlook Johnson's *Greene*. The old Judge was singularly
discursive in his generalizations.[86] Pickett's Alabama [87] can surely
be procured for you in Charleston. See again Russell & Jones.
Prof. Rivers has only written a history of the *Colony* of S. C.

---

[84] Dated by Simms' discussion of books for Dawson to consult in the preparation of his *Battles of the United States*. See letters to Dawson of Feb. 21
and April 23.

[85] Elizabeth Fries Lummis Ellet, *Domestic History of the American Revolution* (New York: Baker and Scribner, 1850) and *The Women of the American Revolution*, 3 vols. (New York: Baker and Scribner, 1848-1850).

[86] William Johnson (1771-1834), brother of Dr. Joseph Johnson, was a
member of the South Carolina legislature (1794-1798), judge of the court of
common pleas (1798-1804), and associate justice of the Supreme Court of the
United States (1804-1834). He was the author of *Sketches of the Life and
Correspondence of Nathanael Greene, Major General of the Armies of the
United States, in the War of the Revolution* . . . , 2 vols. (Charleston: Printed
for the Author, by A. E. Miller, 1822).

[87] Albert James Pickett, *History of Alabama, and Incidentally of Georgia
and Mississippi, from the Earliest Period*, 2 vols. (Charleston: Walker and
James, 1851). Second and third editions were published the same year.

under the *Proprietary* Govt. This has been published.[88] In respect to Tarleton,[89] tho' you may recieve his evidence *cum grano,* you will yet find him useful in suggesting clues to study & inquiry. The critiques of Stedman [90] & Mackenzie [91] are chiefly addressed to the overthrow of T's own pretensions.

In haste, but very truly Yours &c

W. Gilmore Simms

921: To Evert Augustus Duyckinck

Woodlands, March 18. [1859][92]

My dear Duyckinck.

I had fancied several times that I detected your pen in the Century, and your last letter confirmed me in regard to several articles. You are evidently doing its best papers, & I hope you are suffered to touch the *quid.* If not, you are an enemy to the *guild.* This writing our fingers off & brains out, for the benefit of printers & publishers, is the merest folly, and I will none of it. It is very well that you should have an organ, when, for your own objects, you desire to reach the public mind; but it should be only for your own objects, and the organ is always & easily attainable. Publishers are only too glad to get matter from hands that they know to be equally full & *safe,* & you are one of them. I thank Mr. McElrath [93] for his compliments, and may, in my

---

[88] William James Rivers, *A Sketch of the History of South Carolina to the Close of the Proprietary Government by the Revolution of 1719* . . . (Charleston: McCarter & Co., 1856). For Rivers, see note 169, Aug. 2, 1850.

[89] Gen. Sir Banastre Tarleton, *A History of the Campaigns of 1780 and 1781, in the Southern Provinces of North America* (London: T. Cadell, 1787).

[90] Charles Stedman, *The History of the Origin, Progress, and Termination of the American War,* 2 vols. (London: Printed for the Author, and Sold by J. Murray, 1794).

[91] Roderick Mackenzie, *Strictures on Lt.-Col. Tarleton's History "of the Campaigns of 1780 and 1781, in the Southern Provinces of North America"* . . . (London: Printed for the Author, 1787).

[92] Dated by Simms' discussion of Duyckinck's contributions to the *Century.* See letter to Duyckinck of Jan. 29, 1859.

[93] Thomas McElrath (1807-1888), a native of Williamsport, Pa., was admitted to the bar at New York City in 1828 and became a partner of William Bloomfield and Charles Patrick Daly (see note 117, Nov. 24, 1853). In 1841 he was made business manager of the New York *Tribune.* He withdrew from the staff of the *Tribune* in 1857, though in 1864 he again became connected with that newspaper. Late in 1858 he began editing the *Century* (see note 26, Jan. 29, 1859), which soon became a Republican paper.

own time & humour, send him something by way of acknowledgment for his courtesy in sending me his paper; but as for writing
him letters, having sole reference to his publishing success, —
No! No! My dear friend, I trust you are not throwing away your
time & talent in this manner. Make them pay you. Were you to
write gratuitously for a year, and then abandon the concern, the
succeeding Editor would be allowed [94] to slander you, & the gratitude of the publishers would rarely interpose to say 'Hands off
here — this man is my friend.' Now, in this country nothing is
valued unless it commands a money return in the common market;
and the instincts of all people seem to teach them, that, just in
degree with the modest disclaimer of his *quid,* on the part of the
literary man, is the worthlessness of his commodity. They despise
the man who lets them cheat him. And you are not only to exact
your pay, but you are to exact high prices. I have been as great
a simpleton, dealing with publishers, as any man I know; and I
have been wronged, robbed, cheated and abused by them in due
degree with my good nature and simplicity. I have done more
gratuitous work than any man I know, and I have never been,
in any way made aware, that I had even the gratitude of the
parties — save in few instances, to whom the service has been
rendered. Briefly, the moral of the whole country of trade is essentially base. We are a nation of mercenaries. As for Editors,
one half of them are ignorant, impudent, dishonest, — lyars and
knaves and dastards; who will stab at you from behind & skulk
beneath your eye. For thirty years, my experience has been uniform to this effect, and to him who knows what are the sources
of the public moral always, and what are the conditions & history
of social growth in this country, it cannot be otherwise. Let me
entreat you, exact a good price for your labours, or have nothing
to do with the periodical press — never invest a dollar in it yourself, and, if you invest your thoughts, tastes & studies, demand
& exact your pay in good currency, promptly, without letting the
debt grow too large to render its loss an inconvenience. Get your
weekly pay for weekly labour. Talking of periodicals — if you can
pick me up the copies of that work for which Everett writes, do
get & send them to me. I take for granted that the affair is
merely a grand puff, & from what I know of E.'s writings, I feel
very sure that they amount to nothing much beyond details

---

[94] Simms wrote *allow.*

of fact, upon which he flings a rhetoric which is not always classical. He may be pretty, but I do not look to him to be profound, or in any way original. Still I should like to see what he is publishing, and here I see nothing.[95] In a few days I hope to finish my novel [96] which has been so long on hand. I have passed through twelve months of great suffering, my friend, and life has lost no little of its hue & odour to me, & I have lost no little of my wonted hilarity in life. I have sung through life, hitherto, as a bird, now with sad & plaintive, now with gay morning notes; but now I feel that I am losing the wing for flight & the heart for song. Give me your love, my friend, & believe me faithfully Yours

W. Gilmore Simms

P. S. Pray write me. Your letters are always welcome, and if you knew what a charity they are, you would write more frequently. I am very busy planting corn & cotton & potatoes. But I am on my novel which I hope to finish in a few days. But my distractions have been many, and sometimes painful & oppressive. I am a man of many children & — cares. Send me any papers (literary — English or otherwise) which you do not want. My non-intercourse with society, the press & public, — is driving my mind into naked fallow.

922: To WILLIAM HAWKINS FERRIS [97]

Woodlands, (Midway P. O.) S. C.
April 3. 1859.

W. H. Ferris, Esq.

Dear Sir:

I have suffered your letter to remain unanswered, a much longer time than I had designed or should desire, in the hope that each succeeding day would yield me the time requisite for a proper compliance with your wishes; but a continual flow of

---

[95] In the fall of 1858 Robert Bonner (1824-1899), proprietor of the *New York Ledger* (a weekly), agreed to contribute $10,000 to the Mount Vernon Association if Edward Everett (1794-1865), the statesman and orator, would in turn contribute a weekly article for one year to the *Ledger*. Everett contributed fifty-three articles, the first appearing in Nov., 1858. See Paul Revere Frothingham, *Edward Everett Orator and Statesman* (Boston and New York: Houghton Mifflin Company, 1925), pp. 387-388.

[96] *The Cassique of Kiawah.*

[97] See introductory sketch.

company, which, on a Southern plantation, does not imply fashionable calls, — and a pressure of domestic duties which could not
be set aside, have hitherto conspired to defeat my purpose, and
it may be still several days before I shall be able to address myself
to the task. I write simply to mention this & to account to you
for a neglect which is in seeming only. I have another object in
thus writing you. In respect to the poem to which you refer, I
must state that I have a rescension of it, which I hold to be an improvement on the original publication. Now, in the case of poems
to which we have become familiar, the mind sometimes revolts
even at an improvement; even as we should be loth to behold
a change in beloved features, though the change should be really
an improvement in their style of beauty. My question is, do
you prefer to have the poem [98] as you know it, or will you accept
my taste, and recieve the later version? The changes are not
serious ones, of course, & contemplate rather the harmonies of
utterance than any alteration or modification of the thought. I
cover this note in one to Mr. Wallace,[99] who will hand it you,
& am, sir,

Very truly Your obt. servt.

W. Gilmore Simms.

923: To James Henry Hammond [100]

Woodlands. April 9. 1859.

My dear Hammond.

Two of your letters have been lying by me unanswered, for
a much longer time than usual. The first of these, written as you
were leaving Washington, did not reach me till the day after you
had passed Midway. I heard from Jamison [101] of your transit
on that day. Had I got your letter in time I should surely have

---

[98] "The Lost Pleiad." See letter to Gardner of April 15, 1859.

[99] William Ross Wallace (1819-1881), poet and lawyer, was a native of
Kentucky. In 1841 he settled in New York City, where he practiced law until
his death. During the 1840's and 1850's, however, he was occupied chiefly as a
contributor to *Harper's New Monthly Magazine, Harper's Weekly,* the New
York *Journal of Commerce,* and other periodicals and newspapers. In 1860 he
appears to have been on the staff of the *Journal of Commerce* (see Simms'
letters to Ferris of Nov. 23 and to Lawson of Nov. 30).

[100] This letter is a reply to Hammond's of March 13 (written the day before
he left Washington for Redcliffe) and another which we have not located.
Hammond's answer to this letter of April 9 and that of April 11 is dated
April 22. The originals are in the Hammond Papers, Library of Congress.

[101] David Flavel Jamison. See introductory sketch.

met you at the Depôt, especially with the hope to have taken possession of you & Mrs. H. if for a day only. That I have not hitherto responded to you with my wonted promptness is due to a perpetual flow of visitors. I have never had such a continued run, day by day, in my remembrance. And they came at a season when we are all nigh starving. I can neither get fowls nor meats of any kind. It is a spring famine here, always a season of scarcity & especially at this period. Fortunately, I had a present of a wild turkey, succeeded in buying another & a quarter of venison. My pigs are poor in the swamp ranges; and I have no muttons: You may judge how I must have been compelled to use my wits to supply my larder. Add to this, I am reduced to Western Whiskey as my chief & almost sole beverage. Keitt was among my visitors, Aldrich & wife [102] also. Jamison, by the way, was on the point of buying a plantation alongside of me, & would have done so, but for a mischievous speech of yours, which disparaged the property, made him hem & haw, try to get it for $1000 less than was asked, & in the meantime another purchaser steps in & buys. You see the mischief you have done with your despotic tongue & random opinions. You have cut me out of a good neighbour, & him from a good place which would have suited him exactly. It would not suit you, but if you had only reflected that *his* force was a small one, & the place comparatively a large one — 1750 acres — you would have seen that it would afford him ample choice of lands. He works only 23 hands, & could have done here what he never did at his Orangeburg place. This very year the place has yielded 5½ bags to the hand. As soon as he told me what you had said, I knew what to expect. He resolved to offer $1000 less, & was refused. In three days after the place was sold at the amount originally asked, and is thought a bargain. 1750 acres for $10,000. Jamison sold his own in Orangeburg, where he did not make more than 2 bags to the hand, for $12000. It had but 1200 acres. He is now at sea, & regretting that he did not buy. Lands here have been steadily rising. None to be had under $5 to $10 per acre. Yet the same lands, 10 years ago, could have been bought, & were bought, at from $1. to $3. But, enough of this.[103] What with

---

[102] Mrs. Alfred Proctor Aldrich was Martha Ayer, sister of Lewis Malone Ayer (see note 102, April 2, 1847).

[103] In his letter of April 22 Hammond writes: "It is not fair to make me the Scape Goat, in the Jamison affair. I did tell him that I had looked over the place 20 years ago & did not like it. But seeing he wanted it & knowing how agreeable it would be socially to you & him, I toned down my objections

visitors & plantation & other troubles, I have done little or nothing at my desk for three weeks. I have 260 acres of corn up, and am now planting cotton. I have a little cotton up. I have manured this season more than 250 acres, and am about to dress 30 acres of pine land for Cotton, with 2 tons of Guano. Pray for my success. I have been improving things, and have *doubled* the usual crop of my predecessor in two seasons; though still falling very far short of my calculations. I counted last season certainly on 100 bags; but the season was a terrible one on Cotton. For 11 weeks it did not grow one inch. In all that time we had not one drop of rain. With a good season, I am in hope to make 125 bags of 400 lbs. The last year I made but 67 of an average of 400 lbs. How often do you need to buy a gin, & which kind is best? Can you get extra brushes & saws supplied? Or inserted in the old framework? Do you use Guano & how do you dispose of it — in chop, drill or dribble? And what quantity do you put to the acre? There! I have no more vulgar questions. — It no doubt seems to you quite inconsistent with my usual profession & practice to regard politics & place as desirable either to you or to myself. But it is the very extremity of our case that led me to urge your submission should your friends & the good public desire to employ you in the crisis. I believe I know what you are good for in an emergency, and I conscientiously believe that if the country is to be saved from the most terrible of all shocks, if not from ruin, there is no man in it, better capable than yourself to effect its safety. I doubt, indeed, whether it can be saved. I look upon the catastrophe as inevitable; but the event may be retarded by a truly wise man, availing himself of a growing sentiment of conservatism. You, looking upon the case with more favorable eyes than myself, & friendly in sentiment to this conservatism, should not withhold yourself at this juncture; since, I take it, that you, quite as well as any body, and better than most of our Statesmen, can see where & how the momentum may be arrested. I did not wish you to do any thing directly towards acquiring the position; [104] I only sought to render you flexible, and, in fact, to move you to show yourself in an attitude as far as possible from that of an office seeker. It is true, that I concieved the notion that what

all I honestly could & when we parted fully beleived [*sic*] he would buy the next day & am sorry he did not." Jamison eventually bought Burwood, a plantation adjoining Woodlands (see letter to Miles of Feb. 5, 1860).

[104] Of president of the United States. See letter to Hammond of Jan. 10, 1859.

I wished you to do, would be promotive of my desire, if not of yours, that you should be put in the high place for which I thought & think you so eminently fitted; but the process was one, as I fancy, [which] would never subject you or me to any suspicion, on the part of any mind, of such an object being entertained by either. It is just possible, my dear H., that you laughed at the simplicity of my scheme. Most politicians — mere politicians — certainly would laugh. I will not, however, so far offend your *amour propre,* as to argue with you its perfect reasonableness, in spite of its *depths* — or shallows. Let it pass. Acquit me, at all events, of any thought of bringing you into trouble, any wish for lessening the amount of your *dolce far niente* — which, I fear is growing your infirmity & which you excuse by your dyspepsia &c. Only believe that I would have you achieving honorable position, for the purpose of an honorable & enduring fame, & for the public good. I must not talk longer in this vein lest you should suspect me of desiring to establish my own claims as a Patriot. I have, indeed, the notion that we are both men of whom patriots might be made. I am, & can be, in no situation to acquire the character. But it is not denied to you. Aldrich talks still of the nomination of the Convention. I don't see, even should you recieve the Dem. nomination, how that party can do any thing for you.[105] It seems to me doomed to a final defeat & disruption. There must be a wholly new organization, of new elements, before any really great, good or true man can be put into power. My best respects to Mrs. H. Love to Kate, and regards to the Boys![106] God bless you

W. Gilmore Simms

924: To James Henry Hammond [107]

Woodlands, April 11. 1859.

My dear Hammond.

I wish you would sit down & enumerate for me all the American or Southern wines, giving me their names, their localities &

---

[105] For the proceedings of this well-known National Democratic Convention, which met in Charleston on April 23, 1860, and split on April 30 over the party's platform, see note 69, April 9, 1860.

[106] Harry, Spann, and Paul Hammond.

[107] Hammond's reply to this letter and that of April 9 is dated April 22 (original in the Hammond Papers, Library of Congress).

several peculiarities. What they especially merit to be said of them, what are their susceptibilities as well as characteristics, and indicate, where you can, in what they resemble the foreign wines, & which. If you can mention also the names of our domestic grapes, do so. If you have any remarks upon the subject of our grapes & wines, let me have them. You can guess what I aim at, and concieve what I want. The fact is, Redi's poem runs in my head, and if I can find, or invent, high sounding names for our wines & grapes, I propose to incorporate the matter into verse, in the irregular measures, & playful fancies of the Italian poet. If you have not Redi, Harry, perhaps, has seen and has his poem. If not, go to Augusta, & buy a copy of Ticknor & Fields' Edition — in green & gold — of Leigh Hunt's Poems. He has given a loose lively translation.[108] If the Augusta book stores have it not, let them get it for you from Charleston. Russell certainly has it. Write me. I am very sad & drooping; and being thus sad, I propose to write something funnily.[109] God be with you in mercy.

Yours Ever

Simms.

P. S. Add to this information, where you can, the names of all those who make wine in America, local or remote, from Longworth down to McDonald. What of Herbemont? What of your Georgia makers? Who in North Carolina, the source, as is thought, of Catawba & Scuppernong, and Isabella, &c.[110] In short give me every item upon which a rhyme, if not a reason may be hung, or strung.

W. G. S.

P. S. I perfectly understood from your letters that I was to have the young Bull, some good Cotton seed, some grape roots & cuttings, & some Sorgho.[111] You have not omitted any thing. But I have been unable to send for them. It is too late this season.

---

[108] See letter to Hammond of March 2, 1859.

[109] We have found no evidence to indicate that Simms actually wrote this planned poem.

[110] Nicholas Longworth (1782-1863), of Cincinnati, Ohio, was the owner of extensive vineyards and was one of the leading wine-makers of the country. Nicholas Herbemont, who had been professor of French at the South Carolina College during 1807-1817, owned a vineyard near Columbia and was a small producer of wines. We have not been able to identify McDonald. During the 1840's and 1850's *De Bow's Review* published a number of articles on wine-making throughout the United States.

[111] We have not located these letters.

Next, however, I shall try to avail myself of your kindness. Write me soon & frequently. I *need* your letters, and just now the solicitous kindness of my few friends. My head troubles me. My heart is ill at ease. I have frequent fits of extreme depression in which I fancy a thousand subjects of disquiet — poverty, discredit, and — worst of all, the falling off of friends. You need not reason with me in respect to these fancies. When I can be so reasonable as to appreciate the reasoning of my friends, I do not need it. I am thus fully able to know that many of my cares are fancies. But the condition of mind & body which produces the fancy, is the ailment, & this reason does not reach. I have justified myself from keeping from the desk, by a reference to my brain. It has been overworked. It is one of my fancies that it is failing me. I do not feel like work — do not feel like thinking — feel rather like folding my robes about me for a long deep sleep. As soon as the spring is over, always a season of uneasiness with me, I hope to be better. But — once more God bless you. We both need all that he will be likely to accord, of blessing.

W. G. S.

925: To James Gardner [112]

[April 15, 1859]

My Dear Mr. Gardner —

The original of the following poem was written between my eighteenth and twentieth year. It was one of those fortunate

---

[112] We have not located the original of this letter published with Simms' "The Lost Pleiad" in the *Southern Field and Fireside* (Augusta, Ga.), I (June 4, 1859), 10. Since the italics in the date are probably not Simms', we have omitted them.

Gardner (1813-1874), a native of Augusta, was educated at Richmond Academy, Augusta, and Union College, Schenectady, N. Y. He returned to Augusta, practiced law, and was for a time attorney general of Georgia. He was a writer and an orator and the owner of the Augusta *Constitutionalist,* the leading Democratic paper in Georgia. He was the sole proprietor and publisher of the *Southern Field and Fireside* from the first issue of May 28, 1859, until he became associated with John L. Stockton with the issue of May 9, 1863. The periodical was suspended from Sept. 26, 1863, until Jan. 2, 1864, and during this interval Gardner sold both the *Southern Field and Fireside* and the Augusta *Constitutionalist* to Stockton and Co. In the issue of Oct. 1, 1864, Stockton and Co. offers the periodical for sale, and the issue of Oct. 29, 1864, announces that William B. Smith, of Raleigh, N. C., has purchased it and that it is to be combined with the *Illustrated Mercury* (Raleigh). The first issue from Raleigh is dated Nov. 5, 1864. The last issue of the periodical which we have been able to locate is dated Feb. 5, 1865, though under the title of *Field and Fireside* it was still being published at Raleigh in March, 1867 (see the advertisement in the *Crescent Monthly* [New Orleans] for that month).

productions which found popular favor.[113] But it did not satisfy myself. As it has been among the occasional employments of my maturer years, to revise and improve such productions of my youth, as seemed to me to deserve the effort, this, of the Lost Pleiad, commended to me by the favor which it found, as well as by its subject, has necessarily compelled my consideration. A recent application from a correspondent, seeking my autograph, and asking a copy of the original poem, has reminded me of the later *rescension*; [114] and as it has never been re-published, I deem it a proper contribution to your periodical, in compliance with your request.[115] It is always a perilous experiment, upon a production which has already found favor with the public, to attempt its amendment. Its very faults have possibly become favorites; and the mind — happily for humanity — is unwilling to give up an old friend because of his faults, and exchange him for another of even more certain character. We are apt to become sturdy champions of that which we gratefully remember; and it is probable that, with most of those who know the "Lost Pleiad," in my youthful version, there will be much unwillingness to accept any substitute, however excellent. But, more than one generation has sprung into existence since the early publication of the poem, who have never seen it, and will entertain no prejudices in respect to it. To these, then, I commend the present version; while I entreat the forbearance of those who have been pleased to accept the original with favor. *That* has been preserved in my published collection,[116] and may still satisfy its early admirers. This may possibly appeal to a new class, and will, I trust, prove not

---

The editors of the Literary Department of the *Southern Field and Fireside* were as follows: William W. Mann (May 28, 1859—May 18, 1860), John Reuben Thompson (May 25, 1860—Nov. 17, 1860), James Nathan Ells (Nov. 24, 1860—Jan. 4, 1862), S. A. Atkinson (Jan. 11, 1862—Sept. 26, 1863). No literary editor is indicated for the remainder of the issues we have seen.

[113] The earliest appearance of "The Lost Pleiad" which we have been able to locate is in Simms' and James Wright Simmons' *Southern Literary Gazette* (Charleston), I (Oct., 1828), 73-74. Simms was twenty-two at the time.

[114] The *Southern Field and Fireside* prints *re-ascension*.

[115] There can be little question that this correspondent was William Hawkins Ferris. See letter to Ferris of April 3.

[116] *Poems Descriptive Dramatic, Legendary and Contemplative* (New York: Redfield, 1853), II, 13-15. "The Lost Pleiad" is also included in *The Vision of Cortes, Cain, and Other Poems* (Charleston: James S. Burges, 1829), pp. 99-101, and in *Southern Passages and Pictures* (New York: George Adlard, 1839), pp. 69-72.

less successful than the original, in finding favor with its readers. I confess to preferring it myself.

Yours, very truly,

W. Gilmore Simms.

Woodlands, S. C., April 15, 1859.

926: To EVERT AUGUSTUS DUYCKINCK

Woodlands, April 22. [1859][117]

My dear Duyckinck.

Your letter has been lying before me for some time, but a crowd of visitors — in swift succession; the finishing of my book; [118] the business of the plantation, & domestic cares, have all conspired to keep me from my correspondents. Beyond my book, I have been able to do literally nothing at the desk, & fear that much more of this sort of life will force me into miserable old-fogyism. I feel older now than ever I felt before; & need the provocative influences of an old literary correspondent like yourself, to keep me in the mood for art, and fancy, & thought & imagination. I read you, & fancy I detect you in the weekly issues of the Century; but I regret that that journal is lapsing into politics. Why can't we have one work consecrated to pure litera-ture? It is melancholy to think of it. I note the long essays on political subjects in the Century, not only as long and tedious, but as wanting in thought, knowledge and experience.[119] I note what you say of your own connection with the work, and repeat my exhortation, not to peril any thing, even your time, one moment beyond the period when it ceases to compensate in a pecuniary way. There is little reputation and no fame derivable from such sources. The country is inundated with these publica-tions, and there is a multitude of clever young men about town, who can easily execute the dashing, smart, impudent sort of writ-

---

[117] Dated by Simms' discussion of Duyckinck's contributions to the *Century*. See letters to Duyckinck of Jan. 29 and March 18.

[118] *The Cassique of Kiawah.*

[119] Simms was doubtless annoyed at the article entitled "The Present Ad-ministration" in the *Century* for April 9 and the letter entitled "President Making &c." in the *Century* for April 16. The first of these contains the follow-ing remarks: "When will the simple and stupid come to know, that the Southern body are of necessity *always* hostile to intelligent industry. When will they cease to be deceived by the fact that although Northern Democrats are qualified protectionists at home, they sacrifice their private opinion to the will of their Southern masters?"

ings which these publications and their rapidly running & raging class of readers will require. Everett is, of course, employed only because he is in vogue. I take for granted that he will do no more than amplify & illustrate prettily the ancient commonplaces, and round graceful periods to a very old burthen. I begged you, if possible, to pick up & send me some of the sheets of the journal which contains his writings, for here I never see it. I am simply curious to see what sort of elegant haberdashery he serves up weekly. If, without trouble or expense, you can pick up for me a few weeks sheets of Bonner, you will oblige me.[120] — I will not endeavour to lift the sable curtains which overhang your house anew, even to declare my sympathies.[121] It is enough that we both know with what a tender weakness the heart yields to every tale of such privation, where its own fibres have been so frequently wrung as ours by frequent loss. Your sorrows recal my own. May God commend them to our use, while we reap from them the bitter wisdom of humanity — submission, faith, repentance, and the sympathy which forever interposes for the antagonism of mere self. — I read your paper on Milton with pleasure & profit. Masson's book has not reached me. Were you aware that a very good version of the Ode to Diodati was made by Strutt, who has translated all the Latin & Italian poems. His vol. is in my collection, a small 12 mo of 150 pp. London Ed. A. D. 1814. — Jacob George Strutt. His translation is sufficiently close, and his rhyming is very fair, if not elegant. I see you have been wise enough in your translation to make it a perfectly un-ambitious one, — which was right. To attempt more than a simple rendering, would argue a weakness which I should never expect to find in you.[122] — If I can do any thing in season for the blind Lady, I shall be pleased to do it; it is just possible that I may have something on hand which will suit.[123] I will look. Let me know what length of time is suffered. I am quite busy planting

---

[120] For Edward Everett's contributions to Robert Bonner's *New York Ledger,* see note 95, March 18, 1859.

[121] Frances Cooper Panton, daughter of Henry H. Panton and sister of Mrs. Duyckinck, died on March 24. See the New York *Times* and the New York *Evening Post* of March 25.

[122] Volume I of David Masson's *The Life of John Milton* . . . had recently (1859) been published by Macmillan, Cambridge and London; republished by Gould & Lincoln, Boston, Mass. Duyckinck reviews the volume in three articles entitled "John Milton," published in the *Century* for March 26, April 2, and April 23. In the second of these he includes his own translation of Milton's "Elegia Prima," addressed to Charles Diodati.

[123] This is doubtless an anthology of some sort to which Simms was asked to contribute.

Cotton. Season promises to be good. I am almost too busy for any desk labour at present.

Yours Ever truly

W. Gilmore Simms.

P. S. By the way, is it possible to pick up in New York a good copy of Lord Berner's Froissart at a reasonable price. Some years ago, Bartlett & W. had a fine copy for $12.00.[124] I should be glad to get that copy, or one like it, for that price now. Is the thing possible?

927 : To HENRY BARTON DAWSON

Woodlands, S. C. April 23. [1859][125]

My dear Sir:

Your letter of March 25th. and the numbers of your work from one to twelve inclusive have been in hand for some time, but I have been so overrun by visitors for the last five weeks that I have not been able to answer the one, or do more than briefly glance at the other. I shall take an early occasion to go over the History, with especial regard to its Southern portions. As things occur to me, I shall certainly be glad to give you the benefit of any hints, such as they are. In respect to Mrs. Ellet, we shall probably in no particular disagree touching the Lady herself. She is no favorite of mine, and though I gave her the subject of her women of the Revolution, and counselled her in what quarters to seek her materials, she has shown no grateful feeling in return. I can understand your reluctance to recognize her as an authority; but in regard to the volumes which she edited, she is rather a *medium,* & had no motive to misrepresent. The sources of her information in South Carolina were trustworthy. They might be mistaken in many things; they were certainly repeating at second hand of the local & domestic traditions, and you need not be told how apt this sort of authority is to be partial, perverse, and vexed with the *suppressio veri,* and *suggestio falsi,* in individual cases, as partiality or prejudice coloured the mind of the narrator; but allowing duly for all this, and taking the

---

[124] The translation of Froissart's *Chronicles* by John Bourchier, 2nd Baron Berners, was first published in 1523-1525. A reprint was issued by E. V. Utterson in 1812. For Bartlett and Welford, see note 206, June 6, 1845.

[125] Dated by Simms' discussion of Dawson's *Battles of the United States.* See letters to Dawson of Oct. 16, 1858, and Jan. 19, Feb. 21, and March 15, 1859.

books *cum grano,* they must be admitted, if only because they are the best evidence which we can lay hands [on] in respect to certain minor histories.[126]

You have certainly got your hands full of work, especially if you undertake to strip the Northern people of their false Gods in our History. The work of perversion & misrepresentation, of corruption & invention has been going on so long, and has been so profitable in respect to both money & reputation, that Connecticut & some of her sisters may well look with vexation & disgust to such iconoclastic performances as those you threaten. Look at the Pension List for a commentary. Washington's occasional sneers show what he thought of their generals & troops. His commentary so quietly contemptuous, upon the resignation of Deacon Ward [127] being dated at the period when his quarter salary was due, and a number of similar things in his correspondence show what *he* thought of the courage, conduct, patriotism, & selfish meanness of too large a proportion of the public men of New England. You will find him saying something in the same vein about Old Put, but I presume you have possessed yourself of every thing necessary to showing up this old Put.[128] As a fair illustration of the mode in which such reputations have been manufactured, an instance occurred some years ago in N. Y., the facts being fully reported to me at the time, in the case of this very same Putnam. I had written a Life of Marion & one of Smith for popular use, and soon after a Life of Putnam was announced in the same series — by another writer.[129] In this book he resorted boldly to invention & made a ridiculous story of Put, while a boy getting into an apple tree, from which he could not descend, having got off to a branch which was too slender to permit his return. So he bravely required a boy friend to *shoot him off,* i.e. to cut the branch by his bullet, between himself & the trunk of the tree. This most absurd story was a *whole* invention. One asks why Put could not have dropt down without the shot simply by letting go his hold. It was reported to me

---

[126] In his letter to Dawson of March 15, 1859, Simms had earlier suggested that he consult Elizabeth Fries Lummis Ellet's *Domestic History of the American Revolution* and *The Women of the American Revolution.*

[127] Gen. Artemas Ward (1727-1800), of Massachusetts.

[128] In his account of the Battle of Long Island (*Battles,* I, 148-150) Dawson attacks Gen. Israel Putnam for disobeying orders.

[129] William Cutter's *Life of Israel Putnam* and Simms' *Life of Francis Marion* and *Life of Captain John Smith* formed the first three volumes of Cooledge's "Illustrated Library." See note 4, Jan. 2, 1847.

that the author of this most veracious history impudently avowed the invention, and undertook to justify it on the ground that he was compelled to supply a sufficient number of adventures, the *facts* which he had been able to find being quite inadequate to such a reputation as Put had acquired for adventure & daring. So, too, I believe, is the whole story of the wolf in the cave.[130] Did you ever see the Letter of Gen. Smallwood on the subject of the Battle of Long Island, where he says that Washington, himself, & other officers vainly strove by beating the Connecticut troops with their swords, to bring them to the scratch.[131] They fled incontinently without delivering their fire. You perhaps have seen my review of Sabine's work, in which I open the clues to the much vaunted patriotism of the North in the Revolution.[132] Old Graydon's book [133] was unanswerable by them. In haste, but

Very truly Yours

W. Gilmore Simms

Henry B. Dawson, Esq.

928: To R. P. Collins [134]

Woodlands, South Carolina.
April 23. 1859.

R. P. Collins, Esq.

dear Sir:

We have a vulgar proverb in the South, which, I suppose, we inherit from old England — possibly Yorkshire — "A short horse

---

[130] In reviewing *Major-General Israel Putnam. A Correspondence, on This Subject, with the Editor of "The Hartford Daily Post," by "Selah," of that City, and Henry B. Dawson, of White Plains, N. Y.* in the Charleston *Mercury* of June 19 (see note 163, July 8, 1859), Simms writes: "First, we had a wolf story, which came to us through the school books. How he had shot a wolf in a cave, and was drawn out by the heels by a rope, which seems to have been attached to the wrong extremity. The wolf story has been given up; even the cave is doubtful."

[131] William Smallwood (1732-1792), of Maryland, was a colonel at the time of the Battle of Long Island. He was later promoted to brigadier general, and after the Revolutionary War he was governor of Maryland (1785-1788). His letter here mentioned by Simms is printed in Peter Force's *American Archives* (Washington, 1837-1853), 5th Series, II, 1011-1014.

[132] *South-Carolina in the Revolutionary War.* See note 62, June 20, 1853, and note 12, Jan. 11, 1856.

[133] Alexander Graydon, *Memoirs of a Life, Chiefly Passed in Pennsylvania, within the Last Sixty Years . . .* (Harrisburgh: Printed by John Wyeth, 1811). There were several later editions.

[134] Not identified. This letter is reproduced in facsimile in Salley, *Catalogue of the Salley Collection of the Works of Wm. Gilmore Simms*, pp. 24-25.

is soon curried." Your request is so moderate that I find it easy
to comply with it. I very cheerfully send you my autograph.
Would it were more graceful, for your sake, as an exhibitor, &
mine as a scribe.

Very truly Yours, &c.

W. Gilmore Simms.

929 : To Gamaliel Lyman Dwight [135]

Woodlands, S. C.
May 15. 1859.

Mr. Gamaliel L. Dwight.

Dear Sir:

Your application needs no apology. Could I always confer
pleasure upon my readers, by so small an effort of head and hands,
my gratification would be much greater than your own. It is
enough here to say that I find pleasure in complying with your
wishes.

I am, Sir,
Very respectfully
Your obt Servt.

W. Gilmore Simms.

930 : To James Henry Hammond

Woodlands, May 23. [1859][136]

My dear Hammond.

I have been taking some respite from home & the desk, by
paying off certain old social scores: have been down for ten days
into Beaufort, looking out some old friends & localities, and picking up notes for future *'prenting'*. Having shaken off the tedious
burden of a novel which had been lingering too long on my hands,
in consequence of my troubles & toils, I felt like taking a brief

---

[135] Dwight (d. 1875), of Providence, R. I., was a student at Brown University during 1859-1862 and 1864-1865. During the Confederate War he served
first as corporal, then as 1st lieutenant in the 1st Rhode Island Light Artillery.
After being graduated from Brown he studied medicine at Harvard and in
Berlin but never practiced.

[136] Hammond's reply to this letter is dated June 11, 1859 (original in the
Hammond Papers, Library of Congress).

flight in freedom, especially as I have really been suffering physically & morally to an extent considerably beyond my usual experience.[137] When I came back from below, I made the rounds among my wife's relatives in Barnwell; & visited, among others, my old friend Charles Carroll,[138] who has been seriously threatened with a danger which still hangs *in terrorem* over him. He has had two or three slight strokes of palsy, & for a time was deprived of the use of right arm, leg & side. You remember him of course; a really noble fellow, eccentric & capricious; but a Gentleman of high tone & considerable talents. He is better; able to go about, though slightly lame, and as he is comparatively a young man, of no bad habits, in vigorous health otherwise, I am in hopes that the danger will pass away. But I confess I am not quite satisfied with the condition of his mind, in which I fancy I percieve certain unwonted signs of feebleness. This keeps me concerned about him. Carroll was one of the friends of my youth, and at a time when I had great need of friendship & found but

---

[137] *The Cassique of Kiawah a Colonial Romance* (New York: Redfield, 1859), dedicated to William Porcher Miles, is listed among the new works in *American Publishers' Circular and Literary Gazette*, V (May 21, 1859), 248. In his reply of June 11 Hammond writes: "I have read your last novel. As a mere Romance it does not equal the two preceding [*The Forayers* and *Eutaw*]. Yet even as a Romance it has passages surpassing any in them[.] But taking the performance altogether it is perhaps superior in genius & ability to any thing you have done in prose. You nodded some times & some times had a drop too much, & one of your most important scenes was to *my conception* a dead failure. At least I think I could very greatly amend it. I wont tell you which because I think you *put yourself out* in it—(your ability not your genius which explains the failure)—& I should not be surprised to see some reviewer select it as the best passage." The Charleston *Mercury* of June 7 praises the novel highly, though pointing out some crudities of style and remarking that "there are some strong expressions and ideas in regard to the social intercourse of the sexes that are disagreeable, and in our judgment, had better been omitted." The same review also comments: "From the avidity with which it has been sought and read, both here and elsewhere, our expression of opinion may seem to be already anticipated, and the public acclaim of praise awarded." The *Mercury* of June 14 reprints a laudatory review of the novel from the New York *Leader* of May 28. *The Cassique of Kiawah* is also praised by *Godey's*, LIX (Aug., 1859), 180; *Russell's Magazine*, V (June, 1859), 287; *S. L. M.*, XXVIII (June, 1859), 476; *De Bow's Review*, XXVIII (May, 1860), 599; the *Courant* (Columbia, S. C.), I (June 9, 1859), 45; and the *North American Review*, LXXXIX (Oct., 1859), 559-561. This last (reprinted in *Russell's*, VI [Dec., 1859], 276-277) ranks Simms as the greatest of living American novelists and remarks that, though he is often careless and irregular, his writings show "the power of picturesque description, the imaginative conception of character, the nice delineation of its delicate shades, the ability to deal with subtile and violent passions, and the skilful arrangement and development of intricate plots." J. Quitman Moore in "William Gilmore Simms," *De Bow's Review*, XXIX (Dec., 1860), 702-712, also comments favorably on *The Cassique of Kiawah*.

[138] See introductory sketch of the Carrolls.

little.[139] I value him accordingly. We spoke of you. He was with you in College.[140] His son, Dr. Carroll, an amiable young fellow who works a steam saw mill near me, I have asked to visit you with me when next I run up to see you, which will probably be in July, and I may possibly bring my own eldest boy up with me.[141] I wish to interest Dr. C. in the culture of the vine and wish him to get some instructions from you *in pro. per.* On the first of June I propose to remove my family to the city where, however unwilling, I am compelled, *ex necessitate,* to spend my summer, or a part of it. In another year I hope to shake off the city altogether. While I write you, we are all anxious about the safety of another friend — a devoted friend of yours — Aldrich — who is down with Typhus fever. From the last reports we learn that while there seems no immediate reason for apprehension, the Fever is yet quite unsubdued & that no material change has taken place within 24 hours. He is required to be kept perfectly private — no friend permitted to visit him. I have written to Mrs. A. & to James Aldrich; [142] and am hearing from J. A. or from Thompson who reports to me from Blackville.[143] The case is a serious one, & as it affects one whose relations with us have been so intimate & grateful, my concern deepens the more I meditate it. The district could ill afford the loss of Aldrich & his old friends would feel it acutely. Whatever his faults, he was faithful, frank, hearty in his sympathies, and altogether one of the best fellows living. I trust, sincerely, my dear Hammond, that we, at least, may be spared the grief & misfortune of his loss. But the very doubt keeps me miserable. — I am far from well

---

[139] See Simms' letters to Lawson of Dec. 5, 1835, and April 29, 1836, written while he was visiting at Carroll's plantation, Clear Pond, and courting Chevillette Roach at Oak Grove (see note 49, Nov. 4, 1836).

[140] Carroll was graduated from the South Carolina College in 1824, Hammond in 1825.

[141] This visit was not made. See Hammond's letters to Simms of Nov. 23 and Dec. 19, 1859 (originals in the Hammond Papers, Library of Congress). Dr. Francis Fishburne Carroll (b. 1833), physician and planter, married in 1861 Julia Peeples Reynolds, daughter of Dr. William Sims Reynolds, of Fairmount (see introductory sketch of the Reynolds brothers).

[142] James Thomas Aldrich (1819-1875), younger brother of Alfred Proctor Aldrich, studied law in his brother's office at Barnwell and was admitted to the bar in 1842. He practiced law independently from his brother. His wife was Isabel Coroneus Patterson (1829-1902), daughter of Angus Patterson (see note 147, March 26, 1845).

[143] Probably John Houseal Thomson (b. c. 1816), though perhaps William H. Thomson (d. 1868), both lawyers at Blackville and probably brothers. The Barnwell *Sentinel* of April 20, 1861, gives notice of a law partnership formed between Alfred Proctor Aldrich and John H. Thomson.

myself. My head is in bad order. The moment I approach the desk, it seems that I have a tendency to vertigo, and headache follows. I sleep badly. My languor is oppressive. I am restless yet indisposed to exertion, altogether in a very wretched state of mind & feeling. I try to interest myself in the crop, but cannot endure the sun. My Cotton is looking better than ever. I have 290 acres planted and 300 corn. Of the latter I have 60 acres which might be laid by now, & will be at the next working. I can write no more. God bless you all.

W. Gilmore Simms

931: To WILLIAM HAWKINS FERRIS

Woodlands, May 23. 1859

W. H. Ferris, Esq.

Many thanks, my dear Sir, for your present of Steuben.[144] I had not seen the work & have already plunged deeply into it. I may review it, as I have a M.S. Collection of ten or twenty of Steubens original & unpublished letters in my possession. Once more, thanks. Your kind letter has also reached me. I forward, by the same mail with this, a few pamphlet trifles, — thrown off *stans pede in uno,* which, as they are not included in any of my published collections, may be new to you. They are all crude performances under a momentary impulse.[145]

Yours very truly &c

W. Gilmore Simms.

932: To JAMES GARDNER [146]

[May 25, 1859]

My dear Mr. Gardner:

The original of the Ode which I send you, was written and printed in one of our newspapers on the visit of Lafayette to the

---

[144] Friedrich Kapp, *Life of Frederick William von Steuben, Major General in the Revolutionary Army* (New York: Mason Brothers, 1859).

[145] Simms doubtless sent two or more of the following: *Charleston and Her Satirists* (Charleston: Printed by James S. Burges, 1848), *Lays of the Palmetto* (Charleston, S. C.: John Russell, 1848), *Sabbath Lyrics* (Charleston: Walker and James, 1849), and *Michael Bonham* (Richmond: Jno. R. Thompson, 1852).

[146] We have not located the original of this letter published with Simms' "Welcome to Lafayette—Ode" in the *Southern Field and Fireside,* I (June 18, 1859), 26.

United States, in 182 —, and when I was a young versemonger, in my teens.[147] I need scarcely tell you, however, that it has undergone the revision of a much later period, and in the present version, has never been published. I have subdued its crudities and softened its harshnesses, being unwilling to abandon it without some effort at reclamation, as its composition is associated with many very interesting details in my early literary life. It will, I trust, recall gratefully to thousands of your readers the memory of an enthusiastic period in their experience, when the whole country was in a fever of patriotism at the reception of the veteran, who, in old age, came to receive the acknowledgments and tributes of a race whose ancestors he had served with zeal, and at much self-sacrifice. There is, at this time, a tendency to decry the intellectual merits of Lafayette; and, by consequence, the extent of his public services in America. This is all wrong; any such judgment upon his labors would be wrong, and the proceeding is as ungrateful as ungenerous. Without regarding him as a very great man, I am satisfied that he should be recognised as a nobly impulsive, and generously patriotic one, whose contributions to the cause of America are hardly computable at the present day — who made large sacrifices, incurred serious perils, and expended very important sums of money in our cause; and whom, I believe, to have been really moved in his performances by a sincere devotion to human liberty, and an enthusiastic passion for glory, or, at least, honest fame. But I am not now to discuss his merits. It will be enough simply to repeat the hope that this letter may recall to many of your older readers the events in Lafayette's [148] enthusiastic reception in this country, now more than thirty years ago, and convey some idea of the feeling of our people on the occasion, to the more numerous thousands who were not then capable of sharing in it. Whatever the degree of claim on the part of the veteran, the occasion was one full of grandeur, and moral importance. Lafayette was one of the few links between the race then in power and possession, and that by which the Revolution had been achieved. He stood, as it were, the central figure between two imposing epochs of time

---

[147] Lafayette arrived in Charleston in March, 1823. We have examined the Charleston *Mercury*, the Charleston *Courier*, and the *City Gazette* (Charleston) for Feb.–April, 1823, but have not located Simms' poem. It was, however, published as "La-fayette" in *Lyrical and Other Poems* (Charleston: Ellis & Neufville, 1827), pp. 180-181.

[148] The *Southern Field and Fireside* misprints *Laberette's*.

and history, and not unequally united with both. He came to receive the tributes of posterity to the past, and to illustrate the past, for the benefit of the future. This boy's ode may show you in what way the visit of the veteran impressed the new generation that was then on its march to manhood, whatever may be the sort of manhood to which the present may lay claim; and this is quite enough by way of preface.

Yours, truly,

W. Gilmore Simms.

Woodlands,[149] S. C., May 25, 1859.

933: To Armistead Burt [150]

Charleston, June 13. 1859.

My dear Mr. Burt.

It is a long time since I had the pleasure of communicating with you; so long that I half fear you may have forgotten me. We are both in a sort of retirement; but I trust that yours is a pleasant one & that it is prosperous.[151] I write you now to beg that you will help me to some facts in order to the construction of a brief biography, for the Cyclopædia, of Geo. McDuffie. Nobody that I know of is more able to do so. I wish, if possible, the date & place of his birth; the facts in his education & subsequent career; the period of his death; his public services; a mention of his best speeches; of his public connections; his official stations; and all such items as may bring him fully & fairly, however briefly, to the knowledge of future generations. A mere hint, a simple statement, will suffice. I do not wish to be unnecessarily copious or to give you much trouble. One good long letter will probably cover all that is necessary. May I look to you for such a letter — for this information. You are well aware that, could I have obtained the information, I should have written a life of McDuffie. Now, I ask only material enough for a sketch

---

[149] The *Southern Field and Fireside* misprints *Woodbury.*

[150] See introductory sketch.

[151] In 1852 Burt declined to be a candidate for renomination to the United States House of Representatives, and in 1859 he was practicing law at Abbeville, S. C.

— a few paragraphs.[152] Pray let me hear from you soon, & believe me

Ever truly Yours &c

Hon. A. Burt.   W. Gilmore Simms.

934: To William Hawkins Ferris

Charleston, June 14. 1859.

W. H. Ferris Esq.

My dear Sir:

My removal, from the plantation to the city, occasioned some
delay in the reciept of your last favours, & of the copy of the
curious little volume you were so good as to send me. I have
glanced over it with interest & curiosity. It is new to me, and
there are some good things in it. Still, as you say, its rarity &
bizarre design, are its chief recommendations.[153] After recieving
your last letter I looked among my books for a copy of Lacon
which I once possessed — a small Philadelphia edition, bought
when I was a boy. But I have not been able to find it; and if
your copy be indeed a duplicate, I shall welcome it gratefully.
But do not go to the expense of sending by mail. If you will
cover it to my address, and leave it with Appleton & Co, addressed to the care of Russell & Jones, Charleston, it will come
to me without cost and in a short period. I saw Colton in Charleston some 35 years ago — say in 1823 or thereabouts. He published two or three collections of new Laconics in the Charleston
papers. He had the look of a genuine John Bull, was, I think,
under middle height, and carried a short stick, about half the
length of an ordinary walking cane.[154] The pamphlets I sent you
were perhaps only valuable as now quite out of print.[155]

Yours very truly

W. Gilmore Simms.

---

[152] When Simms was planning a memoir of McDuffie for the *Democratic
Review* in 1845, he had written to Burt for information about him. See letters
of April 9 and April 23 of that year.

The cyclopaedia for which Simms was writing in 1859 is *The New American Cyclopædia: A Popular Dictionary of General Knowledge*, ed. Charles
Anderson Dana and George Ripley. See note 81, Nov. 10, 1857.

[153] We are unable to identify this volume.

[154] Charles Caleb Colton (1780?-1832), English gambler and divine, was the
author of *Lacon: or, Many Things in Few Words; Addressed to Those Who
Think*, first published in London in 2 vols. in 1820-1822 and frequently reprinted
in England and in America. He was twice in America: in 1823 and again in
1828. We have not located his laconics published in a Charleston newspaper.

[155] See letter to Ferris of May 23, 1859.

935 : To HENRY BARTON DAWSON

Charleston, June 30. 1859.

Henry B. Dawson, Esq.

dear Sir:

I cover to you a notice which I made of your work in the editorial department of the Charleston Mercury.[156] You will please note that whatever about this article may be found peculiar belongs to a plan adopted in the Mercury, by which to lessen the commonplace baldness of literary notices.[157] I trust that this little paper may not prove ungrateful to yourself, or inconsistent with the objects of your publishers.

Very truly
Your obt. Servt.

W. Gilmore Simms.

936: To W. L. LINCOLN [158]

Charleston So. Caro. July 1, 1859.

W. L. Lincoln, Esq.

Dear Sir:

Your request is so moderate, that I find compliance with it easy, and it pleases me to accept your compliments, and to say that, however briefly, I am,

Your obliged & obt. Servt. &c

W. Gilmore Simms.

---

[156] This clipping, a long review of the first sixteen parts of Dawson's *Battles of the United States* from the *Mercury* of June 27, is still preserved with this letter.

[157] Simms was reviewing books, pamphlets, and magazines for the *Mercury* in a column headed "Our Literary Docket," in which he brings the authors to court and passes judgment on their works. The first of these columns appears in the issue for May 20, 1859; the last in the issue for Oct. 29, 1859. Simms' next column of reviews in the *Mercury* (Dec. 19, 1859) is headed "Current Literature." In it he says: "As 'Our Literary Docket' was designed for the summer months only, and for popular recreation quite as much as criticism, it naturally closed with the season, and with our having cleared the docket of long continued cases."

[158] Not identified.

937: To HENRY BARTON DAWSON

Charleston, July 8. 1859.

My dear Mr. Dawson.

Your letter of June 27. was addressed to me at Woodlands, but I had left the plantation for the city, & did not recieve it until I had despatched a late letter to you. You will see from that & the enclosure, that I had in some degree anticipated your desires.[159] My time is exceedingly stinted, but as occasion serves, I will be pleased to render you my little tribute. Did I ever tell you that I had published a series of long papers in the Southern Literary Messenger, some dozen years ago entitled, "The Civil War, and Revolution in the Carolinas?"[160] Get these papers if you can. The Editor[161] will no doubt provide them. They will help you to supply some of your material, & to settle some doubts. Will you be so good as to suggest to your publishers to supply my numbers of their Shakspeare after 32.[162] Should they also provide me with their publications, they would be justly considered & honestly disposed of in the Mercury.

Yours truly, but
in great haste.

W. Gilmore Simms

P. S. I have seen none of the discussion of which you speak. If your brochure is published, pray let me have a copy.[163] Excuse this soiled sheet, which I commenced scribbling on without noticing. Did you ever see the letter of Gen. Smallwood which states that in the Battle of Long Island, the General officers beat the troops with their swords but could not get them up to the scratch.[164] They fled incontinently without delivering a single fire! — i.e. a large portion of them. I take for granted — speak-

---

[159] See letter of June 30, covering the clipping of Simms' review of the first sixteen parts of Dawson's *Battles of the United States.*

[160] "The Civil Warfare in the Carolinas and Georgia, during the Revolution." See note 367, Dec. 12, 1845.

[161] John Reuben Thompson.

[162] This three-volume edition of Shakespeare's *Works,* issued in parts, was published by Martin, Johnson and Co. (later Johnson, Fry and Co.), New York, during 1855-1859.

[163] *Major-General Israel Putnam. A Correspondence, on This Subject, with the Editor of "The Hartford Daily Post," by "Selah," of That City, and Henry B. Dawson, of White Plains, N. Y.* (Morrisania, 1860). "Selah" was the pseudonym of Abner Clarence Griswold. Simms reviews the work in the Charleston *Mercury* of June 19, 1860.

[164] See note 131, April 23, 1859.

ing of Bunkers &c. that you see Greene's Letters, Washington's, Graydon's Book, and even Thatcher.[165]

938: To WILLIAM HAWKINS FERRIS

Charleston, July 9. 1859.

My dear Mr. Ferris.

Please recieve my thanks for the nice little copy of Lacon which has been duly recieved and placed in my Library.[166] In the matter of the autographs, I may be able to do something for you during the winter. My papers are all at the plantation. I have nothing at my town house but my current correspondence, and current books and a few for study and reference. But I have not found it easy to keep my autographs. They have been annually thinned off by applicants, so that almost all that could be bestowed, have been long since given away. My old friend Tefft, an inveterate autograph monger, with scores besides, have left me no opportunity for accumulation. I will see, when I remove to the country in the winter, what still remains to me, and if possible to find you any thing that can be parted with you shall have the benefit of it.[167]

Yours very truly
&c

W. Gilmore Simms.

W. H. Ferris, Esq.
N. Y.

---

[165] For William Johnson's *Sketches of the Life and Correspondence of Nathanael Greene*, see note 86, March 15, 1859; for Alexander Graydon's *Memoirs of a Life*, see note 133, April 23, 1859. Washington's letters were published in Volumes II-XI of Jared Sparks' edition of *The Writings of George Washington . . .*, 12 vols. (Boston: American Stationers' Company; Russell, Odiorne, and Metcalf; and others, 1834-1837). Benjamin Bussey Thatcher was the author of *Indian Biography; or, an Historical Account of Those Individuals Who Have Been Distinguished among the North American Natives as Orators, Warriors, Statesmen, and Other Remarkable Characters*, 2 vols. (New-York: J. & J. Harper, 1832).

[166] See letter to Ferris of June 14, 1859.

[167] Later, particularly after the Confederate War, Simms sent Ferris a considerable number of letters he had received from various correspondents. A portion of this correspondence is now in the Ferris Collection, Columbia University Library.

939: To John D. Legaré [168]

Charleston July 24. 1859.

My dear Mr. Legaré.

I fully appreciate all the doubts as well as the sorrows of your-self and family in regard to the youthful victim whose fate we both deplore. I trust, however, that neither doubt, nor grief, will operate to prevent you from yielding me the necessary material for the sketch which I propose to make of your son. The record will, I trust, prove a grateful one to all surviving parties. I wish, first, the date of his birth, the place & character of his education; the dates & names of his publications; and a notice of his several inventions, as well as of the degree in which he indulged in the arts. In respect to his poems. I am prepared to speak of his published volumes.[169] What we chiefly desire & need will be an appreciative summary of what he did in art; what discoveries, for example, he had made in cotton & its uses, &c. The facts are especially desirable; the commentary should be brief. The whole of the material you might very well compress within the limits of a single letter. For this I shall be grateful, and if supplied to me, at any time during the month of August, it will be in season.[170] Let me repeat my sincere desire that his family will collect & bind together his various writings, and renew the assurance of my own readiness to contribute whatever aid I can in preparing them for the public eye.

Yours very truly

W. Gilmore Simms.

P. S. Please give the titles of all his *longer* writings, in prose & verse, & especially those which were given to the press. If I

---

[168] For Legaré (1799-1860), see note 202, Oct. 17, 1849, in which his first name is incorrectly given as James.

This letter and a letter of reply (undated) by J. J. Legaré, son of John, is printed in A. S. Salley, "James Mathewes Legaré," Charleston *Sunday News and Courier,* Nov. 1, 1903. Our text is from the original in the possession of Mr. Salley.

[169] Simms had reviewed Legaré's *Orta-Undis* in the *Southern Quarterly Review* in 1849. See note 204, Oct. 17, 1849.

[170] James Mathewes Legaré (see note 202, Oct. 17, 1849) died on May 30. We have not located a sketch of Legaré written by Simms; however, in the Charleston *Mercury* of Nov. 29, 1861, there appears an unsigned article on Legaré entitled "Domestic Resources," which, we think, can safely be ascribed to Simms. It is largely concerned with Legaré's inventions of "plastic cotton," of "a new process for making and coloring the 'encaustic tile,'" and of "substitutes for 'hemp, flax, rope and twine.'" Part of the article, however, is devoted to Legaré himself.

mistake not, he was the author of one work in prose which was anonymously published.[171]

940: To MARY LAWSON

Charleston, July 26. 1859.

My dear Mary.

Your letter of the 14th. was recd. a few days ago, but I was just then about to take a run to the plantation, whence I returned yesterday. There I had the contemplation of Cotton, Corn & potato fields, and scarcely any other object. We have been suffering from drouth, & an intensely hot season, and my crops have suffered in consequence. A good rain of an hour, while I was there, served to freshen & improve the prospect &, I trust, the crops. —

Here we have all our little family with us at this moment. Augusta spends the day with us two or three times a week. Gilmore is here enjoying his vacation. He will return to the Academy [172] in August. Mary Lawson is a fat girl, well developed & growing, with fine bust and pretty face. Chevillette & the younger children are all doing well. Hattie, teething, and drooping occasionally. Our lives, in our little wigwam pass in a somewhat humdrum manner in this horribly hot weather; but the season thus far is healthy, &, for the *discomforts*, my dear, we who have so often suffered from severest griefs, are quite patient with God if he will spare us the *distresses*. May you all learn this lesson of patience under discomfort, without needing to be schooled by the losses and distresses.

You are, no doubt, all comfortable & refreshing yourselves [173] on the Lake of Budd.[174] If my amiable friend Mrs Eggleston

---

[171] In "Domestic Resources" Simms says: "To many of our readers, it is well known that he was the writer of a volume of very delicate and genuine poetry; sweet, graceful, felicitous and classical—not powerful or passionate—but singularly happy in phrase, and pure and exquisite of fancy. He was also a vigorous prose writer—and there is an elaborate prose work of pure invention, never published, in which he sought to realize for the readers the details of that fabulous city, supposed still to exist in the wildest seclusion of South America, which is the tradition with the natives—a faith with the old travellers—but which no one has been permitted to reach, save the Romancer or Idealist. This, and many other of the writings of Mr. Legare [sic], still remain in manuscript."

[172] The King's Mountain Military School.

[173] Simms wrote *yourself*.

[174] Budd's Lake, in New Jersey.

comes, you will find her a genial & unaffected companion. Her husband is a very good fellow too. You will treat them kindly for my sake, untill you come to like them for their own. They are both of excellent, & she indeed, of an old family here, and they have a comfortable dwelling of their own, & a good income. I trust to hear from her, on her return, that you have cottoned together like thieves after a good harvest.[175] It is just possible that I may visit N. Y. before the summer closes. The condition of my affairs & family will prevent me for some time from deciding when, or whether it shall be. But when I determine you shall seasonably hear.[176]

I rejoice that you have the *manliness,* my dear, to avow frankly that you have had no offer yet. Among young ladies, the vanity on this subject, prompts to an immense deal of *lying.* The fact is married life is quite too expensive for thousands of the very best men, and were your Woman's Rights Women, really honest & sensible people, they would, as the greatest boon to young women, devise a scheme for *cheap* living, as the best properest, noblest mean for bringing the sexes together. Untill this is done, matrimony is too expensive a luxury for two thirds of the Masculine gender. Meanwhile, Mary, dear, do not you be impatient. You are perhaps never likely to be nearer happiness than in your present state. Marriage is a very difficult problem. Go farther & fare worse. If you stay where you are, bless God that he leaves you in a condition which is very grateful; surrounded by friends, & with fond father & loving mother. You can scarcely improve your condition by any change. — I hope the Cassique [177] will amuse your hours at Budd's when they happen to be dull. I have only one request to make — that you will lend it as little as possible. As it is pretty generally known, the degree of intimacy between your family & myself, vulgar people are apt to suppose that, when you circulate my books, you are desirous of obtaining favor & praise for me. Let us take care not to give cause of clamour even to vulgar people. — Tell your father he is a goose about the name of Florence. I go for Flor-

---

[175] George Washington Eggleston (1795-1863) was twice married: first, in 1821, to Sophia Heriot (1797-1824) ; and secondly, in 1840, to Martha DuBose (d. 1865), the widow of Philip Porcher (1795-1833).

[176] We are unable to determine whether Simms went North this year. We have found no letters written by him during October or early November; so if he went, he did so at that time.

[177] *The Cassique of Kiawah.*

ence. It is a very pretty name & suits well with that of the family.
Who the devil knows or cares what have been his associations
with the actresses & Florence's Hotel. Out of N. Y. nobody
knows that there is any such vulgar place. Say to him, *I* insist
— for the first time, in my life upon giving the child a name. —
Let it be Florence Singleton Lawson, and I will be godfather,
& send the girl a silver spoon, and give her, when she gets big,
a brooch.[178] Kiss Mama on my account; kick Papa if he is mulish,
& hold me

Ever truly Yours

W. G. S.

941: To John Esten Cooke

Charleston, July 26. 1859.

John Esten Cooke. Esq.

My dear friend.

Your affectionate letter of the 17th. appeals to my affections
with a voice too earnest & impressive for evasion. Believe me,
I most warmly sympathize with you in the appeal, and it will require but little effort of my will to respond to your genial overtures. The sympathies which know fellowship only, & not rivalry, are apt to be rare enough among professional & gifted men.
It is only where the gifts are high, where *the consciousness of
gift* is *an assured and unquestioning one,* that the soul is lifted
above the struggles, the emulations, the envy's & the jealousies,
which are the sure attendants of a selfish ambition. Believe me
to thank you most gratefully for the grace & geniality with which
you lay your bosom bare to the press of mine! I once wrote a
letter to old B. Tucker of your precinct, and closed it with
"Yours *lovingly.*" [179] I forget what were the exact terms of the
old man's response, but it showed that his heart was touched by
the use of a word which men employ femininely only, — and in
their dealings with women. Surely, my friend, in a guild like ours,
which the world never welcomes to *its* love, however frequently
coerced into admiration, — there should be much love among
ourselves! *We,* at least, will try to love one another, at once as

---

[178] Lawson's daughter was named Flora Donaldson.

[179] See letters to Tucker of July 11, 1850; Feb. 7, 1851; and March 2, 1851.

men and authors! And you, surely, have pursued your *rôle* with
an affectionate desire to plant yourself on higher grounds of
heart and soul, than are common to those who write. Your letter
would suffice in proof of this, and nothing could be more genial
& generous than your laudatory notice, in the Index, which has
been copied into some of our papers.[180] It was a most manly &
magnanimous as well as genial tribute, such as our Southern
presses have rarely accorded to our small & scattered flock of
Southern authors. By the way, I have just been applied to for a
photograph & a biography, by Mr. Victor, of the Art Journal

---

[180] We have not located a file for this period of the Richmond *Index* (a
weekly and semi-weekly, which ran during 1859-1860). Cooke's notice of Simms
is reprinted in the Charleston *Mercury* of July 16. Cooke quotes the remarks
about Simms made by William Henry Trescot in his *Oration Delivered before
the South-Carolina Historical Society, Thursday, May 19, 1859* (Charleston,
S. C.: James and Williams, Printers, 1859), p. 23, to the effect that "the State
owes" a debt to Simms "for the fidelity with which he has preserved its memory,
the vigour and beauty with which he has painted its most stirring scenes, and
kept alive in fiction the portraits of its most famous heroes." (Trescot's *Oration*
is also printed in full in the Charleston *Mercury* of May 21.) Cooke then comments: "This public tribute to one of the most worthy and distinguished writers
of the South, found, we are well convinced, an echo in every listener to Mr.
Trescot's admirable essay. It may almost be said of Mr. Simms that he discovered the history of South Carolina; and in declaring as much, we have no
sort of reference to his formal history of the State. We refer to his Revolutionary tales, in which we have presented to us a panorama of the struggle,
wonderfully vivid, picturesque, moving and true to fact and nature. It is an
entire new world which the reader enters as he opens these singularly stirring
romances, and, once read, they cannot be forgotten. . . . Of the lives and
characters and actions of those patriots who lived upon the 'sacred soil' of South
Carolina, Mr. Simms presents us with a picture so vivid and enthralling, that
from the first page of the story to the last line of the volume, there is scarcely
a possibility of the reader's pausing. . . . His books are alive with humor,
passion, incident. In the foray, the assault, the skirmish, the battle, the single
combat, he is truly a master of the brush; and the figures on his canvas stand
out powerfully. He has described a whole world of scenery and character. The
list of his *dramatis personæ* embraces types of all the classes of men who went
to make up the strangely diversified mass which figured in the contest. Everywhere he has woven into the woof of his imaginary history the actual threads
of fact—the personal narrative, the curious anecdote, the entertaining or moving
tradition. Thus, his books are redolent of the South and its modes of life—they
'smell of the soil'—and to us at least, are the best histories that exist anywhere,
of the desperate struggles in our sister State, in the dark and bloody days of
the Revolution. But we did not design a literary criticism upon Mr. Simms'
productions. We wished simply to bear our testimony to the worth and honorable fame of one who has done the South a noble service. For it is the South
that Mr. Simms has ever looked to—which he has delighted to speak of, to
defend, to illustrate, to depict in all its phases. His defence of the part which
South Carolina and the South generally, took in the Revolution, was exhaustive,
final, and conclusive of the question. On a thousand other occasions he has
stood forth in defence of our institutions and our rights—and if we were called
upon to select the one citizen who had done more than any other to foster a
noble pride of lineage and native land, in the rising generation, we should point
to Mr. Simms. May he live many years to illustrate our annals, and to enjoy
the fame which he has secured."

of New York — a quarto of large circulation & much merit.
Of Mr. Victor I know but little, having seen him only twice or
thrice last summer. He is the Husband of Metta Fuller, now
Victor, & a very clever woman, especially in verse. I do not know
but her verse is much better than that of all our lady poets, and
deserves to take rank with that of our best men. For the proof,
see a remarkable blank verse poem, published anonymously, on
the Arctic Discoveries — I forget the title — Arctic Queen, or
something like it.[181] If you have never seen it, probably Thompson [182] can find you a copy. Read it. Well, Mr. Victor wishes my
photograph & a memoir. The former I will send him. In respect to the latter, I shall have to refer to a friend. Professor
Miles here, would cheerfully do it, were I to hint my wishes, but
he has already written a long paper, on the subject, published some
3 or 4 years ago in the Messenger.[183] Paul Hayne is also willing,
no doubt, but his health is feeble & he is just now busy to the
eyes with book & magazine — Poem & what not.[184] It is tasking
your friendship very soon to say, as I do, that I know no one
who could please me better by such a performance, but it must
be a labour of love, for Victor can't afford pay. If you feel in
the vein, you can find adequate material of fact in the paper in
Duyckinck's Cyclopædia;[185] & in the pages of the Messenger, in
the article of Mr. Miles already referred to, & which Thompson
can furnish you with. Your own analysis will supply the commentary; and you may use much of what you have said elswhere, as such a sketch, for such a journal, does not limit you

---

[181] Orville James Victor (1827-1910), author and publisher, was at this time
editor of the *Cosmopolitan Art Journal* (1856-March, 1861). After the Confederate War he edited the *Illuminated Western World* (New York), in which
Simms published "Voltmeier." In 1856 Victor married Metta Victoria Fuller
(1831-1885), author of *Fresh Leaves from Western Woods* (Buffalo: G. H.
Derby & Co., 1852). *The Arctic Queen* (n. p., n. d.) was published anonymously.
Simms had changed his opinion of Metta Fuller's abilities since his review
of *Fresh Leaves from Western Woods*, S. Q. R., N. S., VII (April, 1853),
525, in which he says: "The writer is evidently young, enthusiastic, romantic;
what she needs, is study of the world, reserve, patience, and a knowledge of
the true limits of the imagination. The imagination is a wing, to which thought
is the proper body. Let her brood longer before she attempts to soar. She
must study old men, and older books, if she would properly possess the souls
of young ones."
[182] John Reuben Thompson.
[183] For James Warley Miles' article on Simms, see note 152, June 9, 1851.
[184] Hayne's *Avolio; a Legend of the Island of Cos. With Poems, Lyrical,
Miscellaneous, and Dramatic* (Boston: Ticknor and Fields, 1860) is reviewed
by Simms in the Charleston *Mercury* of July 31, Aug. 1, and Aug. 2, 1860.
During 1857-1860 Hayne was one of the editors of *Russell's Magazine*.
[185] See note 260, Dec. 6, 1854.

to the rigid reserves of a Cyclopædia of biography. Let me hear from you at your earliest leisure on this subject.[186] — I have just written to Gardner, Proprietor of Field & Fireside, in respect to yourself, & suggesting that he should endeavour to secure your Correspondence, referring to that in the Century as the plan. You have by these letters done more for the Century than most of its contributors together. They form the most distinguishing & attractive features of the work.[187] I have said as much to Gardner, and said farther that if he will apply to you, as under my counsel, you will probably be persuaded to work for him at very moderate rates. I have consented to prepare him a novel, to run through 20 chapters, or issues of his work, half a dozen columns to each, for $400. And he pays me the highest price he can afford, &, I fancy, has strained a point to do so. *Keep this matter secret.* I do not begin for months.[188] If he writes you, he will probably apply for Virginia letters; old families; biographical sketches; anecdotica, &c. all of Eastern Virginia. I have suggested this as being probably the most easy work to you. I have counselled him to make you an offer — his ultimatum, — and I beg to counsel you that if at all decent, however

---

[186] Cooke's sketch of Simms was published in the *Cosmopolitan Art Journal* for Dec., 1859. See letter to Victor of Sept.? 1859.

[187] During 1859 Cooke published a series of letters in the *Century* on such subjects as "Early Days of John Marshall," "George Mason," and "Personal Details of John Randolph."

[188] We have examined all issues of the *Southern Field and Fireside* from May 28, 1859, through Feb. 5, 1865, except a few issues missing from the Library of Congress file of Volumes II and III (May 25, 1860—Dec. 27, 1862). Simms did not publish a novel in the issues examined. In addition to the poems listed in note 112, April 15, 1859, note 146, May 25, 1859, and note 3, Jan. 2, 1860, he published the following signed poems in the *Southern Field and Fireside*: "Ballad at Sea," I (May 28, 1859), 4; "Sonnet" (with the motto " 'The *little* dogs,/*How* they bark at me!' *King Lear*"), I (Aug. 6, 1859), 82; "To the Sister of My Boyhood's Friend" (dated "October, 1832"), I (Aug. 27, 1859), 105; "Prophecy of Napoleon" (dated "1830"), published with a prose essay, "Napoleon's Prophecy," I (Sept. 10, 1859), 124; "Marmer's Boat Song," I (Feb. 11, 1860), 296; "Mountain Bugle Song for Battle," I (March 10, 1860), 329—republished (because of an omitted line) in I (March 17, 1860), 337; "Song.—I Have Lived in Fancies" (dated "1834"), II (July 14, 1860), 57; "Ask Me Not Whither," II (Oct. 6, 1860), 153; "Oh! What If the Prospect Be Clouded?," II (Jan. 5, 1861), 256; "Ode—'Our City by the Sea' " (reprinted from the Charleston *Courier*), N. S., I (June 13, 1863), 153; "Ballad— 'Yes, Build Your Walls,' " N. S., I (Aug. 29, 1863), 213; "The Bitter Feud. A Dramatic Sketch—From an Italian Story," N. S., II (Jan. 9, 1864), 3; "Hope Deferred," N. S., II (May 28, 1864), 1; "The Old Man's Reverie," N. S., II (July 23, 1864), 6-7; and "The Sense of the Beautiful," N. S., II (Dec. 10, 1864), 5. Each issue of N. S., II, has separate pagination; the other volumes have continuous pagination.

low, it may be just as well that you should close with him.[189]
It will do you no harm to work freely & frequently in papers
which *do not involve invention*. Your error has been to have
striven to write in fiction with as little reserve as in narrative &
fact — topics. This cannot be done with safety. Fiction requires
invention, more elaborate design, your whole heart as well as
head; and these demand frequent pauses, when the Imagination
may repose, and, looking up catch new inspirations for flight from
passing Eagles — even as Romulus & Remus did — when they
sought for auguries. If I have any secret in this way, & can
teach it, I will do so when you come to Woodlands next winter.
Happy & glad to do so. I am anxious to write the 'Humour of
Glen Eberley', but I am not yet *matured* enough for it. It will require three years more of life in solitude & in the growth of my
own soul, to make the work what I design. For Porgy, in that
work, is to become a Legislator, and he will probably close his
career in its denouement. I must prepare him & myself together
to drape our sunsets with dignity.[190] At present, I am revising
my little History of S. C. for publication in Septr.[191] It is scarce
possible to do any thing else in this hot weather. Do you see
any Literary Dockets in the Mercury. There, I sometimes refer
to you, Greenway Court & the Messenger. Did I hint in my last
that in Greenway you scattered yourself too widely over the
surface; divided the reader's attention among too many person-
ages; did not concentrate yourself sufficiently on any? You have
thus cut yourself off from too many of your own resources; and
your chief success thus far lies in the liveliness & piquancy of
the dialogue, and the saliency of feature in some of your por-

---

[189] The only contributions by Cooke to the *Southern Field and Fireside* which
we have been able to identify are the signed "Recollections of a Contented
Philosopher. Phœbe's Wedding Night," I (Jan. 7, 1860), 257; "The Letter and
the Portrait. A Legend of the Chesapeake Shore," I (Feb. 25, 1860), 315; and
a novel, "The Pride of Falling-Water, a Tale of the Old French War of 1755,"
published in the issues from June 9 through Nov. 10, 1860 (II).

[190] Simms did not write this proposed novel.

[191] The "New and Revised Edition" of Simms' *The History of South Carolina from Its First European Discovery to Its Erection into a Republic with
a Supplementary Book, Bringing the Narrative Down to the Present Time*
(New York: Redfield, 1860) is listed among the new works in *American Publishers' Circular and Literary Gazette*, V (Nov. 26, 1859), 584. Some copies
carry the imprint of Russell & Jones, Charleston. The work is reviewed in
Russell's Magazine, VI (Jan., 1860), 375-376; *De Bow's Review*, XXVIII
(Feb., 1860), 238; *Godey's*, LX (Feb., 1860), 181; and the *North American
Review*, XC (Jan., 1860), 281.

traits.[192] When you come to Woodlands, we will concoct a Virginia Romance together? Eh?—One matter I had almost omitted. Some time ago, at the suggestion of a friend, I took a copy of my poems, & marked those things which I most preferred, & underscored those passages which I thought most quotable. How would you like this copy for your critical uses, & how can I send it you safely?—I would like to see you in Richmond this summer, but doubt whether I can leave home at all. If I do come my trip must be a hurried one, direct for N. Y. and will contemplate only a two weeks absence. I have the plantation on my hands, & make frequent visits to it. Have just returned from one. Have the cares of Cotton on hand; vexed with conditions in corn; perplexed with pease, riled with rice, piqued at my potatoes, &c. To sum up,—this very morning, my wife was threatened with premature labour.[193] She is now easier, but you may readily concieve that I have not my mind in hand at all. You will forgive the meagreness of this scrawl, and genially recognize the will & affection which has made me write, though so ungracefully.

God bless you.
Your friend

W. Gilmore Simms

942: To Henry Barton Dawson

Charleston, July 26. 1859.

My dear Sir:

Your letter, & the proofsheets are at hand. But I have sudden sickness in my family, and can only make a hurried acknowledgement. I suggest one or two trifles. *"Wexhaws,* not *Waxhaws.*["] "Kinlo*c*h not Kinlo*ck*." Should it not be *"Beaulieu"* and not ["]Bieulieu?" Should it not be "Major *Hyrne?* and not

---

[192] Simms' latest notice of *Greenway Court; or, the Bloody Ground,* published serially in the *Southern Literary Messenger* during April-Dec., 1859, is in the *Mercury* of July 12. *Greenway Court* was later republished as *Fairfax; or, the Master of Greenway Court* (New York: Carleton & Co.; London: S. Low, Son & Co., 1868).

In a long article (one and one-half columns) entitled "John Esten Cooke, of Virginia" in the *Mercury* of Oct. 21, 1859, Simms remarks that Cooke "is now one of the most eminent of novel writers in the country," though he criticizes his writings for the same faults that he here mentions in this letter.

[193] Sydney Hammond Simms was born probably on July 27. See note 201, Aug. 11, 1859.

Hyme?["] "Lempriere, not Lampriere." *"Lanneau, not Lenew."*
— These are trifles, but I have not leisure for more.[194] See the
first vol. of Cornwallis's Correspondence, just published by
Ross.[195] Take Tarleton's Memoirs [196] *cum grano*. He lied like a
Hessian. Cornwallis repudiates his book. When you refer to it
for the history of the war in *our* interior, use Roderick Mackenzie's commentary upon his Memoirs, by way of test.[197] He will
afford you some hints even for your siege of Charleston. Where
do you procure your copies of the Diary of Baldwin & the report
of Adj. Bowyer, & whence are your notes of De Brahm.[198] You
do not seem to have my Sketch of S. C. in the Rev. which contains several diaries of the siege, De Brahms & others.

Very truly Yours

W. Gilmore Simms

943: To James Henry Hammond [199]

11 Aug 1859.

My dear Hammond.

I have just got back, after a week's absence from home in
Beaufort District.[200] Within two weeks, my wife has added another
son to my stock; and, as you may suppose, I have been troubled
& anxious for some time past.[201] I am not well besides, experienc-

---

[194] Dawson had sent Simms proof sheets of at least Chapters LIX and LXI
("The Siege of Charleston" and "The Action at the Waxhaws, S. C.") of
Battles of the United States. Dawson made none of the changes Simms here
suggests.

[195] Charles Ross, ed., *Correspondence of Charles, First Marquis Cornwallis,*
3 vols. (London: J. Murray, 1859).

[196] Gen. Sir Banastre Tarleton, *A History of the Campaigns of 1780 and
1781, in the Southern Provinces of North America.* See note 89, March 15, 1859.

[197] *Strictures on Lt.-Col. Tarleton's History "of the Campaigns of 1780 and
1781, in the Southern Provinces of North America"* . . . . See note 91, March
15, 1859.

[198] Col. Loammi Baldwin (1745-1807), of Massachusetts; Col. Henry Bowyer
(d. 1832), of Virginia; and William Gerard De Brahm (1717–*c.* 1799), sur-
veyor general of the Southern District (1764-1770).

[199] This letter is a reply to Hammond's of July 30. Hammond's answer is
dated Aug. 15. The originals are in the Hammond Papers, Library of Congress.

[200] Simms was doubtless visiting the William Fullers.

[201] The family tombstone at Woodlands and Simms' Bible both give July 22
as the date of Sydney Hammond Simms' birth, but he was not born that early
(see letter to Cooke of July 26). In a letter to Dr. William Fuller dated July
28, 1859 (discovered by us after this volume was set in type), Simms writes
that his son was born "yesterday afternoon"; July 27, therefore, would appear
to be the correct date of his birth.

ing, no doubt, the approach of age, precipitated by toils, anxieties, sorrows, a long & wearisome fight for position & justice, in addition to natural infirmities of growing years. You are right & the tone of your letter but too frequently finds its proper response equally from my head & heart. But I cannot write now. I will in a few days. The purport of my present communication is the enclosure. Examine it, & do use all your influence in behalf of the fine young fellow & Physician, Dr. *Peyre* Porcher. Between the parsimonies of Fed Gov. & City Gov. & Med. College, they extort $1000 labor annually from these young physicians, in a public institution.[202] God bless you & all

Yours Ever

W. Gilmore Simms

---

[202] For Dr. Francis Peyre Porcher, see introductory sketch. In his reply of Aug. 15 Hammond writes: "From what you say & the documents you have sent, backed as they are by Dr C[hristopher] Fitzsimons who is here, I should be very happy to do any thing I could for Dr Porcher. But as there would be no sort of chance for him to get any compensation for the *past,* the matter should be considered in reference to the future & without regard to him. The Marine Hospital fund is a charitable one, raised chiefly by the contributions (*forced*) of the poor seamen. The Act of 1802, left its expenditure to the discretion of the President. It is his duty therefore to see that out of it, the proper Hospitals shall be provided at whatever reasonable cost, & if the fund fails to apply to Congress for more. If Dr. Porcher refuses & all other suitable Physicians refuse to attend the Hospital without pay, and this is certified to the President by the proper authorities—the City Council—the Chamber of Commerce—or the Collector of the Port, the President would of course & at once designate a Salary for the post. He could not avoid it. There would be no necessity for me to interfere. But if any *competent* Physician, having in view other objects, than mere pecuniary compensation for this service, would consent to undertake it without pay, then it is equally the duty of the President to accept the offer. And before giving a Salary he should be made fully satisfied, that no one would do this. For he is bound to make this Charitable Fund go as far as it can & to accept all contributions of service or money in its aid[.] You see therefore what must be done before it can be expected that he will make this a Salaried Office. And a little reflection will also show you that if he does make it such an office instead of having it filled by ambitious young physicians, for the honor, for the information to be gained, & for the reputation to be established, it will be certain thereafter to be filled by Jackleg Doctors whose connexions may have influenced to procure it. And then how will the poor seaman fare in his sickness?

"I am not speaking as I said in reference to Dr Porcher, but on the general & you may depend on it, that so long as a competent Physician can be found who will accept the post without pay, it will be infinitely better for all the most interested parties, to take him."

944: To Henry Barton Dawson

Charleston Aug 23. [1859][203]

My dear Sir:

I have read your controversy with considerable interest & amusement. It is a subject upon which we may congratulate ourselves that we are still able to get the proofs — adequate enough — for the conviction of the *Artful Dodgers,* States & Soldiers & Statesmen, — so called — of the Revolution. The rogues have not succeeded in destroying all the old documents, or so forging their counterfeits as to prevent detection. I shall be glad to see your letters in a body. But, if you will allow me, I would counsel you, even in continuing your present controversy to curb yourself, so as never, to lose the command & self control, the dignity of the Historian, & fall into personalities & rudenesses. Though you may have had the provocation, your forbearance will be more honorable, & will tell better in the argument. In Haste, but very truly Yours &c

W. Gilmore Simms.

945: To James Henry Hammond [204]

Charleston, Aug. 24, 1859.

My dear Hammond.

Since I last wrote you, I have been immersed in toils, troubles & anxieties. My wife has brought me another son, a fine vigorous infant, the largest she has had, and which is thought to resemble me. You will hold it as a proof of my old regard, that I have called him Sidney Hammond. We thus blend the names of the two noble little boys I lost last summer, and though it reopens old wounds, with the old memories, yet the memories of these boys are sweet to us, unassociated with pain except in the moment when we lost them. My wife, though fragile is doing well, better than I expected. She was so feeble that I was greatly apprehensive about her untill the event terminated favorably. — I took a week's run to Beaufort, after the affair was safely over; and was taken

---

[203] Dated by Simms' discussion of Dawson's controversy with Abner Clarence Griswold, of Hartford, Conn., on the subject of Gen. Israel Putnam. See letter to Dawson of July 8.

[204] This letter is a reply to Hammond's of Aug. 15 (cited note 199, Aug. 11, 1859).

with fever, accompanied with racking pains soon after my return. I was two days in bed, purging & keeping low. Though up again, and at work, yet I suffer from great languor, depression of spirits, a painful sinking of the heart, & an inexpressible sense of dullness & despondency. My tasks are endless. My drudgeries keep me from better things. I am revising, almost rewriting my history of S. C. which is now in press, & am contributing to the American Cyclopædia.[205] These labours are exacting, consume all my time, keep me from original works, and can do nothing for my reputation, and almost as little for my pocket. My Correspondence too is enormous, & it is in vain that I strive to abridge it. Every body that needs information about the South; about our History; every young author who wishes to be delivered; every beginner that desires to know how to begin; all apply to me; and it would be thought very churlish should I refuse. So every Editor, or Publisher that begins a Cyclopædia or a Magazine, or a Collection of any sort, writes me for succour. What am I to do. I frequently send a batch of 10 to 20 letters to the P. O. It is breaking me down. I long to come & have a few days with you, but till I have got through the history, find it impossible. I must defer my visit till October. It is probable that I shall be with you (D. V.) the first week of that month.[206] — It is a subject of melancholy thought with me to find you writing so gloomily. What is the matter with your physique? Are you drinking, smoking, lying about, seeking nothing, seeing nothing, doing nothing. I half suspect this to be the case. Break off from bottle & cigar & go see after your plantation. Don't physic yourself. Don't leave yourself idle. Move about at all events — & on horseback. Setting aside your physical condition, there is nothing in your political to disquiet you. I hold you to be firmly fixed in your position with the people of S. C. You cannot be touched. It will not be attempted. Your creed is growing in favour — and the danger is that the people will go beyond you — so long as they continue prosperous, — in their resignation to the existing order of things. You see how tame Rhett's speech was; the mere *bis repetit* of his old convictions. It said nothing, answered nothing, & led to

---

[205] *The New American Cyclopædia.*
[206] Simms did not visit Hammond at this time.

nothing.[207] The districts will all be represented in the Convention.[208] Your policy, & that of your most intimate friends, will be
to steer clear of it. You must not think of leaving the Senate —
must go back to it — must be re-elected. It is a shame to skulk
such a position at your time of life. Patch yourself up; live low,
and become a new man, & take no heed of your position. It will
take care of itself. *Will do for you, now, what no exertions* of
your own could do. Leave something to the chapter of accidents,
and all will be well. Get yourself in health if you can. If this
summer you had taken a run to Europe, — only for the summer,
it would have helped you, physically, socially, politically. You
must do so next summer, and if I can raise the money *I* will go
with you! Eh? What do you say to that. Ask your wife. Believe
me, your health is all that troubles me. I attach no sort of importance to your political groaning. This miserable world of men
has always been the same. Will always be the same. You can
never count on any thing, as politically sure, when you have to
deal with a Democracy. The fact is, all the world is in a transition
state, & just entering on the first chaotic phase, in which but a
lurid light shows us the thickest darkness. — Thanks for your
promise touching Porcher.[209] He does not ask compensation for
the past, but a quid for future service. If you can get the office
salaried, pray do so. It is a mean thing of govt. that it should
be otherwise. I congratulate you on your honours. A Grandfather! [210] Well, God bless you in your posterity.

Yours Ever faithfully

W. Gilmore Simms.

J. H. H.

---

[207] On July 4 Robert Barnwell Rhett spoke at Grahamville, S. C. Laura A.
White says (*Robert Barnwell Rhett: Father of Secession*, p. 155) that Rhett's
speech was "a plea for a united South to enter the campaign of 1860 as the
final struggle against Northern aggression, with the clear understanding that
defeat would mean the end of the Union."

[208] The National Democratic Convention, which met in Charleston during
April and May, 1860. See note 69, April 9, 1860.

[209] See Hammond's remarks about Dr. Francis Peyre Porcher in his letter
of Aug. 15, quoted in note 202, Aug. 11, 1859.

[210] Marcus Claude, son of Hammond's son Paul, was born on Aug. 5.

946: To William Hawkins Ferris

Charleston, Sep. 4. 1859.

My dear Sir:

I am still something of an invalid, but one of those invalids who expect to die in the harness. I work and suffer! And try not to complain! In respect to what I said to you, that no agricultural country has ever produced arts or letters, the proof is abundant. Look at the histories from the earliest periods. The secret of intellectual activity is constant attrition. You are right. *Our* only field is the *stump & war — hence we have produced the greatest orators & the greatest warriors of the nation.* Both require *action.* Study the point. It is probable that I shall visit N. Y. in October. If so, I shall find you out & your painter.[211] Excuse this scrawl. I am engaged in a *tour de force,*[212] which leaves me only time to say, God forgive you.

Yours &c.

W. Gilmore Simms.

947: To Marcus Claudius Marcellus Hammond

Charleston, Sep. 18. 1859.

My dear Major

I trust you will esteem it no small proof of my friendship for you, that, with nothing really to say which can interest you, and with labours on hand that keep me at work day & night, literally sleepless, I yet make the effort to give you an occasional scribble, in a moment snatched from cares of the desk, revisions, rewritings, proofs, prose, verse, criticism, &c. if only to show you that you are gratefully remembered and held in sincere & affectionate esteem. It is, as I have said, a period with me of the intensest labour, and so far as the community without is concerned, I know nothing & nothing really is to be known. I hardly leave the house more than once a week to go into the city; and all my respite is at night, when I stroll to a neighbour, to engage in a rubber of

---

[211] Perhaps the painter of the picture which Ferris gave Simms and which was later lost when Woodlands was burned. See letter to Ferris of July 22, 1865.

[212] The revision of *The History of South Carolina.* See letters to Cooke of July 26 and to James H. Hammond of Sept. 18.

whist, & return home, to light lamp in my study and address myself to work. I scarcely read the Newspapers; read no politics;
am literally out of the living world, as this is defined — a world
of bustling butterflies, wriggling monkeys, cunning spiders,
awkward leaping frogs, and any proportion of ants, musquitos
and terrapins, clods & maggots. Charleston, though wonderfully
healthy this season, is ineffably stupid. We have got some three
people who delight in paradox, five lawyers who manufacture puns
& conundrums; thirty six fast women, who would like to do any
amount of whoring if they could escape the consequences; and
who abuse the men terribly because they don't operate, in spite
of their difficulties, though with their free will & consent; and
at the risk of bullet for adultery, & gallows for rape. We know
these things, of course, and know where to lay hands on these
people; but I am no longer ambitious of martyrdom, either by
shot or rope, and I steer clear of the whole fraternity. Several
nefarious attempts have been made upon my virtue, but, like
Joseph, I curbed the lion — what remains in me — and left the
Mrs. Potiphar's to despair and scandal. Meanwhile, I have been
cut by the few real friends whom I would like to preserve. The
General [213] writes me a scribble only once in 2 months, and you,
with nothing to do but to look after the pleasures which you
never find, expect me to answer every letter ere you send another.
Briefly, I am most villainously entreated by those who should
love me most. — I am well *prima facie;* but I suffer from strictures across the forehead; from frequent & severe discharges of
blood — piles — from the sedentariness of my habits, &c. My
legs fail me. I walk but little — *can* walk but little. Get soon tired.
I have just finished brief notices of the Hammonds, yourself, the
General, old Saml & Leroy, for the Cyclopædia.[214] I have been
thus working all my life for people who dont care a damn about
me. My family is well — my wife recuperates slowly. Sydney
Hammond thrives & grows avid to resemble me. I hope Gilm.
S. H.[215] does his duty. Regards to wife & daughter [216] & self.

Yours Ever

W. G. S.

---

[213] James H. Hammond.

[214] Both Samuel (1757-1842) and Le Roy Hammond (*c.* 1740–*c.* 1800) were
Revolutionary soldiers conspicuous in battles in South Carolina. These bio-
graphical sketches of the Hammonds were published in *The New American
Cyclopædia.*

[215] Gilmore Simms Hammond.

[216] Probably Katharine.

P. S. Tell Harry H. that in that famed collection which he gave me, some insects have made their way, & are destroying the leaves, &c.[217] Ask him what I am to do. I wish to save it.

948: To James Henry Hammond

Charleston, Sep. 18. 1859.

My dear Hammond.

I cover you a series of propositions in respect to the subject submitted you — the procuring the Physician of the Marine Hospital in Charleston a salary. Pray do what you can in the matter. The argument seems irresistible.[218] — I am terribly busy, labouring, by a *tour de force,* to get my new edition of the History of S. C. ready by the 1st. Oct. It is now going through the press & I am writing day & night, frequently till after midnight. My labours on the Cyclopædia [219] have also been very oppressive recently. But for these toils I should have been up to see you. My wife brought me another boy last month, an event which added to my anxieties & kept me fettered.[220] She is very feeble. My crop fails to meet my expectations, but will, I think, be a considerable improvement upon that of last year. But I shall have to get another overseer. — In respect to politics we see & hear little here, save through the Mercury; and I find this sort of reading not only unprofitable but disagreeable. You must not heed any thing said about you, but resume your seat quietly & firmly. That you will be re-elected triumphantly, I have no sort of question. The public mind seems quite averse to any excitement whether upon new or old issues. Douglas must part with the South, and is, I suspect, making his count upon conservatism in the North. But, with the exception of a few newspapers, there does not seem in S. C. much interest in the next Pres. Election. I do not hear from you.[221] Remember my toils & write.

Ever truly Yours

W. Gilmore Simms.

---

[217] This is doubtless the unknown collection mentioned by Simms in his letter to Harry Hammond of March 27, 1858.

[218] See letters to Hammond of Aug. 11 and Aug. 24, 1859.

[219] *The New American Cyclopædia.*

[220] Simms had already twice reported to Hammond the birth of his son Sydney Hammond. See letters of Aug. 11 and Aug. 24.

[221] Hammond's latest letter to Simms which we have located is that dated Aug. 15 (cited note 199, Aug. 11). He did, however, write Simms on Oct. 4, Oct. 24, Nov. 23, Dec. 19, and Dec. 22 (originals in the Hammond Papers, Library of Congress). We have not located Simms' letters to Hammond written during these months.

949: To Orville James Victor

[September? 1859][222]

My dear Mr. Victor.

I hasten to send you the sketch of myself which I have just recieved from Mr. Cooke.[223] I might add a good many details, but his summary seems to cover them. You may state, if necessary that I am a Cotton Planter, and reside on the plantation of 'Woodlands,' Barnwell District, some eight months in the year; that I have a wife and seven children living. I have lost seven. I have now four girls and three boys, — the eldest of the former married. Four months in the year, from June to Sept. inclusive my family & self reside in Charleston where we own a residence. We sometimes travel; and I usually make a flying visit north every summer. You may also throw into Mr. Cooke's sketch somewhere, that from my earliest years, I have been a hard student & perpetual reader, rarely even now retiring at night untill the short hours; that I have travelled, in early years, greatly in the South & South West on horseback, seeing the whole region from Carolina to Mississippi personally, and as far back as 1825 when 2/3 was an Indian Country; that I saw the red men in their own homes; could imitate them in speech; imitate the backwoodsmen, mountaineers, swamp suckers, &c. Mr. John Russell, who left Charleston in the Steamer on Thursday, takes on a couple of pictures (photographs) one full face, the other profile, from which you are to choose. Your engraver will need to open the eyes a little. Being once a sufferer from coup de soleil, the least condensation of light upon my eyes, even for a moment, causes the delicate muscles of that region to wince & contract, so that the eye nearly closes, & there is a swelling & corrugation all around it, & the very nose is slightly lifted. To correct this, get the engraved portrait published by Redfield [224] and let the engraver work out from the two. My friends here are of the opinion that

---

[222] The year is established by Simms' discussion of John Esten Cooke's sketch of him (see note 223, below). The date of John Russell's departure from Charleston for New York City would determine the precise date, but the Charleston newspapers do not list him among passengers sailing from Charleston. He is listed as returning to Charleston on the *Nashville* on Oct. 17 (see the *Mercury* of Oct. 18).

[223] Simms had earlier requested John Esten Cooke to write this biographical sketch, published in the *Cosmopolitan Art Journal*, III (Dec., 1859), 212-214. See letter to Cooke of July 26, 1859.

[224] See the frontispiece to Volume I of *The Letters of William Gilmore Simms*.

this engraving would be the best after all for you. You will see that one of the pictures is a profile, which I think will make really the best picture.[225] But suit yourself. You will find Mr. Cooke's article well written & with great spirit. He uses here, a portion of a paper which he published in the South. Messenger.[226] Yours in haste, but

Ever truly

W. Gilmore Simms

950: To Mary Lawson

Woodlands, Nov. 15. [1859][227]

But a few words, my dear Mary, in response to your letter just recieved. I wrote only yesterday to the venerable Jimmy Lawson, your Sire.[228] Better not defer your visit to January or February. Feb. is usually one of our severest months. Before or after that. If here, we can keep you warm, but neither you nor your father should travel in Feb. or Jany. At present nothing could be more delightful than our season. We are just closing the Indian Summer, which has been at once warm, dry & beautiful. It is cooler now, but delightfully so. Do not defer your visit too long. Come, at all events, early in December, when we generally have fine weather. It is perfectly healthy now, every where. Take my counsel & set off between your reciept of this & the first week in December. My letter to your father is full of instructions. Love & a kiss to Mama, and all the young ones.

Yours Ever &c

W. Gilmore Simms.

951: To William Porcher Miles

Woodlands Nov. 26. 1859.

My dear Miles.

I have not heard from you for a long season, and only hear of you through the Newspapers. These tell me that you are now

---

[225] Victor reproduced the "full face." See the picture of Simms facing p. 454 of this volume of Simms' *Letters.*

[226] See note 34, Jan. 29, 1859.

[227] James Lawson and his daughters Mary and Kate were visiting at Woodlands early in 1860; therefore, this letter concerned with plans for their trip South was probably written in 1859.

[228] We have not located this letter.

in Charleston.[229] I never hear from James,[230] who seems to have
cut [me], like every body else in Charleston. He promised to
come & see me before I left the city, but failed. I wrote you when
I heard you were at Saratoga. Presuming that you will hardly
go to Washington, before the 1st. proxo. I hope to shake hands
with you in Charleston, whither I propose to go on or about the
1st. You will hear of me at my daughters, Mrs. Roach, in
Society St. I am an invalid, and almost abstain from writing,
doing just as little as I can. My head is troubled with symptoms
that make me apprehensive, & my liver is out of order. I am under
a cloud; worried & wearied; half crop; worthless overseer; and
find it a hard matter to get a good one. I may have to oversee the
plantation myself. When you go to Washington, please remember
my usual wants.— Documents & Seeds. Send me supplies of all
of these, no matter what their character. My wife sends you her
best remembrances, along with a simple little purse which she
knitted for you; fancying, that, like myself you would prefer
this, as a *porte monnaie,* to the clumsy modern inventions. God
bless you.

Yours Ever faithfully

Simms

952: To John Esten Cooke

Woodlands, Decr. 7. 1859.

My dear Cooke.

Do not suppose that I have forgotten you because I have been
so dilatory in answering your letter. I have had sundry good
excuses — nay, something better, reasons — for being slow to
tell you that I am with you affectionately & faithfully. I have been
an invalid — am still measurably so — and been greatly busied
& troubled besides. Recently, I have had to go to Charleston on
business & lost the better part of a week there. Another reason
for not writing, lay in my desire to cover to you, when I wrote,
a notice of St John. But your confounded Harper's Ferry business,[231] and the business in our Legislature, & the discussion of
rascally politics of every colour, black, white, brown, red, yellow

---

[229] The Charleston *Mercury* of Nov. 15 reports that Miles is back in the
city for a brief season before returning to Congress.
[230] James Warley Miles.
[231] John Brown's raid on Harpers Ferry took place on Oct. 16-18.

&c. have so horribly crowded the newspapers that the Mercury has been able to find no place for that & other articles I have sent them. I trust shortly, however, to see them appear, & as you recieve the Mercury, it is just possible that you will see how I treat you without rendering it necessary that I should cover to you the notice. I do not know that you will find it particularly valuable, but I trust it will please you. As a criticism there may not be much in it. As an expression of sympathy & good feeling — every thing. I find fault, as matter of course; but you will appreciate this, I trust, as only so much Attic salt for the proper seasoning of the stew — the condiment which heightens its flavour.[232] Have you begun another work? Do not be too hurried. Give yourself time enough to contemplate your ground & materials fully, so as to *design* with a better grasp of the *absolute* in your subject. It is the duty of the imagination to grasp the absolute. It is thus that it always shows itself arbitrarily fixed in its object. It must go in one direction — speak in one character — pursue one outline, & has no choice. The Imagination, if not a will itself, seems to work under a will which is imperative as fate, and allows it no caprices. It is the fancy which wanders & has a frequent choice. — I see you still write for the Century, & can understand how you must writhe at the pecunious necessity which forces you to write for such a journal.[233] Fully aware, as you have made me, of your necessities, I still think you will find it your policy to cut your connection with that paper. The present condition of our sections renders it equivocal patriotism to maintain your connection with it. You are to remember that, if you are to succeed in the South, you must beware how you forfeit, or trifle with the sympathies of your people. They will not do justice to your situation, but will reproach your patriotism, or your supposed want of it. Now, it is true, that they themselves may do nothing for you. At present, this perhaps is the case; but in the long run they will probably atone to you, and your repute any how, will be far beyond your pecuniary profits. Think of all this. — I am literally doing nothing in letters — unless letter-writing & occasional notices in the Mercury may be classed in this category. I am still uneasy of brain & anxious of thought, & sad at heart, & wearied with troubles, & full of cares, & fevered by *vigilia*. My interests are hardly more satisfactory than yours, for

[232] See note 17, Jan. 20, 1860.
[233] See note 187, July 26, 1859.

with a large capital, it has been so much neglected, that much time will be required before it can be made to yield an adequate interest. I do not despond; but I am sometimes overwearied with the toil, & temporarily gloomy from defeat. My Histy of S. C. has just been published, but greatly disfigured by typographical errors. I have grown so indifferent to my literary concerns, that I hardly care whether it sells or not; a sign that I am growing prematurely old perhaps, and that some great change impends over me. If I could substitute a higher care than the worldly ones which do oppress me, I should not complain of the world, or myself. Write me soon, and often, my dear young friend, and do not resent my delays to answer. I have many daily & nightly anxieties which drive or call me from the desk. Your letters are always grateful, & I am always & faithfully

Yours

W. Gilmore Simms

P. S.— I wrote this at four o'clock this morning by an imperfect candlelight, & did not observe that I was using a sheet of common MS. paper. I could not sleep, got up, went into my study, & wrote to you.— This P. S. after sunrise, when I can see — but do not read what I have written & on what material.

953: To Return Jonathan Meigs, Jr.[234]

Woodlands, Midway P. O.
South Carolina, Decr. 16. 1859.

R. J. Meigs, jr. Esq.

dear Sir:

I am honoured by the appointment of the Historical Society of Tennessee, to deliver a Lecture before them, and it would give me the greatest pleasure to comply with their & your wishes, so courteously conveyed. But this, I regret to say, is impossible.[235]

---

[234] Meigs (1801-1891), a native of Kentucky, removed to Tennessee shortly after he was admitted to the bar at Frankfort in 1822. He practiced law at Athens and Nashville, was attorney general of Tennessee during 1838-1839, and in 1841 was appointed United States attorney for the Middle Tennessee District. He was corresponding secretary of the Tennessee Historical Society for a number of years. On the back of this letter he wrote "Rec'd Decr. 20, 1859."

[235] Simms had been invited "to deliver a public lecture upon the Literature of the South." After his letter of refusal was read before the Society, he was unanimously elected an honorary member of the Society. See the "Minutes of the Tennessee Historical Society" (MS.) for Jan. 3, 1860.

My domestic cares & anxieties forbid that I shall leave home, and will continue to keep me there indefinitely. My health, besides, is such that I have been compelled temporarily to abandon the desk, and avoid, for a season at least, all mental labours — all, at least, which I can possibly escape. Under these circumstances you will see that I dare not entertain the grateful proposition which you make me, & which, otherwise, I should be most happy to accept. — Be pleased, Sir, to convey to your society my great regrets, & warm respects, and believe me

Very respectfully
Your obt & obliged Servt.

W. Gilmore Simms.

1860

954: To Wheeler, Wilson and Company [1]

[1860?]

Your Sewing Machine is perfectly satisfactory, and I deem it one of the most perfect, as it is one of the most useful, of all modern inventions. It was easily learned, has been thoroughly tried on all kinds of fabrics — coarse and fine — and has not once been out of order, though kept in constant use. Nothing can be better designed for plantation uses, and it is difficult to conceive how we could do without it.

W. Gilmore Simms.[2]

955: To James Gardner [3]

Woodlands, Jan. 2, 1860.

My Dear Mr. Editor:

I send you two Songs for the Season, meant to inculcate faith and hope, old morals in old maxims, and new music, for the benefit of that million who, at the close of each epoch, are naturally inclined to mourn over defeated expectations. They are simple, and though not exactly impromptu, are yet so very nearly such that I should not strain conscience a tithe in so declaring them. Of course they are unambitious [4] performances. The texts

---

[1] This letter forms part of an advertisement for Wheeler and Wilson's Sewing Machines which was published in the Charleston *Mercury* during 1860. Simms' letter may have been written as early as 1858, since the advertisement states that this and other testimonials there included have already been published (we have not discovered where) and one of them signed "A Planter" is dated Aug. 26, 1858. In his letter to Lawson of Feb. 28, 1859, Simms discusses the sewing machine at Woodlands.

Wheeler, Wilson and Company was formed in the early 1850's by Nathaniel Wheeler (1820-1893) and Allen Benjamin Wilson (1824-1888).

[2] The advertisement misprints *Sims*.

[3] We have not located the original of this letter published with "Better Luck Another Year" in the *Southern Field and Fireside*, I (Jan. 28, 1860), 281. "Patience and Shuffle the Cards" was published in *ibid.*, I (Feb. 4, 1860), 289,

[4] The *Southern Field and Fireside* misprints *unambituous*.

are — 1. "Better Luck Another Year." 2. "Patience, and Shuffle the Cards." It is for you to decide whether they shall be warbled in your *field,* or at your *fireside.* Be the smiles of a new dawn upon you and yours at the opening of the Season.

Yours truly,

W. Gilmore Simms.

956: To WILLIAM PORCHER MILES

Woodlands, Jany 18, 1860.

Hon. W. Porcher Miles.

My dear Miles.

I have sensibly felt the kindness and compliment conveyed in the highly distinguished appointment which designates me as Orator at the inauguration of the Statue of Washington, and it is with the greatest pain & mortification that I am compelled to decline it.[5] How eagerly would I have leapt at such an office in other days! But I am now broken down; labouring under a degree of mental frustration, if not physical disease, which involves the utmost danger from any hard work, or close application, or unusual excitement. I dare not encounter either for any length of time. I am not good for half an hour's labour at one time at the desk; and have been doing nothing there, of any consequence, all the winter; those labours only excepted which I could not escape, and which I could perform in brief efforts of a quarter, or half an hour. I am troubled with *vigilia* (irregular & unequal circulation, &c) and any tension determines the blood to my brain, and gives me the most wretched headaches. My mind is too prostrate for exertion. I cannot bring myself to any consecutive or earnest train of thought; and I have none of that enthusiasm, such as I could once boast, and which a man *should* feel who would rise to an occasion so exacting as this to which you call me! My depression is very great, & I weary of all things! Besides, I am in trouble! My crop was a failure, and the very money which would carry me to Washington, & bring me back, I cannot spare! I should feel, while speaking, that people would

---

[5] On Feb. 22 Thomas Stanley Bocock delivered the oration at the inauguration of this equestrian statue of Washington by Clark Mills (1810-1883). See note 34, Feb. 26, 1860.

see that I wear an old threadbare coat; that there would be those in the crowd to say, 'better pay your shoe bill, your tailor, than be splurging here with your grand nonsense!' It matters not, my dear Miles, even to prove to me that I fancy many of my causes of complaint, as some of my friends are pleased to think. My afflictions are not less real even though proved to be only imaginary. Indeed, this class of disorders, is, perhaps the worst; since there is no mode of reaching, or of reasoning with them. The very imagining proves the disease to be real, & in the most dangerous region, the Brain! I have been overworked; I have been unsuccessful all my life; my books fail to pay me; I am myself a failure! In S. C. I am repudiated. A host of enemies have risen up, who regard me as a rival, in possession of the ground, who stands in their way.[6] My histy of S. C. (which, by the way, *you ought* to have with you) which has been entirely rewritten, & is now twice the bulk of the former, has fallen dead from the press. Hardly a newspaper in the State has noticed it;[7] and, while the Legislature

---

[6] In July, 1859, an attack on Simms and his "Literary Docket" in the Charleston *Mercury* was launched by Howard Hayne Caldwell (b. 1831), a South Carolina poet and journalist, who at this time was editing the *Courant, a Southern Literary Journal,* a weekly published in Columbia (May 5–Nov. 10?, 1859). Caldwell's chief ally was John Wilson Overall, a member of the staff of the New Orleans *True Delta.* Paul Hamilton Hayne in a letter to John Esten Cooke dated Nov. 4, 1859, attributes their enmity to Simms' unfavorable reviews of Caldwell's *Poems* (Boston: Whittemore, Niles & Hall, 1858) in *Russell's Magazine,* III (April, 1858), 36-47, and of Overall's *The Funeral of Mirabeau* (no copy located by us) in *S. Q. R.,* N. S., VI (Oct., 1852), 533-534 (see Daniel Morley McKeithan, ed., *A Collection of Hayne Letters* [Austin: The University of Texas Press, 1944], p. 85).

Caldwell took as the occasion for his first attack in the *Courant* of July 21 a review of Poe's *Poems* (New York: Redfield, 1859) in the *Mercury* of July 9, in which Simms defends Griswold's biography of Poe and calls Poe "one of the most morally wretched of gifted men." Overall, in the *True Delta* of July 23 (to which we have not had access), then took up the cudgels and began an attack on Simms even more violent than the *Courant's* (a number of the *True Delta's* remarks, including Overall's first attack, are printed in the *Mercury,* the *Courant,* and *Russell's Magazine*). The *Mercury* and other leading South Carolina newspapers warmly defended Simms, though, as Hayne says in his letter to Cooke cited above, there were detractors of Simms "*even* in the city of *Charleston.*" See the *Courant,* I (July 21, Aug. 4, Sept. 8, and Oct. 13, 1859), 93-94, 110 (misnumbered 200), 149, 189-190; *Russell's Magazine,* IV (Jan. and Feb., 1859), 373, 474; and the *Mercury* of Aug. 9, Aug. 18, Aug. 19, Aug. 29, Aug. 31, Sept. 2, Sept. 12, Sept. 29, and Sept. 30, 1859.

Simms' only reply to his attackers was a sonnet with the motto " 'The *little* dogs,/How they bark at me!' *King Lear,*" published in the *Southern Field and Fireside,* I (Aug. 6, 1859), 82, though James H. Hammond's letters to Simms of Oct. 4, Oct. 24, Nov. 23, and Dec. 19, 1859 (cited in note 221, Sept. 18, 1859), indicate that in his letters to Hammond written during this period (not located by us) Simms complained bitterly about the attacks.

[7] The Charleston *Mercury* of Feb. 7 reprints a notice of Simms' *History* from *De Bow's Review,* XXVIII (Feb., 1860), 238.

could make an appropriation for Laborde's Hist. of the College,[8] there was not a member to move the adoption of my Hist. in the schools. Yet, when you read this book, you will see that I have suffered nothing, by way of clue, suggestion, argument, or fact, to escape me — nothing of the History, nothing of the Principle, which I have not made clear. I hold it to be most necessary to the public man, as to the pupil. Yet the labour is wasted upon a people who have seemingly deliberately decreed that, so far as my living is to depend upon their favour, I shall die! I can appear again on no stage. I have heart for nothing. I am resigned to obscurity, & can struggle no more, except to pay off creditors & feed & clothe my poor little children. You may judge of the terrible depression that weighs me down, when you hear that I have ceased to work. I have done, & am doing nothing, but revising a new collection of poems for the press, with the full conviction that it will pay me nothing; and I print simply to put my works on record, & leave a unique edition which may help my children.[9] And even this revision of old pieces, short lyrics & sonnets, to be made in snatches, is an irksome labour! How can I rise to an oration of any kind? How, before the assembled States, on such an occasion, with such a subject, which is at once so common, so hacknied, yet so peculiarly exacting? On such a subject, how large will be the expectation, & how much is due to *myself,* not less than to the subject! See what I say of it in an article on Thackeray's 'Virginians' published in the Mercury a short time ago — written a month ago. You will there see what I think of the equal difficulties & susceptibilities of the subject.[10]

---

[8] Maximilian LaBorde, *History of the South Carolina College* ... (Columbia, S. C.: P. B. Glass, 1859). LaBorde (see note 52, June 17, 1842) was at this time professor of metaphysics at the College.

[9] This collection was printed as *Simms's Poems Areytos or Songs and Ballads of the South with Other Poems.*

[10] Simms' long review (over two columns) of *The Virginians* (New York: Harper & Brothers, 1859), published in the Charleston *Mercury* of Jan. 5, 1860, is for the most part favorable. He praises Thackeray's "construction" and "design," his "quiet satire," his "keen insight into human frailties and vanities," and his "stripping bare the fraud, and cant, and hypocrisy of pretentious people; whether in society, or letters, the professions, or religion"; but he also says that "there is perhaps too much of it; and the bad and base—the mean and the malignant—are allotted, as usual, too large a proportion of its pages." Simms' chief criticism of Thackeray is of his portrait of Washington: "It needed the most thorough appreciation of the stern, simple, sublime character of Washington—the most admirable knowledge of Virginia details and society, and the most exquisite word painting, as well as moral, to conceive and delineate such a character—needed it not only as a requisite of high art, but as essential to the satisfaction of the American people. It is hardly possible that any portraiture

To do it justice requires a mind at ease, a calm philosophy, a large imaginative grasp, & capacities, in general, which I no longer have at command. I am sick, suffering, despondent, doubtful in hope, wearied with toil, mortified with defeat & disappointment — and good for nothing! If I have the sympathies of friends in my decline, it is all that I can expect; & I can do no more to obtain even this! God be with you! My wife sends her affectionate remembrance, which, with mine, will always be Yours —

                                                    W. Gilmore Simms

957: To WILLIAM PORCHER MILES

                                   Woodlands, 20 Jany. [1860][11]
My dear Miles.

I enclose a letter for Capt. John S. Cunningham, of the Navy, a gentleman whom I do not personally know, but whose kind note, urging me to accept the appointment of Orator at the Inauguration, demands a prompt & hearty acknowledgment.[12] Will you see that it is delivered to him? You cannot concieve the disappointment which I feel at not being able to comply with the wishes of my friends in this matter. The call comes at a period of my greatest prostration, when I am equally sick at heart & in head, harrassed with petty but gnawing cares and anxieties, as

of Washington, in fiction, will satisfy them. But Mr. Thackeray fell lamentably short of himself in the attempt. He was cold, not hearty in his object. He was timid, as he felt his difficulty. He lacked enthusiasm, which is a terrible element of exaction in the moral construction of the American people. He neither felt with them, nor with Washington; nor thought with them; nor knew one-half as much as they did of the character he undertook to draw. . . .

"Such is Washington—not the mere hero of the country—but its sainted model man; the most perfect, performing and truly great, of all the great men to whom we owe the national safety and existence in the days of our greatest peril!

"To afford an idea of the delicacy and difficulty of such a task as Mr. Thackeray undertook, we give but a single instance among the mere minor details. Mr. Thackeray represents Washington as roaring with rage. Roar is the word. Roaring, on the part of Washington! That single word suffices to kill the scene, kill the drama!—in the feeling of the American people! . . . They might not be prepared to deny that Washington was a man of strong passions, and might be made to rage; and they would be quite willing that you should say this, and show this. Nay, we know that Washington had terrible passions, and, sometimes, swore savagely. But they will not suffer—and, in this, they show an instinct of art as well as sentiment—they will not suffer you to use a brutalizing or belittling word, when you speak of his anger."

[11] Dated by Simms' discussion of the forthcoming inauguration of Clark Mills' statue of Washington. See letter to Miles of Jan. 18.

[12] See following letter.

well as troubled with serious fears in respect to my brain. My days are restless & feverish, my nights sleepless, my thoughts vexed & wandering, my life a sort of chaotic dream in which I struggle against deep seas, forever drowning, yet feebly struggling, like a poor swimmer almost spent. God bless you. I get not a syllable from James.[13]

Yours Ever lovingly

W. Gilmore Simms

Your speech is excellent & has given great satisfaction.[14]

958: To John S. Cunningham [15]

Woodlands, S. C. Jan. 20, 1860.

My Dear Sir:

I am greatly honored and deeply touched by the kindness of my friends in procuring for me the appointment to a distinction so honorable as that of pronouncing the oration at the inauguration of the statue of Washington. Suffer me to add that I am

---

[13] James Warley Miles.

[14] On Jan. 6 Miles delivered in the United States House of Representatives a speech "on the Organization of the House," in which he discusses the condition of the North and the South (see *Appendix to the Congressional Globe,* 36 Cong., 1 Sess., pp. 67-69). Both the Charleston *Mercury* and *Courier* of Jan. 14 reprint the speech.

[15] We have not located the original of this letter, published in the *Constitution* (Washington, D. C.) of Feb. 22, 1860. It is reprinted in both the Charleston *Mercury* and *Courier* of Feb. 25, 1860.

In answer to an unlocated letter from Simms James H. Hammond wrote on April 3, 1860: "Cunningham is a native of Charleston & a protegé of [Aaron Smith] Willington [see note 82, c. June 30, 1844]—picked up in the Streets I presume. He was once an editor in Va—transferred to a Clerkship here, & some 3 years ago made a Purser in the Navy. He is very pleasant, amiable, genial, gentlemanly in manners & reminds me of [Christopher Gustavus] Memminger [see note 129, Dec. 19, 1841]—Charleston all over. He seems to have fair abilities & information with much delicacy—a good heart, & is I think reliable. He has a great admiration of you. The only foible I have found is the venial one of vanity, which you may infer from his publication of your letter. He is very quick & active. . . . On the whole he is a genuine So. Ca. I believe (if born in the street) & entitled to be so considered." (Original in the Hammond Papers, Library of Congress.)

Capt. Samuel G. Kelly, of the Division of Naval History, Department of the Navy, writes us that Cunningham was appointed a purser in the United States Navy in 1857 and that at the time of his retirement from service in 1883 he was inspector of provisions and clothing at the navy yard in New York City. He died in 1894.

also greatly touched by your kindness in the solicitude you express
that I should accept the appointment. No ordinary reason, let
me assure you, would have kept me from eagerly accepting so
grateful an appointment — nothing, in short, less than the fact
that I am an invalid, threatened with a disease which forbids that
I should undertake any protracted labor, or encounter any unusual excitement. Under this conviction of my danger and necessity, I have for several months forborne all my customary labors
at the desk, and have been seeking rather to dissipate time than to
employ it. I not only dread the toil and the excitement, but I feel
incapable of them at the present juncture. To meet such an occasion, to treat such a subject, to face such an audience, requires
equally that I should be in good mental training as well as good
physical condition — that I should not only have at command all
my intellectual resources, but that my enthusiasm should so in-
spirit my imagination and provoke it as to enable me to open new
views of a character and subject which have been hackneyed
without being exhausted. None of these resources or stimuli can
I at present command, and it is, believe me, in consequence of my
deep sense of the importance of the occasion, the beauty of the
subject, and the confident expectations of the public at large,
not less than of my friends, that I have been compelled, with
feelings of real sorrow and mortification, to decline so grateful
a duty and so delicate and grateful an appointment. No one can
regret the necessity which makes me do so more than myself, but
I should be doing wrong equally to the public, my friends, and
self, in my depressed condition, to attempt a performance to
which, at this juncture, I feel so wretchedly inadequate; and any
performance of which, however executed, might entail upon me the
most injurious, if not fatal, consequences. It is now with me a
duty of self-preservation to avoid all excitements. With many
thanks, my dear sir, for your kind attention, please hold me,

Very truly, your obedient and obliged servant,

W. Gilmore Simms.

959: To John Esten Cooke

Woodlands,
20 Jany 1860

My dear Cooke.

My house is full [16] — my heart heavy — my head light. I cannot think, or write just now, and I only scribble an introduction to the enclosed notice of your book — full of typographical errors — which I wrote for the Mercury.[17] God bless you.

Yours ever

Simms

960: To William Porcher Miles

Woodlands Jany 26. [1860][18]

My dear Miles.

I take for granted you are *en rapport* with Professor Henry, & will trouble you to have the enclosure conveyed to him. I use you, my friend, to save postage; and would be glad if you would hint to the Professor that you will be pleased to use your franking

---

[16] James Lawson and his daughters Mary and Kate were visiting at Woodlands. See letters to Mary Lawson of Nov. 15, 1859, and to Lawson of Feb. 24, 1860.

[17] Cooke's *Henry St. John, Gentleman, of "Flower of Hundreds," in the County of Prince George, Virginia* (New York: Harper & Brothers, 1859) is reviewed in the Charleston *Mercury* of Jan. 20. Simms praises Cooke's "sectionality," his "lifelike portraits of the great men of Virginia," and his story, "lively, well sustained and interesting, without being deeply tragical, or intensively acting upon the imaginative and nervous systems." But he also admonishes Cooke: "He has done well, so far; but his sinews must be a little more seasoned by the proper exercise; his mind more patient, more deliberate, more sensible of the burden of the task, more grandly stirred within him, by the hourly growing sense of the value of his theme; so that he shall shape it with proper care, with a becoming purpose, and under a severer, sublimer design. We mean by this to convey to him the notion that, in one point, we think him a little too heedless—namely, in design—in the adequate conception *ab ovo*, and in the adequate invention of the appropriate details. This is his chief deficiency, and one which nothing but painstaking will supply. His invention is not only essential to his design, but to the proper topics of discussion, as well as action under it—the one being always carefully rendered proximate and appropriate to the other. He has the adequate endowments for both. Let him beware, lest, in his haste to perform, he neglects the proper matter with which greatly to perform."

[18] Dated by Simms' references to the revised edition of his *History of South Carolina* and to Miles' speech in the United States House of Representatives on Jan. 6 (see letters to Miles of Jan. 18, Jan. 20, and Feb. 5). We do not know what Simms enclosed in this letter.

privilege in covering any thing in the way of books, pamphlets & papers &c. which he may desire to send to your Carolina friends. I am suffering a good deal today, & must write short billets only. Your speech meets here with warm approbation. Keep cool and wait the chapter of accidents & events. Half of the political crises of the world are brought about by what we ignorantly esteem to be casualties. God be with you in wisdom, strength & favor.

Yours truly

W. G. S.

Be sure & read my new Histy of S. C.

961: To William Porcher Miles

Woodlands, Feb. 5. 1860

My dear Miles

Thanks for your frank & fervent letter. You are probably right in saying that I am morbid, but have I not reason to be so, and is this less a malady than dyspepsia? Nay, is it not a part of the malady of all dyspeptics. Do I not know that I am morbid; that my brain is all addled; and is it not this from which I apprehend all my sufferings. But the morbidness has come from real ailments of mind & body, the one overworked disappointed, defeated, anxious almost to despairing, the other dyspeptic, and sore from other sources of annoyance. Brain & liver disordered, and the spirits mournfully depressed, my temperament no longer comes to my relief. I am compelled to be active about the premises, compelled still to hammer at some of the drudgeries of the desk from which I cannot quite escape, — and from the condition of my own & the plantation affairs, which need my constant vigilance & eye — compelled to stay at home. Otherwise, I should be tempted to visit Washington for a month, & make free use of the grateful privileges which you, Hammond & Chesnut have accorded me. But I must not think of it. At present I can have no respite, unless I show myself equally reckless of my engagements, & of my own & children's future. So, I must not look that way. Thanks once more, my dear fellow, for your frank and generous invitation. It is also my necessity that I should not tax any friend for money, for any individual or selfish objects. One of my present miseries is that I owe money which I cannot at present pay. I

had made sure of paying off most of my debts this year. But a
rascally overseer ruined my crop, got drunk, neglected the plantation, let the grass run away with my fields & instead of 125 bales
of Cotton, I made but 50. A still worse disaster accrues from the
failure of the corn crop. I am compelled to buy corn. These mis-
chiefs with others accumulating almost at the same time have
proved the one feather too much for even the back of the camel.
But, I am not wholly despairing. I can still toil, and begin once
more to cherish a feeble little nursling Hope. But my friends
must suffer me to groan sometimes in friendly ears, nor think
the music too intolerable. It is not often that I indulge this vein.
But I am getting old and weak, and the defeat of reasonable
expectations, the mortification of justly founded hopes, the failure
of all proper results from patient industry, the denial of proper
meed for patriotic performances involving much self sacrifice, the
gnawing anxieties belonging to a complication of worldly & domestic necessities — these have conspired to unhinge me, and
make me cast myself down in a momentary paroxysm of despair.
I trust it will not last. I am trying not only to do, but to do
cheerfully. I sometimes write a song or sonnet with a cheerful
moral. I have in press, by the way, a volume containing a selection from my fugitive pieces, song & sonnet, the growings of
thirty years. These almost carry with them a history of my inner
life. They are the gushings of the momentary sentiment, feeling,
impulse; the outbreak of the sudden thought & occasional philosophy. I mean to dedicate this volume to James, your brother,
though he has not sent me a line since I left town, & has failed
to keep his engagement to spend Christmas with me.[19] But, no
more of myself. Your speech,[20] I repeat, gave us all great pleasure,
and I was especially glad of it, in consequence of a warm conversation (entre nous) which I had with Barnwell Rhett (Senior)
about you, some two months ago. He was expressing himself
doubtfully, was dissatisfied, thought you were taking the world
of Washington too easily, &c. I need not tell you what I said in
reply. He is not a person, you are aware, to be easily pleased with
any party who does not recognize himself as the guide. Of course,
he said nothing disparaging, only doubting whether you were
sufficiently alive to your situation, &c. Jamison, who is now my

---

[19] *Simms's Poems Areytos* carries a four-page dedication to James Warley
Miles (pp. iii-vi).
[20] See note 14, Jan. 20, 1860.

next door neighbour,[21] & an ultra secessionist expressed himself also very favorably in regard to your speech — in fact, all who have spoken of it in my hearing. I am glad to see that you mix more in the colloquial debate.[22] That is the best field of training. God bless you.

> Yours,
>
> W Gilmore Simms.

962: To Ed. C. Chapman [23]

> Woodlands, Midway P. O.
> So. Caro. Feb. 8. 1860.

Mr. Ed. C. Chapman.

Sir:

I cheerfully comply with your request for my autograph, & am, accordingly,

> Your obt. Servt.
> &c.
>
> W. Gilmore Simms.

963: To Joseph Henry

> Woodlands, S. C. Feb. 21. [1860] [24]

Professor Jos. Henry.

My dear Professor.

An old & excellent friend, Mr. James Lawson, of N. Y. a Scotch Gentleman of taste & education, of amiable manners & ingenuous character, whom I have known & valued for 30 years, will hand you this. He has with him his two daughters,[25] amiable & accomplished girls, and this is their first visit to Washington.

---

[21] In Jan., 1860, Jamison moved from Orangeburg to Burwood, a plantation which he had recently purchased. See the Charleston *Mercury* of Jan. 19, 1860.

[22] The *Congressional Globe* for this session shows Miles frequently mixing "in the colloquial debate."

[23] Not identified.

[24] Dated by Simms' reference to the Lawsons' visit to the South (see letter to Lawson of Feb. 24 and following letters to Lawson). This letter (preserved with Simms' letters to Lawson) was not delivered, since the illness of his son William Gilmore Simms forced Lawson to leave Washington shortly after his arrival there (see letter to Lawson of March 21).

[25] Mary and Kate.

They are all especially curious to visit the Smithsonian.[26] I venture to beg for them your attention & particularly to ask for the young ladies, that of your fair daughter,[27] to whom & Mrs. H. I beg to be affectionately remembered. Our little Party will probably linger a week in Washington, and will be grateful for that assistance, of the *Cicerone of society,* who will best enable them to see your complicated machinery in W. I have only to add that I shall feel very grateful for any considerate attention to my young friends & their amiable father.

Your kind letter was very acceptable. I shall write you hereafter. At present, I am an invalid, with one of my children quite ill,[28] — and I can scarcely pen equably the few sentences which entreat you above for that consideration to my friends, which you have never withheld from

Yours, &c.

W. Gilmore Simms

964: To James Lawson

[February 24, 1860][29]

dear Lawson

Kates keys were on my table in the study. I cover them in a packet with three letters just recieved, & shall try to send them by Express. If not, by *Mail.* I shall endorse on the packet that if you have left Columbia, it is to be forwarded to Washington, care of Hon. Mr. Keitt. Our child still lies in peril. The fever has lessened today (Friday) — she has slept a little; has had her bowels affected as far as we could wish; and her nervous symptoms are abated; yet the fever is unbroken, and she is still dangerously ill. If the fever increases tonight, & the cerebral excitement returns, it will hardly be possible to save her in her present degree of feebleness. I got two hours sleep last night, but we are

---

[26] Henry was secretary and director of the Smithsonian Institution.

[27] Mary.

[28] Hattie. See letter to Lawson of Feb. 24.

[29] The year is established by Simms' references to the Lawsons' recent visit to Woodlands (see preceding and following letters) and to the illness of his daughter Hattie. Hattie became ill on or about Tuesday, Feb. 21, and was much improved by Feb. 26 (see letter to Miles of that date). This letter written on a Friday should, therefore, be dated Feb. 24.

all worn out. God spare us both, my friend, and spare our precious ones to us.

God be with you & the girls.

Yours Ever

W. Gilmore Simms.

I send by mail, as being most likely to reach you in season, tho' it will cost you more postage. I have but a single post stamp left in the House.

965: To James Lawson

Saturday MG. 7 o'clock
[February 25, 1860] [30]

dear Lawson.

We are at length relieved. Hattie is better. The fever left her last night, & she slept all night. But she is very feeble & as fretful as feeble. She had neither sleep nor food for three days & nights. My wife & self are exhausted. I am sore all over; but grateful I trust to the good God who has spared the child to our prayers. We rejoice to hear that you too are relieved of your anxieties. It was not till yesterday, dinner time, that Mr. Rivers [31] apprised me by note that Kate had left her keys. What a child! I immediately had her chamber searched, but failed to find them, Mary L. S. being of opinion that Kate changing her dress had left the keys in the pocket of the frock she threw off & had thus packed them up in the trunk. But by a mere accident, I found them an hour after amidst a pile of books & papers on my study table. The same day brought me some letters for you. I put all in one packet together and sent at once up to the P. O. — fearing to wait upon the express which I have usually found a slow coach. You will be sure to get them by Monday, & on Sunday if you visit the P. O. that day. Tell Gilmore of Hattie's condition.[32] God bless you & yours.

W. G. S.

---

[30] The year is established by Simms' references to the Lawsons' recent visit to Woodlands and the illness of his daughter Hattie (see preceding and following letters). The Saturday during the critical stage of Hattie's illness was Feb. 25.

[31] Christopher McKinney Rivers (b. 1827?), a planter near Bamberg, S. C., was the husband of Mary Govan Steele, Mrs. Simms' cousin. See note 95, c. May 6, 1849.

[32] Gilmore was a cadet at the Arsenal Academy, at Columbia, where Lawson had gone after leaving Woodlands (see letter to Lawson of Feb. 24).

966: To William Porcher Miles

Woodlands, 26th. Feb. 1860

My dear Miles.

I have been in torture for the last five days. Your poor little god [33] daughter, Hattie Middleton, has been dangerously ill, all that time, with a violent fever which seized upon her brain. I have not slept for 5 nights. She is better, but still suffering & very much exhausted. At one period, for two days, I was hopeless. Am I not a most wretched mark of fate, *mon ami!* You know much! but O! my friend, to have buried seven dear children out of thirteen, and to be always kept trembling for the rest! is driving me to decrepitude, if not to madness! I can do nothing — am nothing! At the very moment when Mr. Bocock was delivering the oration,[34] I was pacing my chamber with the raving child in my arms, momentarily expecting those convulsions which were to bear her from me forever! Ought not vanity & ambition to be rebuked in me forever? But enough! God keep you from such sorrows! — Who is Capt. John S. Cunningham, U. S. N? He writes to me in most affectionate terms, & seems anxious to do me honour. Counsel me, so that I shall not seem cold or ungrateful. I have given a letter, to you, to an old friend of mine, a Scotch Gentleman of N. York, Mr. James Lawson, — one of the most honest, loving & amiable of men, whom I have known for 30 years. He has with him two of his daughters,[35] nice, modest girls, for whom I would entreat your attentions. They are young, & have not seen much of the world; but they are pretty, accomplished & modest. Both musical, and well taught — in music (as I happen to know) at five dollars a lesson, from Maeder, who married the celebrated Clara Fisher.[36] Mr. Lawson is well off; has a Business — Adjuster of Averages — which yields him from

---

[33] Simms wrote *good*.

[34] On Feb. 22 Thomas Stanley Bocock (1815-1891), a member of Congress from Virginia (1847-1861) and later speaker of the Confederate States House of Representatives, delivered the oration at the inauguration of Clark Mills' statue of Washington in Washington, D. C. Though the oration was printed in a pamphlet entitled *Inauguration of Mills' Equestrian Statue of Washington. Oration of Thomas S. Bocock . . . together with a Sketch of the Inaugural Ceremonies . . .* (Washington: W. H. & O. H. Morrison, 1860), Simms probably read it in the Charleston *Mercury* of Feb. 24, which carries the complete text.

[35] Mary and Kate.

[36] Clara Fisher (1811-1898), the English actress, made her American debut in 1827. In 1834 she married James Gaspard Maeder, an Irish composer.

$10,000 to $15000 per annum. Has built himself a noble house in 12th Street, next door to the Mansion given to Gen. Scott by the Corporation of New York.[37] He will welcome any friend of mine to his abode, and is a genial creature. Thirty years ago, when I first knew him, he was an editor & author. He has published volumes of prose & verse, & his plays have run their three nights at the Theatre.[38] He composes verses, and the music which shall accompany them, & his music has been sung by Sinclair,[39] and he himself will play you upon the piano. He is yet a simple, ingenuous creature, not wise, except that he is virtuous and genial, with a kind heart, and a clear conscience. He could tell you much about N. Y. character & politicians — was once, a Politician himself, of Tammany Hall, the co-labourer with Bryant, Leggett,[40] &c. He was one of the first founders of the New York Courier & Enquirer, though now, he does not recognize either Webb or Bennett. He found them out long before the public did. He can tell you much about both.[41] I am quite anxious that you should give his girls every chance in Washington for society & amusement & have commended them to Mrs. Hammond & Mrs. Keitt [42] in similar language. Let me add that while as a witness

[37] Gen. Winfield Scott (1786-1866) was given this house in 1852. See Charles Winslow Elliott, *Winfield Scott the Soldier and the Man* (New York: The Macmillan Company, 1937), p. 647.

[38] Lawson's *Tales and Sketches, by a Cosmopolite* was published by E. Bliss, New York, in 1830; his *Poems, Gleanings from Spare Hours of a Business Life* was printed in 1857 for private distribution (see note 65, July 25, 1857). His *Giordano. A Tragedy* (New-York: E. B. Clayton, 1832) was performed in New York City on Nov. 13, Nov. 18, and Dec. 9, 1828 (see George C. D. Odell, *Annals of the New York Stage* [New York: Columbia University Press, 1927-1949], III, 384).

[39] John Sinclair (1791-1857), the Scottish tenor and father of Catherine Sinclair Forrest (see introductory sketch of Edwin Forrest), sang in America in 1831, 1833, 1834, 1839, and 1842.

[40] William Cullen Bryant and William Leggett. See introductory sketches.

[41] During 1827-1829 Lawson was on the staff of James Watson Webb's *Morning Courier* (New York). In 1829 Webb (1802-1884) merged the *Courier* with the New York *Enquirer* under the title of *Morning Courier and New York Enquirer* and continued as editor and proprietor of the newspaper until he sold it to the *World* in 1861. James Gordon Bennett (1795-1872) was on the staff of the *Enquirer* at the time of its merger with the *Courier* and remained with the merged newspaper until 1832. In 1835 he started the New York *Herald* and was editor and proprietor of that newspaper until his retirement in 1867. Since Webb was an anti-abolitionist, though a free-soiler, and Bennett a strong Southern sympathizer, Simms' dislike of the two men was probably personal (see in this connection the *Herald*'s remarks about Simms and his lecture delivered in New York City in 1856, quoted in note 126, Nov. 21, 1856).

[42] Lawrence Massillon Keitt married Sue Mandeville Sparks (1834-1915), of Marlborough District, S. C., on May 18, 1859.

WILLIAM GILMORE SIMMS

"Perhaps, if I had only great griefs to contend with,— griefs from God — I should bear up more nobly. But, unfortunately, I have others, & petty ones, and I am not capable of a conflict with the flies & gnats, and musquitos. I get out of temper; and naturally exaggerate the evils for which I have no adequate weapon."

(From an engraving in *Appleton's Cyclopedia of American Biography,* V [1888], 533)

MARY LAWSON
(MRS. THOMAS SARJEANT SANDFORD)
". . . and a friend's & fatherly kiss, dear Mary, for yourself.
God keep you all in the hollow of *his* hand!"
(From a photograph in the possession of Mrs. Lawson Sandford, Yonkers,
New York)

& in business matters, Mr. Lawson is equally to be relied on, as
a man of great integrity & good judgment — in literature, the
arts &c. I would not give a fig for his opinions. As respects
Literature, he has not kept pace with it, and for twenty years, on
this subject, his mind is *tabula rasa.* But he believes in me, —
and for 30 years, I have proved him to be worthy of faith &
affection. — Your Speech on Goode,[43] is a very good one, and
shows equal feeling & good taste. I rejoice to see that you are
becoming *practised.* Practise is all that you want to become a
popular & able speaker. Let me beg you to read Grote, Sismondi,[44]
and all that class of writers who treat of the Greek, the Swiss
and the Italian Confederacies, especially where they dip deeply.
Especially would I commend to you the 4 Vols. by the Scotchman,
Finlay, on the subject of Mediæval Greece, Trebizond, &c [.][45]
They will give you the proper material for large generalization
in respect to our country. Russell can provide you. By the way,
the Jewish Empire was a confederacy which Solomon destroyed.
He centralized Jerusalem — ground down the tribes by taxation
to build up the city, and was the first Sultan. He planted the seeds
of ruin in the Empire. Finlay will illustrate to you the processes
by which the Emperors of the Eastern Empire, weaned from them
the provinces, by centralization, & left them free to the invader.
We are apt to stop short in our investigations when we reach the
word centralism, — it is needful to go farther & show its processes. How it works — how it has worked from the time of the
Assyrians, to that of the French — as it works today in Paris,
where the City being the Empire, its destiny & that of the whole
nation, may undergo revolution in a minute. But I am not capable
just now of an argument. I would only suggest the clues to one.
When we meet, if we ever meet again, we will talk over these
things. I am wretched, restless, suffering — can hardly do any
thing & nothing well. I contrive to keep up my notes in the Mercury anent our current literature, which I know so well that it

---

[43] On Feb. 20 Miles delivered in the United States House of Representatives
a speech eulogizing William Osborne Goode (1798–July 3, 1859), member of
Congress from Virginia (1841-1843, 1853-1859). See *Congressional Globe,* 36
Cong., 1 Sess., pp. 845-846, and the Charleston *Mercury* of Feb. 25, 1860,
which carries the text of Miles' speech.

[44] George Grote (1794-1871), the English historian, and Jean Charles
Léonard de Sismondi (1773-1842), the Swiss historian.

[45] Simms had earlier recommended Finlay's histories to James H. Hammond.
See letter to him of Feb. 22, 1858.

only gently exercises my brain.[46] And my contributions to the Cyclopædia [47] are physical rather than mental exercises. All that I am doing [48] is the revision of my fugitive poems, which are in press, & which I propose — though I have not told him — to dedicate to your brother, James.[49] Let me hear from you when you can. I see that Whittaker is in Washington. Beware of him (entre nous) he is an unprincipled & worthless fellow. Had I been present, Mrs. W's ode would have made me vomit. It was more than usually odious.[50] God bless you. My wife sends her regards.

Yours Ever lovingly

W. Gilmore Simms

Hon. W. P. Miles.

967 : To William Porcher Miles

Woodlands, Monday MG.

[February 27, 1860][51]

My dear Miles.

Your little Goddaughter, Hattie Middleton, is thank God, now out of danger, though still feeble & fretful. But she has had a severe gastric fever, threatening the brain, which kept us for four days in terror. We thought of you, dear friend, and of your fond cares for us in hours as dark & more terrible.[52] We thought of you, and bitterly wept over the lost, as over the one dear little one whom we momently dreaded to lose also.

---

[46] During Feb., 1860, Simms reviewed or noticed in the Charleston *Mercury* over fifty books and a considerable number of speeches and issues of various magazines.

[47] *The New American Cyclopædia.*

[48] Simms wrote *doing doing.*

[49] See note 19, Feb. 5, 1860.

[50] "A National Song," by Mary Scrimzeour Furman Miller Whitaker (1820-1906), the daughter of Samuel Furman, of South Carolina, and the wife of Daniel Kimball Whitaker (see note 93, Sept. 20, 1843, and note 168, Aug. 2, 1850), was read at the inauguration of Clark Mills' statue of Washington. The poem is printed in the Charleston *Mercury* of Feb. 24, where Simms probably read it.

[51] The year is established by Simms' references to the Lawsons' recent visit to Woodlands and to the illness of his daughter Hattie (see preceding and following letters). The first Monday of Hattie's convalescence was Feb. 27.

[52] An allusion to the deaths of Sydney Roach and Beverley Hammond Simms. See letter to Hammond of Sept. 24, 1858.

I cover to you a letter to an excellent old friend, a Scotch Gentleman of N. Y. to whom I gave a letter of introduction for you. Please hand him the enclosed in person, if this be possible, & make his acquaintance if he has not already given you the opportunity. He is a kindly Gentleman, a substantial citizen of handsome means, living in good style in New York — a person of amiable simplicity of character in society, & of acute faculties in business. His girls with him are nice girls, accomplished & modest, now for the first time looking out from the maëlstrom of New York.

God shield you my friend.

Yours Ever & Ever

W. Gilmore Simms.

Hon. W. P. Miles.

968: To James Lawson

Woodlands, Tuesday MG.

[February 28, 1860][53]

My dear Lawson.

We perfectly comprehended your reasons for your premature departure. They were such as were naturally dictated by good sense, good feeling & a proper consideration. My wife and self deeply regret that we could not detain you, for your visit with the girls has given us the greatest satisfaction as enabling us to show our affectionate appreciation of the long continued kindness of your wife and self to us & ours. That you have found your visit here, & elsewhere at the South, a grateful one, is a subject of heartfelt satisfaction with us. We should have been greatly distressed had it been otherwise. And we hope, though the first, it shall not be the last. I trust that it will become annual, with some of your flock at least. Hattie is relieved, as I wrote you, of her fever & worst symptoms. But feeble & perhaps febrile still, from teething, she is terribly querulous & gives us a great deal of trouble. Enough, for our great relief, that she is no longer in any danger from the recent attack. God has been merciful to us, my friend, both; and it becomes us to remember it — not with any

---

[53] The year is established by Simms' references to the Lawsons' recent visit to Woodlands and to the illness of his daughter Hattie (see preceding and following letters). The first Tuesday of Hattie's convalescence was Feb. 28.

absurd ostentatious ceremonials of the bigot & sectarian, but with full hearts, fond prayers & gratitude which keeps us continually mindful, & thankful for his benevolence & favor. To feel, as the strongest of us are hourly made to do, that he is the only supreme, is the one lesson which the true religion alone can teach. Let us learn that lesson in our hearts, so that it shall become the law & monitor of our lives.— I am rejoiced that Gen. Jones, and my amiable Scottish friend, Mr. Martin have shown themselves so prompt and attentive in doing the honours to you.[54] But I had no doubt that such would be the case. Nor did I doubt that you would be pleased with Columbia. It is, indeed, a beautiful town. It has not shown itself friendly to me. Untill a recent period, its society was governed by one or two citizens, which I did not conciliate.[55] They showed themselves as hostile to me as they well could, from the moment I commenced my career, even to the present. A change is going on, however, the cliques are broken up, and a new, wiser, less pretentious, and more honestly working population is rising in the ascendant, from which we may reasonably expect better things. Had it been as of old, Gilmore should never have been sent to Columbia.[56] I rejoice that my boy pleases you. I have been solicitous of his thoughts & manners, and as I am one of the freest speakers of his thoughts that you know, and always too earnest of speech to be otherwise than honest, he has heard me often enough to have somewhat shaped his ideas & sentiments to my dicta & opinion. He will be sufficiently independent of character for the formation of his own, as his mind shall ripen. He is ingenuous & manly, warm & tender, sincere & honest, and above all meannesses. I wish to make him a magnanimous performing man. If God spares him to manhood, when he graduates, I will (D. V.) send him to see you. But untill he graduates, he can have little leisure and as little money. He must work for both.— I have sent you all the letters that have been recieved & am glad that you recieved them with the keys safely and in season. Tell my little Kate that she must beware how she leaves her heart about as she leaves her keys; for though, he who

---

[54] James Jones (see note 168, Sept. 5, 1849) and the Rev. William Martin, Methodist clergyman and husband of Margaret Maxwell Martin, to whom Lawson later sent a copy of his *Poems* (see letter to Lawson of *c.* Nov. 23, 1860).

[55] Simms perhaps has in mind William Campbell Preston (see introductory sketch) and Col. Wade Hampton (see note 305, Dec. 11, 1846), James H. Hammond's enemies in Columbia.

[56] Gilmore was a cadet at the Arsenal Academy.

finds it, may be willing for a swap, he will hardly be willing to return it. And I need not tell her that the chances are more than equal that she will gain nothing by the exchange.— My wife will probably write to you at Washington. But you must not calculate on it. She has been so worn & wearied by nursing during Hattie's illness that she can scarcely lift her head in thought — scarcely lift pen to write.— I have written to Col. Keitt, with a message to his wife, to do all she can for the girls. I have no doubt that my letters will serve you efficiently.— And now, my good old friend, God be with you & guard your footsteps all the rest of your journey. That you should find all well, peaceful & loving when you reach home is the prayer of all in the home which you have left. God bless you.

Your friend ever.

W. Gilmore Simms

969: To James Lawson

Woodlands S. C. 3d. March. [1860][57]

dear Lawson.

Presuming that you are safe in Washington & I trust gratefully entertained, I write a scrawl, at midnight, to say that we are in better condition than when you left. Hattie is still an invalid, troubled, we suspect, with worms & teething, an awkward complication; but she is only fretful & puny, & exhibits no such dangerous symptoms as terrified us when you were here. All others are well, except myself. My head this morning distressed me considerably, & I could not well see. But I grew better as the day advanced, & our woods took fire & I was out with the negroes for some hours, sweating like a Bull. The fire seized upon a Bay, which in dry weather, is so much peat. Had it swept the bay, I should have lost my fences & some thousand cart loads of vegetable manure. We saved it, with hard work, and I gave out to the negroes an extra allowance of whiskey & tobacco. This afternoon I rode down to Jamison: He is delighted with your letter, & glad that his served you so well with Jones. We are all quite happy that your sojourn in Carolina was so agreeable to you & the girls. I trust that your letters will secure you equally good

---

[57] Dated by Simms' references to the Lawsons' recent visit to Woodlands and to the illness of his daughter Hattie. See preceding letters.

treatment, or better, in Washington. Today, I sent you off two letters, under cover to your address at Willard's.[58] Write to me when you get home. We hope to hear from you at Washington. My wife and the girls send affectionate regards.

God bless you, old friend, and restore you safely to the bosom of your long abandoned wife.

Yours Ever truly

W. Gilmore Simms.

James Lawson, Esq.

970: To WILLIAM PORCHER MILES

Woodlands 5th. March. [1860] [59]

dear Miles.

Yours just recieved. I write only to say that a letter from Mr. Lawson, mentions that he has been summoned home by telegram, in consequence of the dangerous illness of one of his children. This has probably prevented you from seeing him, and perhaps equally deprived Hammond, Chesnut & Keitt from making his acquaintance. As I have covered letters for him & his daughters not only to yourself, but, as I think, to some of these, will you be so good as to enquire, procure all, & cover them to him addressed

"Mr. James Lawson.
144 Twelfth Street
New York."

I can readily concieve your troubles & toils, their exhausting variety, and uninteresting drudgeries. I did not expect you to read in the thick of the *melée*. I hope you are avoiding all writing or talking in respect to the Charleston Convention [60] — all that you can. I think the probabilities are that it will break up in a row — that there will be found certain irrepressible conflicts there which no soft-sawdering will reconcile. *Nous Verrons!* Do not give much heed to what I may say en passant of politics in my letters. My head is so frequently at fault that I probably write half the time at random.

Á Dios!

W. Gilmore Simms

---

[58] The hotel in Washington.
[59] Dated by Simms' reference to the illness of William Gilmore Simms Lawson. See following letters.
[60] The National Democratic Convention. See note 69, April 9, 1860.

971: To James Lawson

Woodlands March 11. 1860.

Oh! my poor friend, how our hearts bleed for you all. Your dear, noble little Boy — so sweet, so promising, so full of pleasant ways — so precious in a thousand ways! [61] Ah! God be merciful to you, my friend & to your poor wife, & to your dear children all, and strengthen you to bear such a blow as you had never felt before! Oh! may he spare you hereafter, so that ye shall feel no such blows again. May all the dear ones be left to close their parents eyes, when in God's season you shall be called away to meet your blessed little boy. He hath sorely stricken you, my friend. No one better than myself can say how sorely. I have buried seven lovely ones! This is your first great sorrow! Oh! let it teach you such wisdom, and so rapidly, that you will not need again the chastening hand of the eternal father — rebuking pride and vanity, & worldly appetites — for such blows are decreed by the unerring, however inscrutable law, to produce just such effects; — to rebuke the self sufficient — rebuke worldly vanities & lusts — teach humility — make us feel that we are all but weakest children in *his* hands, the father, master, sole great & powerful of this & all other worlds! It is to save the parent that God frequently takes the child. You had set your fond heart upon this dear little boy — he was the very apple of your eye — your secret heart built upon his future with the most ambitious hopes, — and here, in the very citadel of your Hope, and in the very object of your crowning Pride, God smites you to the very heart and soul, and I verily believe for the bettering of the one and the safety of the other. But for such strokes of Fate, we should forget ourselves, and man, & God alike. God deals them that we may not forget either. In our worldly strifes and triumphs — in our daily conflicts and gains — in the full tide of prosperity, — our hearts become hardened through the insolence of our vanities. We become solicitous of worldly things — of worldly triumphs — of the opinions of our neighbours — of position among our neighbours — of the accumulation of wealth,— of the shows of opulence & splendour & wealth & luxury; — and thinking only of our effect upon the market place, we forget God. We forget the short duration of our lives that we shall each be summoned away from the

---

[61] William Gilmore Simms Lawson died on March 5. See the New York *Herald* of March 6.

market place, & that, when gone, not one of all those who sought us in the market place, will undertake a single hour's vigil at our graves, or follow, with fond thought, our passage to the unknown world in which we are to seek, or find, without being permitted to seek, a new position. It is by blows which humble these vanities that God keeps us mindful of himself & of ourselves. And we have better reason to dread the future when we find that God forbears these blows. There is nothing, my dear, good, old, true friend, which is so dangerous to the heart & future hopes of man, as unmitigated prosperity! You will remember with what earnestness, I told you, while you were here with me, the beautiful story of Solon & Crœsus. Take it to your heart, and, so far from repining, as one without hope, thank the Great Father that he has not forgotten you — that he has not suffered you to become forgetful of him — that he has not reserved his chastening for another life. It is a terrible thought to think that any human being shall, for a term of years, & seasons, go free of chastening — be free of sorrow — know nothing but prosperity. What accumulated woes must be in reserve for such a being, & how well he will deserve them. For such are the weaknesses, the vanities & the wilfulnesses of the human heart, that prosperity without check produces drunkenness, defiance, insolence, all the bad passions in a sort of tyranny. The great problem of the uses and the necessity of evil is never so clear as when seen through this medium. You are scourged, you are suffering — simply that you should not forget yourself and God. If you forget neither — if God by his scourgings keeps you properly mindful of both — you will surely recover your dear little (for the present, lost) Boy. Be wise! Be humble! Submit yourself. I do not say, do not weep. Weep freely. Weep your heart empty. Let it fill again & again, & again, weep; not bitterly, but with the sweet memories of how sweet he was, how precious, and with what longing you look forward to the hour when you shall again find him in your loving arms. I enclose you an essay which I published in the Mercury soon after the death of my two precious little boys, Sydney & Beverley.[62] It will show you how I thought if not how I felt, on that dreadful occasion with two dear sons dead before me, and three other children suffering & threatened with the same death, under the

---

[62] Probably "The Morals of Affliction," unsigned, in the Charleston *Mercury* of Oct. 11, 1858. The ideas expressed in it are the same as those Simms expresses here in this letter.

same fearful pestilence which raged through every part of our city. Preserve the article & send it back to me, as I have no other copy. May it lift your thoughts into higher provinces of sorrow — and hope — confidence in God, & sympathy with Humanity. Weep on, dear old friend — good brother — let your heart fill & overflow; but look upward while you weep & seek God as the only true source of comfort. Words of consolation from men are childish & idle things. Go to the one fountain of peace & resignation. Go to God. Humble yourself on your knees, my poor friend, & he will lift you up. For your poor wife, for the mother, the brother & the sisters, I have but tears, as I have for you. Would to God you had all been here with me this winter! Ah, my friend, think — at the very moment when you were so proud, so confident, so happy,— such a blow. Let it teach & make you wise. God be with you & bless you, & reconcile you to his will, so that you shall pour forth your submission in your sorrows, & find your consolation in his will. We weep with you my brother — we weep.

Yours, Yours—

W. G. S.

Jamison writes you today. He feels for you & with you. — But he will tell you all himself.

972: To James Lawson

Woodlands, March 21, 1860.

My dear old friend.

Your letter has just been recieved — it was missent by some wretched postmaster, to North Carolina. You have recieved before this, my letter, and that of Gen. Jamison. My wife wrote to Mary a few days ago. In a letter from Porcher Miles, M. C. recieved today, he writes as follows: " I was very sorry not to meet Mr. Lawson. He left Washington immediately after his arrival, in consequence of the sudden illness of his son, as you are aware. I regret that I did not have the opportunity of showing some attention to a friend of yours so warmly commended to my care. I hope, at some future day, to make Mr. Lawson's acquaintance." Warm and earnest, no doubt, my dear L. will be the human sympathies felt for you by all who know you. I am glad that you bear like a man what you still feel like a father. And so sweet

and noble a boy, so full of life & promise! Ah! my friend — God
giveth, and surely he may take. I trust that his taking, in this instance, will prove to you & yours, a gain of life, rather than a
loss in death. All our afflictions are means of training for the true
life, if we are only wise enough to comprehend them with a loving submission to the will of the great father. We are not forbidden to mourn, to sorrow, to feel humility, to succumb for a
season & be subdued by suffering, for it is this very suffering &
pain that is to season us, and keep our hearts from vanity & our
heads from vulgar & ridiculous pride. In this struggle of life, we
are but too apt to forget what the true life is. The great majority of mankind is born to poverty & toil. Men accordingly
are trained by the commonest necessities, to attach an undue
importance to worldly acquisitions[.] And so gain becomes the
ordinary idea of life with most; and next to this, having acquired,
we address ourselves to the vulgar vanity of exhibiting our state
& wealth & possessions to the world. All this God rebukes; for
all this disqualifies us for those higher essentials of thought, soul
& aim, which constitute the true life of the soul. God can reach
us only through such affections as we have left to ourselves; and
he does this, by giving wings to our riches so that they fly away,
and striking us through our children so that they perish. I have
been a great sufferer [63] in this way — have buried 7, my friend
of 13, and so feel that I have been a great sinner; for though
never caring a straw about money, or worldly shows, I have
had an intense ambition for fame & power. I am getting cured
of that, though mine is a very stubborn case. But every day tends
to wean me more & more from worldly vanities, and when I feel
daily that I have more dear ones (I trust) in Heaven, than I
have on earth — more children — more relatives — more friends,
(I hope) I feel that Death is disarmed of some, if not of all of
his terrors. Your dear little boy has, I trust, met with *my* children. They know how tender has been the tie between their parents. They know each other, in a better world, though they did
not know in this. Ah! my friend, the dear ones, believe [me,]
are about us still. Your little boy is with you, tho' you see him
not. Your great affliction was shown to me — could I have understood it at the time, in the very moment perhaps when the
silver chord was loosed & the golden bowl broken. I am sure of

---

[63] Simms wrote *suffering.*

the soul's immortality, and would try so to live as to be able to rejoin my precious & innocent children. So, do you strive! We will commune on these subjects together, if God shall ever suffer us again to meet. We are to labour in a worldly way — that, indeed, is a spiritual duty, for our spiritual condition will depend wholly upon the use of our worldly gifts & advantages. But bread & meat & drink, and fine raiment, and vanity shows are damnable things, if we live for these alone. We are to keep these desires in modest subjection always to the demands of the soul. And the demands of the soul, are humility, love to man, strict performance of duty, faith in God, in his justice & mercy, and perpetual reference to him as the father — appeal to him in difficulty or trouble — appeal to him in anticipation of trouble. Briefly, we are never to forget God! — in our respect for Mammon, or Eros, or Vanity Fair, or any of the miserable Passions in a state of rampancy. So to your work like a man, but take counsel with God daily. He is the only teacher, as well as comforter. He will not fail you. Mrs. Dr. Steele, who, with all her children, has been spending some weeks with us, has been summoned down in all haste, by the condition of her husband. I expect daily to hear of his death.[64] Love to all & God's mercy upon you all.

W. G. S.

973 : To Henry Barton Dawson

Woodlands, March 22. 1860.

Henry B. Dawson Esq.

My dear Sir:

I regretted very much, while looking over my drawer of Correspondents today, to find that I have suffered one of your letters to remain unanswered from the middle of January to the present moment; — not that there was any matter of moment calling for an answer; for in that event I feel sure it would not have been neglected. But I rarely leave any friendly correspondent without due & usually very prompt acknowledgement. My time has been great-

---

[64] Dr. Edwin Carroll Steele (b. 1827), a Charleston physician, died on Jan. 29, 1861; his wife, Martha W. Porcher (b. 1829), on Dec. 22, 1861. They had two daughters, Ada and Mary, and one son, Edwin, who in the 1880's was rector of the Episcopal church at Orangeburg, S. C. The dates of the elder Steeles are from their tombstones in St. Paul's Churchyard, Charleston.

ly occupied. My house absolutely crowded with guests all the winter, & I have been all the time, more or less an invalid. I have considerably improved, chiefly by abstaining from the desk; and for once my house is empty of visitors. I seize upon the respite to see to my correspondents, and to pray their forgiveness. I have not recently recieved any of your issues & forget just now what was the last number. Whatever it was, the work has been noticed to that date in the Mercury, though it is probable that I have not sent you the notice. I will look it up & have it ready in season for my next communication.[65] Please recieve my thanks for your offered services. Should I visit N. Y. next summer, as I contemplate (D. V.) I will do myself the honour of looking you up.

Yours truly

W. Gilmore Simms.

974: To William Porcher Miles

Woodlands, April 9, 1860.

My dear Miles.

Though I wrote you only on Friday last,[66] yet a letter just recieved from Hammond advises me that a report prevails that somebody in Charleston shows greed for your "Alban Villa" — in other words wants your place.[67] I left Charleston on Wednesday, saw Rhett [68] & others, none of whom hinted at the matter. Hammond is of opinion that you have heard the report from Rhett. I have expressed to him my doubts of this. If there should be any truth in the report — and it is quite probable that there are scores ready & eager to take your place, & all places, if they fancied it attainable — these persons are, none of them, I take it, of the real States rights men; but rather of that mongrel faction who go for the Convention, and possibly for Douglas.[69]

---

[65] In the Charleston *Mercury* of Feb. 25, 1860, Simms reviews Nos. 25-27 of Dawson's *Battles of the United States.*

[66] April 6. We have not located this letter.

[67] See Hammond's letter to Simms of April 3 (original in the Hammond Papers, Library of Congress).

[68] Probably Robert Barnwell Rhett, Sr.

[69] The National Democratic Convention met in Charleston on April 23. On April 30 most of the delegates from Alabama, Mississippi, Louisiana, South Carolina, Florida, Texas, and Arkansas and two of the delegates from Delaware walked out of the Convention in protest over the platform which had been adopted. Most of the Georgia delegation withdrew on April 31. Stephen

Beware of being counselled by any of these. You have faith in Porter;[70] but Porter is a regular party man; is good natured, &, I think, unsuspicious; and may be used, as I am of opinion that he has been used before by more subtle and selfish politicians. Wm. Whaley,[71] or Tom Simons,[72] no doubt, would graciously accept, & so would some half-dozen more of the same calibre and kidney. But, no matter who the party may be, you must beware of falling into the trap which was set for Aiken.[73] A bait which was so successful once may be tried twice, even though the parties to be operated upon may be so decidedly similar. I do not see that any of the persons likely to crave your place, are likely to obtain it, if you keep the field, and I would give you but the single additional counsel, — to return for answer coolly and decidedly to any such correspondent, that you hold the place from your people and mean to keep it, especially at this perilous juncture, against all comers, & just so long as your people are willing to command your services. A decisive tone at the outset will drive off all *feelers,* and discourage adventurers. Can you get & send me a copy of Helper's Book without paying money for it?[74]

Yours Ever truly

W. Gilmore Simms

Arnold Douglas, the leading candidate for the nomination for president, was unable to win a two-third's majority, and on May 3 the Convention was adjourned to reconvene in Baltimore on June 18. See *Proceedings of the National Democratic Convention, Convened at Charleston, S. C., April 23, 1860* (Washington: Thomas McGill, Printer, 1860).

[70] William Dennison Porter. See note 102, July 29, 1848.

[71] William Whaley, a Charleston lawyer admitted to the bar at Columbia in 1837, was at this time a member of the South Carolina House of Representatives.

[72] Thomas Yonge Simons (1828-1878), Charleston lawyer, was a member of the South Carolina House of Representatives for several terms, a member of the Secession Convention, a captain and judge advocate during the Confederate War, and editor-in-chief of the Charleston *Courier* during 1865-1873.

[73] Evidently some professed friend had persuaded William Aiken (see note 326, "Christmas Day," 1846) not to be a candidate for renomination to the United States Senate in 1856.

[74] Hinton Rowan Helper (1829-1909), a native of North Carolina, was the author of *The Impending Crisis of the South: How to Meet It* (New-York: Burdick Brothers, 1857), a violent attack on slavery. In 1859 a fund was raised in the North to print 100,000 copies of the book for use in the Republican campaign of 1860.

975: To James Lawson

Woodlands 9 April 1860.

My dear old friend.

I have just returned home after a weeks absence in Beaufort and Charleston. My wife & self, taking little Govan with us, took the Carriage and, with relays of horses, went through to Dr. Fuller's, 55 to 60 miles, in one day. We were much concerned & apprehensive about Mrs. F. who was in very low spirits. We reached their plantation on the very day when she was safely delivered of a fine boy. Mother & child doing well.[75] I left my wife there & proceeded to Charleston where I spent three days with Augusta, who is fat (weighs 136½ lbs) and well, and her little girl[76] thriving. I came home alone, but sent off next day for Mary Lawson & Chevillette & Hattie, all of whom are here with me now. Our boy-babie[77] is with Mrs. Rivers[78] at Bamberg. Yesterday, (Sunday) I sent off the horses for my wife, and expect her home today. We seized the only respite from company that we have had this winter, to pay this visit; and I am advised of fresh flocks of visitors, among them a newly discovered relation of mine, a rich planter of Mississippi[79] — who will probably keep our house full till June, when we propose to depart for the seaboard. You see, my dear old friend, what a life I live, & how impossible it is for me to save money. Let me say, here, while on the subject of my movements, that I propose (D. V.) to visit you in September. But *L'homme propose, et Dieu dispose!* Who shall say? The sooner, dear friend, we resign ourselves to the will of the Good God, the sooner we acquire peace, if not mortal happiness. That is a boon for which I no longer pray. I pray for mercy, to be spared as much as possible, to let the cup of bitterness pass by, to be taught what is right, & to be endowed with the requisite will, strength and courage, to do it. I have long since been terribly taught that there is nothing mortal upon which mortality can rely — nothing in Science, Literature or Art. These are only agents of good, to

---

[75] Middleton Guerard Fuller (called "Guerard") was born on March 28. He died on June 3, 1910.

[76] Chevillette Conyers Roach (Dec. 8, 1859—June 18, 1907). She later married William McKee (1857-1937).

[77] Sydney Hammond.

[78] Mrs. Christopher M. Rivers, the former Mary Govan Steele. See note 202, Oct. 23, 1846, and note 95, *c.* May 6, 1849.

[79] Not identified.

soothe, not to save — to succour, and elevate, not to secure.
And we must set our *souls* upon no earthly things. They should
exercise, not absorb our affections. Your case, my dear L. has
occasioned the warmest sympathies. My friends Hammond &
Miles [80] have both written me with tender interest, for my friends
would have been theirs. Jamison, W. Roach, my daughter &
her husband, have all felt keenly; Dr. Carroll has expressed himself in grateful terms of sympathy, and my boy Gilmore feels
deeply the loss of the dear boy whom he never knew, his noble
little namesake, to whom, I am sure, he would have always
proved a loving friend. But you must substitute resignation for
grief, dear friend, and always remember that you have still a large,
loving & lovable family of dear young ones, upon whom you must
concentrate all your living love. For whom it will be sweet to toil,
and whom your love may save, and daily succour. You & they
now possess a dear little angel advocate on high, the child of your
loins, whose infant offices, be sure, will be unsparing to watch
over the safety of the beloved ones from whom he has been taken,
to minister to their sensibilities, and welcome them, in turn,
when God shall so will, to the blessed spheres which he has prematurely won. But all this, I have said to you before & trust
that you are in reciept of all my letters. We greatly feel for Kate.
It is temperament. Let her use cold water freely; avoid light
dresses and excitements — have regular employments — take
fresh air & exercise — keep your rooms cooler — expel that
horrid hot air from your house — take wood-fires, or at least
coal, in the old fashioned way, and do not adopt every new
fangled fashionable notion because your neighbour adopts it. 'One
fool makes many!' That hot air does not merely warm the body.
It penetrates the lungs. You must breathe it. Now, the lungs are
not merely a breathing apparatus. They are refrigerators. That
hot air killed Duyckinck's son,[81] is the chief mischief with Mary
& Kate. Look to it in time. — In Charleston, Augusta showed
me a case to my address, said to come from you, & supposed to
contain liquor. It has not yet reached me here. Thanks, my dear
L. for your remembrance. That your heart & thought can, at
such a time, turn to your friends, is a favorable symptom. You
are right in one thing. Keep your mind busy — go to your work

---

[80] James Henry Hammond and William Porcher Miles.

[81] Evert Augustus Duyckinck, Jr., died on Feb. 10, 1857. See note 41,
April 7, 1857.

regularly — do what you can to interest your children, & teach them; but train yourself, however, to the perpetual edict of Cyrus — 'Remember, thou art mortal!' Never let any mere worldly pride, show, vanity, make you forgetful one moment, of the proper sentiments which feed & strengthen a soul for immortality. — Gen. Jones, Chief of the Military Board tells me that Gilmore is remarkably promising, doing admirably, and if he continues thus, will be distinguished at the Head of his Section. I know it will give you, Mary & Kate, who now know him, especial pleasure to hear this, and I know he will be gratified to have you know. He was quite delighted with you & the girls. You, yourself, have made a favourable impression on all my friends whom you had the opportunity to see. Of course, they were prepared to know you, and I had taken due care that they should all know that I had found you, like the Douglas, aye 'tender & true', for the long term of 30 years. We, my old friend, can hardly alter now. We are stedfast. My wife wrote to Lyde just before leaving home. Augusta has also written. It is surprising that any of my letters should have failed. Jamison & myself sent off our letters on the same day. But I think I told you of one of the last recieved of yours, being some weeks on the route. — I must not forget in domestic matters, what is pro bono publico. You heard me on several occasions, put forth views on the relations of North & South which were startling to you. Let me counsel you to get a book just published, entitled "Southern Wealth & Northern Profits" by T. P. Kettell, formerly Ed. of the Democratic Review.[82] You will see by that work, of which study every syllable, that he illustrates by detailed statistics what I dismissed in generalities. He confirms every syllable & principle that I laid down to you. You will see, in that work, what your politicians are dooming you to. To illustrate ourselves & our negroes, — take one fact. You will remember that while with me, I sent off a negro fellow to the city, in order that he should have surgical attendance for a bad hand. He has been absent near 3 months in the city, & *had never been to the surgeon.* — He will probably lose his hand, possibly his life. Yet I have been providing

---

[82] Simms reviews Thomas Prentice Kettell's *Southern Wealth and Northern Profits, as Exhibited in Statistical Facts and Official Figures: Showing the Necessity of Union to the Future Prosperity and Welfare of the Republic* (New York: G. W. & J. A. Wood, 1860) in the Charleston *Mercury* of June 20, 1860. Kettell was editor of the *Democratic Review* during 1846-1851 (see note 214, July 31, 1847).

him weekly with corn & bacon. Such is a negro. God bless you and love to all.

Yours ever faithfully

W. Gilmore Simms.

976: To John Esten Cooke

Woodlands, April 14, 1860.

You and I, my dear Cooke, must not talk to each other of *owing* letters, unless we mean to say something apologetic. It must not be accusatory. Our friendship must not be subjected to any such ordinary tests. You will write to me when the thought of me is pressing, and when no Hard Taskmaster requires you at the hoe; and should you not write, my friendship will say — Cooke is sad, Cooke is sick, Cooke is very busy; he has to work & to suffer like myself, and he is under the hardest of taskmasters, — still like myself — Poverty & the Public. Is it not so. Now, I have been absent from home — I have been straightened for money — I have been harrassed in raising it, and — rather than borrow to meet emergencies — hark in your ear, I have been selling some rare old books out of my Library, and some thousand or two of current ones! Do you not feel like weeping for me. I do not weep for myself. I have got so tired of the lesson that I have forgotten it all. Yet, I could & should weep here, if the eyes did not refuse me. I have lived in my library — among books — among the ancient masters, those loving teachers who counsel you without looking wise, & argue with you without getting into a passion. I have been turning such as these out of doors. I have turned them into corn & cattle. I have been using my brain in like coinage, and but for the aridity of my eyes, I should do any quantity of weeping. I have been collecting my books for quite 30 years. I have imported rare books at rare prices; caught them up wherever I could; and what I had thus amassed has been the sole accumulation left me from my Literary labours during all this time. I had about 12000 volumes. Briefly, for my situation — a day & night laborer, it was too much capital to invest in such unprofitable wares! This year, dreadfully unfortunate in my crop & overseer, I have been driven to the necessity of selling Milton for a bushel of corn, Shakspeare for a bunch of onions, Chaucer for a string of fish, and Bacon for a barrel of beans, &c!! Enough of this poor sickish sort of humour, my friend. It is one satisfaction that I had embalmed them before I let them go — gutted them at all events, of all that I could carry of theirs. I have had other cares, my friend. With so large a family as mine, I am rarely free from apprehension for my children; I have had one of them dangerously ill, & for a week expected to lose her. I have lost so many that the sickness, of one of my children now, is a Terror. I see behind the door a grim shadow casting a deadly dart. God has spared me this time. But a dear friend who, with two of his daughters spent some time with me, hurried home to seal the eyes of a noble little boy, a godson of mine & named after me! [83] To this friend, I gave letters for you & Thompson which his terrible necessity alone, kept him from delivering.[84] He & his family, with scores besides have been my guests this winter. Not a week has passed without company, and I very wretched half the time! But you have had deeper sorrows, greater griefs than cares. I did not learn till lately how grievously you have been a sufferer.[85] Weep if you can, my friend. It will do you good. We are not forbidden to weep — most happy, perhaps, if permitted. Weep. Weep! Try & visit me next winter, and do me the great service of persuading tears into my eyes. I am sorry to say that I only weep when the apprehension is on me. My fountains dry up as soon as the bolt is shot! — I had two brothers, both dead when I was an infant. I never knew them. I lost my mother without knowing her. I was then an infant.[86] I grew up without young associates. I grew *hard* in consequence, hard, perhaps, of manner; but with a heart craving love beyond all other possessions. My friend, it is better to know, & learn to love & lose, — than never to know. Tears are more genial than icicles! But, what need I say more. Come to Woodlands when you can. Let us commune together. We shall be in God's hands even here, my friend, though the world slides by us, possibly in scorn, and we see it not. There is some satisfaction in this. Of

---

[83] James Lawson and his daughters Mary and Kate left Woodlands around Feb. 21, when Simms' daughter Hattie became ill. William Gilmore Simms Lawson died on March 5.

[84] These letters to Cooke and John Reuben Thompson are missing from the collection of Simms' letters to Lawson in the South Caroliniana Library.

[85] Cooke's brothers Edward St. George and Henry Pendleton had recently died. See James O. Beaty, *John Esten Cooke, Virginian* (New York: Columbia University Press, 1922), p. 63.

[86] Simms' older brother was named John Singleton. His mother, Harriet Ann Augusta Singleton Simms, died in 1808 at the birth of her third son, James. See *The Letters of William Gilmore Simms*, I, lx.

course, I will do for your book what I can.[87] Why not [c]ome [88] & spend a month with me, while I talk over all I know, & show you the books I have. My talk would give you twenty times the information which I could impart by letters. Come! Now, I shall be leaving home about the 1st. June, for the seaboard, where I shall spend the summer. Come & stay with me then. You shall have hog & hominy, and the pullets shall lay daily eggs for you. Nay, you shall have the pullet herself. I will have strawberries soon, & peas & snapbeans, &c. And you shall see my wife and young ones for yourself. My eldest daughter is married & living in Charleston. My eldest son is at Columbia, at the State Military Academy.[89] I have here two girls beginning to strum on the piano, & one little girl beginning to prattle; and a boy who has got a bigger head than Julius Cæsar, & the countenance of Lord Bacon on the Bench; and another sad looking boy, born under a sorrowful star, sent, as it were just after the loss of my two noble boys in 1858 as if to replace them, with a blended likeness to both, and, like the elder especially with such deep sad meaning eyes — an infant in the arms. Ah! my friend, you have not yet touched [90] the vast profound. May your children close your eyes, — not you theirs! [91] But come & see. And we will talk together of night & cloud & shadow, and the pall & bier & tomb, and of the star emerging from the cloud, and the shadow passing away and the tomb bursting asunder, and of the spirit freed and on its flight. God be merciful to us both.

Your own

W. G. S.

977 : To Thomas Pennant Barton [92]

Woodlands, April 26, 1860.

dear Sir:

I have made a good many notes on Shakspeare, and have published some on the Tempest, & perhaps some other plays, in

---

[87] Simms had reviewed Cooke's *Henry St. John, Gentleman* in the Charleston *Mercury* of Jan. 20. See note 17, Jan. 20, 1860.

[88] The MS. is torn.

[89] The Arsenal Academy.

[90] Simms wrote *touch*.

[91] Cooke was not married at this time. On Sept. 18, 1867, he married Mary Francis Page.

[92] Barton (1803-1869), of New York City, was a diplomat, bibliophile, and the first important American collector of Shakespeare.

one magazine or other — The Magnolia, Southern Literary Gazette, S. L. Journal, &c. but do not now know where to lay
hands on them. [93] I published in the Orion Magazine four Lectures on Hamlet,[94] but have not a single copy to spare. If you
will see Mr. T. Addison Richards, Landscape Painter, at the
Cooper Institute, he may be able to procure you a copy. I delivered on sundry occasions two lectures on Hamlet.[95] I have
also written for Mr. Forrest, a new version of Timon, altering
the denouëment, & making considerable alterations & additions,
with the view to its presentation on the stage. But this he has,
still in MS.[96] I once proposed a new ed. of Shakspeare, but the
plan did not attract my publisher.[97] I do not now recal any other
labors which I have taken in this field. It would give me real
satisfaction to provide you with copies of these things but this
is impossible at present. I shall find pleasure, when I next visit
N. Y. in taking advantage of your courteous invitation & examining your collection.

Very respectfully &c

W. Gilmore Simms

P. S. I omitted to notice one of your queries. Some of my "Heads
of the Poets["] appeared, first, I think, in a work entitled
"Thoughts on the Poets", or "Oracles from the Poets" — I do
not remember which, edited by my friend, Mrs. Gilman. But
which of them were then & thus first published, I cannot say.
Her book will tell. The rest appeared, I believe, for the first time,
in the vols. to which you refer, and where you now find them.[98]
In some copies of Shakspeare, I have sundry notes, and com-

---

[93] In the *Southern Literary Gazette* Simms published two short articles on
The Tempest: "Errors in Shakspeare's Tempest" (signed "R. H."), I (Nov.,
1828), 186-187, and "Shakspeare—'The Tempest' (unsigned), N. S., I (Sept.
15, 1829), 202-204. In the *Southern Literary Journal* he published two articles
entitled "Shakspeariana" (both signed "Dramaticus"), N. S., IV (Sept. and
Oct., 1838), 184-192, 253-256. No article on Shakespeare was published in
the *Magnolia.*

[94] "The Moral Character of Hamlet." See note 34, Feb. 15, 1844.

[95] See note 3, Jan. 3, 1854, and note 27, Feb. 10, 1854.

[96] See letter to Lawson of Oct. 21, 1852, and following letters to Lawson.

[97] See letter to Lawson of April 30, 1848.

[98] See letter to Caroline Gilman of July? 1848. Simms' two poems on
Shakespeare were probably first published under the title of "Heads of the
Poets" in *Graham's,* XXXIII (Sept., 1848), 170. They are also included in
Poems (1853), II, 155-156.

ments, not only upon the text, but its commentators. These are
still in MS.

Thos. P. Barton, Esq. W. G. S.

978: To James Lawson

[*c.* April 28, 1860][99]

dear Lawson.

You will see by the enclosed that I am still the victim of destiny. My house and furniture destroyed — some 5 to $6000 dol-
lars. No insurance. I had not money to spare, from my daily
needs, to insure. What to do I know not. I go to town by the
next train, to sell out, if I can do no better. I have no means to
rebuild. — I have nothing to tell you. Our little boy, Sydney,
has been very ill — does not thrive. I have no hope that we shall
rear him. My friend, we are thus taught that mortal life is a
small matter in the sight of Deity, & mortal prosperity & property still smaller. Could we only become wise enough to feel
this, it might be better for us. I am becoming indurated, I fear,
by these repeated strokes of Fate & Fortune, and somewhat reckless. May you & my other friends never be subjected to such
trials of fortitude as I am required to endure. — I have recieved
a box from you but know not its contents. Thanks, nevertheless.
It is probably something to keep a man from despair, if drench-
ing freely may do it. Love to all, from all.

God bless & keep you.

W. Gilmore Simms.

979: To William Porcher Miles

Woodlands, May 10. [1860][100]

My dear Mr. Miles.

I have just come back from the city. My House is burnt with
half my furniture. Loss (uninsured) some $4000. The only year

---

[99] Dated by the burning of Simms' house in Charleston. The *Courier* of
April 28 reports that the roof and second story of Simms' "brick residence in
Smith street, a few doors north of Calhoun . . . occupied by Messrs. J. H.
Baggett and W. W. Sale" were "considerably damaged" and "the kitchen en-
tirely destroyed" by fire. The clipping Simms enclosed is not preserved with
this letter.

[100] Dated by Simms' discussion of the burning of his Charleston house (see
preceding letter to Lawson). Trent, p. 243, quotes a sentence from this letter.

(in 40) when we rented it. You will feel a little yourself for a
wigwam, in which you have seen us so bitterly tried.[101] I am
hors de combat. Have no money to rebuild. Dare not borrow;
and must quit the city. — By the way, I saw James at the Library [102] — looking very well, —but complaining as usual. Do
tell me how much he is your senior. I wish to know for a special
reason.[103] In haste, but

Ever truly Yours

W. Gilmore Simms.

My wife sends her regards and remembrances.

980: To WILLIAM PORCHER MILES

Woodlands, May 21. [1860] [104]

My dear Miles.

Thanks for your letter. I should have rejoiced to meet you in
the city, but I had only a week left it, having gone down for that
space of time, to see after the *debris* of my furniture from the fire.
You see how Fate pursues me. There was no Insurance. The
absolute loss, in capital, is about $4000; and then I lose the
usufruct, the rent, which cuts me off from my allowance! I must
now borrow or steal for the summer. I had rented the House for
$500 a year, and the only time we had ever rented it, in 40 years,
it was destroyed! I had just effected arrangements for leasing it
for a term of years. I am deprived of all this resource, & have no
means to rebuild; unless I borrow money for it which I dare not.
The result is that I must sell, and this is my future banishment
from the city. It is the finale to a long struggle against exile! —
from my native place (?) But enow of this. I read your speech
with pleasure, and am glad to see that it was heard with ex-

---

101 Miles was with Simms at the time of the deaths of Sydney Roach and
Beverley Hammond Simms. See letter to Hammond of Sept. 24, 1858.

102 James Warley Miles was librarian of the College of Charleston Library
during 1857-1865.

103 James Warley Miles was born in 1818, William Porcher Miles in 1822.
We do not know why Simms wanted to know their comparative ages.

104 Part of this letter is quoted by Trent, p. 249, who misdates it 1859. The
correct year is established by Simms' reference to the recent burning of his
Charleston house.

pressions of pleasure so decided.[105] I hope it is as you say that our people are united at last; my own opinion is that the people of all the South are monstrously ahead of all their politicians, as the latter will be made to see & feel. It is only the trading politicians that care about a President at all. The *people* of the South want their rights, not office. Those who want office scarcely can understand them. Mark me, the politician now, who would maintain himself long, must endeavour to get ahead of the people, not to arrest their momentum, but to direct it in the very path they are pursuing. I am glad that Hammond's Letter is rightly toned.[106] You have no reason to regret your speech. I believe you are right. We in the South at this juncture can condense all our political creed into one brief formula — "We know but the South and the South in danger!" — And no more tampering with the enemy, no more compromise bolstering up a dwindling party to the ruin of the South. Write me. I need it.

> Á Dios.
> Yours Ever truly
>
> W. Gilmore Simms

P. S. Tell Hammond I am satisfied with his *public* letter and will reply to his private one, as soon as I can feel my head properly posed on my shoulders.[107] But I have been in a fearful maelstrom of trouble & anxiety all the winter. By the way, your little God-daughter [108] is now quite well; with the saddest,

---

[105] The Charleston *Mercury* of May 21 summarizes Miles' address delivered on May 19 at a Democratic meeting held in Hibernian Hall, Charleston. Miles declared himself a *"sectional man"* and said that there was no hope for the South in the Union, since the North was so wholly against her.

[106] The Charleston *Mercury* of May 21 prints the text of a letter written by James H. Hammond from Washington and dated May 15, which was read at the Democratic meeting held on May 19. Hammond says that, if possible, the union of all the states should be maintained, but that it is essential that the cotton states should be kept together in the closest bonds of good feeling. He further says that the forthcoming Richmond Convention (see note 129, June 12, 1860) should not tend to bring about the disunion of the United States, but instead should provide a forum for discussion.

[107] Hammond's letter to Simms of May 11 (original in the Hammond Papers, Library of Congress) is a reply to a letter which we have not located. Evidently the tone of Simms' letter was despondent, for after remarking how shocked he was to hear of the burning of Simms' Charleston house, Hammond attempts to cheer him with a prophecy of lasting fame: "You leave to yours [your children] a name that will be longer & more thoroughly appreciated than that of any one, perhaps, of all your contemporaries in America, certainly second to none. Does not that suffice?"

[108] Hattie.

thoughtfullest face in the world, and destined, (if God spares her)
I think to be a pretty creature & some thing more. My wife with
our eldest girl [109] is now on a visit to her kinswoman, Mrs. Col.
Goodwyn, at Columbia,[110] where she has gone partly to attend
Gilmore's examination at the Arsenal. Once more, God bless you.

W. G. S.

981: To Evert Augustus Duyckinck

Woodlands, S. C. May 28, 1860.

My dear Duyckinck.

I am afraid you will think me neglectful, inconsiderate of past
friendship, and altogether a worldling. But if suffering may excuse a man for the seeming neglect of his friends, I pray you let
it plead for me. My cares, troubles & anxieties seem destined
never to end, and, at a period of life when most men need &
desire repose, my toils & responsibilities seem to undergo increase.
With a large family, I am scarcely ever free from anxiety about
the health of my children. Having lost 7 out of 14, even a slight
sickness of one of them fills my heart with dread. This winter,
I have trembled every moment for one of them, — now happily
recovered;[111] and my youngest boy,[112] now, is in such a condition
that I am satisfied, unless by marvellous favour of God, we shall
not rear him. With family cares, I have those which follow the
keeping of 70 slaves, the most ignorant & troublesome children
in the world. I could give you details, in regard to their dependence, which would confound you. Recently, within a few
weeks, my dwelling house in Charleston was destroyed by fire,
with most of my furniture. No insurance. I have lost between
4 & 5000 dollars; besides the usufruct, or rent, ($500 per annum)
and I had just leased the house for a term of years. I have only
recently returned from gathering up the *debris,* the furniture,
crockery, &c. which had been saved. You perhaps hear what I

---

[109] Mary Lawson.

[110] Charlotte Thomson, daughter of William R. Thomson, was twice married: first, to Dr. Derrill Hart, Mrs. Simms' first cousin; and secondly, to
Col. Robert Howell Goodwyn (1798-1861). She herself was not a blood relation of Mrs. Simms.

[111] Hattie.

[112] Sydney Hammond.

am doing for Appleton's Cyclopædia [113] (Southern Subjects) and
can readily concieve, that I have been able to do very little else.
My health, especially that of my head, has been such as to make
me avoid all possible mental strain. I feel, from various symptoms,
that I have too frequently overtasked myself & this winter I have
undertaken no literary labour for which I was not pledged &
which I could possibly avoid. I am revising for the press my
occasional poetry of 20 years or more; making a final selection
from it, in a volume to correspond with the two already published.[114] This summer I shall endeavour to prepare a new romance, for which the material has been already collected & in
some measure digested.[115] After the 1 July, I shall remove to the
village of McPhersonville, Beaufort Dist. with my family, where
I propose to spend the summer.[116] My address, till that day will
be here. I contemplate (D. V.) a visit to N. Y. sometime in
Sept. when I hope to find you & find you well. I have no literary
news which can interest you. I enclose you a paragraph for your
brother George, penned editorially for the Charleston Mercury,
on his late biography of Taylor.[117] Please give it him with my
regards. Write me all the news, & especially report what you yourself are doing. I am conscious that this is a dull epistle, but if
you knew my condition of mind & body, you would be aware
that it is something for me to write so much, at this juncture,
even to a friend so much valued as yourself. I trust you see the
Lawson's frequently. They have suffered a grievous loss,[118] for
which their previous fortunate experience, had left them totally
unprepared. Lawson will tell you how I live, & how we live
generally in the South. We had no concealments from him; and
he had opportunities of seeing closely & variously. Poor fellow,
he seemed [119] to enjoy himself here, and it is sad to think that

---

[113] *The New American Cyclopædia.*

[114] The format of *Simms's Poems Areytos* is like that of *Poems Descriptive
Dramatic, Legendary and Contemplative.*

[115] Probably "Joscelyn," eventually completed in 1866 and published serially
in the *Old Guard* during 1867. See note 282, Nov. 4, 1866.

[116] As guests of the William Fullers. See letter to Miles of June 12.

[117] Simms reviews George Long Duyckinck's *The Life of Jeremy Taylor,
Bishop of Down, Connor, and Dromore* (New York: General Protestant Epis-
copal Sunday School Union and Church Book Society, 1860) in the Charleston
Mercury of May 23.

[118] The death of William Gilmore Simms Lawson. See letter to Lawson of
March 11, 1860.

[119] Simms wrote *seem.*

his tour of pleasure should be met at its close with so sad a loss. Let me hope, my dear D. that all are well with you.

Yours Ever truly

W. Gilmore Simms.

Evert A. Duyckinck, Esq.

982: To John Reuben Thompson

Woodlands, June 11. [1860][120]

My dear Thompson

I am in reciept of your 3d. No. F & F. of which you will find notice in Mercury some days hence.[121] Your first & second have not reached me — in other words, I have not recd. the 1 & 2 of the 2d. Vol. I enclose you a notice of you made in the Mercury some time ago.[122] You know I do all the literary things for that paper. Pray have 1 & 2 sent me, addressed to "Pocotaligo P. O." S. C. to which I go in a few days. In all probability I go to

---

[120] Dated by Simms' reference to Thompson's "3d. No. F & F." Thompson was editor of the *Southern Field and Fireside* from the issue of May 25, 1860, through the issue of Nov. 17, 1860.

[121] In his notice in the Charleston *Mercury* of June 23 Simms writes: "The third number shows Mr. Thompson, the newly installed Editor, to have addressed himself to his labors *con amore;* and we have several pleasant papers at his hands—graceful, full of vivacity and point, and usually suggestive and instructive. We note that the literary guild of Richmond, Va., gave him a splendid dinner at departure; graced with ode, and lyric, and wit, and sentiment; with *bon mot* and Burgundy. It is probable that the failure of one and two of the new issues of the *Field and Fireside* is the only reason why we do not get, in that paper, the particulars of the 'Reception Dinner' which welcomed Mr. Thompson to Augusta. We hear that it was very brilliant and quite a success. In Carolina, we rather ignore editors and authors. They quib, and sometimes curse—disappear in rage or risibles—and the literary guild gives no sign. There will be certain clubs, that very night, at supper, calling themselves literary; whose members will smile graciously on one another; kiss fraternally; and part lovingly;—abdomen duly distended with pleasantness and peace, peas and porridge;—the parties thus graciously reconciled to each other, to all the world, and to the rest of the Nations. Not a word said about the poor literary editor, just departed;—poet, critic, essayist, biographer, wit and humorist;—though he is ruined in the cause. No body gives him services of plate; goblets of silver, richly chased with laudatory inscription of donor and donee. 'He dies and makes no sign.' They do these things much more handsomely in Richmond and Augusta."

[122] In the Charleston *Mercury* of May 19 Simms reports that Thompson has accepted the editorship of the *Southern Field and Fireside* and says of him: "Mr. Thompson is a ripe scholar, a fine writer in prose and verse, a genial and honest critic, and a gentleman. We shall welcome him gladly to our precincts, and trust that he will make his home hereafter in our sister city of Augusta, where, we are assured, that his fine talents, his courteous manners, and graceful bearing, will make him as grateful an acquisition to its society as his pen will be to its *Field and Fireside*."

Chn. tomorrow.[123] Have the F. & F. sent me to Pocotaligo from which place I shall write you touching contributions.

Yours Ever

W. Gilmore Simms.

983: TO WILLIAM PORCHER MILES

Tuesday Night, June Something.

[June 12, 1860][124]

dear Miles.

Tomorrow I go to Charleston on my way to Macphersonville, where my family will spend the summer with our kinsman Dr. Fuller. My wife & all the little ones left me ten days ago and I have been here alone, drudging day & night to get things into a state of preparation. I shall probably remain just 3 days in Ch. simply to put my poor old wigwam & lot into the hands of the Broker. I am completely at sea, & almost rudderless. My youngest child, Sidney Hammond — named, spite of all omens, after my two dear little boys, has not been thriving, & we have had to consult Geddings.[125] I am in hopes, from what my wife writes me, that the disorder is natural & one easily remedied.[126] I rejoice, amidst my evils, to tell you that my son ranks No 1. at the Arsenal Academy, of Columbia, and is besides a well grown youth, now as tall as his father, brave, gentle, sensitive and generous. He is with his mother now, on vacation. This compensates, my friend, for loss of property; and it is my children's loss rather than mine. At Woodlands, I have a beautiful prospect both Corn and Cotton, but the rainy season has set in, & the struggle before

---

[123] Simms probably left for Charleston on June 13 (see following letter to Miles). He was in McPhersonville by June 23, when he addressed a letter to the Charleston *Mercury* entitled "Passages en Passant" and signed "Il Vagabondo" (published in the *Mercury* of June 27 and omitted from this edition of Simms' letters because of lack of space). In his letter Simms writes of railroads, crops, the weather, and politics.

[124] The year is established by Simms' reference to the burning of his Charleston house (see letter to Lawson of *c.* April 28 and following letters). In his letter to Thompson of June 11 (a Monday) Simms remarks that he will probably "go to Chn. tomorrow." Since he doubtless did not delay his trip for over a week, we have dated this letter June 12.

[125] Dr. Eli Geddings. See introductory sketch.

[126] Simms wrote *remedy*.

us is a hard one.[127] You are hardly planter enough to know the formidable character of Grass, as an Enemy. But if you will remember your Scripture Studies, you will remember that all flesh is grass. Now it is fair logic if all flesh be grass, to assume that all grass is flesh; and if you search farther that it is with the flesh that the devil has most power, you will readily see that the true conflict of the Planter, is with the flesh & the devil. That he does contend with them, after a fashion, is probably the true reason why agricultural life is supposed to be so much more virtuous than any other. Speaking more philosophically & less scripturally it must be so. The Citizen contends with man — this is the reason why he is sharper witted than the countryman. His daily attrition with rival cunning, is the secret of his mental activity & dexterity. The farmer or planter, on the contrary, rarely sees his fellow man, and his conflict is waged with God & the Seasons. Hence, when beaten out of the field, he has only to submit. He thus acquires resignation & so faith, and in truth most planters that I know, are Mussulman-like; in disastrous periods, they fold their arms, in stupid despair, & cry "Allah il Allah![")] They yield. They submit. Hence are they submissionists. This brings me to our present position & the Richmond Convention. You will probably see Jamison, who thinks of going on to Washington. I informed him duly of your desire that he should be a member. He is a good & true man, rather dogged, & not brilliant; but solid, and tenacious of his faith. I have informed him of my views & he concurs with them. The Richmond Convention, if not resolved on *felo de se*,[128] must make a solemn nomination as from the South — putting forward really good men — and whether defeated or not, something has been gained. But their chance is really as good as any, as, in all probability, the election will be carried into the House. The substantial gain to us will be found in the fact that the Cotton States work together. Very soon, the hangers on of the Dem. Party, will discover that the Party is not only dead — but stinks; they will find that nothing is to be gained by connection with a Northern wing which is impotent. Yet these people have had no idea, all their lives, but of

---

[127] The Charleston *Mercury* of June 12, 1860, prints a letter from a "Barnwell Correspondent" (doubtless Simms), dated June 9 and concerned with the crops. In it the writer speaks of the grass being rank and vigorous the next day after being hoed. But he says that his hopes are as "lively as herrings" and his "prospects looking up 'like potatoes.' "

[128] Simms failed to italicize *se*.

President making & office seeking. The Richmond Convention must not deny them their usual exercise. To meet, merely to wait on the Baltimore Convention would be an imbecility & absurdity. Yet they will probably do this, since Politicians have never the courage of the people. Our policy is to get the South working together.[129] My address will be "Pocotaligo P. O." Send your letters to me there. Your public documents, send to me at Midway. Next winter (D. V.) I trust to see you at Woodlands. You know Jamison lives alongside of me. My friend, Dr. Carroll came in as I got to the close of the last page, and took supper with me. We played *double dummy* till 12. at which hour I am closing up this scrawl. I shall not look over it, but trust that you will be able to decypher. I am still something of an invalid — my liver does not act spontaneously. I suppose, troubles of the brain. I have been sorely harrassed, perplexed & defeated. But God is over all. A poet has faith my friend. It cannot be always so; and you will come & see me, when there shall be full granary, & a bountiful board, and a glad smile, & a loving welcome — for are you not one of us, — a brother in our little wigwam.

Adios,

W. G. S.

---

[129] On May 3 the seceders from the National Democratic Convention (see note 69, April 9, 1860), who had met in convention in Charleston after their withdrawal, agreed to meet in convention in Richmond on June 11. When the Richmond Convention met, delegates from ten Southern states were in attendance and all except those from Florida and South Carolina were also accredited to the Baltimore Convention. South Carolina had held a State Democratic Convention in Columbia on May 30-31 and had elected a new delegation, which included Simms' friends Jamison and Aldrich. On June 12 the Richmond Convention, without taking any action, agreed to adjourn until June 26. The Baltimore Convention met on June 18, and on June 21 a secession of delegates took place, after which Stephen Arnold Douglas was nominated for president and Benjamin Fitzpatrick (1802-1869), of Alabama, for vice-president. The seceders met the same night and on June 23 nominated John Cabell Breckinridge (1821-1875), of Kentucky, for president and Joseph Lane (1801-1881), of Oregon, for vice-president. On June 25 (a day before schedule) the delegates from South Carolina and seven other states met in Richmond and ratified the choice of Breckinridge and Lane. Fitzpatrick declined the nomination and was replaced on Douglas' ticket by Herschel Vespasian Johnson (1812-1880), of Georgia. See Charles Edward Cauthen, *South Carolina Goes to War* (Chapel Hill: The University of North Carolina Press, 1950), pp. 17-25; Dwight L. Dumond, *The Secession Movement 1860-1861* (New York: The Macmillan Company, 1931), pp. 55-60, 76-91; George Fort Milton, *The Eve of Conflict* (Boston and New York: Houghton Mifflin Company, 1934), pp. 469-477; and the Charleston *Mercury* and *Courier* for the month of June, 1860.

984: To WILLIAM PORCHER MILES [130]

Pocotaligo, July 2, 1860.

I fancy, dear Miles, you will be in Chston by the time this can reach that city, & that you will soon be home. Yours just recieved. I have no doubt that B. & L.[131] will get the vote of all the South. States. It is enough that Douglas is *suspected* as a foe, — even his friends will be slow to urge him upon communities where he is thus suspected. He can carry *no* Southern State. The contest will substantially lie between Breck. & Lincoln,[132] and were it not for the ridiculous conservative, or, in fact, old line Whig & Federal parties, of the North with their ridiculous Bell & Everett ticket,[133] Breckinridge would secure the whole conservative vote of the North, now in real terror at what they did not believe before — Disunion. Thousands voted the Black Rep. ticket having no such fear. They will not vote it now; and could the wretched *gentlemen* of Boston &c. understand the game, they would see that success could be had by a frank union with the State Rights Dem. as men gather to put out a fire. But there is little hope of them. They will potter & potter, & piddle & piddle, about & over their small significations & sophistications, till there is nothing of them left. In fact, as the contest draws on they will be deserted by their rank & file, small as it must be any how. The common folks will turn to one or other of the controlling parties as the tide seems to set, or as their humours prompt. But, I do not attach any importance to the Presidential Election. Our great gain lies in the fact that we have brought the Cotton States to act together, independently, irrespectively of the North. *In hoc signo vinces!* The blockhead politicians of Virginia, too selfish to see the right, too timid to pursue it, refused us a conference.[134] The convention secures it. We are, in brief, bringing the conflict to the only issue which could possibly rouse our people, or make our politicians honest, — a purely sectional issue.

---

[130] Trent, p. 250, summarizes part of this letter.

[131] Breckinridge and Lane.

[132] The Republican Party nominated Abraham Lincoln for president on May 18.

[133] The Constitutional Union Party nominated John Bell (1797-1869), of Tennessee, for president and Edward Everett (1794-1865), of Massachusetts, for vice-president.

[134] For a detailed account of Christopher Gustavus Memminger's unsuccessful mission to Virginia in Jan.–Feb., 1860, to bring about a conference of Southern states, see Ollinger Crenshaw, "Christopher G. Memminger's Mission to Virginia, 1860," *Journal of Southern History,* VIII (Aug., 1942), 334-349.

The North has 180 votes, the South 120. No chance for ambition, in the South, while the sectional issues last. The only chance, for selfishness, is independence. There will be no motive, on the part of the North, to conciliate any votes of the South, so long as the issue is sectional, & so long as they are 180 to 120. In time, they will divide. Meanwhile, we may get our freedom. Were it our policy to remain in the confederacy, our game would be *'Divide et impera!'* And this by a clever statesmanship could be brought about. But, in the rule of the democracy, & all our parties are democratic, there is no wisdom except for the norm. There is no forethought, no prevision. — You ask what are we to do with a Black Republican President &c. You speak of the humiliation of such a thing. My friend, Humiliation is one of the processes which God employs for renovation. It is sometimes necessary to blister a man to remove his vicious humours — to sting & goad a people into self purification. Religion requires Humility as a first element of reform. Do not despair of Humanity — do not discard your faith in God. If we are base enough to succumb, no more need be said. You cannot preserve any liberty to a base people. But you must not allow your own impatience to move you to mistake Humanity or do wrong to man. You must not expect to reform a race, or recover rights which have been lost for years, in a day. You must not forget that the Union now for 80 years, has had a wonderful prestige. The country has grown to wondrous wealth under it. It is idle that you say to the ignorant man, we are still robbed. He answers, I am prosperous in spite of the robbery. The abstract truth is not for him to consider. He is of the earth compact. Believe me the process for setting him right is wonderfully simple. It consists in habit. We have done all for the present in bringing the Cotton States to act together, & in absorbing so many of the Slave States. Write me here, & hold me ever truly yours

W. Gilmore Simms.

P. S. I am sorry to be obliged to tell you that my poor little family is not at ease, — not at peace — and that we know not how soon we shall be called upon to surrender another member. Our youngest boy, Sydney Hammond, a year old, is in a bad way — a little better now — but in such condition that I have no hopes of ultimate recovery. It is possible that I shall pass through Charleston, to the plantation, in 10 days. If you are there, & I stay a day, I will try to see you. Let me hear from you. Keitt, they tell me withdraws.[135] It is perhaps better, for according to some of his best friends, he could not succeed. God willing, I propose to go to N. Y. towards the last of July. Whither do you go? Advise me, and we may probably find time to prowl in couples in N. Y. — Love to James, & best regards to the family.

Yours Ever

W. Gilmore Simms

985 : To WILLIAM PORCHER MILES [136]

Pocotaligo P. O. S. C. July 15 [1860][137]

Hon. W. Porcher Miles

My dear Miles.

I rejoice to find that your speech is so excellent, and has been so successful.[138] You will, I suppose, have no opposition to Congress; at all events during the term of Breckinridge; and the chances of his election, I hold to be good. The Abolitionists are such an odious tyranny, even among the Northern people themselves that I really believe nothing keeps them now in the ascendant but their own *momentum*. This will be greatly impaired by their rejection of their real leader, & the adoption of a substitute who has no prestige in the popular enthusiasm.[139] There can be no compromise between the *leaders* of the two democratic sections; but there will be a comparative fusion of the masses. I think it probable that in none of the Southern States will an openly avowed Douglas ticket be run — not even in Georgia.[140] They will disguise their support of him, if they give it, under the name of opposition, hoping thus to make a general haul of

---

[135] Keitt did not withdraw from the election for the United States House of Representatives, though in his letter to the Charleston *Mercury* of June 23 (see note 123, June 11, 1860) Simms writes that Keitt is "apparently indifferent" to the election.

[136] Part of this letter is quoted, with minor inaccuracies, by Trent, pp. 250-251.

[137] Dated by Simms' discussion of the forthcoming presidential election. See preceding and following letters.

[138] Miles' address delivered in Charleston on July 9 at the ratification of the proceedings of the Richmond Convention is printed (apparently in full) in the Charleston *Courier* of July 12.

[139] William Henry Seward was Lincoln's rival for the nomination.

[140] Herschel V. Johnson, the vice-presidential candidate on Douglas' ticket, was from Georgia.

WILLIAM PORCHER MILES
"O Friend! who satt'st beside me in the hour
When Death was at my hearth . . .
No brother more devoted! — More than friend,
Beloved evermore, — behold me thine!"
— From the dedicatory sonnet to *The Cassique of Kiawah*.
(From a wood engraving in *Harper's Weekly*, IV [February 11, 1860], 84)

DAVID FLAVEL JAMISON

"Jamison . . . is a man of firmness & character, great calm of temper, & thoroughly
true — intelligent also & familiar with affairs."

(From a wood engraving in *Harper's Weekly*, V [February 2, 1861], 78)

the discontents — Know Nothings, Old Line Whigs, our outsiders seeking seats inside. The truth is the general *instinct* of
the Southern people has become a conviction, that Douglas is
secretly if not openly their enemy. The suspicion generally fastened upon him now, to this effect, will not only drive the masses
from him, but will serve to make the leaders timid in bringing
him forward & urging his claims. I take for granted that Breckinridge will carry all the Southern States, not excepting Tennessee,
for I suspect that as the election approaches, every body will see
that the only effect of Bell's running will be to throw away the
vote of the State or States that may happen to support him.[141]
Nothing is so much dreaded by the American people as being
in a minority, and once apparent, or suspected, they run from
it as the rats from a falling house. Oregon & California, may, I
suppose, be assumed for Breckinridge also; if these things be
true, then it will need but small help from the North & West
to secure the election. Were it not that the Conservatives of New
England are such wretched politicians, hanging all the while between the extremes, too nice to support an out & out Dem. Chief,
and simply wasting their strength on what we may call their
political transcendentalism, I should have no doubt of Breck's
election. If at New York & elswhere, you should teach in all
quarters that if they really desire to save the Union, they must
vote for Breck. They can do nothing with Bell. They can't *ring*
him with the Cope & Sign of royalty. Their votes will simply
be wasted. They should throw him overboard & concentrate themselves upon Breck, as the only hope of giving them victory over
the B. Repubs, and of reassuring the Confederacy. — But, *mon
ami,* what say you now to the action of S. C? Without acknowledging it, she has adopted the policy of Hammond's Barnwell
Speech [142] — nay, gone further. Has given [143] up the threat of Disunion — has resolved to fight the enemy within the Union — nay,
has gone into the business of Prest. Making in order to do so,
& carrying out these purposes, has not only taken up nominees
who do not properly represent her opinions — whose skirts are
not clear of Squatterism — and she even endures internal improvements, in the States, at the cost of the Treasury, & to the
tune of countless millions! And farther, — I, too, have counselled

---

[141] John Bell, the presidential candidate of the Constitutional Union Party,
was from Tennessee.

[142] Delivered on Oct. 29, 1858. See note 288, Nov. 22, 1858.

[143] Simms wrote *giving*.

that she should go into President Making, at the *Richmond Convention,* as the only means of keeping the South together. I had a long & earnest talk with Jamison, begging him to see Rhett & urge strenuously upon him what I should say.[144] I told J. that while I was anxious like himself, for the formation of a Southern Confederacy, I saw clearly, not only that such a declaration would drive our people from us (at this time — the fruit is not ripe) but that we should really retard the final day of deliverance. I showed him that no party, no confederacy can be held together by abstract principles simply. The great body of politicians & people require some symbols which they couple with principles, and which they finally recieve as a substitute for it. These symbols are our candidates for office. It is absolutely impossible to teach our politicians the value of any sort of principles, separate from their candidates. Hence their willingness to take any platform, however self-stultifying — if you will give them the man for office. I counselled Jamison that whether we elect our candidates or not, the great point gained was to get the South acting together, in a *quasi* independent attitude. This is a great step forward. S. C. & Mississippi propose a conference to Virginia. Dreading her own shadow, & in the shadow of her leading politicians, Virginia refuses it, — with a feeling of terror at the thought.[145] And lo! here the bouleversement of the Ch. & Balt. Conventions, gives us the very conference & something more, which Virginia denied with terror. And the incipient measures have been taken, though with no such full approval on the surface, for the formation of a Congress of Southern States. You have to beguile our cowardly demagogues & democrats (— and all *old* parties naturally grow cowardly & dread every novelty of suggestion —) through President Making into Revolution. Do you not see that this helps forward events wonderfully? Do you not see that before we could relieve the South from the usual subsidization, by National Parties, of their chief men, that we have to sectionalize the country? Do you not see that Black Repubn. has done us this great good in the North. That Providence (Quos Deus vult perdere prius dementat) has made the brutal partisans of Douglas, absolutely insane, forcing the destruction of the only national (*soi disant*) party which remained? Do you not see that these things bring us to the condition, when

---

[144] Both David Flavel Jamison and Robert Barnwell Rhett were delegates to the Richmond Convention (see note 129, June 12, 1860).
[145] See note 134, July 2, 1860.

the South & North, standing asunder, & the former in a decided minority, in every trial of political strength, the latter has no longer motive to conciliate the former, becomes reckless, & in its very wantonness of strength forces final & practical issues upon us. The B. R's having no political sagacity, their fanatics being really in the ascendant, must, under the goading insistence of their conscious strength, tear every thing to tatters. No doubt they will split up & divide, in time, & new parties will form which will, one or other, affiliate with the South, or try to do so. But they will first have weaned us from them; they will have destroyed the prestige of Union; they will have taught us to hate if not to fear them; and their very attempts at affiliation then, will teach us their dependence upon us, and how much we may do for ourselves, if independent. We shall learn a thousand things of our own strength in the meanwhile, & our politicians will see that their chances for place & power, will be even more numerous in a Southern than in a confederacy of the whole as before. But the arguments are too numerous for a letter. South Carolina has entire unity in this last business for several reasons.

1. She needed to place herself in the ranks with her Southern Sisters, the moment they took any attitude which promised her redress of grievances, or an approach, however faint, to her long entertained desires.

2. She should do so, lest she wean them from her altogether. Already, her eagerness to be in the front rank made them jealous of a virtue which they had not the self-denial to exercise, and their pride resented a patriotism which their virtues could not emulate.

3. She has to enter into President Making, since a large proportion of her people, whether from policy or appetite, had determined to engage in [it], making her attitude equivocal, & opening the door wide to divisions among her own people. The moment she found that there were no longer men of authority within her limits sufficiently strong or numerous, or popular, to control the tendencies of her ambitious young men, she should have taken the cards out of their hands and played them herself, or through her own well selected representatives, instead of suffering a few small & selfish men, to play not only their own game but hers also.

4. Finding that she could not obtain redress in the Confederacy, yet resolved not to leave it *alone,* and feeling that she

would not influence her Sister States to any movement, by her reasoning, she [was] required to address to them the only motives which could operate upon them — appeal to their partisan habits & promise them like & better results from a Southern Confederacy, than they could hope from the old &c. — The Ch. Convention was a great good so far as it went. But the men who made the movement were not competent to use it. Never did men show themselves more feeble & indecisive. Had Yancey [146] been a wise man as well as an eloquent one — had he not been so much under the bonds & shackles of an old party harness, from which he was not bold enough to cut loose, — and what is said of him applies equally to Bayard,[147] & Meek,[148] and nearly all the rest — they could have done at that time, what now will require four years more of struggle & vexation. But the fruit will mature the better perhaps, & the throes of birth will be less difficult for a new organization. It is to be wished that Mr. Rhett could take no active part in the caucus. The Mercury will do wisely to forbear as much as possible, & so expend its thunders rather upon Lincoln than Douglas. There will be a double policy in this — not only in bringing about the fusion of the people of the two wings, but in showing them that Douglas is not the object of apprehension; thus leading to the dropping of the latter, while concentrating all the hostility of Conservatism as well as Democracy against Lincoln. But I must not bore you any longer with these crude ideas — of which, whatever of truth may be in them, has been made familiar to you no doubt long ago. — I write in order that you may get this letter before your departure for Washington. I make a general calculation to be in N. Y. about the last of July. I shall go by steamer & not take the Washtn. route.

If you hope to be in N. Y. (where I shall be required to linger some 6 weeks) you will hear of me from my publisher, Redfield, 34 Beekman St. I shall spend two or three weeks with a friend

---

[146] William Lowndes Yancey (1814-1863), Alabama lawyer, cotton planter, and newspaper editor, was a member of Congress during 1844-1846 and a delegate to the National Democratic conventions at Baltimore in 1848, at Cincinnati in 1856, and at Charleston in 1860. At the Charleston Convention Yancey was leader of the Southern extremists, and it was his delegation which first withdrew on April 30.

[147] James Asheton Bayard, Jr. (1799-1880), United States senator from Delaware (1851-1865, 1867-1869), was a delegate to the Charleston Convention.

[148] Alexander Beaufort Meek was one of the Alabama delegates to the Charleston Convention.

at Yonkers.[149] If I have money enough & time enough and the weather is not too hot, I may run to Newport & Boston, where I have not been for several years. But all this is very uncertain. My losses by storm, & fire, & failure of publishers &c. keep me terribly poor. I have a volume of my poetical miscellanies in press, corresponding in size with my other volumes, which I shall inscribe to your brother, James.[150] I wish you would say to him that, if he has leisure, & feels in the vein, I should be glad & grateful, if he would do for me what he once volunteered to do — make tables of contents of the two vols. of Poems already published.[151] Say to him that I would have written him, — would write him now, but that my letters would have been too lugubrious. I have had such sick children, such severe losses, such annoyances from want of means, & want of health (six weeks with diarrhœa) and want of peace & want of leisure, that, either I could not write at all, or my letters must have thrown over him a cloud much deeper than any of his own. I am glad to say, however, to you & him, that your godchild [152] is quite flourishing, is quite an interesting little creature, promises to be quite pretty, and will, I trust, prove creditable to all her relatives. My little boy [153] has improved, & there seems no immediate peril, but he is still under medicine, & does not seem to thrive. The case is a peculiar one, & I am apprehensive, argues some thing radically defective in the nervous system. All the rest are well & quite flourishing. My son, Gilmore, at the last examination, Arsenal Academy, Columbia, stood Number 1 in the Institution, is now a tall boy as tall as his father, will probably look down upon him in another year; rides a horse fearlessly, swims the Congaree to & fro, as a breakfast appetizer & as he says, to show the Up Country boys that none of their rivers can stand in his way, and is altogether a hopeful youth — modest, conscientious, clever — without being brilliant or otherwise remarkable. He indicates his desire to study Law. I prattle to *you,* my friend, of my children. I never look at them, or remember them, but I think of you! God bless you, & make you happy someday in your own. My wife joins with me in the sincere expression of this wish & prayer. It is time that, while attending the marriages of your

---

[149] James Lawson had recently removed to Yonkers.
[150] *Simms's Poems Areytos.*
[151] *Poems Dramatic Descriptive, Legendary and Contemplative.*
[152] Hattie.
[153] Sydney Hammond.

friends, you should not be heedless of your own. Pray think of this. *Your position in public will be found to second your aspirations; and as a S. Carolinian, you have an argument, which your individual claims, youth, good looks, manly carriage, honorable conduct, good acquisitions & fine talent, should & will admirably enforce. And your position will help to enforce the claims of these, and so I counsel you to seize the season, while you may,* — i.e. always assuming that you see the desirable object. One of the best secrets of maintaining the political position, is to enjoy such a private one, as to be independent of it! But once more, Àdios! I do not read this long rambling epistle after writing it, & doubt not, that you will find Priscian's head broken more than once in your progress of perusal. My compliments to Mr. Garnett & congratulations.[154] Should Mr. Mason remember me (I dined with himself and Butler some years ago) present me gratefully.[155] To all at home, my best regards especially James.

Yours faithfully

W. Gilmore Simms

P. S. Best remembrances to Trescott.[156] Remind him, if he has not sent me the two copies which he promised me, of Sumner's Speech,[157] to forward them to me here as soon as convenient. I should like to join you on the visit to him.

---

[154] Muscoe Russell Hunter Garnett (1821-1864), member of Congress from Virginia (1856-1861), married Mary Picton Stevens, of Hoboken, N. J., on July 26, 1860.

[155] James Murray Mason (1798-1871) was a member of Congress (1837-1839) and United States senator from Virginia (1847-1861). Simms probably dined with Mason and Andrew Pickens Butler in Feb., 1857, when he was lecturing in Washington.

[156] In June, 1860, William Henry Trescot was appointed assistant secretary of state.

[157] *The Barbarism of Slavery . . . Speech of Hon. Charles Sumner, on the Bill for the Admission of Kansas as a Free State. In the United States Senate, June 4, 1860* (Washington, D. C.: T. Hyatt, 1860).

986: To James Dunwoody Brownson De Bow

Pocotaligo, S. C. Augt. 1. [1860][158]

My dear Professor.

I was in Charleston a few days ago & hoped to meet you, but could hear nothing of your whereabouts.[159] You will have seen my notices in the Mercury of your Review,[160] and I beg to congratulate you on the spirit and ability of its management, and upon your various successes in your energetic progress in life. A friend to your early beginnings, aware of your abilities & worth, I have always been at pains, not only (as you know) to counsel you, but to apprise our public of your merits. It is not possible with me, just now, to write long letters. I am on the wing. I propose to depart for New York, on or about the 10th inst. If you will see me in N. Y. within the next six weeks, or visit me at the plantation, where you will find me after the 1st October, I shall be able to give you my advice as to many improvements in the Review, and in respect to politics & letters in general. I can't afford time to write of these things. My hands are too full of daily duties, for any asides.

I do not know that I could find time to contribute to your Review. I have already quite too much to do. But you hardly

---

[158] Dated by Simms' visit in Pocotaligo at this time and by his reference to his planned trip to New York City. See preceding letters.

[159] In a letter to the Charleston *Mercury* dated "MacPhersonville, Aug. 5," and signed "Il Vagabondo" (published in the *Mercury* of Aug. 8 and omitted from this edition of Simms' letters because of lack of space), Simms writes: "I have been vagabondizing . . . ; made a swift flight to the middle country; passing through your own venerable city into Barnwell. . . . My own plantation, on South Edisto, shows a sorry picture in regard to corn. One field, of twenty-three acres, which I left very beautiful six weeks ago, upon which I thought I could scarcely make less than twenty-five to thirty bushels per acre, will now hardly yield me five! This is the worst, but the old corn is generally bad enough, reducing the chances to, at best, merely half a crop . . . .
"I saw a good deal of General J. [Jamison] while in Barnwell; had from him a detailed account of the Richmond Convention, of which he was a member; with much interesting matter of that sort. . . . There was a public gathering at the Fish Pond Precinct (Barnwell), where Col. Aldrich addressed the people in a vigorous speech, in relation to the Convention chiefly. As there is no issue in this State in regard to the Presidential candidates—as there can be none,— so nobody speaks of the matter. . . . The fact is, that the *momentum* of Black Republicanism must force every body, not avowedly abolition, into resistance. It is such a despotism, even to itself, that it suffers no middle ground to any body. He who is not with it, is against it;—and, on the other hand, we of the South must learn the fact, that he who is not against it, to the very knife, is in some degree of its creed and against us;—certainly gives it help and comfort! There can be no compromise. . . .
"I got back to MacPhersonville on Saturday [July 30]. . . . "

[160] Simms' most recent notice of *De Bow's Review* is in the Charleston *Mercury* of June 29.

need me.[161] You have a goodly squad of contributors, and you might write more yourself. You could & should do more, especially in the Literary department, which is the least imposing of all your provinces. To tempt me to write for any periodical now, it needs that I should have a retaining fee of at least $100. But I repeat, if you will do your own duties, use your own talents, you will need no help of mine. You have reached that age, proved that degree of ability, shown that worth, acquired that position, that nothing is needed for your full success, but your own continued exertion in the way you have begun.

Very truly Yours.

W. Gilmore Simms.

Professor DeBow.

987: TO WILLIAM PORCHER MILES

New York, Aug. 31. [1860][162]

My dear Miles.

I have just heard from Charleston that you have been very ill at Newport, & just seen by the N. Y. papers, that you are recovered.[163] Had I heard sooner of your illness, I should, though bothered here by a volume in press [164] &c. have hurried to see you. My time north, as you may suppose, is very brief, for with family cares like mine, I dare not be long from home; but any how, did I think I could serve you nothing should keep me away. I am here with my poor friend Lawson. The loss of a fine boy kept him from seeing you at Washington & hurried him & his daughters away from that city, & now, while I am with him on the North River, he is threatened with the loss of another child, a lovely creature, of 18 months old — really a very pretty creature, who, teething, has been dragged to the verge of death. If she escapes it will be in spite of physic. But I doubt.[165] My friend

---

[161] Simms did not become a regular contributor to *De Bow's Review.*

[162] Dated by Simms' discussion of Lawson's troubles. See note 165, below.

[163] The Charleston *Mercury* of Aug. 27 reports the serious illness of Miles at Newport, R. I. We have not located the New York City newspaper in which Simms read of his recovery.

[164] *Simms's Poems Areytos.*

[165] Lawson and his daughters Mary and Kate left Washington because of the illness of his son William Gilmore Simms, who died on March 5 (see letter to Lawson of March 11 and following letters). Flora Lawson died on Sept. 19 (see letter to Lawson of Sept. 25).

Lawson bitterly regrets that he cannot say to you — "Come to me!" You would be at home with him; and he will be fond & proud, when the chance shall offer, to seek you out. — I am here, with a big volume of my fugitive poems going through the press. I shall get through it (D. V.) next week, and hurry home (again D. V.) on Saturday, the 8th. I dedicate this volume to your brother James, and at the request of many friends, I include my dedicatory sonnet addressed to you which seems to have found large favour.[166] If you write me, address to "Care of J. S. Redfield, Publisher, 34 Beekman St. N. Y." But I shall be off, if possible, tomorrow week (8th.) [.] I do not care to speak of politics. In good faith we ought to elect Breckinridge, if we can, & throw no disturbing forces into the canvas. After that, and, if we fail, the deluge, if you please. Keitt & Boyce, I am inclined to think, are premature, & are doing mischief.[167] Keitt wrote me a few days ago on the subject. We can do nothing for the South till the Dem. Party is dead, — till all National parties are defunct. Then! Not till then! But you have heard me to this effect, a thousand times before.

Yours, & God bless you

W. Gilmore Simms.

W. P. M.

988: To Benson John Lossing [168]

New York: Sept. 1. 1860.

My dear Mr. Lossing.

I do not know that you have ever seen the enclosed, which I published editorially in the Charleston Mercury. I trust that its

---

[166] "Sonnet.—To W. Porcher Miles," *Simms's Poems Areytos*, p. 364. The sonnet was first published as the dedication to *The Cassique of Kiawah*.

[167] Lawrence Massillon Keitt and William Waters Boyce, members of Congress from South Carolina, had publicly expressed the opinion that South Carolina should secede from the Union in the event of Lincoln's election (see the Charleston *Mercury* of July 20 and Aug. 3, 10, 21, and 22; the Charleston *Courier* of Aug. 20; and Cauthen, *South Carolina Goes to War*, p. 26). The *Mercury* of Aug. 3 quotes the New York *Tribune* (n. d.) on Keitt: "Mr. Keitt, speaking for his few friends, as well as in his own behalf, asserts with impressive solemnity that, in the event of a Republican victory, he means not only to take himself out of the Union—an absconding which would not break our hearts—but that he intends to take South Carolina with him—which we cannot think of *permitting*. . . . All thinking men will agree with us in the opinion, that the South could no more unite upon a scheme of secession, than a company of lunatics could conspire to break out of bedlam."

[168] See introductory sketch.

terms & tenor will not be displeasing to you.[169] I am sorry that you are absent from N. Y. I should have been very glad to see you. It is hardly probable now that I shall do so, for a long time, unless you should visit me in S. C. to which region (D. V.) I propose to return next week. A visit to Charleston might be of service to you in your proposed work on the War of 1812.[170] Several spirited little affairs took place on our coast during the war, & our people prepared for the assailants who menaced Baltimore. I remember the time, & the enthusiasm of all parties. If I can suggest you any clues, I shall be pleased to do so.

Yours, Very truly,

W. Gilmore Simms

B. J. Lossing, Esq.

989: To James Lawson

Pocotaligo S. C. 15 Sept. 1860.

My dear Lawson.

I got home safely. We made Charleston Light about 8 P.M. Monday; [171] but the tide not serving, we lay to till 2 A.M. when we ran up to the city. At 5 A.M. I routed up Augusta, had breakfast at 8 and at 9 I took the Savannah R. Road. At 1 P.M. I was again with my family. All well, except little Hattie who had some little remittent fever. We gave her some medicine & she is now better. Our baby [172] is grown fattish; but exhibits the same remarkable flexibility of limb & muscle which has so much puzzled us. We can do nothing. Only wait. My own & wife's anxiety is now for your sweet little Flory. We are all here warm sympathizers with you & yours; Dr. & Mrs. Fuller being as earnest as ourselves in hope that God may spare the little one to you. Unhappily, we can send you nothing better than our prayers. We are all compelled to feel & know that we are in God's hands only; that we perhaps put too little faith in God & nature, & too much in physic & physicians. Let me add you

---

[169] Simms reviews Lossing's *Mount Vernon and Its Associations* . . . (New York: W. A. Townsend and Company, 1859) in the Charleston *Mercury* of June 13, 1860.

[170] Lossing's *The Pictorial Field-Book of the War of 1812* . . . (New York: Harper & Brothers, 1868) was issued in twelve parts.

[171] Sept. 10. Simms arrived on the *Columbia* (see the Charleston *Mercury* of Sept. 11).

[172] Sydney Hammond.

must have some faith in yourselves, & not seek to devolve your responsibilities upon the art & science of others. Fathers & mothers must learn to study their children, and to prescribe (as they may do) innocently & securely, certainly without doing hurt; probably, by soothing & simple remedies removing all causes of disease & anxiety. We repeat we can only pray God in your behalf & the child's, & we trust in God that your next letter may advise us gratefully of its improvement and safety. She has endured so much, and has been so well sustained by nature; and gives such amazing proofs of vitality; that my hope is strong she will struggle through. If let alone to Nature; if the latter be assisted only; I have strong confidence in her ultimate recovery; especially as the cool change must be favorable to her. On leaving you, you will remember how hot it was. Scarcely had we got to Sandy Hook [173] when it became cool even to coldness, & an overcoat was comfortable; & every day, since I have been home, the weather has been far cooler than any day I have experienced in N. Y. I take for granted that you have experienced the same grateful changes. — I reached Macphersonville in season for a party given by Mrs. Fuller; in which the guests appeared in fancy costume. My poor little wife & self being the only common people present. The house was full; there was a fine supper; tableaux & charades were enacted & all went off merrily. Dr. Fuller appeared as an Italian Brigand or a Spanish Count — I don't know which, & there were, Brigands, Dons, Sailors, Backwoodsmen, &c in any profusion. Mary Lawson was out in some Italian rig, & Chevillette came as a Scottish lassie. The House was full & there was much merriment. Say to Jemmy, that Dr. Fuller sends him an affectionate welcome, & will try to give him pleasure should he visit him, & his wife is equally affectionate in her welcome. She desires that Mary or Kate, or both, will accompany him. I need not say that such also is our desire; but my wife insists that Mary, at least, shall come, as she has no doubt, from Mary's delicacy, that a quiet winter with us, will restore her strength fully, & make a woman of her, — not so fat, perhaps, as Christina, but plump enough to endure, easily, the severe pressure of a hot summer. We have not recently heard from Gilmore, but take for granted he is well, & too earnestly prosecuting his studies for any asides of letter writing. Augusta & baby I found in good condition. Say to Mary

---

[173] New Jersey.

that her purchases have given entire satisfaction. My wife says that in cap & dress, she could not have pleased herself better, & Mrs. Fuller is quite charmed with hers. The girls, M. L. & C. E. are also greatly gratified. Govan & Hattie are not eloquent in thanks about their toys, but the former with his omnibus & horses, keeps the house in a racket, and Hattie purrs over her tea set, untill she is absolutely growing sentimental. I would have written before, but I have been so completely under the weather, that I could not bring myself to the desk. I feel wretchedly jaded, & want a long sleep for recuperation. In a week I shall probably run up to the plantation. — I am now summoned to dinner. God be with you & yours, my dear Lawson, in love & mercy; and restore health & peace to your home, and soften your hearts, & make you all that you should be; and help you to all that is healthful, & needful.

Yours & theirs most lovingly

W. Gilmore Simms.

990: To Israel Keech Tefft

Pocotaligo S. C. Sep 17. [1860][174]

My dear old friend.

I am sorry that we did not meet in N. Y. More sorry that you have not improved in health. I sent a young friend to inquire for you at the Mechanics bank, but got no information — I regretted it much, as it was the desire of my friend, Mr. Lawson, to take you & Mama [175] up to his place at Yonkers for a day or two. Supposing that you have got home (as your letter, which followed me from N. Y. to this place & has this moment been recieved,) advises me that you would leave in 2 days, I now write to say that, if at home again, and prepared to recieve me for a day or two, I will not only visit you myself, but bring my wife with me. Let me hear at once. In the case of old fellows like ourselves, our chief satisfaction in life, lies in the intercourse of old friends who comprehend us, and between whom we expect a more genial intercourse in that future state to which we are both inevitably tending. We have nothing to make out of each other; I have no

---

[174] Dated by Simms' references to his recent visit to New York City (see preceding letters) and to the illness of Tefft (see letter to Ross of Sept. 26).

[175] Mrs. Tefft, the former Penelope Waite.

money to borrow; [176] and for the rest of my life, I suppose, sponge
like, I can suck out of the world sufficient sustenance for life,
and you are equally unselfish in requisition. All we require is
the sympathy of genial natures and pleasant intercourse while
we live. My wife joins with me in regards to Mama & yourself.
God bless & strengthen you.

Yours Ever

W. Gilmore Simms

991: To James Lawson

Pocotaligo, Sep. 25. [1860][177]

My dear friend.

We are just this moment in reciept of the melancholy tidings
you send us of the close of your sweet little one's career. God
is trying you, my friend; and through humility alone can you
find the necessary strength for support; & the means of consolation in thought & prayer & resignation. You have now been made
to suffer twice, as I have been made to suffer seven times. Be not
so stiffnecked as I have been — not so hard of heart — so worldly
— so selfish, thoughtless & presumptuous in prosperity, as to
need, like me, that this terrible scourging should be so frequently
repeated. You, like myself, had probably set your affections too
earnestly upon these dear little idols of the heart; and God is said
to be a jealous God, who will not permit idolatry, & especially
decrees that we shall not so wholly surrender our affections up
to earthly things. You have so much to be grateful for, that you
should speedily make your submission to God; not reproaching
him, with your groans and tears, for what he has taken; but
blessing him, with a cheerful heart & smiling confidence, for
the vast amount of happiness, through other dear ones, whom
he has left you. The spectacle of a firm man, suffering, but standing erect; submissive, but not base in suffering; calm though the
storm rages; capable of consoling other sufferers even while his
own heart is torn & lacerated; this is the spectacle that Gods and
men equally honour when they behold. The brave man struggling

---

[176] Tefft was connected with the Bank of the State of Georgia. He became
assistant clerk in 1822, teller *c.* 1830, and cashier in 1848. He held this last
position until his death in 1862.

[177] Dated by the death of Lawson's daughter Flora on Sept. 19 (see the
New York *Times* of Sept. 21, 1860).

manfully with the storms of fate, and nobly preserving his equilibrium throughout — never shrinking or shrieking, or sinking
back from the helm on which he has set his hand, his eye looking
the while firmly in the eye of the Danger which threatens — has,
in all periods, and by all people, been regarded as the truest of
Christian Heros. Not insensible — feeling keenly (for it is designed by Judgment that he should be made to feel) but still
calm, & firm, with a holy resignation which, acknowledging its
own weakness, throws itself upon the bosom of God, as the only
power which can save & shelter, and through this alliance, derives
the aliment of faith, which is the best secret of Human Strength.
Henceforth, may God be merciful to you and yours, my old
friend. You have in you elements of goodness, which, with due
faith in the wholesome & just purposes of God, will bring you
to peace & fortitude. Exercise your spiritual nature — your reason — your affections — the genial virtues of Charity, Tolerance,
Meekness & loving kindness, and do not suffer mere human successes & human vanities to beguile you from those better hopes
& feelings and faiths of Heart & Soul, through the due employment of which alone, can we recover the lost ones so precious to
your heart. Submit, my friend — entreat your dear ones all to
submission. Be cheerful. You have not lost a child. You have
gained an auxiliary angel who shall help in ministry to your
own hearts, and bring such good succour to you as shall make
your peace with Heaven sure. My wife will write. Meanwhile,
she joins with me, and so do Dr. & Mrs. Fuller, in the expression
of our warm & tearful sympathies. God be with you all.

> Yours
>
> W. Gilmore Simms

992: To ANDREW M. ROSS [178]

Andrew M. Ross, Esq.

Pocotaligo So. Caro.
Sep. 26. 1860.

dear Sir:

I rejoice to hear of the improved health of our friend Tefft.
I was chiefly anxious upon this subject. It would have given

---

[178] Ross, a native of Scotland, was in 1860 a bookkeeper in the Bank of the
State of Georgia, in 1867 assistant assessor of Internal Revenue, and in 1871
a real estate agent (see the Savannah directories for those years). His obituary

myself & wife great pleasure to have accorded him a couple of days; but it was just at this moment, that I could spare the time. Do apprise Tefft when he comes, that I shall be glad to see him and Mrs. T. at Woodlands, any time after the 15th. Oct. when (D. V.) we expect all to be reassembled at home. I go thither myself in a very few days, and henceforth, for the next six months at least, "Midway P. O." will be my address. Please accept my thanks, my dear Sir, for your kind & courteous letter.

Your obt Servt.

W. Gilmore Simms.

P. S. Please say to Tefft that, whenever the Bank can give him holiday, I trust he will take it, and run up to Woodlands, where we have pure air & water, hog, hominy & a noggin of whiskey.

993: To WILLIAM PORCHER MILES

Pocotaligo S. C. Sep. 28 [1860][179]

Hon. W. Porcher Miles.

God bless, & keep, & strengthen you, my friend, for yourself & your friends. We have all been in deep anxiety about you, & our prayer is for your safety. Get well as fast as you can, for at such a time as this, you are especially wanted. Your nomination here for Governor is quite a taking one,[180] & you may be tasked in the noblest manner, at the most exacting time, and we have every confidence in you, and you will prove equal to the crisis. Get well, come home as soon as you can, & nurse your strength. Your constituents will give you every respite. Nobody dare attempt to run against you. If ever man was firm in his position, you are. Let this assure you. It is a very precious conviction to your friends. Entre nous, I am satisfied that S. C. is ripe for withdrawal, even though she goes alone. We are preparing. Even Charleston is working actively, tho' perhaps secretly. Get well & come home, & if you still need respite for recruiting, come to me. You shall be at home with me. I have just heard from J. W. M. I cover to you the proof sheet of my dedication of my new vol.

in the Savannah *Morning News* of Feb. 7, 1876, gives his death on Feb. 6 at the age of sixty-six and says that for a number of years he was a member of the bench of the Inferior Court, Chatham County.

[179] Dated by Simms' reference to Miles' illness. See letter to Miles of Aug. 31.
[180] See the Charleston *Courier* of Sept. 24 and 26.

of Poems to him and the Preludium.[181] It is a vol. of 400 & more pages. I have been greatly distressed for you, my brother, but never dreamed of your danger — thought you were doing well — till on the eve of my leaving N. Y.[182] Once more, God bless you! Get strength & come home. You are wanted. You will be welcome, & to none more than to

Yours Ever faithfully,

W. Gilmore Simms.

994: To James Henry Hammond

Woodlands, Oct. 9. [1860][183]

I don't know how it is, my dear Hammond, that I forgot to say to you [184] that, when on the cars, going up, I met Townsend of John's Island, who expressed a great desire to see & even seek you, but expressed himself bashfully, — feared he might intrude, &c. I did not hesitate to say that I could answer for your welcome, but reiterating the expression of his desires, he still expressed his fears. The truth is, being an *older* man than either of us, there was a conflict between his *amour propre* & his desires. Of course, you well know that Townsend is somebody in our section. He is a man of good natural parts, not original, but of well balanced judgment & acquisitive mind and in his day has been an authority, & still is. His last pamphlet is one calculated to do good — shows more industry than power — but is prepared with no little art & dexterity. It is in progress of large circulation.[185] Now if you

---

[181] The dedication of *Simms's Poems Areytos* to James Warley Miles is on pp. iii-vi; "First Fruits.—A Prelude" (dated 1846) on pp. vii-xi.

[182] On Aug. 31 Simms had read of Miles' recovery (see letter to Miles of that date); on Sept. 8 (around the date Simms left New York City for Charleston) the Charleston *Mercury* reported that Miles' condition was "less favorable" than formerly.

[183] Hammond's reply to this letter is dated Oct. 23, 1860. A number of Simms' letters written to Hammond between his letter of Sept. 18, 1859, and this letter of Oct. 9 are missing from the Hammond Papers, Library of Congress, which contains the original of the above-mentioned letter from Hammond, as well as the originals of letters from Hammond to Simms dated Oct. 4, Oct. 24, Nov. 23, Dec. 19, and Dec. 22, 1859; Jan. 14, April 3, April 8, May 11, July 10, July 29, and Sept. 23, 1860.

[184] Simms had just returned from a three days' visit with Hammond at Redcliffe. See letter to Lawson of Oct. 16.

[185] John Townsend, of St. John's Island, Colleton District, though an opponent of nullification in 1832 and of separate secession in 1851, was the author of two pamphlets distributed by The 1860 Association, organized in Sept., 1860, by a group of Charlestonians to spread secession propaganda. Tract No. 1 of The 1860 Association pamphlets, by Townsend, is entitled *The South Alone,*

will please, you might pen him a note, stating my report of his desire to seek & see you, and that you act accordingly, & that it will be grateful to you to recieve him at any time should he propose to visit your neighbourhood. But this as you choose. I only meant to possess you of the mere fact of his warmly expressed desire, and leave you to decide, without a word of exhortation. Send me that *second* quarto vol.[186] I do not find it here — only four vols of the Globe.[187] I look for my family up on Friday next,[188] and have no small deal of preparation to make. Have nothing yet found or fixed in my library, and have been content to write, as you see, on a rough & rumpled sheet. Got a letter from Keitt yesterday, from St. Matthews,[189] but without postmark, & he does not tell me where to address him, yet eagerly seeks an answer. Wants my opinion of his last letter, and of things in general & politics in particular. I am to Lecture at Cheraw about the close of this month, & shall visit him and wife *en passant.*[190] Best respects to Mrs. H. & the Ladies. Do not forget to save me some of the Egyptian Cotton Seed. I wish to try it in some peculiar land.

Ádios.

Yours &c

W. Gilmore Simms

995: To JAMES LAWSON

Woodlands S. C. Oct. 16. [1860][191]

We are all, my dear Lawson, once more at home at Woodlands, though as yet we have been unable to put things to rights. My

---

Should Govern the South. And African Slavery Should Be Controlled by Those Only, Who Are Friendly to It (Charleston, S. C.: Printed by Evans & Cogswell, 1860). There were at least four editions published during 1860. Tract No. 4, also by Townsend, is entitled *The Doom of Slavery in the Union: Its Safety Out of It* (Charleston, S. C.: Printed by Evans & Cogswell, 1860). The first of these pamphlets, reviewed by Simms in the Charleston *Mercury* of Oct. 20, 1860, is doubtless the one to which he here refers. For an account of Townsend's pamphlets and their probable influence, see Cauthen, *South Carolina Goes to War,* pp. 34-38.

[186] Evidently this volume was discussed during Simms' visit to Redcliffe.

[187] The *Congressional Globe.*

[188] Oct. 12.

[189] Keitt's home was in St. Matthews. In 1860 St. Matthews was in Orangeburg District; it is now in Calhoun County.

[190] Simms delivered two lectures in Cheraw. See letter to Lawson of Oct. 24.

[191] Dated by Simms' reference to the forthcoming presidential election. See preceding and following letters.

wife & children left Macphersonville on Friday last,[192] and came right through Charleston, just stopping long enough to see Augusta. The reason for this rapid transit lay in the fact that some of that annoying disease called "Dengue" or Broke Bone Fever, still lingered in that city.[193] All with me are well. The baby [194] seems quite restored. Augusta is well also, her baby [195] teething, & so, liable to occasional febrile annoyance. Fuller, wife & child [196] were left well, and Gilmore writes in good spirits and is still head boy in school.[197] His monthly reports show him in all departments closely approximating the highest attainable marks; as, for example, in algebra he may reach 60, — he reaches 58 &c. We are already longing for the time when we shall welcome Jimmy & himself together at Woodlands. I left Macphersonville a week before my wife, stayed two days at the plantation, then ran up for three days on a visit to Senator Hammond, on the Savannah river near Augusta.[198] Jamison & Dr. Carroll both well. Our family has just returned from an evening visit to the former. Say to Addison Richards that his old friend, Mr. Jaques & family (though I have not seen them) have passed a healthy summer and are doing well.[199] Gen. Jamison begs his best remembrances to you and the girls,[200] & speaks of you with affectionate sympathy. Last night, while my wife & self were playing backgammon, a knock at the door (9 P.M.) announced a visitor, who soon presented himself in the person of Hon. Mr. Keitt our Member of Congress, who has just been making a

---

[192] Oct. 12.

[193] The Charleston *Courier* of Oct. 16 reports that "the break-bone fever is generally prevalent in Memphis, and has prevailed, indeed, throughout the South and West to an extent never equalled previously, although in most cases in a light and tractable form, when promptly attended to."

[194] Sydney Hammond.

[195] Chevillette.

[196] Guerard.

[197] The Arsenal Academy.

[198] If Simms is accurate in saying he left McPhersonville a week before his wife, he left on Oct. 5, stayed at Woodlands on Oct. 5 and 6, spent Oct. 7, 8, and 9 at Redcliffe, and was back at Woodlands on the evening of Oct. 9 (see letter to Hammond of that date).

[199] Daniel Harrison Jacques (1825-1877), a native of New Jersey, was for a time assistant editor of the *Southern Literary Gazette* (see note 43, March 10, 1851). He returned to the North in 1851, but in late 1859 or early 1860 he again moved to South Carolina and purchased a farm in Barnwell District (see note 317, Dec. 5, 1860). During the Confederate War he lived in the North, but in the late 1860's he came back to South Carolina, where he edited the *Rural Carolinian* (1869-1876), to which Simms was a contributor.

[200] Mary and Kate, whom Jamison had met during their visit to Woodlands. See Simms' letters of Feb. and March, 1860.

speech at Barnwell C. H.[201] He spent the night with us. On the 24th. I leave home for Cheraw for the residence of Hon. I. D. Wilson, at Society Hill — a fine Gentleman now in nomination for the Gubernatorial Chair, who will probably be elected.[202] Next night, I am to lecture at Cheraw.[203] Returning, I shall spend a day with Mr. & Mrs. Keitt in Marlborough, near the Great Pedee, & then home.[204] In reply to Mr. Wilson, of Poughkeepsie, I have invited his sister Margaret, as a Governess, offering her $200 with board, &c. for her services during 10 months in the year — vacation including August & Septr.[205] I look to hear from & possibly see her, every day. I have referred the brother to you touching the region and the sort of life we lead. My crop has suffered greatly from the drought, but I shall probably make enough of corn, to feed 70 negroes, and corn & forage enough, blades, hay &c. for 20 horses & mules, to say nothing of 100 head of cattle, and 200 head of hogs. These small items never find their way into the census. My Cotton Crop disappoints me. Instead of 125 bales as I calculated, I shall make only about 70, which will barely suffice to keep me above water. But I have faith in God, who has never yet suffered me to drown. Our elections are just over, and our State has elected almost the whole Legislature, secession men. If Lincoln is elected, a convention will be immediately called, and South Carolina will secede from the Confederacy, even though she goes alone.[206] But she will not go alone. She will be followed by Alabama, Mississippi, Georgia, Florida Louisiana, & more slowly by North Carolina, Virginia, Tennessee, Kentucky, &c. You may rest assured that all this is going to happen just as I tell you. There is but one feeling at the South now, except among the Yankee agents & shopkeepers and they will need to keep shut mouths. Get in all the money (cash) you can, & keep it safe. Look quietly & cautiously to your investments. And when your agrarians begin to work, as red republi-

---

[201] We have been unable to locate an account of this speech.

[202] Isaac DeLiesseline Wilson (1810-1889), a planter of Society Hill, in Darlington District, represented Darlington in the South Carolina House and Senate for a number of terms. He was a delegate from Darlington to the Secession Convention.

[203] Simms delivered two lectures in Cheraw. See letter to Lawson of Oct. 24.

[204] Mrs. Keitt's family lived in Marlborough District.

[205] Margaret Wilson was the daughter of William Wilson (see note 231, Nov. 28, 1854) and the sister of James Grant Wilson (see introductory sketch). She served as governess for the Simms children from around Oct. 30, 1860, until Aug. 20, 1861 (see letters to Lawson of Oct. 24, 1860, and Aug. 20, 1861).

[206] See note 225, Nov. 5, 1860.

cans & sans culottes, not less than Black republicans, then bring
your flock off to me and live for a season on hog & hominy. Keep
all this to yourself, for tho' matter of opinion only, I would not
have it divulged. Meanwhile communicate to Redfield my desire
to sell my Copyrights of all the books he has in hand. I do not
wish the money, only bond & mortgage, *to you* & in your name,
of Copyrights & plates. I will sell all for $10,000 and he may pay
at his leisure, only paying interest. I will write him also. More
anon. My love to Lide & the girls & a kiss for all. God bless &
keep & preserve you, my old friend, and let the cup of bitterness
pass by us.

Yours Ever

W. Gilmore Simms

996: To James Lawson

Woodlands, Oct. 20. 1860

My dear Lawson.

A letter from Redfield apprises me that my affairs, between
Mess'rs Panton & Widdleton in New York have become more
complicated than ever.[207] Take counsel with Redfield, & weigh
all his suggestions. The balance to my credit on 1st. January,
was over $600. Redfield can give you particulars. I drew last
year for about $300 — & Redfield instructed me to draw on
Widdleton. I did not draw on Panton, and with any connection
between him & Widdleton, I have nothing to do. I authorize you
to proceed, under the Power of Attorney I gave you, as if the
Property were your own; and, if you say so, I will give you a
conveyance of the Copyrights. If you desire legal aid & council,
I wish you to drop a note to Mr. Joseph H. Dukes, of Charleston,

---

[207] We have not located this particular letter from Redfield. Another letter
from him to Simms dated Oct. 18, 1860 (forwarded to Lawson on Oct. 24 and
preserved with Simms' letters to Lawson in the South Caroliniana Library),
sheds some light on Redfield's troubles at this time. Redfield's publishing house
had failed and had been taken over by William J. Widdleton. Henry Panton,
who had been connected with Redfield's firm for a number of years, had acted
as receiver for the firm and may still have been acting as such at this time.
In his letter Redfield accuses both Panton and Widdleton of being "rogues"
and of lying to Lawson about the number of copies of Simms' books printed
and on hand, on which Lawson "should demand a Copyright of 15 pr. ct."
He advises Simms to "instruct Lawson positively to have nothing to do with
them ever." Widdleton, however, did become Simms' publisher. He remained
in the publishing business until his death in 1882.

and an old friend of mine, but now a practising Lawyer of New York.[208] I will write to him to call & see you. Tell Redfield to get duplicate certificates of Copyright, & endorse them, legally, *to you.* You will then be to the public, the virtual owner, & can act without my intervention. Love to all. God bless & keep you my friend.

Yours

W. Gilmore Simms

P. S. I cover to you a letter, unsealed, to Mr. Dukes, which, if you approve, you will seal & forward to his New York address. He is a gentleman, of fine ability, a young man of excellent Charleston family, and a batchelor. He too has written poetry, but like you — has — perhaps wisely — abandoned it for more lucrative employments. I trust you will like, & make a friend of him.

W. G. S.

P. S. I wrote you only a few days ago. — I am looking daily to hear of Miss Wilson, or from her brother.[209] All well. ——— I have addressed to your care a Letter to Redfield.

997: To James Lawson

[October 21, 1860] [210]

My dear Lawson.

I wrote you yesterday on recieving Redfield's letter. I did not think to say that my interests require that if Mess'rs Panton & Widdleton account to me fairly, I cannot refuse to make terms with them, however willing I may be to help Redfield. If they will settle up for the amount due me on the first of January, and now, up to the present date, I owe it to them to continue the same arrangements that I had with Redfield. Let all the parties understand this. If they refuse this settlement, then I require that they

---

[208] Dukes is last listed in the Charleston directories in 1859. In 1860 the New York City *Directory* lists him as a lawyer at 233 Broadway with a residence at Division Avenue, Brooklyn. He is listed in the New York City directories until 1874, though his addresses change during the years. The *Directory* for 1875-1876 lists Marie, the widow of Joseph Dukes. He had contributed "The Charter Oak" to *The Charleston Book* (Charleston: Samuel Hart, Sen., 1845), pp. 298-300.

[209] Margaret and James Grant Wilson. See preceding letter.

[210] Dated by Simms' reference to his letter to Lawson of Oct. 20.

should yield up all use of my publications, except on terms for the future of 15 per cent. I have been kept out of my money now for two years, by their cursed agents & Recievers. As recievers they had no right to keep my per centage. If they do not comply, then you must enjoin them. If they yield compliance make terms with them as before. This seems to me reasonable & right. But how absurd to be selling my books, yet refusing to account, because of lawsuits among themselves. — Act in the matter precisely as if the interest were your own. Show my letters to Mr. Redfield, Mr. Panton, Mr. Widdleton, or any body who has any thing to do with the business. I mean my letters on this subject, & not those which concern our private relations.

Yours Ever truly.

W. Gilmore Simms

998: To James Lawson

Woodlands, 22d. Oct. 1860.

My dear Lawson.

Yours just recieved. You have acted well, and as a man of discretion. I do not wish to take advantage of any man, or even of any woman. If Mr. Widdleton will comply with your requisitions, and the balance due me is paid up forthwith, I authorize you to contract with him on the same terms as with Redfield. I am sorry for Redfield, but fear that nothing can be done for him. I enclose you the letters of Redfield and of Henry Panton.[211] *They must be kept to yourself, but it is necessary that you should use the information they contain.* Send them back to me, *when you have possessed yourself of the contents.* I give you full power to act according to your own discretion. *If you could so manage it as to become the proprietor of my Copyrights,* paying me only whatever interest they yield, I would send you a title for all. If the South secedes, *as it will* in the event of Lincoln's election, I am liable to be pirated. If you were proprietor this could not be done. I would give you titles, acknowledging value recieved, and you by secret articles, could assure me of all the interest derivable from the sales. Consult my friend, Dukes, on the subject. It will be well to get a transfer from Redfield of the three Copy-

---

[211] We have not located either of these letters.

rights, not yet assigned to me, viz: the History of South Carolina, the Cassique of Kiawah, and the vol of Poems.[212] You must
not let him know that I have called for them, but call for them
in your own name, as my attorney. Let the assignment be formally made, before Mr. Walker as a N. P.[213]— You are right in
saying that you cannot be a partisan. But beware of wheedling on
either side. Mr. Panton, as Reciever, for a certain term, must
pay up my percentage; and so must Mr. Widdleton. You see
what Redfield positively states of the printing of new editions.
If Widdleton will deal squarely with you, settle where he owes,
& when Panton shall settle, then it is not possible for you to refuse the former terms to W. But if you can sell to him, for
$10,000. taking for your security, the Mortgage of Copyrights
& plates, then do so, & rest satisfied with the Interest on that
amount. But once more, I leave all in your hands & at your discretion. Secure what you can! I do not see that poor Redfield,
whom I sincerely pity, can do any thing for himself or for me. —
I congratulate you on being home once more. You are wise. Invest nothing in fancy. The South — all the Cotton States first,
& finally all, will secede, as soon as Lincoln is elected. *This is
sure!* I am on the wing, in another day, for Cheraw, where I
am to Lecture.[214] Miss Wilson comes to me by Steamer, on
Saturday next, 27th. Love to all. In haste.

Yours Ever

W. G. S.

J. L.

999: To JAMES LAWSON

Woodlands Oct. 24. [1860] [215]

dear Lawson.

I am just about to take the Cars for Cheraw, where I am to
deliver two Lectures.[216] I write simply to acknowledge reciept

---

[212] *Simms's Poems Areytos.*

[213] Lawson and William Augustus Walker had recently formed the firm of
Lawson and Walker. The New York City directories for this and later years
list them as adjusters at 62 Wall Street. Walker, whose residence was on
Long Island, died on May 16, 1888, at the age of 86. He is the only notary
public by the name of Walker listed in the New York City *Directory* for 1860.

[214] See following letter.

[215] Dated by Simms' discussion of his affairs with Redfield, Widdleton, and
Panton. See preceding and following letters.

[216] In his letter to Lawson of Oct. 16 Simms says he is to lecture on Oct. 25.
We have been unable to discover the date of his second lecture (perhaps Oct.
26) or the subjects of either.

of yours of 19th. with the enclosed certificate. How long & often I have been thus cheated, we may conjecture, but can never know. Here is a barefaced attempt to defraud me of more than $200. by a just operation, & without any contract existing. I leave every thing in your hands. If you can favour Redfield, do so. Whatever his faults may be, & he has evidently been very weak, still I fully believe he purposes to be honest. I cover to you his last letter just recieved. You will note that he speaks of backers.[217] Now, if these backers be good men & true, they can easily protect themselves & him. They will perhaps be willing to buy my Copyrights on the terms proposed — a great bargain, as you will note, when you find that the printing of small editions of only four works yields me more than $200. But I leave every thing in your hands, — use your discretion, just as if the whole matter were your own. We are all well. I shall be back, home again (D. V.) on Monday, & we expect Miss Wilson on Tuesday.[218] Love to all.

Àdios.

W. Gilmore Simms

P. S. One word touching Redfield's Letter, which I enclose, & which you will return to me. He mistakes if he thought while in New York, that I suspected the honesty of either of the parties he names. I confess I was mortified & astonished at Mr. Panton's rejection of my claim for the per centage. But I was willing to ascribe this to some legal difficulty, which, however, I could not well comprehend myself. In respect to Mr. Widdleton, I had no reason to question his honesty *as a tradesman,* and in fact, had no reason to question it as it concerned myself. *But I was satisfied that Widdleton was using Redfield,* & would use him up to the last moment, when, having squeezed the orange, he would throw away the skin. When Redfield told me of anticipated relations with W., I asked him, 'Are you sure of this man; for, were I in your case I should not be.' He (R.) expressed the utmost confidence, & I said no more, but doubted

---

[217] In his letter of Oct. 18 (cited note 207, Oct. 20, 1860) Redfield writes: "Don't let this discourage you from going on with a new book—for I shall now soon be in a position—with some first class house, where I shall be a great deal better situated to look after your interests, than I should have been with this rogue [Panton]."

[218] Tuesday was Oct. 30. Simms had written to Lawson on Oct. 24 that he expected Margaret Wilson on Oct. 27.

none the less. As for honesty among tradesmen, the less we say about it the better. It may be that Redfield has erred & I think it probable; but I believe him to be quite as honest as any of the publishers I have ever had the fate to meet. I have lost, as I know, more than $20,000 by publishers; and if Redfield can resume business, on terms to satisfy you of his securities, then I should rather you should employ him. But, as you please. If his friends will buy my rights & R. has a few others, they can build him up securely & keep the lien on his assets. I will answer his letter with but a word.

Yours &c.

W. G. S.

1000: To James Lawson

[c. November 4, 1860][219]

My dear Lawson

This letter has just reached me. It contains matter which you ought to know. But do not let Redfield know that I forward you this as so much memoranda for your study. I believe Redfield is right about the policy, or impolicy rather, of demanding the price of Copyright merely on printing the Books. He is right, also, touching the impossibility [220] of sale of the Copyrights now. And upon reflection, the Northern people will hardly venture to pirate me, since the Southern can do the same business to greater profit; and when we separate, which Lincoln's election makes inevitable,[221] the two sections must have international copyright.

Yours truly

W. Gilmore Simms

J. L.

P. S. I enclose you a Letter to Redfield, which read, seal & deliver.[222] It is in answer to his within & to others of previous date. As for his Black Republicanism, I do not care a straw for it. Most of the publishers are of his kidney, if they have a political kidney

---

[219] This letter is written on the third and fourth sheets of a letter from Redfield to Simms dated Nov. 1, 1860.

[220] Simms wrote *impossibly.*

[221] Simms, of course, is anticipating Lincoln's election, as he does again in his letter to Lawson of Nov. 5.

[222] Simms neglected to enclose this letter, though he eventually enclosed it in his letter of Nov. 6.

at all. I would not give a fig for the political principles of any of them; and by forcing us into Independence, the Black Republicans are doing us, undesignedly, a most essential service.

1001: To WILLIAM PORCHER MILES

Woodlands, S. C. Nov. 4. [1860][223]

I write, my dear Miles, simply to say how greatly I rejoice that you are once more safely at home, & according to all accounts in an improving state. Yours has been conspicuous, in my own estimate of my afflictions this season. When I left N. Y. the Newspapers reported you rapidly convalescing. But for that I should have run to see you at Newport. Will a quiet retreat like mine be of any help to you now? If so, come, & be at peace for a few weeks. Do not excite or exert yourself. Here my wife & self will nurse you, & all of our children, as if you were one of our own. You will & must believe this. Come, if it is right & safe. But economize yourself in politics. Do not allow yourself to be excited. Our only hope now is in the secession of S. C. *per se!* But you must wait till your individual self is equal to work, & then you will be wanted. Nobody now has a higher reputation for executive work. I was greatly vexed that our friend Bob Gourdin was defeated.[224]

God bless & strengthen you.

Yours Ever

W. G. S.

1002: To JAMES LAWSON

[November 5, 1860][225]

My dear Lawson.

I reenclose you the a/c sent me. Submit it to Redfield. I hold it to be something like an impertinence. At all events, a very great

---

[223] Dated by Simms' discussion of Miles' health (see preceding and following letters to Miles). The Charleston *Mercury* of Nov. 3 reports that, though still feeble, Miles was well enough to take a drive and that he had visited the office of the *Mercury*.

[224] Robert Newman Gourdin (see note 134, Dec. 17, 1853) was defeated for the South Carolina House of Representatives. See the Charleston *Mercury* of Sept. 13 (where he is nominated) and of Oct. 11 (where his defeat is reported).

[225] Dated by Simms' remark that "our Legislature meets this day to elect Electors and . . . *will probably continue in session in order to be prepared for Lincoln's election.*" News of Lincoln's election reached South Carolina on Nov. 7, and by Nov. 10 both houses of the legislature had agreed to a bill (not,

absurdity. I am credited with sales from May 1. to Sept. 22. I
am to be credited with all sales made by Panton since he was made
reciever, and should be credited with all copies on hand, at the
time of selling the stock. My credits, the Bal. due me, as reported
by Redfield on the 1st. Jany last, was over $600. Then, there is
no a/c from January to May. I did not draw on Panton at all.
I drew on Redfield & by his instructions drew on Widdleton,
against the amount due me. See Redfield. Redfield is mistaken in
saying that he told me of Cunningham. I never heard a word of
Cunningham from *him*. But Panton, the last day but one that I
was in N. Y. told me something of that affair; and I inferred
that Cunningham was some new Printer whom R. had employed
to do the work, especially as R. told me that Savage, who had
been his former printer, had left Printing for some other busi-
ness.²²⁶ But, as I employed Redfield, & knew but him in the
business, it did not concern me whom he employed or where he
got his resources. In respect to R's republicanism you surprise me.
I have never heard a syllable from him to lead me to suppose
that he cared a straw for the parties. As for McElrath, taught to
believe that he was unfortunate & under the weather, I consented
to visit him—to accept his invitation through Redfield,²²⁷ which
I should never have done had I supposed him still prosperous, or
still, in any way connected with the Republicans. I still think that
R. is simply indifferent — possibly now, reckless. As for opinion,
in politics, I doubt if he has any. Duyckinck is in the same
category. In politics they are both creatures of habit & association,
& without opinion. In regard to my own affairs, I shall see to
sending you a conveyance of the property, and you will write me a
letter of guaranty, so that if any thing should happen to either
of us, our heirs may arrange affairs, after the rule prescribed by
their fathers. Require of Redfield, the legal assignment of my
Copyrights, as (& give him this reason for prompt action) in his
name, he would be called upon by his creditors to assign them
among his assets. Of course, his assignment to other parties would

---

however, formally ratified until Nov. 13) calling for a state convention to meet
on Dec. 17. This Convention of the People of the State of South Carolina
became known as the Secession Convention.

²²⁶ The New York City *Directory* for 1860 lists three Cunninghams who
were printers: James, Patrick, and Robert. Since Robert, at 191 Water Street,
is the only one of these listed in other years, he is doubtless the printer here
mentioned. For Charles C. Savage, see note 206, Oct. 9, 1855.

²²⁷ During his visit to New York City in Aug.–Sept., 1860. See letter to
Duyckinck of March 15, 1861.

be invalid, since he can show no consideration paid for them, and his taking them out is only a Publisher's habit. But, before you do any thing, get the property legally transferred. In respect to the political future, our excitement grows rather than diminishes. Our Legislature meets this day to elect Electors. *They will probably continue in session in order to be prepared for Lincoln's election.* The moment he is known to be elected, they will call a convention of the people. The Legislature is almost wholly for secession & they are fresh from the people. I have been recently on a journey of 200 miles in our State, on its Northern border.[228] The excitement is great & concentrated. The minute men are forming & arming in all directions.[229] South Carolina is putting her house in order; and my impression is that she will secede *alone,* leaving to the other States to follow. She will await no overt act. Will not wait Mr. Lincoln's inauguration. She will be out of the Union by the 1st. Jany. And I, too, counsel this very policy. So all my friends. Leading politicians of the other States counsel it, & say that the rest will follow. One word more. See to your stocks. *My opinion is that Rail Road stocks in the old states will be the best in all bad conjunctures.* You can readily see why. And they will be bought cheap during a crisis. In respect to Jimmy's visit, there is nothing to fear.[230] My passport would make him safe here, anywhere. There is nothing to trouble him here, in my hands; and you can judge for yourself of the probabilities of Black Republicanism troubling us! I do not fear it! At all events, they will not have the power, till the 4th. March, to do any thing. So do not be alarmed with regard to Jimmy. Tell him that Gilmore's reports [231] are still excellent. He remains first, & is working hard & doing well. Gilmore has already arranged with his friends, to do all he can, towards showing Jimmy our little world favorably. He has designed several excursions for him. Send Mary out too, or Kate, or both. Miss Wilson is with us; an excellent girl apparently; and our children, mine & Jamison's are all in her

---

[228] Simms lectured in Cheraw on Oct. 25 and probably on Oct. 26. See letter to Lawson of Oct. 24.

[229] According to Cauthen (*South Carolina Goes to War,* pp. 46-47), the Minute Men was a state-wide organization "whose declared purpose was to defend the state should secession lead to war." Though its members did some serious drilling, its chief significance was its "contribution to secession excitement through public demonstrations."

[230] James Lawson, Jr., arrived at Woodlands on Dec. 5 (see Simms' second letter to Lawson of that date). On or shortly after Jan. 1, 1861, he left Woodlands for Savannah (see letter to Tefft of that date).

[231] At the Arsenal Academy.

hands. Love to Lyde & the girls from myself & mine. My wife goes to town today for a week.

Yours Ever

W. Gilmore Simms

1003: To JAMES LAWSON

Nov. 6. 1860

Woodlands.

dear Lawson.

I wrote you a day ago, but again omitted the letter of Redfield, which I had proposed to send to him before.[232] He mistakes, if he supposed that I considered either Panton or Widdleton *rogues;* even if I thought so, I never said so, to him or any body else. But, somehow, I suspected that Widdleton was using Redfield, & would use him, up to the last moment; then whistle him off; and when R. told me that he had an understanding with W., I somehow doubted if it would be found binding when the matter was to be closed; & having a kindly feeling for R. whom I believe to be honest but unfortunate — whom I hold to be the tool of more subtle persons, I gave him a hint to this effect & this only. I discovered, briefly, that the understanding between W & Panton was of too close a nature to be quite consistent with Redfield's interests. I am prepared to believe that R. lacks energy, and thus it is that these smart young Politicians, McElrath, Widdleton, Panton, Geo. Duyckinck, *et id om. genus,* have been using him. As for *opinion,* based upon any just knowledge of the subject, or any interest in politics as an essential to society, they know no more than my dog, Banquo. But, tho' lacking energy, I really think that R. means to be honest if New York will let him. I should be sorry to think that he should be found wanting to me; since I have always dealt most liberally & most confidingly with him. Could he now, as he intimates, unite himself with some good business man, I should prefer to have him for my publisher. I need say nothing to you touching Publishers in general. I have tried many, and — found most of them guilty — or worthless. Make what arrangements you please. It is impossible for me to follow up all the rabbit tracks of the gentry, which already distract me, & in which, as you well say, my interests are sacrificed. I

---

[232] The letter which Simms planned to enclose in his letter of *c.* Nov. 4.

put the whole matter in your hands. Tell Redfield this; show him the Power of Attorney; tell him moreover, that you are resolved to become yourself the Purchaser of my Copyrights rather than see me suffer; & point out to him the ruinous effect upon my interests of being for three years in the hands of Recievers — no publications at all — no pushing energies in my behalf, & copies of my books not even kept in the market, to meet demands. You have here good & justifying cause for taking my publications out of the hands of all of them. You will, of course, keep to yourself the enclosure, & the confidential parts of this letter. I have written merely to put you in possession of clues.— Don't fear to send Jimmy. All's right with me. Love to all, and God be with you.

W. G. S.

1004: To James Lawson

[c. November 10, 1860][233]

My dear Lawson.

I send you a Newspaper containing our Governor's Message. Read it carefully.[234] There are no conservatives in our State, such as you describe. All who speak, speak voluntarily. There are not a doz. not in favour of Secession. The South States are not discontented with us. Their chief men entreat us to go on. Those who speak as you think, are not willing that we should do any thing. But all this is too late. Five States will secede before January. The momentum is irresistible. The event is inevitable. There will be no bloodshed unless the North *invades* us! Jimmy is quite safe. I will write the letter to him under cover to Wm. Roach. The Copyright for the Poems [235] is not yet (probably) taken out. Take it out in *your* name. In haste, but truly & lovingly Yrs

W. G. S.

P. S. I wrote to Redfield to get out an edition of the new vol. of Poems. Russell & Jones agreed to take 1 or 200 copies, their

---

[233] This letter was written after Nov. 7, when Lincoln's election was announced in the South Carolina newspapers. Simms' remarks about his copyrights in this letter and in that of Nov. 13 indicate that this one was written earlier.

[234] Governor William Henry Gist's message to the South Carolina legislature, delivered on Nov. 5, is printed in the various Charleston newspapers on Nov. 6. Gist (1807-1874), a native of Charleston who removed to Union District when he was a child, was governor of South Carolina during 1858-1860.

[235] *Simms's Poems Areytos.*

imprint to be used. This is the very time for that vol. in the South, a large portion of the material, being patriotic. He, Redfield, wrote me that now was not the time for publication. In other words he was not in a condition to publish. But there would be a sale of the small edition I proposed, say 250 copies: — as I stated R & J. had alone agreed for 100, or 200., and I wished 50 myself, to give away, resolving that the Publisher should not exercise the right exclusively of giving copies, & meaning to give them to such only as were worthy, & willing to read poetry. What a commentary upon the way I am treated by all these men that after the book is stereotyped, there is no publisher among them. — Redfield furnished me the account. I got none from Zebley, had no correspondence with him, & never knew him in the business.[236] I will look up Redfield's statement, which, on the 1 Jany last, made a balance in my favor of some 650 dollars.

P. S. It is barely possible that I shall be chosen to the Convention. I am in nomination, but am no candidate & shall be sorry to be chosen, as my domestic affairs require all my time, & the Convention may be in session a year or more. It will have on its hands the construction of a new government & negotiations with European States. Disabuse your mind of the notion that there is any party, or body of men, in S. C. not willing for secession. There are not a dozen men. The fact is that it is a complete landsturm, a general rising of the people, and the politicians are far behind them. And every So. State will follow S. C. The people will not suffer the politicians any longer. They are now neither to be deluded, nor coaxed, nor cheated nor cajoled. In this district of Barnwell, which can send 3000 men into the field there is not one who is not a secessionist & preparing his arms. The old men of 60 are forming companies. Never was such enthusiasm seen, from seaboard to the mountains. Of course, we shall try & be decent & dignified. As for our Sister States,— see what our Gov. says of their Counsel & Cooperation. No! Cooperation is a mere dream. The time for consultation has passed. That of Action has come. And you may rest assured of two things, not only that S. C. will secede, & be followed by other States, but that never again can the South be possibly united with New England — probably never with any no-slavery State! As for their con-

---

[236] John F. Zebley, a native of Delaware, was a paper dealer on Spruce Street, New York City. He is first listed in the New York City directories in 1851. He died on Jan. 9, 1881, at the age of 65.

servatism, it is vapour. It is notorious that no faith can be put in their most solemn pledges, or compacts, or compromises, when they attain a majority. They are insolent in power, as they are mean in conciliation. Suppliants today, they are insolents tomorrow, and every concession is construed into weakness & imbecility & is made the pretext for new aggression. The worst is yet to come. The Banks of N. Y. have virtually suspended; the Banks of S. C. redeem in specie. Cotton is bringing us specie daily. We are pacific, mean to be so, but mean to be prepared for all events. If there is bloodshed, it will flow from the effort to prevent secession. Meanwhile, dear old friend, may God's Peace be with you & yours & me & mine.

Yours Ever

W. Gilmore Simms.

My overseer killed a fine fat buck in our swamp two days ago. Today we had the choicest, tenderest haunch of venison. I wished for you. Would we not have washed the burgher down in usquebaugh? [237]

Send me three [238] Barrels of good sound apples, and charge to my account. In my next I will send you a copy of a bill of sundries bought in your city, so as to introduce you to lower prices, even in your own precinct, than you are wont to pay. *Nous Verrons.*

1005: To WILLIAM PORCHER MILES [239]

Woodlands 12 Nov. 1860.

My dear Miles.

I rejoice to hear of your improvement, but beware of too much exertion, and avoid the provocation to too much excitement. This is difficult to forbear at this moment. We are all alive here with eagerness and hope. We shall carry the South, I trust, through what the Germans call the Landsturm. It will be a popular rush, as I always predicted, as soon as the National Party should have perished, the momentum given to the people being such as no popular leader or politician would venture to head, or heading, which would be sure to run over him. We must now see that the

---

[237] This paragraph is written at the top of the first page of the MS.

[238] Simms wrote *one. three.* He was unable to strike through *one* because he had written this paragraph across the text of the first page of his letter.

[239] Part of this letter is printed in Trent, pp. 252-253.

Convention election sends the true men. I could wish that a ticket should be run every where, and that in your section you should have on it Wms. Middleton, Dan. Heyward, one of the Rutledges, a Gadsden, if one can be found of the right lineage & of any decent ability, and in brief as many of the old revolutionary leaders (names at least) as can be gathered together.[240] By the way, the Executive now, of S. C. will be quite another sort of thing from what it has been.[241] It will be, for a time at least, the Presidency of a new Republic, and the Convention itself will have much more work to do besides that of seceding. They will need to organize for a new system, and their session may be prolonged months — a year — possibly more. They cannot secede without putting the State in sure, official position. There will [be] need to digest a thousand matters of detail with regard to the union with other seceding States, arrangements with foreign States, in regard to arming, vessels of war being quite as necessary to be thought of perhaps, as regiments on land — at least to protect us against any mere show of blockade. The Constitution must be revised. A Bill of Rights should precede it, declaring the general principles — future secession of States should be specially provided for, even as we should provide for future admissions, and a most important inquiry should be whether the representation of States should not be equal in the House as in the Senate. Think over this point. The great principle of safety is the protection of minorities, or feeble States. By this rule too we can keep down any overgrowth in numbers of representation. It will have its limits & check all usurpative tendencies on the part of overgrown States. Think of it. There are many things besides, not only of detail, but general principle, which should be prescribed & laid down.— I enclose you a few small pieces from my forthcoming volume of poems, which if they please you & your brother, James, you can have handed into the Mercury for publication. In another packet I cover to you, for the same purpose, sundry other articles of a different class, from the same volume. These are of patriotic character, & may serve to help the present sentiment. I could wish you to ask at the Mercury office if they have not recieved several patriotic lyrics from me of late. These sent them 2 or 3 weeks ago have not yet

[240] Williams Middleton (1809-1883), the son of Henry Middleton, governor of South Carolina during 1810-1812, was a member of the Secession Convention; Daniel Heyward (1810-1888) was not. There was no member by the name of Gadsden or Rutledge.

[241] Miles had been nominated for governor. See letter to him of Sept. 28.

appeared, and should appear now if ever. Do not fatigue yourself with these matters but if you happen to ride in the neighbourhood of the office, put them into your pocket, and deliver them with this query.[242]— I am very busy, very much troubled with my publisher's involvements & with much house & plantation work on hand, I am in no condition for letters or study. My crop was a failure this year from drought. I make just half & hardly that, of what I expected to make. But I trust I shall always have hog & hominy enough for a friend. Be not desponding about your own affairs. We are both straitened. I am poorer than I was at 21. Yet, God's over all. I believe in God. I have a confident faith that he who has kept us both above the waters — though possibly only with our noses out — will not now suffer us to sink. My wife sends her best regards to yourself, Mother, Aunt & James.[243] Try & persuade the latter to give me a week at Christmas. Our children are all well. Your little Goddaughter [244] flourishes, promises to be the prettiest of my girls, & has a good physique. God bless you & yours, my friend.

Lovingly Yours

W. G. S.

1006: To James Lawson

Woodlands, Nov. 13. [1860][245]

My dear Lawson.

A patient is in a paroxysm, the blood determining to his brain, & he on the eve of apoplexy, and you propose to give him water gruel. The ailments of the Confederacy, are not to be healed by any of the remedies you propose. The conservative or Union men of the North are powerless for good. They have been pretending,

---

[242] The following poems published in the Charleston *Mercury* during this period carry Simms' signature or initials: "The Liberty Tree" (Sept. 21), "Ye Sons of Carolina" (Sept. 26), "Battle Hymn" (Oct. 10), "Oh! What If the Prospect Be Clouded?" (Nov. 8), and "Ballad of the South" (Nov. 21). Many unsigned poems published in the *Mercury* during this period are probably also by Simms.

[243] Miles' mother was Sarah Bond Warley Miles (1791-1864), daughter of Felix and Anne Warley and widow of James Saunders Miles. The aunt here mentioned is almost certainly her sister, Anne Eliza Warley (1799-1862). One tombstone marks the graves of both sisters in St. Philip's Churchyard, Charleston.

[244] Hattie.

[245] Dated by Simms' discussion of the impending secession of South Carolina from the Union.

after a fashion, for 20 years. They are discomfited — nay crushed. We shall save & lift them up only by showing to their enemies that they were the true men, & predicted all the present evils. Were we to do as you counsel, there would be no resistance to Black Republicanism. It would be rampant — it would run riot over the land. It would crush your conservatives & crush us. No! The only way to bring them to their senses, is to separate from them. You will have seen that we are in a fair way to do so. We (S. C.) will secede. So will Geo. and so all the Cotton States — in succession. I have been applied to to go to the Convention. I have declined being a Candidate — but will serve if they elect me, which they seem very anxious to do. If elected, I shall aim at but a single object — to separate from a Confederacy in which we are otherwise doom'd to destruction. We cannot wait — must not wait — will not wait one moment longer than we can help. There are overt acts enough, & the election of Lincoln is conclusive. You cannot perform what you promise. If the South submits, the Black Republicans are confirmed in their power, their predictions, their supremacy. Your politicians are childish who think otherwise. You must see, for yourself, that what they have said (the Republicans) will all be verified by our submission. In brief, my dear, good, old friend, they are under the doom of judicial blindness. Having ears they shall not hear — having eyes they shall not see. 'Quos Deus vult perdere, prius dementat.' They have forgotten, if they ever knew, the sources of their prosperity — have waxed fat like Jeshurun & kicked — are resolved to kill the golden goose which has laid them all their eggs, if we are geese enough to let them. We will not let them. Assure yourself of this that on the 17th. Decr. the State of S. C. secedes from the Union. What States will follow, I know not; but if we are firm, all will follow, of the Cotton States, and in process of time, all of the South. It cannot be otherwise. Our people now, have the momentum given them, & the old politicians are powerless. We are here as one man.

As for Jimmy, he shall be safe with me. My letter will be his security. And it will do him good. Will open his eyes, & he will learn from a brief sojourn in the South, that New York is a recipient & distributor of our prosperity — our agent — who has forgotten her principal in her agency, & the prosperity which it has produced. I ought not to say N. Y. City. The merchants there know well enow where their bread is buttered. Send Jimmy on. I will take care of him, & make him safe. As for my Copyrights & Interests in N. Y. let them go to the devil, so that my people get their rights! You have an ample power of attorney. Use your best judgment in respect to it. The South is bound together by the cohesive bond of African Slavery! What binds the North together? Pennsylvania, New York & New England, are all deadly rivals, in the same occupations, for the trade of the South. We have them all at our mercy. We will discriminate between foreign & domestic bottoms. We will throw open our ports, as free ports, to Europe, & shut them, under heavy duties, against the North. We cannot trust a people who have sought to destroy us. Be sure, my dear old fellow, we know our rights, our securities, our advantages, and are not to be compromised any more. Gilmore is still at the head of his school.[246] He has made arrangements with some young associates for the reception of Jimmy, and they calculate on a nice time of it. But Gilmore is full of fight, & has the pluck to take any enemy by the beard. He is rather a proverb among his associates for his promptness to do battle. I heard but yesterday from Hon. Mr. Aldrich, that he & all are bursting with enthusiasm.[247] They long for nothing so much as a fight with the Black Republicans! Send your Webbs, & Raymonds, & Greeley's & Sewards,[248] & you will see some scalping. Love to Lyde & the girls.

God bless you.

W. G. S.

1007: To WILLIAM SIMS REYNOLDS [249]

Woodlands, Nov. 14. [1860][250]

My dear Dr.

Believe me you have my sincere sympathies. Nobody better knows than myself how to feel such bereavements as yours. The

---

[246] The Arsenal Academy.

[247] We have not located this letter from Alfred Proctor Aldrich, at this time a member of the South Carolina House of Representatives.

[248] For James Watson Webb, see note 41, Feb. 26, 1860; for William Henry Seward, see note 216, July 16, 1858. Henry Jarvis Raymond (1820-1869) was editor of the New York *Times,* which supported Lincoln, but which was not abolitionist until after the Confederate War had begun. Horace Greeley (1811-1872) was editor of the New York *Tribune* at this time.

[249] See introductory sketch of the Reynolds brothers.

[250] Reynolds' reply to this letter is dated April 7, 1861 (copy in Reynolds' handwriting in the possession of his granddaughter, Miss Julia Walpole, Birmingham, Ala.).

woman who has lain for long years in our bosom, leaves a terrible vacuum when taken away.[251] But you have sources of solace. You have a lovely family. Nurse them. Fling yourself upon your knees to the good God, for faith in him is the only security, as it is the great solace. If I travel in your direction, I shall surely come to see you.

— As a relief, go more into the world. In especial, take part in the Convention movement. See that you have good men & true, voted for in your section. We have no escape from the necessity. We cannot fly. We must fight, if need be. The fate that threatens us here, threatens all other sections. Give yourself to your people. Overlook the crudeness, the rudeness, in the recognition of the bald, bare, naked humanity; and by identifying yourself with your people, add new links to the chain which binds you to posterity. Come & see me, & bring your girls.[252] Whenever you so incline, write me a few days before, and my carriage shall await you at Midway. My fare is poor, but *mon ami* (and we are boys no longer) your welcome shall be that of a Prince — more — a friend!

Yours truly —

W. Gilmore Simms

1008: To James Lawson

Woodlands. Midway P. O.

S. C. Nov. 20. 1860.

dear Lawson.

I send you the epitaph on the American Confederacy just published in Charleston.[253] The palliatives will all come too late. S. C., Geo, Alabama, Florida & probably Mississippi, will all have seceded before the last of January, and three of them, perhaps, before Christmas. The popular momentum grows every hour, and at such a pace, that Unionism is dead and Conservative Politicians dare not open their mouths. It is here a perfect landsturm, and every days report shows the excitement to be rising higher &

---

[251] We have been unable to discover the exact date on which Julia Peeples Reynolds died. She was the daughter of the Rev. Darling Peeples, of Barnwell.

[252] Reynolds had three daughters: Julia Peeples, who married Dr. Francis Georgiana, who married Ephraim Mikell Carroll and, after his death, William White.

[253] Probably a pamphlet.

spreading broader, and there is no heading the torrent. The Cotton States cannot now arrest themselves if they would. The game is up, and all my predictions to you last winter will be realized to the uttermost syllable! And yet, it is surprising how steady & calm is every thing. Our committees of Safety & Vigilance [254] regulate the most turbulent passions and keep down the most imperious tempers with the courage & decision of a firm will, terribly resolved, yet regulating every movement by law. There are no mobs, and gatherings of thousands, deeply excited, will hold in their breathing for hours, while the orator declaims. They shout! They pause! They hear! Again they shout, as with one soul — then arrest themselves as with a single will, till the new spell word makes them shout again. There is no squabble, no buz, no quarrelling, or rowdyism, — all is patient fervour — a passion regulated by Law, in its wildest rages — the law of a determined will, assured of its objects. Twenty thousand men are now armed in S. C. and there are squads of Minute Men in every precinct. In half an hour 60 volunteered at our little village of Bamberg five miles above me. At another precinct 4 miles west of me, 59 volunteered in the same space of time. And S. C. alone can bring 60,000 troops into the field. Thousands in all the other States from Virginia to Texas have volunteered to support S. C. in the event of war. In Georgia & Alabama, the same excitement prevails. But there will be no war. A war would destroy the whole confederacy of the North, & make that of the South supreme. Give me your ship, my friend, or send her to Charleston. [255] We

---

[254] The purpose of the Vigilance Associations and the Committees of Safety "was to insure the safety of the community against slave disorders fomented by abolitionist agents who were supposedly active in the state," and in some cases "the Vigilance Committee arrested and examined the suspects and carried them before a small Committee of Safety for punishment" (see Cauthen, *South Carolina Goes to War,* pp. 45-46). A Barnwell "correspondent" of the Charleston *Mercury* of Nov. 21 reports that Committees of Safety and Vigilance were organized in Midway Precinct on Oct. 30 and lists Simms, Jamison, and Charles R. Carroll as among the members of the Committee of Safety. The "correspondent" also reports that at this meeting Simms "made a speech of half an hour [a "call for Minute Men"]. Reviewed the necessities of the country; showed what were the duties of the citizen in a juncture like the present; showed what our ancestors had done in all perilous times, from the first colonial period down to the Revolution, and drew from this historical experience the proper example which we had to follow. His speech had the proper effect, and within twenty minutes after it was over, no less than fifty-five gallant young fellows enrolled themselves under the Palmetto banner, ready to serve the country at a moment's warning. In less than twenty minutes they had elected their officers."

[255] Lawson owned a share in the *Edwin Forrest.* See letter to him of Feb. 19, 1861.

will make your fortune. We will discriminate between Northern
& Southern bottoms. We will make our ports free to all Europe.
We will levy our taxes by the poll, or by an export duty on Cotton; and the exports of the South are 270,000,000. We shall have
the revenues hereafter & the carrying trade, and your ships will
require to hail from our ports in order to keep the seas! Send on
your ship to Wm. Roach, as my agent. Come yourself. Settle
here alongside of me, as a Cotton Planter; you shall take trout
from our river weighing 10 lbs.; sturgeon; rock fish, cat fish,
perch, bream. You shall have a cypress canoe, and Mary & Kate
shall be Ladies of the Lake; and we shall eat strawberries daily
in the spring, and melons from June till October, and Green Peas
at Christmas, and you shall revel here in Roses while the benighted heathen of the North, are shivering from the snows, and
shuddering under inadequate blankets. Come. I will get or give
you a farm, and you shall set my verses to music, and your girls
& mine will carol them together under the light & smile of the
sweetest moon that ever carried love, on a silver shaft, into the
deepest avenues of a tender heart. At all events be sure to send
Jimmy as soon as you & he please, & you can spare him. I will
take care of him; and he shall see what a free world is ours, and
how much better calculated to make a man of him than yours! —
A few words about Redfield. *He* did not tell me that he had employed Cunningham to publish my Cassique & History. *Panton*
did, the last day but one that I was in N. Y. But Redfield did tell
me that Savage had given up the printing business, & that the
last volumes had come from another press; and, somehow, I
associated the one fact with the other, & regarded Cunningham as
rather the printer than any thing else. At all events, I took for
granted, up to the last moment, that my works, in the plates,
were under the same general ownership. It does not matter which
owned the plates, or published, since neither Panton nor Cunningham were prepared to pay me. Redfield is right in one thing. I
agreed to stereotype the vol. of Poems [256] myself, the money to be
deducted from the amount due me, which, according to Redfields
a/c was over 600 dollars on the first of January last. Let him
give you his a/c up to date; charge the plates against it; deliver
them to you, & see then what the balance is. The book ought to
be published now. Between these men, I lose every thing. Here

---

[256] *Simms's Poems Areytos.*

you have the facts. You are right in being no Partisan. Use your own judgment. Whoever you contract with, should buy the plates.

Yours lovingly & Love to all

W. G. S.

P. S. Let Redfield transfer the Copyrights, deliver the plates, balance accounts, and let him understand that you insist upon these conditions before you will do anything. If then, he is prepared to resume business, & can procure the whole body of the plates, let him proceed. I do not see how we can do better. As it is clear that Widdleton *decieved* you, it is hardly possible to trust him. If it occurs to you to talk with Duyckinck on the subject, let him know this — i.e. when you are prepared to break with Widdleton. But I doubt all publishers!!!

1009: To JOHN JACOB BOCKEE [257]

[November 20, 1860]

Never was a people so thoroughly aroused and resolute before. . . . South Carolina will secede first, Alabama and Mississippi, Georgia and Florida, in order next, and before the 1st of February, all these States will be out of the Confederacy. South Carolina will be out before Christmas. Her legislature was unanimous, and every member of the convention nominated is for secession unreservedly. South Carolina alone can bring 60,000 men into the field, sixty Palmetto regiments; and we have already 50,000 volunteers from other States, should any attempt be made at coercion. Such an attempt will help us and force all the other Southern States to take their places by our side. . . . The Union had survived its uses, had got to be a mere shop [?] [258] of faction, fraud, and peculation, was no longer a guardian of the feeble, was a bold, impudent aggressor upon the rights of others, an usurper, waxing fat and kicking in its lustihood, and needed to be taken down and driven to short commons.

---

[257] We have not located the original of this letter, printed in part by Trent, pp. 253-254. Trent's date is certainly correct (see letter to Lawson of the same date).

[258] The brackets and question mark are Trent's.

1010: To Simon Gratz [259]

Woodlands, *Midway* P.O.
S. C. Nov. 20. 1860.

dear Sir.

Your letter incorrectly addressed to me at Charleston, was late in reaching my country residence, and arrived during one of my absences from home. Since my return domestic and public duties have equally combined to absorb all my time, to say nothing of cares, troubles & physical ailments. These will account to you for my delay to answer your letter. I published in the Southern Quarterly Review (which you will probably find in some of your Philadelphia Libraries) sometime between the years 1850 & 1854 a long paper on the Baron de Kalb, giving at the same time a number of his Letters.[260] If you will examine this article and tell me which of his Letters you would prefer to print, I will look it up among my papers. But unless you desire the letter itself for lithographing its contents are accessible to you in the Review. I have none of Pulaski, though I think my friend Tefft of Savannah (I. K.) has one or more in his very extensive collection. The article in the Review will tell you pretty much all I could contribute touching De Kalb. I should certainly be pleased to afford you all possible assistance, but that my health is even now suffering from a press of labours from which I cannot well escape, and from anxieties which I find it difficult to combat. I can certainly encounter no additional toils, even though they go not beyond the suggestions which I might make, in regard to your labour, were not the task of letter writing itself, a burden of serious weight in the present condition of my mind & body. I have never withheld myself, in respect to applications such as yours, & I greatly regret that I should now be compelled to show myself in any way costive, or reticent when the subject of inquiry, like yours, contemplates our American Biography & History. I must not forget to say that Mr. Smith of the Maryland Historical

---

[259] Gratz (1838-1925), a graduate of the University of Pennsylvania in 1855, was a member of the Philadelphia bar. At various times he was a member of the Pennsylvania legislature, assistant city solicitor of Philadelphia, and a member of the board of education. He is best remembered for his work with the public schools of Philadelphia and for his autograph collection of between two hundred thousand and three hundred thousand items, now in the Historical Society of Pennsylvania.

[260] "The Baron DeKalb." See note 87, April 5, 1852.

Society published a Lecture on De Kalb,[261] but you will find some
things in my article which were at the time of its publication, new
to the American reader.

> Very respectfully
> Your obt. servt.
> W. Gilmore Simms.

Simon Gratz, Esq.

1011: To James Lawson

[c. November 21, 1860][262]

My dear Lawson

I cover as above a dft on sight upon Appleton & Co, on account, for $150, which I will be glad if you will collect at once,
& hold the money in readiness for my moment order.[263] I may
tell you by tomorrow's mail what I wish done with it. Love to
wife & daughters. We shall look for Jimmy by the 1st. proxo.

> Yours faithfully
>
> W. Gilmore Simms

1012: To James Lawson

[c. November 22, 1860][264]

dear Lawson.

I have drawn upon you for the $150, not for firearms or
powder, but for the ordinary creature comforts. In respect to the
Whiskey to which you refer, I beg to say, that I fancy that which
you sent me to be a far better article than that which I had at
your House, though I well remember you said it was the same.
I doubt. I wish (forgive the mercenary hint) that I had another
demijohn. I have been drinking of this, with the help of com-
petently judging friends, who all approved of it. I told them that

---

[261] John Spear Smith, *Memoir of the Baron de Kalb, Read at the Meeting
of the Maryland Historical Society, 7th January, 1858* (Baltimore: Printed by
J. D. Toy, 1858). Simms reviewed the pamphlet in the Charleston *Mercury*
of May 5, 1858.

[262] At the top of this letter is written "postmarked 22d Novr. 1860" in what
appears to be Lawson's handwriting. The cover has not survived.

[263] Payment for contributions to *The New American Cyclopædia*.

[264] Dated by Simms' reference to his letter to Lawson of c. Nov. 21.

it came as a gift from a venerable Scotch Judge in N. Y., — a Judge of Aqua Vitæ, of Usquebaugh, of Glenlivet & Ferintosh, & that he took oath to its being the best comforter of its order in all N. Y. I have written to Redfield to supply Russell & Jones the amount of their order, 100 copies or 200, of the new vol of Poems.²⁶⁵ It ought to be out before Christmas. I want 50 copies myself for distribution. If it is to come out of my dues, it should be forthcoming. Please insist on it. He need not publish an edition for the North at present. But here it should have been before. Urge the matter immediately. By his own showing he owed me over $600. Let him supply the 100 to Russell & the 50 to me and deliver the plates to you. But get the copies sent before you insist upon the rest. We shall look for Jimmy by the 1st. Love to all.

Yours Ever

W. G. S.

1013: To James Lawson

[*c.* November 23, 1860]²⁶⁶

dear Lawson.

Though I wrote you by last mail, yet, happening upon the within invoice, which was sent me by Wm. Roach, I thought it possible that it might be of service to you in the purchase of groceries. It would be to me, in regard to sundry articles, had I any money. Send it back to me when you have examined it. You may test the propriety of your own grocer's charges by its examination. It strikes me that some of the items are much lower than I have been in the habit of paying & it may be so with you. Mr. Missroon ²⁶⁷ told me, coming on together from N. Y. of the much lower prices than he had paid usually, & I begged for his bill of sundries. This it is. Consult with Lyde on the subject, and if you think as I do, see Mr. Wintringham.²⁶⁸ — I have written to W. R.²⁶⁹ touching Jimmy and his arrival, & covered a letter to his care, for that amiable young man himself. Gilmore is expected

---

²⁶⁵ *Simms's Poems Areytos.*
²⁶⁶ Dated by Simms' reference to his letter to Lawson of *c.* Nov. 22.
²⁶⁷ Henry Missroon, of the firm of Henry Missroon and Co., Charleston. See note 59, Feb. 28, 1859.
²⁶⁸ The New York City directories for this period list Jeremiah Wintringham, a grocer at 4 Broadway.
²⁶⁹ William Roach.

to be with us on Friday next,[270] and we trust and believe that he
still keeps his position at the head of the school.[271] Your copy of
Poems for Mrs. Martin,[272] I sent by Gen. Jamison three days
ago. He has gone up to attend the Session of the Military Board,
by which the Cadets are to be examined. Two of his sons, one a
professor in the Yorkville Military Academy the other a Cadet,
are now, on leave here, at the Genls. plantation, and, with Gilmore, these will make quite a company for Jimmy.[273] Jamison's
eldest son has bought Dr. Sweat's plantation adjoining him,[274] so
that we are getting quite compact. Mrs. Jenkins, his eldest
daughter, is now with him, with her 3 children. Her husband,
who is principal of the Yorkville Academy, has gone on a trip
to Edisto Island.[275] My wife is now away on a visit to Mrs.
Pinckney.[276] We expect soon to have as visitors, for longer or
shorter periods —

　　　Cadet Gilmore Simms —
　　　　"　James Lawson.
　　　Mr. Thompson, Ed. So. Lit. Mess.[277]
　　　　" Paul H. Hayne. Poet —
　　　Dr. & Mrs. Fuller — & baby & nurse
　　　Mrs. Edward Roach, & baby & nurse.

And possibly some half score besides. It is probable that Gilmore
will be able to take Jimmy up to Barnwell C. H. & elswhere.

　　　　Yours Ever with love to Mama & all the girls

　　　　　　　W. Gilmore Simms.

---

[270] Nov. 30.

[271] The Arsenal Academy.

[272] Margaret Maxwell Martin (b. 1807), a native of Scotland, came with
her family to America in 1815. They first settled in Fayetteville, N. C., and
shortly afterwards removed to Columbia, S. C., where, in 1836, she married
the Rev. William Martin, a Methodist clergyman. She was the author of several
volumes of religious prose and verse.

[273] John Wilson Jamison (1839-1886) and William Harper Jamison (1841-
1887).

[274] David Rumph Jamison (b. 1834) purchased this plantation from Dr.
Benjamin Screven Sweat (see note 24, April 30, 1842).

[275] Jamison's eldest daughter, Caroline Harper, was the wife of Micah Jenkins (see note 180, Sept. 15, 1855).

[276] Probably Lucia Bellinger Pinckney (1777-1863), daughter of Edmund
Bellinger, the fourth landgrave, and widow of Miles Brewton Pinckney (b.
1768), brother of Charles Pinckney and secretary to him during his third term
as governor (1796-1798). See note 78, Oct. 27, 1840, where her name is incorrectly given as Lucia Georgiana Bellinger Pinckney.

[277] George William Bagby was editor of the *Southern Literary Messenger*
at this time (see note 299, Nov. 30, 1860). Thompson, whose last issue of the
Southern Field and Fireside is that for Nov. 17, 1860, was doubtless planning
to visit Simms on his way from Augusta to Richmond.

1014: To William Hawkins Ferris

Woodlands, S. C.
Nov 23. 1860.

W. Hawkins Ferris, Esq.

My dear Sir:

I did visit New York in September last, & made several efforts to find you out. Wrote two letters to you through the post office; — searched the Directory; went to the office of the Journal of Commerce, to ask after Mr. Wallace; was treated there by the Clerks, with a cool contempt which made me turn on my heel; wrote to Mr. Wallace; and got no answer from Him or You. You will admit that I took pains enow. We found a W. H. Ferris in the N. Y. Directory, and I addressed him. Got no answer. My publisher (Redfield) interested himself. Could get no clues; & we concluded you had gone off to some of the Watering Places.

In answer to your queries, I am sorry to say that I am doing but little in a literary way — much in letters. My Correspondence is very heavy. My domestic cares pressing. Short crops, from the drought, diminish my resources of the plantation, while the failure of my publisher, & the political troubles of the times, cut off all my means from books. I am weary & troubled, with much work nevertheless on my hands, and but little money. I trust you are more prosperous. — I propose (D. V.) as soon as I can to resume my pen upon a volume; the material of which is all in hand, & my mind, I believe, as ready as need be, but for the fact that there is no policy in publishing just now.[278] I shall **be** pleased to hear from you when you are in the mood.

Yours truly

W. Gilmore Simms

---

[278] Probably "Joscelyn." See note 282, Nov. 4, 1866.

1015: To William Porcher Miles

[November? 1860][279]

My dear Miles.

I trouble you with the enclosed, simply as I wish to save postage to the Mercury which lacks in money. Will you please deliver them.

I have been making stump speeches. Every body right in this region. Minute Men in arms.

Go to the Convention if you can. Of course, Congress is nothing to you now. Identify yourself with the movement. But do not fatigue yourself. — Love to James.

God bless you.

W. Gilmore Simms

1016: To William Porcher Miles

[November? 1860][280]

dear Miles

Hand the enclosed to the Mercury, if you can & please.

I cover to you to save postage, as I am monstrously drawn upon, *pro bono publico,* in the matter of postage, and I propose to tax the enemy for our liberties where I can! Keitt has sent me a package of *franked* envelopes. If you can do the same, I will thank you. Get your pay in full from Govt. before you resign; or let your resignation take date from 3d. March. Meanwhile, as soon as you can go to Washington — i.e. if money be due you, — just take your seat & get your money! On the spot, you may help us somewhat. As Govr. you would make position, and secure

[279] Part of this letter is quoted by Trent, p. 354, who assumes that it was written after the passage of the Ordinance of Secession and that "the Convention" to which Simms refers is the Provisional Congress of the Confederate States, held at Montgomery, Ala. Simms' reference to the United States Congress, however, implies a date prior to the Secession Convention, which is most likely "the Convention" to which Simms refers and to which Miles was a delegate from Charleston. Simms' remark about the "Minute Men" recalls his letters to Lawson of Nov. 5 and 20.

[280] Dated by Simms' reference to Miles' nomination for governor (see letter to Miles of Sept. 28 and following letters to Miles) and by his advice to Miles to "go to Washington . . . take your seat & get your money." When Congress assembled on Dec. 4 Miles did not answer the roll call, but he was there on Dec. 5, his last recorded appearance on the floor (see *Congressional Globe,* 36 Cong., 2 Sess., pp. 2, 7).

capital for the future; be, in brief, in the way for better things. *Verb. Sap!*

Hastily, but ever lovingly, Yours

W. Gilmore Simms

1017: To James Lawson

Woodlands, Nov. 30. [1860][281]

My dear Lawson.

As soon as the Book is ready, send the copies to Russell, & do not ask him. If he returns them (which he will hardly do) well & good. Send in envelopes, with "the Author's compliments, or regards" — the following copies.

To *Charleston* — Care of Russell & Jones.

Hon. W. J. Grayson.

Hon. B. R. Rhett. (Mercury)

Prof. J. W. Miles.

Hon. W. P. Miles.

Paul H. Hayne.

Henry Timrod.

W. B. Carlyle, Esq. (Courier)[282]

Rt. Rev. Bishop P. N. Lynch (Catholic Miscellany)[283]

C. P. Pelham (Columbia Guardian)[284]

Dr. J. Dickson Bruns (Med. Journal.)[285]

J. N. Cardozo (Evening News)[286]

---

[281] Dated by Simms' discussion of complimentary copies of *Simms's Poems Areytos.*

[282] Upon the death of Lewis Hatch in 1858 William Buchanan Carlisle became editor-in-chief of the Charleston *Courier.* He had previously been one of the editors of *Russell's Magazine.*

[283] For Patrick Neilson Lynch, see note 136, July 14, 1849. The *United States Catholic Miscellany* was published in Charleston during 1822-1861.

[284] Charles P. Pelham, formerly professor of Roman literature at the South Carolina College during 1846-1857 and of political economy and history during 1857-1858, was editor of the *Southern Guardian* (Columbia), published as a daily, a tri-weekly, and a weekly.

[285] John Dickson Bruns (see introductory sketch) was editor of the *Charleston Medical Journal and Review* during 1858-1860. In a review of the Jan., 1860, issue of the periodical, Simms writes in the Charleston *Mercury* of Feb. 8, 1860: "Doctor Bruns is no ordinary man. Though young, he is a good scholar, and a hard student, a thoughtful writer, capable of large generalizations, and equally capable of grasping the details of his subjects. He is like all men of real ability, a person of singular independence. He speaks boldly what he thinks."

[286] For Jacob N. Cardozo and his connection with the *Evening News,* see note 181, Sept. 11, 1850.

To Mobile —
   Hon. A. B. Meek.
   Hon. A. J. Requiere.[287]

To Savannah
   T. A. Burke.[288]

To Boston.
   J. T. Fields.
   Hon. E. Everett.

To Philadelphia
   L. A. Godey.[289]

Phil. — Geo. H. Boker.[290]
   T. S. Arthur.[291]

Baltimore.
   Professor N. C. Brooks.[292]

Washington
   Prof. Joseph Henry (Smithsonian Institution)

---

[287] Augustus Julian Requier. See note 119, June 16, 1854.

[288] Thomas A. Burke. See note 192, Oct. 11, 1851.

[289] Louis Antoine Godey (see introductory sketch). A short, favorable notice of *Simms's Poems Areytos* appears in *Godey's,* LXII (March, 1861), 275.

[290] George Henry Boker. See note 233, Oct. 14, 1855.

[291] Timothy Shay Arthur (1809-1885), author of *Ten Nights in a Bar-Room* (1854) and other novels, was the publisher and co-editor with Virginia F. Townsend of *Arthur's Home Magazine,* a Philadelphia monthly. (The title of the magazine varies during the 1850's.) Simms published the following poems in the magazine: "Oh! Welcome Ye the Stranger," III (April, 1854), 309; "Exhortation," VII (Jan., 1856), 62; "Lay of Encouragement," VII (Feb., 1856), 96; "Courage," VII (May, 1856), 278; and "Epigram.—Death," VIII (Nov., 1856), 282. (We have not seen the Feb. and May, 1856, issues, but "Lay of Encouragement" and "Courage" are listed in the index to that volume.) *Arthur's Home Magazine* also published favorable notices or reviews of a number of Simms' works: *The Sword and the Distaff* in II (Aug., 1853), 160, and again in II (Sept., 1853), 240; *The Wigwam and the Cabin* and *Norman Maurice* in II (Sept., 1853), 240; *Mellichampe* in III (May, 1854), 397; *Eutaw* in VII (June, 1856), 379; and *The History of South Carolina* in XV (Feb., 1860), 128. In a long article entitled "William Gilmore Simms," published in *Arthur's Home Magazine,* XIV (Dec., 1859), 277-283, J. Starr Holloway writes (p. 283): ". . . there is not one [of his writings] which does not exhibit the author as a consistent, conscientious, ingenious, thorough, and elaborate writer, whether as essayist, romancist, reviewer, poet, or historian. His works have been called 'a remarkable series.' His fictions alone, independent of his more studied contributions to literature, are worthy the title— as worthy as Cooper's or Sir Walter Scott's. In fact, Simms is the Cooper of the South. . . . There are few of his productions which will not attain a permanent place in American literature, while the South, in view of the author's studied and native preference for her history, her scenery, and her society, must forever regard him and his works with feelings of affectionate interest and reverence."

[292] Nathan Covington Brooks (1809-1898), educator, classicist, and historian, was the author of *A Complete History of the Mexican War* (1849).

New York.

W. C. Bryant (Evening Post)

T. Addison Richards —

O. J. Victor (Cosmop. Art Journal)

Mr. Durand. (Crayon)[293]

Evert A. Duyckinck.

George   Do.

Barry Gray (Home Journal)[294]

Harper & Brothers —[295]

O. A. Roorbach.[296]

N. Y. Day Book.[297]

W. Wallace (Journ. of Commerce)[298]

Richmond, Va. John R. Thompson.

           John Esten Cooke.

           G. W. Bagby, M. D. (So. Lit Messenger)[299]

---

[293] For John Durand and the *Crayon,* see note 257, Dec. 30, 1855.

[294] "Barry Gray" was the pseudonym of Robert Barry Coffin (1826-1886), author of various humorous sketches and assistant editor of the *Home Journal.* The *Home Journal* of Jan. 26, 1861, reprints a highly laudatory review of *Simms's Poems Areytos* from the *South Carolinian* (Columbia), n. d.

[295] *Harper's New Monthly Magazine,* XXII (Feb., 1861), 411, says that Simms' "poetical productions, . . . which are here collected in a volume, evince the genuine feeling of the poet, and powers both of imagination and expression of no common order. Many of the poems in this volume were composed in the author's early years; but they all exhibit a unity of sentiment and purpose which identify them as the offspring of his inmost mind. His versification, though unequal, is vigorous and spirited, and his fancies are usually inspired by a glow of ardent sentiment."

[296] Orville Augustus Roorbach (1803-1861) had been the proprietor of a bookstore in Charleston until 1845, when he removed to New York City, where he operated a bookstore until 1855. During 1858-1860 he was the editor of the *Bookseller's Medium and Publisher's Advertiser.*

[297] John H. Van Evrie, Rushmore G. Horton, and George W. Olney were the editors and proprietors of the New York *Day Book,* published both as a daily (the *Evening Day Book*) and a weekly (the *New York Weekly Day Book*). We have examined the latter for this period but have not found a review of *Simms's Poems Areytos.*

[298] We have examined the *Weekly Journal of Commerce* for this period but have not found a review of *Simms's Poems Areytos.*

[299] George William Bagby (1828-1883) had succeeded John Reuben Thompson as editor of the *Southern Literary Messenger* with the issue for June, 1860. He continued as editor of the *Messenger* through the issue for Jan., 1864. *Simms's Poems Areytos* is reviewed in XXXII (Feb., 1861), 156-159. The reviewer (Bagby?) remarks (p. 158): "Throughout a great portion of the songs in this volume there is a vein of exquisite sadness, which is apt to be the tone of all poetry which is not intensely young; of poetry which has had its boyishness, its huge credulity, its positiveness as to the heroism in man and the angelism in woman rudely chipped, rubbed, scraped off, by observant criticism, and daily contact with a world anything but the creation of a boy-poet. The poetry of Mr. Simms is not the poetry of a hobbledehoy, just mounting Old Pegasus, for his first gallop; but the poetry of one who has made a good day's journey on the faithful beast, whose spirit, although he be winged,

Augusta, Geo.

Field & Fireside.[300]

My whole list for the present, except copies for James & Mary Lawson, with the author's best love.[301] We are looking out for Jimmy. I have sent him a letter to Charleston. No danger! Gilmore has just got home. He ranks A. No. 1. at the examination,[302] & is now tall enow to eat off of his father's head. We have had within 10 days, wild duck, wild turkey & venison, all killed on the plantation. Jamison's two sons are now down here,[303] so that the boys ought to have a merry time. They must take trips to Barnwell & Orangeburg. Dr. & Mrs. Fuller, Augusta & her baby,[304] will all be here in a week. I am nominated for the Convention, but trust that I shall not be required to go. There are scores of *Candidates* — all for secession. I am *not* a candidate — would pray not to go, — as I have a thousand things to do at home. If they elect me, I must go! But it will be serious loss to me, of time & money, to say nothing of works which I feel *called* to do. Of one thing be sure. Nothing less than secession by the South will ever bring the North to its senses. Were we not to secede, they & you & every brave man would despise us. Secession is inevitable. You will remember what I told you a year ago. I warned you of every thing which has happened. I warned you last summer of what would happen, & told you to put your house in order. Spend no *money,* that you can help — buy nothing which you do not want; for, I warn you now, this is no ordinary convulsion. Hold in! God bless & help you & us.

Your friend Ever

W. G. S.

P. S. I have, as written, disposed of 36 Copies of the Poems. Send me the 14 [305] remaining of the 50. Let no other copies be

and has ever and anon renewed his vigor by way-side draughts from the waters of Hippocrene, has nevertheless been sobered by other journeys than mere amblings around the base of Mount Helicon."

[300] A short, favorable review of *Simms's Poems Areytos* appears in the *Southern Field and Fireside,* II (Dec. 29, 1860), 252.

[301] Lawson put checks by most names (indicating, we assume, that the copies were sent), numerals (133, 134, etc.) by others (which we cannot explain), and added after Wallace's name "J S Redfield."

[302] The cadets at the Arsenal Academy were examined by the Military Board. See letter to Lawson of *c.* Nov. 23.

[303] John Wilson Jamison and William Harper Jamison.

[304] Chevillette.

[305] Simms wrote *24.*

sent to any body, without consulting me. There are to be no *Editor's* copies. Let Redfield know, & forward. — I enclose you a letter, just recieved from him.[306] Read & return, & tell me what you think. The whole business seems one inextricable snarl.

W. G. S.

1018: To WILLIAM PORCHER MILES

Woodlands Decr. 5. 1860

A single word, my dear Miles. Do not become excited. Engage in no debate — no dispute. Nurse your strength & come home, able to work for the Lares & Penates of our free Republick. I could wish to see you Governor, and so would & do thousands, but the report of your physical condition, seems to have disarmed your friends, who fear that such labours now, might work fatal results upon you.[307] The Executive Chair is now a seat of equal dignity & responsibility & not, as heretofore, a mere Constabulary. It is difficult to say where the proper man is to be found, who can properly fill it. Some of those spoken of are mere bladdery blatherskites, others again are able enough, but odiously selfish; Maxcy Gregg [308] has been spoken of, but he, though admitted to be bold, brave & able, is yet personally unpopular, I hear. My neighbor Jamison is spoken of, and he is a man of firmness & character, great calm of temper, & thoroughly true — intelligent also & familiar with affairs. He is not brilliant, but sensible. But the Hour brings the man & Jehovah spirit.[309]

God bless you

W. Gilmore Simms

P. S. I need not say to you that the Act of Secession is inevitable. Be prepared to leave Washington at a minute's warning. Get your

---

[306] Not located.

[307] Miles had been nominated for governor. See letter to him of Sept. 28.

[308] Gregg (1814-1862) practiced law in Columbia from 1839, when he was admitted to the bar, until the Confederate War. He was a member of the Secession Convention, and in 1861 he was appointed colonel of the 1st Regiment of South Carolina Volunteers. In Dec., 1861, he was promoted to brigadier general. He was killed at Fredericksburg on Dec. 14, 1862.

[309] On Dec. 17 Francis Wilkinson Pickens (see note 120, Dec. 30, 1842) succeeded William Henry Gist as governor. In the election for the office his chief opponent was B. J. Johnson.

pay, be sure. Strip the Philistines of all you can. S. C. will provide for you, be sure. —

It is just possible that I may be a member of the Convention.
I am put in nomination in Barnwell. But I am no candidate, and
dread the loss of time & money, & peace of mind & comfort, to
which it will subject me. It will be a serious loss, & I can hardly
afford to be a patriot. But, I will not shrink, & neither ask nor
decline. Our district is filled with a herd of scrub candidates, who
are electioneering in all quarters, after the vulgar fashion. It is
quite probable that the delegates in half the country districts, will
be the Dick Smiths, the Sam. Jones, the Absalom Tompkins &
the Tony Simpkins. Fools rush in, &c.

W. G. S.

1019: To James Lawson

Woodlands.

Wednesday 5th. Decr. [1860][310]

dear Lawson.

A single word to say that Jimmy has reached Charleston in
safety according to the Newspapers. We have not heard from
him yet though I looked for himself or a letter today, and sent
the Buggy up for him this morning. We shall also send this ev'ng,
and Tomorrow. And Tomorrow is the day for electing members
of the Convention. All pledged to Secession! I have been named,
but I am no Candidate, do not wish it, trust that I shall not be
chosen, and think it probable I shall not. Love to all.

Ever faithfully

W. Gilmore Simms

J. L.

1020: To James Henry Hammond

Wednesday Night.
[December 5, 1860][311]

My dear Hammond.

I have just read your speech at Augusta. It is the right thing,
in the right vein, and I especially rejoice at it. It confirms all that

---

[310] Dated by Simms' reference to the arrival of James Lawson, Jr., in
Charleston. The *Mercury* of this date lists him as a passenger on the *Columbia.*
[311] Dated by Simms' discussion of Hammond's speech delivered at Hamburg,
S. C. (not at Augusta, as Simms says in this letter), on Dec. 1, 1860, at an

I said of you months ago. I said that all you desired was the result of the vote, the knowledge that it was a movement of the
people & not of the politicians, and that the fruit was truly ripe. That
you would not suffer yourself to be made a tool of, and would
not make yourself ridiculous, by ministering to a flash in the pan.
I told you that the hour had come. I told Orr and his people, at
the Anderson Barbacue, years ago,[312] that it would come, but that
it would not come till the very hour that saw the annihilation of
that Democratic Party which he so much valued, but which I
then denounced as the bane of the South. I told you that the
popular momentum would soon prove not to be withstood, & that
in the death of the National parties, Georgia would go like an
avalanche. It is a great God's blessing that the triumph of Lincoln
was so complete as to leave all national parties hopeless of re-
suscitation. All will be right. I have suggested you for the Convention & trust you will be in it. We want your cool head, and
deliberative mood. I have suggested you to our people here, but the
country is so overrun with Candidates, electioneering on all hands,
that no nomination will avail. It will be a scrub-race. I hope you
will go from Edgefield. They have put me in nomination here,
but I hope in vain, as I can neither afford the time nor money.
I have too much work at home. — Can't refuse if elected, but
dread to think of it. Write me here what you think. I see a great
deal to be done which demands the most farsighted thought, and
the profoundest wisdom & the largest knowledge of affairs.
Meanwhile, there is any quantity of scum politicians in the arena.
God send us the right wisdom now. Once more, I hope that you
will be sent. Should I go, I should desire no better comate than
yourself.[313] Have you sent me a box? And is it wine of your making, and what is its name. I have got one which I suspect is from

"Inter-State Celebration of the People of Georgia and South Carolina." "The
Minute Men and citizens of Augusta" were invited to participate at the meeting
by "the Minute Men of Hamburg." According to the Charleston *Mercury* of
Wednesday, Dec. 5, Hammond's "counsel, a month ago, was for South Carolina
not to take the lead, but to let some other State—Georgia, for instance—but
since then he had seen his mistake. He had feared that the movement had
originated with the politicians and not with the people. He now frankly confessed
that he had been mistaken. He did not see the use of urging upon them the
necessity of secession. So far as South Carolina was concerned, he considered
secession as already accomplished."

Hammond erroneously dated his reply to this letter "Nov. 10, 1860." The
original is in the Hammond Papers, Library of Congress.

[312] On July 24, 1855. See note 166, July 30, 1855.

[313] Neither Simms nor Hammond was a delegate to the Secession Convention.

you. It comes seasonably.[314] Best regards to Mrs. H. & Kate, &
Bet & the boys.

Yours Ever

W. Gilmore Simms

J. H. H.

1021: To James Lawson

Wednesday, Midnight.
5 Decr. 1860.

I write, dear Lawson, simply to relieve any anxiety you may
feel. Jimmy is here & has just retired for the night. He, Gilmore
& Mr. Paul Hayne, who is now on a visit here, sleep in the same
chamber. He, Jimmy, is quite well, looks well, has had no sea-
sickness, and is in good spirits. Tomorrow, he goes with us to
Bamberg to the election.[315] He is already engaged with Dr. Carroll, the young Jamisons & Gilmore, for a partridge hunt, on
Friday. The boys will no doubt make their arrangements day by
day. We are all charmed with the beautiful picture he has brought
us. It is very sweet, & it is really a pity that one who shows such
talent for drawing pictures, should be doom'd to drawing averages. We shall make him a Southron, & you too. I have already,
in my eye, a farm for you, of fifty acres, well wooded, for $500.
where you shall build a fine house for $3000. and cultivate the
grape, and make your own wine, & be a gentleman in a world
of gentlemen. Where your wife shall raise her own turkies, ducks
and chickens, and where your $100,000 shall yield you a better
income than $300,000 in N. Y. Gen. Hammond has just sent me
a box of his own wine. One of his neighbours,[316] from 3 acres,
has sold this season, $4,000 of the *juice of the grape,* to N. Y.
wine makers. He expects to make $10,000. next year. Mr. Jaques
has lived on *his* farm, all the summer, without one day of
sickness in his family.[317] So has Jamison with his dozen chil-

---

[314] In his reply (cited note 311, above) Hammond writes: "The wine I
sent you is the same you tasted here. It is of the Vintage of 1859 & the pure
juice of the Catawba grape. . . ."

[315] The delegates from Barnwell District to the Secession Convention were
David Flavel Jamison, Lewis Malone Ayer, William Peronneau Finley, Benjamin W. Lawton, and J. J. Brabham.

[316] Not identified.

[317] In a review of Jacques' *Hints toward Physical Perfection, or the Phi-*
losophy of Human Beauty and *How to Talk: A Manual of Conversation and*
Debate (no copies located by us) in the Charleston *Mercury* of Jan. 25, 1860,

dren.[318] I am busy, building me a study — a room of 30 x 22, connected, on the East, with the main building by a corridor of arches. I have also altered my portico & steps, am cementing & roughcasting, shingling and boarding up. On Monday next we look for Augusta & her baby;[319] Friday we expect Dr. Fuller, wife & child.[320] You see that Jimmy won't want for company. As the boy was probably tired, and will go with us to Bamberg tomorrow, & come home to a late dinner, and possibly see company all the evening, & go to hunt on Friday, he will probably have little time to write, so I write for him, and trust that you will feel him safe with us, as far as Human Love & friendship can ensure safety. Last night Gilmore & the young Jamisons were Coon Hunting till *one* this morning. Today, they have been practising pistol shooting. There will, no doubt, be something every day, in which they will amuse & exercise themselves innocently. Love to Lyde & the girls, from wife self & our girls. Adios.

W. G. S.

Simms says of Jacques: ". . . he has recently become a resident of our State; having bought a farm in Barnwell District, where he proposes to address himself to fruit and grape culture. Trained originally to farming, from his boyhood in the North [in New Jersey], an early removal, many years ago, to Georgia, and subsequently to Carolina, lifted him into a better consciousness of life and its uses than was quite natural to the unhappy people and the wretched country where his eyes first opened to the light. He found life a different sort of thing in Georgia and Carolina than he ever found it among the Yankee Hyperboreans. There, he found that he could neither enjoy health nor comfort, nor peace of mind, nor piece of meat. A peacable [*sic*] man, of quiet, grave, gentle nature, and delicate constitution, he was bound to go to the wall in the rush and rub-a-dub sort of existence which they only know as life; and very wisely he left them in season, happy in getting away young enough to unlearn the vicious teachings of the moral atmosphere around him, and to imbibe the better lessons of a purer and more genial sky. . . . Here, in Carolina, with a nice little farm, under his own vine and fig tree, we trust to see him bearing goodly fruits for our market—peaches and potatoes; figs and tomatoes; cherries and cabbages; eggs, chickens, pigs, and peanuts; all of which, we believe, are garden products in our generous atmosphere. We shall always instruct our market-man to ask for Jacques' peaches and poultry as soon as we hear of their appearance in market, and hope to get the best cherries and chickens at his hands, at the most moderate prices."

[318] An exaggeration. Jamison had nine children: David Rumph, Caroline Harper, John Wilson, William Harper, Sallie P., Mary D., Elizabeth, Thomas Worth, and Clara. David had married, on Dec. 30, 1858, Ella Elizabeth Zimmerman and was living on a plantation adjoining Burwood. Caroline, who was married to Micah Jenkins, lived at Yorkville, S. C., though apparently she, her husband, and their three children had been visiting her parents (see letter to Lawson of *c.* Nov. 23, 1860).

[319] Chevillette.

[320] Guerard.

1022: To Orville James Victor

Woodlands, Decr. 10. 1860.

My dear Mr. Victor.

You & Mr. Derby were so good as to promise me a copy of the "Shakspeare & his Friends" in place of that which I was so unlucky as to have destroyed by fire. It was told me by Mr. Derby that by calling upon Mr. Taylor, the agent in Charleston, I should have it. But I have not yet recieved it. Your Fallstaff & his Ragged Regiment has been recieved, and for this I thank you. I have been waiting to notice it, in proper terms, in the Mercury, as soon as our political excitements shall have somewhat subsided. Now, it is impossible to do any good by a notice; for not only will the public read nothing but politics, but the paper is so full of these that there is no room for any thing else, unless inadequately mentioned. I now propose, as soon as there is room & reason for it, to notice both pictures together & elaborately, as well as your last issue of the Cosmopolitan.[321] Please direct your future favours to me at "Midway P. O. S. C." I could wish you to say to Mr. Derby that I have recd. none of his publications since I left N. Y. & Mr. Stoddart promised me especially a copy of his volume, The Loves of the Poets.[322] If D. & J. will send me their publications, I beg that they will forward through Russell & Jones, Charleston. In the present turmoil, art & letters stand a sorry chance; but the clouds will break away soon. My respects to Mrs. V. & regards to yourself.

Yours truly

W. Gilmore Simms

---

[321] In the Charleston *Mercury* of Dec. 19 Simms writes: ". . . go to Mr. James H. Taylor, the agent in this city, and procure copies of the 'Shakspeare and his Friends,' published last year; and the 'Falstaff and his Regiment;' both issued by the Art Association of which the [Cosmopolitan] Art Journal is the exponent." Simms promises to speak of "Falstaff Reviewing His Ragged Regiment" later, but evidently this notice was not published. James Cephas Derby (1818-1892) was a member of the firm of Derby and Jackson, New York City, publisher of the *Cosmopolitan Art Journal*. He was later the author of *Fifty Years among Authors, Books and Publishers* (New York: G. W. Carleton & Co., 1884).

[322] Richard Henry Stoddard (1825-1903), the poet, critic, and editor, was in 1860 living in New York City, where he held the position of inspector of customs in the New York Custom House. He was the editor of *The Loves and Heroines of the Poets* (New York: Derby & Jackson, 1861).

1023: TO JOHN JACOB BOCKEE [323]

Woodlands,[324] December 12, 1860.

My dear Mr. Bockee: [325]

I thank you for your letter, and the kindly feelings which it so well expresses. But you are wholly mistaken, equally in your argument and your convictions. *Our safety* is much more important to us than *any Union;* and, in the event of our future union with other parties, we shall certainly look to our safety, with much more circumspection than our fathers did, though they strove to guard their people, with all their vigilance, against the danger equally of a majority and of Federal usurpation. If fortunate in little else, we are now fortunate in an experience far superior to theirs; and we shall deserve the worst of fates, if we do not become wiser and safer for it. We have learned, for example, to value the Union, not according to the hopes of its beginning, but through the wrongs which now demand that we bring it to an early end.

Our case, I admit, is something different from yours — and so is our experience! You at the North may well put the most enormous estimate upon the *value of the Union. You* may well

for nearly eighty years; fattened and flourished, in a degree of lift up your hands and call it *blessed!* You have fattened upon it prosperity unexampled in the history of nations. We can easily conceive the reluctance of your section to see it dissolved. The

---

[323] This letter, printed in the Charleston *Mercury* of Jan. 17, 1861, is an expanded version of a letter (not located by us) which Simms sent to Bockee, to whom he also later sent a clipping of this letter (see letter to Lawson of Feb. 19, 1861). The *Mercury* published the following remarks as a preface to the letter: "'The Blessed Union!' This is the usual cuckoo song of all the Northern people, especially that class of them which more particularly prides itself upon being conservative! We are permitted to publish the copy of a letter, written by a gentleman of this State, in reply to one of his Northern friends, of this class, from whom he had received a most pathetic appeal in behalf of 'this blessed Union!' As it is probable that thousands of similar appeals are written, weekly, by persons of the North, to their friends in the South, it may be instructive to see how such letters may be answered, and how, indeed, they sometimes are answered! It is hardly likely that the recipients of such letters at the North, will venture to seek for them a place in the Northern newspapers. But it is just possible that, after we have given them place in our journals, they may be copied into theirs. We believe the argument of the South, delivered in this fashion, may give them glimpses of the truth, such as the Northern people rarely derive from their own organs. Here follows our friend's letter to his *Northern* friend, as a commentary upon his much eulogized and lamented Union."

[324] Instead of *Woodlands* the *Mercury* prints a long dash.

[325] The *Mercury* prints *B*——

Union, as Daniel Webster once said before the Supreme Court, in reply to young Van Buren, has been the source of all your prosperity. It is your misfortune that, with the usual blind tendencies of all over-prosperous people, you have not sufficiently valued it yourselves. You have perilled it dozens of times, simply because of the insanity of your prosperity. You have, at length, destroyed it.

Understand me. I mean no harsh reflections upon *you,* individually. I do you the justice to believe that *you* would have saved it if you could, and in the only right way — by being just and honest to the South. It is our great regret that, in the measures which we have need to take for our own safety, we must necessarily compromise yours. But in the case of great states, or nations, and their vast and various issues, we are compelled to ignore all individual exceptions. I know that you have thousands, possibly millions, who are in the same category with yourself; who have been friendly to us, and were anxious to be just; but either you were not strong enough in numbers, or warm enough in zeal, or active enough in performance, to secure us justice, by keeping down the fanatical, the foolish, the base and the presumptuous of your section; and it is the law in morals and society, that men should be punished for the bad company they keep! You have not been able to secure us justice or safety, and we must now look out for ourselves. You have allowed our enemies — and I think your own — to triumph; and if you will permit me to say, *now,* your present mistake still consists in the desire, *rather to save the Union, than to do justice to the South.*

Why, my dear deluded friend, do you still desire to save the Union? Of what sort of value, to a Christian man, is that sort of union which persists in keeping men in the same household, who hate and blaspheme each other? And can you be really a friend to the South — a wise one you certainly are not — when you desire *us,* the *minority* States, to submit to the uncontrolled legislation of a majority, which has not only proved faithless to all its pledges, but which has declared its determined purpose to subdue, rule and destroy the minority, and abrogate all its rights and securities?

Suffer me, my dear friend, to hint to you a few other matters. How is it that, in all the trespasses and exactions of the North, upon and from the South, you never wrote such a letter to the aggressors and the trespassers, in behalf of the South, as you now

write to me in behalf of the Union? I never got from you a letter
of indignation, when the North was taxing the sweat and labor
of the South, even to its ruin, by protective tariffs, for the benefit
and greed of the manufacturing monopolists of New England
and Pennsylvania. I never heard from you — addressed either to
me or to the enemies of my people — in anger, at the abrogation
of the Fugitive Slave law by some twelve or fifteen of your States,
your own among them! You never cried out your griefs, or your
wrath, when our slaves were hurried from us by underground
railroads — by wretches, exulting doubly when, robbing the master of his slaves, they succeeded in persuading them to murder
him also; and, when the fugitives from justice were withheld,
and the pursuing owners or officers were seized and mobbed, and
maltreated, and doomed to the penitentiary — why was your
voice silent? Nor do I know, or believe, when, violating the
Missouri Compromise, the hostile and abolition North refused
to the South their recognized rights south of the line of 36° 30′,
that you even made your clamors heard in defence of Southern
rights and privileges, and in the maintenance of a sacred stipu-
lation. And yet, in that very conquest of Mexico and California,
the South sent 46,000 volunteers into the field; the North but
22,000; and with a handsome proportion of the New England
troops refusing to fight when they got to Vera Cruz, alleging,
in the hour of battle, their conscientious scruples about the morals
of war in general, and this war in particular! The battle fought,
the victory won, the territory gained, their moral scruples all
gave way, at the gathering of the spoils! They grasped the whole
territory with the eagerness of a half starved parish boy, blessed
with the unexpected sight of a sudden plum pudding within his
reach! By a majority vote in Congress, they took it all — some
700 miles on the Pacific coast; and drove out the Southern slave-
holders, who had fought the battle! As Edward said to Bruce,
"Have I nothing to do but to win kingdoms for you?" And where
were you, and other friends of the South, while this royal robbery went on? Not a voice was heard in opposition; and I do
not find in any of the frequent friendly letters which I have had
from you, that you even once allude to *our* wrongs at all, or in
the language of indignation. You never seem to have foreseen
that a fatal blow was given to the Union *then* — in that very
hour — in that stroke of a policy so very cunning as to — cut its
own throat!

I look in vain, my excellent friend, among all your excellent letters to me, to find one single expression of your horror at the John Brown raid in Virginia! Your indignation, I suppose, was so intense as to keep you dumb! I cannot, of course, suppose that you were indifferent! Oh! no; your expressions of love forbid that idea! So, too, I see not a word of your wrath and indignation, in any of these letters, at the burnings of our towns, and the poisoning of our fountains, in Texas, by creatures of the same kidney with the vulture Brown! And when Brown is made a martyr of in the North, and his day made a sacred record in the Northern calendar, I do not perceive that you covered your head with sackcloth and ashes, and wrote to me lamenting!

And, when your people *did* rise, after a fashion, and at a very late hour — you among them — to oppose Abolitionism, you had neither the virtue, nor the wisdom, to take issue with the enemy by a manly justification of the South! You only moved *to save the Union* — in other words, *not to lose the keeping of that excellent milch cow,* whose dugs have yielded, for sixty years, so large a proportion of the milk and butter which have fattened your hungry people. You claimed nothing for the South — asserted nothing; asked nothing; had no purpose beyond the preservation of the Confederacy, *as it was;* the South being the victim still — the North the wolf.

I had no pathetic letters from you, touching any of the exactions, aggressions, usurpations, or atrocities of the North! I cannot find a single one in all my collection! and now that you do write of these things, I find that you have but one plea, one prayer, one entreaty — *to save the Union!* to keep the milch cow still within your pleasant pastures; to persuade the lamb not to use his heels, or his watch dogs; but to leave everything to the tender mercies of the wolf!

Ah! my friend, this is very terrible on the part of friendship! Is it malice? Is it mockery?

You now only write to the injured and the endangered party, entreating him to yield himself placidly to injury and danger; to submit to continued outrage and aggression! You do not write when you see *him* in danger. You only write and plead and pray, when you think that the Union, which is the instrument of *his* destruction — as it has been the agent of your bloated prosperity — is in danger! When you see that, driven to desperation by the incessant robberies, aggressions and atrocities of the North, the South is resolved at last to shake herself free from a union which is but the cloak and cowardly shelter, under cover of which her enemies aim the dagger at her breast, assail her midnight slumbers with pikes and fire, and poison the fountains where her women and children drink.

And is such a union desirable, worth preserving, profitable in morals or honorable to either party? What sort of union is it — and with what sort of brethren? It is not a union, surely, of God's joining; but a union of the Devil's joining — to use the strong language of Milton.[326] Is it not a union with hell, and crime, and lust, and vice, and the most Satanic ministry? Surely, as a Christian man, you cannot desire that such a union as this should continue, whether you argue from your section or from mine! If you have any esteem for yourselves or for us, it is surely undesirable to preserve it, unless by such miserable wretches as care not what the crime may be, so that they profit by it. A mercenary tradesman may be pleased to continue such a connection, but an honest, and virtuous, God-fearing man, never!

And what *do* you think of us — and what *should* you think of us — if treated as we have been, we should still be desirous of such an Union, continued on such conditions, with a people who thus hourly entreat their *beloved* brethren with hate, and abuse, and wrong, and robbery in the daily operations of this *beloved* Union? I will not pain you by asking what, in *our* intercourse, has led you to suppose that *I* should be so base as to counsel *my* people to such an utter derilection from all their antecedents — from the precedents given by their fathers — from the principles in which, I gladly believe, they have been educated for eighty years, and from which, I trust in God, they will never depart?

No, no! my old friend, this is as impossible to me as to my people. I am not of this Convention,[327] and can do nothing, and need say nothing. I have not been a candidate — am, as you well know, a candidate for nothing. Have never asked a vote or favor, and, if not a recipient of favors, am no ways taxed for gratitude!

---

[326] In *Pro Populo Anglicano Defensio.* See *The Works of John Milton* (New York: The Columbia University Press, 1931-1938), VII, 170-171.

[327] The Secession Convention.

But the Convention is in good hands. There never was and never will be, a Convention of human peoples, assembled, more calm, resolute, dignified, prudent, and altogether noble, than this. I predict to you that there will be no gaseous exhibitions, no *high* falutin, no *low* falutin, no mere bombastical display of rhetoric and flummery! Our agricultural population is of stern, simple, Spartan character. They are calm; they are determined. They *feel* the necessity which coerces them; and they will ask, not what is to be *said,* but what should be *done!* And they will try to find an answer to this question; and they will then *do* according to their convictions.

It is true that our people have threatened long. But look at their situation. Look at their smallness of State and smallness of numbers. And *they loved the Union!* They really, though possessed of State rights doctrines, entertained a national pride, which was made strong by their reverence for the antique virtues of the past; *and they loved the Union. Had their great men been listened to, they would have saved the Union!* South Carolina threw herself into the breach on several occasions, and had she been properly seconded by Virginia, and other States, her attitude and counsels *would have saved the Union.* It was her modesty that made her waver, in 1832, at the words of Virginia! We need not now ask in what degree Virginia was recreant. It was her misfortune to be a border State; to be too near to Washington; to have given five Presidents to the Confederacy; and the prestige and pap of the Union were too potent for some of her politicians, who had a too confiding constituency. Now, they are all *hors de combat.* They can get no more pap. There is no *prestige* in Virginia which Black Republicanism does not spit upon! Even her chivalry is at discount, in the land of the Puritans, since the raid of John Brown, Esq., the modern martyr.

What will Virginia do? In South Carolina we have long since ceased to ask this question. Her profoundest labors, for twenty-eight years — since Watkins Leigh was her Commissioner to South Carolina [328] — have consisted only in keeping others from performance. She would do nothing herself and, like Ancient

---

[328] In 1833 Benjamin Watkins Leigh (1781-1849), later United States senator from Virginia (1834-1836), was sent by Virginia to South Carolina to secure her withdrawal of nullification.

Pistol, *she ate the leek!* [329] She swallowed her own oaths, under the influence, if not of the cudgel, certainly of the condiment.

As regards South Carolina, I have only now to say to you that, having *tried* co-operation in vain, she will now act for her-self, precisely as if the great danger stood at her own doors only, and there were no Virginia, no other States to suffer in like manner with herself, and to share her dangers. *She will secede* as surely as the sun shines in heaven. She will rely upon the justice of her cause and the virtue of her people. She will invade nobody. She will aggress upon no rights of others. She has never done so. The South has never been the aggressor! We have never meddled in the internal affairs of the North. But we will no longer suffer aggression under the mask of "this blessed Union." We shall tear off the mask, and show the hideous faith-lessness, cupidity, lying and selfishness that lurk beneath. And we shall do this, regardless of all consequences. For these we shall prepare ourselves as well as we can. We have arms, and know how to use them. We can send into the field sixty-five Pal-metto Regiments — say sixty-five thousand men — born to the rifle, and on horseback. We may be isolated by our sister States, though I think not, for *their instincts* will teach them, in spite of all their politicians, that we are fighting *their* battles as well as our own. And on our own ground, in defence of our firesides, and in the assertion of ancestral rights, we shall deliver no blow in vain. We may be conquered, my friend, but we *will* be free!

In five days more South Carolina will have repealed the act which carried her into the Confederacy. And, suffer me to pre-dict, in fifty days more, or less, all of the Cotton States will have withdrawn from a Confederacy which we now begin generally to believe is under the curse of Heaven! The madness that has possessed the Northern States, in their wild rage against their best customers, shows them to be under the doom of judicial blindness! Those whom God seeks to destroy, he first makes mad! Their ears shall not serve for hearing, nor their eyes for seeing; and they but recklessly rush upon their doom. In three months more, all the *Slave* States must follow the *Cotton* States, and withdraw from a Confederacy which would otherwise swal-low them up! Nor these alone. The Southern States are welded together by the one grand cohesive institution of slavery; while

---

[329] *Henry V,* V, i.

New England, New York and Pennsylvania, are deadly rivals, in the same pursuits, for the trade of the South. It will not be easy to suppose that these States can blend together. They must tumble asunder; and it is doubtful which of the two, New York or Pennsylvania, will show most speed of foot in the endeavor to get into the folds of this Southern Confederacy. Meditate the argument for yourself, and see if, according to all reasoning policy, you can come to any other conclusion.

Nor should these things take you by surprise. Your people have been working, against all warnings, to this very consummation! Their purpose was avowed, to make the conflict an *irrepressible* one! What did this mean? Simply that there should be no power capable to repress or still the conflict, until the bitter end had been reached of destroying negro slavery in the South, and reducing the South to a provincial subjection under a wholly irresponsible majority of a section which, for forty years, has been incessant in its hostilities. And they have at length reached a result which served to make their full triumph easy, and to obtain all the fruits which they promised themselves from it. With the Government of the United States exclusively in their hands — the Treasury — Army — Navy — Supreme Court, all, — the cry was already sent up, with demoniac shoutings, "Væ Victis!" Woe to the conquered! Do we not hear them? Are we deaf, as well as blind; base and cowardly, as well as weak? Shall we not take their own assurances, as to what they design; that design being in full harmony with all their past proceedings? Having consummated all their proposed plans, and grasped all the necessary power, shall we doubt that our continuance in the Union is simply submission to our doom!

Ah! my old friend, I fear that you think us equally silly and cowardly, as the Black Republicans seem to have done, if you can suppose that a section possessing four millions of slaves — $400,000,000 of property — and able to send into the field two millions of fighting men, all trained in a high spirit of liberty — trained to arms — all proud of a brave and free ancestry — should tamely submit until the chains are riveted about their limbs, and the knives of the butchers are at their throats! And, even if you could suppose so meanly of us, it is yet a wonder that you should lower us still more in human estimation, by supposing we could *love,* or desire to cherish, a continued union with the people who have been denouncing, reviling, robbing, and finally preparing such a doom for us! In this Union, by cunning acts, protective tariffs, navigation, and other such laws, and the perpetual appropriation of the greater part of the annual revenue, we have been fleeced of our profits for fifty years. In this Union we find neither profit nor honor. We are reviled, as well as robbed, daily. When we ask for our rights under the Constitution and its laws, we are threatened with fine and imprisonment; and maltreated by the licensed mobs of the North when we seek redress in person. The territory for which our money has been paid, and for which our young men have bled, has been wrested from us; and, not satisfied with this, and a thousand other forms of wrong, robbery and aggression, it is now the loving labor of these fraternal States of the North, whose Union is so precious in your sight, to annihilate the sources of prosperity in our actual possession, and deliver us, bound hand and foot, into the meshes of incendiarism. To bring about this unnatural achievement of brotherhood there needed but one crowning act, the election of a President by a section which disdained to ask the approval of the South — which sought to conciliate no support or sympathy in the South — which consulted neither our interests nor our desires — the election of a creature wholly unknown before, save, as it appears, a rail-splitter, in which few well trained Southern negroes cannot excel him; and for a Vice-President who, according to report, possesses no single quality in mind or manhood, so well marked as a streak of the negro in his blood.

Our mutual friend Lawson [330] writes me that I am mad — that our people are mad! We have certainly borne enough to madden any brave people having human sensibilities. It would not be surprising if we were mad. *You* do not say exactly the same thing, though possibly you entertain the same notion. What you do say only seems to suppose us weak and silly, easily cowed into submission, easily gulled by fraudulence, and ready to compromise, with fear, under the meanest trickery of words and promises.

I am sorry, my friend, to think that it is *you* all who are mad! Your Black Republicans to dream that they can ride roughshod over us — your Conservatives to try and persuade us to let them do so: — and *you* to fancy that your plea for Union could avail with one who has long since regarded the Union as the Pan-

---

[330] The *Mercury* prints *L——*.

dora's box of the South, lacking the only ingredient which made the deadly gifts of Pandora at all tolerable to mankind — the buried Hope, which lay dormant at the bottom. The sooner you come to your senses, the better for all parties. Were your present mental condition capable of the use of reason, you would see that the South has no escape for life and safety but in disunion. She is driven to the wall; would otherwise be soon driven into the net of the *retiarius,* and perish, inch by inch, like the tail of the snake whose head had been battered, unless we make timely use of our privilege and right of self-preservation. We must cut asunder the bonds that give you such a fearful power over us. It is through the Union that you have this power.

You ask: "Will this better your condition, or increase your securities?"

I answer: "Yes!" Since we shall then have an open (possibly) enemy, instead of a concealed one. The assailant, then, must strike at us in the attitude of the warrior, not in that of a skulking midnight assassin. And we shall then be better provided with the means of defence, since your treasuries will no longer be filled with the revenues of our $300,000,000 of exports. We shall have *these* in our own treasuries, for our *defence and support,* and not accord them to you, with which to work our ruin. Already your Government is insolvent, and covered with debt. If our mere *resolution* to secede thus fills your trading marts with terror and poverty, what will be the effect of the consummation! And with what shame and horror will you be filled, when — the South driven from you, which was the very breath of life to your industry — your arts, your commerce and trade — you recover your capacity of reason only to know that *your own hands have brewed the bitter beverage of poverty, isolation and overthrow, which your lips must henceforward drink forever!* You were duly warned of all your dangers — of the evils of your course — of the evils which would follow it! The South pleaded, even while she warned! She was reluctant to proceed to extreme measures. The *prestige* of the Union was all powerful with her, not simply because of the war of the Revolution, but by reason of the glories of that of 1812 — that war being urged by the South, especially, for the honor and the safety of the Union. We have made great sacrifices, then — before and since! Virginia and the Carolinas gave up, *without charge,* an immense territory to the North, for the purpose of making new States. The privilege was abused;

and though a limit was placed, by Virginia, on the number of States to be thus made out of this territory, yet that number has been exceeded, to the increase of the political power of the North in the United States Congress. Connecticut — I think you will find — having a certain territory, also, to concede, required and was paid $200,000 for it! Such has been the relative liberality, generally, of North and South, in regard to the wants and wishes of this beloved Union! And an agricultural people is especially a loyal people, tenacious of its habits, usages, and traditions. Nothing but long continued aggression could move them to change; and it is because of this aggression that we secede. The Union has survived its uses, as well as defrauded all its promises. We know it only as the "Daughter of the Horse Leech," whose perpetual burden was "Give! Give!" [331] until, grown insolent by prosperity, its tone changes. It no longer asks and prays, but prepares to seize and take! Well beloved before, when it was modest in claim, and honest in performance, it is now as a despotism, only the object of our loathing and disgust! We not only reap none of its profits, but we are independent of its protection. It does *not* protect us; unless in that style of protection which the Spaniards, under Pizarro, gave to the Incas and Peru — "that of wolves to lambs, covering and devouring them!" We are full grown, and can and must protect ourselves. We believe ourselves able to do so.

You ask — and the question is rather an amusing one, coming from the assailing section — "why should South Carolina be the one, of all the Southern States, to lead in the business of secession?"

Now what should it matter to the North, which of the Southern States should lead?

You hint — evidently taking your *cue* from some of the Northern papers — that, in so taking the lead, South Carolina will so offend the *amour propre* of her bigger and better sister States, as to make them withdraw from her side in the hour of her peril. If *such* could be the effect of this measure, *their cooperation would be valueless to her cause.* But, this is all fudge, and originates only with those "whose wish is father to the thought!" The penny-whistlers of Black Republicanism have been thrusting this suggestion especially into the ears of Virginia, in the hope

---

[331] Proverbs, 30:15.

to provoke her vanity, and move her to give the *cold* shoulder to South Carolina. It was the hope of these people that her pride would interpose to justify and excuse her lukewarmness in a conflict in which, from her ancient reputation, her great size and numbers, it seemed to be required and expected that she should be the first. But the trick is too poor, and the pretence too idle, at such a time as this; and, whatever the faults and shortcomings of Virginia, her people would scorn to avail themselves of any such miserable pretext for hanging back in the present crisis of our fortunes.

But let me ask in return, why should *not* South Carolina take the lead? She is one of the Mother States. Her people were among the first in the Revolution; were the first to beat the British; the first to form a Constitution; have always been the first to check the encroachments of the North; have been always the last to seek the favors of Congress; have been the most tenacious in holding the country to the very letter of the bond; were among the most determined in resistance to the aggressions and wrongs of a protective tariff, and have given to the country, ever since the Revolution, a large proportion of its purest and ablest patriots, statesmen and soldiers. Why should she *not* take the lead in an affair in which you tacitly admit that *some* State should do so, while you doubt the propriety of it in *her*?

My excellent friend, fifteen gentlemen are assailed by an overgrown bully; he has cheated them, vilified them from a distance; stolen their property from safe distances; and, grown bolder from the impunity with which he has done all this, he at length insolently marches upon them; tells them that the conflict is no longer to be repressed, and that he will now take, with the strong arm, what he has hitherto been satisfied simply to steal! Well! — one of the littlest fellows of the fifteen, at once clips him over the mazzard! How laughable if the bully should pick himself up and cry out — "It was not *your* place to avenge this quarrel: *you* should have left it to some one of your fourteen bigger and stronger comrades!" Suppose next, that the fourteen, thus spontaneously represented by the one, should also turn upon the little fellow who has thus promptly resented the common insult and aggression, and indignantly say to him — "You should have waited for us — till we were *all* ready to co-operate with you! You have insulted *us,* in thus presuming to fight *our* battle; even though it be your own. We leave you now to fight it out as well as you can! Our mortified pride will not suffer us to take part in an affair which you have so impertinently taken upon your own shoulders."

Verily, my excellent friend, if such could be the language of Virginia and our other Southern sisters to South Carolina, their co-operation would not be worth a copper; and their wisdom, no less than their chivalry, would be at such hopeless discount, that we might expect, in every county in their domains, a thousand John Browns before the coming of the next Fourth of July.

South Carolina, warned by all the antecedents of Black Republicanism; by its previous thefts and aggressions, and by its recent attitude of power and presumption, well understood that she had no time to wait; that the wretches who had hitherto only cut her purse strings, were now prepared to cut her throat; that the thief had become a burglar, and was already firing her roof overhead, and prepared to desolate her plantations.

But, my most amiable friend, the reproach of not deferring to her Southern sisters does *not* lie at the door of South Carolina. She has positively been looking to them for nearly thirty years; has sought them with fond entreaty; has been prompted to all the steps she has taken by the solemn pledges of *honor* of her Southern sisters, and by their most formidable resolutions; has been sometimes persuaded, by their entreaties, to yet hold back her hands *a little longer;* has sought them in conventions; has found them reluctant to come to the common council board, and reluctant to do anything when they got there; and, only a few months ago, sent an able Envoy-Extraordinary to Virginia to implore her, as one of the great maternal States of the South, to take into her hands the conduct of this great enterprise! I am afraid, my friend, that when the philosophic historian shall review the details of Mr. Memminger's embassage to Virginia, he will be forced to admit that the treatment of South Carolina, by her more powerful sister, was sufficiently cavalier, if not contemptuous, to justify Black Republicanism in the conviction that the game was its own, and that it had only to prepare itself for an easy victory — nay, for the most slavish submission! [332]

Had Virginia and the other Southern States responded, with one voice of manly consent, to the pleadings of Mississippi and

---

[332] See note 134, July 2, 1860.

South Carolina, the *momentum* of the Black Republicans would have been arrested, and the evils of *this* day would not have fallen upon you — would have been averted, at least, for a few brief seasons. Every thinking man in South Carolina discovered, as the result of the failure of that mission to Virginia, that there was but one process of safety left; that co-operation — at all events, a simultaneous moving of the Southern *politicians* — was not to be expected; that the measure had never been successful even in the Revolution; and that *secession* was the only means left for safety, and this involved *the appeal from the politicians to the people.* Sir, my good friend, we have co-operation now, and of the very best kind — that of the people in all the Southern States! It is a general rising! The politicians in sundry States were all opposed to the people — in some, are still opposed to them; but the people have made, and are making, them succumb daily; and it is not improbable that, baffled into irritation by opposition, they will terribly avenge, upon some of their leaders, that tardiness which, whether the result of treachery or cowardice, will soon become too offensive for forgiveness. And then, my friend, they will hang the imbeciles, or — traitors. Hang them justly — as, in truth, through a selfishness the most deliberate and calculating, they have been the very worst enemies of their people, and the real influencing agencies which have given countenance to the encroachments and usurpations of the North. The national parties, Whig and Democratic, by subsidizing Southern leaders, here and there, divided the people upon false issues; kept the truth from their ears, and have thus maintained the Union twenty years longer than the South should have suffered it to last. I predicted, years ago, in a public speech, and frequently in writing, that the people of the South would never obtain their rights until the Democratic party was annihilated; that never would we become sufficiently sectional to be united for defense, until the North should become wholly sectionalized, and the Northern wing of the Democratic party should be so completly absorbed by the Abolitionists as to sectionalize that of the South also. And when, last summer, in New York, I freely said to some of your active Union politicians, that, satisfied as I was we should never have peace within the Confederacy, I was quite satisfied that Lincoln should be elected, as that event would at once bring our difficulties to a final issue, in utterly disorganizing the Democrats, and depriving their politicians of any hopes of power under that effete organization. No blunder could be more extreme than that of the North in the overthrow of the national parties. Through these parties the North had obtained all the objects of power, keeping up the mere forms of the Constitution. They were in the full enjoyment of the national oyster, flinging to the South the shell. Yet, in the full possession of the revenues; realizing a condition of unexampled prosperity, while they kept the South poor, they were perpetually lying to their people against the notorious facts of the case! In one breath they decried the South as worthless, wanting in moral and energy; unprosperous, grossly ignorant, brutal; uneducated, wanting literature, art, statesmanship, wisdom — every element of intellect and manners.

In the next breath they cried out that the South, the ignorant and imbecile, was yet the ruler of the country! How could they reconcile the contradiction — how account for the fact, if it were the fact, in the face of their far superior numbers? They could only do so by making the most shameful admissions against the words of their own people and public men; admissions that might, indeed, be found susceptible of proof when we discover in one single session of Congress more than thirty Northern members of Congress, more than suspected of corruption and some five, I believe, expelled after conviction.

But, if the South *did* govern the country, then the better wisdom of the North, exulting in its unexampled prosperity, should have moved its people to fall, night and morning, upon their bended knees, with a prayer to Heaven that the South might continue to govern the North forever! For thus, under their rule, had the North risen to a prosperity beyond all measure — a prosperity to which its people themselves hourly pointed with exultation, and made the most invidious and offensive comparisons between their condition and our own. The South, then, had ruled the North, magnanimously, to her own great self-sacrifice, and with the most wondrous results of benefit to the latter section!

It is high time that the South should confine itself to its own rule. The Abolitionists have forced this rule upon them, and with its exercise, come independence and prosperity. We, in the South, have all the essential elements for establishing the greatest and most prosperous, and longest lived of all the republics of the earth! We are, indeed, in possession of the philosopher's stone. We reconcile the great problem now threatening all Europe, and all the North, — the struggle between capital and labor. Our labor is our capital. Exporting, now, some $300,000,000 annually (destined to indefinite increase) of the greatest staples of the world — that raw material which all the world consumes, and which we willingly leave to other nations to work up; we employ the world's labor to an enormous extent, and thus hold the world's tacit bond of good behavior and friendship. We have long furnished the freights to nine-tenths of the Atlantic shipping of the North, as all our exports are bulky, no less than valuable. The moment that the South shall discriminate between foreign and domestic bottoms, all that shipping must become ours; and so soon as we shall declare our ports free to the industrial energies and productions of all the world, we subject Northern manufactures, for the first time, to that wholesome competition with the industry of other countries, the absence of which has made her bloated in prosperity, and utterly insane in its enjoyments.

The Southern States are all welded together by the institution of African Slavery — an institution which has done more for philanthropy and humanity in one year than there ever has been achieved by all the professional philanthropists of Europe and America in one hundred years; and this labor, in our genial climate, can be applied to all the industrial arts — to the construction of railroads — to the working of mills — in brief, to all the provinces of toil. Our water power never freezes, and it is abundant; our labor never times itself to short or long hours, and never *strikes,* impatient to share more largely of the profits of the capitalist.

But what, my interesting friend, shall bind the States of the North — New York, Pennsylvania, and New England, together? What does New York ask at the hands of either Pennsylvania or New England? You are all deadly rivals of each other in commercial, mechanical, and manufacturing pursuits, for the trade of the South. So long as you had this, so vast a market and complete monopoly in your hands, you could *all* flourish, and it was a common cause with you to keep it in your hands, and keep the South in subjection. It was enough for all of you, and you have fattened upon it, till, like Jeshurun, you have kicked! This market gone, this monopoly lost, what is it that ye can yield to, or ask from, each other? What bond of union blends you in one? What is the tie? What the interest? You cannot sell to each other, for each possesses in abundance what the other has for sale! Was there ever a more brutal suicide than that of your States, thus driving from them, by constant persecution, their best customers, struggling to strangle the wondrous goose that laid for them all the golden eggs? And how you shudder, when, fastening your hands upon her throat, the goose becomes the eagle! Ah! my friend, God may forgive you — *we* may forgive you — but will you ever forgive yourselves?

There is something more in your epistle which remains to be noticed. You admit our wrongs — you denounce the trespasses of the Abolitionists, and you counsel us to seek our remedy. Where? How? On whom? On the ignorant farmers who sell us onions, cabbages, buckets, baskets, and the ordinary cargo of notions which are brought us in sloops and schooners from Connecticut, creeping along our shores, and slipping into our bays and inlets, wherever they can find a market for their prog! This, surely, my friend, would be a small business for any people, and how wretchedly inadequate as a remedy for that wholesale robbery, which, through the Union, has been spoiling the South for thirty years. For the wholesale appropriation of the resources of the country; for the entire usurpation of Canada; for the loss of thousands of slaves; for the abuse of justice; for the defiance of law; the violation of the Constitution; for contumely and slander; for insurrections, poisonings and house-burnings; and as a security against the power of Lincoln and his satellites, in full possession of the Government — we are to reject or confiscate the onions and cabbages of Connecticut, and drive from our harbors their piddling little crafts and cargos. Verily, my friend, you do but jest! You might as well counsel us to an onslaught, sword in hand, upon their onion beds and cabbage fields! We are to expend our fury upon the ignorant tools, and suffer the cunning scoundrels who have beguiled them to their ruin, to escape. Would you yourself punish those poor devils, knowing as you well do who have been their teachers? These teachers are your leading citizens; your sense keepers, — preachers, editors, — men who profess to keep the intellect and consciences of your people in their hand; who direct their votes and judgments; and who know what the simple farmers do [333] not, that they inculcate crime, under the guise of philanthropy,[334] and

---

[333] The *Mercury* misprints *farmer do.*
[334] The *Mercury* misprints *philanthrophy.*

prompt incendiarism with the view to the usurpation of power.
These must be made to feel rather than the farmers. But all will
feel, good and bad alike, of that punishment which, in such a case
as the present, must fail to discriminate. A people must suffer at
large for the moral of their communities, for the crimes of their
legislation, for the usurpations which they wink at, if they do not
share. But our purpose is to punish none. We aim at no revenges.
We simply seek escape for ourselves from worse evils. As we
cannot live together in amity, we say to you, "let us part in peace.
You take your course — we ours — each on his own ground." It
is the complaint of your people that the responsibility of our institutions rests [335] heavily on their consciences, though they pocket
all of their profits that they can. We would relieve their consciences; we will assume all the moral responsibilities of our
institutions; and the adjustment of the account will then rest
entirely betwixt God and ourselves. I am afraid, my dear friend,
that the difficulty with your people is, that the relief of their
consciences implies a process which somewhat relieves their
pockets also; and the *argumentum ad crumenam* is infinitely a
sorer subject than the argument of conscience.

But I forbear! Were I to speak longer, I might reproach you
for that somewhat humiliating estimate which you seem to make
of me, by supposing that such a plea as yours, in behalf of the
Union, under the present circumstances of the country, could
be tolerable in the ears of any Southron who had not sold his
birthright, of honor no less than soil, for a miserable mess of
pottage. The wrongs we have suffered from the North are a thou-
sand-fold more offensive, dangerous and degrading than any we
ever suffered at the hands of Great Britain in 1776; and, longer to
submit to them, would only prove us capable of any baseness;
would prove our lack of courage as men; our lack of feeling as
gentlemen; our stupidity as politicians; our perfect preparedness
to pass under the yoke! No! no! my friend, it is not for one of the
aggressive section — thriving by the Union; by the abuse of its
privileges; usurping the powers of the Union, abusing its benefits;
baffling and evading its guarantees; and insolent in its usurpations,
to prate of the blessings of the Union to the wronged and suffering
section. You are mad to think it.

---

[335] The *Mercury* misprints *rest*.

Show this letter to our friend Lawson.[336] He has written me just such a letter as yours. He, too, is shocked and horrified at the thought of sundering this *blessed* Union. But, please say to him, as I beg to say to you, that while your plea for the Union is full of fervor, it somewhat lacks in originality. The whole matter is borrowed from a famous history, which, I fancy, is fully a thousand years old. You will find it in the "Arabian Nights," in one of those admirable moral, political and social stories narrated by the Sultana. See the narrative of Sinbad the Sailor. Hear the eloquent exhortations of the old Man of the Sea, as he rode on Sinbad's shoulders. You will find, my friend, that he is the author of your very best passages. "My son, Sinbad," quoth the old Man of the Sea, "let us never break this beautiful connection between us. The bonds of our union are surely consecrated by Heaven. Only see what a dignified and commanding figure I make, lifted so high in the world's eye — on your shoulders! Thus lifted, and with you so docile, I have been able to traverse seas and continents, and gather the spoils of all the nations; to obtain easy victories, add daily to my territory, and reap honors and dominion whichever side I turn. It is possible, my dear Sinbad, that I do gall you occasionally, for I am rather angular of shape, and, when I have a willing steed, I am a hard rider. My spurs rake you, doubtless, a little severely at times, for I am apt to use them indifferently and unconsciously, whenever *I am making most headway*. It is my *peculiar* mode of riding, and *I am not one to spare the spur* when *the horse is a borrowed one*. Besides, I am a person of *peculiar humors,* which I am sure to indulge at every opportunity. In fact, *once mounted,* I cannot deny myself their exercise, even though they may make you uncomfortable. I hope they do not make you lean. Any how, my dear Sinbad, this union between us is, of all things, the most gratifying to *me*. This should reconcile you to any little discomforts to which my hard spurring may subject you. Never let them, my dear Sinbad, prompt a momentary discontent with our alliance; never permit yourself to indulge in the desire to sunder a Union so blessed, so glorious — in which *my* attitude is so imposing, *my* height so great, my pockets so full, my territory so vast, my fisheries so prolific, my manufactories so profitable, and my pride

---

[336] The *Mercury* prints *L——*.

so insolent! No! no! my dear Sinbad, whatever you do, never think to break away from this beloved Union!"

Here, my friend, is the substance of your appeal — those portions only added which show why the Union is so blessed by the one and cursed by the other party.

[*No signature.*]

1024: To ARTHUR PERONNEAU HAYNE

Woodlands, S. C. Decr. 12. [1860][337]

Hon. A. P. Hayne.

My dear Sir:

Mr. B. J. Lossing, an American Historian of ability, is preparing a History of the War of 1812,[338] in which your own part was so honorably distinguished. He proposes a visit to Charleston, with the view to procuring materials for his purpose, and asks of me to guide him to those veterans of the War, upon whom he may rely for information. As I know of no one who may more fully, or who will more justly, make report on this history, in the South and Southwest, I take leave to introduce him to you, assured that you will withhold nothing from him which you can give, which may be essential to the truths in this noble period of our History. You are so familiar with the events of the War of 1812, as well on our Seaboard, as in the Southwest, that it will be no task to provide them, and will enable you to do, what is the legitimate right of the veteran, fight your battles over again, for the benefit of posterity.[339]

Your obt. & obliged Servt.

W. Gilmore Simms

---

[337] Dated by Simms' letter to Laval of Dec. 13, also introducing Lossing.
[338] *The Pictorial Field-Book of the War of 1812.*

[339] Hayne joined the army in 1812 and was a first lieutenant at Sackett's Harbor, a major of cavalry on the St. Lawrence, and inspector general in 1814. He was brevetted lieutenant colonel at the Battle of New Orleans.

1025: To William Laval [340]

Woodlands, Decr. 13. 1860.

Major Wm. Laval.

My dear Major.

This will be handed you by Mr. B. J. Lossing, one of our American Historians, who is now preparing a History of the War of 1812. He desires information touching that portion of it which concerns the conflicts in our precincts, & in the Southwest. As you have won the Honorable reputation of having done brave service in that war, I have presumed upon our long acquaintance, to refer Mr. Lossing to you. You will be able from memory, to give him a clear narrative & just ideas of all that portion of the struggle in which you were personally engaged — the scenes, situations, chief men, & leading events. Let me entreat you to do so, not so much to oblige me, as to serve the purposes of honest History. Let me hope that Time is laying his hands upon you with tenderness, & that with vigorous health and a good memory, you are in the full enjoyment of all the blessings that earth can afford.

Very truly

W. Gilmore Simms.

1026: To James Lawson

Decr. 13. [1860] [341]

dear Lawson.

I have written to Russell. I enclose you Redfield's letter. Of course, I will pay you all liabilities you incur, no matter what is done by Russell. I may not do it today, but you are safe with me.[342] Jimmy went off two days ago with Gilmore, to spend a

---

[340] Laval (1788-1865), of Charleston, was a captain in the War of 1812 until the siege of Pensacola, when he was honored with the rank of brevet major. He resigned from the United States Army in 1822, returned to South Carolina, and later held the offices of secretary of state and treasurer and comptroller general of South Carolina.

[341] Dated by Simms' reference to Jimmy's visit to Woodlands. See preceding and following letters to Lawson.

[342] We have not located Redfield's letter. Evidently Lawson was to pay Redfield for the copies of *Simms's Poems Areytos* which he had printed and had forwarded to Russell and Jones, Charleston, for distribution. Simms, also, had had Lawson send copies of the volume to various friends. See letter to Lawson of *c.* Nov 22 and following letters to Lawson.

few days with some young friends at Barnwell C. H. I have no doubt they will have a pleasant time. He, Jimmy, seems quite well satisfied. But he writes you. He behaves quite well, & we shall make a man of him, without disturbing his morals. I shall write you again, at a moment of greater leisure. My House is quite full, yet I am advised of more coming. Love to all.

Yours

W. G. S.

1027: To Evert Augustus Duyckinck

Woodlands, S. C.

Decr. 17. 1860.

My dear Duyckinck.

Toil & trouble, a house always full of company, and many excitements, have kept me from a host of correspondents, whose favours I have too long neglected, — yours among them. And now I have hardly any thing to say, save what you already have seen reported in the newspapers. We are conscious just now of but one idea, & that is the Secession of the State from the Union, of which I warned you & all my Northern friends long ago, as inevitable from the progress of events. At the very moment while I am writing this (midnight) it is quite possible that the act has already been consummated. It certainly will be within the next 48 hours.[343] You, who have always taken so little interest in politics, will hardly feel excited or depressed by the event. In your placid atmosphere of home in Clinton Place, you hear nothing of the bruit of chariots & horsemen, and if you hear you do not heed or hearken. Living with the ages you eschew the times, and you are wise and fortunate in doing so. I trust that you will send me copies of what you & your brother [344] may print, and an occasional letter on letters, will be always grateful to me as you must know. I left instructions that you should recieve a copy of my new volume of poems,[345] of which a small edition only has been published, for the Charleston Market; rather, in-

---

[343] The Secession Convention met in Columbia on Dec. 17, elected David Flavel Jamison president of the Convention, and adjourned the same day to Charleston, where on Dec. 20 the Ordinance of Secession was unanimously adopted and signed by the 169 delegates.

[344] George Long Duyckinck.

[345] See letter to Lawson of Nov. 30.

deed, to get the book on record than with any hope of sales in
these perilous times of *impecuniosities*. We must wait for calmer
seasons before we hope to find an auditory for any of the singing
birds. In the complication of the affairs of Redfield, my writings
suffer great injury, which I know not well how to redress, or
repair. I have given Lawson a power of attorney to act according
to his best discretion. I am here repairing & building — building a
room for my library & studio, connected with my dwelling by
a corridor. My house is now filled with relatives & friends, not
a room uncrowded. One of my guests is the remarkable musical
prodigy, young Denck — who is a cousin of my wife; and he
plays for us nightly. It is truly wonderful to see a boy of fourteen
so greatly a master of the piano.[346] With best respects to the
family, believe me

Ever truly Yours

W. Gilmore Simms

1028: To James Lawson

Woodlands, Decr. 18. [1860][347]

dear Lawson.

Jimmy got back today from a five days visit to Barnwell C. H.
where he tells me he was well entreated. He spent his time in a
continual round of company, dinner & evening parties, & I believe, is quite satisfied & delighted.[348] He comes back to meet with

---

[346] During his recent visit to New York City Simms acted as correspondent
for the Charleston *Mercury*, signing his letters "Nemo" or "Old South." (We
have omitted this series from this edition of Simms' letters because of lack of
space.) In one of these, published in the *Mercury* of Sept. 28, he writes:
"Joseph Denck, the son of a German gentleman, well known in Charleston as
a successful teacher of music, surprised every body by his infant performances
on the piano. His mother, of one of the best families in Columbia, S. C., was,
like her husband, possessed of rare musical abilities, a passionate fondness for
music, and was besides a highly talented and accomplished young lady; indeed,
something of a leader in the fashionable circles of Columbia twenty odd years
ago. Their son, now a boy of thirteen, inherits their tastes, with probably a
far larger endowment of original genius, entirely his own." Simms then gives
an account of various concerts that Joseph Denck, Jr., has given in Europe
and remarks that he proposes to give concerts in New York City. Mrs. Joseph
Denck was Charlotte Derrill Hart, daughter of Charlotte Thomson and Dr.
Derrill Hart.

[347] Dated by Simms' references to the visit of James Lawson, Jr., to Woodlands. See preceding and following letters to Lawson.

[348] Jimmy writes of this visit in a letter to his sister Christina dated "Barnwell, C H. 14th. Dec. 1860": "Gilmore accepted an invitation for me to visit
his friends the Alriches [the Alfred Proctor Aldriches], who live here, accordingly we left Woodlands on Wednesday morning [Dec. 12] and will

some of our kinsfolk, — Mrs. & Mr. Denck, and their prodigy
of a son, — a musical prodigy, whose performances have astonished half Europe. They are all here with us, & tonight — all
abed now — we had a sort of concert, — Denck, father, accompanying Denck son, — the flute to the violin. Mrs. Jamison [349]
& all her family were present, except the General, who is at the
Convention. This body has adjourned to Charleston, in consequence of the Small Pock at Columbia. Jamison has been elected
President of the Convention. It is a strong body. In 48 hours
the Act of Secession will pass! Prepare for *that*. It is inevitable.
Hold all you can in hand. I enclose you a dft on Harper & Bro
for $25.[350] Get & keep it, untill Russell pays you. I will see that
you sustain no loss. As for sales, we may not calculate on them,
in the present state of the public mind. But you might sell 75
or 100 copies to the Appletons or Harpers.[351] See them, if convenient. Do not send Redfield. I fancy he is quite dead with all the
publishers. — It is with great satisfaction I report that Jimmy
wins favor wherever he goes. He is considered, a fine young
fellow, and while mannish is modest. Gilmore is eager to volunteer
to take the [352] forts.[353] But our policy is to shed no blood: To
throw every thing of responsibility on the Black Republicans. We
urge a legitimate right to secede & will secede. The blood upon
their heads. We have 2,000,000 bales of Cotton, waiting England,

---

probably go back on Monday. I have had a very pleasant time. Mr. Alrich
is a member of the S. C. Legislature and also Mr. [John] Ryan [a prominent
merchant] at whose house we dined yesterday. I have had plenty of dinner
parties, two at Gen. Jamison's (who will be the Governor of the Republic of
So. Ca.) so you see I have been living on the fat of the land. . . . Tonight
the Alriches will have a little tea party. I am very anxious to go to the Convention which meets on Monday, they will vote the State out of the Union
on Tuesday, and I think it will be a very solemn and imposing ceremony. . . .
I have not had any success hunting and shooting. We took stands for deer
the other day but did not start any. I have ridden on horse-back a great deal
since I came South. . . . Barnwell is a very quiet, plain, little town, but there
seems to be very good society here. . . ." (Original in the South Caroliniana
Library.)

[349] The former Elizabeth Ann Carmichael Rumph, Jamison's first cousin,
whom he had married in 1832.

[350] Doubtless payment for his "King's Mountain.—A Ballad of the Carolinas,"
Harper's New Monthly Magazine, XXI (Oct., 1860), 670-671. A correspondent
signed "L." reviews the poem at length in the Charleston *Courier* of Sept. 27.
"L." objects to Simms' prefatory note to the poem, which says that the Battle
of King's Mountain "constituted a turning point in the war of the Revolution
in the South."

[351] See note 342, Dec. 13, 1860. We have not located copies of *Simms's Poems
Areytos* with the imprint of either Harper and Brothers or D. Appleton and Co.

[352] Simms wrote *the the*.

[353] Fort Moultrie, on Sullivan's Island, and Fort Sumter, in Charleston
Harbor.

who must have it, & will open all blockades for it. Georgia will follow S. C. & so will Alabama, & Mississippi, & Louisiana & all the Cotton States, & so will [354] Virginia & Maryland & even New Jersey. We will precipitate no struggle if let alone. If vext, we shall discriminate against the North, in importations, and if blockaded, we will let loose a thousand privateers, under letters of Marque, and — England — must have our Cotton. Peace is the best policy for all parties. But we are prepared for war. Must have free ports — free from blockade. Once more: Jimmy is doing well, expressing himself gratified, &c. But he will write you. One thing. He had better, when he goes home, take the land route from here. Georgia will secede, as well as S. C. God be with you all. Would you were here with us.

Yours Ever

W. G. S.

1029: To James Lawson

Woodlands, 19 Decr. 1860

My dear Lawson.

I wrote you yesterday, covering a small dft for $25 on Harper & Brothers. Today, I cover you a letter just recieved from Redfield.[355] I wrote to Russell, touching your claim, and I suppose he will attend to it as soon as possible. You can apply, in the meantime, the $25 to your own uses, and, if you think proper, use it for having bound up the remaining copies. These, if you please, might be sold by some of your booksellers. Consult Redfield. If Russell does not seasonably pay you, I will do so. Fortunately, the amount will not break either of us, though in these palmy days, it swells into dignity in spite of its size. Before this can reach you, our act of Secession will have taken place. It has passed probably even before I write. Our friend, Jamison, is President of the Convention. Jimmy got back, highly pleased, yesterday. He sits by me now while I write, busy reading. He has been to dinner & evening parties, and behaves himself handsomely. His manners are gentle & easy, & he carries himself with a modest grace which is the very rose in the chaplet of youth. My house is already full, yet today, we have advices of another accession shortly. I wish all your folks were here now, & away

---

[354] Simms wrote *will will*.
[355] We have not located this letter.

from the winter, — a winter of discontent, if nothing worse — in New York. I killed 3 Beeves on Monday, each weighing about 400 lbs & 2 of them solely for the negroes. This morning we killed 6 Hogs. Tonight we shall have sausages. I have Corn enough in store to last me till next October; have 200 Hogs — 60 head of Cattle, 30 Turkies, 100 fowls, Geese, Ducks, &c. so that, if you should get to starving times in N. Y. you have only to ship your woman & children to me, *prepared to eat hog & hominy,* and live in dry walls away from the chariots & the horsemen. I am building my library, making a wing to the house, connected by a corridor. The new room, is 30 by 22, and the ceiling 12 feet. The corridor presents a series of small arches. I have also altered the front steps of the House, introducing a balustrade in place of the heavy brick wall front, and otherwise greatly improving the front, which is done with rough cast & cement. All the steps are cemented producing the appearance of stone. I have done most of this work with my own workmen; made my own brick, & cut the timber from my own woods. I have spent but little money; simply on paint, window glass, locks, bolts, hinges & cement. All the rest is home-made. I have found little leisure for other employment, and this alone has saved me from the exhaustion produced by the intense excitements of the times. As I am in no position, I can do nothing but fret with impatience, like a Bear chained to the stake — or like a fiery sword cutting through its own scabbard. Had I been exercising at all for the last 30 years as a soldier, I should now surely be in the field, fighting on my own hook. Love to all.

Yours Ever

W. G. S.

1030: To WILLIAM PORCHER MILES

Thursday MG.

[December 27, 1860][356]

My dear Miles.

By the Adams Express I send you today a scarf which my wife has wrought for you & with which she desires that you shall keep neck & shoulders warm, during the Convention & the

---

[356] Dec. 27, a Thursday, is a probable date for this letter about the scarf, mentioned again by Simms in his letter to Miles of Dec. 31.

winter. It is a modest thing, in good taste, which it will not discredit you to wear. She joins with me in affectionate remembrances to yourself, Mother, Aunt [357] & James. God speed your work; but do you economize yourself. When you have respite & feel like a run up here, you are welcome

Yours faithfully

W. Gilmore Simms

W. P. M.

1031: To James Lawson

Woodlands, 31 Decr. 1860.

My dear Lawson.

Jimmy is preparing to go to Charleston, and thence to Savannah. I have just had a long talk with him. The Charleston Steamers are stopt. Possibly, within the next 3 days, the Savannah Steamers will be stopt also. Possibly, this very night, an attempt will be made upon Fort Sumter. I have said to Jimmy — "You can go to Charleston & to Dr. Fuller, and the cost will be trifling, & the risk nothing. But, if the Savannah Steamers, as well as the Charleston have stopt running, you must go home by land. In that event, come home, *here,* to *me*; & go hence by the Wilmington R Road. *Your father's son shall have the means,* though I steal 'em; but your father's son must not have a hair of his head endangered." Accordingly, I have *ordered* him, if there be any fighting on the Seaboard, "do you come back to *me.*" I will give him letters of credit to Charleston & Savannah,[358] for such small amounts as he will need, enough to keep & carry him home; even though his father's credit should fail; which is not likely. It is to you much more important that the boy should be safe, than that he should be in a hurry to get home. He is safe with me, and under my counsel. We are on the eve of war, and our boys are not to be kept bridled much longer. A dirty trick has been played upon us; Mr. Buchanann pledged that the forts should be kept in their present *status.* And while we have kept faith with him, the *status* has been changed.[359]

---

[357] Probably Anne Eliza Warley. See note 243, Nov. 12, 1860.

[358] See letter to Tefft of Jan. 1, 1861.

[359] Buchanan had tried to keep his agreement with South Carolina to maintain the *status quo,* but on Dec. 26, 1860, Maj. Robert Anderson (see note 16, Jan. 13, 1861), without orders from Washington, removed his command from Fort Moultrie, on Sullivan's Island, to Fort Sumter, in Charleston Harbor.

In brief, the Federal Government, is one of dirty rascals, with [360] whom no faith should be kept. The *Venue* changed, we shall have harder work; and with the loss of more lives. We could have captured all the forts weeks ago, — but we wished the work to end peaceably. This is denied. War is inevitable! And — God defend the right! I know not what is to be done. I am not in a position to know or to do any thing, and I am a small volcano in a canebrake: ready to boil over & burst; but without doing more than making the canes explode. Gilmore has been suddenly summoned back to Columbia, to drill the other boys.[361] Head of the first class,[362] he is thus thrown back. He chafes; is anxious to go to Charleston — anxious to volunteer; will fight like the devil, if I will let him; but *I* cannot afford it. He is the last hope of the family. Fortunately, he is an invalid. He has been afflicted, ever since Jimmy came on, with blood boils, or tumours, on his neck, which have kept him in the house, with head awry, with constant poultices, from which he is not yet freed. Sooner than he shall enter into the fray, I will go myself! — In respect to Jimmy, it is with pleasure that I tell you that all parties speak of him with favour. He is an intelligent boy, and a modest boy, and wins his way with grace and propriety. We are all fond of him, & would keep him longer. If I find that there is any difficulty in Charleston, by the papers tomorrow, I shall probably not suffer him to go thither. I shall keep him out of danger. He shall stay *here,* till I hear from you. Here, there is no danger. — He, & Carroll,[363] Gilmore & myself have been playing whist till this

---

Immediately Governor Pickens charged Anderson with violating South Carolina's agreement with Buchanan and demanded his return to Fort Moultrie. Upon Anderson's refusal Pickens gave orders for the immediate occupation of Castle Pinckney and Fort Moultrie, demanded the surrender of Fort Sumter, forbade all communication between Fort Sumter and Charleston, and ordered the erection of batteries on Morris Island and Sullivan's Island to prevent if possible any attempt to reinforce Fort Sumter. The South Carolina commissioners sent to Washington to negotiate for the transfer of Federal property to the state (Robert Woodward Barnwell, James Hopkins Adams, and James Lawrence Orr) demanded that Buchanan order the return of Anderson to Fort Moultrie. On Dec. 31 Buchanan replied that his first impulse had been to order Anderson's return, but that he had then received information of the occupation by South Carolina troops of Fort Moultrie and Castle Pinckney and that he must, therefore, refuse to withdraw the troops from Fort Sumter. For an account of the various negotiations, see Cauthen, *South Carolina Goes to War,* pp. 92-101.

[360] Simms wrote *with with.*

[361] At the Arsenal Academy.

[362] At the Citadel Academy, in Charleston.

[363] Dr. Francis Fishburne Carroll. See note 141, May 23, 1859.

moment. All are gone to bed but myself, & as I have several letters to write tonight, I bid you God E'en[?], & God be with you.

Yours ever

W. G. S.

1032: To WILLIAM PORCHER MILES [364]

Woodlands, 31 Decr. [1860] [365]

dear Miles.

Keep yourself warm with the scarf. My wife will never forget you, nor will I. God bless you & yours. — We are all here on the *qui vive* of expectation, & today the rascally mails failed us, & we have neither Mercury nor Courier. I have written to Jamison. It was an oversight to let Anderson transfer himself from Moultrie to Sumter. I told Jamison, long ago, that Ft. Sumter held control over all the forts in the harbour, & must be had first, to secure the rest. Your *Guarda Costas* should have been flying between, day & night. Now, so far as I can see, you have but two processes left you. You must either starve out or smoke out the garrison. You should certainly not suffer them to mount a cannon; but by incessant cannonade, from the landside, wear them out. In the smallness of the garrison is your hope. Do not attempt *escalade,* until all other means have failed. I am here, like a bear with a sore head, & chained to the stake. I chafe, and roar & rage, but can do nothing. Do not be rash, but, do not let this old city forget her *prestige.* Charleston is worth all New England.

God be with you!

W. Gilmore Simms.

---

[364] Part of this letter is printed in Trent, p. 255.

[365] Dated by Simms' discussion of the forts. See letter to Lawson of Dec. 31.

1861

1033: To Israel Keech Tefft

Woodlands, S. C.
Jany. 1. 1861.[1]

My dear Tefft.

This will be handed you by Mr. James Lawson, a youth, the son of an old & much respected Scotch friend in New York. I have been intimate with him for 30 years. The young man has been spending the last month with me. He wishes to visit your city,[2] & thinking he may go thither, I commend him to your attentions. Should he need some thirty to fifty dollars, in these perilous times, pray help him to them. His father is good, & I will be your bondsman to that amount, and see that you are paid. Much love to Mama;[3] tell her that Augusta & her baby[4] are with us, & meditate a visit to her in February.

Yours truly as Ever

W. Gilmore Simms

1034: To William Porcher Miles

Woodlands, S. C. Jan 12. [1861][5]
Midnight.

My dear Miles.

I sent you, a few days ago, by Dr. Fuller, a copious letter which I was especially desirous that you should instantly recieve. He writes me that he failed, after several efforts, to find you, and dropt the letter or letters, for I think there were two, into

---

[1] Simms erroneously dated this letter *1860*. The correct year is established by the visit of James Lawson, Jr., to Woodlands (see preceding letters).

[2] Savannah, Ga.

[3] Mrs. Tefft, the former Penelope Waite.

[4] Chevillette.

[5] Dated by Simms' discussion of the fortification of Charleston Harbor. See following letters.

the P. Office. As the Dr. is a countryman, it is quite probable
that he did so without putting on the penny stamp. Should you
not have recieved it, enquire at the P. O. and do not be satisfied
until you know that *all* of my letters have been recd. for, in the
last four days I have written you half a score or more.[6] Fuller
writes me, to my great surprise, that from what he could learn
you have only *three* guns mounted at Fort Morris, and no new
batteries elswhere, except at Ft. Johnson. This, after your long
working would seem to be a most lame & impotent conclusion. I
am in hopes he is mistaken, & that you have 30 rather than 3,
as I fondly hope still. With but 3 guns at Ft. Morris, & none
elswhere for the covering of the channel, except Moultrie, I do
not see what is to prevent one or more vessels getting in, provided several are sent, enough to keep Fort Morris employed & to
pass Moultrie while Sumter plays upon that fort. I am satisfied
that you should have several batteries to open on Sumter, the
moment she opens on Moultrie; & the guns well addressed to her
embrasures, from several quarters, would give such distracting
employment to her small garrison as to baffle aim, and prevent
deliberation. You have a wide semi-circle from which to choose
your position for battering Sumter, & may so choose it as to
enfilade her guns in the rear, from several quarters, while your
own are measurably free from her aim. I would rather you should
have six small than one large battery. For breaching, 42, or 36
prs, or Columbiads should be employed, if you have them, while
your *oblique* batteries, & gun boats, could address themselves
especially to the portholes. I confess my anxiety lest, from the
knowledge obtained of our port through the coast survey, a light
draught steamer, taking the flood, should force her way through
Wappoo Cut, & thus get to Sumter, unsuspected. This should be
seen to. I also fear that landing by boats may be effected, in the
rear of Forts Johnson & Morris, and unless we have camps on
the island, of riflemen & flying artillery, these forts may be surprised. Enfilading batteries are all important in operating on Ft.
Sumter. Shot entering a port hole will be apt to kill every man
at the guns. When I wrote before, I was under the impression
that there were sundry *pivot* guns, working on the barbette at
Sumter, & not under cover. I am still under the impression that
such is the case on the island side. I see, however, from one of

---

[6] We have not located any of these letters, all doubtless concerned with the
fortification of Charleston Harbor.

the newspapers, that all of the guns are casemates. It may be so, but I doubt. If covered, your showers of grape could do no hurt except in the area. There, a combustible such as I suggested, if such can be prepared would no doubt be of infinite service. At any rate, the great point is to bring, at the same time, as many guns to bear upon Sumter as possible, & from as many different quarters. Once fully employed, the garrison would have little leisure to notice the quiet approach of scaling parties, on rafts, or in gun boats. When you do move, it should be with an overwhelming force as well as determination. A half moon battery, between Moultrie & Sumter, constructed of earth & logs, faced with iron bars, & sufficiently high as well as thick, would cover that garrison. I am in such ignorance of what has been done that it is quite probable that I blunder at every step in my suggestions. — If not employed, & your health does not improve as rapidly as you wish, why not give me a few days up here?

Your friend

W   Gilmore   Simms.

1035: To William Porcher Miles [7]

Sunday Night, 12 P.M.
[January 13, 1861][8]

I am sleepless, my dear Miles, & must write. If you should be sleepless also, it is not improbable but that my letters will help you to a soporific condition. — It seems to me that you will have a little respite. The opening fire upon the Star of the West, changes materially the aspect of things to the Federal Government, & they will hardly think to send supplies to Sumter, except under cover of armed vessels, which is the inauguration of open war upon the State which the President & Cabinet will hardly attempt unless under Authority of Congress.[9] Congress, alone,

---

[7] Most of this letter is printed in Trent, pp. 255-261.

[8] Dated by Simms' remark: "By the Mercury it is said that some negotiations are on foot which [will] prevent bloodshed. The inference is that Ft. Sumter will be given up." The Charleston *Mercury* of Jan. 12 (Saturday) says that it is understood that communications have taken place between the authorities of the state and the commander of Fort Sumter "which, it is hoped, may save the effusion of blood, and secure to the State the possession of that fortress."

[9] On Jan. 9 Maj. P. F. Stevens and a detachment of cadets from the Citadel Academy, occupying the battery on Morris Island, fired on the *Star of the*

I believe, has the power to declare war. There is no telling, however, what may be done when the power is under the hands of
a weak administration, counselled & governed, in fact, by a person
whose whole training has endowed with military ideas as paramount to all.[10] We must, of course, prepare for two dangers —
treachery & assault. But, it strikes me that the *unexpected* fire
of Fort Morris, will compel a pause in the Federal Councils, for
the better maturing of plans, & some respite for preparation will
be allowed you. Not an hour should be lost in preparation. To
have numerous guns to bear, equally upon an assailing squadron
& Ft. Sumter seems to be the necessity. Looking at the map, I
note that Mount Pleasant is distant from Fort Sumter some two
miles, while I estimate Moultrie to be 1¼. A battery at Mt. P.
cutting the Western angle of Sullivan's island, seems to be in
direct range with Sumter; and if within range of heavy cannon,
then a battery of earth at this point, with half a dozen 32 prs
might operate successfully against it, at all events compel a very
useful diversion of its fires. So, I find that on the sandhills, below
Ft. Johnson, & on the sandhills, at the extreme Western verge
of Ft. Morris, batteries of say 3 heavy cannon each, might face
Ft Sumter, formed of logs faced with iron & filled in with sand,
which could contribute largely to its distraction, if not its injury.
On these sandhills also, you possess an advantage in their elevation, which will tend to reduce the superiority of Sumter in height.
Two of these batteries along these hills & at these points, mere
bastions, having two or three guns each, of heavy calibre, could
be thrown up very suddenly, assuming, as I do, that you can
command, from the popular patriotism, any amount of slave
labour. I would have them so planted as not to face the port
holes of Sumter, yet be able to take them at an angle. Shot entering a port hole obliquely would be more mischievous, perhaps,
than if direct, since the zigzag course they would pursue would
be likely to kill every man at one side or other of the guns,
besides abrading the embrasure very seriously. In reference to
Wappoo cut, let me mention that as the obvious entrance to that
cut is by the Stono, there is an old fort, once thought a pretty

---

West, an unarmed merchant steamer sent from New York City with men and
supplies for the relief of Fort Sumter. Maj. Anderson (see note 16, below)
failed to support the *Star of the West,* which returned to New York City. See
Cauthen, *South Carolina Goes to War,* p. 102.

[10] Gen. Winfield Scott, at this time commander-in-chief of the United States
Army, exerted a strong influence on Buchanan's administration. See Elliott,
Winfield Scott, pp. 672-691.

strong one, at the mouth of the Stono, on Cole's island. This might be manned by volunteers from the precinct, officered by some good military man. It covers Bird Key, & is very well placed, though still, I think, it would be good policy to stop up Wappoo cut, or keep an armed schooner, in Ashley river, at the mouth of it. I am writing, you percieve, without the slightest knowledge of what *has* been done, and it is quite probable that all my suggestions have been anticipated. If, however, you fancy there is any thing in them, communicate with Jamison & any military friends on whose judgment you rely.[11] Ranging timber [12] properly morticed might be prepared by the mechanics of the city, and the iron bars laid on, if desired, before shipment to the desired points. It is my impression that old Ft. Johnson ranges Moultrie in the same line with Sumter. If so, it is a question how far it would be proper to use the former place with heavy cannon which might range across the strait. You should employ all the heavy cannon you can. Jamison told me that you had an abundance. Unless Fort Morris has numerous pieces, she could hardly play any efficient game with many assailing vessels. I do not know where Ft. M. is placed, but suppose it to be fronting equally the ship & the 12 foot channel. In that event, unless the sand hills interpose, it is under the range of Ft. Sumter, provided the distance be within 3 miles, as I suppose it to be. I should have said 4, but for the threat of Anderson to fire on Morris. A battery between Ft. Morris & the Light House, on the edge of the sand hills might rake the ship channel with a *plunging* fire, yet I should think be out of range & even sight of Ft Sumter. I think I said, in a previous letter, that in sighting the guns for long distances, telescopes should be used; [13] of course, I meant only the ordinary ship spy glasses, of which a sufficient number for each battery could be obtained in the city. With another battery to second Ft. Morris, each of 12 guns at least, &

---

[11] On Dec. 30, 1860, Governor Pickens' nominations for his Executive Council were confirmed by the Secession Convention. David Flavel Jamison was appointed secretary of war, Andrew Gordon Magrath secretary of state, Christopher Gustavus Memminger secretary of the treasury, A. C. Garlington secretary of the interior, and William Wallace Harllee (the lieutenant-governor) postmaster general. See *Journal of the Convention of the People of South Carolina, Held in 1860, 1861 and 1862, together with the Ordinances, Reports, Resolutions, Etc.* (Columbia, S. C.: R. W. Gibbes, Printer to the Convention, 1862), pp. 136-137.

[12] Timber suitable for use as cross timbers in the construction of a house or ship.

[13] We have not located this letter.

heavy ones, you could give a telling account of all entering vessels. They might all be sunk with good gunnery. But two shot only taking effect, out of 18 fired,[14] would seem to show that the gunnery was not sufficiently practised. I write only from report. Tonight, I learn that (on dit) there has been a mutiny in Ft Sumter, & that Anderson has had to shoot one of his men, & put ten more in irons; & that *this* was the reason why he did *not* fire on Fts. Morris & Moultrie.[15] By the Mercury it is said that some negotiations are on foot which [will] prevent bloodshed. The inference is that Ft. Sumter will be given up. This is hardly probable. I suspect treachery. We should suspect nothing else. Anderson wishes communication with the city. If opportunity is allowed him to see what we are doing or to hear of it; or if he is allowed to corrupt mercenaries, we shall have worse mischief. We must not be too confiding, too easy of faith, too courteous even to an enemy, who, if he had the right feeling would at once resign his command & throw up his position on the distinct ground of his Southern birth & associations.[16] He should be kept corked up closely, until we are quite ready to draw him off. If he still keeps his position, and we are to have an attempt by the war-steamers, Ft Sumter must & will take part in it; and the vital point is how to neutralize her action in the engagement. I see but the one suggested; to keep as many batteries at work on him, breaching & otherwise, and a cloud of vessels & men ready for scaling, as will effectually divert his regards from those forts which are designed for the defence of the harbour. And unless Fort Morris be made strong in guns, I see that vessels of heavy dft in deep water, may shell it ad libitum, while the smaller craft presses in. I am very doubtful whether a fort on the East end of Sullivans can do more than cover the Maffit & the Ratlsnake channels,[17] if these. It can hardly do much mischief to vessels entering the ship channel. Something will depend upon the calibre of its guns. Do, if you can spare a half hour, write me, in charity,

---

[14] When the *Star of the West* was fired upon. The Charleston *Courier* of Jan. 10 says seventeen shots were fired.

[15] We have found no confirmation of this rumor.

[16] Maj. Robert Anderson (1805-1871), of Virginian descent, was born near Louisville, Ky. His wife was Elizabeth, daughter of Gen. Duncan Lamont Clinch, a Georgian. Anderson had been sent to Fort Moultrie when the secession of South Carolina seemed imminent. In 1861 he was promoted to brigadier general, and in 1863 he retired from active service.

[17] The Maffitt and Rattlesnake channels.

how we stand & with what degree of preparation, and believe me

Ever truly Yours

W. Gilmore Simms

W. P. M.

P. S. Should there be thought, at any time, that a proper moment for escalade had come, rafts, constructed in Ashley river, the two head ones to be covered with thick plank and tin painted dark, could be set afloat in a dark night, towed over to James Island, where with ropes men might keep them close to shore, until they had reached the rear of Fort Sumter, where they might be lodged silently anchored and chained together, & reaching from the fort to the shore. The two head ones, covered, would protect from hand grenades. With batteries in the rear, at two angles of the fort, a mile distant, with guns, loaded for breaching & others for grape, the garrison could scarcely attempt any thing against the rafts which would form, at low water, an almost solid bridge. But I still think that escalade should not be attempted; certainly not, till the breach was made ample & pretty low. The battering from several points, concertedly, would, I think, neutralize the action of the garrison against other forts, & so long as we can keep the shipping out, so do we gain. The garrison will be worn out & must suffer before long. The great point is to keep them from doing mischief. So long as we can effect this, & keep them in a state of seige, there is no discredit to the State. We should do nothing rashly now, to the peril of our brave young men, which we can possibly avoid. But you will think me interminable. Once more, Good Night.

W. G. S.

1036: To David Flavel Jamison

Woodlands, 15 Jan 1861.

My dear Jamison.

I had just written to you a night ago, when, last night, I recieved yours by private hand. I had foreborne writing more frequently, as I well knew how much you would be distressed by business, and I did not wish to add even a feather to the camel's back. But I had many thoughts, & as I fancied, some new notions of value, in our present troubles, so I wrote copiously to Miles, with the request that, if he thought the matters suggested important, he would lay my letters before you. I presume that he has done so.[18] There is one point which I concieve to be a discovery, or rather the application of a discovery in a new direction & use, hitherto unthought of. I mean the employment of ranging timber in the construction of defences, *and the facing them with plates of rail road iron.* This, if the English opinion of the new French vessels of war, thus plated with iron, be correct,[19] is a discovery even more available for fortresses by land (especially extempore ones) than for vessels at sea. The iron is impenetrable & there is no splintering of the timber. Even picquets, filled in with earth, & faced with these plates, must defy the bombardment from the heaviest cannon in use. The ranging timber, well put together, in strong & frequent sections, bolted & braced, & filled in with sand, then faced with the iron bars, laid on perpendicularly or diagonally, would it seems to me furnish a fortress at once cheap, readily built & secure. The advantage of the palmetto logs lay in the spongy character of the wood, which did not fracture, and scattered no splinters. Faced with iron bars such as the rail roads use, even the flat ones, (and perhaps they may be the best[)], the ranging timber, which is more easily to be procured than the palmetto logs, would, thus faced, answer as good a purpose, perhaps better as these logs may be procured of greater length & breadth than the palmetto. The bars need not be placed nearer than 4 inches to each other, or 3 inches, as the size of the balls employed against such a fortress are not likely to be less than 12 or 18 pounders. If placed diagonally thus / / / / / / the pressure of the ball will be distributed over a larger surface, & make the least direct impression. The whole claim for the use of the iron here, rests on the truth of the statements given in the British periodicals, & the experiments made on the newly scabbarded war vessels of the French. If a ship thus laced with iron can resist & throw off a 32 lb shot, how much more effectually would this be done by a fortress from 16 to 25 feet thick, & filled solidly in with earth. There is another use to which these timbers, thus covered

---

[18] Jamison's failure to return these to Miles would account for the many letters written by Simms to Miles during this period which are missing from the William Porcher Miles Papers, Southern Historical Collection, University of North Carolina. Doubtless they were lost when Jamison's home, Burwood, was burned by stragglers from Sherman's army.

[19] See "Iron-Clad Ships of War" (unsigned) in *Blackwood's Edinburgh Magazine,* DXXXVII (Nov., 1860), 616-632.

with iron may be put. The embrazures, or port holes, nay the whole platform may be roofed over with logs, thus scabbarded, their planes inclining inward, so that shot would glance off & shell explode without mischief. Even were the plane *upward,* on the interior, & this may be the best, the shot would ricochet, & flying upwards, would pass over the rear walls of a small fortress without harm. The iron plates, driven down with heavy spikes, would also serve to strengthen the whole fabric. I am assuming that you have much to build & in the hope that you will be allowed sufficient time to do it. The *old* iron of the rail road would answer just as well as the new. You should seize the Columbia & Nashville also. But as no two are in the port at the same time, and as the seizure of the one will be telegraphed instantly, & the other prevented from leaving port, so it may be well to practise a little *ruse* in your operations, & only seize the one at the hour when she is about to leave the wharf, & have the telegraph wires cut above Branchville, for a couple of days, so that the N. Y. Steamer shall be fairly out at sea, & beyond recall, before the news can reach that city. By such means both vessels can be secured.[20] With strong & heavy beds, they can be made to carry the heaviest cannon, and if you please their bulwarks may be also faced with iron down to the bends. You will need to have signals with such sea captains as are trustworthy; at least should be prepared with your steamers to overhaul & examine all vessels before they are suffered to come in. How if American War Steamers should approach with the British or French flags flying? I hope you have strengthened Ft. Morris sufficiently to enable her to take the whole game on her hands, in the event of a bombardment from several vessels. A fort upon the sandhills contiguous would give Ft Morris increased security, & have the advantage of elevation for a plunging fire on the enemy. Such a fort as I suggest might be constructed in a few days, & mounted with three heavy pieces would be formidable. Forgive me, for troubling you in military matters with my suggestions, and ascribe to my zeal what would otherwise be an impertinence. But civilians have furnished many of the most admirable suggestions & discoveries to the military — gunpowder, shelling, percussion powder, &c. all came from the closet of the civilian. So far by way of apology. You will find also, in my letters to Miles, a suggestion by which the space between

---

[20] The *Nashville* was seized after the fall of Fort Sumter and was eventually fitted out as a cruiser.

the shore & Fort Sumter may be effectually bridged so as to be accessible to escalade whether at high or low water. This is by a series of rafts, built with a floor & in sections. In each section a bale of cotton, & all floored over with slabs. A roofing on the first two or three rafts of slabs coated with iron, would effectually protect from hand grenades, & even heavy artillery. These rafts drifting down Ashley river in a dark night, at the ebb of the tide, must cross to James island, & towed by ropes from the shore (no oar or paddle in the rafts — only poles) to the rear of Fort Sumter, and one by one ranged from the mole to the shore, chained together, and an anchor dropt from each. Even if heard, the fire of the fort would be of little danger in the darkness, while the two or three covered rafts next the fort, would defy hand grenades. A battery on shore, with guns ready to rake the rafts, in the event of any effort at their destruction, would be advisable. Ft. Johnson might do this. Her guns ought to be heavy; and were you to have a battery, nearer & on the S. W. of Ft. Sumter, the several fires, with those from Pinckney, Moultrie &c. would give them enough to do. But see the letters to Miles. Consult with Magrath [21] who is too shrewd & longheaded & able a man, not to see, at a glance, whether there be any thing valuable in a suggestion. Unlike myself he combines the military man with the civilian, & is thus doubly armed for a proper conception of the subject. But God grant that your hopes of a peaceful solution of the difficulty may be well founded.

Yours Ever

W. Gilmore Simms

1037: To James Lawson

Woodlands, 19 Feb. 1861.

My dear Lawson.

While I have wondered that my two last letters to you remained unanswered, I find you thundering at me for my silence. I owe a letter to Jimmie, but none to you. You are still my debtor to the extent of one scribblement. Yours of the 7th. was recieved during my temporary absence to the city, whither I went to transact some

---

[21] Andrew Gordon Magrath (see introductory sketch) was at this time secretary of state in Governor Pickens' Executive Council. See note 11, Jan. 13, 1861.

business, (anent taxpaying &c.) to hear the news & see the
batteries, and the fight, for which I had supposed all the parties
ready. I was there a week. Our taxes, in consequence of the new
condition of things, have been increased about one third, and I
had to see my factors [22] about the money, which I must get them
to advance. I have still a few bales of Cotton to sell, and have laid
in most of my supplies to last the family & negroes till next harvest, and stand a siege if necessary. I have cured 55 hogs, 4 beeves,
have made 3000 bushels of Corn, 100 rice, a few barrels of flour,
& there are peas & potatoes & poultry, and I have some 80 head
of Cattle, & 200 of Hogs at large in the swamp. My negroes are
all fat, and satisfied with the prospect before them. Briefly, I have
calculated the calibre of each portly paunch, and fancy that they
will say at every sunset *quant. suff.* But I have no money! There
will be some for me in Appleton's hands, some 2 months hence,
I fancy, say $400 to $500.[23] But I fear the account of Widdleton
will be a Flemish one. Your letter does not inspire me with
hope from that quarter! As for Duyckinck, he probably acts wisely
in not suffering himself to be embarrassed with the affair. I have
not said a word to him about it, since I prefer, in the case of one
so amiable, not to disturb & for no good reason, the pleasant
relations which have existed between us. You will do wisely to
adopt this plan also. My legal friend is Joseph H. Dukes, Esq.
He is a smart fellow and will be disposed to work for me faithfully. I believe the poems [24] sell a little. I heard of one person
taking 7 copies. At this rate they would soon go off. But people
here breathe nothing but war, & read none but military books now.
Gilmore is at the Citadel, doing more *practical* than *theoretical*
work — making cartridges & cannons, & percussion caps, &
mounting cannon, & drilling daily, as a Zouave. He is eager for
a hand in the fight, but I tell him — No! not till you are called.
He is only 17, and I wish him to get his growth and education.
You are aware, perhaps, that it was a detachment of the Cadets
that fired on the Star of the West? [25] All the devils could not have
kept their hands off. We do not intend to do any thing rashly. We
crave peace. But we prepare for the war that is threatened & in

---

[22] Probably the firm of Robinson and Caldwell (J. K. Robinson and J. M.
Caldwell), factors and commission merchants at Atlantic Wharf. See note 20,
April 10, 1862, and the Charleston *Directory* for 1860.

[23] Payment for contributions to *The New American Cyclopædia.*

[24] *Simms's Poems Areytos.*

[25] See note 9, Jan. 13, 1861.

which the North will more effectually cut its own throat than it has ever done yet; for in that event, we shall declare our ports *free* to Europe & shut them to the North; and France & England will raise our blockades, without which they will not get a bag of Cotton, and we shall issue Letters of Marque *ad lib.* & Yankee commerce will be the prey of Yankee Privateers; so look out for the Edwin Forrest. Sell out your share & pocket the money. If we are let to go in peace, we shall not discriminate against the North, and our trade will still be accessible to her industry & enterprise. Jamison told me of your writing him. I have been daily closeted with him, Magrath, & the other Secretaries, & Pickens & myself are old intimates.[26] We served together in the Legislature.[27] I saw them all daily & nightly in long discussion. The employment of rail road iron on ranging timber, in shore & marine batteries is my suggestion, which they have adopted to some extent, though I did not plan the forts, or the water battery.[28] I have been writing every night for six weeks, till 3 in the morning, on public affairs, for the Mercury or for some of the Secretaries.[29] They are all busy day & night. I went down with Jamison to examine the forts for one day, & saw some 2000 of our boys in armour, eager to smite Black Republicanism, & wishing for nothing so much as the appearance of Scott.[30] On our several batteries we now have some 200 guns mounted, ranging from 24's to 65's — Mortars & Columbiads. Had there been enough cannon powder in the magazines, it is probable that the war would have broken out long ago. But all our leading men are busy keeping the peace. We want peace! And nothing but the utter insanity of the North

[26] For Governor Pickens' Executive Council, see note 11, Jan. 13, 1861.

[27] During 1844-1846. Simms was in the House, Pickens in the Senate.

[28] In an unsigned article on seacoast defense published in the Charleston *Mercury* of July 9, 1861, Simms gives detailed specifications for the construction of the water or marine battery and discusses the use of such batteries. For the success of the battery under fire, see the accounts of the bombardment of Fort Sumter in the *Mercury* of April 13 and May 2, 1861.

[29] During 1861, Simms wrote a great many editorials for the Charleston *Mercury* on "public affairs." All are unsigned, and only those on the subject of seacoast defense can be conclusively identified: in his letter to Hammond of Nov. 18 he says that he has written "nearly all" the articles on this subject that the *Mercury* has "published . . . for the last 8 months," and his are easily distinguished from those written by others since in them he repeats the same ideas he expresses in his letters to Miles, Jamison, and the Hammonds written during this time. Simms also continued his critical notices in the *Mercury* and contributed to the newspaper occasional poems, articles (see, for example, "Domestic Resources," cited in note 170, July 24, 1859), and letters "to the Editor" (see, for example, the letter cited in note 54, March 2, 1861).

[30] Gen. Winfield Scott.

(*Quos Deus vult perdere, prius dementat!*) could entertain the idea of coercing into subjection 6 States, with 300,000,000. of Exports — raw material (employing 6 million of European Laborers) and with a government already established? But I warned you a year ago — years ago — of every thing, just as it has happened. I told you that the North was committing suicide — trying to strangle the goose that laid them all the golden eggs. I told that silly fellow McElrath, and he treated it lightly — till I got angry.[31] I counselled you to sell your real estate a year ago — last summer.— You will admit that I indicated every step that has been taken both by North & South. — Did you get my letter, sent to Bockee, with instructions that it be sent to you? After I had written it, I read it to Jamison who pressed me to publish it. I expanded the letter to five times its size & sent it forth through the Mercury. I sent Bockee a copy of it, also. Get him to show it to you, for though very different from what I wrote to him, it is still based on the same premises.[32] I shall look for your tragedy; but revise, in the spirit with which we did some of the scenes.[33] When you send me one — have it *interleaved* that I may hint at each page what I think necessary. My House [34] is done 30 x 22 a large room,— corridor of 20 feet with arches, connecting with the main building. Next year (D. V.) I shall build the other wing. Come this summer, or next winter, & taste the inspiration. I did not mention that the Mercury has just sent me 5000 cigars & a barrel of Monongahela. I am ready for a siege & who knows but my house may be made a citadel. With a revolver the other day, I planted 5 bullets at 20 paces within 1½ inches of the center.

Àdios.

W. G. S.

---

[31] During his visit to New York City in Aug.–Sept., 1860. See letter to Duyckinck of March 15, 1861.

[32] See letter to Bockee of Dec. 12, 1860.

[33] In 1861 Lawson had 100 copies of *Liddesdale: Or the Border Chief. A Tragedy* printed for private distribution.

[34] Simms means "My Library."

1038: To WILLIAM PORCHER MILES [35]

Woodlands, Feb 20. [1861] [36]

My dear Miles.

Do not forget the interests of Literature in the formation of the new Government.[37] Have it decreed that all Nations, States or Confederacies in amity with this Gov. and giving to its people the privileges of Copyright, as possessed by their own, shall enjoy the same rights & securities as our own people — *but no other States!* The leading men of letters at the North are all abolitionists, with very few exceptions. Such a measure will astonish them! Let the Copyright be accorded to the author for fifty years, or during his natural life, with right of renewal to his wife & family, his heirs, for 50 years longer. *An author's copyrights,* if he be a man of original faculty, are generally most valuable when he is dead. In degree as he is profound & original,[38] is he unappreciated during his natural life. It is only when he can no longer offend the *amour propre* [39] of rivals, that the public are permitted to form a proper judgment of his merits.[40] We ought to frame no organic law touching the slave trade. We may express a sentiment, if you please. But no law. Either negro slavery is a beneficient, merciful, Godchartered institution, or it is not. If beneficient, why limit it? Is it better for the negro to be a barbarian & savage in his own country, than to work out his deliverance in this? If better, why be at the pains to cast censure on the morale of the institution. Regulate the trade, but do not abolish. Neither deny nor admit. It is quite a mistake, if by

---

[35] Part of this letter is printed in Trent, pp. 262-263.

[36] Dated by Simms' discussion of the provisional and permanent constitutions of the Confederate States. The Provisional Congress of the Confederate States held its first session in Montgomery, Ala., from Feb. 4 through March 16. The delegates from South Carolina were Miles, Robert Barnwell Rhett, Robert Woodward Barnwell, Lawrence Massillon Keitt, James Chesnut, Jr., Christopher Gustavus Memminger, Thomas Jefferson Withers, and William Waters Boyce. Withers (1804-1865), of Camden, was a lawyer and former editor of the Columbia *Telescope.*

[37] On Feb. 9 the Provisional Congress of the Confederate States appointed a committee to draw up a permanent Constitution. The committee reported on Feb. 26, and on Feb. 28 Congress began its consideration of the report. The Constitution was adopted on March 11. See *Journal of the Congress of the Confederate States of America, 1861-1865* (Washington: Government Printing Office, 1904), I, 25, 41-42, 87, 851-896.

[38] Simms wrote *orinal.*

[39] In going from one line to another Simms failed to italicize *propre.*

[40] An act "to secure copyrights to authors and composers" was passed by the Provisional Congress and was signed by President Davis on May 21, 1861. See *Journal,* I, 113-114, 194, 247, 264.

abolishing, you suppose that you conciliate England. The conscience of England is commercial — a sort of moral caoutchouc, she cannot help herself. Only leave her sufficient room to dodge the direct issue, between profit & principle.[41] And why adopt the 3/5 rule in regard to the representation of slaves, — a rule forced upon us by a people who were about to abandon slavery, and, in surrendering to which, we gave them the power to conquer us?[42] There is only one motive to this — to conciliate Maryland, & Western Virginia, Missouri, Kentucky & Tennessee.[43] Yield the point here, & they overslough us. They will soon hold the same relation towards us which the North held to the South. Briefly, we do not want these States at all. We can do without them. They bring us no help. They are simply dead weights. They will take out of the treasury ten times what they bring in. I grant you, we should *look* more formidable, as 15 States than 7 or 8, & might thus, overawe the North so as to compel recognition. But we gain nothing by it. Better meet the worst issues now, than yield in a point so vital to our future safety & success. Better that the Border States should form a Middle Confederacy, as they must do, if they do not take up with us. Our policy is *now, not* to report a permanent Government; but to make the provisional sufficiently strong for defence. We must, or should, stave off the report, & consideration of the terms of the provisional Government, *till after the fourth of March,* untill, all Compromises & Peace Conventions having failed, the temper of the Southern people & politicians, is so roused, that a rupture becomes inevitable. The Black Republicans *cannot recede until* they are in full possession of the offices. If they do, it seals the fate of their party & forfeits the spoils. The spoils will keep them together untill they are in power. We may hold out *lures* to the Border States. It may be as well to suffer them to see that the Committee

---

[41] The South Carolina delegation opposed the clauses in both the provisional and permanent constitutions of the Confederate States (adopted respectively on Feb. 8 and March 11, 1861) forbidding the "importation of negroes of the African race." See *Journal,* I, 35-36, 868-869.

[42] When the Provisional Congress voted on the permanent Constitution, Keitt made a motion that the entire slave population rather than only two-thirds of it should be counted for purposes of representation and taxation, but his motion was lost. See *Journal,* I, 861-862.

[43] By Feb. 20 no other state had joined the six seceding states of South Carolina, Georgia, Louisiana, Alabama, Florida, and Mississippi, which had united on Feb. 8 to form the Confederate States of America. Texas was admitted on March 2, Virginia on May 7, North Carolina and Tennessee on May 16, and Arkansas on May 18. See *Journal,* I, 39, 97, 193, 234-235, 244.

reports the 3/5 rule; but beware how you adopt it. Its adoption seals the fate of the Cotton States. Your *weak* point is just here, & here it becomes necessary to play the politician with most effort. Count the votes for yourself & see where, in a few years, the Cotton States would be with such an arrangement. On one hand, Virginia, Maryland, Kentucky, Tennessee, North Carolina & Missouri, *versus,* S. Carolina, Georgia, Florida, Alabama, Arkansas, Louisiana & Texas. *Verb. Sap.* I am sleepy. It is 2 o'clock in the morning. All well here. God be with you.

Yours Ever

W. Gilmore Simms.

1039: To WILLIAM PORCHER MILES [44]

Woodlands, Feb. 22. 1861.

My dear Miles.

I wrote you only yesterday,[45] but write again if only to emphasize what I indicated in my previous letter, that we are attaching far too much importance to the alliance with the Border States, and I am afraid are prepared to pay too great a price to secure it. If we move steadily forward, they cannot help themselves & must come into our fold & on our own terms. *We should make no organic law, and pass no provision under it, having their case in contemplation at all.* I would rather have a compact empire than a very extensive one, and our future secret of safety & success must depend wholly upon the homogeneity of our society & institutions. Were the territory occupied by the Border States an inland sea, a waste of waters, it would please me better. You see, so petty is the interest of Maryland in negro property that the scheme of the abolitionists is to buy her out, and she would perhaps be willing to sell out were Virginia not between her & the sea; & the interest of Va. in slaves is too large to be bought out. We might conciliate Western Virginia & Maryland by adopting the three fifths rule of representation for our slaves, but that would be suicidal; would ruin Charleston & Savannah & Mobile & New Orleans as great ports & yield the ascendancy to Norfolk & Baltimore. In a few years, we should have the same trouble

---

[44] Part of this letter is printed in Trent, pp. 263-265.
[45] The preceding letter dated Feb. 20?

with these states which we now have with the North. The 3/5 rule of representation not only discredited our institution, but has done as much towards ruining us as any thing else, & that we should voluntarily adopt it, when our sole object is alliance with Slave States like our own, seems to me the most egregious folly. It plays the devil with the *status* of So. Caro.— will injure Georgia, Mississippi, Louisiana, Arkansas, Florida & finally Texas; and all for what?— To conciliate States into our alliance, whom we shall have to support just as we have supported New England. It is idiocy to think of it, & especially when the Border States can urge no possible pretext against the recognition of the slave in full, all having the same property. If they do make objection, it is clear that they will do so, only because the recognition gives us a degree of political strength which will enable us to resist their domination. The hostility of the Border States to the slave trade, is grounded partly on this very political issue; quite as much so as upon their interest as slave breeders for the Cotton Market. Now, my dear Miles, it is a God's Providence for us that has kept the Border States from prompt action, enabling us to make & prescribe the conditions of Union. If they never come in, I am satisfied. Their only use now will be to make an imposing front, which *might* discourage the hostility of the North. Any how, they will serve as a breakwater. Let us not permit, in any organization, other States to look into our private concerns, and require us to surrender a political right because of a peculiar social condition. The *present* is not enough for the Statesman. He must regard the future. In 30 years, Mississippi, for example should have 1½ millions of Slaves to 1 million of Whites (at least.) In process of time all Mexico is destined to be civilized through the medium of negro slavery. Nor need we doubt that the Border States will come in, however tardily. In a connection with the North, they will possess no political power. As a separate confederacy, Tennessee & Kentucky, are both tributaries to the Maritime States on the Atlantic while Arkansas & Missouri are like tributaries to the Gulph States. They will follow the destiny that makes them tributary. The truth is, we shall be much more troubled with the question hereafter, — "Who shall we keep out," — rather than "How many will come in?" In this latter question, it is our ignorance & fear that speak, not our need. The difficulty will be how to keep out New Jersey &c. The true line of demarcation, geographically imposed, will be the

Hudson & the Lakes. Even Kansas & Nebraska will be rather apt to go with Missouri, while California in three years will set up for herself, probably in connection with Oregon which she will not need. It is impossible to concieve the extent of spread of this Southern Empire of ours, if we keep ourselves free from entanglements & blunders. We only need to be firm, to be independent, and only need to be Independent to be the most prosperous nation of the Earth. But if we yield in these points, it is difficult to say what troubles will enure to our children. Let us not bother our heads to please England & the North on the score of negro slavery & the slave trade. They have already voted us barbarians. But we have them in our power. Let us not bother our heads to please the Border States. They, too, are in our power. We are reducing the whole question for their people to a very simple formula. We say — you want a Union — you are desperately fond of a Union. You have always been accustomed to a Union & you can't well do without it. Well, we will oblige you. Here is a choice of unions — with a kindred people, on the one hand, having the same interests with you, — and on the other, here is a people who have been always bothering you & vexing you, with whom you have no sympathy, and who have declared that your destruction is the only guarantee for their peace of conscience. Can you doubt what the popular instincts will decide, when it is reduced to this question, and when all their trading politicians show themselves at fault? Continue the duties on tobacco, on sugar & molasses — for the present — put the duties on negro clothes at 10 per cent. Let in the wines of France at the smallest rates. Let in R. R. iron at the same. Isolate Pennsylvania. New York will fall from her on the Morrill Bill.[46] Precipitate the event. But keep your secrets. It is vitally important that the *Permanent* Confederacy should not be formed, until the Border States have failed utterly in their Peace & Piddle Conventions. Let the rupture be complete. Do nothing beyond preparing for War! Appoint your Commissioners [47] — let your Government be

---

[46] The Morrill Tariff Act passed the House on May 10, 1860, the Senate on Feb. 20, 1861, and became law on March 2, 1861. It restored *ad valorem* duties to about the level of those in the act of 1846 and gave increased protection in the specific duties.

[47] On Feb. 13 the Provisional Congress of the Confederate States had passed a resolution to send representatives "to the Courts of England and France and other European powers." On Feb. 15 it had passed a resolution to send "a commission of three persons . . . to the Government of the United States of America, for the purpose of negotiating friendly relations between that Govern-

filled in all its departments, so that you can negotiate with other nations, and — stop there. Put off the decisive topics & results, and let your discussions upon the New Organism be wholly private & do not publish except in cases which can do no harm. An agricultural people is necessarily more ignorant than any other, simply because it has less mental attrition. There is hardly an element in this subject of statesmanship, which is at all understood by ten men in Kentucky, Tennessee, Arkansas & Missouri. *And these people have never yet learned to go alone. The same ignorance* led to the blunders of the Constitution of the U. S. Let us try not to perpetuate them, and the argument against them is equally strong in the case of all the States in our present Confederacy. It is *not* so strong as regards the Border States, and hence their coldness & tardiness on the subject of secession. Hence the necessity which will kick them into our arms. But let us not be too eager in our embraces, and especially let us avoid those miserable fears and doubts which may prompt us to make great & vital sacrifices for an alliance which is really not worth a tinker's d — n to us or our cause. Consult with your friends. If what I have said, strike you favorably, see Davis himself.[48] He is a man of affairs, an able man, and a brave one. He must see. Let us not sell our substance for a mess of pottage. If I had money, I would run to Montgomery & see how you come on. But I am as poor as Job's turkey, or, to use a less biblical illustration — as poor as a mouse of the Swedenborgian Church. All other mice, of all other churches, are supposed to be full fed. But, though I have no money, I have meat & bread, hog & hominy, enough to stand a siege. I have killed 55 head of Hogs, corned down four beeves, made 3000 bushels of corn, 100 of rice, &c. And I insist that you do not pass Woodlands, on your return, without stopping for awhile, as long as you please.— My depôt is "Midway," some 64 miles from Augusta. Let me know a few days before, and my

---

ment and the Confederate States of America, and for the settlement of all questions of disagreement between the two Governments." William Lowndes Yancey, Pierre A. Rost, and A. Dudley Mann were appointed commissioners to Europe; André Bienvenu Roman, Martin Jenkins Crawford, and John Forsyth were appointed commissioners to the United States. See *Journal of the Congress of the Confederate States of America*, I, 45-46, 49, 52-55, 85-86, 89, 93, 114-115, 375.

[48] Jefferson Davis was elected president of the Confederate States on Feb. 9 and was inaugurated on Feb. 18. See *Journal*, I, 40, 63.

Carriage shall meet you at Midway, where you will only be 1½ miles from my dwelling.

Ever your friend

W. Gilmore Simms.

P. S. It is now 3 oclock in the morning, and writing as I do to you, to Jamison & scores besides, to say nothing of my profession, I rarely go to bed before this hour. Judge whether I should not be weary of head & weak of hand.

W. G. S.

1040: To WILLIAM PORCHER MILES

Woodlands 24 Feb. [1861][49]

My dear Miles.

I am afraid I bore you, but the points I have endeavoured to make are quite too serious, according to my notions, to be left unconsidered. We must beware lest the Border Slave States overslough us. Their destiny involves more rapid changes than ours. They will become manufacturing. The matter most important is that we should be able, as Cotton States, to neutralize the numerical force of such states as Virginia, Maryland, N. C. Missouri, &c. Believing, as I do, that for the next 50 years, more or less, the natural division line will be the Hudson & the Lakes, and that N. Jersey & Pennsylvania will both prefer a connection with the Cotton than the New England States, we must provide against their preponderance of numbers. We *must* make our *negroes* count as an integral of our society & on equal terms with all. We must take the decisive ground that the quality or caste of our population is not a matter for the discussion of our Sister States. *Now,* we have the power to do so, & the right. A month hence, and we may not have this power, & a new revolution, some 25 years hence, will be the consequence. If now, I could persuade the Floridians to divide Florida, as in old times, into East & West, I would do so, as a corrective, in the Senate chamber, of the preponderance of the Border States. It is my notion that God means nothing to be permanent which is merely mortal. It is therefore the part of wisdom, not only to meet the emergency, but to look forward & guard the avenues of the future. Florida

---

[49] Dated by Simms' reference to his preceding letters to Miles.

has twice the territory of S. C. Yet vanity of territory may make her sacrifice the most important securities. If her politicians are reasonable men, a hint may be of service. As for Virginia, she is necessarily very sore. Her *prestige* required her to be in the first rank. She has faltered. In her case, we see the effects of 40 years of bribery. Tennessee & Kentucky & Missouri & (measurably) N. C. must all follow Virginia. Keep your eye therefore upon *her.* Keep back your permanent constitution, untill she is fairly committed, for or against, the North. It matters not much which side she takes. A big body, with a little soul. If she is made angry, & there be no loop hole of evasion, she breaks from the North. But that does not mean that she will come with us. She will still endeavour to maintain her ascendancy by a league of border States. *Here,* her prestige will fail her; for it will then be evident to Kentucky & Tennessee, if not to Maryland, that she only seeks to maintain her ascendancy, and not a common cause. She would *now* come promptly into the Southern Confederacy if she could make it appear she led. Our policy is so to manage that she will have no recourse. To do this, we must be heedful to make no provision touching the slave trade, or the ratio of representation in the provisional government, and to keep the scheme of the permanent government in abeyance, until she is fairly committed against the common enemy. We shall then have her on the hip. If we now show our hands, she will certainly try to set up the Middle Power. Here she will fail, for the instincts of the people of N. C. Tenn. & Kentucky, will be too strong for her *prestige.* But this will give us trouble for the time, & lessen the force with which we shall appear among the nations. There is no need to force forward the plan of a permanent government. Let the Committee wait.[50] The provisional Govt. can make all necessary provision for defence, and for recognition. Things will work right, if we let God have a chance. If in our apprehension, our eager timidity, we make concessions now, conflicting with our rights & securities, we leave the same trouble to our children, which now brings us to the bayonet.

Yours Ever truly

W. Gilmore Simms.

---

[50] The committee to draw up a permanent Constitution. See note 37, Feb. 20, 1861.

1041: To WILLIAM PORCHER MILES

Woodlands, S. C. March 2. [1861][51]

dear Miles.

My friend, Major M. C. M. Hammond, the Brother of the Senator, wants a military appointment. He is an honored graduate of West Point — has served in Florida, Texas, & the West — was the author of the excellent Military Reviews in the Southern Quarterly of the War in Mexico — was President of one of the Examining Boards at West Point, — made the Report & delivered the Oration,[52] & has been urged for the office of Secy of War. Something conspicuous ought to be had for him. At one time he dissipated in Brandy & Cigars. He is reformed; has given them up; and wants to be doing. Is it possible to do any thing for him? See Chesnut and Keitt & others. A colonelcy might be got. He has himself written to Stephens. (V. P.) [53] Again, I urge keep back the discussion on the Permanent Constitution and let it be in *secret* — at least until the imbroglio at Washington will reach a head. As for Export and Import duties both, what nonsense.[54] A simple duty for Revenue, of 10 per cent. would suffice. We should be tenacious of an economical Govt. In the ex-

---

[51] Dated by Simms' reference to "the discussion of the Permanent Constitution" of the Confederate States. See preceding letters.

[52] Hammond's oration was published as *An Oration on the Duties and the Requirements of an American Officer. Delivered before the Dialectic Society of the United States Military Academy at West Point, N. Y., June 5, 1852* (New York: Baker, Godwin & Co., Printers, 1852). At the time of its delivery Hammond was president of the Board of Visitors of the Academy.

In giving M. C. M. Hammond advice on how to write an address, his brother James remarks of Simms in a letter dated May 15, 1852: "But the *points* may be treated well in twenty minutes: and the whole art of speaking & writing is to make *strong points well knit together*. Discursiveness & diffuseness suit only story telling & may be greatly abused in that as Simms does." Again, in a letter dated May 20, 1852, he writes: "Composing is like tunnelling—one must not advance an inch without clearing every thing away behind & securing sides & arch, & ascertaining that you are preserving line, grade, & every thing necessary to bring you to your exact point on the other side, & to enable any body to follow you right through with safety, pleasure & profit— Simms & such generally scramble through any way." (Originals in the South Caroliniana Library.)

[53] Alexander Hamilton Stephens (1812-1883), of Georgia, elected vicepresident of the Confederate States on Feb. 9, 1861 (see *Journal of the Congress of the Confederate States of America,* I, 40). Hammond did not receive an appointment (see letter to him of Nov. 9, 1861).

[54] Simms discusses this subject at length in a letter, signed "Gossypium," addressed *"to the Editor of the Charleston Mercury"* and published in the *Mercury* of March 2 (omitted from this edition of Simms' letters because of lack of space). "Gossypium" is a pseudonym Simms frequently used in publishing poems in the *Mercury* during 1861 (see, for example, note 30, April? 1863).

cess of the Treasury, is born the devil of republics. My wife sends her regards. Do not pass us going home. We shall look for you at Woodlands with such welcome as unaffected friendship & a simple state of society can give. God bless you.

Yours hurriedly

W. Gilmore Simms.

W. P. Miles.

1042: To James Lawson

Woodlands, 3 March. [1861][55]

dear Lawson.

The article of Mr. Brower is so sound and sensible that, on recieving it, I at once prepared an introduction for it, and sent it to the 'Mercury', where, *if it appears at all,* it will appear editorially. My doubt arises from the great length of the article, & the crowded state of the columns of the paper, from the pressure of daily news, of more present interest. The argument of the writer has been long familiar to the mind of South Carolina.[56] Tell Mr. Brower that if he can lay hands on "the Crisis" of Robt. J. Turnbull (Brutus) a volume of 200 pages, it will help him in further studies of the question. The book was published in Charleston in 1832 by A. E. Miller, Publisher there.[57] The great evil of the North is that it (as a people) studies nothing beyond the question of numbers; and nothing seems to offend them more than that you should interpose the Constitution as a veto upon the claim of a majority. I have been astonished to find that the Literary men, are generally, almost wholly ignorant of politics, the Constitution, the debates at the formation of the Confederation, and, briefly, of all the principles & issues which were involved in the establishment of the Confederacy. Mr. Calhoun's replies to Mr. Webster

---

[55] Dated by Simms' references to "the counsels of the Southern Confederacy" and to Fort Sumter. See preceding and following letters.

[56] If this article was published in the Charleston *Mercury,* it appeared after March 17 (see letter to Lawson of that date). We have not been able to identify it; nor have we been able to discover any information about Brower, whose initials may have been J. M. B. (see the above-mentioned letter to Lawson).

[57] For Robert James Turnbull, see note 16, Nov. 27, 1833. Most of the essays in *The Crisis: Or, Essays on the Usurpations of the Federal Government* (Charleston: Printed by A. E. Miller, 1827), published as by "Brutus," had appeared originally in the Charleston *Mercury.*

were conclusive; [58] but the people of the North, who live by rages & impulses, regard with no favour, & will not read, an argument which conflicts with their desires; and made insane by prosperity and insolent by a belief in their power of numbers, they mock at argument, deny right, & so far as their relations with the South are concerned, they have resolved themselves into a settled despotism. Nothing but secession could open their eyes, and nothing but the evils accruing from it will ever coach them, and it will be quite too late for their own good, when they are made to see. They have committed the greatest political & social suicide that History has ever shown. Never was such blind ignorance so insolent, never good fortune so blind, never presumption so riant and imbecile at the same moment. But you can teach them nothing by argument or reason. They do not listen to reason and argument only offends vanity. They are so accustomed to run riot in their periodical rages, that any attempt to arrest these by argument, is offensive to self-esteem. The whole body of the people seems corrupted by prosperity & the abuse of power, incurably, and nothing but great suffering can ever produce that degree of Humility which will allow even moderate exercise to common sense and reason. Of all the North, I doubt if there are 25 of their politicians who could have argued out the paper of Mr. Brower, or would have known where to look for its materials, or could show themselves capable of disabusing themselves, or of being disabused by others, of their habitual reference to the majority as the only source of Confederate Power. I shall do my best to get Mr. Brower's argument published, but there will be doubtless some delay in doing so. You will have seen that the counsels of the Southern Confederacy have been marked by the utmost soberness & forbearance. Nor have we in S. C. failed to exhibit an inflexible calm of mood, keeping back our more passionate men, and some ten thousand of our youth who have been boiling with the desire to fling themselves on Fort Sumter. There are now 20,000 volunteers drilling daily & nightly in the State; and there are no less than 5000 actually in arms in & about the harbour of Charleston. The Cadets [59] have volunteered. Gilmore came up to see me on furlough to procure permission to do

---

[58] For an exposition of Calhoun's reply to Webster on Feb. 26, 1833, "a conspicuous parliamentary triumph," see Charles M. Wiltse, *John C. Calhoun Nullifier 1829-1839* (New York: The Bobbs-Merrill Company, Inc., 1949), pp. 186-195.

[59] Of the Citadel Academy.

so. But while making ourselves ready, nobody desires war, and we see no necessity for it. We reluct at bloodshed. Nothing but invasion will bring us to it, and the refusal to surrender our forts. Then if it comes, we shall let loose all our tigers, & carry the attack into the enemy's country. We shall declare our ports free to the trade of all friendly powers, & issue letters of marque & reprisal, and arm a thousand privateers if possible, and hurry forward our own navy, for which we are now preparing. The consequences be upon the heads of those who would not suffer us to be at peace in the Confederacy, nor leave us at peace when we withdrew from it; whose consciences made them wretched at an alliance with us, yet when we relieve their consciences of all responsibility, who are unwilling to be relieved, and resolve that the victims whom they have so long robbed and reviled shall not escape them. But a truce to this. We are in the enjoyment of May weather. All our trees are blossoming, and a return of cold & frost, would lose us all our fruit. But you & Mary & Kate & all, should see our woods now, while putting on their morning glories. I could wish, too, that you could see my improvements. I have altered my portals so that I have made my old brick steps as handsome an entrance as any in the State. I have rough cast them, cemented the whole flight, introduced an open balustrade at the front, along the first platform; have painted & whitewashed and added my corridor and the new library building: this is 30 x 22 — a single large room. The corridor, connecting it with the main dwelling covers 20 x 12, with four arches in front; and cemented

floor. The building presents some such appearance as this — that is the mere elevation. In this outline, I have not regarded the relative proportions and only seek to give you some idea of the general plan which contemplates a corresponding wing & corridor on the opposite side. The main dwelling is 50 feet front, the corridor 20, the library building 22, thus covering a front of 92 feet. When I complete the opposite wing, which (D. V.) I contemplate to do next winter, the whole front will be 184 feet. We have set in front of the house some fine shrub trees — the English laurel, the Italian & other cedars & a variety besides. We have also set out numerous roses & flowers. I had a present of about 100 dollars of fruit & shrub trees, and have set out 1000 grapes Catawba & Warren, and shall set out (D. V.) another 1000 in a week.[60] Love to all. God bless you. Gilmore brought up some daguerreotypes, one of which I will keep for you.

Yours Ever truly

W. G. S.

1043: To WADDY THOMPSON [61]

Woodlands, Midway P. O.

Hon. Waddy Thompson   So. Caro. March 3. 1861

My dear Sir:

Can you, in a short space of time, furnish me briefly with such particulars in your life as you would desire to make public, as would enable me to provide a paragraph concerning you in the Cyclopædia now publishing by Appleton & Co. of New York.[62] The work is an elaborate & important one which will make some 16 vols. large octavo. I desire that South Carolina should have a good showing in it, and will be pleased to indicate to the public the facts in your career, such as belong, at least, to your public life. A few pages [giving] [63] period of birth, public appointments, the transactions in Mexico, date of the publication of your Book, & names of publishers,[64] with such other personal details as you may be pleased to give, will suffice. May I hope to hear from you at your earliest leisure. I write to you at Greenville, somewhat at random, since, when I last heard of you, you were in Florida, but at what place, I do not know. I shall request the postmaster to forward this letter, should you not be at Greenville.[65]

Yours very truly,

W. Gilmore Simms

---

[60] James H. Hammond had sent Simms the grape cuttings. See his letters to Simms of Jan. 10, Feb. 6, Feb. 23, March 5, and March 23, 1861 (originals in the Hammond Papers, Library of Congress).

[61] See introductory sketch. Thompson's reply to this letter, dated March 15, is in the Charles Carroll Simms Collection, South Caroliniana Library.

[62] *The New American Cyclopædia.*

[63] The MS. is torn.

[64] *Recollections of Mexico* (New York and London: Wiley and Putnam, 1846). Thompson was United States minister to Mexico during 1842-1844.

[65] Thompson owned land in Florida and a home on Paris Mountain, near Greenville, S. C.

1044: To Benjamin Franklin Perry [66]

Woodlands, Midway P. O.
So. Caro. 3 March 1861.

Hon. B. F. Perry.

My dear Col.

It is a long time since you & I have conversed together, perhaps for the very sufficient reason that you have been mingling with public life while I have been retiring from it.[67] And it is your life that I now seek, though with no unfriendly intent. I could wish to get from you such heads of topics as will enable me to give you a paragraph in the New American Cyclopædia, in course of publication by the Appleton's. You will know what I desire without further explanation. The space allowed is brief, but I desire S. C. to have as good a showing in the work as possible. It is an important & valuable publication, and our record should be made. I have just written to Waddy Thompson to a similar effect. Should he not be in Greenville, to which place I have addressed my letter, will you be so good as to instruct the P. M. where to send it. I need hardly say to you that my wife & self both remember our pleasant time with you in Greenville,[68] & I trust, should occasion serve, that you will not pass by Woodlands, without looking in, upon your old confrere, & obliged Servt.

W. Gilmore Simms.

1045: To William Porcher Miles [69]

Woodlands, S. C. March 7. [1861] [70]

My dear Miles

Mr. Robert Martin, a native of Charleston, but resident of Barnwell District, whom you will perhaps remember as once one of your pupils in the Charleston College is desirous of procuring

---

[66] See introductory sketch.

[67] Perry was a delegate to the National Democratic Convention which met in Charleston in 1860 and was one of the two South Carolinians who kept their seats after the bolt of most of the members of the Southern delegations. He was a Unionist until the secession of South Carolina, but, like many other Unionists in the state, he then became a loyal Confederate.

[68] In 1842. See letters to Lawson of Aug. 22 and Oct. 7 of that year.

[69] Part of this letter is printed in Trent, p. 265.

[70] Dated by Simms' discussion of the defenses of Charleston.

a Captaincy in the Southern army. There are two reasons, perhaps, why such a man should be encouraged, & in seeking, find
what he seeks. First, Mr. Martin is a man of fortune, one of the
wealthiest in our district. We are to infer from this that he seeks
the army with an honorable ambition. Second, he is considered
by those who know him to be singularly competent as a Militia
officer — is at once brave, circumspect, intelligent, & very temperate. He, perhaps, needs but little training to reach excellence,
and with the opportunity would most probably distinguish himself, and do service to the cause, and credit to the country. I have
several reasons besides for desiring him to recieve the appointment; but if this be not possible, I presume that he will not object to a First Lieutenancy. Am I asking too much of you to beg
that you will see the persons in authority, and use your influence
in Mr. M's favour.[71] Well! You see Lincoln is simply about to
realize his fate, and confirm our good fortunes.[72] We must go
through a trial, not merely to confirm us in Independence, but
to force the real necessity of their case upon our Southern bretheren. I shall rejoice that they do not come in until our System is
determined. But I earnestly adjure you to every possible effort to
realize the lowest possible amount of duties — not more than 10
per cent (and this on every thing, with few exceptions)— and
see that our representative ratios are founded upon the recognition of the slave, as a person in minority — in lifelong minority
— and not as a slave. In 1835 I took the ground, in my pamphlet on the Morals of Slavery,[73] that our Institution was not
slavery at all, in the usual acceptation of the term, which implies
some wrong done to the party, but that the negro in the South
was a minor, under guardianship — forfeited no right — was
recognized in all his attributes of humanity — was distinctly in-
dividualized, & protected in all his rights & privileges, through a
representative master. We should fight this matter, & the first
named, to the last. It is perfectly monstrous that a great producing
people, and very slightly a manufacturing people, should deliberately tax themselves for the benefit of foreigners, and of in-

---

[71] Martin attended the College of Charleston in 1852. He was appointed
captain in the Palmetto Sharpshooters.

[72] Lincoln's inaugural address, delivered on March 4, is printed in the
Charleston *Mercury* of March 5.

[73] *Slavery in America, Being a Brief Review of Miss Martineau on That
Subject* (Richmond: Thomas W. White, 1838) was first published in *S. L. M.,*
III (Nov., 1837), 641-657. See note 39, Aug. 30, 1837.

terests entirely dissimilar to their own. — Well! Mr. Lincoln has spoken! And we are to have war. Let us not *declare* it. Hostilities may exist without war. Let us simply meet the issues as they arise. In Charleston, they are daily expecting the struggle. I know nothing precise, but from what I hear, a few days will probably confirm these anticipations. God be with our people. I have been writing my counsels, night after night to Jamison, and am now engaged in trying to make a new, simple, cheap, & facile adaptation of the sword bayonet to the old musket. I have made the model, & expect a smith tomorrow to see if he can work my plan into ship shape. I find that Jamison has adopted my suggestion of using ranging timber with facings of R. R. iron for batteries; but I am not satisfied with the shape of the battery, nor with the manner in which the iron is laid on. The shape of the battery (profile) is this:

It presents too long a plane surface to a plunging fire. Besides the rails are not spiked down. I counselled that they should be spiked, but loosely, so as to allow some working of the rail under the shock of shot or shell. My plan would have presented this profile:

so that no shell or shot could strike without glancing upwards & over, or, if striking in front, beneath the angle, then recoiling into the sands, below. And I would have had the structure solid, filled up with sand. Who are these men whom you have sent as Commissioners to Washington? Forsyth is the only one I ever heard of, and he, though a smart fellow, has the reputation of being a sharper politician than we need.[74]

> Yours lovingly, but in haste
>
> W. Gilmore Simms.

---

[74] The commission of the Confederate States to Washington (see note 47, Feb. 22, 1861) was terminated on April 10. Nothing was accomplished.

1046: To WILLIAM PORCHER MILES

Woodlands. S. C.
March 12. 1861

My dear Miles.

You are to take a recess.[75] You must give me at least one night on your way to Charleston, if, as I suppose, you will wend your way thither. You have never been at Woodlands. Come now. You may never, otherwise, see me again. I am sinking into the sere & yellow leaf, & have grown in the last two years, as grey as a badger. You will hardly know me. It is just possible that though no professional politician, I may have some hints for you. Come! I am exactly in your route. Take your ticket at Augusta for Midway, and with a days notice, my Carriage shall meet you at the depôt which is only 1½ miles from my house. An you love me, come.

Yours Ever,

W. Gilmore Simms.

1047: To EVERT AUGUSTUS DUYCKINCK

Woodlands, S. C. March 15. [1861] [76]

My dear Duyckinck.

In the whirl & excitement of the life that I have been living for the last few months, I am at a loss to say whether I returned an answer to your last letter or not. I have been busy day & night on the plantation, building & planting, but night & day engaged at the desk also, now writing to politicians, now to military men; planning books & batteries; belles lettres & bayonets. Verily, my life, though secluded, is by no means an idle one. Ask Lawson & he will give you some idea of the necessity which is upon me, without holding office, to be in constant communication with officials. But you are not forgotten. On the contrary, I always think of you with kindness & regard, & sorrow for the delusions, in which I fear you shared, which have re-

---

[75] The Provisional Congress of the Confederate States took a recess on March 16 and reconvened in Montgomery on April 29. See *Journal of the Congress of the Confederate States of America,* I, 158-159.

[76] Dated by Simms' discussion of his financial troubles with Redfield, Widdleton, and Henry Panton. See letter to Lawson of Oct. 20, 1860, and following letters to Lawson.

sulted in the destruction of this once grand Confederacy. If you will recal our frequent conversations, you will find that I predicted every thing which has happened. I predicted all to Lawson a year ago, when he was here, & last summer when I was with him. I predicted every thing in the Southern Review — see that work — in 1851.[77] I discovered, to my surprise, that, regarding the majority as the Law, very few of the Literary men or Editors of the North, knew any thing of politics or Government. New York, had but one idea on this head. How shall we so arrange as to get the offices — gut the treasury. You & I, were too careless of this seeking of the spoils, and knew but little of the game. It is now up, — and forever. There may be peace between our sections — there can be no profit to either party from war — but there will be no reunion. The South has made a marvellous escape from destruction. But I must not trouble you with politics, which I know are not to your taste. I only sought to account to you for my possible neglect of your last favour. — I have been in much trouble & anxiety, and short of provant as Dugald Dalgetty [78] would say. For three years, I have been able to get no returns from Redfield. I thought him a good fellow, & I was easy. Panton was friendly, & I was easy. But with 6 or 800 dollars to my credit on the books, I could get nothing. Well, Widdleton bought out the establishment; yet would make no returns to Lawson, whom I appointed my agent, and denied having printed new editions of my works, when we had the Printers certificate to the contrary. I wrote to Panton. I could see no reason why an assignment of Redfield's effects, should affect my percentage; that was mine, not assignable. There we stand. You will see that I cover you a notice of Widdleton's publications, with, I trust, a grateful reference to yourself. I feel kindlily disposed to this young man. As for Redfield, I thought him a good fellow; but feared that he was quite done up. Lawson now writes me that he is a Black Republican, following in the wake of McElrath. I never suspected even McElrath of being such a fool, & took supper with him last summer. — But all this is nothing to you. Enough that you see in my paragraph that I feel with you as ever, and would like greatly to see you do yourself justice by some energetic performance of your own. There

---

[77] Simms is probably referring to the unsigned article entitled "The Prospect before Us," *S. Q. R.,* N. S., III (April, 1851), 533-541.

[78] In Sir Walter Scott's *A Legend of Montrose.*

must be many writings of Trench in the periodicals uncollected.
Are they traceable? Was he not Richard Chenevix, before he
became Trench? These worked up by proper classing, with proper biographical introduction would enable Mr. Widdleton to make
his edition unique & complete. And nobody could do this work
better than yourself.[79] I shall look with interest & curiosity for
the volume you are engaged upon of Eminent Americans.[80] A
work of this sort could be made a great improvement upon those
of our editors generally, who get all their material at second
hand, know not where to look, or what has been done, & thus
omit from their collections many of their most admirable histories & subjects. Send me a list of your subjects. I sympathise
with you sincerely at the loss of our old friend, Francis. His geniality & bonhommie must be greatly missed from your circle.[81]
— Occasionally I get a copy of a flash weekly from our ancient
acquaintance Cornelius Mathews. But his labours seem to be light
& worthless, and the paper a very ordinary one. I suppose he
has written his mind out, as well as down.[82] I suppose that literary affairs generally are, at this period, no where considered.
Do not publish your book till the question is settled, of peace or
war, between the sections. It is just possible that the habitual
lying of your newspapers about the South will provoke war. All
their stories touching South Carolina are gross as invention and
palpable enough as lies. For our markets, see our prices current
of Charleston. Beef is 12 cts a lb. & so in proportion all other
edibles, meats & vegetables. *In the country, there is scarce a
planter who has not meat & bread for himself, people & slaves,
to last one year.* I have, for example, — & my crop was a shorter
one than that of most of my neighbours, — about 3000 bushels of
Corn; 8000 lbs Bacon, 200 head of Hogs, 80 of Cattle; 25 Goats,
22 Sheep, 100 of poultry, besides rice, potatoes, & other *stores.*

[79] In the Charleston *Mercury* of March 13 Simms notices four volumes of
the writings of Richard Chenevix Trench (1807-1886) recently published by
Widdleton. He writes: "We presume that the publisher will soon follow these
up with the other writings of Trench, especially such as have not yet been
collected from the periodical press. The collection, thus made complete—a sketch
of the author's life from the facile and graceful pen of Mr. Duyckinck—would
greatly commend the edition to the lovers of pure literature."

[80] *National Portrait Gallery of Eminent Americans: Including Orators,
Statesmen, Naval and Military Heroes, Jurists, Authors, Etc., Etc.,* 2 vols.
(New York: Johnson, Fry & Company, [1862]). When the work was repub-
lished in 1868 (?) a sketch of Simms was added, I, 513-520.

[81] Dr. John Wakefield Francis died on Feb. 8.

[82] We have not identified the weekly for which Mathews (see introductory
sketch) was writing at this time.

And we are now planting corn which will be ready for use in the last of July or middle of August. I have 150 acres of rye & oats growing; have several tons of Fodder & Hay cured & put away. So much for starvation. All the accounts of forced loans are absolute inventions — totally false. Not a case of the kind has occurred! The N. Y. Times publishes a letter full of this sort of stuff from one Judge (Something — I forget what) — no such man or Judge is known in S. C. The State never had a Judge of his name. A Mr. Pearson of N. Y. has just published there that he fled from S. C. to escape being drafted, that every third man had been drafted. Now, there has been no draft — not a man has been drafted. All are volunteers. We have more volunteers than we want or care to feed. More than 30,000 have volunteered in S. C. alone, & in the Confederacy, there are more than 200,-000 ready to take the field & eager for a call. The tax on negroes in S. C. is reported to be $160.00 per head one fifth the price of the negro. The tax bill requires but $1.26 one dollar & 26/100 per head. Mr. Pearson announces the Marine battery to be a failure; to have fallen to pieces & partly sunk at launching. The Marine Battery never sank, never fell to pieces, was launched successfully, is now afloat, finished, armed with 42 Pounders, & yesterday fired a salute in honor of the Confederacy. But the task would be endless, to correct all these falsehoods, meant to gratify a vulgar spleen, which delights to believe that we are suffering.[83] On the contrary, never were a people better satis-

---

[83] The New York *Times* of March 8 reprints *"From the Waco (Texas) Gazette"* a letter "from Judge Lyon, of South Carolina, to a Friend in Texas," dated "Abbeville, C. H., Thursday, Jan. 24, 1861," and signed "Robert Lyon." "Lyon" (we have been unable to locate any such person, and doubtless Simms was right in saying that there was not any such person) writes: ". . . I can remain here no longer. . . . Everything is in the wildest commotion. My bottom land on Long Cane, for which I could have gotten $30 per acre, I now cannot sell at any price. All our young men nearly are in and around Charleston. Thither we have sent many hundreds of our negroes (I have sent twenty) to work. Crops were very short last year, and it does now seem that nothing will be planted this coming season. . . . We have no money. A forced tax is levied upon every man. I have furnished the last surplus dollar I have. I had about $27,000 in bank. At first I gave a check for ten thousand, then five thousand, then the remainder. It is now estimated that we are spending $25,000 per day, and no prospect of getting over these times. . . . Many are leaving now . . . and before long one third of the wealth of South Carolina will be in the West." The *Times* of March 12 reprints from the Albany *Evening Journal* of March 11 an account of "Charles Pearson . . . just returned home [Albany], after several months sojourn in Charleston." According to the account, Pearson "left to avoid being drafted into the regular army of the Southern Confederacy," which is drafting "about every third man." This same article remarks that "the much-talked-of Floating Battery is abandoned as a total

fied than those of S. C. We cordially approve of the elections at
Montgomery, and lest it should be thought that our patriotism
was tainted by personal ambition, it was generally understood
that no South Carolinian desired office & that none would seek
it.[84] We have no domestic anxieties. It is for the Govt. at Washington & the people of the North to say whether we shall continue under the pressure of a foreign anxiety. Our recognition
by the European States is certain. The whole secret of our policy,
and of the events, was known to us in S. C. 20 years ago. I fancy
you may recal the arguments which, scores of times, I gave you
in N. Y. on this subject. But I trespass, and I know too well
that you take no interest in politics. I think this was your error.
Your habit at the North is not only to leave every thing to ma-
jorities, but to suffer to the masses the exclusive keeping of the
public soul & conscience.

Your friend Ever

W. Gilmore Simms.

1048: To JAMES LAWSON

Woodlands, March 17. [1861] [85]

My dear Lawson.

Only a few days ago, I penned a long screed to Jimmy; but
your letter recieved yesterday prompts another to you. I take for
granted you have done what is necessary in the case of Mr.

---

failure. Mr. Pearson was present when Gen. Beauregard first saw it. The
General laughed at it; and soon after it was launched it capsized and sank."
The Charleston *Mercury* of April 13 gives the following bulletins about the
marine battery under its baptism of fire:

9 A. M. April 12,	"The Floating Battery has been struck eleven times, but the balls failed to penetrate."
10 " " ",	"Anderson has concentrated a heavy fire on us. The battery stands well."
11 " " ",	"One ball struck on the edge of the roof and perforated the planking. When a ball strikes the battery, the shock is not perceptible."
2 P. M. " ",	". . . the fire of Sumter is principally directed against the Floating Battery, the Four Gun Battery, and the Dahlgren Battery on Sullivan's Island, with little apparent effect."

[84] Davis, of Mississippi, was elected president; Stephens, of Georgia vice-
president; Davis appointed Robert Toombs, of Georgia, secretary of state;
Christopher Gustavus Memminger, of South Carolina, secretary of the treasury;
and Leroy Pope Walker, of Alabama, secretary of war.

[85] Dated by Simms' discussion of the plans for the defense of Charleston
Harbor.

Widdleton. Are you sure that the books *were* burned. It seems to be my luck to be always in danger of fire. My plates destroyed by fire in Harper's vaults;[86] my House destroyed by fire;[87] my books in Widdleton's hands by fire; my books (Areytos) in Redfield's hands destroyed by fire.[88] What the d——l does it mean? Here is a chapter of mischances, all in my case, which should hardly occur in the case of any three other persons. I fancy this fire is sometimes a false fire and an invention. See if Redfield approves of this faith in fire: If he believes in Widdleton's fire. It is certainly very strange that I should be peculiarly subject to these fiery fortunes! — You must certainly come, & bring Lyde, to see Woodlands. I trust, unless burnt up, that I shall have things in proper trim to show her ladyship. The new library is completed; but will not hold all my books. I shall still have to keep some 2000 in the outer building. We shall have peace some day, and you shall come. But we do not believe in peace & are still preparing for war. The report of the delivery of Fort Sumter seems to me a mere *ruse de guerre,* meant to disarm our vigilance.[89] I have written to our public men to believe nothing of the kind, but to put themselves in condition to meet an assault both by land and sea. If they come, be sure of this; but few of them will ever get back. We have been prudent & forbearing. Have kept our young men back, who would have stormed Fort Sumter, long ago. But we wished no blood shed. My counsel has been to keep Fort Sumter under blockade, and while we could keep it passive, to keep ourselves patient; but be ready, the moment it showed its teeth, to overwhelm it with shot & shell. We have now probably 40 pieces, Mortars, Columbiads, 42's & 32's bearing directly upon it. You are hardly to believe a syllable you read of us in the N. Y. papers. Never was such audacious & in most respects ridiculous lying. There are no forced loans. The story of Judge Lyon is a hoax. There never was such a Judge as Judge Lyon in S. C. The region from which he is said to write knows no such person. There has been no draft for troops in S. C. The Mr. Pearson who fled from S. C. to escape a draft is a liar by wholesale. We have 30,000 more

---

[86] In 1853.

[87] See note 99, *c.* April 28, 1860.

[88] Evidently these were recent fires.

[89] At this time the New York City newspapers were reporting that "there is little doubt that the Government will order the evacuation of Fort Sumpter [*sic*]." See, for example, the *Times* of March 11-15.

volunteers than we can feed, or are disposed to feed, & the Gov. is daily compelled to decline their services. The Marine Battery was not sunk in launching & is not considered a failure. She is now afloat, with her guns mounted, & fired a salute for the Confederacy a few days ago. It is reported in the N. Y. papers that the tax on negroes is one Hundred & sixty dollars, each, one fifth the price of the negro. By the tax bill, it is one dollar & 26/100. Last year it was $1. Our taxes have been increased about 25 per cent. In one breath they report the forced loans by the thousands, tens of thousands & hundreds of thousands. In the next breath they point to the Loan called for by Law — $675,000 for which 7 per cent. is offered; and they sneer at our want of resources as this loan is not yet wholly taken up. If we can get forced loans, why call for this amount & pay interest upon it. Not one of these lies but is patent, transparent, conveying on their face the proof of the falsehood, and capable of easy refutation, *if it were not the wish of the Northern people to believe them.*[90] It is a great delight to persuade themselves that we are suffering. You get from the same wretched sources the notion that South Carolina has been treated ill by the Confederate Congress, & that we are discontents. As the Herald elegantly phrases it, our nose is out of joint.[91] But we ourselves are not conscious of it. We are not discontent. The elections have given general satisfaction. The Constitution, though not considered perfect, is admitted to be the best in the world. We think that the Congress has made some unnecessary sacrifices to conciliate public opinion abroad, & this has been its error. We think it has been influenced too much by the old tariff notions of the U. S. Congress. We would have had a nearer approach to free trade. But altogether, we congratulate ourselves upon a singular success and a great improvement in our future security & prosperity. I enclose you the comments of the Mercury on the Constitution, which cover all the

---

[90] See note 83, March 15, 1861.

[91] The New York *Herald* of Feb. 12 in an article entitled "South Carolina's Nose Out of Joint" says of South Carolina: "She has lost her independence. It has been swallowed up in the superior power and authority of the United States South. She cannot now make war or peace, or send ambassadors, or attack forts. She must do as she is ordered, or be squelched; and this time she cannot get out of the Union. . . . In avoiding imaginary evils, she has fallen upon evils she knew not of. It is out of the frying pan into the fire. She can no longer strut about with a little petty, brief authority, and she must be exceedingly civil to the new federal power."

objections that are made here, & in which I concur.[92] As for office, South Carolina was especially careful neither to seek, nor desire, and, if possible not to take office. We prefer that our course should suffer no imputation of selfishness. In this country, it is not easy to persuade politicians that there is such a virtue as patriotism. But, if you will remember, South Carolina, for 30 years, has discouraged all the attempts of her people to obtain office, and wherever individuals sought or got it, it was only to incur a certain degree of odium at home. Be assured that our reported discontent is only another weak invention of the enemy. I fancy Mr. Brower's article, with my introduction will be published in the Mercury as soon as space can be found.[93] Another article, on a like subject, which I ascribe to the same pen, *has* been more recently republished in the M. from the Jour. of Com.[94] I shall look with eagerness for your drama.[95] Send your copy to Gen. Jamison, with mine, through Wm. Roach. Send one to the latter also. Gen. J. *at present* will hardly find time to read, much less criticise; but the drama is not his province. He is still in the city, as busy as ever, with forts, & batteries & guns and mortars. I have been experimenting in the effort to improve the sword bayonet & have a model now at the workshop. Did I tell you that the plan was mine of building forts of ranging timber & scabbarding them with rail road iron. These materials have been adopted in the construction of one of the batteries of Columbiads on James island, 1254 yds from Sumter; but the shape of the fort is not mine, & I am not so well satisfied with it; but believe that ranging timber thus coated with R. R. iron T or U Rails, will be invulnerable, if put together properly. We have 5000 men in arms in & about Charleston, yet the streets are as calm as those moonlight nights when, as young lovers, we used to serenade our sweethearts. If the storm blows over, Lyde & yourself had better run down to Charleston & up here this spring. Miss Wilson goes on a visit to town the last Sunday this month,[96] chiefly to recieve the sacrament. Did I mention that her presence

---

[92] This clipping from the Charleston *Mercury* of March 15 is still preserved with this letter.

[93] See note 56, March 3, 1861.

[94] "Bella! Horrida Bella!," signed "J. M. B.," "*from the New York Journal of Commerce*," is published in the Charleston *Mercury* of March 4. Brower (?) says that the Republican Party is going "to force the country into a civil war" and predicts as the result the ruin of the United States.

[95] *Liddesdale.* See note 33, Feb. 19, 1861.

[96] March 31.

in my house, as Teacher, is reported to be the cause of my defeat for the convention.[97] It is the feeling of the common people towards Northern teachers. But do not mention this. Of course, we never let her suspect it. She seems a good girl; looks the Scotch lassie and seems faithful to her duties as Governess. We are all quite well. Gilmore is in the Citadel, but has his knapsack ready, and is eager to get a crack at the enemy. Augusta has just gone on a visit of a week to Mrs. Fuller, in Beaufort district, and will extend her journey to Savannah, & stay some days with the Teffts. I will send you a daguerreotype of Gilmore as soon as I can get a chance. He is now about 6 feet high, some 2 inches taller than his father I fancy, or nearly so. He is very popular, and is a good boy. I lost a fine negro wench the other day; have another just recovering from a broken leg. Today (Sunday) I gave out a molasses allowance. Thus, I feed, physic, clothe, nurse & watch some 70, and have to live from hand to mouth myself — the mere steward of my negroes. Love to Lyde & all.

Yours

W. G. S.

1049: To William Porcher Miles [98]

Woodlands, S. C. April 2. 1861

Hon. W. Porcher Miles

My dear Miles.

It is highly probable (D. V.) that I shall make a flying visit to Charleston next Saturday.[99] In that event, I shall make an effort to see you & your brother James especially. I shall reserve what I have to say in respect to politics to the period of our meeting. As W. F. Dessaussure [100] once said to the people, talking of the Temperance Question — "there is much to be said, my friends, on *both* sides of the question." I have just written to Keitt touching some of the public Documents of the former U. S. in which my setts are deficient. It is probable that you may from extra copies help me in supplying the deficiency. For example, the quarto publication, one of the most interesting *to*

---

[97] The Secession Convention.
[98] Part of this letter is printed in Trent, pp. 266-267.
[99] April 6.
[100] William Ford DeSaussure. See note 258, Nov. 24, 1846.

me, in 10 volumes, of "Explorations for a route from the Mississippi to the Pacific" — of this sett I need 4 vols. — the 3d, 4, 6 & 8.[101] If you have duplicates of either of these, pray let me have them. Of the last Congress (U. S.) in which you engaged, I could wish to get every publication which, in any degree, related to the Secession Mouvement. I wish to fortify myself especially in regard to the controversy, as well from the opposite standpoint as from our own. If, at your leisure, you can find any of the publications of the late Cong. which you do not need, let me have them. Keitt would do so no doubt, if he could remember a request half an hour after hearing it.

Yours ever faithfully

W. Gilmore Simms.

P. S. I suppose you have seen how quietly all my agency in the suggestion of the battery of rail iron & ranging timber has been ignored.[102] In my letters to you & to Jamison (and the letters to you were all transferred to him) I planned batteries for land & water, went into details, showed all the advantages, showed how the structure should be made casemate, bombproof, how the plane should be inclined to the rear, how the *"rat trap"* in the rear might be made to improve upon every thing hitherto used. In your letters to me you professed to know nothing of these things, & to have no such intimacy with military men as to justify you in approaching them on the subject. In Jamison's letters, he spoke of the great difficulty which he had in persuading military men to consider the subject — all seemed to doubt & to distrust every thing which was *novel,* & from the hands of a civilian.[103] But, gradually, as public opinion *abroad* began to speak of the conception as working a revolution in such structures, I find the battery a subject of great attraction, and all my poor agency in it ignored wholly. And yet my plans & suggestions covered this & the floating battery, & covered other schemes for temporary

---

[101] *Reports of Explorations and Surveys, to Ascertain the Most Practicable and Economical Route for a Railroad from the Mississippi River to the Pacific Ocean* . . . , 11 vols. (Washington, 1855-1859).

[102] This postscript was prompted by a letter in the Charleston *Mercury* of April 2, signed by Maj. P. F. Stevens and dated April 1, giving the credit for the plan and construction of the iron-clad battery at Cumming's Point, Morris Island, to C. H. Stevens, cashier of the Planters' and Mechanics' Bank, of Charleston, and later colonel of the 24th Regiment of South Carolina Volunteers.

[103] We have located only one letter from Simms to Jamison (Jan. 13) and not all of those to Miles. We have not located a single letter to Simms from either Jamison or Miles.

structures, by which I proposed a covered approach, to the walls of Sumter, which should be as secure against hand grenades as against cannon. Well! — It is not much. More: If there was any strategic device for the relief of Fort Sumter, I argued & anticipated it in my letters to Jamison written almost nightly for months! Enough! Yet one feels a little sore that there should be no record of a patriotism & a devotion to his country, which has left him little time or thought for any thing else, ever since the moment of secession, & for years before. In my labours of political literature, I had the same fate. And this, my long experience of 30 years, makes me feel nothing but scorn & contempt for 7/10 of those who wear the feathers & who make the fuss! Adieu. If I write longer I may grow splenetic.

Yours Ever

W. G. S.

W. P. M.

2. P. S. I will thank you to mention to Gen. Jamison whom I suppose you see every day, that I hope to be down on Saturday next, & will try to see him that evening at the Mills House,[104] if I am not too much fatigued or indisposed.

1050: To MARGARET MAXWELL MARTIN [105]

[c. April 15, 1861][106]

I have just returned from an eight days' absence in Charleston, where I witnessed the bombardment of Fort Sumter.[107] I con-

---

104 A hotel in Charleston.

105 We have not located the original of this letter. Our text of this fragment is from Mrs. Martin's "Celebrities That I Have Seen. Gossiping Sketches.— No. IX.—William Gilmore Simms," *New Monthly Magazine: A Literary Journal* (Nashville, Tenn.), II (Oct., 1871), 278.

106 The year is established by Simms' remarks about the bombardment of Fort Sumter. In his letter to Miles of April 2 Simms says that he plans to go to Charleston on April 6; since he herein says he has "just returned from an eight days' absence in Charleston," we have dated this letter *c.* April 15.

107 On April 11 Gen. Pierre Gustave Toutant Beauregard (1818-1893), who in March had assumed command of the whole coast of South Carolina from Georgetown to Beaufort, sent a demand to Maj. Anderson for the surrender of Fort Sumter. Anderson first refused, then later agreed to evacuate the fort on April 15 unless controlling instructions or additional supplies were received before then. Beauregard's aides who received this last reply considered it unsatisfactory and ordered an attack on the fort on the morning of April 12. The bombardment continued on April 13, when Anderson surrendered and agreed to evacuate the fort the following day. See Cauthen, *South Carolina Goes to War*, pp. 130-132.

gratulate you on the expulsion of the enemy from the sacred soil of Carolina, now *doubly* sacred to you since your first-born was one of the first sacrifices in its redemption.[108] May his memory blossom anew in your hearts with love, to mature hereafter to a glorious ripeness, while it remains enshrined in the tender regrets of his countrymen! God is surely with us, my dear friend, thus far, in our progress to independence. May we never, by any vain exultation leading to presumptuous confidence, forfeit the powerful favor of the mighty King of all nations who hath thus far been our shield and strength in the day of our trial. But in times like these words fail us, and, as you say, prayer itself sometimes becomes impossible. Certainly, all such prayer as seeks utterance in mere words must be feeble as idle. But silent thought is perhaps the most valuable form of prayer — that thought which blends with feeling and wings its way to God through tears and truthful emotions, through an imagination which soars above the earth, and seeks only to spread its wings of rejoicing directly under the living sunlight, and in the generous smile of heaven. We do not the less pray, my friend — the heart being right, and the purpose just and true — though we speak never a word, and though we breathe with a difficult delight. Rapture, when at the highest, grows dumb, and all our finer pleasures are inarticulate things. Let us only feel how great are God's mercies to us, and so act as not to forfeit them, and the ordinary thought of our waking hours is prayer sublimed for heaven.

1051: To WILLIAM PORCHER MILES [109]

Woodlands, Wednesday Night.
April 17. 1861

My dear Miles.

I assume you to be very busy, but must trouble you with what I have to say for two reasons. You are *now* associated with military men, and may be called upon for opinions, & may

---

[108] William Maxwell Martin (1837-1861) was a school teacher at the time that he joined the Columbia Artillery. His company left for Charleston on Jan. 2, 1861, and on Feb. 21 he died at Fort Moultrie from typhoid fever. He was the author of *Lyrics and Sketches* (Nashville, Tenn.: Printed at the Southern Methodist Publishing House, 1861), published posthumously.

[109] A few sentences of this letter are quoted by Trent, p. 265.

have opportunities for expressing them,[110] while Jamison is probably about to leave the city, where his duties are no doubt at an end.[111] I shall be excused for writing on military subjects, in consequence of the natural solicitude which we all feel for the safety of the good old city, & the brave young cause. The principles urged by me for the use of ranging timber and R. R. iron for batteries, have been in some degree proved to be right. I was satisfied that neither shot nor shell could harm logs, 12 inches thick, plated with iron. I doubted the iron more than the timber, fearing fractures when the bolts were driven, & suggesting, accordingly, that they should not be spiked too tightly, but should have a little play. The only use of the iron was to protect the timber from fire & splintering — otherwise, the logs themselves would have a power of resistance which no 65 lb shot or shell could disparage. I take for granted that Gen. Beauregard will so change the face of this & other batteries, as to bring them to bear upon an approaching enemy. I assume, also, that he is throwing up small redoubts, south of the Light House, so as to cover the approach of boats in the rear. The batteries in the channel might easily be connected with timber & rail road iron. Fort Sumter itself might be roofed in like manner against shells hereafter; the roofing so constructed as to enable us to build the quarters of the Garrison under the same cover, and to man with heavy pieces the barbette bearing upon James island. The Boomarang (Marine Battery) should now be moored on one of the sandbars covering the channel, so as to have long range. Supposing we have to contend with an adventurous enemy & a large fleet, we cannot too soon put Castle Pinckney in the best fighting condition. This fort too may be completely roofed & casemated, her barbette being really her most valuable battery. As it would be the policy of an enemy to cover the city with his guns & thus neutralize the forts, & in fact have them at his mercy, he might try to run the gauntlet of the batteries. It is just possible that some of his ships might escape them, & run

---

[110] On Feb. 12, 1861, Miles was appointed chairman of the Committee on Military Affairs of the Congress of the Confederate States (see *Journal of the Congress of the Confederate States of America*, I, 44). He also held the rank of colonel as a volunteer aide on Gen. Beauregard's staff (see *O. R.,* 1st Series, I, 15, 35, 37, 63-66).

[111] The second session of the Secession Convention had adjourned on April 10. Jamison, as secretary of war in Governor Pickens' Executive Council, had doubtless remained in Charleston to see the outcome of the negotiations with Maj. Anderson and the bombardment and surrender of Fort Sumter.

up Ashley & Cooper rivers, in which event the city would be defenceless against mortars & cannon. A water battery, running along the east face of Schute's Folly (Castle Pinckney island) covering the harbour would not be amiss, & this might be made of timber & iron in short time. I think the mistake in our present rail road battery consists in two respects. It presents too much of a plane to shot, especially from an elevation, & it limits the elevation, if not the depression of the guns. My plan would be to present some such front as the following, to an enemy.

Front. the Rear.   rear.

The rearward structure is a *rat trap,* or barrier against explosives falling in the rear. It might be pierced for musketry. Roofed & faced with iron, with an inclination upward from front to rear, shot & shell would rebound & glance or ricochet, as quickly as if upon a wall of ice, especially where the ridges of the iron, as in the U. & T. iron present the arch, or a fluted ridge to the missle. By planning the rear of the front structure, so as to overhang (as it were) the back structure, it is scarce possible for a shell to fall between them. In making roofs for the forts, I am of opinion that (the framework being sufficiently strong) 3 inch plank would suffice, covered with the iron, & that a single thickness of the iron would suffice also. The uprising ridge or arch effectually prevents the shot from striking the flat parts through which the bolts or spikes are driven. By a layer of welded sheet iron, *beneath* the planking, you have an effectual covering against rain. Shutters may cover the embrasures. The planking & iron may also be employed in a sort of hanging mantelets or shields, suspended by chains from the parapet, which, if stout rolls of hay were let in between, would effectually keep the brick work from abrasion by shot. Another advantage of the wood & iron structures is that they constitute a temporary barracks. The rear structure, or rat trap, pierced for musketry, would be an excellent protection from surprise in the rear, as well as from bursting shells. It is highly necessary that the links should be frequent in the chain of posts connecting Fort Johnson with the forts on Cole's island. Of course, at the present moment, you have your troops covering every part; but should the troops be withdrawn, & the war continue, the mouth of the Stono will need to be kept up as a place of defence, & ought to be made very strong. Cummings Point & all that reach of sand covering the Channel where the Star of the West Battery lies, should be made very powerful, and the structure of wood and iron would be excellent for cover from shot & shelter from the weather. Indeed, during war, a good fortress at this point would be advisable, and if the war were to be a long one, a rude rail road would be important for reaching it promptly from Fort Johnson. I am a little doubtful whether the guns at Fort Johnson afford sufficient command of the bay, assuming the passage of Fort Sumter. But, I speak only from memory, & from a map which is far from satisfactory. I am afraid we shall need gunpowder. If it is in your way to speak to any chemical capitalist, do insist that villainous gunpowder, ordnance &c. as a manufacture, will sooner lead to fortune now than any other. The political questions now occur. Will Lincoln, by war, insanely triple his enemies? Can he expect that, called upon to fight, the Southern States will war with each other & not with him? Is not his course working for us, & to his utter overthrow? If not, then all auguries must fail, however based on the best probabilities. I see that N. C. has sent to us for heavy cannon.[112] Can we spare them now? Does N. C. really need them, at any time? She has no seaport of any consequence, & even the possession of her seaboard forts cannot affect her interior, as it would ours. We must hold to our arms if we would make good fight. Our first object should be to build up a navy. Had we *that,* all would be easy. Again: Unless our enemy assails us in Charleston, where would he assail us. The accessible points, besides, are Georgetown, North Edisto & Beaufort. If he attacks or penetrates these, it must be in marauding expeditions, to carry off negroes, or foment insurrection. If he designs more — a march upon Charleston, it will be from Beaufort, and an enterprising General, such as you have, I doubt not, in Beauregard, would cut him off in detail in the thousand defiles of the country, before he could march 30 miles. I am very glad that we have Beauregard. I like him. He inspires confidence; & this strengthens brave men to enterprise, & encourages the timid to be firm. Should you see or write to Pryor, of Va.[113] say to him that I am *en route,* when

---

[112] The Charleston *Mercury* of April 16 reports that "several heavy guns will be spared to North Carolina, in obedience to the request of Governor Ellis. They will be forwarded immediately."

[113] Roger Atkinson Pryor (1828-1919), former newspaper editor and congressman (1859-1861), held the rank of colonel as a volunteer aide on General Beauregard's staff (see *O. R.*, 1st Series, I, 15, 35, 37, 63-66). In July, 1861, he became a delegate to the Provisional Congress of the Confederate States (see *Journal of the Congress of the Confederate States of America,* I, 279),

he passes either to Charleston or Virginia, and that I have
Monongahela, hog & hominy & a loving welcome. Say this to
any of your friends. Midway, you are aware, is my depôt. Today,
my dear Miles, I am 55! But my grey beard is 65. I have grown
very old in 2 years. God bless you, my friend.

Yours Ever.

W. Gilmore Simms.

1052: To JAMES LAWSON

Woodlands, S. C. May 8. 1861

James Lawson, Esq. (New York)

My dear Sir:

At sight, please pay to the order of Miss Margaret Wilson
(of Poughkeepsie, N. Y.) Sixty Five ($65) dollars, and charge
to your obliged friend & servt.[114]

W. Gilmore Simms.

1053: To WILLIAM PORCHER MILES

Woodlands, S. C. May 11. [1861][115]

My dear Miles.

Jamison having abandoned his Excellency, Gov. Pickens, Magrath having pretty much done the same, since, *inter nos,* he took
no counsel from either, and made all his appointments, not only
without consulting them, but in spite of them, I have nobody to
write to, capable of taking advice or acting wisely under it.[116]

---

but soon resigned to enter military service as colonel of the 3rd Virginia
Regiment. In 1863 he was promoted to brigadier general, but resigned his
commission and fought as a private in Fitzhugh Lee's cavalry. After the war
he moved to New York City, where he became a prominent lawyer and justice
of the supreme court of New York.

114 On the back of this letter Margaret Wilson wrote: "Mr. James Lawson
will please pay the within draft to the order of George S. Wilson of Poughkeepsie and oblige Margaret Wilson Woodlands S. C 9th. May 1861." Under-
neath this notation is the signature "George Sibbald Wilson."

115 Dated by Simms' reference to "the fall of Sumter" (see preceding letters).
At this time Miles was in Montgomery attending the second session of the
Provisional Congress of the Confederate States (April 29–May 21).

116 The Executive Council (see note 11, Jan. 13, 1861) was abolished by an
ordinance of the Secession Convention on April 8, effective as soon as in the
governor's opinion public affairs should permit (see *Journal of the Convention
of the People of South Carolina, Held in 1860, 1861 and 1862*, pp. 511, 775;

I know not, my friend, if I am capable of giving it, but the position of the country, & of our State, keeps me dreadfully anxious, & though my own family is a subject of anxiety, that which I feel, touching our affairs, will not suffer me to be silent. I have been reasoning, or trying to reason, out the projects & plans of the U. S. Govt. It is difficult to reason in the case of a desperate party, which knows that if once the excitement sleeps, the thought of the people awakes. The Black Republicans can only save themselves by keeping up the excitement. How are they to do it. The plea of Washington menaced has been more potent than any thing besides. The vanity of the North has been sorely hurt by the fall of Sumter. In the first rages of the people the mob is in the ascendant. But, meanwhile, they get 25,000 at Washington. What to do with them? As the summer approaches, active operations in the South are almost impossible on the part of Northern men. But their policy will be to quarter their troops in the South, at healthy situations. I have no doubt that Scott has arranged to hurl 10,000 men upon Beaufort, establishing a camp, occupying the country, & giving him a base of operations at once against S. C. & Georgia. A detachment will occupy Bluff-town. In November, they will be prepared with 15,000 more, to act upon Charleston & Savannah, and to ascend to Augusta & Columbia. For the details, you must use your conjectures. You will note that the points where quarters might be established during summer, south of Virginia, will be Beaufort & Wilmington, N. C.; Beaufort & Blufft. S. C. & probably Brunswick, Georgia. S. C. is especially an object of detestation. If it be the purpose of the U. S. Govt. to invade, the most assailable & profitable point will be Beaufort in S. C. Hence they can pass even in summer, to Bluffton, establishing themselves on the Savannah. In Nov. they will calculate to march upon Charleston, &c. In a conversation with Jamison he expresses the belief that Beaufort is provided with defences. I am afraid that he & others say this anticipating only marauding attacks of small vessels. But what if a fleet should come, of 10 sail, with 10,000 men in transports. What is our power to resist them. What to dislodge them? Having no faith in the wisdom of Pickens, & as I know him to be without coun-

---

the Charleston *Mercury* of April 9; and Cauthen, *South Carolina Goes to War*, p. 142n). We have been unable to discover the exact dates on which Jamison and Magrath resigned, though the Charleston *Mercury* of May 8 publishes a correspondence between Jamison and Pickens in which Jamison requests to resign and Pickens refuses to permit him.

sellors, & with none but toadies & flatterers about him, I must appeal in some other quarter.[117] I see that some of the Newspapers talk about a landing on Sullivan's island.[118] This movement is not one likely to succeed, & not one which Scott would favour. He would prefer a landing 30 miles S. of Charleston on the Edisto, — if it were winter. In summer, contending with General Summer & General Malaria, he would aim at a healthy position for a *coup d'appui*; and Beaufort would be his best base of operations. The question to be asked is not whether Beaufort has one or more batteries, but what will Beaufort do, & what are her defences against 10,000 men, with numerous light draught vessels. I know that she has batteries, but as I said before, I believe that these are designed only to baffle any attempt of a small force at marauding & burning. Now, we are establishing camps at Aiken, Columbia & other places in the middle country. Why not, if spots can be found equally healthy, place them nearer the seaboard. Should a force of the kind I mentioned suddenly appear in the waters of Beaufort, they may get full possession before our troops could be brought by R. Road from the interior; and when they reach the nearest point to Port Royal on the Savannah & Charleston R. Road, they have still before them a march of 18 miles, with an arm of the sea to cross before they could reach Beaufort. A single small vessel of the enemy assuming Beaufort to be taken, could cover the crossing at the P. R. Ferry,[119] destroy the boat, and all boats approaching. I know not if any sufficient reconnaissance has been made of the precincts, & I write now only that you may confer with our friends & the powers that be, who, if there be any plausibility in my suggestions & suspicions, would still no doubt be in time for preventive & protective measures. Rhett & Barnwell ought to be quite familiar with all the approaches to Beaufort and could decide much better than I can. In all probability, should an attempt be made on Charleston, the plan chosen would be precisely that of the British in 1779 — make first a lodgement at Beaufort, & turn at pleasure to Savannah & Charleston. Bluffton, as a place notoriously salubrious, would be also an object as suited for a camp.[120] — I had written the 2 first

---

[117] Pickens was being criticized throughout the state. See Cauthen, *South Carolina Goes to War,* pp. 140-141.

[118] A correspondent of the Charleston *Mercury* of May 11 who signs himself "Senex" warns that the United States will attempt to land on Sullivan's Island in order to take Fort Moultrie.

[119] The Port Royal Ferry.

[120] Simms was something of a prophet. See note 166, Nov. 7, 1861.

of these pages when I had a visit from Jamison, whose answer at first was that given me before, "We have taken the necessary precautions for Beaufort." But when I suggested the probability of an overwhelming force, with the view to taking & holding possession, he seemed much less assured. He, by the way, returned last night to Charleston in consequence of a despatch by Express, requiring his immediate presence, under a call of Pickens.[121] He had no conjecture as to the reason for the call, but was in hopes that it was nothing more than some petty little snarl, about appointments, into which the Good Govr. seems constantly inclined to fall. — You will hear of the matter, no doubt, before I shall. God be with you. Regards to Keitt & other friends.

Yours Ever faithfully

W. Gilmore Simms.

P. S. My little daughter Chevillette has been sick with Bilious Remittent for 20 days. The fever still clings to her & has assumed the typhoid aspect. We hope & fear. Pray for me & mine, my friend. Your little Goddaughter [122] is quite flourishing.

1054: To WILLIAM PORCHER MILES

Woodlands, June 8, 1861.

My dear Miles.

I write you at random, not knowing where you are but address you at Richmond.[123] My heart and head are so full that I cannot help but write, though perhaps I shall say nothing of value. Even now, I have a sick family, & your little God Daughter is down with fever. But not, I trust, seriously. I write at midnight. All are sleeping. I cannot sleep. I have just closed up two large batches of editorials for the Mercury,[124] which, I am sorry to see, is beginning that sort of fire upon the Confederate Govt. in the management of the army, which it kept up, on our own, before the taking of Sumter. This sort of writing, is the cause of great in-

---

[121] This remark indicates that Jamison was still secretary of war in Governor Pickens' Executive Council.

[122] Hattie.

[123] After the second session of the Provisional Congress closed on May 21 Miles again served as colonel on Beauregard's staff. Beauregard had assumed command at Manassas, in Virginia, on June 1. See *O. R.*, 1st Series, I, 446, 478, 500, 522, 896, 901.

[124] See note 29, Feb. 19, 1861.

dignation among many here. It is wild, mischievous & idle. I have faith in our officers & soldiers & fear not.[125] Still, my friend, as you know me to [be of] a restless mind, anxious to be doing — not permitted to do — striving to teach some thing which may help our poor country, you will understand why I write. I have some suggestions to make, which, if you please, you may empty into the ears of Gen. Beauregard. I would have him pick ten men for each company in every regiment, have them well officered, painted and disguised as Indians. They will inspire terror. They should be habited in the yellow Hunting Shirt of Cotton — they should be turbanned, — armed with rifle, bowie knife & hatchet, and each company, thus formed, should be attached to its own regiment as an auxiliary force. Once produce disorder in the enemy's line or column, & let these fellows put in for close action. But the officer should be a rare fellow, & should know his business. These should be your Seminole Zouaves. It should be made as public as possible that every regiment has its band of Indians. The tumeric will dye the garments — the blood root, — *poccoon,* or *sanguinaria canadensis,* the face, hands, arms & neck. If there be any thing which will inspire terror in the souls of the citizen soldiery of the North, it will be the idea that scalps are to be taken by the redmen. Encourage this idea. You will have in your masses thousands, I trust, who will be familiar with the Indian mode of warfare. Beauregard, himself, will know all about it. Your Texans should be freely employed in this fashion, and for your officers you should have live, daring, reckless fellows — the boys chosen should be at once bold & expert.

Scott has an inveterate idea of invading by separate columns, to act in concert under given circumstances. It may be presumptuous in me to give an opinion. But *entre nous,* I have always regarded Scott as a Humbug, but one of the most fortunate blunderers of the age. To march 3 separate columns into so large a state as Virginia, is to expose each of them to the fate which, I trust, awaits them; viz — to be cut off in detail, by the concentra-

---

[125] On June 1 the Charleston *Mercury* began its well-known attack on the Davis administration by saying: "By assuming the position of the defensive we have lost Maryland, endangered Missouri, neutralized Kentucky, and are now making Virginia our battlefield. Is this wise statesmanship? Is it efficient generalship? Fabian tactics are out of place. We trust that the war policy of the South is about to become aggressive and efficient. It is time. . . ." The *Mercury* had also severely criticized Governor Pickens for not attacking Fort Sumter earlier than he did. See Cauthen, *South Carolina Goes to War,* pp. 106-107, 200 ff.

tion upon them, severally, of overpowering masses.[126] This, I take to be the game about to be played. I can only conjecture the amount of force which you now have in Virginia, but suppose it far to exceed, in numbers, the calculations & conceptions of the enemy. I doubt the report of your making an attempt to recover Alexandria.[127] *Cui Bono?* So long as the enemy having the shipping, which controls the river, the possession of Alexandria will do you no good. The secret is either to destroy the enemy in masses, or to prolong the war upon the borders, untill he is worn out. Already, I fancy, the symptoms of exhaustion begin to show themselves.

But, if you can destroy his columns, then you must take Washington, destroy it, expel the conqueror, rouse up Maryland, & penetrate Pennsylvania with fire & sword. A merely defensive war, dealing with the most presumptuous & aggressive people in the world, is simply child's play. You must *dictate* a peace, & this you will only be enabled to do, when you have obtained two or three decisive victories, & when the European powers shall be implicated in the war. In less than six weeks, I expect to see Great Britain in the field. There will be an *ex tempore sea fight,* in which *she will be worsted.* Then comes the rest, & the rest will be conclusive. But you have hardly leisure to regard my generalizations. Jamison is home, alongside of me. He was at my house today. I need not say to you that I feel like a bear chained to the stake. I can neither ride nor march. I can only pass sleepless nights, fuming to my friends, of what I think may be done. May the Great & Good God shelter you, dear friend, & render you to us in safety.

Yours Ever faithfully

W. Gilmore Simms.

---

[126] Confederate forces evacuated Alexandria, Va., on May 5. Union forces occupied Alexandria on May 24; Newport News, Va., on May 29; and Grafton, W. Va., on May 30. See *O. R.,* 1st Series, II, 23-52.

[127] The Charleston *Courier* of June 3 prints a dispatch from Camp Davis, Manassas Gap, dated May 27, which says that "Alexandria has been taken possession of by the Federal troops and we are ordered there immediately to retake it. We leave here at 2 o'clock today. . . ." Simms was right to doubt the report.

1055: To James Henry Hammond [128]

Woodlands 14 June 1861,

My dear Hammond.

My House for the last 2 months has been something of a Hospital. I have had three children down, seriously, with Bilious remittent, in one case running into typhoid.[129] They are now better, but my anxiety & suffering have been great, & I now tremblingly watch against relapse. Half a dozen little negroes sick also, one of whom will probably die tonight. The rest doing well. I, too, have been suffering from (I suppose) both mind & body; with nothing to console & every thing to distract me. No more books to make — no money — some debt, — and plain living. Othello's occupation is gone for the present, and my copyrights, worth $20,000 — the whole of my life earnings — not only temporarily valueless to me but liable to confiscation! The North takes away from me, and the South has never given! Jamison is at home again. Pickens is such an ass that he will drive away from him every decent counsellor. Jamison, Magrath, Frost, all have left him, and all, I believe, in disgust.[130] He never consulted either in his appointments, & I told Jamison that he should have put his foot down imperatively, & required that all his appointments should be weighed in Council. Neither that of Bonham, or Dunovant, or McGowan would probably have met the approval of his Council. But the appointments were known to the public as soon as to his private advisers.[131] His vanity throws him open to the

---

128 Simms' latest letter to Hammond which we have located is that of Dec. 5, 1860. Evidently a considerable number written during this period are missing from the Hammond Papers, Library of Congress, which contains the originals of letters from Hammond to Simms dated Nov. 10, 1860 (probably an error for Dec. 10, 1860), and Jan. 10, Feb. 6, Feb. 23, March 5, March 23, May 1, June 9, July 17, and Sept. 28, 1861.

129 Chevillette and Hattie (see letters to Miles of May 11 and June 8) and probably Sydney Hammond, who died shortly after this date (see letter to Lawson of July 4, 1861).

130 On April 4 Edward Frost (see note 152, July 17, 1854) had succeeded Christopher Gustavus Memminger as secretary of the treasury in Governor Pickens' Executive Council (see *Journal of the Convention of the People of South Carolina, Held in 1860, 1861 and 1862*, p. 243). He, in turn, was succeeded by Wilmot Gibbes DeSaussure (see the Charleston *Courier* of June 4). For Jamison's and Magrath's resignations, see letter to Miles of May 11.

131 Governor Pickens had appointed Milledge Luke Bonham major general in command of the Volunteer Forces of South Carolina and Richard G. M. Dunovant and Samuel McGowan brigadier generals. In April, 1861, Bonham was appointed brigadier general in the Confederate States Army in command of the 1st South Carolina Regiment of Volunteers, and at the date of this letter he was serving in Virginia. Dunovant had command of Sullivan's Island

most contemptible advisers. All who will flatter, can rule him. He has caused the most infinite degree of blundering & has offended many. I heard it said, that he had given *one pack* of field pieces — probably the very one which as Govr., you laid hands on, to no less that *four* different applicants, — too flexible to refuse any, and not remembering 10 minutes after what he had done. Hampton,[132] I believe, gets it finally. He is at times, too flexible, to say no — at other times, too mulish to say 'yes' though every argument called for it, & all the Counsellors. His proclamations are public, & so the absurdity is patent. It is a terrible thing that such a man should be Executive at such a moment. He & Gibbes[133] (*par nobile fratr.*) are unitedly enough to make any revolution absurd, were not the people so unanimous. I am disposed to think that the worst is past — i.e. if we have no serious disaster in battle. I am satisfied that our policy is to protract the war. It will be the mean, not only to exhaust our enemy but to confirm our independence. I agree with all your views, on the question economically considered.[134] It is an economical question between

---

during the attack on Fort Sumter (see *O. R.,* 1st Series, I, 33) ; he later was a colonel in the Confederate States Army (see *ibid.,* IV, 1). McGowan (1819-1897), a lawyer in Abbeville, S. C., and a member of the state legislature for a number of years prior to the Confederate War, was in 1862 appointed colonel of the 14th South Carolina Regiment of Volunteers. In 1863 he was promoted to brigadier general and assumed command of Maxcy Gregg's famous brigade.

[132] Gen. Wade Hampton (1818-1902), son of Col. Wade Hampton (see note 305, Dec. 11, 1846), was commissioned colonel by Pickens and directed to raise his own command. The Charleston *Courier* of May 3 contains his call for volunteers. On May 23, 1862, he was appointed brigadier general in the Confederate States Army; on Aug. 3, 1863, major general; and on Feb. 14, 1865, lieutenant general.

[133] Probably James Guignard Gibbes (see note 80, June 27, 1865), who proposed all sorts of schemes for the aid of the Confederate States.

[134] Hammond writes in his letter of June 9: "Credit is pretty well at an end every where North & South. Every thing of consequence is cash in Augusta, & Savannah & I presume in all towns. This is rather a god send for us. An Agricultural People should have no credit system at all & can at any moment introduce by law specie & cash payments without material loss. But Credit is the Chief Capital of a Trading & Manufacturing people & when that ceases they are paralyzed & specie hides. Where will *money* come from to spend at the rate of a million a day? They have about $1 mill. per week from California (if they get it) & of all their other Exports they have nothing upon which they can realize cash at home or abroad save grain & meat if there are hard times abroad[.] With the breaking down of their credit system their strength vanishes. Breaking down ours is really a blessing. Then we have cotton, tobacco, rice & naval stores, which at *all* times, good or bad, can & do *command specie* from every spot on the Western Hemisphere (cutting the Globe in two) & even elsewhere. These constitute a mine in our hands, producing more specie annually than all the metal mines of the earth. Half of our $200 mills. exports, probably three fourths of it we can, without ultimate loss to us, put at the disposal of our Govt. & they can readily make it as available as gold. Thus our Treasury will have in it virtually $1 to 150 mills by

us, as nations, & so one of strict policy. I wish you were somewhere in position. Without irreverence, I say with John Bull — "D — n your eyes! What right have they to fail you now!" But you must suffer me to say that, with your general health tolerably good, the affection is purely local, — and your *best policy is not to use your eyes at all, and above all, not to use them with glasses.* Let my fair friend, Kate write your letters, & translate to you. Give your eyes holiday, & bathe constantly in cold water, the eyes & back of the head. Not one of my grape-cuttings has sprouted. All that you sent me have failed.[135] They must have been trimmed at the wrong moment, & laid by too long. — As Beauregard is now in command at Manassas Station, your anxieties should lessen.[136] I do not think him brilliant, but he is well drilled, experienced, cool, steady & singularly cautious. Bonham would, I doubt not, head a brilliant charge of Cavalry, but he has no head, I fancy, for any thing beyond. Let me hear from you when you can. Best regards to Mrs. H. & Kate.

Àdios
Yours   Ever

W. G. S.

1056: To James Lawson

Woodlands, July 4, 1861.

My dear Lawson.

Your letter, through Wm. Roach, has just reached me, but how the d——l am I to answer it. We have not a single U. S. stamp in all this precinct. But I write at a venture, & will see tomorrow, if the Adams Express Compy. can find me the necessary U. S. stamp, in addition to that of the C. S. Your volume [137] was recieved by both Jamison & myself & has been read by both with pleasure. The General tells me that he is quite grateful to you, not only for the compliment of the copy, but for the gratification had in its perusal. He is not given to Poetry, & knows little of the Drama; has none of our literary tastes. But he is a man of good sense & judgment, & when he writes will no

October *without taxation.* If we can hold our own until the crops come in the North cannot by any means or from any quarter raise then one tenth of that sum."

135 See Hammond's letters cited in note 128, above.

136 See note 123, June 8, 1861.

137 *Liddesdale.* See note 33, Feb. 19, 1861.

doubt prove satisfactory. At present, I have counselled *him,* not to write to *you* at all. He would otherwise have answered your letter months ago. In better seasons he will write. And I think his judgment upon your drama will be even more favorable than mine. I am nothing, you know, unless critical; and I will wait for my *interleaved* copy, before doubling you up. I may say, however, that your print reads much better & more easily, than your M.S. and I see many more merits in the vol. before me than I did in the angular lines of your mercantile scrawl. When your interleaved copy comes, see what I shall say. I will search you thoroughly & enable you, I think, to make this work your most classical performance. But literature, poetry especially, is effectually overwhelmed by the drums, & the cavalry, and the shouting. War is here the only idea. Every body is drilling and arming. Even I practise with the Colt. I am a dead shot with rifle & double barrel, & can now kill rabbit or squirrel with the pistol. Our women practise, & they will fight, too, like she wolves. Your Yankees are converting our whole people into Unionism. If you ask me about myself, I have only to say that I am sad & sick & suffering. Gilmore is feverish to buckle on armour & go to Virginia. We have lost our youngest son, the boy Sydney Hammond, 2 years old, teething, — and, I think, with a spinal affection.[138] Betsy [139] has been very sick, but is now better. All the rest are well. Mrs. Fuller has another son.[140] All doing well. Fuller has volunteered for seacoast defence.[141] Crops are good — mine never better. We shall make abundance of corn, & the Cotton crop will probably exceed that of last year by 300,000 bales. The seasons have been very favorable. We have been eating at Woodlands, for months, strawberries, green peas, green corn, okra, irish potatoes, snap beans, squashes, radishes, blackberries, June berries, artichokes, &c. &c. My wife sells $2 of butter weekly. Her pocket money. We have milk, butter milk, curds, clabber, spring chickens & eggs in abundance. But we want peace! We are invaded! Every hour widens & deepens the breach between the two sec-

---

[138] We have not been able to determine the exact date of Sydney Hammond Simms' death, also mentioned by James H. Hammond in a letter to Simms dated July 17, 1861 (original in the Hammond Papers, Library of Congress). Simms' family Bible and the family tombstone at Woodlands both give the incorrect date of July 22, 1861.

[139] Chevillette.

[140] William Henry Fuller was born on March 30. He died on June 2, 1867.

[141] Dr. William Fuller enlisted on Aug. 1, 1861, and was commissioned 2nd lieutenant in Company F, 11th Regiment of South Carolina Volunteers.

tions; and passion is succeeded by Hate, & Hate by Vindictiveness, and if the war continues, there will be no remedy. Your city will be utterly ruined by the Black Republicans who dare not think of peace, and who, if the people once come to their senses, will be torn to pieces. You, perhaps, do not think all this. But you had warning of every syllable a year ago & last summer. The cowardice of your conservatives is the secret of your evil. You have no moral at the North. The mob rules you. If the war is persevered in, it must be a war of extermination. Our people will fight to the last! You do not mention whether the Wilsons applied for the money.[142] Miss W. has had no advices from home on the subject. I have just had a letter from the Appletons, & shall (D. V.) resume my work for them tomorrow.[143] Gilmore is still at the Citadel. If called out, it will be for local defence. We have 10,000 men in Virginia; 10,000 here waiting orders; and some 40,000 drilling & arming. Every body is eager for fight, and such is the feeling that I much fear, in a contest with the Yankees, no quarter will be given. Hosts of our people are fighting without pay. The Cotton crop will probably all be hypothecated to the Government, and not a bale be suffered to depart save through our own ports & by *bona fide* foreign bottoms. The crop will be large — probably larger than last year — and will be likely to reach 5,000,000 bales. The seasons have been eminently favorable. I have not had such a good stand of Corn & Cotton for ten years, and such is the case every where. The wheat crop is also enormous. The blockade does not trouble us at all, for if we do not sell a bale of Cotton, we have still abundance for support. Cotton is our *surplus* crop. If you would read "Southward Ho!" you would comprehend all this.[144] I have now in store corn enough for my family & people till Nov. of the crop of last year. The crop of Corn, of this season, is already made; we are giving it its last working now. I calculate to make 4000 bushels. I have on hand 300 weight of beef, smoked & corned, for the negroes. I have also 5000 lbs Bacon. In December I calculate to kill 100 hogs, averaging 125 lbs each. Some will reach 250. I have several acres of rice, 5 perhaps, 5 to 7 acres of Potatoes, and probably 40 of peas, growing. I have just cut

---

[142] See letter to Lawson of May 8.
[143] Writing articles for *The New American Cyclopædia*.
[144] See the discussion of the life of the planter versus that of the manufacturer and the life of the cotton farmer versus that of the textile worker in *Southward Ho!* (New York: Redfield, 1854), pp. 166-174.

30 acres of oats & 60 of rye. My gardens are 2 acres. I am eating of almost every vegetable, and we milk 14 cows daily. My wife sells or gives away several dollars of butter every week. This is her perquisite. Flour has fallen in our markets to $6. per barrel. Judge in what degree the blockade troubles us. I trust, for one, that it may not be removed in a hurry — at all events not until Europe finds it necessary to seek our Cotton, cash in hand. God bless you & yours, my old friend, and give us peace in our old age.

Yours Ever truly

W. Gilmore Simms.

1057: To ALFRED PROCTOR ALDRICH

Saturday Afternoon, Woodlands.
[August? 1861][145]

dear Aldrich.

Did I, or not, see you on the Cars this morning at Bamberg? I should have preferred seeing you at Woodlands. How long will you remain in the State? Do you go back? Shall we be allowed to see you? I long to have a talk from you touching affairs in Virginia.[146] There is a battalion muster near Fishburnes [147] on Thursday of next week in the hope to get up some martial & patriotic spirit. Jamison & myself are invited to be present. We shall accordingly (D. V.) be at Fishburne's on *Wednesday* night of next week. Can't you meet us there? Fishburne (I answer for him) will give you hearty welcome, as in olden times. If you can, join us, & give the boys a speech at the Muster Ground. You will be authority, as you come fresh from the scene of action.[148] I have been half a dozen times on the point of writing to your wife during your absence; but I have been so distracted, having had more trouble in my family — having buried another son — and

---

[145] Dated by Simms' references to the death of his son Sydney Hammond and the illnesses of his daughters Chevillette and Hattie. See preceding letters.

[146] Aldrich was a colonel on Bonham's staff and had been serving in Virginia.

[147] Dr. Francis Beatty Fishburne (1807-1883), son of Mary Cussings Bellinger and Maj. Francis Beatty Fishburne and brother of Sarah Fishburne Carroll (b. 1805), wife of Charles Rivers Carroll, lived at Orange Grove Plantation, about five miles from Bamberg on the road to Allendale. His wife was Caroline Legaré Roach (1809-1885), daughter of Nash Roach's half-brother William.

[148] We have not located an account of this battalion muster.

having had two of my daughters down with typhoid fever &
seriously ill. You are aware that I am engaged in the experiment
of living on the plantation this summer. It is not a matter of
choice. Thus far, since the summer set in, we have been healthy.
I trust that God, who forces the necessity upon us, will mercifully
spare us. Let me hear from you. It is barely possible that Jamison
& myself will run up to Reynolds' [149] on Tuesday next. With best
respect to Mrs. A. I am

Ever truly Yours

W. Gilmore Simms.

Col. Aldrich.

1058: To James Lawson

Woodlands. 20 Augt. 1861.

James Lawson, Esq.

My dear old friend.

Miss Wilson will leave us today, for New York, by a circuitous
route, which will probably keep this scribble some two weeks on
the road. Her year is out & her mother [150] commands her return
home. She professes to have been well satisfied here, and we have
paid her up in full. We could do no more. We have no money,
though we have plenty of bread & bacon, chickens & beef, ham &
eggs, wheat, rye & corn & oats, potatoes and peas, and certainly
the most wonderful crops of corn & Cotton upon the ground. If
present prospects continue, I shall make twice the Cotton that has
ever been made upon the plantation. My Corn Crop is prodigious,
exceeding every thing for 20 years. We are really in the enjoyment of abundance. We don't care to sell Cotton at all. I am
living solely from the plantation. Our sugar is plenty. Our coffee
& tea are all that we have to buy. My stock of Hyson is 6 lbs.
of Black 4 lbs. I have 100 lb. Coffee. I could feed all your family
a year and never feel it. I have 5000 lbs of Bacon in the Smoke
House; 100 lbs Smoked Beef. I shall kill (D. V.) 100 head of
Hogs in December, & probably 4 beeves between this & then.
Today, I have half a *shoat* for dinner, (the other half sent to Mrs.
Rivers) a string of trout & perch from the Edisto, and a pair of
Chickens. We have curds cream & clabber & buttermilk in any

---

[149] Fairmount, Dr. William Sims Reynolds' plantation.
[150] Mrs. William Wilson, the former Jane Sibbald.

quantity, and my wife, who has this among other perquisites in making money, by selling Butter every week at Midway or Bamberg. The health of the plantation is excellent. I have not a case of fever on the plantation, though this is the sickliest month of all our year, and we have 70 negroes and some 10 whites. If you see Miss Wilson, she will report. She seems to be an excellent girl, is modest & proper, & intelligent; plays with taste, and is wonderfully possessed of a passion for whist. I have been teaching her, & have referred her to you, to finish her off. Jamison has written to you anent your tragedy.[151] He has been with me all this morning. (Sunday) My wife has gone up with most of the children to Bamberg. But they all think of you & the girls, & w'd send love were they here. We should really be glad to see you & Lyde, & all the girls here with us, and, I trust, when this war, at once brutal & ridiculous ceases, we shall have you here again. Oh! how your foolish city has been cutting its own throat. Only think of a people making war on their best customers. What suicide. Your *accounts* are not such as reach us of the events of the war. Our Government is not one to suppress reports of the action; to seize upon telegraphic despatches; to alter reports for the press & telegraph — in brief to do what it pleases, in violation of Constitution, law & rights of the Citizen. Whether you will hear the truth until the war is ended, is very questionable. But you ought to be shrewd Scotchman enough to guess it for yourself, when, after all the mighty preparations of the North, they still tremble for the safety of Washington, & every step in Virginia has lost them blood & treasure. We do not exult in this. We wish for peace. We desire no war, but are prepared for the worst. We are resolved on Independence. We have been persecuted for 30 years & will stand it no longer — from our brethren. By this time your thinking men see the sort of game that is before them. Let them grow wise before it be too late. Every battle, thus far, has resulted in a Southern Victory. — Sumter, Bethel, Bull Run, Manassas,[152] Harpers Ferry & Missouri, — all tell the same tale. Your Generals are cashiered.[153] Your army demoralized. Your papers are at a loss where to cast the blame. They will be at no

---

[151] *Liddesdale.* See note 33, Feb. 19, 1861.

[152] Simms wrote *Manassah.*

[153] Probably Simms has in mind the removal of Gen. William S. Harvey from command of the Department of the West and the removal from field service of Gen. Irvin McDowell, in command of the Union forces at the Battle of Bull Run.

loss before long. They will see that their cause is bad. We have now 200,000 men in the field, with 250,000 in preparation for it. We can feed our armies from the fields, without buying any thing but guns & ammunition. We shall make 4,500,000 bales of Cotton. We will look at the piles & if need be, burn them. We do not need to sell a bag. Of all this, you, among others, were well warned long ago. I do not blame *you* for this war. I know that you desired peace. We offered peace. But your people have sacrificed the country for the sake of a party that had no other object in view, than the monopoly of office. Office without revenue! Where are your democrats? Where were they at the passage of the Morill tariff,[154] for the benefit of Pennsylvania and New England. Between these two, New York is in ruins. We are prepared for a long war — preparing for it. It will fully establish the independence of the South. We are now manufacturing guns, cannon, rifles, powder, shot, oils, machinery, wool & cotton clothing, percussion caps, sewing machines — every thing. Three years of war will be the making of our people; and they are all beginning to percieve it. Not a bale of Cotton will be sent to the seaports. Hardly one off the plantations. Our young men are all profitably employed. Our old men are keeping things straight at home. Our crops are abundant, and we are willing that the vile petty conflict of 30 years, should close, at last, in a final issue of battle. Every day of delay in the conflict strengthens us, & every man feels that our cause is just & that God is with us. Troops for Virginia & our Sea Coast are pouring in daily. New regiments are in constant formation, and such a *personnel* for war is rarely witnessed in any nation. —

You will recieve a letter from my neighbour, Jamison, who speaks in very complimentary terms of your Drama. He has finished his Life of Bertrand de Guesclin and is now revising it.[155] He is making a good crop this year. Two of his sons volunteer for Virginia this week.[156] For my part, I am literally doing nothing in letters. I am so much excited in the present condition of things that the labour of the desk is irksome — I go to it with reluctance, and leave it on the slightest pretext. All that I have

---

[154] See note 46, Feb. 22, 1861.

[155] Jamison's *The Life and Times of Bertrand du Guesclin* was published in 1864. See note 72, c. Aug. 1, 1864.

[156] John Wilson Jamison was aide de camp to Gen. Micah Jenkins. William Harper Jamison was commissioned 2nd lieutenant in Company A of Lucas' Battalion of Artillery.

been doing is on the Cyclopædia. In a late letter, Mess'rs Appleton & Co admitted a Bal. due me to April 18. 1861 of $22.75, but beg that I will not draw for it until they advise me. I however cover to you a draft for this amount, *payable at their earliest convenience*. It is so small a matter that they will probably pay it at once. If so, put it to my credit. I have also referred them to you & Duyckinck for any personal or literary details in regard to myself, for, tho' furnishing them with some facts, I have utterly refused to write the notice of myself. I suggested that probably our friend Richards, the Painter, might do it.[157] Miss Wilson is anxious to secure employment here in the winter; but neither Jamison nor myself is willing to incur a debt which we may lack the means to pay. We shall have bread & meat in plenty, but possibly no money. I am already picking Cotton; and we shall pile it up in pyramids, with piles of light wood beneath it, ready to be fired as soon as your fierce Yankees penetrate the country. We shall admire daily the piles as they grow, and they will make a splendid conflagration, lighting up the country for miles, and showing the bright armour of the enemy on his march. But war is a sad subject for jesting upon & to us, old fellows, it is hateful. You & I might have adjusted the whole issue — i.e. if despotic powers for 24 hours had been given us. Love to Lyde & all.

Ever truly Yours

W. Gilmore Simms.

1059: To Benson John Lossing

Woodlands, S. C.
Aug 20. 1861.

B. J. Lossing, Esq.

My dear Mr. Lossing.

I cannot suffer Miss Wilson to leave Woodlands for home, without reminding you that I still live, and that I remember you with friendly sentiments, spite of the fact that we are forced to be

---

[157] We do not know who wrote the article on Simms in *The New American Cyclopædia*. Two letters from George Ripley (one of the editors) to Lawson dated Dec. 11 and Dec. 20, 1861 (originals in the South Caroliniana Library), indicate that Lawson read the article in proof and made certain corrections which were accepted by Ripley.

enemies.[158] I trust you now percieve the propriety of my counsel that your visit South should be foreborne during the present state of affairs. I take for granted that you concur with me in the desire that we may soon have peace on terms honorable to both nations, and favourable to the grand interests of civilization.

> Very truly & respectfully,
> Your obt servt.

> W. Gilmore Simms.

1060: To FRANCIS PEYRE PORCHER

Woodlands, 23 Augt. 1861.

My Dear Dr.

I am glad that my hurried notice of your essay gave you pleasure.[159] I wrote at midnight, recalling, as rapidly as possible, all I had heard or knew in relation to your subject, which I really wish that you would pursue. You will probably induce many to turn their experiences to good account in these blockading and hard times. I don't know that my experiences & suggestions will be of any value to you, but think it possible that something may be made of them. Your chemical analysis will decide that. Of course, there are a thousand subjects of which we might have spoken. The soap made of the Pride of India Berry, is, by the way called "Poor Man's Soap," among the country people. At intervals, I recal many items, but before I can set them down on paper, forget them. There is the supple Jack, the cane, the osier, all of which may be worked into excellent mats & baskets. If they make cartridge boxes as they used to, of a soft wood, bored with small augur holes, the Tupelo is superior to any other wood, being at once, very close, & almost as light as cork. It is commonly used as a substitute for cork, throughout the country. There are, I think, two or three varieties of the Broom Straw — Planta Genista — one of which is found to make excellent brooms. But you have probably thought of all these things. Should any occur to me, I will suggest them. I would commend to you to give an

---

[158] Lossing was an intimate friend of the William Wilsons and later edited Wilson's *Poems* (Poughkeepsie: A. Wilson, 1869).

[159] Simms' review of Porcher's "Resources of the Southern Fields and Forests," *De Bow's Review*, XXXI (Aug., 1861), 105-131, is in the Charleston *Mercury* of Aug. 13.

occasional reciept for making things, in connection with your reports upon the native substances. For example, the simplest reciept
for making Vinegar; the Home (get it from the Professor) [160]
process for manufacturing Wine. This year, the grape is abundant.
It is possible that in the upper country, cherries are only ripening
now. They are done with us. Cherry Bounce, I have made in this
wise. I fill a demijohn with cherries, & add 4 quarts of whiskey
to every gallon of cherries. I drain off the whiskey, & add a thin
syrup, boiling, one pint to every pint of the juice. A thick syrup,
boiling, poured over the cherries themselves, then taken out of the
liquor, will make the Brandy Cherry.

Of the uses of the oak, for ship building, I need say nothing;
but it might be urged now, that Charleston, Beaufort, Savannah,
St Mary's & other places in Florida, might be all put in requisition
to season oak for naval purposes at home, and even now to build
gallies & gunboats for the shoal waters. All the winged seed trees,
like the Ailanthus, are, I think, designed for the recuperation of
worn lands, which have been denuded of their fibrous matter.
The berries of the Pride of India are also useful for this purpose.
These shrub trees not only restore the woody matter, but they
serve to disintegrate the soil where it is tough. They are hard to
exterminate, & in this lies one of their merits. They do not oppose
much resistance to cultivation & though perpetually springing up,
they are easily cut down. I have said that the May Apple will
make beer & vinegar. In making the latter, would you allow the
fruit to ripen fully, or take it when sourest & while the pulp is yet
tolerably hard. Turnips make Jersey Champagne, — why not
vinegar also? Good reciepts for vinegar, wine, preserves, pickles,
might all be given in your articles. Enquire into the uses of the
Cassina which was employed for tea in the Revolution, & into
the uses of the Sumach & the Ginseng.

All of these are, I believe, native. Should you feel disposed to
extend your researches, run up & see me & look about *our*
woods.[161] I have reason to believe the region perfectly healthy. As
yet, we have had but a single case of fever among 70 negroes. My

---

[160] Not identified.

[161] In 1863 Evans and Cogswell, Charleston, published Porcher's *Resources
of the Southern Fields and Forests, Medical, Economical and Agricultural.
Being Also a Medical Botany of the Confederate States; with Practical Information on the Useful Properties of the Trees, Plants, and Shrubs* (see letter
to Porcher of April 14, 1863), in which he adopts a number of the suggestions
Simms here makes, frequently accrediting Simms with them.

family has all been healthy during the summer. The season is now showery, as we may expect in August. Our crops thus far are good. We shall — have made — corn in abundance. My cotton crop promises far better than usual, and I have commenced picking. I can give you plenty of hog, hominy, milk, eggs, fresh butter, & vegetables, with a broiling chicken daily; and a friend's welcome! There!

Make my best respects to our Virginia friend, your wife; [162] and tell her that I fervently hope that her tidings from her native State will continue grateful.

Yours Ever truly

W. Gilmore Simms

1061: To William Gilmore Simms, Jr.

Woodlands, Thursday Afternoon.
[November 7, 1861] [163]

You had better, my dear Son, get a belt and pocket of leather, for your revolver, and not burden yourself with carrying the box. It will not be necessary to you. If you have enough of bullets, even the bullet mould & all the appurtenances of powder flask &c. may be left with the box. The same flask from which you load your musket, will afford you powder for your pistol. But as in the musket you may probably use cartridges, then carry the powder flask of the pistol. But be sure & strip yourself of all unnecessary incumbrances, which the Romans called *Impedimenta*. Be as lightly armed as you can. It would be better that I should provide you with moulded bullets than that you should carry mould & lead with you. Leave box, mould & all that sort of thing with your sister.[164] Advise me, as soon as you can, of your whereabouts & the mode of reaching you, in the event of our desiring to send you any thing. See that your provision for clothing is warm & sufficient. Leave every thing that you do not need, with

---

[162] The former Virginia Leigh, daughter of Benjamin Watkins Leigh, of Richmond.

[163] Dated by Simms' discussion of "the attempt on Beaufort" (see note 166, below). The Thursday during the attack was Nov. 7.

At the time of the writing of this letter Gilmore was a cadet at the Citadel Academy. After the attack on Port Royal the cadets were ordered to support the Washington Artillery, stationed at Wappoo Cut (see Col. Oliver James Bond, *The Story of the Citadel* [Richmond: Garrett and Massie, (1936)], p. 63).

[164] Augusta.

your sister; and remember that nobody is more lighthearted than he who has fewest cares, whether of brain or body. Your bowie knife may be very useful. You are to remember that you are to defend your mother country, & your natural mother, from a hoard of mercenaries & plunderers, and you will make your teeth meet in the flesh. The less you fear for yourself, the more your security. 'He who would save his life, the same shall lose it!' This is a biblical warning against that lack of firmness, that over-caution, always trembling at consequences, & calculating chances, which was the infirmity of Hamlet, and which is fatal to all heroism. And this audacity & courage are not inconsistent with the utmost prudence and circumspection. All generalship, in fact, is so much military prudence, as reconciles valour with judgment & wisdom. Mere inconsiderate rage is not so much valour as blindness, ignorance, presumption & insanity. Obey orders, do your duty faithfully & cheerfully & patiently, and wait your time, & watch your time, and keep your head so, that where your leader may falter, you shall be able to keep him up, counsel him on, & where he falls, take the lead yourself. A strong will, a brave heart & clear head, in the moment of danger, these constitute the es-sentials of heroism. Let nothing, at any time, divert your mind, from the immediate duty which is before you. This is *first* & therefore *over* all. It will be time enough tomorrow for other matters. But I will not bore you with laws and maxims. Be a man, my son, faithful & firm, and put yourself in God's keeping. All that the love & confidence of parents can do for you will be done. Yourself, with God's aid, must do the rest. We are in his hands, all of us! Pray to him. It will not lessen your strength & courage to do so, even on the abyss of battle! We are all well except your father. I am suffering from neuralgia in the head, from ear ache, and tooth ache, all at once. The latter will probably compel me to visit the city on Monday next,[165] & I may go to the Mills House or Charleston Hotel. I trust you have the dressing case by this time. Better take out of it a single razor, get it *set* by the Barber, take a small box of the ointment & the Brush & leave the case with your sister. It would only encumber you. A mere pinch of the ointment is put upon the face, and the brush, wet with water is then applied briskly. In laying the razor to cheek or chin, let it be as flat as possible. It will then cut the beard

---

[165] Nov. 11. Evidently Simms delayed this trip until Nov. 15 (see letter to Hammond of Nov. 18).

better, and will be less likely to cut the skin. Besides, it will keep the razor longer from being dulled. — The news which reaches us is exciting without being satisfactory. I have for six months predicted the attempt of the enemy on Beaufort, with a formidable force, with which they would expect to make Beaufort a base of operations, against Charleston & Savannah equally. I expected them in September.[166] What our troops will need is numerous small steamers & boats so as to have ready access from one island to another. What I fear is the cutting off of small bodies on isolated spots. We require, now, that we have made the issue on the sea islands where the naval force of the enemy can be employed, to sustain our batteries against launches landing infantry & light troops. Any small bodies landing, we can cut off. To concentrate our troops in sufficient bodies against a formidable force will be more difficult, and, in the end, in all probability, we may be reduced to a guerilla warfare along the main fronting the sea islands. Write when you get a chance. God be with you, my son,

Your father

W. G. S.

1062: To MARCUS CLAUDIUS MARCELLUS HAMMOND [167]

Woodlands, S. C. Nov. 9. 1861

[Dear Major]

[I return] to you the letter of Northrop.[168] If [his ideas were] followed out, friendship would [have no vir]tues. It would be a mere name. [It makes me] think all the Bellinger & Northrop tribe, [to be me]n of *kinks,* notions. This man has some [merit]. He is honest & fearless. But, from all I [h]ave heard & seen, he

---

[166] A fleet under the command of Commodore Samuel Francis Du Pont 1803-1865), carrying an expeditionary corps of 12,653 men under the command of Gen. Thomas West Sherman (1813-1879), arrived at Port Royal on Nov. 4. On Nov. 7 the Northern forces captured Forts Beauregard and Walker and had possession of the area (see *O. R.,* 1st Series, VI, 3-20, 185-186). Simms had doubtless seen the Charleston *Mercury* of Nov. 7, which reports a cannonade at Port Royal between the United States fleet and the Confederate States fleet under the command of Capt. Josiah Tattnall (1795-1871). Simms had prophesied the attack in his letter to Miles of May 11.

[167] The MS. of this letter is badly mutilated.

[168] Lucius Bellinger Northrop (1811-1894), the son of Claudia Margaret Bellinger and Amos Bird Northrop, of Charleston, was commissary general of the Confederate States Army from March 16, 1861, to Feb. 16, 1865. He was a brother of Claudian Bird Northrop (see note 257, Nov. 24, 1846).

is rude, usurpative and suspicious — perhaps jealous also — in fact labor[s] under a disease which we may call a morb[id] self-esteem. In respect to Davis's treatment of yo[ur] application, I can say nothing, as I know nothing of him. *You have probably been misrepresented, or u[n]favorably represented,* and your faults & foibles magnified into crimes & vices: or your application never reached him.[169] I am unwilling to believe that a man who has shown himself to possess so many distinguishing qualities, should have petty prejudices, mean spites & small jealousies. But you need not depend on him or any man. In your present position, you may make an undying reputation. While I write you, South Carolina is attack[ed] by a formidable fleet & army. On dit 30,000 [me]n. We have probably 10,000 all told, of what [*about three words missing or illegible*] ourselves. We have some 13,000 in [rese]rves. Our *young* men are all gone off. If the contiguous states do not come forward, she must [be] crushed, and, under the same policy, all of t[he] States [wil]l be crushed in detail. *You should volunte[er]* to put yourself conspicuously forw[ard. The North] has the notion that by the invas[ion of S. C.] we shall be compelled to with[draw our troops] from Virginia. This invasion has a[s its purpose] to compel us to withdraw our troops & [to obtain a] Cotton port, under their control, to Eur[ope. I] do not concieve it possible that we shall be [able] at a day's warning, to concentrate 30. or 4[0,]00[0] troops for the defence of any one port. You see [ho]w vital it is that we meet them with concentrating [arm]ies from 3 states at least, and without withdrawing [an]y troops from Virginia. The U. S. Congress, is really [an]xious of its next session in Washington, and it is, I suspect, the policy of Davis, to invade Maryland, above & below Washington, as soon as the Congress fully assembles. But, aside from general politics, you are in position to help yourself to superior position, if your health will suffer. What to you will be a seat in Congress, in comparison with military prestige. *That* will secure you a seat any day hereafter and you are a military man especially. If elected, resign your seat and volunteer to lead a Brigade to the defence of South Carolina. — Enow! My head aches, & my heart sickens at the loss of our b[att]eries. I counselled against any defences exposed to [the] enemy's shipping. I preferred to devastate & [ab]an[don our] coast & fight them on

---

[169] See letter to Miles of March 2, 1861.

the main. We plant pe[tty] batteries, armed by a mere company, or at most a sm[al]l brigade, just where their shipping, with the [superior weigh]t of metal, can be brought to [bear on the]m. The Hilton affair is but [the consequence] of that of Hatteras.[170] Not so bad, [but bad enou]gh, as showing the incompetence of [our Engine]ering & Generalship. To plant batteries [in such] situations, is just to invite the enemy [to at]tack where we are weak & they strong. But the event will be of service, in rousing the spirit of the people. I have been writing f[or] six months, editorially, in the Mercury [on] our coast defences. Nobody listened. But [a] few days ago, somebody — some sage [*one word illegible*] said in my hearing, "they will not attempt South Carolina." Yet S. C. was the very state they were bound to attempt, & I indicated that Beaufort was the point at which they would aim, & long ago mentioned that they would seek to plant a corp d'armee of 25,000 men there, as a base of operations equally against Charleston & Savannah. Besides, to keep steamers from passing batteries, you must bl[ock] the channel, so as to give sufficient time to [the] batteries to do their work. But all's lost upon the poor imbeciles in office. God bless y[ou.] I can write no more. Best regards to wife and young ones.

Your friend

W. Gilmore Sim[m]s

P. S. If the enemy approac[h here,] I shall send my wife & chil[dren to] you at Athens,[171] and blow up [my] establishment. They shall have not[hing] that I can destroy.

1063: To James Henry Hammond [172]

Woodlands, 18 Nov. 1861.

My dear Hammond.

Date Obolum Belisario! I do not exactly want an obolus, nor am I exactly a pauper; yet I need some succour. I went to town

---

[170] On Aug. 28-29 Confederate batteries at Hatteras Inlet, N. C., had been captured by Northern forces (see *O. R.,* 1st Series, IV, 579ff). Fort Walker was located on Hilton Head Island in Port Royal Bay (see note 166, Nov. 7, 1861).

[171] Georgia.

[172] Hammond's reply to this letter is dated Nov. 26. He again wrote Simms on Nov. 29. The originals are in the Hammond Papers, Library of Congress, which also contains the original of an undated letter from Hammond to Simms which appears to have been written sometime in Nov., 1861.

on Friday last,[173] seeking a Hogshead or a couple of barrels of molasses. Not a gallon was to be had in Charleston, the troops having consumed every thing. And as the troops continue to accumulate, & as we can get nothing except by the slow coach, over the land route, it is almost impossible that things should be more favorable to my wishes a month hence than now. Meanwhile, I wish to feed my negroes, & through sweets, keep them in sweet temper. It is probable that the article may be procurable in Augusta. Will you endeavour to buy me a Hogshead of the cheapest, or a couple of bbls, (which I should prefer) and, as I am not known perhaps, as a man of substance, to the *solid* men of that town, endorse me as good for the nonce. If you can, do so as soon as possible. I hold it to be important, & suggest it to you, that our negroes should, especially just now, be taught to feel that their owners are their best friends. Mine are very docile. I have 70, and most of them are born on the place, and have grown up with my children. I have lost my overseer — gone to the wars. My son, the only one able to do duty — just 18 — is in camp & eager for an opportunity.[174] But for my helpless little ones, I should be very much disposed, though I can neither ride nor march, to set off for the seaboard myself, for I can still see to shoot. What have you done for negro clothes and shoes? Or have you been more provident than your friends & laid in a supply of both while it was possible. Will you let me know whether a good thick cotton stuff, of sufficient weight as a substitute for woollen, can be got from your Augusta factories, and at what prices, and whether I can get credit, to the extent of a couple of hundred Dollars, or whether they will take pay in cotton and at what prices? Do see to these matters for me as soon as you conveniently can. I would run up and see about the matter myself, and visit you at the same time, but that I have nobody on the place but myself.[175] I took the opportunity, while my overseer was still with me, to go to Charleston on Friday last; and he went off with his troop on Saturday, and before I could return. I saw Pickens; went to see him about this most atrocious proclamation or order calling out

---

[173] Nov. 15.

[174] See letter to Gilmore of Nov. 7.

[175] In his reply of Nov. 26 Hammond writes: ". . . I . . . am surprised that you who write so *really* wise about coast & other defences should have neglected to defend your family to this extent at least. I have always maintained, that though a Poet & Novelist (Your true *forte* was Statesmanship) you were a man of sound sense & judicious action & that the old foggyism of good old Mr Roach overshadowed you."

the militia, and licensing them indiscriminately, to take horses, carts, wagons, provisions at pleasure — in other words authorizing every squatter to help himself to a fine horse, and all that he might desire.[176] The result was instantaneous. In Orangeburg, as soon as it was known, stables were broken open, and in some instances, 3 & 4 of the best carriage horses were carried off, while the fattening hogs in the pen were shot down. Pickens denied that he had ever authorized any such order; countermanded it, & Schnierle, who issued the order, resigned, & is said to assert that Pickens forgets, or forswears, his own handwriting.[177] So the matter stands. Our engineering along the coast, under Trapier,[178] has been wretched, & without science or judgment. The planters on Edisto, under the lead of Jenkins Mikell,[179] have applied the torch to their cotton. The Yankees have not attempted to approach the main, and are stepping very cautiously from island to island. I fancy that their whole aim is to get foothold, some where in all of the Cotton States, with two objects — first, to open Cotton ports to Europe, under their auspices, & in the hope that high prices will tempt the planters to send their cotton; next to be able to boast to the world that their flag once more flies in all the seceded states. I saw Miles who tells me that Lee is the *beau ideal* of a Great Captain, and fine warrior.[180] He says that Beauregard has but 38,000 men in the Army of the Potomac, while Mc-Clellan [181] has 120000. But he adds that Beauregard said to himself emphatically, just before he left him, that he wished for nothing but that the enemy should come on, as his ground was so well chosen, his entrenchments so admirable, his troops all so

---

[176] Pickens' proclamation of Nov. 11 is printed in the Charleston *Courier* of Nov. 12.

[177] The Charleston *Courier* of Nov. 18 reports the resignation of Maj. Gen. John Schnierle, commander of the 2nd Division, South Carolina Militia, and remarks that he has been considering a resignation since Dec., 1860, for reasons "involving his self respect and the proper discharge of his duties."

[178] James H. Trapier (1814-1866), a graduate of the United States Military Academy in 1838, resigned from the United States Army in 1848 and was a planter at Georgetown, S. C., until the organization of the Confederate States. With the rank of captain of engineers he served in the construction of the Confederate batteries for the attack on Fort Sumter and was engineer-in-chief on Morris Island. In Oct., 1861, he was promoted to brigadier general in command of the Department of Eastern and Middle Florida. He later served in Alabama, Mississippi, and South Carolina.

[179] Mikell's sister Eliza Adeline was the wife of Bartholomew Rivers Carroll, Jr. (see introductory sketch of the Carrolls).

[180] Early in Nov., 1861, Gen. Robert E. Lee was sent by Davis to organize the defenses of the South Atlantic seaboard.

[181] In Nov., 1861, Gen. George Brinton McClellan (1826-1885) succeeded Scott as commander-in-chief of the United States Army.

select and well prepared that he was ready to stake, his honour, life, reputation, his *head,* all that was precious to him, on the result.[182] Write me soon. Make my best regards to Mrs. H. and to Cattie [183] when you see her, in which request my wife joins. My eldest son is with the battalion of State Cadets. He is eager for the fray. Tell Mrs. H. that my daughter Augusta, is again a Mother, with a fine little boy.[184] She is doing well, but is feeble. I expect her to be with us in a couple of weeks. By the way, and before I forget it, the Mercury has been making itself very odious every where in S. C. in consequence of its course towards Davis & the Gov.[185] *It is now doomed,* I confidently believe. It was doing well, after secession and promised fairly to become one of the most powerful organs of the South. But the Rhetts cannot bear prosperity, and they have kicked over the milk tub of theirs. I scarcely write for it now. The last article was one on our coast defences, about a week ago. I wrote nearly all that they have published on this subject, for the last 8 months.[186] But with such men in authority as Pickens, Schnierle, Trapier, *et id. om. ge.,* I was fated like Cassandra to speak the truth with nobody to listen. My plans would most effectually have kept the enemy from breaking in at Port Royal. It is not the Yankee race alone that needs purging & scourging. We too need punishment to destroy the packed jury, & old family systems, the logrolling & the corruption every where. Ah! were you but a well man, & both of us, young ones! Harry, I see is with

---

[182] Miles was "Chairman of a Special Committee . . . to examine into the condition of the Quartermaster's, Commissary's and Surgical Departments of the Army" and report to Congress. The Charleston *Courier* of Oct. 29 reports that since the adjournment of Congress (Sept. 3) the members of the committee have "visited the Army in Western Virginia and are now with the Army of the Potomac."

[183] Hammond's daughter Katherine, usually called "Kate."

[184] Gilmore Simms Roach (called "Simms") was born on Nov. 3. He died on Jan. 22, 1865.

[185] See note 125, June 8, 1861.

[186] See note 29, Feb. 19, 1861. The article to which Simms here refers is "Our Coast Defences" published in the *Mercury* of Nov. 13. In this "last article" on the subject Simms writes of the "disaster at Beaufort," reviews the advice he had been giving in his editorials for many months past (the same as he had earlier this year given Miles and Jamison), repeats many of the ideas expressed in his letter to M. C. M. Hammond of Nov. 9, remarks that he had "spoken and prophesied with the fate of Cassandra," urges the planters along the coast to burn their cotton in order to keep it from falling into the enemy's hands, and advocates that South Carolina "strike a blow [at the enemy] as soon as we can" as "our best social and military policy."

Jones.[187] Jones is a cool, longheaded, person, & will employ his regiment judiciously, & will economize it. Where are Spann & Paul.[188] Do write me. I am very desolate and disconsolate — able to do little — very much curtailed & cut down. My copyrights, worth $25,000 are, I suppose, all confiscate!

Yours Ever

W. Gilmore Simms

1064: To James Henry Hammond

Monday Night, Decr. 2. [1861][189]

My dear Hammond.

I wrote you on Saturday.[190] Today, I recieved your letter. Thanks for what you have done. You have recieved mine, by this time, and today, I was advised of 306 yards of twill, from the Columbia Mills of Gibbes & Co.[191] at 25/100. The fact may be of some use to some of your friends. I am to pay in Cotton at 8 cents & a fraction. I shall need some cotton for under clothes & shall await Jamison's report. I subscribed 20 bales to the Confederate Govt. I have made a corn crop adequate to my own use; but expect Dr. Fuller's negroes as soon as the enemy shall land upon the main. He has 40 or more, & perhaps, 8 or 10 mules & horses. I shall have to feed them. He owes me $1000 now, and perhaps will be never able to pay. But he is a connection, & if he never pays, it matters little. We shall all settle off our scores before long. Your subscription of 200 bales to the Conf. Govt. binds you to that extent. But, if you will

---

[187] Harry Hammond held the rank of assistant commissary in Gen. David Rumph Jones' brigade. Jones (1825-1863), a native of Orangeburg, S. C., and a graduate of the United States Military Academy, was commissioned major in the Confederate States Army shortly after his resignation from the United States Army on Feb. 15, 1861. He was Gen. Beauregard's chief-of-staff at the time of the surrender of Fort Sumter, and in June, 1861, he was promoted to brigadier general.

[188] Spann Hammond had been on Bonham's staff at Manassas, but at this time he was not in the service. At this time Paul Hammond was on Gen. Edmund Kirby Smith's staff.

[189] Hammond's reply to this letter is dated Dec. 12, 1861. The original is in the Hammond Papers, Library of Congress.

[190] We have not located this letter of Nov. 30.

[191] The Saluda Factory, across the Saluda River from Columbia, owned by James Guignard Gibbes (see note 80, June 27, 1865).

let me counsel you, I would sell as little Cotton at 8/100 as possible. *You* need not. I go with the old trimeter

> "Never quake,
> Make or break,
> All upon the single stake!"

With Cotton at 24 in Liverpool, and 25 in N. Y., I am disposed to wait events, especially as the crop is a short one. I believe that England only waits a *political* necessity, to give her a pretext to elude & escape her philanthropic proclivities. She has been costive, in respect to the Confederate States, simply because she has never regarded the breach as irreparable. We have been mouthing & crying wolf so long — have been so long threatening disruption — that it is now hard to believe it. But, *necessitas non habet legem.* And England is evidently restive. The capture of our Commissioners is evidently an imbroglio devised for her benefit & digestion.[192] It will give her a pretext. I have come to the conclusion that their capture was a profound trap laid for the Yankees by Davis. Were it really of importance to send these Commissioners & send them in safety, then the Confederate Govt. & the Commissioners themselves played the silliest game in the world.

1. The Government should have kept their appointment a profound secret till they were fairly off for Europe, but it was published as soon as made.
2. The Commissioners had themselves trumpeted in Richmond as on their way to Charleston.
3. In Charleston they were trumpeted & feted, and it was no secret that they were to go out in the Nashville. This vessel took on coal, & was firing up, and the Commissioners made their preparations to go aboard; when advised of all, the Yankees sent two more of the fastest sailing steamers to complete the blockade of Charleston. So that scheme exploded.
4. Then they slipt out in the Theodora & got safely to Havana. There, instead of remaining incog, and lying perdu, under

---

[192] The Confederate States diplomatic commissioners to England and France, James Murray Mason (1798-1871) and John Slidell (1793-1871), left Charleston on the *Theodora* on Oct. 12; disembarked at Cardenas, Cuba, and travelled by land to Havana; left Havana on the *Trent* on Nov. 7; were seized at sea by Capt. Charles Wilkes (1798-1877) of the *San Jacinto* on Nov. 8; and were taken to Fort Monroe on Nov. 15 and to Boston on Nov. 24. They were released on Jan. 1, 1862.

Simms published an article entitled "Our Commissioners to Europe" in *De Bow's Review*, XXXI (Oct. and Nov., 1861), 412-419.

the names of Jones or Tompkins, British subjects, they had the trumpets blown, & walked the highways en grand, & were feted by men & women, & crowned with laurels.

5. Now first to last they were ostentatiously engaged in giving publicity to a proceeding which should — to be successful — have been kept as the closest of possible secrets. — Ergo, I conclude that Davis designed them for capture, in the very way the thing was done — torn by violence from a British vessel, sailing from & to a neutral port, and on the High Seas.

My hope is that Great Britain will be glad to seize upon the ground of quarrel which this outrage offers her. She cannot be undesirous of the dismemberment of the late Confederacy — cannot be desirous of the perpetuation of a Union which was in conflict with all her interests — to her shipping, trade, manufactures & institutions — of which she was jealous — which she at once feared & despised — cannot be indifferent to Cotton supply, or regardless of the free trade with 10 millions of people, who do not conflict with her in any way, but on the contrary, as purely Agricultural, are her natural allies. I should not be surprised to find her at war with the U. S. in less than 3 weeks. *Nous verrons.* That she has not acted before, is due, I suspect, to her fears of Napoleon, against whom she is nursing all her strength, which makes her reluctant to be embroiled with a powerful maritime region like the North. But our Commissioners should have been able to show her that this great maritime power of the North is due to her exclusive monopoly of the carrying trade and manufactures of the great staples of the South, and that the successful establishment of our Independence, transfers the great bulk of her shipping to the South. But all these things are more familiar to you than to me. — Did I tell you in my last that the report is that Ripley & Drayton have had a terrible quarrel touching the late disaster. On dit, that R. denounced D. for incompetence! Ripley is supposed to be the cleverest officer they have got, next to Lee. Of Dunovant & Dessaussure, it is said they are brave enough, but lack every thing like head.[193] Of Lee, Miles who

---

[193] On Aug. 21, 1861, Gen. Roswell Sabine Ripley (see note 175, Aug. 18, 1852) was ordered to assume command of the Department of South Carolina (see *O. R.*, 1st Series, VI, 267). For his report on Gen. Thomas Fenwick Drayton (1808-1891), who commanded the defenses of Port Royal at the time of the Northern victory in that area, see *O. R.*, 1st Series, VI, 13-14. For

knows him, speaks in the very highest terms, as the model equally of a Gentleman & soldier. — I have written to the Major to volunteer a Brigade for S. C.[194] He says he can get 5000 men. But he declines, alleging neglect and bad treatment on the part of Davis. I suspect that the Major has been shabbily treated by some of his *professing* friends. — Jamison has now been 10 days in Columbia, ostensibly for the examination of the Arsenal boys, & those desiring admission; but I suspect he is kept there by the politicians who are endeavouring to get the Convention called together. To call them to do nothing, is to do mischief; but I fear that they will enact some positively mischievous thing if they once get together.[195] What we now need is men. But the political influences of the last 30 years in S. C. has served to lay on the shelf the able men, & to demoralize the younger aspirants. We have been living most of that time under packed juries. It is melancholy to look about and see how resourceless we are in intellectual power. God send us relief & rescue. It is hardly to be found in our men. As soon as I can get off, I will positively take 3 days & bestow myself upon you. But I am sadly harassed.

God bless you all.

Yours ever

W. Gilmore Simms.

1065: To WILLIAM PORCHER MILES [196]

Woodlands 22 Decr. 1861.

My dear Miles.

Dr. J. Dickson Bruns,[197] whom you very well know, has written you already on the subject of his application for *full* Surgeon's

---

Gen. Dunovant, see note 131, June 14, 1861. Col. Wilmot Gibbes DeSaussure (1822-1886), of the 1st Regiment of Artillery, was in command of the batteries on Morris Island during the bombardment of Fort Sumter.

[194] See letter to Marcus Claudius Marcellus Hammond of Nov. 9.

[195] The third session of the Secession Convention met from Dec. 26, 1861, through Jan. 8, 1862.

[196] On the back of this letter is written: "W G Simms as to Dr. Brun's [*sic*] Dr Brn's [*sic*] Letter given to Surgeon General 27 Dec CRM [Charles Richardson Miles (see note 5, Jan. 15, 1862)]." Samuel Preston Moore (1813-1889) was surgeon general of the Confederate States Army; Robert Wilson Gibbes was surgeon general of South Carolina. It is probably the former to whom Miles here refers.

[197] See introductory sketch.

appointment in the C. S. A. He has Chisolm's [198] endorsement & that of Gen. Evans,[199] who is desirous to place him on his staff. He begs for my endorsement also. Of his *great cleverness, & full competence,* neither you nor I have any question, and his chief defect, that of a self-esteem which is quite too *prononcé,* is one which will perhaps be less perceptible in the discipline of a camp. At all events, his vanity, is in his case, sufficiently *excused* in recognition of his real ability. He is a good companion besides, and I have found him a *clever* fellow, and believe him to be a warmly devoted friend. Gen. Jamison joins with me in my endorsement of his ability and genuine worth, while he smiles at the *one* prominent defect of his character — viz: the self-esteem which makes him at times, almost as garrulous as myself. Let me beg that you will give this young man your support. I know him to be really superior to a very large proportion of those who seek place with audacity and find it, as frequently through pretension as worth.[200] — I had feared, my dear Miles, when called upon yesterday, to write you today, that I should, if I wrote at all, have to do so with streaming eyes and a broken heart. My beautiful little girl, your Goddaughter was seized 2 days ago with Scarlet Fever. Yesterday she was delirious, and our apprehensions were very great. Though she still has fever, the worst seems to be over now, and the Drs. declare her improving. We have to watch and still apprehend, but with growing hope. You will unite in prayer with us that she be spared us still. She is a very lovely child, lovely in person, with a noble ·head, and a very quick generous mind & nature. She is remarkably well developed for her age. Pray for us, my friend.[201] — Alas! that we should need to pray, and perhaps, sweat tears of blood for our poor country. Our curse is the incompetence of those parties who at present

[198] John Julian Chisolm (1830-1903), surgeon and oculist, was professor of surgery at the Medical College of the State of South Carolina when he received the first commission issued by the Confederate States to a medical officer. He attended the wounded at Fort Sumter, was later chief surgeon of the military hospital at Richmond, and then directed the plant for the manufacture of medicines at Charleston. After the Confederate War he returned to his professorship, and in 1869 he moved to Baltimore and was on the faculty of the University of Maryland for a number of years.

[199] Nathan George Evans (1824-1868) was appointed major and adjutant general in the South Carolina Army in Feb., 1861. In May he was appointed captain of cavalry in the Confederate States Army, and after his victory at Ball's Bluff in Oct., 1861, he was promoted to brigadier general.

[200] Bruns later received the appointment of surgeon at the Citadel Academy. See letter to Hammond of Dec. 4, 1862.

[201] Hattie died on Dec. 25. See letter to Miles of Jan. 15, 1862.

have our destinies in charge. The curses against Pickens are equally loud; deep & general.[202] And he is not alone. Never was our poor State so sadly deficient in becoming & able men. But you know all as well as I do. I feel that even if my poor counsels, as delivered incessantly in the Mercury & otherwise, in respect to our coast defences, had been followed, the miserable disasters at Port Royal, might have been escaped. Now! — But, why need to prate of this or any other matter, when the deafness of inordinate vanity, imbecility and the *dolce far niente,* as natural to the people of our Southern Seaboard as to the Italian, prevents all hearing on the part of those, who heed no counsel lest their own pretensions should be suspected & fathomed.

God be with you, & us, & our suffering country, in guardianship & mercy.

Yours Ever & Ever

W. Gilmore Simms.

---

[202] See Cauthen, *South Carolina Goes to War,* pp. 140-143.

1862

[January, 1862?]¹

My dear Thompson.—

Accompanying you have some of the things, in the way of political song & sonnet, which I have dashed off during & before our secession movement. They were all published in the Ch. Mercury. They might make a chapter in the Messenger, and are, I think, worthy of publication in the projected vol. of Professor C. I shall forward a similar batch, as soon as I can get them copied, and shall send you some besides which have never appeared in print. If you see, or communicate with Cooke, give him my remembrance & benison. Let me hear from you & believe me

Ever truly yours

W. Gilmore Simms.

The signature used with these pieces was mostly "Tyrtæus." Use that signature, if any, & if you credit a paper let it be the Mercury.

---

¹ Dated by Simms' reference to "the projected vol. of Professor C." This volume (evidently never published) is certainly that described in *S. L. M.,* XXXIV (Jan., 1862), 70: "Prof. Chase and Jno. R. Thompson, Esq. of Richmond, have undertaken the worthy task of rescuing from newspaper oblivion, the many excellent little poems which the war has called forth." The poems Simms enclosed with this letter are doubtless "The Ship of State. Sonnet" (signed "Tyrtæus"), published in *S. L. M.,* XXXIV (Feb. and March, 1862), 127, and the poems (signed "W. Gilmore Simms") published under the general title of "Odes, Sonnets and Songs, for the Times" in *ibid.,* 101-105: "The Soul of the South. An Ode," "Sons of the South, Arise. Ode," "Morals of Party. Sonnet," "Beauregard. Song," "The Border Ranger," "On, Advance!," "The Oath for Liberty," and "Shades of Our Fathers. An Ode." All of these had earlier been published in the Charleston *Mercury,* some as by "Tyrtæus," a pseudonym Simms used in the *Mercury* as early as 1859.

During 1859-1864 Simms was an infrequent contributor to the *Southern Literary Messenger,* and other than the above-mentioned poems we are able to ascribe to him only two signed poems published in the *Messenger* during these years: "Dedication Sonnet. To Hon. W. Porcher Miles, M. C.," XXVIII (June, 1859), 460, and "Oh, the Sweet South!," XXXII (Jan., 1861), 5.

1067: To WILLIAM PORCHER MILES

Woodlands, Jany 15. 1862.

Alas! yes, my dear Miles,

Our chief guest, on Christmas Day, was Death.[2] He found his way, without warning, and tore away our precious little one. The dear baby has arisen. I, who have so frequently been made to groan and shudder at his coming, am not a whit better prepared to meet him now, when he thus bears from us, each new bud of promise. No sooner have new tendrils closed over the old wounds, than they are rent away, and the scars reopen, & the old hurt bleeds afresh. This child was very sweet & dear to us. She had served, my friend, as you rightly intimate, to add new chords to those ties which linked you & ourselves so gratefully together even over the still unburied corses of my two noble little boys.[3] And, in herself, she was so surpassingly lovely. You can have no idea how tall she had grown, & how beautifully. Her form was perfectly developed; her face very fine & her forehead & whole head were cast in a mould of peculiar intellectual strength and beauty! Alas! Alas! — And scarcely had we laid her in the grave before I was again made to shudder with most awful terrors, when her brother, Govan, a year older, was taken down with the same loathsome & cruel disease. But God has been merciful in his case, & the boy has been spared. Yet you can well concieve my own & the agonies of his poor mother. Ah! my friend, to think that of 14 children, we have now buried nine! And all of such wonderful promise. Five are yet left us, but for how long — how long? I have no longer any sense of security. My days & nights teem with apprehension. I wake from fearful dreams. I walk musing with my fears & terrors. It affects my health, my happiness, my habits, my performances. I no longer read or write with satisfaction, or success. Briefly, my dear friend, I am under these successive shocks, growing feebler, rapidly aging, and shudder with a continued sense of winter at my hearth. My occupation utterly gone, in this wretched state of war & confusion,

---

[2] Simms' family Bible and the family tombstone at Woodlands give Dec. 24 as the date of Hattie's death. But the date appears to be erroneous (as are others in the Bible and on the tombstone), since Simms in this letter and the Charleston *Mercury* in its issue of Dec. 30 both report that Hattie died on Christmas Day.

[3] Sydney Roach and Beverley Hammond. See letter to Hammond of Sept. 24, 1858.

I have no refuge in my wonted employments from the intensive apprehensions engendered by so long & so dreary an experience. Could I go to work, as of old, having a motive, I might escape from much of the domestic thought, and in foreign faring, quiet the oppressive memory. But nobody reads nowadays, and no one prints. My desks are already filled with MS.S. Why add to the number — the mass, — when, I so frequently feel like giving these to the flames? My will is not strong enough, even in obedience to the calls of my mind, to engage in new labours which are so wholly motiveless. I can still continue the work of self-development, though I no longer put pen to paper, or book to print. But I will not press this egotistical matter upon you any further. Touching yourself. When we saw that a *Pliny* Miles was sick almost to death, we had no interest in the matter, never once thinking that you were the person.[4] But one day, Dr. Bruns came hither, and then for the first time, we were taught to apprehend for your safety. He told us of the error of the press, and that Porcher & not Pliny Miles was in danger. He added that your brother Richardson [5] had gone on to you. I need not assure you how keen were our anxieties untill we heard that you were out of danger. And now what do you propose to do — where to travel? You cannot now travel, with any profit or benefit in this country. If you were willing to try this, you would find hundreds of warm firesides thrown open, and would be welcomed by thousands with affection & regard. If you can get to Europe, then should you make interest to procure a foreign appointment, — to Spain for example — for that Empire is one with which our new Confederacy should especially desire to cherish relations as friendly, as they will assuredly be intimate. It appears to me that your friends ought to be able to obtain you such an appointment, & you should not have any scruples in seeking it, considering the importance of the object to yourself, and the conviction that your friends must universally feel, that, perhaps, there is no one better competent to the Mission than yourself. If I knew any thing that *I* could do to promote this object, I should spring at once to the

---

4 See the Charleston *Mercury* of Jan. 1. Miles became ill while in Richmond attending the fifth session of the Provisional Congress of the Confederate States (Nov. 18, 1861—Feb. 17, 1862).

5 Charles Richardson Miles (1829-1892), a Charleston lawyer admitted to the bar in 1851, was Isaac W. Hayne's partner. During 1862 he was acting district attorney of the Confederate States for the District of South Carolina, and during 1882-1886 attorney general of South Carolina.

performance. Pray, if you have not already thought of this matter, give it proper heed. At all events, let me know what you design. I have lately seen Hammond.[6] He speaks of you with something more like affection than mere praise. He said these words — "Of all the public men with whom I have ever had commerce, I believe Miles to be one of the purest, the most faithful, noble & unselfish. He is a man & a Gentleman!"

On the subject of the war, I can report nothing new to you, and my opinions would be comparatively worthless. Yet, though the notion seems to be that this Burnside expedition is designed to act against Virginia & Richmond, in cooperation with Mc-Clellan's forward movement, I am much more apprehensive of an attempt upon Georgetown (S. C.) and the subsequent attempt, after landing to penetrate the N. E. Rail Road, & thence have the routes open to Charleston & Wilmington. I have for a long time wondered why they did not strike in this direction. Now, there are actual embarrassments to a progress from Georgetown to the mainland, & to the R. Road; but our personnel, I fear, is sadly deficient in that section, & our N. C. brethren should be on the alert.[7] We should need from 10,000 to 20000 troops for successful resistance here, and none, I fancy, could be made of Georgetown proper, against the numerous gunboats of the enemy. As to our forces, I hear only of Gen. Harllee's Brigade,[8] or rather Regt., say 1200 men recently levied & organized, & our Genls. are so reticent that I can only guess at the number of our forces along the seaboard. S. C. has now between 30 & 40,000 men on duty, a proportion of nearly 1 in 7 of her white population. It is difficult for her to send more into the field without leaving the country at large without patrol protection. But, all this you know as well as I. Once more, dear Miles, I beg to hear from you. Every step you take will be of great interest to my little flock.

---

[6] Simms' visit to James H. Hammond at Redcliffe was made between Dec. 22, 1861, and Jan. 8, 1862 (see Hammond's letters to Simms of those dates, originals in the Hammond Papers, Library of Congress).

[7] An expeditionary force under the command of Gen. Ambrose Everett Burnside (1824-1881) with a fleet commanded by Flag Officer Louis Malesherbes Goldsborough (1805-1877) left Hampton Roads, Va., on Jan. 11; arrived at Hatteras Inlet, N. C., on Jan. 13; and captured Roanoke Island on Feb. 8 and New Bern on March 14. See *O. R.,* 1st Series, IX, 72ff.

[8] William Wallace Harllee (1812-1897), lieutenant-governor and a member of the Executive Council (see note 54, Dec. 4, 1862), had raised a brigade, known as the Pee Dee Legion, and had been commissioned brigadier general by Pickens. At the time that he was preparing to enter the field, he was appointed to the Executive Council.

We all pray your speedy & full recovery, & God's blessing on your life & fortunes.

> Ever truly & lovingly Yours.

> W. Gilmore Simms

1068: To William Porcher Miles

> Woodlands, Jany 31. 1862

My dear Miles.

I wrote you at Richmond, on the reciept of your letter from that place, but a very short time after, discovered that you had reached Charleston. I take for granted that the letter will be forwarded you in event of your having left before it reached [you]. In that letter I spoke of my own & family condition at full, & will now simply add that we are all in good condition at present. My wife sends her regards to your mother, self & James. For myself, I am dong nothing except losing time. My occupation seems gone, like Othello's — I trust for the present only. I have ceased writing for the Mercury, not being altogether satisfied with our relations. I employ myself as well as I can, in grounds & garden— overseeing the overseer — a troublesome task, and sowing peas & potatoes. I have been building an addition to my house — a wing, connected with the main dwelling by a corridor. This wing which is 30 x 22 is devoted to my library. The Corridor is a series of 4 arches, and constitutes a good piazza. The whole establishment being of brick, it is cool in summer & warm in winter. Last summer, we did not suffer one day from heat. Our nights were invariably cool, & fresh buckets of water from a deep well, need no ice. We do not miss it. I am now clearing some new land for corn — shall plant a full crop of corn & a small one of cotton — a decision generally made by our people. But not to be carried too far. We should have an adequate supply of Cotton, at least, to afford us foreign exchange, which we shall need largely as soon as the war is over. Of this, however, the prospect is at present doubtful. It will need that we should give the Yankees one crushing defeat to arrest their insanity. Should they give us one, it will undoubtedly revive their hopes & prolong the struggle. I trust that we are prepared for them sufficiently along the coast from Georgetown to Savannah. I confess my apprehensions were great from the Burnside expedition, addressed, as I thought it would be, to Georgetown, & thence against the junction R. R. at Florence or thereabouts. This would subject their troops to a longer & more difficult march, but through a more defenceless country, where we should find it not easy to concentrate large bodies of troops very suddenly. I hope that the expedition will give us but little trouble in any quarter. If you can give me any clues as to the conduct and condition of the war, pray do so, in an early [9] letter. The papers are wholly useless for the formation of opinion, their meagre details being doubtful in most cases. A friend in Virginia, in a *par parenthese,* writes me that "Jenifer was the person who fought & won the battle of Leesburg." [10] Is there any ground for this? I have been suggesting a scheme of a Library of the Confederate States, to include only Southern writers in all departments, publishing a *single vol.* monthly. It will comprise Lives, with selections, of & from Calhoun, McDuffie, Hayne,[11] Bev. Tucker, Jefferson, Washington, Randolph, &c. with the miscellaneous writings of Hammond, Grayson, &c. and be interspersed with original writings as they offer. I merely propose & will not edit. I am revising Hammond now for the press.[12] There is a firm of West & Johnson, in Richmond, who seem disposed to establish the publishing business in that city for the South. I could wish you to see them & talk over the subject.[13] To enable you to do so, I will instruct an old correspondent *au courant* in literary business, J. R. Thompson, of Richmond, to call upon you & make your acquaintance. He was formerly Ed'r of the Messenger, & is a man of fine tastes & talents, — a good fellow — somewhat desultory & something of a dilettante. He will introduce you to the Publishers, and you can give them encouragement. I need not say to you that the Publishing business

---

[9] Simms wrote what appears to be *ealy.*

[10] For Colonel Walter H. Jenifer's report of the Battle of Ball's Bluff, near Leesburg, Va., on Oct. 21, 1861, see *O. R.,* 1st Series, V, 368-372. Jenifer was in command of cavalry. We are unable to identify Simms' "friend in Virginia."

[11] Robert Young Hayne. See note 86, Dec. 1, 1840.

[12] See James H. Hammond's letters to Simms of Dec. 12, 1861, and Feb. 18, 1862 (originals in the Hammond Papers, Library of Congress). This volume of speeches was not published, though doubtless Simms' revisions were made use of in *Selections from the Letters and Speeches of the Hon. James H. Hammond, of South Carolina* (New York: John F. Trow & Co., 1866), and Simms may have prepared this published volume for the press (see, in this connection, Simms' letter to Harry Hammond of Jan. 24, 1865).

[13] This project was not carried out. For an account of the publishing house of West and Johnson (John M. West and Thomas Johnson), founded in 1860, see Andrew Morrison, ed., *The City on the James. Richmond, Virginia . . .* (Richmond, Virginia: George W. Englehardt, 1893), p. 258.

is one *per se,* and not to be confounded with that of the Printer. In the whole South we have never had a single publisher who ever had the slightest notion of his business & its requisitions. My copyrights, I suppose, are all confiscated at the North. I propose to bring out new editions secured in the South.[14] When Peace is won, we shall then, no doubt, be enabled to effect an International Copyright. But while the grass groweth, the steed starveth. My brain is seething with some new conceptions, but surrounded with MS.S. as I am, I ask myself why add to the mass? I can now publish nothing. I propose a work to open all my revolutionary series, with the very dawn of the Revolution in S. C. It will need to be a work of very great painstaking.[15] But I will not bore you further. Mr. Thompson, by the way, who is quite an accomplished litterateur & writes nimbly both prose & verse, & is altogether a good companion with the advantage of European travel, besides being a good classic, is a candidate for the Secretaryship of the C. S. Senate. If you can assist him with Barnwell & Orr,[16] & have no committals, pray oblige me & do so. You will find Thompson grateful. Let me add that he is a gentle & amiable man. Should you meet with John Esten Cooke, a brother author, now Captain of a gun in the Richmond Howitzers approach him in my name, & at my request. You will like him. And now dear Miles, with love to James W. believe me

> Ever Yours
> W. Gilmore Simms.

W. P. M.

1069: To RICHARD YEADON [17]

[*c.* March 27, 1862][18]

You have heard, I take it, of our continued losses. We have buried nine of fourteen children. For myself further, I need not

---

[14] This project was not carried out.

[15] Evidently this novel was not written.

[16] Robert Woodward Barnwell and James Lawrence Orr were Confederate States senators from South Carolina.

[17] We have not located the original of this letter, of which a paragraph is included in an article entitled "A Worthy and Distinguished [Citizen] Overwhelmed with Calamity," published in the Charleston *Courier* of March 31, 1862, and concerned with the burning of Woodlands (see following letters). Richard Yeadon, who was senior editor of the *Courier* at this time, was doubtless the recipient of the letter, as he was of that from Jamison included in the same article (see note 20, April 10, 1862).

[18] The *Courier* says that this letter was received "just before the recent disaster" (March 29). If this remark is to be taken literally, March 27 would be a likely date.

tell you that my copyrights and plates are all confiscated and lost — some $25,000 — the whole earnings of my life, save my library. I realized annually from my copyrights, from $1200 to $1800. "Othello's occupation's gone!" and Cotton is not to be sold. But I do not regret the loss — present or to come — or the privation; if I can bestow upon my children the more precious inheritance of independence.

1070: To WILLIAM PORCHER MILES [19]

Woodlands in Ruins.
April 10. [1862][20]

Thanks, dear friend, for your kind letter. It is the most perfect solace I have, to find gathering to me at this juncture, troops of friends. Your words are most precious among them. You have

---

[19] Part of this letter is printed in Trent, pp. 270-272.

[20] Dated by the burning of Woodlands. In a letter to Richard Yeadon dated "Burwood, March 29, 1862" (printed in "A Worthy and Distinguished [Citizen] Overwhelmed with Calamity," Charleston *Courier*, March 31, 1862), David Flavel Jamison writes: "I have just returned from witnessing a scene of ruin that has impressed me more painfully than any similar incident which has occurred within my recollection. The fine residence of W. Gilmore Simms, Esq, at Woodlands, now presents the sad spectacle of an unformed mass of brick and rubbish, with the gaunt chimneys, standing out against the noble oaks of the still beautiful grounds. On visiting the scene of the disaster, it was a saddening sight to behold the old homestead, where a liberal and almost lavish hospitality had been dispensed for thirty years, incapable of longer affording shelter to its generous owner.

"How the accident occurred, one can only conjecture. About three o'clock, this morning, the inmates of the house were awaked by a bright light, which proceeded from the burning roof; and, as the fires had been extinguished as usual, at bed time, it was not easy to account for its breaking out at that late hour. After it was discovered, the progress of the flames was rapid and irresistible. The negroes of the plantation promptly assembled on the alarm, and, under the cool and judicious direction of the owner, worked actively, faithfully and devotedly, and saved much of the furniture, though in a damaged condition. A number of handsome paintings were lost, and among them was a beautiful head of a peasant girl, painted for Mr. Simms by Sully, and which probably owed its fate to its not being framed, as the servants, in removing most of the other pictures, in the same room, esteemed of little value a painting without a gilded frame.

"Fortunately, by extraordinary perseverance and good management, the fine library, containing some eight or ten thousand volumes, which was connected to the dwelling by a corridor, was saved, with its contents; only some hundred and fifty or two hundred volumes, scattered in different rooms of the mansion, were consumed with it.

"This is a heavy blow to a most estimable and distinguished man, especially in such times as these, when, even to the affluent and prosperous, it would be difficult to replace the loss. This is the third house that Mr. Simms has lost by fire. Within the last two years his town house was destroyed, which drove him from your city, and now his last place of refuge is gone from the same cause.

been beside me in previous, and, I think, worse trials. Gladly now would I give my dwelling & all that I have saved, for the restoration of my two boys. And since then, a third boy, & a girl, your own protege, and, I think, one of the most promising & lovely of my children. Truly, I am pursued by a hungry fate! But I will not succumb. It may crush, but shall not subject me, no more than Yankeedom shall subject our country. I am happy to tell you that I have saved all my MS.S. and nearly all my library. I fortunately built, only the last year, a wing to the dwelling, connected by a corridor, 20 ft in length. The wing was saved. But for this removal of my books, they must have been all lost, and only a few days before the fire, I gathered up all my M.S.S. — matter enough for 50 vols. and packed it into trunks, not knowing how soon, I should have to fly — thinking more of the Yankees, than of midnight fires, & wishing to be ready. Had I lost my library & MS.S. the blow would have been insupportable. As it is, I mean to die with harness on my back.

My family is occupying my Library, & two outhouses. I write you this letter from a corner of my carriage house. I am building two rooms in a board house which will afford me tolerable shelter from the summer, and if the Insurance Compy will pay, as I am promised 75 in the 100, I shall get enough with my own brick layers & workmen to rebuild the walls & roof of my old mansion. But to restore is impossible. My loss in money is about $10,000. I have lost the best part of my furniture — every bedstead but one — half of my bedding, bed & other clothes — drawers, wardrobes, crockery, medicine case, and pictures, statuettes, candelabras, ornaments, & a thousand toys, ornaments, mementos, such as can never be replaced — the accumulations of two or three families, for five generations. All the stores in my pantry were destroyed. Luckily, my meat house & other outhouses were saved. My negroes worked zealously, & with a loving devotedness which was quite grateful to me. I had them on the roofs of corridor,

---

"I am informed that the house was partially insured, in one of the Charleston Companies [the Fireman's Insurance Company], of which Mr. [Samuel Yöer] Tupper is President, but I fear, from the losses, occasioned by the late disastrous fire in your city, that this resource may not avail Mr. S. much, if anything. The policy, I believe, is in the hands of Messrs. Caldwell & Robinson. My chief object, in writing to you, is to obtain your aid in ascertaining, as soon as practicable, what assistance Mr. Simms may expect from that quarter. It would be a handsome thing, even if the stockholders were not legally liable, for them to raise up, from his present prostration, one so worthy of their generosity, and one to whom the State really owes so much."

library & kitchen; narrowly escaped myself by a ladder from an upper window, while the floors overhead were falling in. I do not despair — do not despond — but verily, it tasks all my courage & strength to endure such repeated strokes of fortune. It would seem as if I were pursued by a Fate which no sacrifice — no submission pacifies. As yet, my mind is all chaos. I can only meet the calls of the moment. I have long since ceased to write for the Mercury, as perhaps, you may have seen. And, I have no other medium, even if I had any thing to say. I wrote to a friend in Charleston, to communicate certain notions of mine, for the defence of Charleston to Ripley — but he writes me in reply that R. is unapproachable, — fenced in by a triple wall of brass — vanity & conciet.[21] You are aware of the difficulty of making myself heard about our iron battery.[22] Trapier told Jamison that if required to build it, he must have a positive order in writing, for that if it proved a failure, as he felt it would, he would be blamed, & if successful all the credit would enure to another. Yet tho' the balls of Sumter fell harmlessly on that structure, it was never tried again, though such a battery might be improvised in a week on every headland; and my plan for floating batteries is precisely that of the Virginia.[23] The Yankees too have caught it up & built their gunboats after the same general model.[24] Othello's occupation seems every where gone. Yet, by the way, — ask your army men, why artillerists should not be armed with pikes, instead of short swords which are of no use. Pikes in the hands of artillerists could protect a battery against any dash of cavalry; while the ordinary short sword is of no manner of use. It falls within your province to consider this, or to inquire into it. The art of war is no more perfect than any other art, and is susceptible of a thousand improvements, which are not to be expected from the mere soldier of drill & routine. Even commissioned officers in battle might better carry a good musket or double barrelled shot gun than the idle utensil called a sword. This, is now a holiday weapon; the use of gunpowder superseding it except as

---

[21] Gen. Roswell Sabine Ripley was in command of the Department of South Carolina. His headquarters was at Charleston. We are unable to identify Simms' "friend in Charleston."

[22] See Simms' letters written to Miles and Jamison during Jan., 1861.

[23] On March 29, 1862, Capt. Josiah Tattnall assumed command of naval defenses in the waters of Virginia and took the *Merrimac,* which he renamed the *Virginia,* as his flagship.

[24] Simms is doubtless speaking of the *Monitor.*

lance or bayonet. All our mud or earth forts could be made case-mate by iron roofings — in the centre above, the iron being laced, as in cancelli — thus ✕✕✕✕✕ letting in the air, & excluding fragments of shells. The hexagon, when this mode of extempore casemating shall be adopted will be the proper form of earth works or small batteries, — or three sides of the hexagon on a promontory or isthmus. But I trespass upon valuable time, to say nothing of your patience. Yet, let me add that against cities or shipping, fire balls of tow or cotton, saturated in bitumen, or gum resin, with a due admixture of burning fluid, would probably approach the Greek fire, & with a certain proportion of the gun cotton could be made explosive, would scatter, stick where it fell, and could not be extinguished.

Yours lovingly

W. Gilmore Simms

1071: To JAMES HENRY HAMMOND

Woodlands in Ruins. April 10. [1862][25]

We, my dear Hammond, who have speculated so often in spiritualism,[26] have arrived at certain conclusions in favour of the Hebrew notion of Demonology. At all events, both of us have had personal experience which inclines us to believe that there are certain persons who seem to be perpetually pursued by some angry Fate, which haunts his steps, & dogs his career, as tenaciously as ever the Furies clung to the heels of Orestes. It seemed to me, a few months ago, when Death became my guest at Christmas, — the day that is usually hallowed to happiness in every porch — when he tore away one of the loveliest & most promising of my little brood — it seemed to me then, that the insatiate archer Fate, had achieved his crowning victory over me, and would be thenceforth satisfied. It seems not. I am still as bitterly pursued as ever, & can now only await patiently and in expectation for other strokes, each perhaps more heavy & more deadly than the last. Now that my homestead is in ruins, it would

---

[25] Dated by the burning of Woodlands on March 29 (see preceding letter). Evidently a number of Simms' letters to Hammond written during this period are missing from the Hammond Papers, Library of Congress, which contains the originals of letters from Hammond to Simms dated Dec. 12 and Dec. 22, 1861; Jan. 8, Feb. 18, and March 15, 1862.

[26] See letter to Hammond of Dec. 30, 1856.

seem that the next shaft would properly be aimed at the Master.
Well, my friend, I who have been required to endure so much,
should, by this time, be prepared for any fate. To a certain extent
I am; and perhaps the chief regret which I should feel, at being
suddenly summoned to the great account, will be at leaving so
many helpless ones for whom I have mostly striven, and who
have constituted at once my principal cares & joys. That a Fate
has pursued me for more than 30 years of loss, trial, trouble
denial, death, destruction, in which youth has passed rapidly to
age, & hope into resignation that is only not despondency. It is
my chief consolation that I have been able to endure so well;
and if the Fate smites, the God strengthens. Even under this
severe calamity, which it would have been terrible to me to anticipate, I am patient. I have lost none of my energy & courage,
though I may have lost some of my cheerfulness & elasticity. I
am bracing myself to bear, and to repair. To restore is impossible.
As you say, there are losses in such a calamity as can never be
restored. The accumulations of self & family, for 100 years, in a
numerous household like ours — several families amalgamated
into one, of which mine was the general store house — were
wondrous large. As yet we know not the full extent of our losses.
Half of the furniture was destroyed outright. What is saved, is
partly ruined. We have but one bedstead left of 9 or 10, and that
happened to be sent out of the house, the day before, to be cleaned.
Five or six chests of drawers, wardrobes, trunks all full of bed &
other clothing — sofas, tables, chairs — 2/3 of my pictures,
among them a portrait of myself, done by Bowman,[27] when I was
but 21, and when I was considered a handsome youth, — a fine
picture by Sully,[28] copied from Rembrandt, and perhaps some
30 more — dozens of daguerreotypes — scores of volumes for
parlour tables of costly character, — candelabra — statuettes,
&c — all gone. The garret was all lost, & a part of the upper
story, before we were awakened at 3 in the morning. The negroes
had to be summoned from the negro quarter, a third of a mile
off. They worked admirably when they came, with the most eager
zeal & the most perfect devotion. *That* fact, my dear H. is to me

[27] James Bowman, Charleston portraitist. In the *City Gazette* (Charleston)
of Feb. 19, 1831, Simms published a poem entitled "Lines to Mr. Bowman, on
Receiving from Him the Portrait of the Author," signed "S."

[28] Thomas Sully (1783-1872), the portraitist, who painted in and around
Charleston for a number of years.

full of consolation. And when in a moment of personal danger, —
for I had to escape from an upper window, while the floor above
was falling in — had you heard their passionate cries from below,
to save myself, & seen the wonderful efforts which they made to
bring a heavy ladder to my relief — you would have been gratified at the tacit proof thus given, that there was no lack of love
for their master. I had not been down three minutes before the
cornice above the window came crashing down, with the fall almost literally of a thousand brick. My loss in the building, in
furniture & stores, cannot be less than $10,000. I am now building
a wooden house in the rear of the dwelling, to consist of two
chambers. This will be of rough boards. It will suffice, with my
library room (30 x 22) and two outhouses within 40 yards, for
my family during the summer, and meanwhile I must meditate
the future. Fortunately, I own 2 bricklayers, and can rebuild
cheaply. I was insured for $3000 in one of the Insurance Comps
of Charleston; but that is now in liquidation. They are about to
sell out their assets, and if these are well sold, I shall probably
get something over 2000. With $3000 and my own resources in
workmen & labour, I can rebuild, partially on the old walls; and
this I may attempt before winter. As for finishing & furnishing,
this must be the work of time. As for a subscription, as proposed
by the Mercury, it looks too nakedly a charity for my acceptance.[29]
It must not take that form at all events. But I do not think it
will come to any thing. The country is too poor at present to do
any thing handsome, and its pride will not suffer it to lapse into
an abortion; so, I take it, the measure will die out quietly. — We
are all grateful to you for your generous tender of Home, Hog
& Hominy; and if we could accept of any of the numerous invitations to the same effect which we have had, yours should be
the preferred. But it is impossible for *me* to leave here, and my
wife will not leave me; and we are both unwilling that the few
children left us, should be scattered abroad. But some of us may
visit you for a few weeks in the summer. Thanks for the $100
which comes seasonably. I had laid in my stores, and unhappily,
much of them was in a pantry of the house. These were all destroyed. I had just had made 10 or 12 dozen tallow candles from
a fine beef killed this spring. They were destroyed, with all my

---

[29] A subscription for the rebuilding of Woodlands. See the Charleston *Mercury* of April 1, 3, and 14 and letter to Bruns, Gregg, Hammond, and others
of June 27, 1862.

kerosene oil. My whole bureau of medicines was destroyed; and but for a neighbour we should not have had a candle, or a dose of salts. I shall charge myself with the hundred & use it for immediate wants; and trust some day, my dear H., not only to repay you, but to show you how sensibly I have felt, & feel, the uniform kindness which you have shown me for more than 20 years of our acquaintance. — If you can spare me 2 or 3 dozen of your *commonest* whiskey, *one* bottle of brandy & *one* of red wine, — for *sick* persons the two last — send me them; and if you have a dozen or two more of your Catawba to spare, they will be acceptable. My son was home on sick leave,[30] when the fire took place. He had had chill & fever, at intervals for 3 months — he was away, on a visit to Carroll & Mrs Pinckney,[31] the night of the fire — improved daily here, and yet, the very day of his going to town, had a return of chill & fever. Should he be compelled again to leave the Citadel, I will send him up to you. Should I do so, invite him to wine at the table, but no other time. He is a tall boy who now looks *down* upon his father. Once more, my dear H. many thanks. My wife joins me in respects to Mrs. H.

Yours Ever truly

W. Gilmore Simms.

P. S. We must not despair of the world, when misfortunes bring forth evidences of virtue. I had just finished my letter to you, when one of our plain farmers rode into the yard — one of the Jenningses of Edisto river — a mill owner — owner of two mills, &c. and a man well off. He said, "I am truly sorry to see your ruins. You are building. You are buying lumber. I have a large quantity, such as you want, at Cannon's Bridge.[32] I have rafts on the river. Haul off what you want. You shall have 15,000 ft. and I will not suffer you to pay a copper for it. Your house has been a public house, & you are a public man without pay; and you shall have my lumber to rebuild — all that you want, — and you shall *not* pay me." Was not this handsome? And nothing but my promise to send for the lumber, would satisfy him.[33]

W. G. S.

---

[30] From the Citadel Academy.

[31] Dr. Francis Fishburne Carroll (see note 141, May 23, 1859) and probably Lucia Bellinger Pinckney (see note 276, *c.* Nov. 23, 1860).

[32] Across the Edisto and about two miles from Woodlands.

[33] John S. Jennings. The *Daily South Carolinian* (Charleston) of Jan. 10, 1866, contains a short obituary of Jennings doubtless written by Simms: "The

1072: To Richard Yeadon [34]

Woodlands, June 17, 1862.

Richard Yeadon, Esq.:

My Dear Yeadon, —

I should have written you while still at Richmond, after hearing of the melancholy tidings of your loss, but supposing that event would hurry you home, I awaited your reported return before doing so.[35] And now that I do sit down to write, it is scarcely possible to say anything. All attempts at consolation, from any degree of friendship, must fail in such a case as yours. The ordinary language of sympathy is so completely stereotyped that it sinks usually into the baldest common-place; and in an extreme instance, the last loss, the greatest grief, sorrow and sympathy equally find themselves speechless. Were I with you I should probably do nothing more than silently squeeze your hand. To say anything would seem impertinence. One hoods himself in the house of mourning and takes a silent place beside the desolate hearth, or broods for a moment over the face of the dead,

---

Districts of Orangeburg and Barnwell, especially along the region of the South Edisto, have lost one of their most excellent and worthy citizens in the death of the late Captain John S. Jennings. He was a public worker, a public and private benefactor, always seeking to be useful, always generous and just, a man of great enterprise and the most judicious of workers. He died on the night of the first of January of the present year. . . ."

The Charleston *Mercury* of April 14, 1862, in an article about the proposed subscription for the rebuilding of Woodlands, says: "In a letter to a friend [perhaps John Dickson Bruns, who was collecting subscriptions (see note 42, June 27, 1862], Mr. Simms relates this noble piece of generosity on the part of one of his neighbors: Mr. Jennings, who lives on the opposite bank of the Edisto—probably one of the heirs of the great Jennings' property in England— a large timber cutter, and the owner of two or three mills on the Edisto, rode over to see Mr. S. after the loss of his house, and said, 'I feel very much for your losses; you wish to rebuild; you must not buy lumber; you *must* take mine; I *will* not receive a cent of money from you for it. Send and haul away 15,000 feet, or as much more as you want. I have a large number of rafts in the river; they shall be landed where it is most convenient for you. You *must* and *shall* take them. You have been a public man, without pay. Yours has been almost a public house, and we have been proud of it. You must rebuild, and if I had my own way, you should rebuild without a dollar of expense. My lumber you shall have, and whatever you want that I have not got sawed send me an order for to Graham's [Graham's Turn Out, now Denmark, S. C.], and it shall be cut at once. I am determined to do this much towards showing my gratitude for your labors, and I will not have money mentioned.' "

[34] We have not located the original of this letter, published in the Charleston *Courier* of July 10, 1861. The omissions are the *Courier's*.

[35] Richard Yeadon's adopted son, Richard, the son of his sister Harriet and her husband, Phineas Franklin Smith, principal of the Morris Street Public School, had recently been killed in action in Virginia. See the Charleston *Courier* of June 10, 13, 21, and 24.

and weeps silently with the living mourner, and so goes drooping
to his own habitation, dreading the hour when the case shall
become his own. I who have buried so many dear ones, know well
how idle are all attempts at consolation, and but too frequently
how painful and offensive. In your case it is not only your affections that are stricken. Your pride is crushed also. This lost boy
was your nephew, and your *heart* feels the loss of a dear kinsman,
the eldest son of the last surviving sister. But he was your adopted
son also, chosen to bear your name, to perpetuate it, to maintain
your position in society, to gratify your ambitious hopes for the
future, and to represent your fortune. In his fate all these calculations are baffled, and these hopes mortified with defeat. Yet
had he been spared to you, the promise which he gave was
eminently grateful and strong, in behalf of your expectations. He
seems to have been chosen well. His letter to you, in which he
accepts the name and destiny which you would have assigned him,
is equally modest, manly, circumspect and sensible, showing just
and noble sentiments, and a calm, considerate judgment, blended
in proper degree with gratitude and affection.[36] It is not easy to
replace such a boy; not easy to repair the loss, or fill the gap,
equally in pride and love, which his fate must occasion, as well
in the mother's heart as your own. I feel quite as much for
Harriet [37] as I do for you; for while her pride was almost as
much interested and as active as your own, her heart is naturally
a greater loser. There, no doubt, if not alone, he reigned sovereign.
An eldest son, just at the threshold of manhood, already a brave
performer, graceful, manly, sensible, warm, ardent and dutifully
affectionate, and on a sudden cut off by the "abhorred shears" [38]
of fate. Yes, my friend, your sister will feel the vacancy of bosom,
the immense void, even longer than yourself, if not more keenly
at the first. You will have the world as a refuge. In its strifes,
triumphs, ambitions—in the cares which your very wealth must
impose upon you, and in the earnestness of your mind, your love
of labor, and your variety of resource, you will find a refuge which
is rarely awarded to woman. You will need to choose and find
another son. You must find another who will bear and represent
your name and family, and use your fortune wisely, after you
have folded your robes about you in the sacred slumber. And you

---

[36] This letter, dated March 1, 1862, is printed in the *Courier* of June 13.
[37] The *Courier* prints *H* * * * * * *t*.
[38] Milton, *Lycidas*, line 75.

will choose one as like to the boy you have lost as possible, and may God grant you to choose as wisely, and more fortunately to retain. For him who has gone you have a two-fold consolation, in the fact that he died young, ere he had much suffered, and while he was yet pure; and that he perished gallantly striving in battle for the independence of his country. It may not be amiss to refer you now to the uses, to yourself, of this great affliction. Without undertaking to justify the ways of God to man, it is yet only reasonable to assume that he has a purpose in this, as in all other of his providences which we may not readily fathom. This purpose, no doubt, contemplates your ultimate benefit. You, my friend, are at this very moment in as great peril as ever at any moment in your life. You have reached that dangerous state of which the Gods themselves are said to grow jealous.

*　*　*　*　*　*　*

The rebuke and chastenings of the Deity are no doubt provided to correct evil tendencies growing out of the elation incident to great prosperity; to subdue the pride of the mortal to a humility becoming humanity; to lift the intellectual man to permanent performance, to elevate his objects, and school his heart to toleration and greatness, patience and sweetness of temper. Let me refer you to Schiller's beautiful ballad of the "Ring of Polycrates", of which Bulwer and several others have given translations.[39] There is a better story than this of the same kind, told of Solon, in his exile at the Court of Croesus, King of Lydia, with a superior moral still; but I know not just now where to refer you for it. You will very probably find the source of it in Plutarch.[40] I would look it up for you, but as yet I cannot get at my books. They illustrate the case of danger which I would indicate to you. They confirm the beautiful moral growing out of adversity. For my own part, I have learned to thank God for all his punishments. They have hurt my house frequently; but I do honestly believe they have helped my heart! May the good God so deal with our hearts and heads, my friend, as to make one hard lesson serve us, and not render necessary its frequent repetition.

---

[39] "The Ring of Polycrates. A Ballad," *The Poems and Ballads of Schiller,* tr. Sir Edward Bulwer Lytton (New-York: Harper & Brothers, 1844), pp. 181-184.

[40] See Plutarch's life of Solon.

You may expect me at Kalmia sometime during the season,[41] and we shall look for you here. Take what I have said to you, as the fruit of thoughts and experience, growing for more than forty years, growing, too, in a hot bed of suffering, which, I fear, has left me still liable to more severe schooling. * * * * *

Yours ever faithfully,
W. G. S.

1073: To John Dickson Bruns, William Gregg, James Henry Hammond, and Others [42]

Woodlands, June 27, 1862.

Messrs. ——— ——— ———:

Gentlemen and Dear Friends:

Sincerely and most gratefully do I feel the regard which dictates your letter, and the liberality which prompts your gift. A

---

[41] Yeadon had a home at Kalmia, near Aiken, S. C.

[42] We have not located the original of this letter, published in both the *Mercury* and *Courier* of July 8, 1862. A clipping of the letter from an unidentified Columbia newspaper of July 10 is in one of Simms' scrapbooks in the Charles Carroll Simms Collection, South Caroliniana Library. All three newspapers print long dashes in place of the names of the recipients of the letter and italicize *Messrs.*
All three newspapers also print the following letter to Simms:

> A few friends, sympathizing deeply with you in your recent losses, and mindful of the important services which, as her novelist, historian, and poet, you have rendered to South Carolina, have subscribed the enclosed sum of $3,600, to aid in rebuilding your hospitable and honored homestead, recently destroyed by fire.
> Had not the exigencies of this unhappy time prevented, we doubt not that the whole State would have joined us in a spontaneous and hearty tribute—more substantial than words—to your great public worth. But the evil days on which we have fallen have temporarily deprived us of the means of liberality, even where our feelings are most strongly excited, and no one can appreciate better than yourself the heavy sacrifices which are every day being made in the sacred cause to which all of us have pledged our fortunes and our lives.
> We offer the accompanying trifle not as a donation, but simply as an assurance—in an hour of peculiar distress—of the high esteem in which you are held as a man and as a writer. We trust that you will accept as cordially as it is tendered, this moderate instalment of the large debt which the State has so long owed you; its existence is universally recognized, though none would attempt to measure its value.
> With sentiments of the highest regard, we are faithfully yours,

——————— ———————.

Charleston, June 20, 1862.
James H. Hammond writes in a letter to Simms dated July 10 (original in the Hammond Papers, Library of Congress) that among the contributors were himself, Gregg, Gourdin (Robert ?), and George A. Trenholm, and that Bruns had written to him to subscribe.

sympathy so warm, ready and generous — a movement so spon-
taneous and unsolicited — touches me deeply, and lifts me greatly
above the sense of privation and discomfort. But for the kindness
of friends, their soothing attentions and genial service, I might
have been discomfited by fortune — might have been utterly
cast down by the repeated disasters and severe trials to which,
in the last few years, I have been subjected; followed finally by
the crowning evil of the destruction of my homestead. But my
feelings of humiliation are relieved by a new sense of pride, as
I find, from so many noble sources, not only the warmest solicitude, but aid and succor so generously tendered as greatly to
divest misfortune of its sting. My immediate neighbors, old
friends and associates, at the first tidings of my distress, came
promptly to my relief with tenders of money, labor, material, and
mechanical assistance, and there are others, personally unknown
to me, who have made offers of help and service. Such tributes,
with now the generous addition of yours, made in spite of the
worse conjunctures of evil times, are matters of pride to me, and
not humiliation. They prove to me, and in the most conclusive
manner, that I have not lived or labored in vain — that the forty
years of my life which I have devoted to the fame and interests
of our people — their reputation and securities — have not failed
to win their confidence, their affection and esteem. They do me
the justice to believe that I have wrought for my country with
zeal and fidelity, and some success. I feel that I can transmit to
my children no better testimony in behalf of my public services —
though always rendered in a private capacity — than that which
is contained in your letter, signed by those, who, in their several
sections, are known to be among the ablest and best men of the
country.

Thus persuading myself — I trust with a pardonable egotism —
I turn to a noble passage from the prose writings of Milton (in
his "Second Defence") where, with that equal blending of pride
and humility, which constituted so marked a feature in his character, he indulges in a like boast of the friendships which succored
his need — of the sympathies which soothed his sorrows — of
the generous comforts which cheered his declining years. Though
not strictly a parallel case with mine, and though I dare not
arrogate to myself such claims upon my country as those which
the great Englishman had upon his, yet I will quote the passage

without mutilation, still pleased and proud to think that some portions may apply, and thus justify my appropriation of it:

"To this" (his condition, his claims) *"I ascribe the tender assiduities of my friends; their soothing attentions, their kind visits, their reverential observances; among whom there are some with whom I may interchange the Pyladean and Thesean dialogue of inseparable friends. This extraordinary kindness which I experience cannot be any fortuitous combination;* and friends, such as mine, do not suppose that all the virtues of a man are contained in his eyes." (He had been reproached with his blindness as a judgment of Heaven.) *"Nor do the persons of principal distinction in this commonwealth suffer me to be bereaved of comfort, when they see me bereaved of sight, amid the exertions which I made, the zeal which I showed, and the dangers which I ran, for the liberty which I love. But soberly reflecting on the casualties of human life, they show me favor and indulgence, as to a soldier who has served his time; and kindly concede to me an exemption from care and toil.* They do not strip me of the badges of honor which I have once worn; they do not deprive me of the places of public trust to which I have been appointed; they do not abridge my salary or emoluments; which, though I may not do so much to deserve as I did formerly, they are too considerate and too kind to take away; and, in short, they honor me as much as the Athenians did those whom they determined to support in the Prytaneum, at the public expense, &c."

There are, as you will see, many noble lessons in this passage, for those who administer the affairs of a republic.

I have held no offices, and sought for none, and receive no emoluments from the public. Nor, in fact, have I needed them; nor do I need them now. If I did, the want would be more than supplied by that generous care of friendship, which, in my case, has been so prompt and tender and assiduous. Nor shall I dismiss myself from the task of patriotic labors, so long as God shall vouchsafe to me the life, the energy and vigor still to perform in those fields with which I have grown familiar, and in which I seem to have found favor with many friends.

To you, my friends, knowing your generous purpose, I am persuaded that it will afford the greatest satisfaction to learn that you have enabled me to do, at an early day, that which, otherwise, I might not have been able to accomplish for years, if ever — to

restore my ruined habitation — rebuild it as it stood of old —
recalling the banished *Lares familiares,* not even forgetting my
ancient chimney cricketer. This duty is now before me to perform; a duty which I owe hardly less to you than my wife and
children. To this, in spite of the condition of the country, I design
sacredly to address myself as soon as possible, and as though it
were the last duty of my life. Not that I despair or doubt of that
providence of God, which has so long sustained me, and which
I trust will enable me to execute other works and achieve other
labors equally honorable to myself and to our country.

With great regard and respect, and with every feeling which
should become me under relations such as ours, I am, good friends
and gentlemen,

Very faithfully, yours,

W. Gilmore Simms.

1074: To the Editors of the Southern Illustrated News [43]

[September 20, 1862]

To the Editors of the "Illustrated News:"

Gentlemen, —

I have endeavored, though hurriedly and imperfectly, to comply
with your wishes, in sending you a contribution for your periodical. These "Sketches in Greece" were originally written many
years ago. I now revise them, for the first time, for publication.
I trust they will prove acceptable to your readers.[44] At this time,
it is not easy to do anything of length, involving much elaborate
design. You have well adverted, in your editorial department, to
the difficulty of engaging now in literary composition. To do

---

[43] We have not located the original of this letter, published in the *Southern
Illustrated News,* I (Oct. 11, 1862), 2. The first issue of the *Southern Illustrated
News* (Richmond, Va.), a weekly, was published on Sept. 6, 1862 (dated Sept.
13), the last on March 25, 1865. Ayers and Wade were proprietors and publishers
of the periodical throughout its existence; they are first listed as editors in the
issue of July 4, 1863 (II, 4), and this listing continues through the last issue.
We have been unable to identify the editor or editors before that date. Each
issue has separate pagination.

Since the italics in the date are probably not Simms', we have omitted them.

[44] Simms published six poems under the heading of "Sketches in Greece":
"Arcadia" and "Salamis," I (Oct. 11, 1862), 2; "Castaly" and "Thessaly," I
(Oct. 18, 1862), 3; "Actium" and "The Temple of Minerva, at Sunium," I
(Oct. 25, 1862), 7.

justice to the public, or to one's self, in letters, implies a perfectly calm mind, much leisure, and freedom from distracting occupation. Your whole mind must be concentrated on your subject. But who can give his whole mind to, or concentrate his thoughts upon abstract topics, when the whole country is heaving with the throes of a mighty revolution — when we are arming our sons for battle — when every dwelling presents daily a scene of parting — and when, from so many thousands, a voice of wailing is sent up from mothers and sisters, weeping for the beloved one, and refusing to be comforted? All our thoughts resolve themselves into the war. We are now *living* the first grand epic of our newly-born Confederacy. We are *making* the materials for the drama, and for future songs and fiction; and, engaged in the actual event, we are in no mood for delineating its details, or framing it to proper laws of art, in any province. This must be left to other generations, which, in the enjoyment of that peace and independence for which we are now doing battle, will be able to command the leisure for those noble and generous arts by which nations best assert their claims to independence, and secure a proud immortality for fame! We shall need to leave this labor to them. For my own part, in addition to the same anxieties which fill the national heart with care, and our eyes with tears, I labor under embarrassments of situation and circumstance, almost peculiar to myself. Household troubles press upon me. I lack conveniences for study and composition. I am now busied in rebuilding my house, lately destroyed by fire, and am living amidst the din of saw and hammer, and in hourly communion with my workmen. Still, in a little time, I trust to find myself re-seated at my old desk, in the resumption of familiar labors. I send you these trifles from my pigeon-holes, rather to assure you of my sincere wish to serve you, than with any hope to satisfy the expectation of your patrons. It is not impossible, however, that some of your classical readers will be pleased to have re-called to them their ancient memories of classical lore and tradition; and as the histories of Greece, in the conflict of that Confederacy with the Median invader, are not very dissimilar, in detail and character, to that which our young Republic is waging with our enemy, these poems may be found not so far foreign to our present moods as the general topic might seem to suggest — may embody

the thoughts and language of patriotism, at least, as fully as they
do those of the muse.

With due respect,
Your obd't serv't,

W. Gilmore Simms.

Woodlands, S. C., Sept. 20, 1862.

1075: To James Henry Hammond [45]

Woodlands 28 Oct. 1862.

My dear Hammond.

I cannot remember whether I owe you a Letter or not; but if
you had known my situation, it is probable that your sympathies
would have prompted one to me. For a month my eldest son has
been lying dangerously ill with typhoid fever contracted in camp.[46]
Fortunately, he got home before the disease had fully declared
itself. Had he not done so, he must have perished. We have been
watching day & night, his poor mother never once leaving his
bedside, till she was taken in labour a few days ago. She has been
safely delivered of a boy & mother & child are now doing well.[47]
My eldest son, though not yet free from the fever, is yet free from
its most dangerous symptoms; and we now have only to wait
upon the malady, & watch carefully against any imprudence. He
is feeble to the last degree; cannot rise, or turn himself in bed;
and it must be weeks before he can leave it safely, & perhaps
months ere he can regain his strength, and take the saddle. But
the worst of my anxieties being over, I write you, — devoting
the day & night to my long neglected correspondents. In the midst
of my troubles I had to dismiss my overseer for some barefaced
peculations; and my crop is yet to harvest, moderate, as it is,
from his rascally neglect & falsehood. I am building, also, & with
negro mechanics, have to see to every brick laid, and every door

---

[45] Hammond's reply to this letter is dated Nov. 2. Evidently a number of
Simms' letters written to Hammond since April 10 are missing from the Ham-
mond Papers, Library of Congress, which contains the originals of letters from
Hammond to Simms dated May 17, July 10, Aug. 29, and Sept. 30.

[46] In the spring of 1862 the Citadel cadets formed "The Cadet Company"
and joined (as Company F) Col. Hugh Aiken's 6th Regiment of South Carolina Cavalry. M. B. Humphrey was captain of the company and Gilmore was
3rd sergeant.

[47] Charles Carroll Simms (see introductory sketch of the Simms family)
was born on Oct. 20.

frame planted. My brains are half bewildered with the variety of my cares & the pressure of my anxieties, and I meditate a visit to you, as soon as I can feel safe in leaving home, in order to find some little respite. I will write to advise you, as soon as I can feel any tolerable certainty, as regards the condition of my family.

And what of the condition of the country? The expedition of Lee into Maryland was a flash in the pan, and Bragg seems to have done as is rhymed of one of the Kings of France, who, having marched up a hill, — marched down again. There may be something latent in these transactions which I do not fathom, or they are sad failures.[48] — It is cheering to know that our boys in the Yemassee country have done so well.[49] The odds were very great against them. But why such odds? What are we to do, if a really formidable force of 30,000 or 40,000 are brought against us. And their march coupled with a sea attempt on Charleston? — I confess I feel very anxious on this score, especially as I see no reason to believe that our harbour has been yet brought into any admirable state of defence. Our gunboats were to have been ready to smash the Blockaders a month ago. We hear of their getting christened and all that nonsense [50] — in which, the worst is that every thing is published to the enemy — but beyond newspaper twattle & idle ceremonies, nothing of moment seems to be done or doing. Then again, with the full knowledge of the fact that the enemy is making his most desperate preparations for invasion every where, and with 600,000 fresh troops, Davis calls for a conscription between 18 & 40 — when we shall need every biped from 16 to 50, all of whom should now be in training for the field.[51] Is there something behind the curtain? Is the curtain to be suddenly drawn up? Do we build on conflicts in the Yankee Wigwam, or disaster & crash in their money markets? Or upon foreign intervention. I fear that our Govt. is calculating upon some such scores as these — one or all?

---

[48] Simms here refers to the Maryland campaign of Gen. Lee during Sept. 3-20 and the Kentucky campaign of Gen. Braxton Bragg (1817-1876) during Aug.–Oct.

[49] The Charleston *Mercury* of Oct. 23 reports that the Confederate forces were successful in defeating two Union forces at Mackey's Bend, near Pocotaligo, and at Coosawhatchie.

[50] The *Palmetto State* and the *Chicora* were launched at about this time. See John Johnson, *The Defense of Charleston Harbor, Including Fort Sumter and the Adjacent Islands, 1863-1865* (Charleston, S. C.: Walker, Evans & Cogswell Co., 1890), pp. 32-33.

[51] See note 61, Dec. 4, 1862.

Can you give me any clues? — I am far from well myself. I feel jaded & fagged, yet have been doing nothing at the desk. If I could get back into the old traces, my brains & bowels would both be better. — My best regards to Mrs. H.[,] Bet, & whoever you have with you of your own flock. God be with you in mercy.

Yours Ever.

W. G. S.

J. H. H.

1076: To James Henry Hammond

Woodlands, S. C. Decr. 4. [1862][52]

My dear Hammond.

I have just got back from Columbia, whither I went on Saturday last.[53] I saw Aldrich & a number more, pretty capable of judging how things will go. Aldrich got your letter while I was with him. There is no chance of any member of the Convention or Council being elected.[54] You & Jamison preemptorily decline.[55] *Aldrich applied to Jamison to consent,* — with what motive Heaven only knows, as they have not, for some time, been on the best of terms, & Aldrich well knows there is no chance for him. There is no chance for any truly able man, unless Orr, & they are endeavoring to persuade him, simply to put Pickens in his seat in the Senate.[56] If he consents, he will be elected without difficulty.

---

[52] Dated by Simms' discussion of the forthcoming election for governor of South Carolina. Milledge Luke Bonham was elected, the final vote being Bonham 79, Manning 63, Preston 3, Trescot 6, and scattered 7. For details of this election, see Cauthen, *South Carolina Goes to War*, pp. 162-163.

[53] Nov. 29.

[54] The Secession Convention or the Executive Council. By an act of the Convention the ordinary executive power of the governor had been vested in a council composed of Governor Pickens, Lieutenant Governor Harllee, and three elected members (William Henry Gist, Isaac W. Hayne, and James Chesnut, Jr.). This council, which was also given almost unlimited war powers, had first met on Jan. 9, 1862. Almost immediately Governor Pickens' supporters started a campaign against the Council, and although for the most part the Council's work was good, popular resentment was so high that it was abolished by an act of the legislature on Dec. 18, one day after the Secession Convention was dissolved by its own act. For a detailed account of the work of the Executive Council, see Cauthen, *South Carolina Goes to War*, pp. 138-162.

[55] In his letter to Aldrich dated Nov. 27 Hammond declines to be a candidate for the office of governor, giving ill health as his reason. The original is in the Hammond Papers, Library of Congress.

[56] Orr was elected to the Confederate States Senate in Dec., 1861, and served until the fall of the Richmond government.

If he declines, then, it is said & thought that the feeblest man in the field will be chosen. Chesnut told me that Manning's chances are about the best of any. He is said to be busy, morning, noon & night, electioneering.[57] Chesnut declines — having no chance. But there is an alternative presented which it will shock you to hear, as exhibiting the large strides which we have taken & are taking towards anarchy. It is said that Pickens desires to be re-elected; that, his friends, should they fail to elect Orr, will cast blank votes, prevent all election & so, under the Constitution, Pickens holds over *untill his successor* shall be elected. One of his notorious *strikers,* it is said, (Magrath told me that he got it from his own lips) one Major Harris,[58] told *him* that they already counted 70 votes which were to be cast *Blank,* should they find their policy in doing so. The Legislature is reported to be the feeblest body known there for fifty years. There are some 96 new members, each eager to fire off his popgun at Convention & Council. These, as you well know, only need a topic. The Council, as an anomalous body, readily affords them one. This Council affords Pickens the most fortunate escape from office, into sudden popularity. All the blunders, errors & evils of his administration are fastened upon the Council & shifted wholly from his shoulders. I am told that every measure of which the people have complained, was *his* measure. I found Chesnut very sore & angry, & in that mood which will prompt him to sieze upon the first pretext for fixing a personal quarrel on some of his assailants. I suspect that this is Hayne's feeling also. As for Hayne, his fate is certain. The Council has killed him. The greed which tempted him to hold the office, having already that of Atty Gen., will lose him both; and so time brings his great revenges. Were it the fate of the Council only, there would be no great matter; but this struggle is to inaugurate the birth of two fierce factions in which all our conservatism & securities are destined to be torn to pieces. Not that Pickens will be able to hold any party long together; but the struggle for place & pension, for corruption & intrigue, so long restrained in our State, having found a beginning is destined to

---

[57] John Laurence Manning (see note 235, Nov. 17, 1846) had promised to support John Smith Preston (see note 184, Sept. 15, 1855) for governor; but Preston had defended the Executive Council, and Manning decided to stand for the office himself. See Cauthen, *South Carolina Goes to War*, pp. 162-163.

[58] Perhaps Maj. David B. Harris (1813-1864), a native of Virginia, who was chief engineer of the Department of South Carolina, Georgia, and Florida during 1862-1864, with headquarters at Charleston.

go on, &, mark my words, with more intensity & heat, & appetite
& passion than in any other State in the Confederacy, — & for
several reasons — the long restraint put upon faction; — and the
absence of any strong bold, man, of equal courage & ability,
among the competitors. It appears that Pickens having sent our
reserves — all from 18 to 50, though [pledge]d [59] only to send
them from 18 to 40, his Adjutant General [60] allows no exemption
of overseers unless they be over 60. By what rule or reason he
so decides, it is difficult to see.[61] — There is much in this letter
that you will keep to yourself — much that should not be reported
except on good testimony. I give you the matter for what it is
worth. It is midnight & I am tired. By the way, our friend Bruns
has been elected Surgeon of the Citadel, which will help to make
fire under the poor fellow's cookpot.[62] My best regards to Mrs.
H. & Bet. My folks are all doing well.

Yours Ever truly

W. Gilmore Simms

1077: To Margaret Maxwell Martin [63]

[December? 1862][64]

Now that I have at last provided a shelter for my family, before
the winter, I am more at ease; but, in place of domestic evils, we
have those of the country, and the doubtful prospect before us,
to keep anxiety wakeful and the heart sore. Only a couple of
weeks ago I had a letter from poor Maxcy [65] Gregg, exulting in
the thought of future associations with his friends in Carolina,
when our independence should be secured, and now he lies silent

---

[59] The MS. is torn.

[60] A. C. Garlington.

[61] The second Confederate conscription law of Sept. 27, 1862, extended the
draft age to forty-five and called for those through the age of forty. The
Confederate exemption law of Oct. 11, 1862, exempted one overseer or owner
for each plantation and an additional person for every twenty slaves on two
or more plantations within five miles of each other. See Cauthen, *South Carolina Goes to War,* pp. 146, 167, and *O. R.,* Serial No. 128, pp. 73-75, 156, 176-177.

[62] Bruns was surgeon at the Citadel Academy during 1862-1864.

[63] We have not located the original of this letter, of which this fragment
is published in Mrs. Martin's "Celebrities That I Have Seen . . . William
Gilmore Simms" (see note 105, *c.* April 15, 1861), pp. 278-279.

[64] Dated by the death of Gen. Maxcy Gregg at Fredericksburg on Dec. 14,
1862.

[65] "Celebrities That I Have Seen" has *Maxcey.*

forever to all human senses. How has our poor little State suffered in this war! Nothing but independence can compensate us for all; and this is a boon so precious, so necessary to our children and their children, that we must needs stifle our moans.

1863

Woodlands, S. C.
Jany 10. 1863.

Jno. R. Thompson Esq.

My dear Thompson.

Fancying that I see some of your handiwork very frequently in the "Illustrated News" I assume that you are still in Richmond, and not invalided.[1] Under this assumption I write to you to entreat a little favour at your hands. Having concieved the idea that a series of my minor tales or novels, such as Martin Faber, Castle Dismal, Helen Halsey, The Maroon, Marie de Berniere, &c. would be good selling books especially now, & for reading in camp and along the highways — [( )]small volumes each of 150 to 200 pages, — & bringing from 50 to 75/100) I wrote to that effect to Mess'rs West & Johnson. To this letter I got no answer. There is a Mobile publisher[2] with whom I had some correspondence before the war, respecting a series of Southern publications; but Mess'rs W & J. seem to have got the start of him, and as I believe that one good publisher is quite as much as we need at present, I am unwilling to open negotiations with any other, till I hear from these Gentlemen. Will you then do me the favour to see them, and ascertain if my letter was recieved. If recieved, their silence, is perhaps sufficient answer.[3] — And now pray tell me how things fare with yourself. I presume you to be busy, & I trust successfully so. The several poems I have seen from your

---

[1] At this time Thompson was assistant secretary of the Commonwealth of Virginia and as such had a share in the administration of the State Library, then under the direction of George W. Munford.

[2] Sigmund H. Goetzel, a native of Austria, emigrated to Mobile, Ala., in the early 1850's and established a publishing house with offices in both Mobile and New York City. Alexander Beaufort Meek was his chief Southern author, and during the Confederate War he was the South's leading publisher of foreign works. For an account of Goetzel, see Richard Barksdale Harwell, *Confederate Belles-Lettres* (Hattiesburg, Miss.: The Book Farm, 1941), pp. 14, 20.

[3] Neither Goetzel nor West and Johnson published editions of any of Simms' works.

pen, are all sweet & felicitous; and with your variety of resource, facility of expression, and admirable taste, you should find your hands full of employment, especially with one or more active presses alongside of you. For my part, I have done little or nothing in literature for two years, — done little more than revise some old things for the Illustrated News — rather in compliance with the desires of the Editor, than with any desire of my own to publish.[4] In fact, my domestic cares & labours, have been sufficiently — and too frequently painfully, employing my brain. Last year my House was destroyed by fire.[5] I am now busy rebuilding it. In September, my son came from camp with typhoid fever, was 50 days in bed, & has not yet recovered his strength.[6] My wife, two months ago brought me another boy [7] — my overseer I had to drive off for peculation; and with the plantation to see to, 3 families [8] to provide for and 50 refugee negroes besides my own to watch, — with bricklayers & carpenters to superintend, — I have almost forgotten how to write — Indeed, as my library is now our parlour, dining & frequently sleeping room, I have hardly a place to write in. I am now trying to do something — working up an old story for the Illustrated News, but the work is uphill entirely.[9] I need leisure, repose & my wonted conveniences for composition. I need not say to you, also, how much a man of my excitable temperament may be kept from his tasks by the condition of the Country. It will need a year of peace to bring me back to that calm of mood which Literature demands. — And how is our friend Cooke.[10] I trust he is still safe, and in good physical condition.[11] Is it true, as I see stated in the Newspapers, that Florence James, the daughter of our excellent G. P. R. is keeping a school in New York.[12] — What of your old journal, the Messenger. I

---

[4] Ayers and Wade, the proprietors and publishers of the *Southern Illustrated News* throughout its existence, are first listed as editors of the periodical in the issue for July 4, 1863 (II, 4). We are unable to identify the editor or editors prior to that date. For Simms' contributions to this weekly, see note 44, Sept. 20, 1862, and note 9, below.

[5] See letters to Hammond and Miles of April 10, 1862.

[6] See letter to Hammond of Oct. 28, 1862.

[7] Carroll.

[8] Simms' own, Augusta's, and probably William Fuller's.

[9] "Paddy McGann; or, the Demon of the Stump," I (Feb. 14, 21, 28; March 7, 14, 21, 28; April 4, 11, 18, 25; May 2, 9, 16, 23, 30), 4-5, 4-5, 4-5, 4-5, 4-5, 4-5, 4-5, 6-7, 6-7, 4-6, 5-7, 5-7, 5-7, 5-7, 5-7. This novel has never been republished.

[10] Simms wrote *Cook*.

[11] For Cooke's military career, see Beaty, *John Esten Cooke*, pp. 76ff.

[12] We have not located this newspaper account. We also have been unable to confirm the report. She is not listed in the New York City directories for the 1860's.

infer from what Dr. Bagby says editorially, that he is doubtful of its continuance. I trust sincerely, for auld lang syne, that
he will renovate it.[13] The News is reported to be prosperous. Were
you the Editor now, I should scarcely doubt that it would retain
or procure an ample patronage. Apropos to nothing; but while
your hand is in, you can say to Mess'rs W & J. that I have never
recieved the publications which they were so good as to promise
me.[14] I might help them somewhat in our precincts. Let me hear
from you, my good fellow — a long screed, with as much news
as you can pick up & bind together.

Yours Ever truly

W. Gilmore Simms

1079: To CORNELIUS KOLLOCK [15]

Woodlands, 27 March. [1863][16]

Dr. C. Kollock

My dear Dr.

Yours of the 20th reached me two days ago, and gave me great
pleasure. It is very long since I have heard from or of you, and
I very much appreciate your kindness in remembering me at last.
I am glad that you find something to please you in my "Areytos".
I trust that your Lyceum will in course of time teach a more
general taste for poetry and the fine arts to your people. Poetry
is the foundation of the fine arts, and has no little to do with the
work of invention even in the mechanic arts; and it is in these
particulars that our agricultural states & all agricultural states
are mostly deficient. We have to lift their tastes, & cultivate their
fancies, if we would carry on the work of enlightenment. Where
the Imagination & Fancy remain without cultivation, the morals,
as well as social progress of the people must be low & slow. But

[13] In *S. L. M.,* XXXIV (Nov. and Dec., 1862), 687-688, Bagby writes at
length about the condition of the periodical and announces the commencement
of the "Cash System": "No Messenger will be sent for the next year, unless
the money has been paid in advance."
[14] We are unable to identify which of West and Johnson's rather considerable number of publications Simms here refers to.
[15] Kollock (b. 1824), of Cheraw, S. C., was graduated from Brown University in 1845 and from the Medical Department of the University of Pennsylvania in 1848. He was one of the most distinguished physicians and surgeons
in the state.
[16] Dated by a letter from T. P. Lide to Kollock dated May 18, 1863 (original
in the possession of Mrs. Alexander Gregg Kollock, of Darlington, S. C.),
written in answer to Kollock's inquiry about Col. Kolb.

I must not write an essay. You do not say a word about the Lyceum. What progress does it make, or any, during the War? Have you had any Lectures this winter? I met our friend Wilson [17] in town some month or so ago, & proposed to him a series of questions, touching Col. Kolb,[18] Cheraw, and the Peedee Country, & especially begged him to consult you on the topics indicated. I am looking for his answer every day. The truth is, I am pledged for a short novel to a periodical, & would just as readily lay my foundation in your precinct, as any other part of the world, provided I were quite as secure of my ground, my facts, &c.[19] I wish you then to assist Col. Wilson in procuring me answers to the following questions. 1. What portion of Dromgoole Simms Book [20] is historical, or rather of local tradition. Does he give the particulars of Kolb's murder correctly, and what other facts. 2. What was the personal character, the education, influence, family & circumstances of Col. Kolb. 3. How many *real* persons are introduced into Simms's Book. 4. The number of his children, age & sex. 5. What camps, British or American, were established in the precinct, and by whom officered, and how long maintained. 6. What traditions of fights, or skirmishes. 7. The names of other parties concerned in the War in that neighborhood, on which side, and how distinguished. 8. Sketch me a rough map of the country for 20 miles around Kolb's plantation, marking courses of the roads, of the River, of any conspicuous streams, or any remarkable places. Give no other details, and mark no other points than Kolb's House, Society Hill, Cheraw, Darlington, & the course of the Peedee, & the roads used in the Revolution, unless they be camps, forts or places some way important by the facts in their connection or by certain peculiarities of scenery. 9. Any details that you think may be used profitably in a work of fiction — remarkable incidents or characters.

If you can answer any or all of these questions, and suggest anything of fact besides, suitable for fiction you will oblige me, & probably enable me to bring out [at] an early period a story of your Peedee Country. You ask for my Photograph. My dear Dr. you know not what you ask. Could you see me now with long

---

[17] Isaac DeLiesseline Wilson. See note 202, Oct. 16, 1860.

[18] Col. Abel Kolb, an officer of Marion's brigade, was on April 28, 1782, surrounded in his home at Welsh Neck, Cheraw District, by a party of Tories. He surrendered after being assured that he would be treated as a prisoner of war, but he was immediately killed in the presence of his wife and child.

[19] We have not located a novellette with this setting written by Simms.

[20] Alexander Dromgoole Sims' *Bevil Faulcon.* See note 175, Sept., 1854.

gray beard like a Jewish father, or a Swedenborgian, you would
dread the idea of seeing me hung in your parlour. I have long
since ceased to sit for the Photographer. I have sat so often, &
show so shockingly through his medium that I feel reluctant to
see myself served up with such villainous presentments. My eyes
are singularly sensitive to the light bearing upon them, & they
resolutely shut themselves up when I am sitting. I am quite willing to oblige you, however, should an opportunity ever occur
again, but I rarely visit Charleston or Columbia, and then for a
day or two only, with head crowded with business & hands with
bundles. Still, I repeat, I shall remember your request when an
opportunity occurs. By the way, should not your Lyceum make
a Gallery of all your Lecturers.[21] This alone might inspire domestic art. I am told that this is done in some of the Northern
Lyceums. I know that some of them keep a book of autographs.
Make this, too, a department in your Institution. Excuse the hurry
of this scribble, which I trust is not quite illegible. I write with
quill pens only, & my pen knife is almost worn out, my pen's down
to the stump, & my fingers weary after a long day's work. Write
me soon and believe me

Very truly yours, &c

W. Gilmore Simms.

My regards to Macfarlan [22] & other friends.

1080: To Francis Peyre Porcher

Woodlands, 14 April. [1863] [23]

My dear Porcher.

I have recieved & examined your volume with equal care &
satisfaction, and I fully concur in the opinion of Mr. Ravenel, of
whose capacity, as a Judge in Botanical subjects, I am well
aware.[24] Your book shows wonderful industry, and great variety

---

[21] Simms had lectured in Cheraw in 1856 and in 1860. See letters to Chesnut
of March 7, 1856, and to Lawson of Oct. 24, 1860.

[22] Col. Allan McFarlan, of Cheraw, a lawyer enrolled at the bar at Columbia
in 1845.

[23] Dated by Simms' discussion of Porcher's *Resources of the Southern Fields
and Forests, Medical, Economical, and Agricultural. Being Also a Medical
Botany of the Confederate States; with Practical Information on the Useful
Properties of the Trees, Plants, and Shrubs* (Charleston: Evans & Cogswell,
1863). In his revised edition published in 1869 Porcher follows many of Simms'
suggestions and quotes (pp. 228, 432) part of this letter, which he dates 1863.

[24] Henry William Ravenel (see note 230, Nov. 28, 1849) aided Porcher with
his work.

of resource; & should prove an exhaustless mine of information, not only to the scientific, but to the great body of our people. I am glad to see that you have endeavored, & not in vain, to give it a popular character, by simplifying your material as much as possible, & by the introduction of all such domestic & household details, of a practical sort, as will render it highly useful to the plain housekeeper. You might increase its value, & diminish its bulk, by throwing out, in future editions, all reference to authorities. The brackets & italics cumber & disfigure the page & occupy a great deal of space which might better be accorded to material topics. I am aware that there is a large class of grave blockheads in the world to whom you can only make approach by being clad in the armour of authority; who are only to be overawed by the solemn externals of science; who listen to you if you speak in a dead language, but turn a deaf ear when you wag the modest vernacular. But this book is not designed for this class, but especially for popular use, and if you will content yourself with simplifying & condensing for them, your book will be a living one, to be thumbed by honest fingers for ages to come. The domestic subjects which I suggested to you for treatment in a separate work might be grafted upon this in new editions. What a vast improvement in health & morals would be the result of a substitution of wine, beer and ale making, for the ordinary produce of the still. Under the several heads of malt liquors, ale & lager, or laid beer, you include not merely the several processes, step by step, but the agents, — their kinds, their characters, modes of cultivation & the preferable kinds of soil. Thus for the benefit of the Southern farmer, you borrow the simple domestic practice of the English farms, in all of which (I believe still) small & strong beer are familiar preparations, as regularly made, as the crops are regularly planted. You show the several kinds of beer, ale, porter — beginning with the culture of the barley, hops, &c — the preparation of the yeast, &c. and rejecting all terms of science, you teach precisely as you talk to any plain man whom you wish to help in his business. Half of the failures to learn, arises from the pretension of the teacher, who prefers to be obscure, in order to seem wise, and to confound, and who thus, through mere vanity, cuts the very throat of his own purpose. We must deal with the very ignorant as we do with children, taking special care that their first lessons do not terrify them, and for whom we make the elementary steps as simple as possible. I would suggest to you, for example, in any future publication of this class, to put

first the vulgar name of the subject, & not the learned one. The
first word that catches the uneducated eye, should be one that will
appeal to his understanding or his recollection. His curiosity will
be pleased afterwards to see by what name the scientific call it.
Pardon these general suggestions. They are designed only to assist, in a small way, to the promotion of your object. It has escaped me, if in your book, you speak of the Ground nut, called at
the North, Ground pea, or Pea nut, as a prime material for making chocolate. I see where you speak of it as a substitute for
coffee. But as coffee it is a very inferior thing to its use as chocolate. Are you aware that the manufacture of chocolate cakes, out
of the ground nut alone, & without a particle of cocoa, is an immense & most profitable part of Yankee manufacture? We make
it, in my family of a quality not inferior to any you buy, and you
will hardly believe me when I tell you we impose it on every body
that drinks as the bought chocolate. To prepare it for the table,
it is beaten in a mortar. At the North, I have been told that the
hulls are ground up with the nut, and I do not doubt that this is
an improvement as qualifying the exceeding richness of the nut,
which I have usually found too rich, prepared as chocolate in our
way, for my stomach. What you say of the Cassina, or Yupon,
as a *tea* of the redmen — and, by the way, of our Carolina ladies
during the Revolution, — is quite correct; but I think there is
some mistake among the authorities you quote, when they assert
this to be the material out of which the Indians manufacture the
famous *"Black Drink"* used at their most solemn festivals, and
which I have always understood, while travelling among them 40
years ago, to be compounded of *various roots,* by decoction, and
acting as a powerful emetic. The leaves used moderately as we use
tea, have never, as I believe, acted thus upon the system. — In
your notice of the Poke weed, I percieve that you make what I
concieve to be a very serious omission. You say nothing of the
Poke as a *spinach,* as a substitute for spinach, which will decieve
most *feeders,* that is, if the plant be used when young & tender, &
subjected to a second boiling. I relish it as much as I do spinach.
In my boyhood, it went by the name of Jew Poke in Charleston.
Why, Heaven only knows, unless it be that the Jews, more knowing than the Christians had discovered its proper uses, and had
it duly honoured in their kitchens. Suffer me to draw your attention to the May apple, & to what you call the *"May Weed."* You
have these under the same classification, but if so, there is a
serious error in the ascribed qualities which I will illustrate by

an anecdote. A venerable kinsman of mine, a Planter,[25] who had studied medicine with Dr. Edward North,[26] of your city, simply that he might physic his own negroes, returning to the plantation in October, discovered some of his negroes gathering the *May apple weed* in baskets. He asked their purpose, & was told that they used it as *greens* & for making soup. He bade them throw it away, & forbade the use of it, telling them it was poisonous. He extended the orders to his driver, who laughed heartily, saying, "Ef 'tis pison, Maussa, we all ought to be dead long ago, for jest so long as I kin member, we bin using it for bile wid our meat." My venerable relative went to his books, and there found it gravely recorded that the fruit was pleasantly sweet & innocuous, but the leaves & weed, as he had said, were poisonous. And though the books still continue to denounce it as poisonous, the negroes still, as I believe — for I have not inquired lately — continue to use it, without feeling their intestines any the worse for wear. Enquire into the matter, & see if you do not need to make a new classing of the May apple weed, & the '*May weed.*' Any how, the name of the latter seems very indefinite; May being the prolific mother of many weeds. — I am, my dear Porcher, at the bottom of a big sheet, which I trust will not exhaust your patience to peruse. I repeat, I have found great interest, & I believe that our Southern public will find great & good uses, in your book. What I have suggested may be of service to you in future editions. I might make other suggestions, but fear that I may only weary you. When we meet, I shall be glad to talk with you touching sundry other heads. Our best regards to Mrs. P. and an old man's blessing on the babies.

Your friend Ever

W. Gilmore Simms

---

[25] Not identified.
[26] Dr. Edward Washington North. See note 174, Dec. 30, 1856.

1081: To the Editor of the Magnolia Weekly [27]

[April? 1863][28]

To the Editor of the Magnolia:

Dear Sir:

I send you a trifle, in verse, from my portfolio, on a subject which we are much more apt to identify with commerce and manufactures, than with poetry. And yet, what sight is more pure and beautiful than a visit to a cotton field in full *blow,* and what history can be more interesting to humanity than of an obscure weed, from which Human Art draws the resources, which, in clothing millions, feeds as many millions more? An ingenious and imaginative writer, taking a single cotton seed in his hands, and pursuing its culture, the working, picking, ginning, packing, vecture or carriage, its subsequent manufacture, till it passes from the loom into the apparel of a Beauty, or grows into a sheet of rosy paper for beauty's *billet doux,* might work the whole history into a beautiful romance, or into a series of sketches, such as Dickens manufactures, for his "Household Words," in which the utilitarian and the romantic are exquisitely blended; which instruct labor and industry, and present pictures that de-

---

[27] We have not located the original of this letter, published with Simms' "Cotton" in the *Magnolia Weekly,* I (May 9, 1863), 161. Since the italics in the salutation and in "Woodlands, S. C." are probably not Simms', we have omitted them.

The first issue of the *Magnolia a Southern Home Journal!* (Richmond, Va.), a weekly, is dated Oct. 4, 1862. The title was soon changed to the *Magnolia Weekly,* and the last issue which we have been able to locate is dated April 1, 1865. Charles Bailie was the proprietor of the periodical until his death in Dec., 1862 (see the issue for Dec. 27, 1862, I, 50). He was succeeded by his "kinsmen" and "friends" (see the issue for Jan. 3, 1863, I, 54), who in turn were followed by Oakley P. Haines and William A. J. Smith (see the issue for March 7, 1863, I, 88), who altered the title to the *Magnolia Weekly.* Smith became sole proprietor with the issue for July 4, 1863 (I, 224), Smith and H. C. Barrow with the issue for Jan. 9, 1864 (II, 116), and Smith and Robertson with the issue for July 30, 1864 (II, 284). Haines was probably the editor of the *Magnolia Weekly* at the time of the publication of Simms' letter. Later James D. McCabe, Jr., and Charles P. J. Dimitry served successively as editors and H. C. Barrow was an associate editor for a short time.

Simms' poetic contributions to the *Magnolia Weekly* are the above-mentioned "Cotton"; "Dreaming and Waking," I (Aug. 8, 1863), 268; "While the Silent Night Goes By," II (Nov. 28, 1863), 65; and "The Prayer of the Lyre," II (March 26, 1864), 206. The last three are signed "Adrian P. Beaufain, Esq.," one of Simms' favorite pseudonyms. His major contribution to the *Magnolia Weekly* was "Benedict Arnold" (see note 57, July 29, 1863). Simms is the subject of two articles by William Archer Cocke entitled "Sketches of Southern Literature," II (Nov. 7 and Nov. 14, 1863), 47, 54.

[28] It is probable that this letter was written only a few weeks before publication.

light the taste and fancy.[29] If my verses on this humble but fruitful subject, should serve to inspire some more elaborate artist, to attempt a more imposing illustration of the history, I shall be well satisfied. They are unstudied lines, almost an *impromptu,* and have already been printed in a newspaper, but with so many imperfections that I revise them for your columns, and shall be pleased if you find them worthy of your reading.[30]

Your ob't serv't,
W. Gilmore Simms.

Woodlands, S. C.

1082: To PAUL HAMILTON HAYNE

Woodlands, 22 June 1863.

My dear Paul.

It occurs to me, after the reading of your last letter, to ask why your mother,[31] wife [32] & self, persist in living at such enormous charges in poor & obscure up-country villages, when you can live more cheaply and comfortably in Charleston? In respect to climate, the middle country is far superior to both seaboard & up-country. I have been living for two summers at my plantation enjoying better health than usual, self & family, no malaria, no musquitoes, and I have not yet felt a *hot* day — never feel one in our *house,* it being of brick. I counselled you several years ago, having some regard then to your constitutional liabilities (which I suspected) to persuade your mother & wife to settle on a small farm in our middle country, where your capital would yield you ten times the health and comfort which you can find in the city; where you can raise your own peaches, grapes, pears, apples; all your vegetables; poultry, pigs; your own corn & fodder & hay; and all upon 100 acres, which you can buy for $1000; and where you could build for $2500 as large a dwelling house as you have in the city; and all this near a rail Road depot, directly on the route to Charleston, Augusta, Columbia, Richmond, &c. Barnwell & Orangeburg afford you all these opportunities now, and, in either of these districts you could find a hundred

---

[29] *Household Words,* which ceased publication with the issue for May 28, 1859, contains many articles on science and invention.

[30] "Cotton" was published as by "Gossypium" in the Charleston *Mercury* of Aug. 30, 1861.

[31] Emily McElhenny Hayne, the widow of Paul Hamilton Hayne, Sr.

[32] The former Mary Middleton Michel, of Charleston, whom Hayne had married in 1852.

precincts, like that pleasant region where John Torré [33] finds refuge, and perhaps the only sure prolongation of his chances of life. It is not too late. I tell you that after travelling all over the country; to mountain sides & watering places; there is no region where you can find so great a degree of health, comfort, profit & pleasure, as in this beautifully wooded middle country of these districts. Any where in Barnwell, from Midway up to Aiken, you can find delicious spots, for small farms, at 10 or 12 dollars per acre, having all these advantages & susceptibilities. Even now, when all things are so expensive, land is tolerably cheap and bargains are to be had. You can get near villages which have 2 or 3 country stores, postoffice, daily mail, and some few respectable & pleasant families. Such are Midway, Bamberg, Graham's,[34] Blackville. All these precincts are *pleasanter* than Aiken — less hot, better wooded — better water — and cheap, — not at the *fancy* prices which make Aiken one of the dearest places in the State. Think over what I tell you, & consult your mother & wife. I report simply the result of my own observation & experience. Where you are, you are out of the pale of civilization. Ours is far the better region for the enjoyment of the *dolce far niente,* the great luxury of a Poet, when the sacred vapours are dissipated from his brain. In haste, but

> Ever truly Yours
>
> W. Gilmore Simms.

1083: To Paul Hamilton Hayne

Woodlands July 4. 1863.

I have just read your Poem, my dear Paul, in the Illustrated News, and hasten to congratulate you upon it.[35] It is a very felicitous performance, chaste, graceful, fanciful, and very happily versified throughout. You have done singularly well, in handling a subject, which required very nice skill, discrimination, tact, & the appreciation of effects and characteristics. Indeed, I see nothing to find fault with, unless it be a want of fullness, and the too vague sketchiness of certain verses, here and there. I would recommend you now, to expand it, giving the characteristics, where you can, more definitely, supplying some other names,

---

[33] Not identified.
[34] Graham's Turn Out is now called Denmark.
[35] "The Southern Lyre," *Southern Illustrated News,* I (July 4, 1863), 6. The poem is reprinted in Richard Barksdale Harwell's "A Confederate View of the Southern Poets," *American Literature,* XXIV (March, 1952), 56-61.

bringing in the woman kind (perhaps in a group) and accompanying the Poem with tolerably copious notes. With this expansion, the notes, and a selection from your hitherto uncollected pieces, you have the material for a new volume, of which this poem may be made a leading feature. It appears to me that you should not omit Farmer,[36] tho born an Englishman. He might be described as/one who toyed beside the stream,/Beheld the Muses in his dream,/and took from fancy all his theme;/capricious sporting with the lyre;/but not with deep intense desire;/his fancy cooling still his fire, &c/And why omit Holland,[37] —/ who, with more labour might have wrought,/and found in stern, severer thought,/a better fame than ere he sought;/whose martial lyrics might have grown/to strains which lead an army on,/By sea & land, to victory won, &c./There were two Halls of S. C. — one Wm. the other Robt. both very clever lyrists who published volumes which I have.[38] You speak of Simons, meaning Wm. Hayne, and totally omitting his brother James W. who had more power & passion, less grace & fancy.[39] There is young Sass,[40] and perhaps, we might find others whom you could group together as neophytes just putting on their singing robes. Think of these suggestions. In respect to myself, you will remember that I discouraged the reference to my doings at all; but if you would write such a poem, of course you could not have omitted me without subjecting yourself to reproach if not suspicion. My objection lay in the conviction that the characterization would be erroneous & exactly in the respect in which I think you have made it so.[41] In my poetry, I make Fancy the subordinate of Imagination and Thought. I do *not* exclude her; on the contrary she appears on every page, but her attitudes are more humble. She is a page or nymph in waiting. It is the great mistake, I

---

[36] Henry Tudor Farmer. See note 233, Dec., 1854.

[37] Edwin Clifford Holland (1794-1824). See letter to Duyckinck of May 5, 1854.

[38] William Hall (see note 223, Nov. 27, 1854) and Robert Pleasants Hall (see note 51, Feb. 24, 1852).

[39] For William Hayne and James Wright Simmons, see introductory sketch of the Simmons brothers.

[40] George Herbert Sass (1845-1908), of Charleston, was at this time a frequent contributor to the *Southern Field and Fireside*.

[41] Hayne's lines on Simms are as follows:

And He, whose rugged presence shows
A soul whereon the tempest blows
Have left at last a stern repose;—

Whose songs, with weightiest meanings fraught,
And trenchant measures, strongly wrought
In strains of olden English thought,

think, of most of the present race of poets, to make her supreme. They deal in nothing but fancies; lack the eye & beak and strong wings of Passion & Imagination, and even make the thought a lay figure upon which they lay the colours of the rainbow. Their songs do not rise to power or grandeur, but are a sort of pleasant twitter, capriciously issuing out of a leafy bower, and using up a little sunshine and moonshine, and flowers & bowers, through all the hours; never mounting with their powers, to the height of mountain towers, &c. &c. But I must be content. Take all that I have said in good part. Some day we will talk over the subject of fugitive poetry, upon which you have mistaken me altogether. The specimens of *successful* fugitives to which you refer me, are *not* fugitives at all. They are mostly remarkable *improvisations,* refined subsequently by exquisite art — *Happy inspirations. I object to studies of art* in a province which implies improvisation — lyrics really being bird gushes — involuntaries — unpremeditated. But you *deliberately sate down to manufacture a long series of provocative & exciting events into lyrics* — this labour implying a total mistake as to the nature of the lyric. But I must not glide into an essay, & I am at the bottom of my sheet. God be with you in mercy.

Your Ever truly

W. Gilmore Simms

1084: To Marcus Claudius Marcellus Hammond [42]

[Jul]y [1863] [43]

dear Major.

I have been for a week [daily] expecting from Mr. Wagner [44] an account of the sales of your three Bales Cotton. I wrote him

---

Please not our fancy's lighter hour,
But fair with health, and rife with power,
Rain 'round us in a fruitful shower!

"Poet of Woodlands!" men will see
More clearly what they owned in Thee
When thou, oh Bard! hast ceased to be!

[42] The MS. of this letter is torn and several words and parts of others are missing.

[43] The year is established by Simms' reference to "the exciting events in & around the Harbour of Charleston" (see note 49, July 17, 1863). Simms' remarks about the sale of Hammond's cotton indicate that this letter was written during the second week in July.

[44] Theodore D. Wagner was a wealthy Charlestonian of the firm of John Fraser and Co. It was due to Wagner that David Flavel Jamison was able to publish his *The Life and Times of Bertrand du Guesclin* (see note 6, Jan. 8, 1866).

instantly on the reciept of your last letter, & have delayed my reply to you, in daily expectation of one from him. But I suppose that the exciting events in & around the Harbour of Charleston has put a stop to all business. My belief, however, from what Mr. Wagner said to me when I was last in the city, say about [the] 27th June, is that your Cotton wa[s] then sold, & at about 40 cents. [I] had 5 Bales in his hands about [the] same time, & h[is ins]tructions were [that] he should sell yo[urs] & mine at the highest market p[ric]e, *before the 1[st] July.* I had another lot engaged to him at the market price, *in transitu,* which I held to be sold before the same day, & for the same reason, viz. to escape the tax in kind & pay that for money on hand. I look to hear from Mr. W. that all this has been done, & my calculation is that neither of us has got less than 40, which was the market price when my instructions were given. As soon as I hear & am authorized to draw, I shall have the money deposited to my credit, & send you a dft for your portion. I have no reason to think [that] Mr. W. *will speculate upon us* [*him*]*self,* or be so indifferent to our interests, as to suffer any one else to do so. Set your mind easy on that score, and assume that your Cotton was sold before the 1st. instant. It is probable that when you, your Brother & Yeadon, advise me that peaches are melting in the mouth, and in abundance, I shall pay you a visit all round, bringing with me one or both of my daughters.[45] But this will depend on the state of affairs along our seaboard. We are all in too much anxiety to think of pleasures or peaches, or visits of pleasure. Best regards to all & believe me

Eve[r tr]uly Yours

W[. Gi]lmore Sim[ms]

1085: TO JOHN REUBEN THOMPSON

Woodlands July 17. 1863.

John R. Thompson, Esq.

My dear Thompson.

I am really very glad to see that you have been translated to the Editorial chair of the News.[46] Your fine tastes, & ample

---

[45] Mary Lawson and Chevillette.
[46] Evidently this report of Thompson's becoming editor of the *Southern Illustrated News* was erroneous, since in his letter to Hayne of July 29 Simms speaks of him as editor of the *Record* and remarks that "it affords him no field, for his nice taste & happy talent."

knowledge of the history of Literature will enable you to do for that work what it very much needed; and I trust that you assure yourself with a competent salary. All the old standards of compensation must be abandoned, in the wide waste of our present currency, and in the monstrous rate of charge for every thing. Take care of yourself. While doing this, please take care of me a little. There are a number of my "Sketches in Greece" — metrical — which lie in the hands of your publishers,[47] which I desire to see in print, especially as I had grafted upon them allusions to the present condition of our affairs, which would be lost, if not put to present use. I suppose the publishers have delayed their issue, as they lacked the aid of rhyme — the cunning artifice of octosyllabic jingle. In one of his last letters he promised their early publication. There are 6 of them. They ought not to be published, in connection of numbering, as a series. Nothing serial ought to be published in an *American* Weekly. But please put them forth, each, individually, omitting the general title of "Sketches in Greece" — & under its individual name. The poems are grave, moral, political & descriptive. The first six of the series which were published, were so wretchedly misprinted, that it was scarce possible to read them. Let me entreat you to call for the remaining poems & put them forth at intervals, as so many several contributions, with my name. And if you will yourself read the proofs, you will greatly oblige me.[48] — I write in haste & under great anxieties of mind, as even while I write I hear the heavy booming of the cannon in our harbour — 72 miles off — the enemy making his approaches both by land & water.[49] We are in the hands of God, & I do not despair, though my anguish & anxiety are very great, for our poor old city, & our gallant boys — the best blood of the country confronting the vilest scum of Europe & the North. My eldest son, the only one grown, is on the coast, in the cavalry & has been two years; and with every shot that I hear I tremble, and think of him. You probably have drunk deep of this experience in your own Virginia. God give us his shield, and interpose, since that poor beast of imbecility — Lord J. Russell — always an imbecile — is cutting

[47] Ayers and Wade.

[48] For Simms' "Sketches in Greece" published during 1862, see note 44, Sept. 20, 1862. The other six "Sketches" were not published in the *Southern Illustrated News*.

[49] On July 10 Union forces under the command of Gen. Quincy A. Gillmore launched an attack on Fort Wagner on Morris Island. Fort Wagner was eventually captured on Sept. 7. See *O. R.*, 1st Series, XXVIII, Pt. I, 199ff.

England's sinews while suffering ours to be cut.[50] Let me hear
from you, & God be with you in mercy.

Ever truly Yours

W. Gilmore Simms

P. S. Russell was always a poor devil — upheld only by his
family name and his peerage. He is by nature weak, timid, indecisive — a mere measured gentleman of small nice proprieties.
Even when a young man these were his characteristics. Turn to
Moore's apostrophe (Tom Moore) to him, 40 years ago, to remember his family, name, ancestors, & not skulk his duties.[51] You
can make a good Editorial paragraph on the subject & select the
poem. He has no mental character. Even in literature, his editorship of Moore is disgraceful to the manhood of the one, & to the
moral, if not the reputation of the other.[52] In the mismanagement
of the Crimean War, he was proverbial and as a politician, he
has always balked where he should have gone forward, & stam-
mered where he should have spoken, and tottered, where he should
have been firm as a rock.

1086: To Paul Hamilton Hayne[53]

Woodlands. 29 July. 1863.

My [dear] P[aul.]

Your [las]t letter represented you as about to move, and I
think to Greenville, but I have mislaid the letter, and address
you now, somewhat doubtfully, at that place. I had hopes that
you would write me, when fairly settled down in your new abode.
Wherever it be, I trust you find it more grateful & less expensive
than the last. I myself, after a long experience, prefer the middle
to the mountain country at all seasons, and in summer the seaboard. You will find the middle country, as I have already repeatedly urged, far preferable for your constitution. Since our
last writing, you see that our poor old city has been & is seriously

---

[50] Lord John Russell, the 1st Earl Russell (1792-1878), was at this time
foreign secretary of England. He attempted to maintain a strict neutrality between the North and the South.

[51] See "Remonstrance after a Conversation with Lord John Russell . . . ,"
Poetical Works of Thomas Moore, ed. A. D. Godley (London: Oxford University Press, 1924), p. 530.

[52] Russell edited the *Memoirs, Journal, and Correspondence of Thomas
Moore,* 8 vols. (London: Longman, Brown, Green, and Longmans, 1853-1856).

[53] The MS. of this letter is in bad condition with several words completely
torn away. Part of the letter is printed in Trent, pp. 275-276.

menaced. Our people, so far as I can learn, have shown, if they do not now exhibit, a singular degree of apprehensiveness, not warranted by the circumstances, and not creditable to their manhood & resolve. They are recovering from it, but there is still too much of doubt & despondency among the citizens not to give us great concern. My trust is that as the pressure begins to be seriously felt, and as anxiety & suspense give way to the certainties of conflict, they will rise above the crisis, and prove successful in the encounter with it. It will probably resolve itself into a final trial with the bayonet on James island. You have seen that our friend Ramsay has got himself honorably wounded in the fight at Wagner's, but I trust not fatally, and that he will emerge from the fall as vigorous & more resolute than ever. He is said to have shown beautiful pluck, highly creditable to the historical name he bears.[54] — I got a letter yesterday from Thompson, who is now editing a paper in Richmond called "The Record" — an eclectic, which embodies the documentary history of the day & country. It affords him no field, for his nice taste & happy talent, unless in the propriety of his selections; and, as he writes me — probably apprehending that I might seek an organ — he has no literary patronage to bestow.[55] But my heart is too full of anxiety to suffer me to write, and though I have a contract for some $200 worth of prose,[56] I find myself unable to divert my thoughts from the crisis in which the country trembles in suspense. What I write is in a spasm — a single burst of passion — hope, or scorn, or rage or exultation. If, where you are, you can abstract your mind from the present, & throw into the far land of the past, or poesy, do so for your own relief. I cannot! I have sent the last instalments of my dramatic essay on 'Arnold' to the 'Magnolia,' and it will

---

[54] Maj. David Ramsay (1830-1865), the son of Dr. James Ramsay and the grandson of the historian David Ramsay, all of Charleston, was wounded on July 18 as he commanded the Charleston Battalion at Battery Wagner, on Morris Island. Ramsay died on Aug. 4. See the Charleston *Mercury* of July 20 and Aug. 5, 1863, and the Charleston *Courier* of Aug. 6, 1863.

[55] The *Record of News, History and Literature* (Richmond, Va.), a weekly, ran from June 18 through Dec. 10, 1863. The firm of West and Johnson was the publisher. No editor is mentioned in the periodical, though evidently Thompson was the editor throughout its lifetime (see following letters to Thompson). The first issue announces (I, 4) that the *Record*'s "literary material will be eclectic, not original—though sometimes it may offer an original paper, essay or poem." The following poems by Simms were reprinted in the *Record* from the Charleston *Mercury* of Aug. 1, Sept. 9, Oct. 24, and Nov. 11: "Fort Wagner," "Sumter in Ruins," "The Angel of the Hospital," and "Grayson," I (Aug. 13, Sept. 24, Nov. 26, and Dec. 3), 73, 133, 217-218, 225. The first two are signed; the last two are not.

[56] Doubtless the novellette mentioned by Simms in his letter to Kollock of March 27, 1863.

soon be finished. But the business of revision had become a drudgery with me long before it closed, and the horrible corruptions & blunders of the press, had disgusted me with every column.[57] I have no news. I have had a child [58] very sick with worm fever, & my wife has been suffering severely with neuralgia in the face. They are now better — but who can be well, while this terrible war lasts, and while so many whom we love are in danger. Present us gratefully t[o y]our w[ife] & mother, & believe me

Ever truly [Yours]

W. Gilmore Simms.

[*About one word missing*] Br[uns] [*several words missing*] is full. He is too busy to write.

1087: To PAUL HAMILTON HAYNE

Woodlands, Sep. 23. [1863][59]

My dear Paul.

I am under the impression that I answered all your letters. I have a vague notion that our two last letters crossed on the route, & I left it to you, as the youngest, to reopen the correspondence. I perfectly recollect the remarkable event you refer to,[60] in respect to poor Ramsay — on these subjects, as you are probably aware, I am not an incredulous man. The spiritual world is in close contact with us. I believe that my beloved dead are ever with me, and I would not willingly give up the belief. — I have been ill, my friend, I may say dangerously ill, from the moment when I was struck down by the heaviest bolt of all that ever shattered my roof-tree.[61] I was, I think, insane. I neither slept nor ate for four days and nights. Fever seized me, and I should have gone mad but for the administration of timely opiates. I am once more on my legs, but very weak. Today, is the first that I have given to the desk, and this I could do only in snatches of brief period.

---

[57] "Benedict Arnold: The Traitor. A Drama, in an Essay" was published in the *Magnolia Weekly*, I (May 16, 23, 30; June 6, 13, 20, 27; July 4, 11, 18, 25; and Aug. 1, 1863), 165-167, 173-175, 186-187, 194-195, 202-203, 210-211, 218-219, 226-227, 234-235, 242-243, 250-251, 258-259. See note 21, Jan. 25, 1850, for further discussion of the history of this work.

[58] Probably Govan.

[59] Dated by the death of Mrs. Simms. See note 61, below.

[60] Simms wrote *you refer to you*.

[61] On Sept. 10 Chevillette Simms died after a short illness (probably acute appendicitis). A notice of her death is printed in the Charleston *Mercury* of Sept. 10 and an "In Memoriam" in the *Mercury* of Sept. 23.

I move about the house & try to see to things. But every thing seems blank, & waste, & very cheerless. I am alone! Alone! For near 30 years, I had one companion in whose perfect fidelity, I felt sure. To her I could go, and say, 'I suffer!' — or 'I am glad,' always satisfied that she would partake the feeling with me, whatever its character. Your eulogy is not mere varnish & gilding. She was all that you describe, — a dutiful wife, a devoted mother, and the most guileless of women. Ah! God! And I am lone!

We live too much for the world, my dear Paul. It is a poor affair. This ambitious struggle after greatness, is a vanity. Our sole justification must lie in the will & wish to *do,* irrespective of the profit and the loss. What does Milton say in Lycidas — I half forget the passage —

> 'But not *the praise,*
> Phœbus replied, & toucht my trembling ears —
> Fame is no plant that grows on mortal soil —
> &c. [']⁶²

Write me, my young friend. The old man has grown much older — much feebler — & it is becoming, the ministration of you, the younger brother of his guild, to assist his palsying eylids, and point his sight, and say — 'here place your staff — set your foot here, & now — sit. There is a prospect before you of a glorious valley, purple in a generous sunset.' God be with [you] & yours in mercy.

Your old friend

W. Gilmore Simms

1088: To John Reuben Thompson

Woodlands, Midway P. O.
S. C.   Oct. 15. 1863.

My dear Thompson.

I thank you very much for your kind & genial expressions of sympathy. The tender solicitude of friends have done much in the way of soothing, under a great sorrow which the mercy of the Good God alone can lighten. I have not been able to write to you before. I have just risen from a bed of protracted sickness, and am still very feeble. The terrible shock of my great calamity — so totally unexpected, & for which none of us was prepared — fell upon me like a bolt from a clear sky. I sank under it. Fever

---

⁶² Lines 78ff.

threatened my brain, & for four days & nights I neither ate nor slept. Then followed the disturbance of the biliary secretions, which have kept me in fever, at intervals more or less prolonged, for a full month. In brief, I suffered more physically in this one month than in all my experiences of ailment, put together, for 50 years before. As already said, I am up, and at my desk, trying to make Thought a refuge from brooding & reverie — to "wreck Thought upon expression" as Byron phrased it.[63] The work is not easy. Every thing, house, grounds, garden, children — all forcibly present me with the image of my sole close companion & confidante of 30 years — the woman who had borne me 14 children. The sense of desolation is a solid weight upon eyes & heart & thought, and it is to the Good God alone that I must look for support & succour. I will try — I am trying — to throw the work of resistance upon my mind, & propose, as soon as I shall have answered an accumulated Correspondence — to address myself to some literary labour. But, what with my own lon[e]liness,[64] & constant reverie, — what with the terrible anxieties which oppress me in regard to our poor country — it is not easy to divert the mind to the regions of the ideal. I have for some time past done little more than write patriotic odes & ballads for the Mercury. Most that you see in that paper are mine.[65] But that you must have conjectured. I recieved the first 4 numbers of your "record." [66] Can't you let me have the rest. I have little or nothing to read, & can't study. With many thanks,

Yours truly

W. Gilmore Simms

---

[63] See *Childe Harold,* Canto III, Stanza xcvii, lines 2-3.

[64] The MS. is torn.

[65] During 1863 Simms published a considerable number of poems in the Charleston *Mercury,* among them "Fort Wagner" (Aug. 1), "Beauregard—A Lyrical Ode" (Aug. 3), "To Alfred Rhett" (Aug. 26), "Sumter in Ruins" (Sept. 9), "Passage of the Red Sea" (Oct. 14), and "The Angel of the Hospital" (Nov. 11). The Charleston *Courier* of June 22 contains his "Ode—'Our City by the Sea,'" which the *Mercury* of June 25 calls "one of the noblest and most elegant tributes, ever penned, by poet or historian, to a city triumphant and jubilant with victory."

[66] See note 55, July 29, 1863.

1089: To Francis Peyre Porcher

Woodlands, Oct. 20. 1863

My dear Porcher.

Your letter is grateful & consolatory. It finds me just recovering from a severe fit of illness, more severe than I have suffered in all the preceding 50 years of my life. When the sudden & terrible calamity of my house fell upon me, like a bolt out of a clear sky, I was seized with mental paroxysms of great violence which threatened the integrity of my brain. For four days & nights I neither ate nor slept, and but for opiates successfully administered, I should have gone mad. This attack was followed by a general derangement of the biliary organs; and I was prostrated by fever for more than a month. I am up again, but very feeble. In order to change air & scene, & attend to some business, I visited the city a week ago, & could scarcely lift myself in & out of the cars. I could not walk 200 yards without exhaustion; and I recuperate slowly. I am very desolate; but duty to my children & to my own mind, finds my will to do, unimpaired; and I propose, as soon as possible, to subject my mind to some continuous task. I congratulate you on the continued success of your book, the reputation of which seems firmly established. You must now lose no time, and spare no labour, in improving its contents, and enlarging them where this is possible & desirable.[67] Two or three items, which I have lately picked up may be of service to you. I have seen some beautifully dyed stuffs, of a rich purple brown, the dye made of the *roots* of the China briar, with a little copperas. A lady of my acquaintance uses *peach* leaves, as a substitute for Hops, in making the yeast biscuits for bread. I suggested my fears that the prussic acid in the leaves might be deleterious; but she said that some of her oldest neighbours had been in the habit of so using the peach leaves all their lives, and suffered no ill effects. Recently, up at Bamberg, I saw some very beautiful bonnets for ladies, manufactured *in the loom,* and out of the *common wire grass,* by two young ladies, who told me that they had cost them only the labour of *half an hour.* Such bonnets would sell in Charleston for $20 or $30. In the same way, & with the same material, rich curtains, dyed with all the hues of autumn, might be wrought, and so the matting for floors, in an incon-

---

[67] In his revised edition of *Resources of the Southern Fields and Forests* published in 1869 (see note 23, April 14, 1863) Porcher adopts many of the suggestions Simms makes in this letter, frequently accrediting Simms with them.

cievably short space of time. These facts, if you are not already possessed of them, are worthy of your note book. — In respect to the condition of things in the city, I can report but little. The military & people are of opinion, that it may be partially destroyed but not taken. Our Generalship [68] there has been very wretched, in my opinion, & our [*remainder of letter missing.*]

---

[68] Gen. Beauregard was in command of the Department of South Carolina, Georgia, and Florida. Charleston was in the 1st Military District, in command of Gen. Ripley. Other generals commanding in and around Charleston at this time were States Rights Gist, Thomas Lanier Clingman, and James H. Trapier.

1864

1090: To James Ryder Randall[1]

Woodlands, S. C. Feb. 1. 1864.

James R. Randall Esq.

My dear Mr. Randall.

I regret your failure to visit me, but ascribed the disappointment to the right cause. You, perhaps, sustained no loss, since the creature comforts, known of old, on our plantations, are seen now only at angel intervals, yet we could have done better for you than at the Hotels, for it was the Hog killing period, when sausages daily smoke on the breakfast tables, and when every negro is heard whistling, and seen with a greasy mouth. We had still some show of the good old times, and a roast turkey would have reminded you that the Christmas period was not wholly over. Let me trust that you will, hereafter, *en passant,* and without ceremony stop at Midway & take a night with us at least. At Midway you are but 2 miles from Woodlands, & my boy & horse (buggy at times) are always there on the arrival of the trains.

With great respect, Yours truly

W. Gilmore Simms.

1091: To Marcus Claudius Marcellus Hammond[2]

Woodla[nds, *c.* February 15, 1864][3]

[Dear Ma]jor.

[It i]s lucky for me that [I am a poor man. I]f my books were safe, [I would not fear, for] I have little of my own at the [plantation. Fear is] for you men who talk daily of you[r wealth, you]r half million, & millions — your for[tunes in c]otton, tobacco,

---

[1] Randall (1839-1908), journalist and poet, was the author of "Maryland, My Maryland." On Dec. 14, 1864, he married M. C. M. Hammond's daughter Katharine.

[2] The MS. of this letter is torn, water-stained, and frayed at the edges.

[3] This letter was written between Feb. 12 and 18. See notes 4 and 5, below.

sugar & whiskey, which only [keep you] in a tremor. It is to
hide away the currency [from the] spoiler — how to convert this
currency, into B[onds which] shall give you 8 per ct. in good
money after [the war is] over, and with goods down to old prices.
Ah! [I know] the problem is not easily solvable, & is simply [an
im]possibility. Work as the financier may, he cannot [conver]t a
currency which he has amassed by the million & from trifles light
as air, into gold, or any substantial, without suffering [a] large
decline in [i]ts value. Reconcile yourself to that. If Congress
could & would fund the whole at 5 per cent, & keep faith with
the people, we could throw the debt on posterity & still be
moderately well off. But Congress is a many headed ass, the hundred heads only differing from each other in the extent, length
& breadth of ears — & tongues. Flour you say is $130 per bbl.
You dread lest it should rise to $400. The matter don't concern
me! I have not bought a morsel for three years. We eat corn.
But flour at $400 is [ju]st as cheap & reasonable as nails at $300.
My plan is to buy nothing or as little as I can. I have nothing
to sell but 10 bags of Cotton & that is $125. If I could get
transportation, I would sell, pay off all my debts & snap my
fingers at the whole chapter of chances. — I have just got back
from the city where I have been kept for several days in great
anxiety. Gilmore was in the fight on John's Island.[4] His company
had the [*half of a line missing*] fight, [*two-thirds of a line missing*] with a [*two-thirds of a line missing*] is almost [*two-thirds
of a line missing or illegible*] in turn by [*two-thirds of a line
missing or illegible*] we could get no [*almost half of a line missing
or illegible*] [I got] home on Sunday, tired out. [I advise you to
stick] to your farm. These short cuts to fortune [*one-third of a
line missing or illegible*] And you are getting too old now to [be
kept in a p]erpetual fever by the caprices of Fortune [and b]lock-
ade running. Mr. Randall would be better [off on a] farm alongside of you, though he had but [one n]egro. There are several
of my poorer neighbours [doing w]ell, thriving, not only living
decently, but making [a crop] small as it is, and without a
negro. — So you have be[en] reading Wordsworth. You are
hardly yet in a condition of mind to do him justice. He is the
greatest of all the tribe of contemplative poets. From 15 to 40 a
man of blood enjoys Byron & Moore. After that he asks for the
food of thought, and not of passion. Politics do not commend
themselves to me. They disgust. I can do nothing, and would

---

[4] On Feb. 9-12.

rather not know the evils which I cannot avert. — You should visit Redcliffe. You must go there with me when I come up. I hope to do so in March. I am to go [to] Smyrna on Thursday next to lecture for the benefit of the soldiers.[5] — I will remind Gilmore of your desires, as to the l[a]nd in question. But, with the owners generally absent it is hardly possible to get details. To procure the names of owners & their factors, is all probably that he will be able to do. — The war will end this year. — Mr. Randall told me that he had got the Abbot [6] from you, & that it kept him up during his journey. Let the girls write a few days before hand, when they propose to come. Ask Starnes about the Lectures.[7] Best regards to Mrs. H. and the demoiselles.

Yours faithfully

W. Gilmore Simms

1092: To Jacob Keith Sass [8]

[February 23, 1864]

My Dear Mr. Sass —

I have great pleasure in remitting to you the sum of two hundred dollars, the proceeds of a Lecture which I delivered recently at Smyrna Church, in the pleasant precinct of Allandale,[9] in our District of Barnwell. You will see by the accompanying letter of the Hon. Mr. Lawton, our Senator from Barnwell District, that this fund has been confided to me for the benefit of our soldiers or people. As I am not in a situation to do this in person, I beg to confide it to you, as much more experienced in this pious and

---

[5] Simms lectured at Smyrna on Saturday, Feb. 20. See letter to Sass of Feb. 23.

[6] Simms' *Father Abbot*. See note 206, Oct. 17, 1849.

[7] Evidently Simms was planning to lecture in Augusta.

[8] We have not located the original of this letter, published in the Charleston *Courier* of Feb. 29, 1864. Accompanying it is a letter to Simms from Benjamin W. Lawton dated "Allandale, Barnwell District, February 22, 1864," which says that at the conclusion of Simms' lecture "on Saturday last [Feb. 20], a voluntary contribution, amounting to two hundred dollars, was raised to aid any benevolent enterprise connected with our present struggle" and that "as it was raised entirely through the instrumentality of your lecture before our people, and as you are more directly in communication with the wants of our soldiers than I, I prefer to enclose the amount to you."

Sass (1813-1865) was president of the Bank of Charleston. Benjamin W. Lawton (1822-1879) was a member of the South Carolina legislature for a number of years and had represented Barnwell District in the Secession Convention.

[9] The name of this town is now spelled *Allendale*.

patriotic work, and much better acquainted than myself with the most deserving and suffering subjects. To your discretion, therefore, as almoner of the liberal people by whom it has been given, I transfer the fund, fully assured that your disposition of it will be judicious of aim and useful in application.

Ever truly yours, &c.

W. Gilmore Simms.

Woodlands, February 23, 1864.[10]

1093: To Edward Roach

Woodlands, 28 March. [1864][11]

My dear Edward.

I wrote you yesterday, to be forwarded by Wm.,[12] a letter containing $25 in money, to be added to other sums in your hands, making $100, and with this to secure a Bond in the event of your not being able to make any purchase with it. Today, however, I recieved a demijohn by the cars, which, I take it, contains the gallon of Brandy. If so, the $25 sent, and the $15 of Chevillette's, which Augusta has, may be kept for awhile, and we can see what may be got with it, as the whole amount is in fives. Hereafter, if necessary, we may have to fund it; but, in all probability, the girls will find it easier to spend it — & more grateful. — I write this at night in my study, the Jamisons, bringing a guest with them, driving up just as we had sate down to a game of whist. I have left them playing some girls game in place of it. Tell Augusta I shall be glad to see her soon. Washington gives a Birthday party to her children tomorrow, and all our little folks are to be there.[13] Corn cake & dumpling are the go. Corn & peas are $15 per bushel in Augusta. Instead of 200,000 bushels of Corn, as reported, Hammond [14] made 43,000. I hear that he is complained of as not selling below the market price. But why should he be required to do what his neighbours refuse to do. While the planters are fleeced

---

[10] The *Courier* misprints *Woodlawns*. Since the italics in the place and date are probably not Simms', we have omitted them.

[11] Dated by Simms' references to Augusta's forthcoming visit to Woodlands (see following letter) and to James H. Hammond, who died later this year (see letter to Spann Hammond of Nov. 20).

[12] William Roach.

[13] Evidently Washington Fuller was staying in Bamberg with her sister, Mary Rivers.

[14] James H. Hammond.

on every hand, & taxed & tythed from head to foot, they can only
save themselves by getting all that their wares can command in
the markets. Once more, love to all.

Your affect. father

W. Gilmore Simms

1094: To Edward Roach

Woodlands. April 15. '64

My dear Edward.

I have drawn upon you, in favor of James W. Gray, Esq.
Master in Equity,[15] for $55. which please pay on presentation of
the dft. Tomorrow I set out for Barnwell, seeking some $200
which I have there. I have told Augusta that I will take your
certificate of 4 per cent, give you one of $100, which you will
need for taxes and give you my bond besides for $400 paying you
7 per cent interest. With this addition to my own funds, I may
scrape through with the taxes. I wish you to keep in mind that
I shall probably need a number of the coarse bags for cotton picking; and as I hope to make from 70 to 100 bushels of wheat, I
shall also need a number of such condemned bags as will serve
to hold it, after one patching. I would be glad if you, or Wm.
would see Mr. Chafee,[16] & ascertain what he will sell a gallon of
Jamaica for. I have lately been suffering much from depression,
& fear that I may have a return of my chill & fever. If I could
procure a small supply of any good liquor, I should probably escape these attacks altogether — at all events during the summer.
If I can get the liquor at any price within my means, I will make
a tincture of the Cherry Bark & Dogwood, as a tonic, taking so
many spoonsful through the day. But to pay an enormous price
for the wretchedest rot gut, revolts equally my gorge & pocket.
I have just written to Gilmore. His last letter speaks of his departure as certain, but not *instanter*. I do not know what the
poor fellow will do for a horse. No news here. The crops are
backward. Seasons unfavorable. Your wife and children have continued well since they came up, and are still so. — I have made

---

[15] We have not had access to the Charleston *Directory* for 1864. The *Directory* for 1860 gives Gray's residence as the corner of Lynch and Beaufain
streets.

[16] William H. Chafee (d. 1893) was a wholesale grocer and commission
merchant at 207 East Bay Street, Charleston. See the Charleston *Directory* for
1866-1867.

some very good Ink. Will send you a Bottle when Augusta goes down. I have sold 4 doz Pints at $12 per doz. to Burke & Sease.[17] Buy me another pound of Copperas. This is one of my Ingredients. Make my respects to your mother [18] & Wm.

Yours Ever affectionately

W. Gilmore Simms.

1095: To EDWARD ROACH

Woodlands. 28 April. [1864][19]

My dear Edward.

I sent you by yesterday's mail, $150. I enclose you in this, today $60 more, making $210. It is probable that I will send you another small sum on Monday, all of which I wish you to dispose according to the directions in my last letter. I met Dr. Fuller yesterday at Midway who told me that he expected his wife up today, & that Mrs. Roach [20] would possibly accompany her. As no message has reached us today, I think it doubtful, their coming. Tell Augusta that I have just returned from a pic nic party at Jennings' Mill.[21] We had quite a smart repast. I left the girls at Mrs. Patterson's,[22] where they are to spend the evening. There are a dozen young cadets in attendance. I only went to escort the girls & was very tired. Mrs. Jennings [23] asked very kindly after Augusta & regretted her absence. Gilmore expects a furlough early in May. He danced all night at Mrs. D. Rowe's [24] & marched by

---

[17] James Burke and John Sease operated a general store at Midway.

[18] Esther Ann Conyers Roach, the widow of Edward Roach. See note 225, July 19, 1858.

[19] Dated by Simms' reference to Gilmore's probable appointment "to the artillery Regt. of Rhett." See note 26, below.

[20] Edward's mother.

[21] Near Woodlands.

[22] Hannah Frizzell Trotti Patterson (1804-1889), daughter of Francis Trotti and widow of Angus Patterson (see note 147, March 26, 1845), lived at her father's plantation, Briarwood, after her husband's death in 1854.

[23] Mrs. John S. Jennings.

[24] Sarah Keziah Moss Rowe (1814-1884), daughter of Stephen and Ann Erwin Moss and wife of Donald Christopher Rowe (1809-1876), all of Orangeburg District. Mrs. Rowe was distinguished for her ministering to the hungry, sick, and wounded throughout the Confederate War. Almost every morning she would board the train from Orangeburg to Kingville, then to Branchville, and then in the evening back to Orangeburg, "bearing baskets and boxes of food, medicines, bandages, and other comforting articles for the soldiers." It is recorded that "she was kind and generous to Northern soldiers and prisoners as well as to her own loved boys in gray." For an account of Mrs. Rowe, see Mrs. Thomas Taylor, Mrs. A. T. Smythe, Mrs. August Kohn, Miss M. B. Poppenheim, and Miss Martha B. Washington, eds., *South Carolina Women in the Confederacy* (Columbia, S. C.: The State Company, 1903), pp. 147-149.

daylight in the morning. Isaac [25] has gone up to Columbia to carry one of his horses, and bring another back. Miles, in a letter to me, recd. this day, mentions that his appointment will now be made very soon — that he is next but one in line on the list. He will probably be appointed to the artillery Regt. of Rhett.[26] Mrs. Jenkins is recovering, but one of her children is reported to be sick today of pneumonia, & Mrs. Jamison's Clara has been ill for several days of the same disease.[27] Frank Carroll's two children are also reported to be very sick, & it is feared of the same disease.[28] Dr. Fuller is, I believe, in attendance. Salley Pinckney goes to St. John's as a Governess. I dined with the P's yesterday, at their most pressing invitation. Dr. P. is at home. They are fitting up the carriage factory as a residence.[29] Nothing more that I can think of to interest either of you. All well here, thank God! Love to Augusta & regards to Wm. I look to hear from you soon. If Wm. can bring up the gun for me, I shall try to feed awhile on squirrels. The rabbits, doves, and partridges, as well as squirrels are in abundance. I see them whenever I walk or ride.

Yours Ever affectionately

W. Gilmore Simms

1096: To EDWARD ROACH

Woodlands, 3 May. [1864][30]

My dear Edward.

Yours & Augusta's letter was recd. during my absence at Columbia whither I went [h]earing [31] from him [32] that he would get no furlough[.] But this was an error. He has got one & came home with me today. He has had a gay time in Orangeburg &

---

[25] Isaac Nimmons, Simms' body servant. See introductory sketch of the Negroes at Woodlands.

[26] It was not until the autumn of this year that Gilmore was commissioned 2nd lieutenant in the 1st South Carolina Artillery, under the command of Col. Alfred Rhett, son of Robert Barnwell Rhett (see letter to Gilmore of Nov. 14, 1864). During May–June of this year Gilmore served in Virginia in Aiken's 6th Regiment of South Carolina Cavalry (see letter to Thompson of May 15).

[27] Mrs. Jenkins is Mrs. Micah Jenkins. Clara is the David Flavel Jamisons' youngest daughter.

[28] Julia Peeples Carroll (b. 1862) and Charles Rivers Carroll, II (b. 1863).

[29] Salley Pinckney was the daughter of Dr. Hopson Pinckney. St. John's, Berkeley Parish, is located just north of Charleston.

[30] Dated by Simms' reference to having gone to Columbia to see Gilmore. See letter to Hayne of May 8.

[31] The MS. is torn.

[32] Gilmore.

Columbia, and he & the girls have gone down to a Party at the Patterson's tonight. I am here, playing watchdog till midnight, & answering my several correspondents. A small packet for Augusta was sent by Rebecca, who spoke of her affectionately; she, Mr. I. & all her girls are well.[33] She expresses a wish to visit you when she can. Thanks for the leeks. All of the onion family are grateful to me. I will see to saving & returning the bag, and will have the others looked up, though I should rather you would charge them to me, as soon as you can ascertain the price. As I am in no hurry for the bags — they will answer in June or July — you can invest the money in the new currency. I send you Twenty Dollars more, making $230, and in a week more, will probably send you some farther amount. I dare not venture on the liquor at such prices. Gilmore will probably have 10 or 12 days, & in that time, may run down & see you for a day. In that event, he will bring the package from Rebecca. I know not what it contains. My garden is improving, though we had a slight frost, & a sharp snap of cold this morning. Green peas in blossom. Potatoes looking well. Snap beans, asparagus, lettuce, spinach, tomato, cucumbers, melons, & corn all growing. We gave Mrs. Pinckney [34] a handful of strawberries this evening. They promise to ripen fast, and I wish you could be up here to enjoy them. We have had several messes of asparagus, some spinach, and our lettuce is fit to eat, but without mustard & oil, nobody cares for it. The wheat is improving, & I shall be able, if it continues to do well, to send a bag for Augusta, or more. Our sweet potatoes are at an end, or nearly so. Every bank is demolished. The girls took Claudia [35] over to see your mother, who pronounces herself far better than when in town. On the cars today, we encountered Mary Roach.[36] Gilmore had three ladies of his acquaintance to escort — a Miss Stock, an

---

[33] Rebecca M. Giles Isaacs (1824?-1906), wife of George E. Isaacs (1824-1888), of Columbia, who after the War became a conductor on the Columbia and Greenville Rail Road, was a relative of Simms' first wife, Anna Malcolm Giles. The Isaacses had three daughters: Georgie A. (1850-1902), who married Lawrence N. Zealy; Lizzie, who married James M. Morris (1844?-1882); and Florence, who married W. H. Scott. At the time of Sherman's march through South Carolina Simms and his family were staying with the Isaacses. Augusta Simms Roach's children called Mrs. Isaacs "Aunt Rebecca," but it seems likely that she was a cousin rather than an aunt.

[34] Mrs. Hopson Pinckney. Mrs. Pinckney was a relative of the Kelloggs of Great Barrington, Mass.

[35] Claudia Roach, Edward's sister.

[36] Mary Cussings Fishburne Roach (1809-1868), sister of Dr. Francis Beatty Fishburne (see note 147, Aug? 1861) and widow of William Roach (1799-1838), Nash Roach's half-brother, lived on a plantation in Barnwell District.

old maid, Miss Bee & Miss Chisolm.[37] There is a rumour here today, of severe fighting in North Carolina. I expected it on Sunday last. It will be Lee's policy to endeavour to defeat or destroy the Yankee columns in North Carolina, so as to prevent himself from being flanked from that quarter. God send us victory. I trust that Beauregard was fully prepared for the encounter.[38] The children of Carroll & Jamison are all recovering. My own, thank God, are well. With the exception of Augusta, & yours, they are all with me, and I should be grateful to God that he has spared them to gather around me still. I must put my faith in him & not nurse my anxieties. May he keep you & yours, in the safe sheltering hollows of his hand. Love to Augusta & kisses for the children. Regards to Wm.

Your affect. father

W. Gilmore Simms

P. S. Do you know Mr. T. A. Burke [39] in the Qr Master's Office?

1097: To Paul Hamilton Hayne [40]

Woodlands, May 8. 1864.

My dear Paul.

I hurried, on a brief visit to Columbia to see my son before his departure for Virginia, expecting him to go without delay. I was agreeably disappointed to find that he had got a two weeks furlough, & was enabled to come home with me. I saw Timrod and was glad to find him in better health and spirits than he has had for years before. Temperance & employment are doing him good. If his situation lessens his opportunities for verse writing, it at all events gives him the creature comforts & with a young

---

[37] Miss Bee was probably Valeria North Bee (b. 1848), the daughter of Rebecca Hutchinson Stock and William Cattell Bee. She later married, in 1872, Laurens North Chisolm (b. 1848). We are unable to identify conclusively Miss Stock and Miss Chisolm, since there were several families of those names in Charleston at this time. Doubtless Miss Stock was Valeria Bee's cousin, and possibly Miss Chisolm was her future husband's cousin.

[38] These engagements around New Bern and in Albemarle Sound did not take place until May 4-6. See *O. R.,* 1st Series, XXXVI, Part II, *passim.*

[39] Thomas A. Burke. See note 192, Oct. 11, 1851.

[40] Jay B. Hubbell in *The Last Years of Henry Timrod 1864-1867* (Durham, North Carolina: Duke University Press, 1941), pp. 21-25, published this letter from two garbled copies of the original made by Hayne's son, William Hamilton Hayne, and from a portion of the letter as printed by Trent, pp. 277-278. Our text is from the original (in the South Caroliniana Library), to which Professor Hubbell did not have access.

wife,[41] he has need of all he can earn in these parlous times. Besides, he is making himself a fine prose writer, & the practice, in a daily newspaper, will improve his energies, without materially disparaging the proprieties & grace of his style. His tendency is to the essayical, but a daily newspaper will modify this. A daily newspaper in a village like Columbia, is far different from that of a great commercial city, & the very limited space accorded by our papers now, lessens the strain upon the mind. The labour is not exhaustive, nor very various. He has only to prepare a couple of dwarf essays, making a single column, and the pleasant public is satisfied. These he does so well, that they have reason to be so. Briefly, our friend is in a fair way to fatten, and be happy, though his muse becomes costive & complains of his *mesalliances*.[42] I met Mr. de Fontaine [43] for the first time. He seems a pleasant & intelligent gentleman & treated me very courteously & kindly. They sent me their paper, & I have tried to pay them in kind. I sent them several little lyrical things which I had on hand, & which you may have seen — one or two of which I thought well of, as the piece called "A dream in Spring" or something like it.[44] I did not meet with Tim's wife, though he gave me an invitation to see her. But the walk was too much for me. I am scarcely good for a mile heat now-a-days — & besides I had not the time. — I am not so sure that the verses in the Mercury, which you ascribe to me, are always mine. Poor Bruns has furnished several — poor fellow — expressive of his sorrows. The piece called "Drift" — a mournful cry out of the sea-wilderness, is his.[45] But I have sent

---

[41] On Feb. 16, 1864, Timrod had married Katie Goodwin, an English girl then living in Columbia with her brother George, who had married Timrod's sister Emily. See Hubbell, *The Last Years of Henry Timrod,* pp. 12, 16-17.

[42] The *Daily South Carolinian* (Columbia) of Jan. 13, 1864, announces the transfer of its ownership and control from Robert Wilson Gibbes to F. G. DeFontaine and Co. and the securing of the services of Timrod as an associate editor.

[43] Felix Gregory de Fontaine, or DeFontaine (1834-1896), born in Boston, the son of an exiled French nobleman, was the proprietor and editor of the *Daily South Carolinian*. He was also the author of *Marginalia; or, Gleanings from an Army Note Book* (Columbia, S. C.: F. G. DeFontaine & Co., 1864), published under the pseudonym of "Personne." Several years after the Confederate War he went to New York City, where he worked for three years on the *Telegram* and for the remainder of his life on the *Herald*.

[44] "The Dream of Spring" (unsigned) was published in the *Daily South Carolinian* of March 30. We are unable to identify as Simms' any other poem published in the newspaper around this time. In the issue for Oct. 13, 1864, he published "The Lions of Mycenae" (signed), and in the issue for Nov. 19, 1864, "The Temple of Ægina" (signed "Adrian Beaufain").

[45] John Dickson Bruns' "Drifting" was published in the Charleston *Mercury* of April 25, the *Tri-Weekly Mercury* of April 26, and the *Daily South Carolinian* of May 6.

sundry to the paper, mostly old compositions. I am trying, in this way, to clear my desks. As a matter of course, some of these are very poor — perhaps flat failures.[46] As for the poem on Stonewall Jackson, it remains in status quo. I am waiting for the *vates* to finish it. I think it fine of conception, & good, thus far, of execution; and it is because I think so well of it, that I await the proper mood for resuming it. It is long, but I have not counted the lines — they are already several hundred, I think.[47] I should not forget to say that recently I finished what I think a very creditable poem, entitled, "Midnight Chaunt in Autumn." It was begun several years ago, and shortly after I had lost two noble boys, in one day, by yellow fever. But *then*, after writing a dozen stanzas, my heart failed me, if not my head, and the M.S. was thrown aside. Happening recently upon it, & under similar circumstances of suffering & season, I finished it. It makes some 80 verses — quatrains. You will like it, I think, though whether it sees the print in a hurry is very questionable.[48] With the plantation upon me, the cares of the family, anxieties without number, tithes & taxes to be provided, and a still heavy burden of correspondence, life seems escaping from me, frittered away in small things and wretched details. Add to this that I have recently had a return of my chill & fever, needing the necessary stimulus to keep it off. Whiskey, or Jamaica, I only get occasionally, and when Rhett [49] is pleased to send me a gallon. I require at least a gill per diem for my proper digestion, tho' half a pint would answer better. — I congratulate you that you are working, & I trust successfully. You have no excuse for not working. But why, good prose writer as you are, do you not contract with Field & Fireside, or some other weekly, & write a series of sketches, essays, short delicate things, like Irvings & Goldsmith's. Your old Editorials might be profitably worked up into Essays for which these periodicals would [pay] you tolerably, and from which you might derive reputation. Adopt some *nom de plume,*

---

[46] The Charleston *Mercury* for this period is filled with poems by Simms, some signed with his name or initials, some signed with his various pseudonyms, and some unsigned.

[47] Two incomplete versions of this poem, both entitled "The Death of Stonewall Jackson," are in MS. in the Charles Carroll Simms Collection, South Caroliniana Library. We have been unable to discover whether it was ever completed or published.

[48] We have been unable to discover whether this poem, inspired by the deaths of Sydney Roach and Beverley Hammond Simms, was published. The MS. is not among Simms' papers in the South Caroliniana Library.

[49] Robert Barnwell Rhett, or perhaps his son Robert Barnwell Rhett, Jr.

& try the experiment.[50] Be sure of this, that our people are not prepared for poetry, & you must beguile them into it through prose. I shall be very glad to *see* your poem [51] when complete, more glad to *hear* it read by yourself. Why not run down & spend a week with me. You ask about feeding in these times. We have no variety, but enough. We can give you pickled beef, and some bacon, hoecake & rye bread, & we are beginning to get asparagus and strawberries, and lettuce. Of course we have corn & peas, some rye flour, &c. but our potatoes are all out. The war will end this year. The papers just arrived report the fighting in Virginia, and our success thus far.[52] I can write no more.

Yours Ever truly

W. Gilmore Simms

1098: To JOHN REUBEN THOMPSON

Woodlands, S. C.
[May 15, 1864][53]

John R. Thompson, Esq.

My dear Thompson.

My son starts for Virginia tomorrow. He is one of Humphrey's Company, Aiken's Regt. of Cavalry, Hampton's Brigade.[54] I have instructed him, if opportunity offers, to present himself to you in Richmond as one of his father's friends. He is just 21, has behaved well in several small actions & is recommended for pro-

---

[50] We have been unable to ascribe to Hayne any of the essays published in the *Southern Field and Fireside* after this date.

[51] Not identified.

[52] The Charleston *Mercury* of May 7 reports an engagement in Spottsylvania County, about twenty miles below Orange Court House, in which "our forces repulsed the enemy handsomely, capturing 981 privates and 40 commissioned officers."

[53] Since Gilmore's orders were to report to Columbia on May 16 to join his company, which was to proceed immediately to Richmond (see note 54, below), Simms' remark that "my son starts for Virginia tomorrow" indicates that this letter was written on May 15.

[54] Gilmore was in Capt. M. B. Humphrey's Company F of Col. Hugh K. Aiken's 6th Regiment of South Carolina Cavalry, which on reporting to Virginia formed part of Gen. Matthew C. Butler's Brigade, a part of Gen. Wade Hampton's Division. Aiken's Regiment left South Carolina for Virginia in two detachments. The first left Columbia on May 5 and arrived in Richmond on May 29; the second, ordered to report to Columbia on May 17, and arrived in Richmond on May 23. (See *O. R.*, 1st Series, XXXV, Part I, 535, and 1st Series, XXXVI, Part III, 852-854.) Since Gilmore was at Woodlands on furlough on May 8, he was in the second detachment.

motion. You will find him amiable & intelligent, though 3 years in the army, has abridged his educational advantages very materially. Your counsel & countenance may serve him materially in your city, and I will thank you, should he find you out, to give him the address of John Esten Cooke, and a note of introduction. If you can give *me* his address, I will write him myself. While my hand is [in], asking kindnesses at yours, let me beg you to see the publishers of the Southern Literary Messenger, and say to them that I think it ungenerous that one, like myself, who has been a regular, & frequently gratuitous contributor for more than 30 years — and who would still occasionally contribute gratuitously — should be suddenly cut off as a dead head. Since the new publishers have come in, I have recieved no copy of the Messenger. If they will send me the last four numbers & continue the work to me, I will send them an occasional poem, with the use of my name.⁵⁵ Hurriedly, but every truly

Yours as ever

W. Gilmore Simms

1099: To Marcus Claudius Marcellus Hammond

[May 15, 1864]⁵⁶

I shall have to pay here, is $3. per bushel. The 4 bushels will weigh 200. I am pl[eased] that the 'Areytos' reached you safely, [and] hope that you will find in its pages many pieces deserving the ears of your damsels. The first difficulty in your reading is want of *clearness*. Poetry is *not* prose, & is to be read as poetry; in other words as thought delivered in music. It is thought, born of Beauty, nursed by Passion and Fancy, suckled on [*one word*

---

⁵⁵ In Dec., 1863, Macfarlane and Fergusson sold the *Southern Literary Messenger* to Wedderburn and Alfriend. Frank A. Alfriend became the editor of the *Messenger* with the Feb., 1864, issue, and edited the magazine through the last issue of June, 1864. The only poem published in the *Messenger* during this time which may be Simms' is "Imitations of Horace," signed "Il Penseroso" (a pseudonym frequently used by Simms), XXXVI (May, 1864), 281. But Simms' remarks about the *Messenger* in this letter lead us to think that "Imitations of Horace" is not his.

⁵⁶ The handwriting of these two fragments, the stationery on which they are written, and Simms' remarks about poetry in each indicate that they form part of the same letter. The year and month are established by Simms' references to his "plough men [having] gone off to work on the fortifications" (see note 57, below) and to having "the fever" (see letter to Magrath of Jan. 9, 1865); the exact date is then determined by his remark that Gilmore "leaves . . . tomorrow" (see letter to Thompson of May 15). We cannot explain why Simms was so late in sending Hammond a copy of *Simms's Poems Areytos*.

WILLIAM GILMORE SIMMS

"I have sung through life, hitherto, as a bird, now with sad & plaintive, now
with gay morning notes; but now I feel that I am losing the wing for flight &
the heart for song."

(From a photograph made probably in 1859 and now in the South Caroliniana Library)

JOHN ESTEN COOKE

"Believe me to thank you most gratefully for the grace & geniality with which you lay your bosom bare to the press of mine!"

(From a wood engraving in Evert Augustus and George Long Duyckinck's *Cyclopædia of American Literature* [1856])

missing] [a]nd Sentiment, and to be produced [*two or three words missing or illegible*], Harmony, Tenderness, [*one or two words missing*] and Animation. But you must read it over slowly, with due earnestness & emphasis, and with a tongue clear as a bell, not thick as a German tongue, or a bottle of [*two or three words missing or illegible*] — Read nightly, and leave off sw[ea]ring & drinking, & smoking, and all other vices. In reading the Drama, you read it as an essay, and not as one delivering himself in an intense dramatic situation — under a passionate & pathetic vision. — Did you recover your horses. Gilmore reached home when I did. Last night he sallied out with a young assistant, rode some 20 miles, till 3 A.M. & succeeded in capturing a des[er]t[er.] He leaves with him tomorrow.

[*End of first fragment.*]

[w]eeks [*almost a line missing*] Confederate Fortifications [*two or three words missing*] if any thing will be left me. [I wan]ted to plant an adequate crop of co[rn, but] my land not being good corn land — n[ow] I have nothing to sell. With 10 bags of [corn] only, I can get no transportation for i[t. I am] offered 1.15 in Charleston, but cannot g[et] mules & people *now,* to haul. One fourth of my plough men gone off to work on the fortifications![57] — Had the fever ever since my return. Make my best regards to Mrs. H. and the girls. Exercise your voice at nights for their amusement & instruction. Revive your own innocent tastes in Poetry, & awaken theirs for the divine art. It is the music of Thought, as all other music is that of the Senses.

Yours Ever truly

W. Gilmore Simms

1100: To Anna Augusta Singleton Simms Roach

Woodlands, June 2. 1864

My dear daughter.

The report is that Mike Carroll and Anna Reynolds, are to be married tonight. I know not how true; but he is here, & the news comes to Claudia in a letter from Julia. It may be true or

---

[57] Simms evidently complained of this impressment of labor in a letter to James H. Hammond which we have not located. Hammond writes in a letter to Simms dated "June 12, 1863 [1864]" (original in the Hammond Papers, Library of Congress): "I sympathise fully, with you in your annoyances, for they are mine. They took 6 of my primest fellows on 4th April for 30 days— kept them over 60—all the time *under fire*—in Sumter & on Sullivans Island."

not.[58] I delivered your money, letter & packages to Julia in person. All are well here. My crop is promising. I wish Edward to select me 25 of his best bags & send them by the first opportunity. The Wheat & Rye are both ripening fast. In another week I shall probably cut, & then the bags will be needed. I wish you would get Edward or William to see what Rye will bring. I shall probably have 25 to 35 bushels to sell. I have been selling here, at $10 per bushel — bushel measure, and see no reason why I should sell at less. We cannot weigh — no scales — & must sell by measure. Let that be understood. I can probably, by waiting, sell here all that I care to sell. If Charles Simons wants any let me know, how much & what he is willing to give.[59] I will not stickle at a trifle in serving him or any farmer on the Neck; but they must pay freight. I deliver at the Midway Depôt. Let Ed. or Wm. make all these things clear to the purchaser beforehand. Gilmore is now in Richmond. If you write him promptly, he will probably recieve your letter before going to the seat of war. He will probably join Lee's army. Think of his forbearing to call on Miles, Orr & Farrow,[60] all my friends, to whom I had written beforehand of his coming — because he had no clothes but those of a trooper. I have had to send him $30 new currency. Government is paying nobody. I went over part of the upland crop this morning. The stand is good but irregular. Prospects fair. Had Mrs. J. Aldrich & all the Patterson girls, & Juby to dine on Monday.[61] That night 3 of the cadets came to supper. Annie Tuper [62] has got back. Is well. Mary Rivers went home Tuesday. Isaac gone today to Barnwell. There, you have my whole budget. Will send you the rye shortly. Love to Ed. & the children. God bless you.

Your affect. father

W. Gilmore Simms.

[58] Georgiana Reynolds, daughter of Dr. William Sims Reynolds, did marry Ephraim Mikell Carroll, son of Bartholomew Rivers Carroll, Jr. (see introductory sketch). We have been unable to discover the exact date of the marriage. Claudia and Julia are Edward Roach's sisters.

[59] Simons is not listed in the Charleston directories for 1860 or for 1866-1867.

[60] James Farrow (1827-1892), a native of Laurens District, S. C., was admitted to the bar in 1848 and began practice in Spartanburg in 1849. During 1856 he was a representative from Spartanburg District of the South Carolina House of Representatives. He was elected to the Confederate States House of Representatives in 1861 and served during 1862-1865.

[61] Isabel Coroneus Patterson Aldrich, wife of James Aldrich (see note 142, May 23, 1859), her sisters Marion (1838-1917) and Julia (1842-1920) and her brother Jabez (1840-1873). Monday was May 30.

[62] Annette Elizabeth Tupper (1849-1929), daughter of Virginia Martha Davis and Samuel Yöer Tupper (see introductory sketch), was an intimate friend of Mary Lawson Simms.

1101: To ANNA AUGUSTA SINGLETON SIMMS ROACH

[*c.* June 20, 1864][63]

My dear daughter.

Gilmore is wounded seriously — but in the hand. I trust that the wound is not such as to endanger the limb. I can write nothing more. If the Jamison girls come on Saturday Mary L. must come with them. She had better be at home now. I have not heard from Gilmore since the 6th. and if seriously wounded, I suppose he will be coming home. Poor fellow. He has had no pay for months, & but for $30 which I sent him, he would have no means to get home.

Your affe father,

W. Gilmore Simms

1102: To JAMES HENRY HAMMOND [64]

Woodlands, 28 July. '64

Hon. J. H. Hammond.

My dear Hammond.

I have just returned from Charleston, whither I went to take my son down to the surgeon and procure him some clothes. On my return, I find a telegram from Jamison, expressing himself with great anxiety lest you should have got into collision with the authorities in respect to the Impressment of your corn.[65] He

---

[63] Dated by Simms' discussion of Gilmore's wound. Gilmore was wounded at the Battle of Trevilians, in Virginia, on June 12, but it was not until Saturday, June 25, that the Charleston *Mercury,* which doubtless got its information from Simms, reported: "We have been deeply pained to learn that this brave and patriotic son of our distinguished author has been severely wounded in one of the recent cavalry fights around Richmond. He left the Citadel Academy, where he was a student, to enter the service, distinguished himself in more than one fight in defence of our city, and was shot down a few days ago while doing his duty nobly. God grant that his life be spared for his own sake, and for the sake of his noble and devoted sire." See also the *Daily South Carolinian* (Columbia) of July 21, 1864.

[64] A considerable number of Simms' letters to Hammond written during 1863 and 1864 are missing from the Hammond Papers, Library of Congress, which contains the originals of letters from Hammond to Simms dated Dec. 30, 1862; Jan. 6, Feb. 19, March 26, April 15, April 28, May 28, Aug. 27, Sept. 13, Sept. 17, Dec. 14, 1863; Feb. 21, April 16, June 12 (misdated 1863), and Aug. 24, 1864.

[65] Impressment had been authorized by the Confederate States Congress on March 26, 1863, and the law had aroused considerable protest in South Carolina. For an account of the effects of this law in South Carolina and of Hammond's clash with and eventual partial acquiescence to the impressment officers, see Cauthen, *South Carolina Goes to War,* pp. 184-187, and Merritt, *James H. Hammond,* p. 144.

wrote from Savannah, where it seems that the report is current,
that you have expressed your purpose to resist the Impressing
officer by force of arms. He is in so much earnest on this subject
that he has naturally impressed me with it, and I write (though
I trust unnecessarily) to exhort you to a patient submission to
the extortion & injustice which we may expect, & which we cannot easily escape. You are such a marked man, and, without any
miserable flattery, so far preeminent over all your fellows, that
every defiance in your case, of the authorities — every denial of
help to the cause, however justifiable as a private right, will be
made to show enormously odious. This odiousness you might
well brave & despise on your own account. You have little to ask
& perhaps quite as little to fear. But the worst is the mischief will
not fall upon your shoulders only, but will be entailed through
life & for generations to come upon your progeny. Your children will be made to feel the odium in all the relations of Life.
Your sons will be cut off from all the distinctions — nay, from
all the associations of society, and this will not be confined to
South Carolina, or the little precinct in which you live. It will
pass into history, & be made the topic of debate among all that
class of persons who grovel at the base of eminence, seeking its
overthrow by sap — men who

"Distort the truth, accumulate the lie,
And pile the pyramid of Calumny." [66]

For the sake of your children & grandchildren, you must not
incur this danger, or give occasion for this sort of malignity to
work. Nor (however little you may value life) must you incur
the risk of losing yours, in a miserable brawl. Better lose the
money. It is lucky that you can afford to lose it, better than anyone I know. Yield gracefully & loftily. No one better knows
how to do this than yourself. And believe me, dear H., I speak
from my heart to you. I have never, I believe, counseled you in
any way inconsistently with your dignity & honour. I think that
I do not now. Refer my letter to your wife. Take the woman's
counsel with that of your friend. I look upon your wife as a rarely
good woman, & a rarely *good* woman is perhaps far wiser in
such a case, than a rarely endowed man. Were you as rarely
good as you are rarely endowed, you would be one of the most
perfect men living. It is your passions, your impetuous & too
frequently stubborn will, that neutralizes some of your noblest
gifts. Forgive me for saying so now, but I have always thought

---

[66] Not identified.

this, & a thousand times said it to yourself. Believe me that this is one of the very cases where I would have you sacrifice your passions along with your interests, to that humbler wisdom which God employs for chastening the one, and keeping the other from getting wholly the better of heart and head. No man knows more thoroughly than myself, the crimes, blunders, indecencies & robberies, of the incompetent, dishonest, and cruelly corrupt character of thousands of the creatures employed in this war, as agents of those in power. But their crimes & blunders must not be suffered to disparage the labour & character of the army, and we must be content to sacrifice interest, even to the spoiler, & to waive a natural & just indignation & resentment, in regard to the safety of paramount interests, which our defiance might endanger. And it is a wise selfishness which makes us fear that unjust odium, entailed upon our children, which we have not deserved ourselves, but from which, in a struggle with the blind passions & prejudices of the multitude, we may not be able to relieve ourselves. Pray, my dear H. take all these things to heart. Let your friend, as I may fearlessly claim to be, prevail with you. Let your wife decide, for once, in a matter, which, while it is business, becomes a question of selfish policy in which she is deeply interested for her children & grandchildren. — I will try & run up to see you next month.[67] It is possible that my son may anticipate my visit, & bring one of his sisters on a week's visit to Mrs. H. — that is, if you are not already crowded. My son is doing well; and I too am improving. God preserve you all & keep you wise.

Yours Ever truly

W. Gilmore Simms.

---

[67] Evidently Simms did not make this trip, since Hammond's letter of Aug. 24, an answer to this letter, would not have been necessary if Simms in the meantime had visited him.

1103: To Paul Hamilton Hayne [68]

[*c.* August 1, 1864] [69]

My dear Paul.

Bruns told me of your poem,[70] and reports it as the finest thing you have done. Finish and publish. Publish as fast as you finish, if the thing be possible, and begin again *de novo*. As for the trifle that Bruns told you of, as mine, it is a mere nothing — a Ballad of the mystic school, which I sold for $50. When it appears in print, if I have an extra copy, I will send you one, provided it shall read then to my liking.[71] Jamison's book is simply a narrative. He was fettered by the Chroniclers, and being an unimaginative man, he *acknowledged* his fetters.[72] But you are to take it as a narrative merely. It is for you to work out poetry from it; — and I do not know but that you may extract a fine story from it some of these days.

You mention Davidson. Who is Davidson? I see that he has settled your case & mine to his own satisfaction, & with no small complacency. But — who is Davidson? Is he in the wars? Is he not one of Caldwell's Clique, with Overall, who killed me off & made Butcher's meat of me several years ago?[73] Ah! — Where's

---

[68] This letter is printed, with minor inaccuracies, in Hubbell, *The Last Years of Henry Timrod,* pp. 25-28.

[69] The year is established by Simms' references to Gilmore's wound (see preceding letters) and to Davidson's articles (see note 73, below). It was certainly written after the publication of at least the first part of Davidson's article on Simms and after Simms' return from Charleston on July 28 (see his remark in this letter about Bruns and see letter to Hammond of July 28). His remarks about trips to Columbia and Charleston in this letter and in his letter to Hayne of Aug. 20 indicate that this letter was probably written around Aug. 1.

[70] Not identified.

[71] "Isadore" (see letter to Hayne of Aug. 20) was not published in any of the Confederate periodicals we have examined; it was perhaps published in the *Illustrated Mercury* (see note 73, below) of Aug. 13, which we have not seen. "Isadore" was later published as "The Ballad of Isadore" in the *New York Mercury* (see note 10, Jan. 8, 1866).

[72] David Flavel Jamison's *The Life and Times of Bertrand du Guesclin: A History of the Fourteenth Century,* 2 vols. (Charleston: John Russell, 1864), dedicated to Simms, is reviewed (probably by Simms) in the Charleston *Mercury* of June 25.

[73] James Wood Davidson (1829-1908), a native of Newberry District, S. C., was a contributor to various periodicals, the author of several books, and after the Confederate War a member of the editorial staff of the New York *Evening Post*. At this time he was writing for the *Illustrated Mercury* (Raleigh, N. C.), a weekly edited and published by William B. Smith. We have had access to only a few issues of the *Illustrated Mercury,* among them those for July 30 and Aug. 6, 1864, which contain the second and third parts of Davidson's article on Simms, which forms part of a series entitled "Litterateurs of the South." Presumably the first part of this article was published in the *Illustrated*

Caldwell & Overall, *et id omne genus*? All I can say for myself, is simply that I have not written for these people, & that in publishing I simply put myself on record. If there be good in what I have done, 'the world will find it after certain days.' The very periodicals in which these men scribble are all the time dying, and they die with them. What can we think of writers who live only by what they abuse. They make no record. They simply plead to a small mean passion in their own bosoms. And, if they find response any where, it is only in bosoms like their own. My writings are not to be estimated by things of a clique or of a day. Get what you can out of these weeklies, make them pay you in money for all you write, and whenever they permit you to be abused in their columns, double your prices. For every thing I furnish to this paper hereafter, I shall charge just double. Do you the same.[74] *But, keep your secret. Do not blab!* This letter is especially private. Do not correspond familiarly with any man who blabs. — When are you coming to see me? You can get a passport now. On Friday [75] I visit Columbia on business. I hope to see Timrod. He has paid me a visit, and is improved. He seemed to spend the time here pleasantly enough. I still have some hoecake & bacon, and expect to be again at home on Tuesday of next week. And hope to have a supply of the famous Barnwell Eau de vie. My son is with me, & his wound in the hand is rapidly healing. He has lost one finger. His other wounds were deadlily aimed, but narrowly missed being fatal. If you come, bring your poem with you.

Yours Ever Truly

W. Gilmore Simms

Mercury of July 23. None of the issues to which we have had access contains Davidson's article on Hayne, certainly part of the same series and probably published in the *Illustrated Mercury* of July 16.

For Howard Hayne Caldwell's and John Wilson Overall's attacks on Simms in 1859, see note 6, Jan. 18, 1860.

[74] The *Illustrated Mercury* of Aug. 27, 1864, lists Simms as a regular contributor. A signed poem entitled "Flown" was published in the issue for Oct. 22, 1864. Doubtless Simms published other poems and possibly articles or short stories in issues which we have not seen.

[75] Aug. 5?

1104: To Paul Hamilton Hayne

Woodlands, Aug. 20. [1864][76]

My dear Paul.

I have just got back from a visit to the city after 4 or 5 days absence, & really forget whether I answered your last letter or not. My impression is that I did, & somewhat at length. But should it not be so advise me. I saw John Bruns, busy yet bright as usual. Nothing stirring. Some cases of Yellow fever in the city, & Small Pock also reported. The Poem of 'Isadore' by the way is atrociously full of typographical errors. The recurring rhymes of which you speak, were *purposely* introduced, with the view to certain *weird* effects. Of course, I know the objection to such *recurrences* on ordinary occasions. When you can come down do so, & bring your Poem. All well here. I trust that all are so with you.

In haste, but truly

W. Gilmore Simms

1105: To Paul Hamilton Hayne [77]

Woodlands, 19 Sep. 1864.

My dear Paul.

A very hurried letter must suffice, & answer all the leading matters in yours. I am tired down, worn out & sickish. Have just returned from a week of toil in Columbia & at Orangeburg, whither I went, following to the grave the last remains of my poor & long tried friend Jamison. He died of Yellow fever in Charleston, in a few hours, a most insidious & malignant case.[78] The disease is all over Charleston, and is generally fatal. Your mother's house [79] is within range of the enemy's cannon. Their shot reach beyond John & Vanderhorst Streets to St. Philips, & on a lower line, even to my old residence in Smith St. It is probable that the city will be attacked by Farragut, by the 5th. Oct. He will run the Batteries, may have half of his vessels sunk,

---

[76] Dated by Simms' references to his own "Isadore" and to Hayne's unidentified poem. See letter to Hayne of *c.* Aug. 1.

[77] This letter is summarized by Trent, p. 279, who misdates it Sept. 17.

[78] Jamison died in Charleston on Sept. 14 and was buried in Orangeburg (see the Charleston *Mercury* of Sept. 15). An unsigned sketch of Jamison published in the *Mercury* of Dec. 8, 1864, is probably by Simms.

[79] The Charleston *Directory* for 1860 gives Mrs. Hayne's address as 8 Alexander Street.

but with the rest, he will bombard the city *from the inner harbour.* His shot will then traverse the whole city — will sweep through whole blocks as if through so much pasteboard.[80] You cannot look to a return to Charleston. Make other arrangements. The middle country, will be more secure. Aim at the Camden & Sumter precincts. The fall of Atlanta is nothing *per se.* But it is much that our armies should be confided to Generals who, however meritorious as fighters, are capable of very little generalship. Hood has been miserably outgeneralled by Sherman. Unless Johnson is sent back, or Lee or Beauregard takes command of the army in Georgia, the enemy will penetrate to Macon, Augusta, Andersonville, &c.[81] The militia of Geo. could not be brought to a charge. There had been no previous drill or discipline of Gov. Brown's [82] 15,000 pet exempts, & they were found wanting at the crisis. To use the old English expression, coarse but significant, they hung an a——e at the last moment, and so will it be with our reserves, unless Bonham sends them into camp at once. The crisis of the interior will be upon us in 3 months, that of the seaboard most probably in 3 weeks. At this moment, Wilmington is menaced by a concurrent attack by land & sea. Beauregard is there in command. It is probable that a simultaneous attempt will be made on Charleston. All can be saved, if the exempts, detailed men & skulks can be brought promptly into the field, & subjected to timely discipline.[83] Otherwise, we shall die by inches like the tail of a snake. Imbecility in office, civil & military, is tolling on the young life of our country, our youth, to unproductive peril & sure destruction. We are made daily to sup on horrors. The war will probably be of continued duration till both parties are exhausted, — unless God shall more emphatically interpose —

---

[80] Rear Admiral John Adolphus Bernard Dahlgren (1809-1870) was in command of the South Atlantic Blockading Squadron. He was not reinforced by Rear Admiral David Glasgow Farragut (1801-1870), who was chosen to command the naval forces that were to be employed in the reduction of the defenses of Wilmington, N. C., but was relieved from the assignment because of ill health.

[81] On July 17, 1864, Gen. Joseph Eggleston Johnston (1807-1891), in command of the Army of Tennessee, was replaced by Gen. John Bell Hood (1831-1879). Hood was incapable of stopping the advance of Gen. William Tecumseh Sherman (1820-1891), and on the night of Sept. 1 he evacuated Atlanta. Sherman's army marched out of Atlanta on Nov. 15 and on Dec. 21 occupied Savannah.

[82] Joseph Emerson Brown (1821-1894), a native of South Carolina, was governor of Georgia during 1855-1865.

[83] Charleston was occupied on Feb. 18 and Wilmington on Feb. 22, 1865.

how he may, or will do so — we may conjecture, but none can predict. Put your house in order. God be merciful to you.

Yours Ever truly

W. Gilmore Simms.

1106: To Marcus Claudius Marcellus Hammond [84]

Satu[rday]
[October, 1864] [85]

[Dear Major]

[*Several words missing*] with [*several words missing or illegible*] $1000 duly recieved [*several words missing or illegible*] $100 at once paid [for t]he freight of 5 Bales of [cotton fr]om Midway to Granitevill[e. I had] the pleasure of meeting H[arry] and Spann on the cars at Midway and took the liberty of broaching to the latter the idea you entertained of his taking the F. & F. & thus securing himself exemption from the duties of the field. I told him that even if he lost a few thousands by it, it would probably save him from a broken constitution. He seemed to incline to the idea. Should he do any thing, or you, I refer you to previous counsels & suggestions. One matter. When I spoke of subscribers (good) being each worth $1, I referred to *old* currency, that being the amt. paid, in old times, to collectors, for each subscriber brought in. Briefly, 5 times as much in the *present* currency, would be as smal[l as you can offer. But] the object — the [real object — is] Spann's exemption. [If the true o]bject were suspected [by the propr]ietors of the F. & F. they [might ex]tort. It would be well [for you to] agree to make the pro[position th]at you should negotiate, [writ]ing in your own character, & seemingly with reference to Randall. Spann should neither be seen nor heard of in the business. If you could get a good practical printer to take an interest in the work, so much the better. [86] If possible, I will run up & see you in a week or two.

---

[84] The MS. of this letter is in bad condition, torn, water-stained, and frayed at the edges.

[85] Dated by Simms' remarks about the *Southern Field and Fireside* and McClellan's nomination for president of the United States (see notes 86 and 87, below).

[86] In the issue of Oct. 1 Stockton and Company offers the *Southern Field and Fireside* for sale. The issue of Oct. 29 announces that William B. Smith has purchased it and that it is to be combined with the *Illustrated Mercury* (Raleigh). See note 112, April 15, 1859.

At present, very busy getting in the crop, — and that a poor one. It is possible that I shall make corn enough to do me, & — no more. Even that is very doubtful. I am nearly starved out. My bacon is at its last gasp & gash. What with thieves & Cholera, I shall hardly have more than ½ doz Hogs to [slaughter this year.] We are now [going to be releg]ated to syrup & [corn-bread, and a]nother year will [bring a] taste of Famine. I tru[st that you a]re right in your calcu[lations of the t]rend of the war prospect. [May Go]d help us. Man does l[ittle] but rob us. The Govt. & its agent[s] show themselves decidedly hostile to the farmer & planter. It is slavery that they strike at. I suppose that McClellan means to lie after the fashion of Party, in his Letter of acceptance. His party seems to understand it so. Lincoln's defeat is fatal to the Abolition Party proper; and the character of the future administration will depend on the temper of the people at large. Our calculations are more safe when we base our hopes on the Western, than on the Eastern States.[87]

Ever truly Yours

W. Gilmore Simms

1107: To William Gilmore Simms, Jr.

Woodlands. 8 Nov. 1864.

My dear Son.

I have just recieved from Evans & Cogswell,[88] a present of books of their publication. Among them are the following: viz: 1 & 2 General Orders from Adj. & Insp. Genls Office, C.S.A. 3 Marshal Marmonts "Spirit of Military Institutions.["] 4 Casey's Infantry Tactics, Vol 3. 5 Nolan's Cavalry; its History & Tactics.

---

[87] At the National Democratic Convention in Chicago during Aug. 29-31, 1864, Gen. McClellan was nominated for president. He was informed of the nomination on Sept. 8 and in his letter of acceptance he repudiated the Party's platform, which called for the "cessation of hostilities, with a view to an ultimate convention of the States, or other peaceable means, to the end that at the earliest practicable moment peace may be restored on the basis of the Federal Union of the States." See John G. Nicolay and John Hay, *Abraham Lincoln a History* (New York: The Century Company, 1904), IX, 253-261.

[88] The firm of Evans and Cogswell (B. F. Evans and Harvey Cogswell), Columbia, was formerly the firm of Walker (J. C. Walker), Evans and Cogswell, Charleston. The firm removed from Charleston to Columbia either in 1863 or in 1864 (see note 89, below).

6 Mahan's Course of Permanent Fortification, & of the attack & defence of Permanent Works.

7 A digest of the Military & Naval Laws of the C. S.

8 Gilchrist's "Duties of a Judge Advocate on Court Marshal["]

9 Andrew's Mounted Artillery Drill.[89]

Several of these volumes may be equally interesting & useful to you, and should you think it so, send me a list of such as you may desire. I should suppose that the books of Marmont, Andrews, & Mahan would be useful. On Friday, the 11th. I expect Dr. Bruns & shall send your shoes & some books by him. Should your reply reach me in time, I would include any of these that you require. Nothing new here. All well. No further tidings from Gen. Hammond.[90] On the 28th. (D. V.) I am to be in Columbia.[91] God bless & preserve you.

Your affect. father

W. Gilmore Simms

1108: To William Gilmore Simms, Jr. [92]

Woodlands, Monday MG.
Nov. 14. 1864

My dear Son.

Dr. Bruns goes down tomorrow, and will carry your trunk, with whatever articles we can get together for your uses & in reply to your requisitions. There will be a quilt, a mirror, a pair of shoes and a variety of books. I have ordered search for a

---

[89] We have not been able to locate a copy of Evans and Cogswell's edition of *A Digest of the Military and Naval Laws of the Confederate States.* Copies of the other books here listed are in the South Caroliniana Library. Those dated 1864 give Columbia as the place of publication; those dated earlier give Charleston. The authors, titles, and dates of publication are as follows: *General Orders from Adjutant and Inspector-General's Office, Confederate States Army, in 1862* . . . (1863); *General Orders from Adjutant and Inspector-General's Office, Confederate States Army, from January, 1862, to December, 1863* . . . (1864); Auguste Frédéric Louis Viesse de Marmont, Duc de Raguse, *The Spirit of Military Institutions* . . . (1864); Silas Casey, *Infantry Tactics* . . . (1864); Lewis Edward Nolan, *Cavalry* . . . (1864); Dennis Hart Mahan, *Summary of the Course of Permanent Fortifications and of the Attack and Defence of Permanent Works* . . . (1862); Robert Cogdell Gilchrist, *The Duties of a Judge Advocate* . . . (1864); and Richard Snowden Andrews, *Andrews' Mounted Artillery Drill* . . . (1863).

[90] James H. Hammond died on Nov. 13.

[91] To attend the meeting of the Board of Visitors of the Arsenal and Citadel academies. See letter to Hayne of Nov. 21.

[92] Gilmore had recently been commissioned 2nd lieutenant in Col. Alfred Rhett's 1st South Carolina Artillery. This letter is addressed to him at Battery Marion, Sullivan's Island.

small shallow tub or cooler, and if there be one it shall be sent you. If not, I will have one made for you by Old Jim.[93] But I sent you a tub, in your box, designed for this very purpose, and I really do not see to what other use it can be put. It was filled with potatoes at the bottom of your box, & possibly you have not discovered it. The shoes are very good ones. — I have just learned that there is no tub sufficiently small to be got into your trunk. In desiring to know what money you would need, my purpose was to supply *all* your deficiencies of uniform, and to prevent the necessity of your getting any thing on credit. If you have enough, I am satisfied. Do not stint yourself in respect to any necessary purchases for yourself, by any regard to the girls. I will provide them. My purpose in writing to you, in lessons of economy, were to prevent you from wasting money, or your pay, when you happen to have it. Neither you nor I can afford to be guilty of waste or luxury, having all these children to provide for, and having to provide against the contingencies of an obscure & very uncertain future. In the diseased unrest of your mind, your desultory & purposeless mode of life, it is easy to expend money in the attainment of the means of temporary excitement. It will need that you should exert all your will & moral force, to subject your mind to patience, so that you may reach a wholesome condition of the blood, — calming yourself to methodical & regular movements, & so toning down your moods, as to get rid of that feverish impatience of the staid & prosaic, which your present & recent mode of life has naturally engendered. It is a great misfortune to find yourself forever in a hurry — forever seeking change — and feeling as irksome, the restraints of place or duty. Think how monotonous will be any mode of life to you, after the war is over — unless you can now gradually subdue yourself to some method in your daily walks, & to a patient dogged determination, to do the work before you, and this done, fold your hands quietly for such meditations as should naturally occur to one in your situation, having a future purpose of self-development, and cogitating upon its plans. It was painful to me to witness in you, the irritable & feverish restlessness which marked all your movements while here — the impatience of the uniform — the fidgetting & nervous desire for change of scene, place & action — all of which, if indulged, must lead to a frivolous

---

[93] Jim Rumph, Sr., one of Simms' slaves (see introductory sketch of the Negroes at Woodlands). According to his tombstone at Woodlands, he died in 1922 at the age of 112.

future — unsettled, unmethodical, without aim or purpose, beyond the mercurial impulse of the moment. Of course this habit has been engendered by the life you have been leading; but you must not let yourself be mastered by such a life, or your whole future will be lost. To concentrate your thoughts, aims & powers — all your faculties — should be your paramount effort now, in order to neutralize, as far as you can, the exhausting influences of your situation — its levities, momentary impulses, — vague consideration of all objects, & the fruitless expenditure in air of all your faculties. It is for yourself to do this. I can only counsel. I see the ill effects (for the future) of your present life, and I deplore them. Bring your own will to bear. Address yourself only to duty. Study thoroughly all that belongs to the military tasks in which you are engaged, and make yourself a master, — not a mere drudge. Allow nothing to divert you from these studies, except at infrequent intervals, & when a consideration of mental & physical health shall require relief and amusement. Do not address yourself to cock fighting or raising chickens. It does not become manhood — a resolute will — a gentlemanly purpose. Begin to be an earnest man — earnest of aim, — concentrative of effort — your eye fixed on your purpose, and all your powers concentrated in the one direction for its attainment. When you write, write on both sides of your paper, & send a half sheet rather [than] a whole sheet but half written, and when you send off two letters on the same day, one to me and another to the girls, put in one envelope. We judge of great things by small. — Paper is 25/100 per sheet. Each letter postage is 10/100. Why — when we have so little money, waste 100 per cent, on every letter that you write. If you do not economize your resources you will not economize your powers. In wasting the one you betray characteristics which will make you waste the other. And see to your pay. Take the proper steps. Write & act promptly; and when you recieve your pay, get E. R.[94] to keep the bulk of it for you. If you keep it in camp, with your disposition, you will never keep it long. I wish none of it, nor for the present will your sisters need it. Nor is it for the sake of the money that I would have you economize; but because in the waste of money it becomes the melancholy agency for the dissipation of your best mental & moral qualities. The dissipation of money is a process, for the dissipation of time, & thought &

---

[94] Edward Roach.

performance. Dr. Bruns will take the trunk to his quarters which are in Rutledge Street, & within fifty yds. of the House of Ro. Fishburne to which your sister will remove, if not already removed.[95] You must apply for it there; though, if not applied for, he will send it over to Augusta as soon as she does remove. He lives with the mess of Mr. Chisolm & Dr. Huger,[96] nearly opposite to the residence of the Misses Rose, which is, I beli[eve,] [97] one or two doors off from Fishburne's house, on the same square & street.[98] We have nothing new to report. Gen. Hammond still lies dangerously ill, & with some very bad symptoms. I very much fear that he will never recover. The Pattersons, Jamisons, Bruns & Fuller had a deer hunt & killed a buck in our swamp. We shall dine on it today. We shall have the Jamisons, F. Carroll, & Fuller, to play whist & take supper with us tonight. I would you were here, but pray that you be well & happy where you are. God bless you.

W. Gilmore Simms.

1109: To Edward Spann Hammond

Woodlands, Nov. 20, 1864

My dear Spann.

Language fails me in any effort to embody my feelings in words. I will not speak of my loss, in comparison with that of your mother — you — all of you.[99] Yet your father was my most confidential friend for near twenty five years. Never were thoughts more intimate than his & mine. We had few or no secrets from each other — we took few steps in life without mutual consultation. We had, — I am sure I had — perfect confidence in him. I believe he had in me. I felt that there was something kindred in our intellectual nature. Certainly, there was

---

[95] We have not located a Charleston *Directory* for 1864. The directories for 1860 and 1866-1867 do not list Robert Fishburne (1842-1883), captain of the Palmetto Guards during the Confederate War. The cover of Simms' letter to Augusta of Jan. 13, 1865, gives her address as "Calhoun & Rutledge Strts."

[96] Dr. William Harleston Huger (b. 1826), a prominent Charleston physician, entered the Confederate States Army as a surgeon, but during most of the time he was in the service he was in charge of "Soldiers Relief" in Charleston. We are unable to identify Chisolm among the many men by that name living in Charleston in the 1860's.

[97] The MS. is torn.

[98] The *Directory* for 1860 lists a Miss M. L. Rose on Rutledge Street, as well as a number of men with the same surname, also living on Rutledge Street.

[99] James H. Hammond died on Nov. 13.

much, very much, in common between us. Never did man more
thoroughly appreciate his genius — its grasp — its subtlety — its
superiority of aim. And most deeply did I sympathize with him,
under that denial of his aim, and the exercise of his powers, —
which, permitted, I verily believe he would have lived to a mature
old age — lived for far higher triumphs even than those which
he achieved. But the will of God be done. His faith & mine,
recognized the future as compensative — regarded immortal life,
as enabling us to develope fully those immortal endowments to
which this mean under world denied opportunity & occasion.
So let us all hope, for our own sakes, not less than his. — I
would have liked much to have been with him in his last days
— not his last hours — for I could not well have borne to witness his loss of consciousness — to behold that intellect wandering, which so often spelled my own — to hear meanin[g]less [100]
words from lips that were ever so governed by the magnetic
mind. I should have been with him, and purposed to do so —
made an engagement with Gregg, and even wrote of my coming
to your father; but a letter from Gregg advised me that he
could no longer see his friends. From the first intimation of his
case, I feared the worst. This day, I feel doubly alone. I have
seen committed to the grave, year after year, children, wife &
friends. The fiery circle of Fate is drawing rapidly around me.
We shall meet before many days, and, I trust in God, that we
shall meet not only for the renewal of old ties, but for the
exercise of those faculties, in which I felt proudly that we were
kindred. Preserve all his papers. I hope some day to render a
proper tribute to his memory. We have no chance for this now.
There is no organ. There are no means. Do not suffer his
revised publications to be mislaid. Have them carefully preserved,
compactly put up & sealed against mischance. With God's blessing, I hope to put on record my appreciation of his claims and
to illustrate them by his works. And I propose, if possible, some
time this winter to visit you, when your minds & my own heart,
are more reconciled to this dispensation. I trust that your fears
in respect to your mother are ill founded. She is too strong
a woman, too pure & pious a Christian, to forget that she has
now double duties to perform — Children & Grandchildren to
watch & to rear, to admonish, counsel & console. Besides, she
has no reproach upon her conscience. Never have I known a

---

[100] The MS. is torn.

woman more tenderly & thoroughly devoted to her husband. She has consecrated her whole life to his — to his need, his want, his very existence, with all a woman's tenderness & a wife's love. Let her turn to the All Consoler, & she will be strengthened. Her own soul at peace, from the conviction of cares nobly borne, and duties piously done, it only needs that she should cast herself upon God, to be rendered strong for the duties which lie before her. I fear nothing for her. If ever woman was nobly strengthened during life for her mission, and duly sensible of it, & rigidly observant of all its requisitions, your mother is that woman. And shall she falter now. I hope not, and believe not. — But I write with painful effort. I have been too much staggered by recent events fully to command the resources of my mind. I cannot *will* myself to thought. I can only fold hands, & wonder, and perhaps pray. What awaits us in the future, is perhaps foreshown to us by our Past, of trial and loss and suffering. Or it may be that God designs that we should surrender in sacrifice our choicest possessions, that we may become worthy of the great boon of future Independence. Yet while I write, and hope, and pray, the day grows more clouded. I trembled & had sore misgivings when Johnson [101] was removed from the army, & Hood put in his place. I predicted evil then to your father & to others. He concurred with me. And when Hood removed from Sherman's front, I then declared my opinion that if Sherman had the requisite audacity — it did not need Genius, — he would achieve the greatest of his successes, by turning his back on the enemy in his rear, & march boldly forward towards the Atlantic coast. I fear that such is his purpose. If so, — what have we to oppose him? I dare not look upon the prospect before us. It may become necessary for you, for me, & all to prepare as we can, for the overrunning of Carolina! All's very dark; — doubtful, perhaps; but the probabilities are as I relate. Commend me with affectionate sympathy to your mother, and God be with your household in mercy.

Your father's friend & your own.

W. Gilmore Simms.

---

[101] Gen. Joseph Eggleston Johnston.

1110: To Paul Hamilton Hayne

Woodlands, 21 Nov. [1864] [102]

My dear Paul.

I have not heard from you for a long time, & but for Bruns
would scarcely have heard of you. He tells me that you design
to spend the winter with Pickens.[103] If so, it will be easy to pay
me a visit sometime during the winter, — i.e. if Sherman does
not smoke us out of our domain. While with Pickens get him to
report to you his reminiscences of the remarkable men whom
he has met, at home and abroad. He is full of interesting anecdotes
which will not only afford you pleasure to hear, but afford you
materiel for future use. Bruns tells me that your last poem [104]
is the best that you have done. Whenever you visit me, be sure
to bring it along with you. I am busy getting in my crop, which
is, as usual, a very sorry one. Another year of war will deprive
the Planters of the power to produce any thing. I have lost 2
Horses & 2 Mules in a year, & cannot replace them; and all our
agricultural implements are worn out! In Literature, I do little if
any thing. A few short poems are all that I have done for 18
months. Did you see a thing of mine in the Field & Fireside
called "The Old Man's Reverie," — & another in the Carolinian
called the "Lions of Mycenæ" — full of misprints.[105] These and
a dozen others, unpublished, make up the sum of my labours at
the desk. On Monday next,[106] I go (D. V.) to Columbia, as one
of the Board of Visitors of the Military Academies.[107] I should
like to meet you there. When do you propose to leave Greenville?
There is no fear now in visiting any part of our country except
the city. We have had ice several times. In the city Yellow
fever still lingers; and it is expected that the Yankees will shortly
subject us there to a new trial of strength. My son is now a Lt.
in Rhetts Artillery on Sullivan's island. I have no news, & write

---

[102] Dated by Simms' reference to Gilmore's appointment as 2nd lieutenant in
Rhett's Regiment. See letter to Gilmore of Nov. 14.

[103] Francis Wilkinson Pickens, at Edgewood, his estate near Edgefield, S. C.

[104] Not identified.

[105] "The Old Man's Reverie," *Southern Field and Fireside*, N. S., II (July
23, 1864), 6-7, and "The Lions of Mycenae," *Daily South Carolinian*, Oct. 13,
1864.

[106] Nov. 28.

[107] Simms succeeded David Flavel Jamison as a member of the Board of
Visitors of the Arsenal and Citadel academies.

rather with the view of showing you that I am still in existence, & that I remember you, than with the hope to interest you.

God be with you in mercy.
Yours Ever

W. Gilmore Simms.

1111: To Edward Roach

[November? 1864] [108]

My dear Edward.

Of the above Draft, four Hundred & Twenty four ($424) belongs to your wife, and I suppose you understand from her what is to be done with it. The remaining $100. I send to be put to the credit of Gilmore. He wants an overcoat or cloak. He says it will cost about $60 or $75. I wish you to get it for him after communicating with him. He is now (I suppose) at Fort Sumter. I enclose a note for him which I beg that you will send as soon as possible. I suppose that boats go to Sumter nightly. Write to him yourself, get his instructions — procure the coat, & forward him by safe hands. But let him advise you how all this is to be done. All well here. Your wife & children arrived safely.

Your affect. father

[*Signature cut.*]

1112: To William Gilmore Simms, Jr.

Woodlands, 27 Decr. '64

My dear Son.

I had already anticipated the purport of your last letter. I have made arrangements to remove the children (D. V.) to Columbia, on Friday next.[109] I have commenced shelling corn &c. in order to forward after them the necessary subsistence *for one year*. I am now packing up M.S. &c. & tomorrow, Albert & Sam [110] set to work making boxes for my books. The question

---

[108] Since this letter is written on the same kind of paper (some sort of receipt forms) as Simms' letters written to Gilmore during Nov., 1864–Jan., 1865, it seems likely that it was written between those dates. His reference to Augusta and her children (Chevillette and Simms) implies a date prior to Dec. 30, when Simms planned to send his family to Columbia.

[109] Dec. 30.

[110] Two of Simms' slaves.

is whether I shall be able to get them off after they are boxed. To wagon the books is impossible. I may have to wagon the provisions to Columbia, and this will be a serious job considering the smallness of my force in mules, & the badness of the roads in winter. Still, it must be done. I have determined to hire out half a dozen of my fellows to the R. Road, as affording me money for current expenses, & lessening the drain upon my crop. I propose to see the girls safely in Columbia, deposit them, my money & M.S.S., then return to the plantation, & urge forward the rest of my preparations with all possible speed. The probability is that Sherman will leave us very little time for loitering. At present he is hardly able to move, & will not untill largely reinforced from the army of Grant. I have no doubt that corps of this army are already *en route* to join him,[111] & think that the probabilities are that Lee & Grant will both measure their strength, in a winter campaign on the plains of S. C. or Georgia or both. Neither will go into winter quarters in Virginia when such great work is opened to them in the South. The progress of Sherman, & the disaster of Hood, all justify the course of Johnson,[112] & show the equal criminality & stupidity of the Government which removed him. I predicted these consequences in the moment of his removal. To remove a General in the fullest confidence of his army, was a great blunder; to send Hood to Tennessee, flanking Sherman, & cutting him from his base, without previously putting 20,000 men in readiness & reserve betwixt him & the coast, was to *compel* his movement on Savannah. In shutting the one door on him, we left open the other. This has brought the war to our doors. [*Remainder of letter missing.*]

---

[111] Gen. Ulysses S. Grant did not reinforce Gen. Sherman.
[112] Gen. Joseph Eggleston Johnston.

1865

1113: To Andrew Gordon Magrath

Woodlands, Jany 9. 1865.

His Excellency
Governor Magrath.[1]

My dear Governor.

After writing you a long epistle a few days ago, I had not
thought so soon to trespass upon your time and good nature,
especially as at this juncture you can have but little leisure
for any asides from your important public duties. But a selfish
necessity, of a kind most serious to myself, makes me obtrusive,
if it does not justify the trespass, and I write frankly to ask
of you whether you do not regard me as a proper subject of
exemption from military duties. For twenty years, I have been
held to be exempt, in consequence of ext[reme][2] physical dis-
abilities; and when I state the facts in my case, I trust that
you will percieve the propriety of my continued exemption. At
59 years of age, and entering my 60th. I am yet aware that
your call holds me in the class required for service, and no
doubt that a large proportion of this class will still be found
able to endure the fatigues of the service.[3] But not only has a
sedentary life at the desk, for more than 40 years, deprived me
of the usual degree of physical vigour; but this infirmity has been
still more increased by ailments which are now chronic. For 30
years I have suffered from hemorrhoids which were duly &
greatly increased under circumstances of fatigue, exposure and
excitement. Even now, when I have little blood for waste, cold,
exposure fatigue, uneasiness, or unusual excitements, occasion
copious discharges of blood, which leave me for a time utterly

---

[1] Magrath was elected governor of South Carolina on Dec. 13, 1864.

[2] The MS. is torn.

[3] The Charleston *Courier* of Jan. 12 carries Magrath's special order: "The
Legislature of South Carolina has declared that all free white men between
the ages of sixteen and sixty shall be liable to military service. . . . All will
come forth; all must come forth."

exhausted. In addition to this, I have suffered for more than 10 years, from an enlargement of the left testicle, occasioned by some hurt on horseback, I believe, which, if I walk or ride, becomes increased in size, & subjects me to great pain. Hence, for many years, I have not ridden on horseback, — have not walked, except when in the cities, and then only for short distances at a time, and find my locomotion only in car, carriage or buggy. Though, for the last year, the overseer of my own plantation, I have not once been able to visit the remoter fields. A week of walking, drilling, campaigning or camp life, would I am sure, shorten a life, which, tenderly economized, and in customary labours of the desk, may be prolonged to the usual limit accorded to man. If you could find me some bureau occupation in Columbia, as a secretary or assistant, I would cheerfully accept it, and might be useful in such a department, where I could be of little use in the field. Last year, suffering mentally from a great calamity in my household, I nearly succumbed from a nervous attack which threatened to become brain faver. You may have seen the condition to which I was reduced, when, at poor Jamison's request, I changed the scene, & spent a week with him in Charleston.[4] This attack, which let me down wofully, was followed by a long spell of chill & fever, which racked and enfeebled my whole system. For the whole of the present year, under the advice of Drs. Bruns & Faust,[5] I have been taking prophylactics of cherry, dogwood and quinine, and only in May last, I suffered severely from a return of the chills which are now almost certain to follow from any undue exposure. If needful, I can probably procure adequate certificates from Geddings,[6] Bruns & Faust, all of whom know my condition. My sensibilities have shrunk, and I still shrink from the idea of exposing my person to the examination of a Board of strangers. You will readily understand this feeling, & the delicacy of those sensibilities from which it springs. To a man of honour & delicacy, these sensibilities are at once most sacred and imperious, and I do not know but that, before submitting to such exhibition, I should prefer to take the field, even though assured of a fatal termination to a very brief campaign. But I have said enough. It is in your power to give me a

---

[4] We are unable to date this visit. Mrs. Simms died on Sept. 10, 1863, and Jamison on Sept. 14, 1864.

[5] John Dickson Bruns and Christian I. Faust. Faust (1825-1884) lived and practiced medicine near Graham's Turn Out (now the town of Denmark).

[6] Dr. Eli Geddings.

dispensation, and for this I shall be most grateful. I need not add any thing touching the ruinous abandonment of my place, my library, furniture, negroes, every thing, for all which & whom, I have as yet been able to make no provision. I may be of service to you, as a Secretary in your Bureau, or in some other — any, will suit, which will give me *writing* to do, and men should be chosen for their adequacy to their tasks.[7]

Very truly Yours, &c.

W. Gilmore Simms.

1114: To Anna Augusta Singleton Simms Roach

[January 13, 1865] [8]

precious to my children. I am resigned to whatever happens. I hope that Gilmore will be with you tomorrow or Sunday.[9] If so, the pig will be a good roast. Cook half of it, and let him take the other half with him. I would have sent him grist, but that we have to wait on the mill till tomorrow night. In a week or so, if nothing happens, I will try & send him a box of provisions. Mrs. Roach & Claudia are still here. Clara is sick in Aiken.[10] Mrs. W. R.[11] has given the girls to understand that the room they now occupy, is destined to the use of Dr. Henry Fuller.[12] They have failed, thus far, to obtain situations. Mary Rivers is with us, but goes home tomorrow. Mrs. R., *through her,* has asked me to haul up her chattels to Midway. It will be a day's work. But shall be done. I do not learn that they have got rooms yet, or when they expect to depart. It is probable that I shall make an effort to go to Columbia on Monday. No newspapers today. God bless you all.

Your afft. father

W. Gilmore Simms

---

[7] On the back of this letter is written: "W. Gilmore Simms A. I. G. O Jany 9/65 Whether he is exempt & asking some employment." This notation is followed by another: "Ex: Dept: Jany: 20th 1865 Exempt Henry Buist Lt: Col: & A. D. C. Exemption issued Jany. 21st 1865." Buist was in charge of the Department of Detail and Exemption.

[8] This fragment is dated by Simms' letter to Gilmore of Jan. 13, in which he also discusses the pork roast for Sunday dinner and refers to this letter to Augusta.

[9] Jan. 15.

[10] Edward Roach's mother, Esther Ann Conyers Roach, and his sisters Claudia and Clara.

[11] Mary Cussings Fishburne Roach. See note 36, May 3, 1864.

[12] Youngest brother of Dr. William Fuller and a physician in Beaufort, S. C.

1115: To WILLIAM GILMORE SIMMS, JR.

Woodlands. 13 Jany 1865

My dear Son—

I am in hopes that Wm.[13] will meet you in town. He is to go down tomorrow. I send by him, 2 bags potatoes, 1 of peas (2 bushels) and a good shoat. One of the sacks of potatoes is for Augustas children, & you will give her one half of the Pork for roast on Sunday. I have authorized her to this extent. We have no grist & can get none from the mill till Saturday night. Next week, God willing, I hope to send you a box. Let me hope that what Wm. takes down will reach you safely, and help to relieve your appetite. It is not improbable that I shall run up to Columbia on Monday next. Isaac [14] returned today, having carried up 4 cows & calves, & a wagon load of poultry, in safety. He represents all as quite well & the children delighted to see him. But the girls have not written me for a week. Tomorrow, I hope to send off the car, for which I have been for 10 days accumulating the contents. *It will contain provision for all mine & Mr. Isaacs family* for one year, & include Augusta's.[15] She will read you the memorandum in her letter.[16] I see that you have perforce been compelled to have another execution on the island. I trust you did not have to officiate at a scene so painful.[17] I have written to Mr. Miles,[18] to cause them by the proctors to recieve pork instead of Bacon, & to cure it in camp or feed it out as corned pork. If they delay till the farmers can cure it, vast quantities in the border districts, may fall into the hands of the enemy. Yet, even cured as Bacon, & brought in now, the tythe recievers *refuse to take it* — yet the soldiers are starving. This is all very shameful & pitiful. Nothing stirring here, except that Capt. Patrick [19] has been nearly beaten to death by 3 runaway negroes, whom he had captured & was conducting from Midway

---

[13] A slave.

[14] Isaac Nimmons, Simms' body servant.

[15] Simms had sent his family to Columbia (see letter to Gilmore of Dec. 27, 1864), where they were staying with the George E. Isaacses (see note 33, May 3, 1864).

[16] This memorandum is missing from Simms' letter to Augusta of Jan. 13.

[17] The Charleston *Courier* of Jan. 12 reports: "Privates Mac Dillon, Samuel A. Robertson, A. H. W. Robertson and N. M. Robertson, all of Company D, First S. C. Artillery, were shot to death with musketry at 12 M. Wednesday [Jan. 11] on Sullivan's Island, for desertion."

[18] William Porcher Miles.

[19] Capt. George A. Patrick, at this time in Company B, 5th Regiment of South Carolina Volunteers.

to Bamberg. With his gun in hand, & pistols, on horseback, instead of compelling them to keep ahead of him, he let them divide on each side of his horse, whence they pulled him, beat, & left him for dead! I think I mentioned to you that I had invited Gen. Jackson [20] to visit me & had got a polite answer in return. We hear of Conner's [21] Brigade & Hoke's [22] going on to Charleston & tis said that all of Longstreets [23] division is to be sent. I wrote to Miles & Ayer,[24] to say, that if they concurred in opinion with me, our delegation would demand that Joe Johnson [25] be put at the head of our troops in S. C. Good troops, as well as bad ones require a good general, & he, I think, is our best. Who is the Col. Anderson now in command of Charleston? [26] I did not attend muster, being quite unwell, & taking mercury within, & smearing with mercurial ointment & sulphur without. I have had a week of constipation, & been taking the blue pill nightly. It is not improbable that I shall have to take the field. It is a relief to me to think that I shall tomorrow be able to get off the supplies for the family at Columbia. I have hired 6 hands to McMillan, at Grahams,[27] for the R. Road, at $40 per month. Wm. goes to you, that is 7. Young Jim [28] is working as a Cobbler at Bamberg, at $25 per week, — 8. Hannahs 3 children & Champion are at Columbia, — that is 12 disposed of, off the plantation. I shall probably send off 4 mules & the Pony to Col. Wilson,[29] & for those who remain, there will be ample provision & they have their instructions how to proceed, in case of the appearance of the enemy. All the furni-

---

[20] Perhaps Gen. William Hicks Jackson (1835-1903), who had led the left wing of the Confederate States Army in the defense of Atlanta.

[21] James Conner (1829-1883), son of Henry Workman Conner (see note 118, Aug. 10, 1848) and former United States attorney for the District of South Carolina during 1856-1860, served throughout the Confederate War and on June 1, 1864, was commissioned brigadier general. In Aug., 1864, he assumed command of Kershaw's Brigade.

[22] Robert Frederick Hoke (1837-1912), a native of North Carolina, was commissioned major general in the Confederate States Army in April, 1860.

[23] Gen. James Longstreet (1821-1904).

[24] Lewis Malone Ayer was a member of the Confederate States Congress during 1861-1865. For an account of Ayer, see note 102, April 2, 1847, in which his father's name is incorrectly given as Hartwell Ayer. His father was Lewis Malone Ayer.

[25] Gen. Joseph Eggleston Johnston.

[26] The Charleston *Mercury* of Jan. 9 carries an order dated Jan. 7 and signed by Col. E. C. Anderson, announcing that he has assumed "command of the Post of Charleston, including all the troops and batteries in the city."

[27] We have been unable to identify Mr. McMillan of Graham's Turn Out.

[28] Jim Rumph, Jr., one of Simms' slaves.

[29] Col. Isaac DeLiesseline Wilson.

ture that could sell well, or be useful, has been sent off — the house is stripped of all that is possible for me to send & tho' much of value remains, yet the loss of it would not be seriously felt — except my library. This, if time is left me, & I can get a place for its reception, I shall also try to send away. In thinking out all these matters, picking up & packing, I am broken down. But having done thus much, I am comparatively at ease in mind. Having done all that was in my power, I fling myself upon God. He will do the rest. He has kept me from drowning for 59 years, and will not suffer me now to sink. But I am weary, my son. God send you happy sleep, and a bright awakening in a more cheerful day.

Your affect father

W. G. S.

1116: To William Gilmore Simms, Jr.

Woodlands, 16 Jan 1865.

My dear Son.

I am sorry to tell you that I am very much under the weather, from a complication of evils. I have been in fact, quite unwell for a week, using the blue pill nightly. I suffer from indigestion & constipation, always sure to follow great fatigue or great anxiety. For two days I have had headache, & today, a tooth troubles me in addition. I have caught cold & am sore, as if beaten; — all my bones ache. I have been working very hard to get the car packed for Columbia, and the labour has been too much for me. I did not break down, however, till the work was done. The car is now ready, but unluckily, the freshet in the Congaree has carried away a portion of the R. R. bridge or Trestle work, and we know not how long it will be before freight can be sent across. Meantime, however, I had sent Isaac up with a wagon load of poultry, and 4 cows & calves, all of which arrived safely, though Isaac & the wagon had to make a considerable *detour* in order to get back. They were 7 days absent. In the meantime, though lacking Isaac's help I have succeeded in loading the car with supplies which ought to be ample for our own & Augusta's family, if not Rebecca's [30] also. I have sent 100 bushels Corn including 10 of grist, 20 bushels Peas, 20 of Rough Rice, 10 of ground nuts, 5 bushels clean rice,

---

[30] The family of Rebecca Isaacs. See note 33, May 3, 1864.

one bushel wheat flour, 1 or 2 of rye for Coffee, a jar of Lard
& 460 lbs of Pork. These supplies, with the milk & butter from
one or 2 cows, ought to enable our poor little flock of exiles to
keep famine from their door for a year at least. There were also
sent 27 head of turkies & 57 of fowls. — I sent you by Wm. on
Saturday, a good fat shoat, 2 bags of potatoes, & a 2 bushel bag
of peas.[31] See that you send all bags to Augusta. Some of them
belong to Govt. We had no grist from the mill — it not being
able to do the amt. of labour forced upon it. Yesterday (Sunday)
I met Dr. Keller [32] at Midway, who promised to take down the
grist for you if ready. I sent at daylight to the mill this morning,
but have not yet heard (12 M.) whether the grist was obtained
soon enough for the Dr. who departs today. It is probable, if not
sent, that I will make you up a box in the course of the week.
Eat your potatoes rapidly: They are beginning to sprout. I told
Augusta that you would share the supply with her. Poor thing,
I fear she suffers in Charleston, and will not speak. You were
right to get the overcoat. I would supply you with the money to
pay Edw.[33] but it is better that you should pay it yourself. I am
probably better able to keep money, for future exigencies, than
yourself. — I have no idea that the enemy design any direct
demonstration on Charleston, or, from the coast, direct on
Branchville. Should they do so, considering the character of the
country, they would give our army great advantages. My notion
is that Sherman means to take Augusta first, then seize upon the
R R. send a column down upon Branchville, & press directly
across the country for Columbia. *Nous verrons.* If he succeeds in
opening the river navigation his Gunboats can run up & take
Augusta.[34] — Do not bother now about the overseer. I have hired
6 prime fellows to the R. R. at $40 per month. Young Jim works
as a shoemaker in Bamberg at $25 per week. Six of my mules I
propose, as the enemy demonstrates, to send over to Col. I D
Wilson, at Society Hill who has offered to work them & feed
them. The rest of the negroes (men) I will try & get out of the
way of the enemy. And for the small crop which may be made
under the circumstances, we can do without an overseer. I have

---

[31] See letters to Augusta and Gilmore of Jan. 13.

[32] Dr. Joseph Keller lived in St. Matthews Parish. He later gave the Keller
Building to Newberry College, Newberry, S. C., as a memorial to his son, who
died when he was about to be graduated from the College.

[33] Edward Roach.

[34] Gen. Sherman's army left Pocotaligo on Feb. 1 and entered Columbia on
Feb. 17.

60 acres sown in rye, 23 in wheat, shall sow next month 20 of oats; shall plant rice largely, which requires hoe work only. And I have cleared up 100 acres of old land in the swamp for corn. I wait to hear how my cows have sold in Columbia, & if well, may send ½ dozen more. We will see about the mare hereafter. You will hardly, as an artillerist, be sent into the field. So long as we retain Charleston, the batteries on the island must be maintained. I will cheerfully yield you any thing you desire, but doubt [*Remainder of letter missing.*]

1117: To HARRY HAMMOND

Woodlands. 24 Jany 1865

My dear Harry.

Yours has just been recieved. The enclosure only adds to the long continued proofs which I have enjoyed, equally of the liberality & the affections of your father.[35] It is my consolation, under his loss, that I have endeavoured heartily to requite the regards which I shall never cease to feel. — Your suggestions touching certain letters, are dictated by a very wholesome prudence. I cannot[36] now refer to the particular letter to which you refer; but I think it quite probable that you yourself will be able to do so, before this reaches you. I have only within a few days covered two packages, addressed to your mother, and made up solely of his Letters. These, I sent by Mr. Moore, or Mr. Redheimer, with an endorsement to the care of Mr. John Bones. They were delivered to the conductor by Dr. Fuller, I, being too sick at the time to leave the house, and I requested that the conductor would either deliver them to Mr. Bones in person, or get Mr. I. W. Meredith to do so as soon as possible. I presume they have already been delivered, but if not, then let inquiry be promptly made of Mr. Bones, or, he failing, of Mr. Meredith.[37]

It is not one merely of your father's letters which contains matter not to be published. Where he confided in his correspondents, he wrote with the singular frankness with which he spoke. Hence it was that I suggested, in previous communications that

---

[35] Doubtless James H. Hammond had left Simms a bequest of some kind.

[36] In going from one line to another Simms failed to write *not,* though *can* has a hyphen after it.

[37] John Bones, of Augusta, was an old friend of James H. Hammond (see note 191, July 15, 1847); probably I. W. Meredith was also. We are unable to identify Moore and Redheimer: if the former was a conductor on the railroad, he was probably not Henry P. Moore, of Augusta (see note 50, May 6, 1857).

we should reserve his correspondence for some future volume, whenever events should suffer us to prepare it for the press. His letters contain some of his most valuable writings & the cream of them should be put on record. Wm. D. Porter [38] told me that he had recieved some of especial value, & regretted their destruction in the great fire of Charleston three years ago. The family of James M. Walker [39] ought to possess many if they have preserved them. So ought M. C. M. H.,[40] Pinck. Starke,[41] James S. Clarke [42] of Columbia, Waddy Thompson, Frank Pickens,[43] perhaps Dr. Bruns, and many other parties whom you will perhaps be more able to designate than myself. In turn, as opportunity offers, all these persons should be addressed on the subject, & I need not say to you, how willing I shall be to examine what we possess, and address them & other parties on the subject, whenever the family shall deem it a proper time, to prepare an additional volume. It may be well, too, to incorporate these extracts throughout the progress of a memoir, corresponding with the several periods of his life.[44] Meanwhile, you will among you, be better able to preserve & conceal them than myself. Your mother would be the most proper custodian. She & Bet will be better in a city than on a plantation, whenever you find the country approached by armies or infested by marauding parties. Sell your stock, if you cannot run it; get your mules & horses out of the way. They will not otherwise escape our own troops. The domestic impedimenta convey to Augusta. That town will probably be pleased to share the fate of Savannah, but this will be no reproach to your wife [45] and mother. — I am here trying to rescue what I can from the wreck. With the exception of my son, Gilmore & Mrs. Roach, all my children are in Columbia in an obscure dwelling, sheltered by humble but excellent people,[46] who are connected by marriage

---

[38] William Dennison Porter. See note 102, July 29, 1848.

[39] James Murdock Walker. See note 264, July 10, 1845.

[40] Marcus Claudius Marcellus Hammond.

[41] Col. William Pinkney Starke. Starke was the author of a sketch of the early life of John C. Calhoun, abridged and published in J. Franklin Jameson's edition of the "Correspondence of John C. Calhoun," *Annual Report of the American Historical Association for the Year 1899* (Washington, 1900), II, 65-89.

[42] James L. Clark. See note 237, Dec. 17, 1849.

[43] Francis Wilkinson Pickens. See note 120, Dec. 30, 1842.

[44] One volume of Hammond's papers was published: *Selections from the Letters and Speeches of the Hon. James H. Hammond, of South Carolina* (New York: John F. Trow & Co., Printers, 1866). The originals of most of Hammond's letters to Simms are in the Hammond Papers, Library of Congress.

[45] The former Emily Harford Cumming (1834-1911), whom Harry Hammond had married on Nov. 22, 1859.

[46] The George E. Isaacses.

with my eldest daughter. For myself, I apprehend, though I can neither walk nor ride, I shall become a peripatetic — possibly untill the war is over. With strong symptoms of age, & failing health, I dread fatigue & exposure, & want rest. I begin to congratulate those fortunates who have escaped this crisis, and whom we still, perhaps unwisely, deplore. Present me affectionately to your mother & wife, & believe me always willing, whenever able, to serve you all.

Very truly, Harry, their friend & yours.

W. Gilmore Simms

1118: To BENJAMIN FRANKLIN PERRY

Columbia 6th. March '65.

Hon. Judge Perry

My dear Perry.

Mr. Isaacs, who will hand you this, will tell you fully of the fate of Columbia, & of its present condition.[47] I am here, perforce, in a sort of durance, with my little family, & cannot, for the present, get away; & know not the fate or state of my plantation. Several reports lead me to apprehend that my house & every thing has been destroyed.[48] Can any small cottage, however

---

[47] Gen. Sherman entered Columbia on Feb. 17 and shortly after dark of the same day the city burst into flames and was almost completely destroyed. One of the best accounts of the destruction of Columbia is Simms' *Sack and Destruction of the City of Columbia, S. C. To Which Is Added a List of the Property Destroyed* (Columbia, S. C.: Power Press of Daily Phœnix, 1865). The account was first published in the Columbia *Phœnix* during March–April, 1865.

[48] In the Columbia *Phœnix* of April 12, 1865, Simms published an account of the burning of Woodlands evidently written by himself and derived largely from a letter from Mrs. Hopson Pinckney, in whose charge Simms had left the house when he went to Columbia ("Mrs. Pinckney . . . her family, a friend and two children" stayed at Woodlands), and "partially from circumstantial details furnished subsequently from other and trustworthy sources." In this article, entitled "Woodlands," he writes: "When the enemy reached the neighborhood, Mrs. P. addressed a letter to Gen. [Francis Preston] Blair, requesting protection for the dwelling and library, and suggesting the enormity of the crime which could destroy books, especially such a collection—some ten thousand volumes—made with great care, during a period of forty years, and constituting, perhaps, the most valuable library, to a literary man, to be found in the Confederacy. Before an answer could be received to this application, bands of stragglers had penetrated the house and begun the work of robbery. The trunks and bureaus were at once broken open. In the midst of this scene, the guard sent by Gen. Blair made its appearance, and relieved the house of the plunderers. The General himself, with Gen. [Oliver Otis] Howard and other officers, visited the estate, and spent some time in the examination of the library. They took away a collection of maps, including Mills' Atlas of South

humble, be bought in your precinct, with our present currency?
Of this, & in bonds, I can command some $15,000. How much land
can this procure? I am at a place of refuge, and care not much
for the rudeness of the dwelling, if there be a moderate, but sufficient, quantity of land along with it — say a few acres. Will
you interest yourself for me in these questions, & report through
Mr. Isaacs, who will advise you, no doubt, of the period of his
return to Columbia. I will also thank you to procure for me a
small supply of *candles,* for which I will pay you at a future day.
We are here, and my money is mostly in the Union Bank, which
has gone Heaven knows where — probably to Charlotte. We
have only an occasional voice from the outer world, and there is
not a shop left in Columbia. Fortunately, I had made provision
in *meat & bread* for my family, and though some of it was burned,
I have still enough to last us awhile longer. But of small comforts,
such as candles — almost indispensable to me, with my habits —
matches, medicines, weapons, firewood &c. — we are almost
utterly stript. The incendiary & Robber have done their work

Carolina, and perhaps a few other volumes. They also carried off a couple of
double barrelled guns and a rifle; but nothing besides of any importance, and
their deportment was courteous and becoming. They left a sufficient guard
behind them, and the building was saved while this guard remained on the
premises. But, with their departure, frequent attempts to burn the house at
night were made, and the ladies became so much alarmed and wearied with
night watching, that they fled, and sought refuge for themselves and family at
the neighboring hamlet of Midway. With their departure, the fellows succeeded in their design. The house, a very extensive, newly built one, and only
partially finished, but with six habitable rooms, besides the library, was fired
at four several quarters, and when the flames were discovered by the servants,
at daybreak, they had reached a degree of height and intensity which made
all efforts impossible to save. The library, in a separate wing, connected with
the main dwelling by a corridor, was the first to burn. Not a volume was saved.
From the other wing, and the centre building, the servants rescued some of
the bedding and furniture. Some idle stories have imputed the destruction of
the property to the slaves of Mr. Simms, and one of these, his body servant
[Isaac Nimmons], who was the chief laborer and the most indefatiguable in
his efforts to save the property—who did, in fact, save the most of those things
which were rescued from the fire—was arrested, on some vague conjectures,
and actually tried for his life before a court of freeholders. He was unanimously
acquitted. The slaves, themselves, all testify that the incendiarism was due to
small squads of white stragglers, following in the wake of the main army—
miserable bands of plunderers, who usually lurk behind with this very object.
. . . The larger and better portions of the furniture had been previously sent
off to other places. The library shelves were left full, and sixteen large boxes
of choice books besides had been packed away by the author, and would have
been sent away, could transportation have been obtained. This was found to be
impossible. In addition to the dwelling, the incendiaries destroyed the kitchen,
the carriage house, gin house, threshing house, stables, barns and various other
buildings; carried off four or five horses, and three oxen, with wagons and
buggies. They also carried off some twenty-eight or thirty negroes." Woodlands was burned in February, but we have been unable to determine the
exact date.

most effectually with the wretched people of this town. No less than 8000 persons are depending for their daily food, upon a short ration of meal & lean beef, distributed by the Authorities. Half of the population, male & female, have been robbed of all the clothes they had, save those they wore, and of these many have had overcoat, hat & shoes taken from them. Watches & purses were appropriated at every corner; and the amount of treasure & wealth, in cloth, gold, silver & other booty borne away by the Huns & Vandals of the Century, is incomputable. Seven-eights of the best portions of Columbia have been destroyed. In fact, what remains unburnt are, almost exclusively, the suburban precincts. All is wreck, confusion & despair. With best regards to your family, & the renewal of old pledges, believe me

> Ever truly Your friend
>
> W. Gilmore Simms

P. S. A little good smoking tobacco would be very acceptable. Here we can only get a villainous substitute of stem & weed, for that glorious plant which Spenser calls "divine." [49] Mr. Isaacs will probably be soon coming down in person, and will be pleased to bring any thing you may send me. I am lodging in his House, where my *little* flock of *seven*,[50] enjoys two rooms. The humble-ness & obscurity of our abode, constituted its security. It held forth too little promise to the plunderers, and so escaped the fire. Few of the finer dwellings of the city have escaped, & but one small house remains on the whole length of Main St. from Cotton town, inclusive, to a point considerably beyond the capital!

> W. G. S.

---

[49] *The Faerie Queene,* Book III, Canto v, Stanza 32, line 6.

[50] Evidently the following members of Simms' family were with him: Mary Lawson, Chevillette, Govan, Carroll, Augusta, and Augusta's daughter, Chevillette. Augusta's son, Simms, had died on Jan. 22, 1865.

PAUL HAMILTON HAYNE

"Write me, my young friend. The old man has grown much older — much feebler — & it is becoming, the ministration of you, the younger brother of his guild, to assist his palsying eylids, and point his sight, and say — 'here place your staff — set your foot here, & now — sit. There is a prospect before you of a glorious valley, purple in a generous sunset.'"

(From a wood engraving in *Frank Leslie's Illustrated Newspaper*, February 2, 1861)

WILLIAM GILMORE SIMMS
"The spirit was within him, & he strove,
Unqualified by base desire or deed,
Most nobly though perchance he never won,
The golden goal he sought."
— Simms writing about himself in a manuscript poem
given to Julia Sands Bryant and now in the Goddard-
Roslyn Collection of Bryant papers.

(From a wood engraving in the *New York Mercury*, XXVIII [October 6, 1866], 4)

1119: To ANDREW GORDAN MAGRATH [51]

To His Excellency.
A. G. Magrath, Esqr. Gov. of the State
  of South Carolina.

Columbia, S. C. April 15, 1865.

[S]ir Your Excellency.

I have endeavoured, to the best of my ability, and [wit]h the few and inferior agencies which I have been able to [co]mmand, to comply with the wishes of Your Excellency, & to prepare such a report as would fully enlighten the public mind, in [r]espect to the details of the enemy's late progress through our [S]tate. I regret that the time allotted for the task has been so [li]mited as to prevent, in great degree, the reciept of such com[m]unications in answer to my own, as might have supplied the [n]ecessary information. The rapidly approaching assemblage of the [L]egislature, and your expressed desire to have the material supplied [in] season for the uses of that body, require me to furnish you only [wi]th the crude & imperfect narrative which follows, and this I [ha]sten to do, with the hope, that, however, imperfect in its details, [it] will be found trustworthy in general, and constitute a sufficient [ba]sis for reasonable conjecture as to the extent of the mischief [do]ne by the invasion, & for a sufficient estimate of the loss sus[tained]. This understood, & the needs of the country at all times fully [in mind,] it will be less difficult for yourself & the General Assembly [to de]termine in what manner, & to what degree, the people who [hav]e suffered along the route of the enemy, may be succoured [by l]egislation of the State.

We are told that the plan of the enemy's campaign [contem]plated the movement of the two corps, the 14th. & 20th. under General Slocum,[52] along and up the Savannah River in [the] direction of Augusta, which place they were to threaten [at] least, if not capture, while the Right Wing, under Genera[l Sher]man himself, moving from Beaufort, was first to make a feint towards the city of Charleston, so as to keep our ar[my] confined to that precinct, while he should, by a subsequent rapid

---

[51] We do not know whether this letter was actually sent to Magrath; our text is from a first draft (?) in the Charles Carroll Simms Collection, South Caroliniana Library. The MS. is in bad condition, torn, stained, and frayed at the edges. Our reconstructions are based to a considerable extent on the various reports of Sherman's campaign given in *O. R.,* 1st Series, XLVII.
[52] Henry Warner Slocum (1827-1894).

change of direction, push forward directly for the int[erior] and the State Capital. The enemy does not seem to have made any concealment of his real plans, which he may be said to have pursued inflexibly from the beginning rendering it easy for any reflecting mind to conjecture his objects. His plan seems to have been to avoid battle so long as possible, in order to economize his army with the paramount view to its concentration, in full force, upon the flanks of Gen. Lee. Auxiliary to this was the cutting of all the railway communications of the interior with the cities of Charleston and Richmond. The feint of Sherman in the direction of Charleston, was to be followed by the mixed local troops under Gen. Foster,[53] who, n[o] doubt had his instructions, to lie contiguous to the city, in waiting for the resu[lt] of Sherman's progress in destroying the railway commun[icat]ions. It was quite as well understood, no doubt, by the en[emy] Generals, as by our own, that Foster's force, whether by sie[ge or] by assault, would prove quite unequal to the task of t[aking] Charleston, so long as we were willing to defend it, an[d t]hat its evacuation and surrender must promptly follow [a] successful attempt to cut off its supplies from the count[ry.]

That the city might have been held, & sti[ll he]ld to this moment, is not a question with us, and whether [it] was not a vital policy with [th]e [Co]nfederate Government that i[t] should be held, even at a great [sa]crifice of m[en and] materiel, is as little questionable. By an ac[cu]mula[tion of] three or six months provisions, by the stern expulsion [of] all the inhabitants not necessary to the garrison, & [espe]cially the slave population, there is littl[e] question [of their] capacity to have kept it secure, not less against assau[lt] than against its temporary isolation from the destruction of the railways. Thi[s] is a q[ues]tion which is not necessary for discussion [he]re. It i[s o]ne, however, of large importance to military statesmanship — a blending of two requisites for government in ti[m]e of war, [w]hich, perhaps, recieve but too little of the public attention. [Had] the policy thus suggested been pursued, it is very cer[tain th]at Gen. Foster could not have captu[r]ed the city, and [it] is ver[y] doubtful that General Sherman w[oul]d have suffered [hi]mself to pause, and turn aside from his progress towards Virginia, to u[nder]take either the siege or the assault of Charleston. He [would] have satisfied himself with the sundering of the com-

---

[53] John Gray Foster (1823-1874).

[munica]tions, and calculated confidently on [t]he result predicated, [by] [*one word partly missing and partly illegible*] military men, from the silent operation of this perfor[m]ance, [any o]ther yie[ld]ing sufficient time to the preparations of [t]roo[ps for def]en[ce a]s well as to his own. General Sherman [i]ssued [orders for General] Slocum [a]t Sist[er's ferr]y on the Savannah [river to cross into South Carolina, and he] himself crossed [by Port Royal ferry on Broad river.] I estimate his [wh]ole for[ce a]t the beginning of this invasion, at about [4]5,000 men. Of these I assume the proportion to hav[e] been, — of infantry 35,000; [artille]ry and cavalry 10,000; in[cluding] K[i]lpatrick's,[54] not exceeding 7000. I cannot per[suade mysel]f [f]rom such facts as we have been able to re[cieve] that their army exceeded 50,000; though, according [to th]e habit of exaggeration, so general with the enemy, [they] themselves rat[e]d their numbers as ranging from 60,000 to [65,]000.[55] With their columns thus entering Beaufort District, by the Sister['s] ferry on the Savannah, and from Port Roya[l] ferry on Broad river, and converging to a meeting, their advance enabled them to traverse, as with one embodied front, the whole interval of Country from the Savannah to the Combahee and their march may be traced, as laid out by a swathe [of] fire. All property was plundered or destroyed. Houses inva[ded] which were temporarily abandoned, though filled with fur[niture and] the proofs of re[cen]t occupation; and in numerous instan[c]es, fami[li]es were dispossessed, and driven forth, while their dwellings were fired. By this process the work of plunder was carried on without annoying obstruction from the proprietor. Cattl[e,] horses, mules, a[ll] stock of much use or value, was carried off [by] the army; all provisions; and where not taken, destroyed; in [no] instances was the food left for the families, even for the slave[s], quite adequate to their needs. Cotton, & Cot[to]n Ho[uses,] Gins, threshing mac[hi]nes, mills, wagons, [*one or two words missing*] we[re] destroyed. And the [*two-thirds of a line missing*] progress of Sherm[an] [*several lines missing*] district wholly, and [*almost a line missing*] the invaders, — the tract of devas[tation measuring from w]est to e[ast] an average [of forty miles,] expanding to fifty, when [they wanted to at]t[ac]k & destroy favorite settlements[, and mer]ging to fif-

---

[54] Gen. Hugh Judson Kilpatrick (1836-1881).

[55] The strength of the Northern forces was 60,079 officers and men. See *O. R.*, 1st Series, XLVII, 42.

teen, where the passes wer[e too difficu]lt, or when concentration
was essential fo[r a con]flict with our troops. Unhappily, thes[e
conflicts were] neither frequent, nor of a sort to com[pel]
[*several words missing or illegible*] the caution of the enemy.
[*several words missing*] defile, of narrow causey, & [*several
words missing*] the intervals between our river[s], seem [to have
been to]tally unemployed for the purposes of [defence. Opposi-
tion] appears to have been presented on[ly at the cross]ings of
the rivers. It may be remar[ked that no bett]er country could be
found for [a small force to defend itself] against a large one; its
close [*several words missing*] [d]efile & contiguity of swamp
fores[ts provide innumerable] covers, where a courageous [&
bold force, well] officered, might make continual [attacks on]
an invading enemy always in [motion and uncertain] of his route,
& so harrass, anno[y] [*several words missing*] to achieve a conquest, such [*several words missing*] the employment of the
[*several lines missing*] gifts and resour[ces] & adapt [their warfare to the] characteristics of their country [*about two-thirds of
a line missing*] [b]ut calculate [*about two-thirds of a line missing*] were not ambitious of a display [of the tactics of E]uropean
warfare, in [a] co[u]ntry [whic]h [in no way rese]mbled
Europe. It was thus that they [could have engaged the g]enerals,
the military art, and all the material r[esources of the U]nited
States, for a longer period than that in [which they would be]
engaged in fighting the same power [in Europe; & they would
have] withdrawn, in consequence of [the delay. Our w]arfare,
[hav]ing a like country to defend with [*several words missing*],
migh[t] have been, nay, must have been, [*several words missing*]
that of the red men, had we been wise. [We should] have conducted the war upon their principl[es & tactics, be]ing confirmed
& as it were consecrated by [their usage by o]ur chieftains of the
American Re[volution.]

[Beginnin]g a march of devastation the tr[oops of General
Sherman] passed from Beaufort into Barnwell [district. They
enco]untered on the Salkehatchie [Rive]r Bri[dge a smal]l force
of our army, when a sharp at[tack was made. Our] troops confined themselves mostly [to the area] of a well known crossing
po[int since they were w]holly unequal to a protracted [*several
lines missing*] impassable. This [*about two-thirds of a line missing*], and the enemy pressed f[orwar]d[, followed by th]e
cavalry of Kilpatrick moving [tow]ards [Blackville] [*one or two
words missing*], followed by the infantry command of Gen. Jeff

[Davis,[56] w]hile Shermans columns inclined to the right, and [moved dire]ctly for the South Carolina Railway, & the Edisto [river. The] progress of all these columns was marked by the [most uni]versal devastation. The country was swept as by a [forest] fire, making a tract of desolation more than forty [miles] in width. No unoccupied houses in this tract were [spared]. All were given to the flames. And those which were [occupi]ed by the aged, by women & children, were plundered, & the [oc]cu[p]ants treated with brutality & blows. Women were [ass]aulted with horrid oaths, while the pistol muzz[l]e threat[en]ed their breasts, and the bowie knife & sabre flourished above [th]eir heads. All valuables that could be found portable we[r]e [s]tolen; mules & horses & vehicles; gold & silver; watches & jew[e]ls; and the negroes in large numbers, beguiled away, or [ca]rried off by violence. These latter were chiefly vigorous & [a]ble-bodied men, & young & likely negresses. The beautiful pre[c]inct of Allandale was nearly all destroyed. The fine plan[t]ations of the Hon. Mr. Lawton, of Major Martin, General Er[w]in, and, indeed, all, with few exceptions, were plundered & [g]iven to the flames; they were stript of stock & cattle, mules [&] horses; their vehicles were carried off or destroyed, & the supply [of] provisions left (in most cases hidden away too securely to be [foun]d) was too scant for the sustenance even of the negro population. [The region around the Salke-hatchie] Bridge shared the sa[me fate. No house was allow]ed to remain which could [be used as a] dwelling. Passing on to Barnwell Court Hou[se, des]troying as he went, Kilpatrick entered this ill[-fated town] driving in our outposts at Salke-hatchie Bridge F[our] miles distant. There was no fighting, nothing to [rouse the] passions of the soldiery; yet scarcely had they en[tered the] village, when the torch began the work of destru[ction, the] plunderer & the burner being equally busied in a[ll quar]ters. No house was spared by the former, & but f[ew by] the latter. No privacy was respected. The chambers of [the] women were burst open by the licentious invaders; a[nd] what was left unstolen was destroyed. The Court Ho[u]se[,] Jail, the M[as]onic Hall, two taverns, & the shops, were the first to burn, private dwellings followed. Though promised by Kilpatric[k] that private property should be respected, & that no houses which were occupied should be destroyed, yet, on the arrival of the

---

[56] Jefferson Columbus Davis (1828-1879).

infantry, under Davis, a few days after, the work of destruction was renewe[d] and the wretched women & children were awaked in ra[in] and cold, at day light, to fly from the crackling & blazing roofs of their dwellings. More than one hundred buildings, the best in the village were destroyed. Every body w[as] plundered. Neither meat nor bread, nor clothing, was left to the starving mother, or the naked child; and they openly avowed their purpose to subjugate the men of the country, by depriving the women & children of their means of life. The wine of the sacred vessels in the churches was drunk by their offic[ers.]

[Leaving B]arnwell Village, Kilpatrick's Cavalry p[ressed forward] in the direction of Augusta. Following slowly [after an] interval of three days, the infantry of Davis, [tak]ing several routes, made their way to the S. C. R. [R., des]troying it for several miles below Williston and [White Pond], and cooperating with the troops of Sherman, which [then p]ursued a progress to the right, after effecting the passage [of th]e Salkehatchie, and made their way to the same line [of] railway, destroying, in like manner, upwards, untill th[e ru]in was complete, from Midway to Blackville, a space of twenty miles. The progress of this latter column had been in like manner marked by destruction. No unoccupied house escaped the flames. None of any sort escaped the plunderer. The estates of Mrs. Lucia Pinckney, Mr. Charles R. Carroll, Dr. Fishburne, Mrs. Roach,[57] &c. all were burned, along the Springtown & other roads. Along the Edisto those of the late Hon. Angus Patterson, of Hon. D. F. Jamison, President of the Convention, of Mr. W. Gilmore Simms, were all burned [an]d ravaged. From the plantation of the latter 28 negroes [we]re taken off or beguiled away. The villages of Black[vi]lle, Grahams, Bamberg, were more or less given to the [fla]mes, and Aiken was about to share the same fate, when [Kil]patrick was encountered, even as the spoiler had begun [his] work, by the cavalry of Wheeler,[58] and driven back to the succour of his infantry. All the intermediate country was swept of its possessions — destroyed or bor[n]e away. A [le]tter now lying before me, from [a we]althy planter, & an emi[nent law]yer and public man of Barnwell District,[59] w[ho writes] from his own experience of loss, and personal obser[vation will] illustrate the present devasted condition of the whol[e district.] After narrating the

---

[57] Mary Cussings Fishburne Roach. See note 36, May 3, 1864.

[58] Gen. Joseph Wheeler (1836-1906).

[59] Perhaps Alfred Proctor Aldrich.

ravages of the enemy in the village [of Barn]well, he proceeds thus: "The enemy overran about tw[o-thirds] of the district, burning all the houses left unoccupied at [their] approach; burning the fences generally, gin houses, barnyards [and] all the machinery and implements on the plantations; dri[ving] off or killing all the work animals & stock cattle & hogs; bu[rn]ing the cotton & provisions, in some places leaving none whatev[er,] in other places, a mere pittance hardly enough to support the negroes, with a stinting economy till the production of another crop. In general *all* the meat was carried off, and such of the negroes as they could persuade to go; others were forced away. The loss to the district is, at least, one-third in buildings; three fourths of the fencing, ¾ of the provisions including corn & meat; ¾ of the stock including horses, mules, oxen, cattle, sheep, hogs, &c. Whether willingly or not, a great many negroes were carried off, & many have, since their departure, found their way to Beaufo[rt] and Savannah. The enemy's line of march, in the district, extended from its base to the Upper Three Runs, & along the railway track from the Edisto Bridge to the town of Aiken[.] In the village, I lost three houses, and my law library, which [was] equally large & well chosen, the accumulations of more than [*numeral missing*] years. At my residence, just without the village, my Barns & Stables [wer]e burned, all my stock of every description killed or carried [off] except a few hogs that w[ere] in the woods; the fences destroye[d and my] provisions & groceries of every sort consumed or [destroyed]; not enough left to maintain the family for ten days. [My furn]iture was greatly abused; all the blankets, quilts, [sheets,] bolsters, pillow cases &c. carried off; every closet & drawer, [and bu]reau, broken into & pillaged; the secretaries of my wife & [self] were broken open, & the private papers scattered to the winds; [they] covered the floor, yard & highways. The books were taken from [my] Library & thrown about the yard, or carried off to camp; [so]me 40 pieces of plate, a gold watch, the violin & guitar of my [s]ons & daughters, were stolen or broken to pieces. Nearly all the glass & crockery was destroyed; all our shoes, of self, wife and children, stolen; in short every thing is swept away, the accumulations of a life time; and that I have a house left is due to the vigilance of my wife and a faithful negro; for the fiends set fire to the dwelling four several times while the women and children were in it; but not till they had plundered it [c]ompletely. At my plantation on the Edisto we lost 7 negroes. The Gin House,

Blacksmith Shop, with all the fencing; 100 bales [o]f Cotton; some 2000 bushels of Corn; about 3000 lbs of Bacon; 100 bushels of rice; 18 horses & mules; 52 head of Cattle; 100 head of sheep; 100 of Hogs; all the poultry; all the wagons & carts; briefly every thing [w]as either burnt or stolen. In fact, all that was saved for the [n]egroes was about 150 bushels of Corn, and this was only yielded at the urgent [e]ntreaty of the negroes themselves; as they had already set fire to the barn which contained it; and it required strenuous exertions to rescue what was thus saved."

This narrative will suffice as [a] sample of the universal [ruin] of this most brutal and savage foray. But it did [not] finish here. The enemy cutting the rail way along the [South] Edisto pressed forward from Binnaker's, Cannons, & [the] New Bridge at Blackville into Orangeburg District, [and] again their course was marked by plunder & fire. T[hey] left Branchville, where our defences indicated some prep[aration] for fight, to the right, and with a strong column proceeded [at] once to the village of Orangeburg. The destruction of all th[e] business portions of the town followed, including the Court House and Jail. One half of the place was destroyed; ever[y] portion of it was plundered. Crossing the Rail way, pressing forward right and left, destroying the road in their progress, they reached the Congaree with one column, while with another they traversed the district of Lexington. In their progress into th[is] district, their columns penetrated by way of all the bridges, over the bridg[e] south or east of Merrills on the Two-Notch Road, and, by North Edisto, over all the bridges south of & including Gunter's, which [is] at or near the Sand Dam, to Orangeburg C. H. They thus occupied a[ll] the public & private roads from both these rivers, leading i[n] the direction of Lexington C. H. & that of Columbia; & but few places in the woods escaped unvisited by one or other of their predatory bands. The right wing of a portion of the army came up the state road, & passed through the Sandy Run Ar[ea] on the Congaree, one of the most populous, wealthy, & prosperous portions of Lexington District. It was probably the left [win]g of this colu[m]n that passed along Thom's Creek through the [Gei]ger neighbourhood & Majo[r T]hreewits. This latter force crossed the Sal[ud]a just below the [Sa]luda Bridge on [pontoons] and over the Broad, at or near Geiger's Mill, on pontoons als[o, an]d skir[m]ishing with our troops began about Thom's creek, & continued throughout their progress, till they entered Columbia[.] The right wing of the enemy crossed the Congaree

at or nea[r G]ranby. The 14th. & 20th Army Corps, with the
larger portion of Kilpatrick's Cavalry, covered the rest of Lexington District up to the Two-Notch Road as far north as Lightwood
Cre[ek.] After the passage of that stream, it scattered & extended t[o the] west, striking the Augusta road from Columbia,
10 miles ab[ove] Lexington village and thence to Saluda, along
the Waters ferry ro[ad] to the neigh[bo]urhood of Heallya.
Ferry. These forces arrived at Lexington Village on Wednesday,
the 15th. Feb. and remained un[till] the 17th. The Pickets, however, were not withdrawn untill [the] 18th. They crossed the
Saluda on pontoons at Youngiers [Ferry] about 5 miles above
the Saluda factory, & then cro[ss]ing [the] whole of the Dutch
Fork, marched north & crossed Broa[d] river at Freshley's,
nearly opposite Lyttleton on the Greenvi[lle] R. Road, on Monday th[e] 20th. A portion of their forces, mov[ed] west, far
above this point, striking the Newberry Line above Hope's Station, on the same Rail road, but on the w[est] side of Broad river.
A small portion of the Fork, lying a[long] Bear Creek, which
empties into Saluda river above [*one word missing*] ferry, on
the north side of it, escaped the[i]r ravages. [From] that portion
of Newberry on [t]he [north] side of Saluda al[ong the] Waters
ferry road to Lightwood Creek [and] Two N[otch] r[oad]
[*several words missing*] of said roads, escaped t[h]em, bu[t]
these [are] ex[tre]mely small belts, and for the most part very
[po]or. The [b]urning of the Saluda Factory was the heaviest
[in]dividual loss in Lexington District. In the march of the enemy
[no]t a mill was spared, unless accidentally, and by being [o]ver-
looked, not found. Two or three more were saved, by [sto]ut
individual exertions, after being fired & left. To ge[t a] list of
the private dwellings given to the [f]lames, would [be] impossible; few worth saving were suffered to remain. All [tha]t
were unoccupied were destroyed. So were all the fencing, [a]ll
the farming implements, workshops & gin houses. All the
[ho]rses, mules were carried off; all the cattle, sheep & hogs,
[sa]ve those which were shot down & left to [die.] Scarcely [a]
carriage, wagon, buggy, or vehicle of any kind, has been [left]
in the district. The dwelling houses were all pillaged, [*one word
missing*], and the furniture destroyed, even where the house [it-
self] was spared. The clothes of women & children seemed to
[be a]s much coveted by the robbers as those of the men. Every
[mou]thful of provisions, of every sort, was stolen or destroyed.
[The] people have been living since, [u]pon the offal left by [the

men] in their camps, or by their horses where they fed. For [wee]ks after their departure the wretched inhabitants thus [plu]ndered might be seen daily — old men & women & children — [pa]infully gleaning from the closely-scraped earth, the mis[erable] refuse of gr[a]in which the improvidence of the robbers had [let] waste upon the g[round.] The [ne]gro[es] were treated as brutally [as their masters an]d were eq[u]ally robbed of th[ei]r small possessions. [Nor did] their brutality limit itself to a plunder of posses[sions. In one ins]tance, certainly, a young lady of respectable family [was ra]vished. But the criminal did not escape. He was slain by [the ha]nds of some of the lady's kinsme[n], at Bouknights Ferry, [where] he now lies buried. The whole country, even as we [write] is [sti]ll fœtid with the stench of decaying animals, in [various st]ages of putridity. For days after the departure of the [enemy] bleating calves might be seen, along the track [which] they pursued, moaning about their dead dams, while [ot]h[er]s but a few days old, were feebly sucking at the teats of the slain mothers. Mares with young had their throats cut or their brain[s] blown out. But why continue the loathsome catalogue. Suffice it that the District of Lexington, in almost every part is a vast ruin; its possessions destroyed; its fields ravaged; fences burned; means of culture all gone; and famine threatens its wretched inhabitants on every hand.

At the Court House, the mills, including saw, & grist & Bark mi[lls] of Mr. Meetze, Commissioner in Equity, were all destroyed; the tanned leather & the untanned hides; his dwelling, including a Library of 1500 volumes, and all of his papers, in‐ cluding those of his clients; the law office of Col. Boozer, with all his books & papers; of Col. Forts; of Bauskett & Caughman; the dwelling [oc]cupied by C. W. Crouch; the Carriage Factory of D. Rawls, with steam engine and all necessary fixtures; the Jail; t[h]e Court House; &c. The sheriff saved some of his books; t[he] c[l]erk the records, but lost the papers; [*several words missing*] is a total lo[ss] to the Commissioner [*several words missing*] the recor[ds.] The [Luth]eran Church was burned after the melodion [had been] literally beaten to pieces; the bell of the Chu[rch was] tolled by the enemy while the village was in fla[mes;] the Fair House, fencing, stalls, &c. was consumed; th[e hall] of the Sons of Temperance; with all their book[s,] p[apers &] regalia; Dr. Caughman's office, with all his me[di]cin[es; the] ware houses of Hendrix & Co;

Hendri[x] & Brother, [*several words missing*] Hendrix, with his ware houses; the store house of Ca[ughman] & Co, with large dwelling & ware house; the Commissi[oner's] store house, (property of Meetze); Hendrixs Hotel, w[ith] all the outbuildings; R. Hannan's Hotel, &c.; W. N. Hendrix' mill seat & dwelling; Corley's d[we]lling, &c.; [*man's name illegible*] dwelling, &c.; J. E. Hendrixs dwelling &c.; John Hendrix' dwelling; Mrs. M. Frank's dwelling &c; and, briefly, the whole business portion of the town, with many other houses. But little has been spared whether of village [or] District.

T[h]e approach to Columbia was not suffered without some show of resistance. The enemy was encountered at Thom's Creek on the [*blank space left by Simms*],[60] and skirmishing continued untill the [time] when our troops recrossed the Congaree burning the bridges be[hin]d them. There was no force on our side for adequate resistance. Though the army of Virginia depended for all its supplies upon the Carolinas & Georgia, and though Charleston was the only s[e]a port accessible to [o]ur vessels, no serious ef[fort] was made for [the protection] & maintenance of [the port. The] enemy [pressed forward] and cr[ossed the river, and began the] work [of plun]der almost as soon as [they entered] this town. This continued during their whole sta[y of fo]ur days. On the night of the first day the city [was] fired. The act was a deliberate one. More than 1400 [buildings] were consumed. All the public stores and buildings appr[opri]ated to Confederate purposes; all the public buildings of the State; the old capital; the arsenal; the armory, powder mills, &c. The injury done to the work prepared for the [new] capital & upon it, has alone been computed at one million [of] dollars. No estimate can be made of the losses of the [State] in public & private property. But as copious statements of [the dev]astation & robbery of the city have already been put [in pri]nt, and accessible to all, we need not pause for [the menti]on of details here. — Alarmed by a reported disaster [near Lancaster] to his cavalry, under an attack of Hampton, [the en]emy precipitated his departure from Columbia, pressing forward in this direction. His columns spread widely, as before in his progress, on either hand. On the left, they struck the corner of Newberry District t[o] & including Pomaria, where they are described as indulging in

---

[60] The date was the 15th.

their usual brutality & gratifying to the full their appetite for plunder. Still on the left, they passed through Fairfield, partially destroying the [to]wn of Winnsboro, which was also plundered. On this line, [def]le[c]ting to the right, they overswept Kershaw, partially des[troyin]g & fully plundering the town of Camden; swept through [the district] of Lancaster, traversed Chesterfield; burned a consid[erable por]tion of the town of Cheraw, & crossing a section of [Darl]ington & Marlborough, [*about one-half of a line missing*] [for]ty miles from right to left, finally passe[d out of this] State and into the neighbouring counties of Nor[th Car]olina.

[No signature.]

1120: To JAMES LAWSON

[May 25, 1865]

dear Lawson.

I need some succour of friends. Can you, & will you, honour my draft for one thousand dollars, at 3 days sight? Get Duyckinck to see Harper & Brothers, and see if they will advance me money on works to be furnished hereafter. I have written you by private hand already. Gilmore survives the war, though several times wounded. I have 6 children living. Telegraph me at once. Love to all. In haste, &

Ever truly Yours

W. Gilmore Simms
Columbia, S. C., May 25, '65

1121: To JAMES LAWSON

Columbia, S. C. June 13, 1865.

My dear Lawson.

I have a chance of writing you, but only a few moments. I have written you repeatedly, by parties going north, mostly returning soldiers, but half doubt whether you have recieved any of my letters. If you have not you have yet to learn that my house, newly rebuilt, has been destroyed by Sherman's army; my stables, carriage house, barns, gin house, machine and threshing houses; in short every building of any value; my mules, horses, cattle driven off & carried away, or butchered; my wagons, ploughs, implements, all destroyed; and I am here, temporarily destitute, without money to spare to telegraph you. I am sleeping in a garret, so are my daughters, Mary L. & Chevillette. Augusta, with her own daughter, & my two little boys are living with Mrs. Rivers at the little village of Bamberg, with barely bread enough to support life. I earn here a small pittance weekly, by editing a paper, newly started in this place, which does not yet pay.[61] Two weeks ago, I was summoned by telegraph to my son, Gilmore, who lay dangerously ill, in the town of Chester, some 65 miles off. He had typhoid fever. I had to borrow the money, a trifle, to eke out the little I had, in order to get to him — had to travel in a wagon, all the railways being destroyed. I found him delirious, raving, & without sleep for 5 days. By the blessings of the Good God he is spared; and the crisis terminated favorably. I left him convalescent & out of all danger, but too feeble to travel, and had to leave him, to see to my duties here & my other children. Thirty of my negroes were carried off by Sherman's Army; the rest are at work, after a fashion, but greatly needing my presence & help; and I have still my lands, and some of my property to see after. Yet I lack the means to get home again. The railroads destroyed, the horses & mules carried off, it is only at long intervals that an opportunity offers for travel, and it requires money — which I have not. Can you help me to any? You are aware that I have rarely taxed my friends for help of this nature, & nothing but the direst necessity compels me to call upon them now. I wish to borrow from you $500. If you can spare me this or any sum, send it to me here by the Adams Express Company, taking the usual precautions. To re-establish myself properly again, I shall need about $2000. I wish you, therefore, to see the Brothers Harper, who will probably help me in consideration of past & future. See them yourself or get Duyckinck to do so. I know of no good reason why he will hesitate to exercise all his influence

---

[61] The first issue of the Columbia *Phœnix* is dated March 21, 1865. It was a tri-weekly, published on Tuesdays, Thursdays, and Saturdays, until April 10, when it became a daily. On May 15 the title of the newspaper was altered to the Columbia *Daily Phœnix* and on July 31 to the *Daily Phœnix*. Julian A. Selby was the publisher, and Simms was editor until Oct., 1865 (see letter to Duyckinck of Oct. 1), though his name does not appear on the masthead of the newspaper.

In addition to writing editorials and news items for the *Daily Phœnix*, Simms also published in the newspaper his *Sack and Destruction of the City of Columbia, S. C.* (see note 47, March 6, 1865), a considerable number of poems, and a series of laconics.

in urging my wishes. I wish to get an advance from them, as much as they may be willing to spare, on account of future writings. I have two or three articles on hand, suitable for their monthly and which I deem very good.[62] These, I will revise in a few days, & forward by the next opportunity. You need hardly assure them, for they know me almost as well as you do, that I will faithfully work out the debt according to my best ability. My health is good, my strength unabated, and my mind, I think, in its best condition, at once vigorous & mature. Ask Duyckinck also to see the Publisher of my books.[63] There ought to be a very considerable sum to my credit during the last four terrible years, in which I have not had a cent from that source. I have about $20,000 in Confederate paper!! You have been apprised that I am a widower; that I have lost the one precious companion of 27 years. I have 3 boys & 3 daughters left. Gilmore has had several narrow escapes, & bears the marks of four desperate wounds, & has lost the middle finger of his left hand. But of all these miserable details hereafter. You have the will to succour me, I believe; I trust you have the ability also & that your family & fortune have suffered no loss in the terrible interval of time which has thrown an impassable chasm between us — impassable till now. Write me fully when you can, and by any opportunity offering. Mr. Selby,[64] the Publisher of the paper here, will probably seek you out. He left for the North during my absence, or I should have written you by him. Telegraph me as soon as you have resolved to send, or procure me any assistance. The telegraph works, though the mails do not. Tomorrow, we have a public meeting here, for the purpose of restoring the State to the Union.[65] I would that I could come to you for a few weeks; but this is seemingly impossible at present. You can send a letter or letters by the Express Company. Tell Duyckinck that I will write him by the next opportunity — would write him now, but that no time is allowed me for more than

---

[62] Nothing which we can ascribe to Simms was published in *Harper's New Monthly Magazine* until 1870. *Harper's* for October of that year contains his "How Sharp Snaffles Got His Capital and Wife," XLI, 667-687.

[63] William J. Widdleton.

[64] Julian A. Selby (b. 1833), printer and publisher of Columbia, was the author of *Memorabilia and Anecdotal Reminiscences of Columbia, S. C., and Incidents Connected Therewith* (Columbia, S. C.: The R. L. Bryan Company, 1905).

[65] Simms was appointed to a committee of twenty-one men to communicate to President Johnson the desire of South Carolina to return to the Union. See "Return to the Union—Public Meeting," *Daily Phœnix*, June 15.

this letter to you. Telegraph me as soon after the reciept of this as you can, as to what I may expect or hope, & as to what can be done. Among my losses is my library, 10,700 vols! My books! My books! My heart is ready to break when I think of them. I have had nothing new, in the way of books for four years. My friends here, by the way, the very wealthiest are incapable of helping me, or I should not call upon you & my friends at the North. They have the will, but are as helpless as myself. But enough. I will tell you all, when I am more calm. My love to Lyde and all the children. I think of them as fondly & tenderly as ever — think of you all a thousand times a day, & have had you all in my prayers. I sincerely hope that Jimmy is spared to you also — that he has not been forced to engage in the war; and that peace & love, & prosperity are still in your possession making the happiness of your household. And now, old friend, God be with & bless you still. My girls send their love. They will probably prepare a letter for Mary & Kate in readiness for the next opportunity. Once more, à Dio.

Yours Ever as Ever,

W. Gilmore Simms.

1122: To Evert Augustus Duyckinck [66]

Columbia, S. C. June 15. 1865.

Evert A. Duyckinck Esq.

My dear Duyckinck.

An opportunity by a traveller, at length gives me a chance of communicating with you, and I assume that you will not be displeased at the prospect of a resumption of our ancient and grateful intimacy. You have probably been apprised already of the destruction of my house and plantation, by your army under Sherman. The house had been recently rebuilt. It is completely destroyed; all my furniture, and — my library! — not a volume was spared. You can form, from what you know, a sufficient idea of the value of the collection which numbered some 10,700 vols. My carriage house, stables, kitchen, barns, machine house,

---

[66] This letter is printed, with minor inaccuracies, in Alfred Taylor Odell's "William Gilmore Simms in the Post-War Years," *Bulletin of Furman University*, XXIX (May, 1946), 5-8. The original of Duyckinck's reply to this letter, dated July 1, is in the South Caroliniana Library.

threshing house, wagons, implements of husbandry, — all shared the same fate. Eighteen mules & horses were carried off, and how many head of cattle, hogs, poultry destroyed, it is impossible to say. Thirty one of my negroes were carried off. Some 45 remain, of whom 5 are over 70, as many over 60, and perhaps 10 are children less than 10 years of age. Their provisions were all taken from them, and they, like myself, are almost destitute. There are 17 now at work on the place, but these, without tools, implements, mules, wagons &c. will hardly be able to earn their bread. I, at all events, can derive nothing from their labour, & what they shall make is yielded to them wholly. My family is temporarily scattered among relatives & friends. Two of my girls are with me here.[67] We are all sleeping in garrets, and my only present resource is a few dollars per week, derived from contributions to a petty County Court Newspaper; and how long this source of revenue will continue is very doubtful. Meanwhile, our railways are all destroyed — but few beasts of burthen are left in the country, and these are all absorbed in the cultivation of the present crop. It is accordingly impossible for me at present even to get back to my plantation, lacking equally in money & the ability to walk. The Pedestrian now is with us almost the only traveller. Money is so scarce that one's richest friends cannot give him succour, to the amount of ten dollars, without considerable self deprivation, and I have only been kept from telegraphing you & Lawson, by sheer inability to pay for the telegrams. I am, under these circumstances, constrained to ask what my friends in New York & elswhere can do for me. I need present succour, and such pecuniary help as will enable me to start anew the operations of my plantation, though on a greatly reduced scale. I have written to Lawson, by the same conveyance with this, to lend me a small sum of money & forward it by express. (There are no mails now.) I do not address the same request to you, but wish you to serve me in another way. I wish you to see Harper & Brothers, and get them to advance me whatever sum they can or please, on the strength of future writings, either in their magazine or in separate volumes. A like bargain may be made with any other publishers whom you may know, of liberal character. You & they know enough of me to believe that (D. V.) I will faithfully fulfil my pledges of repayment, in the process of time, and as soon as opportunity is

---

[67] Mary Lawson and Chevillette. See letter to Lawson of June 13.

allowed me. I wish you next to inquire into the condition of my copyrights, and ascertain what is due me on the sale of my books, upon which I have not for five years recieved one copper. The sum ought to be a considerable one. Whatever you may obtain from these several sources, much or little, I will thank you to forward, or have forwarded, as soon as possible by the Express Company, taking all the usual securities. I have a few articles in hand now, suitable for Harper's Magazine, which I will revise & forward them by the next opportunity. I have written to Lawson to put himself *en rapport* with you in regard to these matters. As I shall need to gather from all sources, in order to even the most partial reestablishment of my affairs, I would like to know from you, if a private subscription could not be obtained, for an illustrated octavo containing my complete poetical works. This stereotyped might afford me a prolonged (even if small) source of income.[68] And I could wish to have some books sent me, through John Russell, of Charleston. I have had nothing to read for 4 years, and the publishers might well make up a collection for an author whose own contributions to literature have been so various and extensive. I know your influence & the good taste & judgment with which you could prosecute these objects to a successful result, if your old feelings and sympathies have survived the terrible war which has prostrated me & mine.[69] What you do, in respect to the money advances, please do quickly, as I wish to escape the humbling necessity of incurring petty debts at the shops of strangers. I wish to break away, get home, & go to work in solitude & quiet, if not in peace & happiness. Of my domestic circle hereafter. Enough that I am a widower & have buried 9 out of 15 children. My hair & beard are quite white, and I am verging on 60, but I am healthy, comparatively vigorous, & with my children present ever to my eyes, I feel that I have many years of good work in me yet, — if my

---

[68] This volume was not published.

[69] In his letter of July 1 Duyckinck writes: "I have seen Mr Widdleton who has now the publication of your novels. Of course the war has *greatly* impeded their value; but he has done what could be done to keep them in the market and something, say $100, may be expected from this source. He will make up the account at once. I will see the Harpers immediately with Lawson and trust to accomplish something there. Lawson is over head and ears in business now during the few hours he can be in the city. . . . Widdleton & Scribner, and doubtless others, will be happy to send you parcels of their books. It cannot be long before the railways will be in operation for Prince Cotton, if not for you and I, when you may doubtless enjoy a resumption of your old literary activities."

friends will help to rescue me from my shackles. Excuse this hurried epistle, which is written *stans pede in uno,* & with the momentary expectation that it will be called for. Besides, all my old familiar conveniences of desk, table, portfolio, good pens &c. are gone. I am literally the inhabitant of a garret, such as Grub Street would recognize from family likeness, & such as Goldsmith so well describes.[70] Half of my study & bedroom is piled up with old lumber, boxes, trunks & bedding. Telegraph me whatever you do, as soon after the reciept of this as you conveniently can. — And believe me Ever, with the old time regard.

Your friend &c.

W. Gilmore Simms

1123: To Evert Augustus Duyckinck

[June? 1865] [71]

My dear Duyckinck.

I enclose a poem which I trust you will be able to commend to our venerable friends, Harper & Brothers, as blending, in happy relation, the sensuous, thoughtful, & imaginative. Pray see them at once, & what you do for me, do quickly. I have no reason to doubt that H & B. feel for me as kindly as ever.

Yours &c

W. Gilmore Simms.

1124: To Edward Roach

Columbia, June 25. 1865.

My dear Edward.

The girls & myself have repeatedly written to you, Augusta, and Mr. Rivers, and I suppose, by this time, you have been fully advised of every thing that concerns us here.[72] Gilmore, I

---

[70] See "A Description of an Author's Bedchamber."

[71] This letter was probably written shortly after June 15, when Simms wrote to Duyckinck that he had "a few articles in hand now, suitable for Harper's Magazine, which I will revise & forward them by the next opportunity." We are unable to identify the poem Simms enclosed.

[72] Augusta, Edward, and their daughter, Chevillette, were living with the Christopher McKinney Riverses in Bamberg.

left convalescent & out of danger, but too feeble to travel. He
was a mere skeleton after the fever left him, but with a good
appetite & tolerably cheerful. I have heard of, but not from
him, since my leaving him, and he was reported to be still improving. Mr. Isaacs has gone up for Lizzie [73] & I trust he may
be able to bring Gilmore down with him. I wait his arrival
before coming down to Barnwell, & hope that his presence will
enable me to make my meditated trip. But I shall not leave here,
until perfectly assured of his safety by his arrival. When I come
down, I hope to adjust the affairs with the negroes. Meanwhile,
I could wish that you & Mr. Rivers would procure some help
from your neighbours, at least to haul up from Woodlands, the
bedding, bureaus & whatever else has been saved. Say to Isaac
that I shall expect him Edward & John [74] to drive up the cow
or cows, & whatever else you & Mr. R. may think proper to
bring away. Say to these three men that if they do not obey, I
shall have them tried by the Yankee officers for disobedience &
misconduct. Find out from Tench, & Isaac, & Edward, what
butter & other things have been sold by Diana & to what persons.[75] I wish you also to make inquiries as to the opinion entertained of the burning of the House &c. I propose to have
the incendiaries tried for the crime, under the charges made by
Mrs. Pinckney, — i.e. if the opinion of the neighbours is against
them. Let Augusta sound Tench on the subject.[76] You cannot
sell your Bond at present without great sacrifice, and it will all
be ultimately good. As for the money issued by the Town Council
it does not seem to be much taken here, but I may, at all events,
get the interest on the Bond in this money, & see what I can
do with it. I am in hopes to get some money from the North
before coming down, & I propose buying with it enough of
corn, flour, bacon &c. to last the family at Bamberg through
the year at least, and as much beyond as possible. I enclose a
power of attorney to Mr. Rivers, and he will please get Charles
Carroll & Dr. Fishburne to examine it, and if they think my

---

[73] George E. Isaacs' daughter.

[74] Former slaves.

[75] Tench and Diana were also former slaves. Isaac was Isaac Nimmons,
Simms' body servant.

[76] For Simms' account of the burning of Woodlands, see note 48, March 6,
1865. Evidently he had recently heard reports which led him to believe that
perhaps the slaves did have something to do with starting the fire. Simms'
children, however, said that ultimately he completely exonerated the slaves and
laid the blame on stragglers from Gen. Sherman's army.

terms fair, then request the United States officers, on the spot, to give it their sanction and explain it to the negroes, and make them sensible of the liberality of its provisions. I will make no agreement beyond the present year. He will also request the U. S. officers to expel from the plantation all negroes that do not belong to it, making them seek their former places of work or abode. It is not easy for me to get away from this place. I have but $7. in money, and shall be required to pay something more than this to get Gilmore down. By next Saturday[77] there will be $10 due me; but even this will not suffice, even if I use none of it here, to enable Gilmore & myself to get down to you. I am therefore looking *with all anxiety,* to succour from abroad. I trust that the Good God will come to our relief in due season, and enable us to lift the burdens that now so oppressively rest upon our hearts & shoulders. Mr. Selby is absent at the North, & it will probably be two weeks more, before he returns. I would not willingly leave his paper until he does return. The girls will write Mary[78] & Augusta. We are all glad to hear that Mary is recovering. She has suffered long enough. I am not well. Have been suffering ever since I left Chester, from the water of that place. On Saturday, I was on the eve of being arrested for an article in the paper. The article of arrest was made out; but, cited to appear before the General in Command, I satisfied him that his arrest would be an error.[79] Love to Mary & Augusta.

---

[77] June 31.

[78] Mary Rivers.

[79] About forty years later Julian A. Selby wrote of Simms' threatened arrest in *Memorabilia and Anecdotal Reminiscences of Columbia, South Carolina* (Columbia: R. L. Bryan Company, 1905), pp. 24-25: "During my absence on one occasion, Mr. S. ventilated Gen. [Alfred S.] Hartwell (formerly Colonel of a colored regiment), who commanded this department, and warmed him up pretty thoroughly. A corporal and squad of soldiers waited on Mr. Simms that day, with a summons to appear at once before the offended General, at his headquarters, northwest corner Bull and Gervais streets. Of course, the order was obeyed. Entering the room where military law was being dispensed, Mr. Simms embraced the opportunity of a temporary lull in the proceedings, to request to be allowed to seat himself, as he was well advanced in years; and he was permitted so to do — an orderly quietly handing him a chair. His turn soon came. Mr. G. [*sic*] was placed directly in front of the General, and the trial began. In a very short time the charge was dismissed, and Mr. S. was invited to partake of an elegant luncheon in an adjoining room, which he politely accepted. When Mr. Simms returned to his quarters, it was in Gen. Hartwell's carriage, with a large basket filled with champagne and canned delicacies. The General expressed himself to Col. [Nathaniel] Haughton (of the Ohio Veteran Volunteers) the next day, to the effect that if Mr. S. was a specimen of the South Carolina gentleman, he would never enter into a tilt with one of them again. 'He out-talked me, out-drank me, and very clearly and politely showed me that I lacked proper respect for the aged.' 'I

Kiss them & the children for us. Best regards to Mr. R. and God's blessing on you all.

Your affect father

W. Gilmore Simms.

1125: To James Lawson

Columbia, S. C. June 27. '65.

My dear Lawson.

This will be handed you by the Hon. Mr. J. G. Gibbes, Mayor of the City of Columbia.[80] He is on a mission to Washington, as our representative to apply for the restoration of S. C. to the Union. He will extend his visit to New York, where he has business. He is a man of education, energy & intelligence, a business man, and you can be of much service, in making him familiar with places & persons of business in your city. Let me beg you to do so. He will report to you the condition of things here, &, in some measure, my own condition. On this subject, I have already written you at large, & look daily, with hope, to hear of & from you. I need the succour of my friends. They may enable me to recover something from the wreck; to renew my work, if not restore my house. Mr. Gibbes will bring on letters and any small packages for me. If you can help me in any degree, you will do so. Perhaps, there may be other friends to cooperate with you in doing so. Pray write me soon. A telegram from you, as letters are slow & circuitous, would be grateful. Money can

---

told you so,' was Haughton's reply." If an affront to Gen. Hartwell was, as Selby reports, the occasion for Simms' summons, it was an imaginary affront: the only mention of Hartwell in the Columbia *Phœnix* for two weeks prior to June 25 (Sunday) is in the issue for June 22, which reports merely that he has returned to Columbia from Orangeburg. What Simms' offensive article was we do not know; perhaps it was "Taveau Has the Floor," in the issue for June 23, in which Simms discusses a letter by Augustin Louis Taveau (see note 191, Dec. 15, 1848) recently published in the New York *Tribune* and, in so doing, attacks the Northern newspapers for their treatment of the South.

[80] James Guignard Gibbes (1827-1903), born in Columbia, was graduated from the South Carolina College in 1847. Prior to the Confederate War he was the chief engineer in the building of the Columbia and Greenville Rail Road and the New Orleans, Opelousas, and Georgia Western Rail Road. During the Confederate War he was sent to Europe and successfully negotiated a cotton loan for the Confederate States. He then enlisted for active service in the Confederate States Army, but was detached to take charge of an Augusta factory to make cloth. He became mayor of Columbia the day after Sherman's army burned the city.

be forwarded — Greenbacks — by the Adams Express Company. Get Duyckinck to see what the Publishers of my books owe me, and see what Harper & Bro. will advance me on the strength of articles to be furnished them hereafter. Love to all as Ever, & Ever as Ever Yours, — & in haste.

W. Gilmore Simms

1126: To Evert Augustus Duyckinck

Columbia, S. C. June 27, '65.

Evert A. Duyckinck, Esq.

My dear Duyckinck.

This will be handed you by the Hon. J. G. Gibbes, Mayor of the City of Columbia. He will be able to give you all information about my condition & the condition of things here. He is a man of business & of great energy & large intelligence, especially in business affairs. He goes specially from our Committee of the people here, to present our application to the President for the restoration of South Carolina, to the Union. But he also has business in New York, & you may be of much service to him in affording facilities to his acquaintance with men of business. May I beg that you will promote his objects where you can possibly do so. He will bring back letters to me, & probably be able to bring any small packages. I have written you at length already by other opportunities, & trust that you have recieved my letters & will be pleased to do for me the services requested. Your influence with the publishers will procure me books. I have had nothing new for four years; my library is destroyed; my house, furniture, property, and I and my children are the occupants of rooms in a garret. Enough. And — God bless you.

Yours ever truly, but in haste,

W. Gilmore Simms.

1127: To E. C. Doughty [81]

Columbia, S. C. June 27 1865

E. C. Doughty, Esq.

Sir:

I comply with your wishes from a home in ashes, with heart sore and stricken, under the scourge of a Fate which I trust will never visit your roof-tree in your old age.

Your obt. Servt.

W. Gilmore Simms

P. S. This will probably be handed you by the Hon. Mr. J. G. Gibbes, Mayor of the City of Columbia, a man of character & business, to whom, if you are a business man, you may profitably render some attentions.

1128: To William Hawkins Ferris

Columbia, S. C. July 22. '65.

W. Hawkins Ferris, Esq.

dear Sir.

I have ordered the Phœnix newspaper to be sent you by the Publisher. It is a small sheet & will hardly interest you. I have no concern in the publication save as *quasi* editor, and do not expect long to continue in this position.

I thank you, my dear Sir, for your kind sympathies so warmly expressed. They are very grateful to one suddenly made homeless, stript of nearly all his possessions, and after a life and condition of comparative ease, compelled, in his old age, to sleep in a garret, which, during this terrible heat, is like sleeping under the leads of a Venetian prison. I regret to mention that among my losses by the destruction of my house was the beautiful painting you were so good as to send me.[82] It has shared the fate of 76 others.

Yours very truly

Wm. Gilmore Simms

---

[81] The New York City directories for 1864-1871 list E. C. Doughty, a book-keeper living in 1865 at 155 Duffield Street. Directories for different years list him variously as E. C. Doughty, Egbert C. Doughty, and Edward C. Doughty.

[82] In his letter to Ferris of Sept. 4, 1859, Simms had written: "It is probable that I shall visit N. Y. in October. If so, I shall find you out & your painter." Perhaps Ferris' "painter" was the artist who did "the beautiful painting" lost when Woodlands was burned.

1129: To Benjamin Franklin Perry [83]

[July 28, 1865] [84]

My dear Governor.

The preceeding letter speaks for itself. Mr. Boatwright, the writer, is the son of the well known physician of Columbia, of the same name, whom I take for granted that you have long & sufficiently, as well as favorably known. He is a fine & promising young man of 22 years, who has lost four most important years of his life in the late wretched war. These four years, passed in training, would have probably found him now in the pursuit of some profitable profession or occupation. As it is, he is stranded on a desert shore, like too many of us, without being able to get into his proper element. If you can do any thing to give him present occupation, implying mere support, I could wish that you would do so. Mr. Boatwright, as you will have seen by his letter, writes a good hand, & composes very well. I may add that he is a fine looking young man, with a most proper grace of manner, well blended with modesty, that rose of youth. I commend him to your favour. —

I have been hoping, my dear Governor, for your presence in Columbia, having much to say to you, & hoping to hear from you much more. If you have seen the little paper which I have been conducting in this city, you will see that I have not been forgetful of our old friendship of a Hundred Years ago.[85]

With best regards to your family, believe me,

Very truly as Ever,
Your friend &c

His Excellency,
Hon. B. F. Perry.

W. Gilmore Simms

---

[83] On June 30 President Johnson appointed Perry provisional governor of South Carolina. He served as provisional governor until James Lawrence Orr was inaugurated governor in Nov., 1865.

[84] This letter is a postscript to a letter from John H. Boatwright, Jr., to Perry dated "July 28, [1865]." Boatwright, the son of Dr. John H. Boatwright, who lived at the corner of Sumter and Washington streets in Columbia, was a cadet at the Citadel Academy earlier this year.

[85] In the *Daily Phœnix* of July 8 Simms writes of Perry: "Mr. Perry, a distinguished lawyer, a man of fine morals, excellent character and sound, manly sense, has been through life a consistent Union man. . . . He was opposed resolutely to the secession of the State, and regretted the measure to the last. . . . We regard Mr. Perry as really one of the most unexceptionable persons who could be presented to the United States authorities [for the position of provisional governor of South Carolina]." See, also, the *Daily Phœnix* of July 7, July 14, July 17, and July 22.

1130: To EVANDER McIVOR LAW [86]

Columbia, S. C. Aug. 12. 1865.

Gen. E. M. Law.

My dear General.

I presume that, before this, you have seen the humble tribute which I prepared in the Columbia Phœnix, editorially, seeking to honor the memory of our friend, Mr. Latta.[87] I had a copy addressed to you after its publication, but as I was then about to hurry off to Barnwell & Orangeburg, to which two regions my family had already gone, I had no time to answer directly your painfully interesting letter.[88] I employed its contents, however, in preparing my notice, and greatly regret that the materials were so scanty. I could only guess at his age, and, from ignorance, had to forbear details which it would yet have been very interesting to publish, as contributing to the completeness of the notice. Still, I trust, with all its defects, that it will afford a melancholy satisfaction to Mrs. Latta,[89] and her & your family. It embodies my conviction of his great & many excellencies of mind & heart, and is, I think, at once sincere in opinion, and honorable to the subject. Mr. L. had been always a kind & amiable friend to me, and more than once had expressed an earnest wish to serve me in important respects, especially when he knew that I was suffering from domestic afflictions & large material losses. I felt that he was sincere in all these expressions, & have no reason to question the fidelity with which he welcomed me & mine to his home & heart. I shall not soon forget his frequent

---

[86] Law (1836-1920) was graduated from the Citadel Academy in 1856 and taught at the King's Mountain Military School, Yorkville (now York), S. C., and then at the Military High School, Tuskegee, Ala. In 1861 he recruited a company and was commissioned captain in the Confederate States Army. He was promoted to lieutenant colonel in 1861, to brigadier general in 1862, and to major general in 1864. He was in command of Columbia when Gen. Sherman approached the city. After the Confederate War he was a planter in Tuskegee and Yorkville, where he resumed connection with the King's Mountain Military School (then called the King's Mountain Military Academy) until it closed in 1884. He later established at Bartow, Fla., the South Florida Military and Educational Institute. On March 9, 1863, he married Jane Elizabeth Latta, daughter of William Albert Latta, of Yorkville.

[87] William Albert Latta, Law's father-in-law (see note 181, Sept. 15, 1855), died on July 7. Simms' obituary of Latta appears in the *Daily Phœnix* of July 26.

[88] In an editorial in the *Daily Phœnix* of Aug. 12 Simms says that he has "just returned from a ten days' absence in the Districts of Orangeburg and Barnwell."

[89] The former Anna Clark Clark, of Winnsboro, S. C.

kindnesses, his warm entreaties, the pleasant hours I passed in his household, the grateful trip together into North Carolina, & the invitations he gave me to still farther rambles in his company & carriage.[90] You have said but the simplest truth when you assure me that in his death, I was the loser of a faithful friend. It is our loss that we need to lament; not his; — for in the case of one so pure & simple-hearted, so truthful, innocent & liberal, I take for granted that the final change from time to eternity, must have been an exceeding gain [91] to him. I shall hold his memory dear to me, while any memory is left. He has escaped much painful & depressing experience in worldly affairs. If I can afford you any counsel at any time, be so good as to believe me a true friend of the family, prepared to yield you from my experience & thought & labour, any service which you may need. Have you applied for a pardon? And will this not be essential to your usefulness in managing the affairs of Mrs. Latta & of the family generally. Do not regard me as impertinent in this suggestion. I presume that it has occurred to you already. Had Mr. Latta lived, he too would have needed to have sought a pardon for the treasonable offense of being wealthy beyond a Procrustean standard. In the division of his property, it may not be necessary to seek it for the widow & his children. But it is probably absolutely essential to you in all your own future performances. Not to procure it, may greatly embarrass your usefulness, to others as to yourself. Please present me affectionately to Mrs. Latta, to your wife, and all members of the family. Should you or any of them visit this town, pray have me sought out. I am still conducting the Phœnix paper, which yields me a miserable stipend, hardly the wages of a Journeyman printer. I do not expect to retain the situation beyond the summer months. By the timely assistance of a couple of friends at the North,[92] I obtained money enough to send my two youngest daughters to their relatives in Orangeburg, there to pass a couple of months, until I can find them some humble shelter of my own. My eldest daughter, with her husband & child, and my three sons, I have sent to Barnwell, where they have found a temporary shelter also. My dwelling was completely destroyed, and I must wait for the accumulation of a few hundred Dollars, before I

---

[90] See letter to the Charleston *Mercury* of Sept. 15, 1855.

[91] Simms wrote *exceeding game* or *exceeding gaine.*

[92] One of these friends was Lawson. See letter to Duyckinck of Aug. 12.

can rebuild a small wing of three rooms, into which I must try & crowd them all as winter comes on. For my own part, I need only to find respite from present necessities to resume my profession, and if my right hand has not lost all its cunning, I trust to extort from Fortune, tho' now 60 years old, an adequate means of living decently to the end of the chapter. I shall also try, when we get again under civil regulation, to procure some modest office in the State which will enable me to perfect my history of So. Caro. and put on record some few more of these domestic histories, as fictions, by which I trust to identify my name with hers, for a long future.[93] I trust that you will send good sensible & legal minds to the *Convention*,[94] and send to the Legislature the most modest, sedate, thoughtful & circumspect *Representatives*. Of the Senator you need not be too tenacious; but we should have shrewd, thoughtful & sagacious men in the House, capable of new ideas, and of comprehending the necessity for a radical change, or changes, in our domestic policy, corresponding with our changed conditions & new interests. I do not know whether you see the Phœnix, but, if you do, you will see that I have thrown out hints for future legislators, of those subjects which must come up for consideration.[95] — How do mules & horses sell in your precinct. I need one or more, but those offered here, though low in price, are generally low in flesh & high in years. I lost, in all, 17 mules & horses carriages & buggies, carts & wagons in proportion. Write me soon, if you please & can, and especially inform me as to the health & prosperity of Mrs. L. & family, hers and yours, to whom I commend myself as a friend most respectfully & earnestly.

Very truly Yours

W. Gilmore Simms.

---

[93] The last edition of Simms' *History of South Carolina* published during his lifetime is that dated 1866. See note 139, July 1, 1866.

[94] Delegates to the State Convention for the revision of the Constitution of South Carolina, elected on Sept. 4, assembled in Columbia on Sept. 13 and adjourned on Sept. 27. Simms was not a delegate. See *Journal of the Convention of the People of South Carolina, Held in Columbia, S. C., September, 1865. Together with the Ordinances, Reports, Resolutions, Etc.* (Columbia, S. C.: J. A. Selby, Printer to the Convention, 1865).

[95] Simms appears to have written most, if not all, of the editorials in the *Daily Phœnix*.

1131: To Evert Augustus Duyckinck

Columbia, S. C.
Augt. 12. 1865.

My dear Duyckinck.

Since your first letter, I have had no other from you. I have written you two in reply to it, and now address you the third.[96] All these letters have to be despatched by private hand, as we have neither post office nor regular mails. It is quite probable that the hurry & remissness of the parties, by whom my letters were sent, may have occasioned their failure. One of them, addressed to Godey, has been returned to me through the Charleston P. O. in consequence of the nonpayment of stamps. Not a stamp is to be had here for love or money.[97] Cover me a few, if you please. Our only communications with the surrounding country, are by a few miserable wagons; and it is only now & then that we hear of a citizen going to the North. I forward this by a hand, which, I trust, will secure its safe delivery either to yourself in person, or at your post office. He[98] promises me to procure the stamps when he shall reach some town where they are to be had. In my first letter I sufficiently described to you my wretched situation.[99] I have lost every thing but my lands. I have barely a sufficiency of clothes — chiefly homespun — for decency; and with 9 persons to support,[100] my whole income is but $10 per week, and, until I can get means to get away from this place, & to find a comfortable shelter for my little ones, I can do nothing better. With a little help from Lawson, I have sent off all my family to Barnwell, where my eldest son is striving to make some outhouses habitable. My eldest daughter, Mrs. Roach, with her husband and one child, and with my two youngest boys, are about to go thither in a few days. I have succeeded in buying them 50 bushels of corn, & hope to procure a little bacon for them, and with this they must make out. Nearly all my hogs & cattle have been destroyed, by Sherman

---

[96] We have not located these earlier two replies to Duyckinck's letter of July 1 (cited note 66, June 15, 1865).

[97] Doubtless Simms had written Godey asking to contribute to *Godey's*. We are unable to ascribe to Simms anything published in *Godey's* after this date.

[98] Not identified.

[99] See letter of June 15.

[100] Evidently Simms here counts himself, his six children (Augusta, Gilmore, Mary Lawson, Chevillette, Govan, and Carroll), Augusta's husband (Edward Roach), and their daughter (Chevillette).

first & the negroes afterwards. My two other daughters, one 18
& the other 16 are with friends & relatives in Orangeburg. I
have no home for them, & cannot support them here. My first
object is to procure enough money to make a house comfortable
for them & myself before the approach of winter. Hence the
solicitude expressed to you & Lawson in my first letters. You
may concieve the growth of my anxiety since from neither of
you do I hear a syllable, since your first writings. Though quite
confounded to hear of the small sum mentioned by Mr. Widdleton
as coming to me from Copyrights,[101] yet even this is too important to my present necessities to make me indifferent to it,
and I could wish, if not too much taking your time & sympathy
that you would get his accounts & the money immediately, &
get Lawson to put up & forward by express. He (Lawson) is
practised in the business & would spare you this part of the
trouble. — It would be much to me, if Harper & Brothers could
be persuaded to remit me a few hundred dollars on the strength
of papers, tales &c. for their magazine, which I would proceed
to prepare as soon as I can get things decently settled at the
plantation.[102] Here, I write in a borrowed room. My chamber
in a garret, being under the *leads,* as in Venice, is almost killing,
day & night. In fact, I mostly sleep in an open piazza, on a
mattress spread on the floor, and free to the incursions of the
musquitos, to say nothing of other insect invaders. Verily, that
I can write or think at all, is wonderful. I need a few hundred
dollars to buy lumber, for building 3 rooms at the plantation —
need a couple of mules for hauling lumber & material — need
crockery, clothes, bedding, &c. My hat, a vile thing, cost me
$400. My shoes, the commonest farmers, which pain me as
I walk, cost $300. My son, just recovering from typhoid, comes
home to me naked. But you can concieve all. If the publishers
could make me these advances, I could begin the world anew,
and set my wheels & springs in motion. I am conscious of no
diminution of powers. My health is good — my frame vigorous,
and, once restored to peace of mind, — freed from the terrible
anxieties about my children, which now afflict & keep me sleepless, I believe that I could do better things in letters than I have
ever done before. I have my brain seething ever and anon, with
fresh conceptions, over which I brood at intervals, with a loving

---

[101] $100. See note 69, June 15, 1865.
[102] See note 62, June 13, 1865.

mood of meditation which makes them grow upon me, until the images become as familiar to the eye, as they have been to the mind. You suggest to me a part in politics. It may be that I shall take your advice.[103] My neighbours have applied to me to go to the Convention.[104] This I have declined; but have told them that if sent to the Lower House in the Legislature, where much good & fresh work is to be done, I will go, provided they do not ask me to canvas the country.[105] I have schemes for revolutionizing the whole industrial system of our country, which I have long regarded with distrust & suspicion. But, I have no room to explain. Meanwhile, you will see, from all that I have said, that my first care, is my poor little flock of fugitive children. I have 9 of these, including grandchildren,[106] whom I have to support now on $10 per week! See if your publishers & patrons of Literature have magnanimity enough to give present employment, and a small credit, to one, who after 40 years service in the field of letters, may well consider himself a veteran — one not broken down in the service, but wretchedly out of repair. — I am also greatly in need of Books, — have had nothing to read for 4 years. My library gone — & no books for study. Can you not have some sent me — "Care of John Russell, Charleston" — to await my orders. Please write to J. T. Fields [107] on this subject. — But, I pause. I hesitate! May I not be trespassing too much on our ancient friendship? Has the war chilled you towards your Southern friends? Has politics killed Literature? Where are you? Speak! What are our present relationships. At all events, may God forgive & be with you in mercy.

Yours as Ever.

W. Gilmore Simms.

---

[103] In his letter of July 1 Duyckinck writes: "You may . . . find politics a more inviting field than literature for some time to come. I would not intrude advice; but I cannot help recurring to the thought that men of ability, integrity and patriotic lovers of the Union may by their timely efforts *now*, immensely hasten the reconstruction and development of the South on a firmer, more assured and more profitable basis of prosperity than ever."

[104] The State Convention. See note 94, Aug. 12, 1865.

[105] Simms was not elected to the South Carolina legislature.

[106] Chevillette Roach was Simms' only grandchild alive at this time.

[107] James Thomas Fields, of Ticknor and Fields, Boston. See note 16, *c.* Jan. 18, 1854.

1132: TO JAMES LAWSON

Columbia, Sep. 9. 1865.

My dear Lawson.

I omitted from the Letter to you yesterday, the Enclosure of which I told you, from the publishers Street & Smith. I send it now. You will ascertain what you can about these parties & advise me what you think it my policy to do. Were I in New York, I could perhaps go to work at once, and earn the money.[108] But it is doubtful when I can get to New York, unless, indeed, I accept a proffered appointment from the Masonic Lodges of this place who wish to send a Commission of Three Masons to N. Y. Phil. & Boston, to try & make collections for the relief of the Fraternity in this place, the restoration of their paraphernalia & buildings. Since I saw you last, I was persuaded to join the Masons, & hence the prospect of my appointment.[109] But my presence will perhaps be needed at Woodlands, especially if I can procure means to rebuild any portion of my dwelling. If not, I shall have to hire some cottage at Bamberg or elswhere, and go to work as well as I can, in a wigwam. It is just possible, again that my people of Barnwell may wish to send me to the Legislature. I have been already applied to on the subject, and though I can ill afford the time, yet I should have to serve, if elected. I trust that this will not be the case, though Duyckinck counsels me to go into public life. I sent to him a poem which I hoped that he might dispose of to H. & B. or some other periodical publisher, procuring me some decent *quid* for it.[110] But I do not hear from him (with one exception) more than I hear from you. He has written me twice. Writing you so recently, and so much at length, I have nothing more to say, save that it is very difficult to write at all. The weather is so terribly hot, and my chamber & studio, all in one, are just under the sloping roof, briefly an old fashioned garret. I have hardly a comfort left, & shall enjoy no freedom of any kind untill I get home. Is Mary married yet? You did not tell me the name of her suitor. If not

---

[108] Simms may have been a contributor to *Street and Smith's New York Weekly* (see letters to Duyckinck of Sept. 9 and to Dawson of Oct. 2), though we are unable to attribute to him anything published in the periodical during this period or later. Francis S. Street and S. Francis Smith were partners in the firm of Street and Smith.

[109] See following letters.

[110] See letter to Duyckinck which we have dated June? 1865.

already married, I trust to be present when the affair comes off.[111]
My girls have written to her & to Kate, but have had no replies.
You are all as silent as the Cable, though not so deep I imagine.[112]
Love to all.

Yours Ever as Ever

W. G. S.

1133: To EVERT AUGUSTUS DUYCKINCK [113]

Columbia, S. C. Sept. 9. 1865

My dear Duyckinck. —

I enclose you a Letter which I have recieved from one of your
N. Y. Publishers. I meant to enclose it in one addressed to
Lawson, but find that I closed his letter without doing so. Will
you do me the favour to hand it to him & confer with him upon
the subject. I am at present here, fettered against my will, but I
hope to escape during the present month. I have given notice to the
Publisher of the Phœnix Newspaper that I will leave him by the
first of Oct. It is possible that I shall go hence to N. Y. Lawson
will tell you of those details which I need not repeat. My first
necessity is to put my children under shelter. That is my difficulty, and implies the necessity of some money — not a great
deal; but some is necessary. I am looking to Mr. Widdleton to
send me all he can; all that is due me. See Lawson's letter for
my expectations on this score. A few months ago, I had a volume
in press here. The advent of Sherman was fatal to its publication.
The book was considered a good book & so pronounced in your
journal. It is entitled "Tom Nettles; or as Good as a Comedy."
You will probably remember the story. It made about 250 pp.
duodecimo in Carey & Harts Library of Humourous Literature.
I propose that Mr. Widdleton should republish it, in connection
with another tale, though with this one title, uniform with my
other books. It will probably help the sale of the others.[114] I have

---

[111] According to a clipping of Mary Lawson's obituary from an unidentified
newspaper (now in the Charles Carroll Simms Collection and probably
formerly belonging to Simms' daughter Augusta) she was married on Oct. 26,
1865, to Thomas Sarjeant Sandford.
[112] During the summer of 1865 an unsuccessful attempt was made to lay
the Atlantic Cable. It was successfully laid the following year.
[113] This letter is printed, with minor inaccuracies, in Odell, "William Gilmore Simms in the Post-War Years," pp. 8-9.
[114] *As Good as a Comedy* (see note 79, March 28, 1851) has never been
republished. Perhaps the other "tale" Simms here has in mind is "Paddy
McGann" (see note 9, Jan. 10, 1863).

other materials which will be used in other volumes, & it is important to him that the works should be uniformly published. I do not see that in his advertisement, he has announced either the History of South Carolina, or the Cassique of Kiawah.[115] Of these two works, the History will always sell in the South, & the Cassique is one of my most interesting romances. In the conflict of interest between Redfield & other parties, I do not know where I am.[116] But it is the interest of all parties that the series should be published complete, in an unique edition. Will you enquire into the subject? I propose, if I do not at once come to N. Y. to proceed to the plantation & prepare a new romance, under the persuasions of Smith & Street, which I think I can make equal to any thing I have yet done. Is it possible for you to procure me a History of the Pyrates, the 2 vol. 8 vo. Edition?[117] This, with all my books, has been destroyed. It gives me great material, which I have long desired to work up into a standard romance of Pirate life & practice.[118] Any books which you may procure for me, you will be so good as to send to the "Care of William Roach, Mercht. of Charleston, S. C." Say to Mr Widdleton, that the set of my own works, handsomely bound, given me by Mr Redfield is lost. He may well send me a copy. I also need a Shakspeare, and whatever works he will be pleased to supply. Mr. Henry B. Dawson has written me to tender his aid in procuring me the beginning of a new library, & a ream of the paper which I write upon, and a corresponding supply of envelopes, with my name, has been sent me by a New York citizen whom I have never seen.[119] I do not despair. Let me hear from you & believe me

Ever truly Yours,

W. Gilmore Simms.

The portrait of your brother is very happy, and presents him to the life in his best aspect. I shall always remember him grate-

---

[115] Simms wrote *or the Cassique of Accabee.*

[116] See letter to Lawson of Oct. 20, 1860, and following letters to Lawson.

[117] Probably Capt. Charles Johnson (*pseudo.?*), *A General History of the Pyrates* . . . , 2 vols. (London: T. Warner; T. Woodward, 1724-1725).

[118] Simms started a romance entitled "The Brothers of the Coast" (see letter to Duyckinck of Feb. 20, 1866, and following letters). The MS. (173 pp.) of probably all that he wrote of it is in the Charles Carroll Simms Collection, South Caroliniana Library.

[119] A Mr. Seymour, whom Simms later came to know (see letter to Ferris of March 7, 1867). We are unable to identify him among the various Seymours listed in the New York City directories for this period.

fully.[120] If you can supply me with his several volumes, I shall be glad. I could also wish for a complete copy, or as much as you can supply, of the Literary World.[121] I have lost all except a few loose numbers. Thank you for the portrait. Procure me all the books you can. Without books, the life on a plantation, to a man of my tastes & habits, is terribly exhaustive. Mess'rs Appleton [122] might supply me liberally & lose nothing by it. Write me soon, & — ["]*de omnibus rebus*," [123] — for I have heard nothing for five years.

1134: To WILLIAM GILMORE SIMMS, JR.

Columbia 20th. Sept. 1865.

My dear Son.

I have paid over to Capt. Whetstone [124] One Hundred Dollars, which he is to hand over to you as soon after he goes home as possible. Fifty Dollars of this money belong to your sisters, Mary L. & Chevillette. It is the money sent them by Miss Kellogg.[125] The other fifty is my own, to be kept carefully, and expended only to meet exigencies on the plantation. I have notified Mr. Selby that I shall quit the Phœnix at the close of the present month. I propose then to run down to the plantation & see how you are getting on. After that, it is highly probable that I shall go to the North to see after my affairs in that quarter. There is some prospect of my being appointed one of the Commissioners on behalf of the Masons in this city, at the Northern cities, to which they have addressed a Memorial soliciting aid & assistance. If so, my route will be by land to Washington, Baltimore, Philadelphia, New York & Boston. They are to pay my expenses.[126] But of all this I shall report to you fully hereafter. In consequence of what was said in Augusta's & Edward's letters, if not your own, I have been expecting John Whetstone [127] & yourself in the wagon at Columbia. Capt. W. is doubtful about the matter. Your own letters have come to me very sparingly, and you write too

---

[120] George Long Duyckinck died on March 30, 1863.

[121] For Duyckinck's editorship of the *Literary World,* see note 34, Feb. 2, 1847.

[122] The president of D. Appleton and Co. was William Henry Appleton (1814-1899), son of the founder, Daniel Appleton (1785-1849).

[123] Simms failed to italicize *rebus.*

[124] John M. Whetstone (1809-1870), who lived near Midway.

[125] Nancy Kellogg, of Great Barrington, Mass.

[126] See following letters.

[127] Capt. Whetstone's son.

costively to give full satisfaction in regard to your several objects, plans, performances or desires. I am anxious, of course, to do & contribute all I can to your progress, but I am still more anxious that you should begin to do for and develope yourself, & the resources within you. Were I to die tomorrow, you would have devolved upon you the care for yourself & your sisters & brothers. I prefer to devolve this upon you now, while I still live to counsel & assist you. Do not allow your eagerness to be doing to make you precipitate in any case, where the result may be a serious loss or evil. You must temper your ardour with discretion. I shall not be surprised or vexed even if you blunder; but I shall be sadly mortified if you so greatly blunder as not to be able to recover quickly. Beware of committing yourself to the negroes. Entertain no large schemes for the future. Make your calculations simply to live & endure for awhile, untill we can see our way clearly. I bought a double barrelled gun at auction a day or two ago, which has been badly used but which I think may be made to do good service. If Edward [128] goes to town let him procure you a keg of powder, and a bag of squirrel shot. We ought to be able to live on squirrels this winter, though we shall try to lay in sufficient stores to be independent of them. It is the day of small things, and the wise man will make the most of small things. You should write me what you desire me to get here & bring or send down. If I dared send money by letter you should have had it before; but Capt. Whetstone will probably be too late to supply you before Edward goes. I have not heard from you for ten days. It is very important that I should know whether you design coming here or not, with the wagon. Should you come, I could buy certain articles here which the family will need; and the difference of cost would not probably be material. Your fellow Charley [129] has played you a shabby trick. I gave him $5 and upon that he has probably been tempted away, having got within a stone's throw of you. There is but little faith to be reposed in the generality of men, especially when they have lived loose lives, or a life of adventure. But we need waste no words on him. I shall silently make my preparations, and hope to be down with you the first week in October. I get no letters, & know nothing about you or the girls or the children. When letters come they are 10 days old. God be with you all in mercy.

Your aff. father

W. Gilmore Simms

---

[128] Edward Roach.
[129] Not identified.

1135: To Evert Augustus Duyckinck [130]

Columbia, S. C.
Oct. 1. 1865.

My dear Duyckinck.

Thanks for your several letters and your attention to my petty commissions. I know not whether my letters reach you regularly or not, &, doubting, I may have to repeat something already expressed. As yet we have no regular mails, and need to employ chance travellers to some city or town, whence the mails go. Thanks, by the way, for your supply of poststamps. Please hold me your debtor for them. We could, & even now, can get none here, there being no postoffice, & but a nominal postmaster. This day, I resign the Editorial chair of the Phœnix Newspaper. I created it, & have already made it the best organ of opinion in the State. In the end, it will be a fortune to its publisher.[131] At present, it gives too little compensation to justify me in bestowing any farther care upon it. It has answered my purpose in giving me employment during the summer, & bread & meat. That is all. In the course of the week, I propose to go down to the plantation, where I shall stay some week or 10 days, return, & proceed from Columbia to the North. I hope to be in N. Y. & to see you somewhere about the 20th. or 25th. inst. I told you in previous letters that I had been appointed by the Masonic bodies of this place, the Chairman of a Commission to represent them in the Northern cities in the hope to procure some assistance. I prepared their memorial, a copy of which I will send or bring you. They are to raise the necessary funds for the Commission — not so easy a matter in a place so utterly stript of resources.[132] Lawson authorizes me to draw on him for $100 — the amt. of a dft from Widdleton. Wretched as this return is, the money enables me to send off by wagon, all the little luggage, clothing, bedding & furniture which I have here, to my children on the plantation. Of 16 Bedsteads, I have 1 left; so, in proportion of mattresses & feather beds. We have not a chair or a table. Not a knife or fork; hardly a cup or plate or tumbler. And such things we cannot buy. Our

---

[130] This letter is printed, with minor inaccuracies, in Odell, "William Gilmore Simms in the Post-War Years," pp. 9-11.

[131] Julian A. Selby. The *Daily Phœnix* of Oct. 3 announces that W. B. Johnston is one of its editors. Simms still contributed at least poems to the *Daily Phœnix* (see the issue for Jan. 24, 1866, which contains a signed poem entitled "The South").

[132] See preceding and following letters.

basins for washing are of tin, made out of tin, saved amid the ruins of Columbia. We have literally nothing left us but our lands, & how to dispossess the negroes is the problem. They will no longer work. They steal. We can scarcely keep a horse or mule, unless in a lodge directly beneath your chamber, under the muzzle of a gun. They are perishing by thousands of exposure drunkenness, starvation & all brutal practices. The old are deserted by the young. Sons abandon their fathers, mothers their infants, all to crowd to the cities where they quarter themselves for rations on the Government. They are daily convicted of robbery, & murders are frequent. But I will tell you all when we [133] meet. I will endeavour, before I leave Columbia for the plantation to correct & copy out for you a few favorite pieces of verse, written during the last year, which I think well of, & for which, if possible, I wish you to procure me as much compensation as you can.[134] If you knew my straits, you would find much merit in the pieces. At all events, they will I think neither discredit me nor any publisher. I saw a number of Scribner's Magazine yesterday. He needs some help from other hands than those which he has employed.[135] After four, nearly five, dreadful years, it will give me the greatest pleasure to meet with you again. But say as little as possible to me about the war, and my miserable Country. Did I say to you that the portrait of your brother is admirable.[136] Poor Boy! Alas! Alas! We are mere cherry stones in the hands of Fate who delights in flinging! God bless you

Yours as Ever

W. G. S.

1136: To Evert Augustus Duyckinck

[c. October 2, 1865][137]

My dear Duyckinck.

I send you two favorite pieces of mine written during the last year, for which I could wish that you would find a market. I think

---

[133] Simms wrote *we we.*

[134] Certainly the unidentified poems which Simms sent in his letter which we have dated *c.* Oct. 2.

[135] The first number of *Hours at Home,* published by Charles Scribner and Co., is dated May, 1865.

[136] See postscript to letter to Duyckinck of Sept. 9.

[137] At the bottom of this letter is written (evidently by Duyckinck) the date "Oct. 1865." Since in his letter to Duyckinck of Oct. 1 Simms says he plans to leave for Woodlands "in the course of the week" and "will endeavour

them good and do not see but that our friend, Harper or Scribner will be pleased to pay for them on moderate terms. Will you see & take what you can get — and as much as you can get, for it is the day of small things with me now. You can sign my name to them if this be desirable.

Yours Ever truly

W. Gilmore Simms

1137: To Henry Barton Dawson

Columbia, S. C.
Oct. 2. 1865.

My dear Mr. Dawson.

I have already written you, in reply to your kind letter, and trust that mine has been recieved. I now write simply to tell you that I hope to visit New York about the 20th. Oct. — this month. I have resigned the Editorial chair of the Columbia Phœnix, shall this week revisit my plantation, and after a ten days absence shall return here, to proceed to N. Y. It is my hope to meet you in that city. I shall have business there of my own, with the publishers; but I have been appointed the Chairman of a delegation, from the several Masonic Lodges of Columbia, who are applying to the Fraternity of the North for help & succour. I have drawn up their memorial. This mission will consume 3 weeks or a month of my time; — which I very much grudge, for the necessities of my family are such that I must needs go to work with all possible speed, in order to enable them to live. When I tell you that we have not a single chair or table left, that my children are hutting it, in a low log cabin, without a bedstead, and hardly a plate, basin or tumbler, you will readily concieve to what straits we have been reduced. I have a *quasi* contract with a N. Y. Publisher, for a new Romance; and I hope to perfect the contract, profitably, while I am in N. York.[138] But you, by this time, know of what materials Publishers are made. After five years of interval, in which I never recieved a copper, the present publisher of my works sends me $100. Such a result might well discourage the author

---

. . . to correct & copy out for you a few favorite pieces of verse . . . for which . . . I wish you to procure me as much compensation as you can," we have dated this letter *c.* Oct. 2. We are unable to identify the poems Simms enclosed in this letter.

[138] Doubtless this "*quasi* contract" was with Street and Smith. See letters to Lawson and Duyckinck of Sept. 9.

from ever again putting pen to paper. It is clear to me that I shall need to adopt some better system for dealing with such people. Living in affluence hitherto, I have been very easy with my publishers, & have *not* regarded the money profits from my writings. It is now a necessity with me that I should do so. Pray let me see you in N. Y. when we can talk over History & Politics and Author policy together. You will hear of me through Mr. James Lawson (of the firm of Lawson, Walker & Lawson,[139] Average Adjusters, Wall Street, N. Y.) an old friend of mine for 30 years. Please see him, *ad int.* and let me see you when I arrive.[140] Meanwhile, my address is still at Columbia, "Care of Mr. Julian A. Selby, Publisher."

Yours Ever Gratefully

W. Gilmore Simms.

1138: To WILLIAM HAWKINS FERRIS

New York: 9th. Nov. [1865][141]

My dear Mr. Ferris.

The enclosed may be of interest to your children at some future day, and may interest you now. See the endorsement on each. You may guess from these specimens how rich I might become, could I make but these blue backs green, and can readily understand from these same specimens why I am as poor as Job's turkey now.

Yours truly

W. Gilmore Simms

Put them into your collection — they will grow in value.

W. G. S.

---

[139] James Lawson, Jr., had joined his father's firm of Lawson and Walker.

[140] Dawson, who was editor of the *Gazette* (Yonkers) during 1865-1866, says in the *Gazette* of Nov. 4: "Wm. Gilmore Simms, the historian, of South Carolina, is now on a visit to the North, and is at present the guest of our esteemed friend and townsman, James Lawson, Esq. While here Mr. Simms desires to interest the Masonic fraternity in behalf of their destitute brethren in his State, who have been reduced to poverty through the fortunes of the late war. We commend Mr. Simms, and his praise-worthy mission to the fraternity in Westchester County, and throughout the State."

[141] After the Confederate War Simms was in New York City in November only in 1865.

1139: To WILLIAM CULLEN BRYANT

St. Nicholas Hotel.

10th. Nov. 1865.

My dear Bryant.

In the destruction of my house & library, I lost all the copies of your books which bore your autograph. Can you supply them, from your publishers, with any thing new which you may have published since 1859. In writing you so frankly, you will readily concieve that I have undergone no change as a person or as a friend. But the position of our poor Southrons is such just now, that self-respect forbids that we should put ourselves in any equivocal attitude, and I must await, and cannot seek my conquerors, albeit the friends of ancient days. Please present me gratefully to Mrs. B. and Julia, and to Mr. & Mrs. Godwin [142] should they be with you.

Ever as Ever

W. Gilmore Simms

Wm. Cullen Bryant, Esq.

1140: To HENRY BARTON DAWSON

New York, 30th. Nov. [1865] [143]

My dear Mr. Dawson.

I write simply to bid you a (temporary) farewel. I sail this day for Charleston, and greatly regret that circumstances should have prevented our frequent meetings. But I hope for better things in the future. I shall be glad to hear from you at your earliest convenience, & hope that our correspondence will become regular. My address will be "Charleston, S. C.— Care of Wm. Roach, Esq." until farther notice. With best wishes & regards, believe me

Very truly Yours &c

W. Gilmore Simms

Henry B. Dawson, Esq.

---

[142] Frances Fairchild Bryant, Julia Bryant, and the Parke Godwins. Mrs. Parke Godwin was Bryant's daughter Fanny.

[143] This is the only year after Simms began his correspondence with Dawson in 1858 that he appears to have sailed from New York City on Nov. 30. He arrived in Charleston on Dec. 4, the ship having been delayed by "head winds & seas" (see letter to Lawson of Dec. 5).

1141: To James Lawson

Charleston, Decr. 5, 1865

My dear Lawson.

Safe you see! But we did not get into Port untill Monday,[144] having encountered head winds & seas, & being too heavily freighted. With the exception of the too tardy progress, we had a pleasant passage. Tomorrow, I expect to proceed to Woodlands, where I hear that, at last advices, all are well. Edward Roach is in town, and doing business with his Brother, Wm. At present their toils are light, & their profits lighter. But they hope, & so consent to live a little longer. Augusta still remains at the plantation, and is doing well. I have no news. Shall probably be absent for a week from the city; then come down to work as the Fates may decree or permit. Wm. & Ed. R. send their best remembrances. I shall write you from the plantation. Love to Lyde & all the girls, and best respects to Mr. Sandford [145] and Jimmy.

Every truly & affectionately Yours.

W. Gilmore Simms

1142: To Evert Augustus Duyckinck [146]

Charleston, Decr. 19. '65.

My dear Duyckinck.

I am writing you from the desk of the South Carolinian Newspaper, where I do a daily amount of drudgery for my own & the good of the public, with the hope, at least, that both parties shall be well benefitted by the occasion.[147] I have been up to my planta-

---

144 Dec. 4.

145 Thomas Sarjeant Sandford, Mary Lawson's husband. See note 111, Sept. 9, 1865.

146 This letter is printed, with minor inaccuracies, in Odell, "William Gilmore Simms in the Post-War Years," pp. 11-12.

147 The first issue of the *Daily South Carolinian* (Charleston) is dated Nov. 17, 1865. The masthead of this and following issues lists Felix Gregory de Fontaine as editor and publisher and Simms and Timrod as associate editors. We have had access to only a broken file of the newspaper from Nov. 17, 1865, through April 23, 1866 (in the Boston Athenaeum), and have, therefore, been unable to determine the exact date on which Simms began his contributions. His major work for the newspaper appears to have started about the date of this letter to Duyckinck. He severed his connection with the *Daily South Carolinian* sometime in May, 1866 (see letter to Lawson of May 25 of that year).

In addition to writing editorials and news items for the *Daily South Carolinian,* Simms also occasionally published poems, short stories, and prose articles

tion where I found my family quite well, tho' in very humble state & unsatisfactory condition. My eldest son was trying to extract some little work out of the negroes, but to little profit. Of 50 who still remain on the plantation, he could only hire 3 to do any thing. The negroes have been taught to believe that the lands of the country are to be divided among them, and they are no longer willing to work on any contract. They are most effectually ruined as laborers forever.[148] But enough of this. I hope shortly to begin my 'Sensation' Story, of the progress of which you shall have periodical report.[149] I do not find that any publications but those of Appleton & Co have reached me in Charleston. In the bundle sent by Widdleton & brought by myself there were none of his own publications except a sett of my own writings, and a volume of Sydney Smith and of Kit North which he handed [150] to me in New York. Nor had any package from him been recieved at Russell's. Harper & Brothers and Scribner had sent nothing. Now I do not wish to harass any of these parties, but if a reminder from you would have the effect of prompting their liberality, I should be obliged to you for using it. Having charge of the Editorial department of the South Carolinian, it will be in my power greatly to extend the chances of their publications attaining a proper notoriety.[151] May I ask you to see Scribner, and obtain from him the MS. of the Poem called "The Sense of the Beautiful", which I was to obtain before my departure, but failed to do so. When you get it please hand it over to our friend Lawson, to whom I have written instructions

---

in the newspaper. Two signed poems entitled "At the Burial of the M. W. John H. Boatwright, Grand Master of South Carolina" and "The Morals of the Cotton Plant" (earlier published as "Cotton" [see letter to the editor of the *Magnolia Weekly* of April? 1863]) are in the issues for Jan. 16 and April 13, 1866; a poem signed "Werter" (one of Simms' pseudonyms) and entitled "Love Song in Spring" is in the issue for April 14, 1866; Chapters x-xiii of "Gleams after Glooms; or 'Joy Cometh in the Morning,'" a short story, are in the issues for Dec. 27 and 28, 1865; and Parts I and IV of an article entitled "The Valley of the Edisto" and Part II of an article entitled "On the Wing" are in the issues for April 14, 17, and 23, 1866.

[148] Simms discusses this subject in an editorial entitled "What Is the Need?" in the *Daily South Carolinian* of Dec. 23.

[149] Simms probably has in mind "The Brothers of the Coast" (see note 118, Sept. 9, 1865), which at this time he appears to have designed for *Street and Smith's New York Weekly* (see note 108, Sept. 9, 1865).

[150] Simms wrote *hand*.

[151] Simms reviewed Duyckinck's edition of the *Wit and Wisdom of the Rev. Sydney Smith . . .*, first published by Redfield, New York, in 1856, in the *Daily South Carolinian* of Feb. 3, 1866. He reviewed Mrs. Mary Wilson Gordon's *'Christopher North,' a Memoir of John Wilson . . .*, published first by W. J. Widdleton, New York, in 1863, in the *Daily South Carolinian* of Feb. 1, 1866.

in what way to dispose of it.[152] I could wish also that, if Mr. S.
has appropriated any money for the pieces left with him, you
would let me know the amount. Pray try also to sell the Copyright of the Mother Goose for cash.[153] I am greatly straightened
for means, as you may suppose when I tell you that I now sleep
in a chamber which has been shattered by shells, with orifices in
the walls through which the winds stream & the rains beat; sleeping on a pallet on the floor, and without a single article of chamber
furniture except my trunks. I am in hopes today to secure goblet,
basin &c. For the furniture I await a cheap set from N. Y. to
be had on credit. — Should you be able to move the publishers
to any liberality in my case, I could wish to have some of the
best books put forth during the war. Please prompt the Harpers
to send me the various works by military men describing the
events of the war, especially of Sherman's Campaigns. I wish to
obtain from Appletons copies of Wordsworth, Tennyson, Dante
&c. — i.e. if they publish them. Your general acquaintance with
the publishers will enable you to extend the area of supply, no
doubt sufficiently to meet all my needs if not desires. In an occasional letter, you may enable me to report the doings of our
Literary friends in N. Y. & increase the value of the information
by your own commentary upon their performances. These will
always be acceptable at the office of the South Carolinian. There
is a new Poem on the model of the Greek Drama, "*Somebody* in
Calydon", of which I have heard loud mention. If you can procure me a copy from the publisher, I should be glad.[154] Hurd &
Houghton [155] might be persuaded to send me some of their publications put forth during the war. All these books, though published four years ago, are new to the Southern people, who, during
all that time, have had no books to read. Literary notices now
would draw attention to them. This is a point upon which you
may properly dwell. Do not forget to collect for, and send me,
the numbers of the Literary World which you may have to spare.
I trust that while I thus trespass upon your time and kindness,

---

[152] This poem was published as "A Dream of the Beautiful" in *Hours at Home,* II (Jan., 1866), 211-212.

[153] Simms was unable to find a publisher for this work (see his letters to Duyckinck written during 1866-1867). The MS. of at least part of it is in the Charles Carroll Simms Collection, South Caroliniana Library.

[154] If Simms reviewed Charles Algernon Swinburne's *Atalanta in Calydon. A Tragedy* (Boston: Ticknor and Fields, 1866) in the *Daily South Carolinian,* he did so in an issue which we have not seen.

[155] The partners in the firm of Hurd and Houghton, founded in 1864, were Melancthon H. Hurd and Henry Oscar Houghton (1823-1895).

you know enough of me to believe the assurance, that I shall be most happy to requite you, in kind, on all possible occasions. With best respects to Mrs. D. hold me

Ever truly Yours

W. Gilmore Simms

1143: To Evert Augustus Duyckinck

[December, 1865?][156]

My dear Duyckinck.

Accompanying I send you a fine poem, ballad fashion, upon Schiller, giving the characteristics of all his several writings, good & true criticism in musical verse. The poem is by Dr. J. Dickson Bruns, one of the most brilliant young men of this city. He sends it with the view to Scribner's Magazine, or any other which will accord him the *quid*. He is needy, and will accept what ever may be given.

Yours Ever truly,

W. Gilmore Simms

---

[156] This letter was written between Dec. 4, 1865, when Simms returned to Charleston from the North, and April, 1866, when Bruns' "Schiller" (unsigned) was published in *Hours at Home,* II, 506-507.

1866

1144: To William Hawkins Ferris

Jan 2. [1866][1]

My dear Mr. Ferris.

Accompanying, I send the M.S. of Mr. Timrod's poem printed in the Carolinian of Sunday last. I must remind you that as this was copied for the use of the printers, and designed to be particularly legible, the handwriting is not that of Timrod ordinarily, but is a sort of broadfaced schoolboy hand which rather discredits the writers usual penmanship. I may add that the poem is not worthy of his pen. He has been, & still is, an invalid, and he has evidently written doggedly, & under the rule which old Sam Johnson laid down for himself, and without the proper inspiration.

Yours ever

W. Gilmore Simms

W. Hawkins Ferris.
Ch. Hotel.[2]

1145: To Evert Augustus Duyckinck

Charleston, 8th. Jan. 1866.[3]

My dear Duyckinck.

Thanks for your kind letter, which reached me yesterday. Believe me, I gladly reciprocate the gentle and loving sentiments which you express. We are both of a temper to bear meekly our several crosses, and to submit cheerfully to the dispensations of the great Lawgiver of all the nations. We may cherish regrets without becoming querulous over them, and may remember wrong

---

[1] Dated by Simms' reference to Timrod's "1866. Address to the Old Year," *Daily South Carolinian,* Dec. 31, 1865.

[2] Charleston Hotel. Ferris with his family had spent Christmas at Woodlands (see letter to Lawson of May 25, 1866) and was evidently on his way back to the North.

[3] Simms erroneously dated this letter *1865.* The correct year is established by his remarks about various recent publications.

doing with indignation, without desiring revenge. With those who love us and entertain us with kindness, we have means of requital in a love which finds in cherishing gratitude, one of the most grateful securities for conscience. You have my hand, my dear Duyckinck, over the sea, that now divides us, and it has been almost a reproach with some of my biographers that I have carried my heart too much within my hand. At all events, I have never suppressed the one, while I extended the other, whether in the direction of friend or foe. The aspect of God in Mercy be turned upon you & yours in the year which is before us! Selah! Thanks for all that you have done, and all that you propose to do for me. From the Harpers I have recieved nothing. From Appleton & Co. Merivale's Roman Empire, Derby's Homer, & Baxley's Voyages and "At Anchor["] ; from Scribner, Forsyth's Cicero, Froude's England; from Widdleton a set of my own novels, a copy of Gordons Kit North & your Wit & Wisdom of Smith.[4] *Voila Tout.* Russell & Courtenay [5] both deny that they have recieved any thing. It is probable that the unsent package at Appleton's will supply much that I have been anticipating, with eagerness & hope of profitable reading. Should you find the publishers liberally disposed towards me, you may represent my entire destitution of books, that aliment which was almost as necessary to me as my daily food, & indicate the further fact that, during the last five years, our section got no books at all, and are still in ignorance of what is on the record. In respect to all such books, retrospective notices may be of as much service here, in our newspapers, as if the books were only recently sent forth I am happy to say that I have been able to procure copies of Jamison's Bertrand du Guesclin, for yourself & James Lawson. The books are perfect, though the covers are somewhat stained by damp on the voyage. Mr. Wagner has a box of them which he desires may be sold for the benefit of the authors widow, who

---

[4] Charles Merivale, *The Conversion of the Roman Empire* . . . (1865) ; Edward, Earl of Derby, tr., *The Iliad,* 2 vols. (1865) ; Henry Willis Baxley, *What I Saw on the West Coast of South and North America* . . . (1865) ; *At Anchor. A Story of Our Civil War,* written "by an American" (1865) ; William Forsyth, *Life of Marcus Tullius Cicero* (1865) ; and James Anthony Froude, Vols. I-IV of *History of England* (1866). For Widdleton's two publications, see note 151, Dec. 19, 1865. Simms reviewed Merivale in the *Daily South Carolinian* on Feb. 1, Derby on Jan. 26 and 27, Baxley on Feb. 3, and Forsyth on Feb. 15. He doubtless reviewed *At Anchor* and Froude in issues missing from the file of the newspaper to which we have had access.

[5] John Russell and Samuel Gilman Courtenay, Charleston booksellers. Courtenay (1825-1867) was for a time in partnership with his brother, William Ashmead Courtenay, also a Charleston bookseller, who later gave a portrait of Simms to the Charleston Library Society.

is in great distress, & if you will be so good as to propose to
Appleton or Scribner to take at a moderate price, a number of
copies each, it would be a kindness and a substantial charity. The
edition was a small one, & several of the consignments were lost
while running the blockade. Such as were recieved here, were
given away wholly in the South; the book has hardly been seen
at the North, & will not be unless through the medium of Mr.
Wagner or myself. It will be out of print with this edition; and
though not a remarkable book, as the mind of the author though
studious, painstaking & logical, was not philosophical, or capable
of any large grasp of the subject, it is still a valuable contribution
to the library, and supplies some of the historical deficiencies of
the period. The research in the old French Chronicles & Spanish,
has been considerable.[6] The two copies sent you, in one package,
will be shipped by the Steamer Moneka, to depart next Wednesday. I shall have the packet confided to the personal charge of
Captain Marshman, & will beg you to visit the ship as soon after
her arrival as possible & procure it.[7] It is addressed to yourself.
In the fly leaf of each first vol. I have written the presentation
inscriptions for Lawson & yourself, so divide accordingly.
Scribner has *not* sent me his Magazine, though I have seen it, &
find the "Dream of the Beautiful" correctly printed.[8] Have you
seen my "Fancy in Siesta," with its illustrations (These are said
to [be] by Darley, and they are happy) as put forth in the Sunday Mercury?[9] Look it up. I find that I have among my papers

---

[6] Jamison writes in the "Advertisement" to *The Life and Times of Bertrand
du Guesclin,* I, xi: "After completing the revision, I placed the MS. in my
escritoir, to await more peaceable and happy times; and the work would not
now have seen the light, but for the kind offers of one whom I am happy to
call my friend—of Theodore D. Wagner, Esq., a distinguished member of the
patriotic and princely house of John Fraser and Co. of Charleston, and Fraser,
Trenholm, and Co. of Liverpool." The volumes were printed in England and
some copies carry the imprint of Trübner and Co., London, as well as that
of John Russell, Charleston. We have not located any copies with the imprint
of D. Appleton and Co. or of Charles Scribner and Co.

[7] C. P. Marshman was the captain of the *Moneka* (see the advertisements
of the New York and Charleston People's Steamship Co. in the *Daily South
Carolinian* during 1865-1866). Wednesday was Jan. 10.

[8] See note 152, Dec. 19, 1865.

[9] The *New York Mercury. A Journal of American Literature* (New York),
a weekly, was at this time edited and published by William Cauldwell and
Horace P. Whitney. The issues from Jan. 6, 1866, through July 13, 1867, are
the only ones to which we have had access. During this period Simms pub-
lished four signed poems in the periodical: "Shadows," "Fancy in Siesta,"
"Spectres of a Household," and "The Ballad of Isadore," XXVIII (Jan. 6,
Jan. 13, Feb. 3, and June 16, 1866), 5, 4, 4, 4. The issue for Oct. 6, 1866
(XXVIII, 4), contains an unsigned article about Simms entitled "Photographs
of Popular People. William Gilmore Simms," illustrated with a woodcut of
Simms (see the illustration facing p. 487 of this volume of Simms' *Letters*).

several more of the Mother Goose MS. which I will forward you anon. I am still troubled about that little roll of M.SS. which I thought I had left with you. It occurs to me as highly probable that, walking with you, I may have handed it to Scribner to keep for me, and that he or one of the Clerks may find it in his Desk. Get him to look for it. The pieces were on rough sheets, & some one or two of them were unfinished. There were also some of them in print, as for example, a ballad called "Isadore".[10] Enquire at Widdletons also, for an untied roll of MS.S. I have ordered the South Carolinian to be sent to you & to Lawson, free of charge. You will percieve that its dimensions & advertisements leave me little space for dilation, — and it is well. I extract but a slender amount weekly from the work. Enquire for it at the P. O. I shall write to Dawson & have our paper sent him. Please say to him that any packet by the Steamers Moneka or Emily Souder, confided specially to the care of the Captains,[11] addressed thus — "W. Gilmore Simms, care of William Roach, Shipping Merchant, &c."[12] will not only reach me in safety, but probably without charge. I shall try & secure one of these copies of Bertrand for Dawson, & have the newspaper sent him. Regards to Mrs. D. &c

Yours Ever truly

W. Gilmore Simms

---

[10] See note 71, *c*. Aug. 1, 1864.

[11] R. W. Lockwood was the captain of the *Emily B. Souder*. See the advertisements of the New York and Charleston People's Steamship Co. in the *Daily South Carolinian* during 1865-1866.

[12] William Roach's advertisements in the *Daily South Carolinian* during 1865-1866 say that he is a "General Commission Merchant and Agent of Merchant's Line of New York Sailing Packets." They also state that he is "Late Henry Missroon & Co."

1146: To Robert Macoy and Daniel Sickels [13]

Charleston, S. C. Jany 16. [1866] [14]

Mess'rs Maccoy & Sickles.

Friends & Bretheren.

This will be handed you by Mr. F. G. de Fontaine who is the Publisher of the South Carolinian newspaper of this place, in which journal I write. He is not only a Brother Editor, but a Brother Mason, though, perhaps, like myself, not so diligent a working brother as he may become & should be. He will be pleased to make your acquaintance, & it is quite probable that your counsels may help his innocence amidst the snares of your wicked city. I am glad to say that Bro. Bruns [15] & myself are both quite well, & cherish grateful recollections of our late visit. Bro. Fontaine will be able to report upon my case.

Ever fraternally,
Yours &c.

W. Gilmore Simms

---

[13] Macoy (1815-1895) and Sickels were members of the firm of Macoy and Sickels. The New York City directories for the 1860's list the firm variously as publishers, dealers in books, and dealers in Masonic regalia. Both Macoy and Sickels were editors of several books about Freemasonry. In 1866 Macoy was one of the editors of the *Masonic Eclectic* (New York), a periodical published monthly.

[14] Dated by Simms' reference to his work on the *Daily South Carolinian.* In *My Own Story with Recollections of Noted Persons* (Boston and New York: Houghton Mifflin Company, [1903]), p. 310, John Townsend Trowbridge, a Northern writer who made a tour of the South in 1865-1866, writes of meeting Simms early in 1866: "I found him in a printing-office, doing some sort of work on a daily paper; a man of sixty, with shortish iron-gray hair and roughish features,—not at all my idea of a great writer who could harrow up the souls of boy readers. He was quite ready to talk to me, particularly upon one topic, namely, the damage the Yankees had inflicted upon his beloved State and idolized city.

" 'Charleston, sir,' he said, with a level fixity of look, 'was the finest city in the world; not a large city, but the finest. South Carolina, sir, was the flower of modern civilization. Our people were the most hospitable, the most accomplished, having the highest degree of culture and the highest sense of honor, of any people, I will not say of America, sir, but of any country on the globe. And they are so still, even in their temporary desolation.' "

[15] Robert Stewart Bruns (1834-1874), a native of Charleston and one of the most distinguished Masons in South Carolina, had accompanied Simms to New York in 1865. In 1866 he formed a partnership with William Y. Leitch, auctioneer, broker, and real estate agent of Charleston.

1147: To Evert Augustus Duyckinck [16]

Charleston — 10 Feb. '66.

My dear Duyckinck.

I shall send you next week by one or other of the Steamers a brochure of Hon. Henry Laurens, the President of Congress, comprising his Diary of Travel in Europe, just before the Revolutionary War. It strikes me that with your manipulation, it would constitute a very proper volume for that series of *quasi* private publication which is so much affected among you at present. It will show things in a lively way from 1772 to 1774 in England & the Continent; the modes & cost of travel, cost of things &c. H. L. was a keen business man, who itemizes every thing according to the requisitions of the Day Book, & may be relied on for the strictest accuracy. The book would probably amuse even in Europe. Examine it. It will need very little manipulation, yet might be provided with notes.[17] I have just recieved my papers from Columbia, but have not yet had time for their examination.[18] The truth is, I am & have been for the last ten days greatly under the weather. We have had very bad weather here, & I have taken a severe catarrhal touch which has penetrated all my bones. I am really suffering. When I get strength & spirit for the effort, I will devote an early moment to the examination of these papers, & see what can be done with them, and probably send you others. Be so good as to enquire at the Steamer, whenever Moneka or Souder shall arrive, for packages for your address. A letter from Mr. Richardson proposes for the Southern Poetry of the War; but, needing money as I do, I could much prefer taking even a small price, to wait upon the lingering returns of sales for one or more seasons. I will write to him to this effect; but refer him finally to you; and you are at liberty to use your own judgment in the matter. Knowing my needs, you will do your best.[19] So, I could wish you to treat as soon as possible for the Mother Goose — selling the Copy right if you can, tho' not at too great

---

[16] This letter is printed, with minor inaccuracies, in Odell, "William Gilmore Simms in the Post-War Years," pp. 12-14.

[17] This "Diary" was in manuscript (see letter to Duyckinck of Feb. 20, 1866). We can find no record of its publication.

[18] When Simms moved his family to Columbia during Gen. Sherman's march through South Carolina he took with him a number of his more valuable manuscripts, including his collection of Revolutionary letters and documents.

[19] Charles Benjamin Richardson was a publisher at 540 Broadway, New York City. In 1866 he published Simms' *War Poetry of the South* (see note 295, Nov. 29, 1866).

a sacrifice as I regard the work as one likely to obtain a long possession of the market. At all events, I shall do my best to make it do so. Still, I very much need money. Even could we succeed in making any contracts with negro labour, the want of means among the planters, for the purchase of mules & material, would utterly prevent the employment of any but a small proportion of the original force. For example, I owned 80 negroes; 40 of whom worked; the rest were aged or children. Now, it is not easy to procure the labour of 4. And if I could procure the return to work of the whole 40, I should require a capital in horses, mules machinery & implements of at least $10,000 to enable me to give them proper employment. My son has engaged several squads, not one of whom has kept his engagement. If we arrest and put them in prison, they wish nothing better. They remain idle, & we support them in prison. The prospect is utterly hopeless.[20] It is not likely that I will remain long in this city. The pay does not compensate, fritters away my mind & time, and keeps me from higher & more enduring performances. I seriously meditate my own individual remove to New York, where in some obscure chamber, I can live at moderate cost, & have the press at my command. My eldest son, with my son in law, Major Rowe,[21] has charge of Woodlands to do with the land & timber what they can; my eldest daughter, Mrs. Roach lives with me here in the city, with her husband, and has with her my second daughter Mary L. and my two youngest boys. I can give very little help to the young men on the plantation, and what I am able to do for the rest of the children here, I can even more efficiently do in N. Y. than Charleston. But the privation involved in leaving my young children, even for a season, and the exile from my native land, in this its hour of utter humiliation & misery, "these are thoughts we cannot bridle — Force their way, without the will." [22] Enough that I now seriously meditate some leading change in my location & manner of life. And, whatever step I take need money. None of my friends here can give me help. They are all equally prostrate. — Upon reflection, I will send you with Laurens' notes of travel, another little book, containing his running commentary, as for a review or speech, in Congress, of

[20] Simms writes at length on this subject in an editorial entitled "Touching Free Negro Labor and the Contracts," *Daily South Carolinian,* Jan. 6, 1866.

[21] On Dec. 25, 1865, Chevillette was married to Donald Jacob Rowe (d. 1905), son of Sarah Keziah Moss and Donald Christopher Rowe (see note 24, April 28, 1864).

[22] Not identified.

Silas Deane's famous report.[23] It will interest Mr. Bancroft especially & perhaps afford him some clues. It will also please Mr. Dawson to examine it. You must use your own discretion in showing it, for these curious little antiques must not be lost.

God bless you & yours

W. Gilmore Simms

1148: To JOHN A. MCALLISTER [24]

Charleston, Feb. 19. 1866.

dear Sir:

The war poems of the South are still daily coming in to me, a large proportion of them in M.S.[25] I have not yet attempted classing them, nor do I know what duplicates may be found, nor have I yet decided what selections I shall make from them for publication. It is at present impossible for me to say what I have and what I might wish to have, especially as it is impossible for me to know what things may be scattered over the country to be brought to my knowledge only by accident, or the occasional contributions of persons like yourself making collections. As I propose to publish at the North, it will possibly form a part of my plan to stop in your city & go with you over your collection. It will certainly afford me pleasure to yield you copies of all or any that I have[,] provided the copyist can be obtained who will undertake the task *con amore*.

Yours &c.

W. Gilmore Simms

Jno. A. McAllister, Esq.

---

[23] This "little book" was also in manuscript (see letter to Duyckinck of Feb. 20, 1866). Silas Deane (1737-1789) was sent as a commissioner to France during 1776-1778. His "report" is *An Address to the Free and Independent Citizens of the United States of North-America* (Hartford: Printed by Hudson & Goodwin, 1784). There were several other editions of his *Address*.

[24] The cover of this letter has not survived, but since the original is in the Ridgeway Branch of the Free Library of Philadelphia, it is possible that McAllister was a Philadelphian. The Philadelphia *Directory* for this year lists John A. McAllister, an optician at 728 Chestnut Street with a residence at 114 South 21st Street.

[25] In the *Daily South Carolinian* of Dec. 15, 1865, Simms announces his plan for *War Poetry of the South* and asks collectors to send him poems. The same issue of the *Daily South Carolinian* contains an editorial on Simms' project.

1149: To Evert Augustus Duyckinck

Office of the Carolinian.
Charleston, Feb. 20. '66.

My dear Duyckinck.

I sent you by one of the Steamers, — advising you first by mail of my intention — two MSS. in one packet, from the pen of Prest. Laurens.[26] I am naturally anxious that they should reach you safely. Please advise me accordingly to that effect. Prior to the reciept of your last letter, an engagement had been made with Mr. John Russell, Bookseller, of this city, for the sale of Jamison's volumes.[27] The money was desirable at the time, for the benefit of the widow, whom the war has utterly ruined. She had, like myself, some eighty slaves. They are lost; and the noble mansion [28] built but a short time before her husband's death was burned by the army at the same time with my own. She has lost every thing, and with some 10 children, now lives in a log house through which the winds & rains make their way. I will consider what you say, touching a sketch of Jamison, in connection with a rèsumé of his volumes for Scribner. It is possible that I may do it.[29] At present, & during the absence of Mr. De Fontaine, the publisher of the Carolinian at the North, I am kept exceedingly busy. The whole Editorial charge & much of the labour devolves upon me. What is called the local department devolves upon subordinates, though I not infrequently write for this also, as the humour prompts & the topic offers. I am also engaged upon my romance, called "The Brothers of the Coast" of which more hereafter.[30] I find that I have with me here several of the ballads & jingles of Mother Goose, and cannot say whether copies of them are also to be found in the collection left with you. Of course, all shall be provided in the event of a publisher being found, and I shall also be glad if you will indicate to me those peculiarly Northern topics which I should be pleased to illustrate, in order that the Book should be most thoroughly national. Let me hope that you will press it on some good man of the trade, & dispose of the Copyright, outright, for whatever it will command. My needs are so many, & so urgent, and my resources so much reduced,

---

[26] See letter to Duyckinck of Feb. 10.
[27] *The Life and Times of Bertrand du Guesclin.* See letter to Duyckinck of Jan. 8.
[28] Burwood.
[29] This abridged edition appears not to have been published.
[30] See note 118, Sept. 9, 1865.

that I should take far less money for a Copyright now than I should have done at any preceding time. — I recieved, at the same time with yours, a letter from Mr. Richardson, which I have somehow mislaid. Do me the kindness to see him, and say that I shall be quite willing that he shall have the book;[31] but that I should much prefer to dispose of the Copyright, for the reason already given. I will write him as soon as I can lay hands upon his letter. The book will be quite creditable. There will be a very large mass from which to select. Still, I should be pleased to know the several titles of the poems in Dr. Emmet's [32] collection. I find the demand for these things very considerable, North & South; and have recieved letters from collectors & librarians begging duplicates & annoying me by a fruitless correspondence. In case you should succeed in making an arrangement for either or both of these volumes, please refer the parties to Lawson for the completion of the sale, your arrangement being always to be complied with. You can suggest, — and I beg that you will do so, — to Mr. Richardson, the goad of that necessity which makes money so precious to me at this moment. Thank Mr. Richardson, also, for his promise of books. They will be very grateful. I have recieved nothing from Appleton, Scribner or any body else since I last wrote to you. You will see in the Carolinian notices of *all* the books I have recieved — Forsyth's Cicero; Froude's England, Derby's Homer, the Ingoldsby Ballads &c; Praed's Poems; Sydney Smith; John Wilson (Gordon) and perhaps one or two others.[33] These are all. Nothing from Fields, or Harpers, or any body save Appleton, Scribner & Widdleton. Tell the latter that he neglected to include a set of my poems,[34] in the set of my works sent me. If he has a bound copy, I should prefer it. If these notices in the 'Carolinian' have escaped you, let me know, and I will send you them. I see, by the 'Post' of today, that

---

[31] *War Poetry of the South.*

[32] Thomas Addis Emmet (1828-1919), born near Charlottesville, Va., was a physician and antiquarian. In the 1850's he went to New York City and was for a number of years Dr. J. Marion Sims' assistant at the Woman's Hospital. In 1861 he was appointed surgeon-in-chief at the Woman's Hospital, and he held this position until 1872, when he was made visiting surgeon.

[33] Simms reviewed Richard Harris Barham's *The Ingoldsby Legends . . .*, 2 vols. (New York: W. J. Widdleton, 1865), in the *Daily South Carolinian* of Feb. 10. He reviewed *The Poems of Winthrop Mackworth Praed . . .* (New York: W. J. Widdleton, 1865) in an issue of the newspaper missing from the file to which we have had access. For his reviews of the other books here mentioned, see note 151, Dec. 19, 1865, and note 4, Jan. 8, 1866.

[34] *Poems Descriptive Dramatic, Legendary and Contemplative.*

Freneau has at length appeared. I trust you will not forget me.[35] Did you not promise to secure me, if possible, the volume of Dr. Francis.[36] I surely ought to have one for 'Auld Lang Syne.' Let me know anent the Laurens' MS.S. and what you think of their fitness for the series of which you spoke. I do not hear from Lawson. Has the anticipated Spectre yet entered his household? [37] With best respects to Mrs. D. I am as Ever Yours

W. Gilmore Simms

1150: To EVERT AUGUSTUS DUYCKINCK

Carolinian Office.
Charleston, March 5. [1866][38]

My dear Duyckinck.

Accompanying you will find a genuine, original & interesting letter of George Washington, which you will find worthy of a frame in your Library. I am glad that the MSS. of Laurens reached you safely. I note what you say touching the Laurens papers, & the use which may be made of them, & when I next visit N. Y. will bring them with me. The materials are ample. At present I am busy day & night, writing for the bread of the day. I have written some 150 pp. of a MS. romance anent the Pirates.[39] But I get on too slowly for my impatience, tasked as I am with the sole Editorship of the Carolinian, & writing for that Journal some 3 columns per day. I shall cheerfully assent to any arrangements you may make for the publication of these papers. At present, in the condition of Lawson's family, he can be called upon for nothing.[40] It is just possible that I may come on at an early day myself. Say to Widdleton that in giving me a copy of my own writings, he omitted the Poems. Should he

---

[35] The New York *Evening Post* of Feb. 10 carries an announcement of the publication of Duyckinck's edition of Philip Freneau's *Poems Relating to the American Revolution* (New York: W. J. Widdleton, 1865). Simms reviewed the volume in the Charleston *Courier* of June 29, 1866.

[36] John Wakefield Francis, *Old New York: Or, Reminiscences of the Past Sixty Years . . . With a Memoir of the Author, by Henry T. Tuckerman* (New York: W. J. Widdleton, 1866).

[37] Kate Lawson died on Feb. 24, 1866. See the *Gazette* (Yonkers) of March 3, 1866.

[38] Dated by Simms' reference to the Laurens MSS. See letters to Duyckinck of Feb. 10 and 20.

[39] "The Brothers of the Coast." See letter to Duyckinck of Feb. 20.

[40] Simms probably had not heard of Kate Lawson's death on Feb. 24. See letter to Lawson of March 5.

have a copy of these to spare in the neat binding in which I once
had them from Redfield, I should be pleased to recieve one of
these. I presume you have seen in the Carolinian what I have
said of Sydney Smith, John Wilson, Doran's Stage &, in brief
of all the books recd. from him, Scribner & Appleton.[41] I have
recieved nothing since; nothing at all from Harper, & nothing
since I left N. Y. from either Appleton or Scribner. The latter
does not even send me his Magazine.[42] I shall look with keenest
eyes of expectation for your Freneau, and Tuckerman's Francis.[43]
From Fields nothing yet. I especially desire the biographies of
his publication, including Wordsworth, &c. No packet from the
Harpers ever reached me from the St. Nicholas.[44] I should be
pleased if Appleton's could be persuaded to send me a copy of
their Cyclopædia.[45] I was largely a contributor & have not a
vol. left. They had only sent me a part when the war took
place. I wrote to Fletcher Harper to beg for copies of Anthon's
Latin & Classical Dictionaries & an English Dictionary; but got
no answer.[46] I tried in vain to verify a quotation from the
Paradise Regained, but had no copy. I am sadly destitute of the
poets & dramatic authors; and with no longer resources of my
own for purchase, I must look to the charities of Publishers.
God knows I have been working long enough for the trade, to
find some favour now at their hands. I am very rapidly accumulating the war poetry of the South. It comes in to me daily, and
much of it will take high rank. Let me know what general
arrangements you may agree upon in regard to this volume,
& Mother Goose. I need present cash for present necessities, and
any arrangement which will give me that, will be welcome. *I*

---

[41] See note 151, Dec. 19, 1865; note 4, Jan. 8, 1866; and note 33, Feb. 20,
1866. John Doran's *"Their Majesties' Servants." Annals of the English Stage,
from Thomas Betterton to Edmund Kean. Actors—Authors—Audiences,* 2
vols. (New York: W. J. Widdleton, 1865), is reviewed in the *Daily South
Carolinian* of Feb. 3.

[42] *Hours at Home.*

[43] See notes 35 and 36, Feb. 20, 1866.

[44] The Saint Nicholas Society of the City of New York was organized in
1835 largely through the efforts of Washington Irving. Its membership was
restricted to natives or residents of the City or State of New York prior to
1785 and their descendants. It is still in existence.

[45] *The New American Cyclopædia.*

[46] Fletcher Harper (1806-1877), of the firm of Harper and Brothers, was
the son of Elizabeth Kolyer and Joseph Harper and the brother of James,
John, and Joseph Wesley Harper. The dictionaries Simms here requests are
Charles Anthon's *A Classical Dictionary . . .* and *A Latin-English and English-
Latin Dictionary, for the Use of Schools,* of which Harper and Brothers pub-
lished many editions.

have no shelter of my own, in which I can lay my head, & my children, at present, are living at the plantation in negro houses. A few hundred dollars now would enable me to *restore one wing* of my dwelling there, and give me a tolerable habitation. If I can procure this aid from these two volumes, I should feel comparatively at ease. I should then have an abode where I could live cheaply, write cheaply, & dying, be buried with little cost, among my kindred. Do you not get the South Carolinian regularly. It is regularly mailed to you. Mr. De Fontaine who is now in New York, has a Letter to you. He is a smart, active, intelligent little fellow, amiable & genial, and sufficiently pushing to make his way in the world. He is preparing to enlarge his paper, the better to engage in the competition with his rivals. I am half meditating a total transfer of my individual self to New York, with the view to the more profitable exercise of my wits. I am off the course, when my rivals are already off, & making the circuit. I have one or more dramas partly written which I contemplate for the stage.[47] But for the starring system, we might have a drama. But starring is death to authors as well as good stock companies. — My best respects to Mrs. Duyckinck, to Panton,[48] &, as the Backwoods people phrase it, "other inquiring friends.["] God be with you in mercy.

> Yours Ever truly
>
> W. Gilmore Simms

1151: To William Hawkins Ferris

Charleston 5th. March. [1866][49]

My dear Ferris.

I cover to you an original Letter of Washington. By framing it with glass on both sides, it can be completely read. I wrote you some time ago to beg that you would procure me some fish Hooks. Today I recieved from my son-in-law, Major Rowe, the memorandum which I enclose, of the kind he prefers. I am better, but far from well, & so busied that I have little leisure for correspondence, besides being wearied of pen & pencil. I shall write

---

[47] We do not know which of Simms' several "partly written" dramas he was still contemplating "for the stage."

[48] Henry Panton. John Albert Panton died in 1863.

[49] Dated by Simms' reference to de Fontaine's absence in the North. See letter to Duyckinck of March 5.

you however very soon. Mr. De Fontaine's continued absence seems to increase my labours daily, & my uneasiness in equal degree. Love to wife & children from all here. Yours in haste, but ever truly

W. Gilmore Simms

P. S. Your long & grateful letter just come to hand. Thanks, many thanks, for your & your wife's kindness.[50] At present, I can say nothing of my plans. I can only decide after delivering up to De F. his establishment, and I am accordingly impatient for his return. — Just heard from Woodlands where all are well. It is possible that Mrs. Roach may have something to write so that I will leave this little scribblement unsealed till she comes in. — Once more, God bless you. Mr. Simms sends back her kiss to Josie,[51] in order that it may be put to interest. Explain the process to her.

W. G. S.

1152: To James Lawson

[March 5, 1866][52]

dear Lawson.

I send you a genuine autograph of Washington. The letter is written, as you will see by what I have written, by the celebrated Col. John Laurens, the favorite aid of Washington.[53] It is worth framing for your collection. — We are all tolerably well here, except myself. I am overworked, & kept busy day & night. I have about 150 pp. of my new romance[54] written, but get on

---

[50] An invitation to visit them in Brooklyn. See letter to Lawson of March 5.

[51] Ferris' daughter.

[52] This letter is postmarked March 6, and it is likely that it was written at the same time as the two preceding letters to Duyckinck and Ferris.

[53] On a sheet of paper accompanying the letter from Washington (both still preserved with this letter to Lawson) Simms wrote: "The within Letter of George Washington was written by Col. John Laurens, the confidential aid of Washington, & the person whom he selected to proceed as Special Commissioner to France, in order to procure that succour which Dr. Franklin had failed or neglected to secure. Laurens, directly from the army was better able than Franklin to declare its necessities. The history of this Mission was a particularly important one, and was marked by an incident of striking & impressive character, showing Laurens to be one of the most remarkably endowed young men of his age. He was called the Bayard of America, & led the storming party of the Americans, at the siege of York. He was killed in a skirmish at Combahee, South Carolina. This letter is in his hand writing. The signature is that of Genl. Washington. The letter is thus doubly valuable to the Collector. W. Gilmore Simms."

[54] "The Brothers of the Coast."

more slowly than I otherwise should, if my health & spirits were better. — I am looking anxiously to your quarter & to hear from you. May the Good God reconcile you to all his providences.[55] — A letter from the plantation today reports Gilmore, Chevillette, & her husband all well, & all at work. — Another letter recieved today from Mr. Ferris gives me a pressing & very well expressed invitation to visit him at Brooklyn and spend some time with him. — My love to Lyde, the Girls, Jemmy & Mr. Sandford. Augusta & Mary Lawson join in affectionate regards to you, Lyde & the young ladies.

Ever truly Yours & theirs

W. Gilmore Simms.

James Lawson, Esq.

1153: To EVERT AUGUSTUS DUYCKINCK

Office of the South Carolinian

Charleston, S. C.

March 21. 1866.

My dear Duyckinck.

This will introduce you to Dr. J. Dickson Bruns, one of the most brilliant of the young men of South Carolina. You have heard of him before. He writes well, equally in prose & verse; he is an experienced Surgeon & Physician, has edited one of the best Medical Journals, ever issued from the American Press;[56] is altogether a singularly able & well endowed Gentleman. He is on the way to Europe for the summer, & pays his way as a correspondent for the newspapers.[57] If you can, in any way, promote his objects, let me entreat you to do so. He will remember, & be grateful, & perhaps may be able to requite. At

---

[55] Simms appears not to have heard of Kate Lawson's death. See preceding letters.

[56] The *Charleston Medical Journal and Review*. See note 285, Nov. 30, 1860.

[57] On March 30, 1866, Timrod wrote to Hayne: "Bruns . . . has been writing the book notices of the Courier, with his accustomed ability. He has had a medical class—has been appointed Extra-ordinary Professor of the Theory & Practice of medicine [at the Medical College of the State of South Carolina]— and is going to start for London next week (stopping two weeks in Philadelphia) with the purpose of devoting a summer to the study [of] pathological anatomy" (see Hubbell, *The Last Years of Henry Timrod*, p. 62). Bruns left Charleston on April 5 (see the *Daily South Carolinian* of April 6). His "European Correspondence" was published in the Charleston *Courier* during June–Sept., 1866.

least, let me entreat, as a favour to me, that you will do all you can for him.

Yours Ever truly,

W. Gilmore Simms.

Evert A Duyckinck Esq.

1154: To William Hawkins Ferris

Office of the South Carolinian

Charleston, S. C. March 24. [1866]⁵⁸

You have broken me, New York, or yourself, my dear fellow, in the wonderful supply of lines & hooks you have sent me, enough for taking captive of all the finny tribes from the Potomac to the Rio Grande. What could you have been thinking of. Why, I can manufacture cordage enough out of your lines (which are almost as interminable as the tender lines I get from the Ladies about war,) for the hawser of a British Three Decker. Tomorrow, I hope to take a run for a week at Woodlands, and will carry up my precious burden to the boys,⁵⁹ who will no doubt devour it with their eyes, of such delight, as to concieve the perch, bream, cat & trout, already struggling at every extremity, on the tenter hooks of apprehension and feeling the application of the cook to their gills, and scales & tails with no remorseful fingers. Thanks, my friend, for your attention; but pray keep in mind that I cannot let you break yourself because my sons are eager to be bobbing in fishy waters. Keep a memorandum of what you expend on their & my behalf, so that I may reimburse you, & save you from exposure in the Gazette. My treasury, indeed, is not so mockingly replete with Greenbacks as that which you daily contemplate; but I must see that you do not make me bankrupt in gratitude; and I shall hold you to strict account when we meet, to report the extent of your accounts on my behalf. — Thanks for your kind letters, to one of which, at least, I have already replied. I fancy indeed, that you can no longer reproach me with being your debtor for a Letter. But, if so, say so. Yet you will please keep in mind, that I have the daily task of writing 3 or 4 columns in the Newspaper, answering a large

---

⁵⁸ Dated by Simms' remarks about the *Daily South Carolinian*.

⁵⁹ Gilmore and Donald Rowe. Govan and Carroll were with Simms in Charleston (see above).

Correspondence, editing the War Poems, and writing at snatches, when I can, a chapter of my new Romance, which has reached its 9th. chap. & 173d. page.[60] I have besides been exercising myself under a three weeks influenza, which has kept my head stuffed as with a hundred lbs. of upland Cotton; my nose employed busily in the use of 2 or 3 pocket Handkerchiefs daily, out of a stock of half a dozen of infinitesimal dimensions, and my temper in that state which exhibits little veneration for Gods, Columns or Magazines. — Our paper is (*entre nous*) in a bad way, and I shall be very glad to get rid of the burden of it, which works me incessantly and does not compensate. Mr. De Fontaine still lingers at the North, doing, Heaven knows what, and delaying heaven knows why. "What does he in the North, when he should serve his paper in the South." As an organ of opinion, it is acknowledged here as the superior Journal;[61] but it is in vain that you expend mind & character in a contest against money. Mammon still prevails, when the proper Deity fails. Its tasks keep me from my own; but I am reluctant to quit, while the Publisher is absent, especially as he has left nobody to take my place. Mr. Timrod has done nothing to assist me for five weeks.[62] My plan is, in May or June, or possibly before, to present myself suddenly before my friends in N. Y. saying 'ecce homo.' Here I am. By that time, I hope to have my book of War Ballads mostly ready for the press, & possibly be able to start the serial publication of my piratical romance. *Nous verrons!* I have other

[60] The only MS. of "The Brothers of the Coast" known to us (that in the South Caroliniana Library) consists of exactly this part of the romance. On April 13 Simms wrote to Ferris that he had "some 200 pp. of MS. written," but on April 27 he wrote to Lawson that he had only "some 170 pages." Thus "some 200 pp." appears to be an exaggeration. There is no evidence in Simms' later letters to lead us to believe that he wrote any more of this romance.

[61] The *Courier* was the only other newspaper published in Charleston at this time.

[62] Professor Jay B. Hubbell in *The Last Years of Henry Timrod,* pp. 51-56, prints a letter from Timrod to Hayne dated "Columbia March 7th 1866," in which Timrod writes: "Since I last wrote you I have had a long and painful fit of illness—having been confined for three weeks to my bed, and for more than a month to the house." But this letter should be dated 1867; thus Timrod's "fit of illness" does not account for his failure to assist Simms in editing the *Daily South Carolinian.* (The correct date of Timrod's letter of March 7 can be established by a close comparison of the letter with Timrod's letter to Hayne dated "March 26th [1867]," which Professor Hubbell prints, pp. 74-77. Conclusive evidence of an 1867 date is Timrod's reference in the letter to Bruns' "emigration to the west": Bruns did not go to New Orleans until Oct., 1866 [see Simms' letter to Hayne of Oct. 22, 1866]. Professor Hubbell writes us that we are certainly correct in redating the letter on the basis of the above-mentioned evidence.)

plans in projection, but still can say no more than *'Nous verrons.'*
I shall then, D. V. take you at your word, and divide myself
for the few weeks I propose to stay between some two or three
or four good fellows like yourself, taking for granted that I
shall find out your cigar box, & the last demijohn of Bourbon.
My point of special anxiety is to procure money enough to rebuild one wing of Woodlands, which with the outhouses I have
will afford my whole family refuge, should the Cholera or
Yellow fever visit the city. Even as it is, I propose, should I go
North & when I do so, to send Mary Lawson & the two little
boys up to Woodlands, there to remain for the summer or
untill I return. But I am at the bottom of my sheet, and without
well knowing what I have written. My head is still terribly
addled by this wretched Influenza. My special love, and thirty
kisses with interest in advance for Josie. Make my best regards
to Madame & hold me ever truly, though in gray frieze,

Your friend &c

W. Gilmore Simms

1155: To William Blake Trask [63]

Charleston. S. C. April 3. 1866.

Wm. B. Trask, Esq.

Sir:

A temporary absence from the city has delayed my answer
to your letter. You were misinformed in respect to the death
of the Rev. Thomas Smyth, D. D. I saw him some two or three
weeks ago, & conversed with him. Some two Sundays ago, he
was announced to preach to his Congregation in his own pulpit.
He is in feeble health, but not more so than has been the case
with him for several years. His address is "Charleston, S. C."
for the present, and your application to him will no doubt
result in his supplying you with the facts wanting to his biography
in Redfield's Collection: I am inclined to think that I furnished
the sketch of him in that work, and it is likely that I procured

---

[63] Trask (b. 1812), the Massachusetts antiquary, was historiographer of
the New England Historic-Genealogical Society during 1861-1868.

from Dr. S. himself, the facts which he was disposed to impart.[64] Your simple application to him would ensure you such other *materièl,* as regards his subsequent writings, as may have accumulated since. It gives me pleasure to furnish you with the desired clues.

Yours respectfully

W. Gilmore Simms

1156: To Evert Augustus Duyckinck

Charleston, April 5. 1866.

My dear Duyckinck

I have been absent from the city for a week at my plantation, which has kept me from making prompt answer to yours of the 19th. ult. Since I have returned, I have been suffering from some derangement of the system, arising from catarrh, and have not yet recovered my equilibrium. As I am considerably in arrear to my Correspondents, you must forgive me if I am brief. — I shall be able to prepare a proper historical or biographical introduction to any papers that I am prepared to publish. The simple question is, in what degree these papers (Revolutionary) are valuable. I hope to see you early in June or before, when all these matters may be discussed & settled.[65] — I trust you will have better success with Mother Goose than your experience seems to warrant. An *original* & *American Mother Goose,* is not only something characteristic, but seems to be wanted. The Poetry of the South, during the war, will possess (I think) a much higher character, than any thing that has yet been published. I wish you would, if able, send me Cooke's address, which I had but lost. His "Stonewall Jackson" has just reached me, but save this, I have recieved no books whatever from New York, since the date of my last acknowledgments to you, — one pamphlet from

---

[64] Smyth (1808-1873), born in Ireland, was pastor of the Second Presbyterian Church in Charleston from 1834 until 1870, when he resigned. "Redfield's Collection" is *The Men of the Time or Sketches of Living Notables* (see note 84, April 5, 1852).

[65] Simms later edited *The Army Correspondence of Colonel John Laurens in the Years 1777-8 Now First Printed from Original Letters Addressed to His Father Henry Laurens President of Congress with a Memoir by Wm. Gilmore Simms* (New York: [Bradford Club], 1867). Simms' "Memoir of John Laurens" is on pp. 9-54.

Richardson excepted. Cooke's "Surrey" *not* recieved.[66] — From
Harper & Bro. nothing, from Scribner nothing, not even his
Magazine [67] — from Widdleton nothing; that packet so long lying
in Appleton's bunk, not yet come to hand — from Ticknor &
Fields nothing of all the good things promised. Your Freneau
not yet at hand, nor Tuckerman's & Francis book.[68] The Captains
of the Steamers Moneka & Emily Souder [69] will both be pleased
to bring me packages direct to the office, nor need they wait to
send them through any bookseller here. — Dr. Bruns, who is on
his way to Europe will hand you a letter from me. Welcome
him & make much of him. He is not only an honorable gentleman,
but one of the best endowed and educated of all the young men
of the South, for the last 20 years. He is Professor in our Med.
College,[70] & has been, before the war, Editor of one of the
ablest Medical Journals (monthly) in the U. S.[71] — We have
just had a flying visit from J. P. Kennedy. I spent an hour with
him today. He has been to Cuba for salubrious airs & a genial
temperature, & is now on his way to Europe — will be in New
York about the 5th. or 10th. of June.[72] Enquire of Derby after
a *promised* Copy of "Irving & his friends" — the Picture.[73] — I
have written 170 M.S. pages of "The Brothers of the Coast"
my new Romance. God be with you in mercy.

Yours Ever

W. Gilmore Simms

---

[66] The *Daily South Carolinian* of Feb. 9 reprints from the Richmond *Enquirer* (n. d.) a review of John Esten Cooke's *Surry of Eagle's Nest* . . .
(New York: Bunce and Huntington, 1866). An excerpt from Cooke's *Stonewall Jackson* . . . (New York: D. Appleton and Company, 1866) is printed
in the *Daily South Carolinian* of Feb. 13. Simms reviewed these two works
in issues of the newspaper which we have not seen (see letter to Cooke of
May 4, 1866). The pamphlet here mentioned is Augustus Wood Clason's *The
American Conflict* (New York: C. B. Richardson, 1866), reviewed by Simms
in the *Daily South Carolinian* of April 4.

[67] *Hours at Home.*

[68] See notes 35 and 36, Feb. 20, 1866.

[69] C. P. Marshman and R. W. Lockwood.

[70] The Medical College of the State of South Carolina, at Charleston.

[71] The *Charleston Medical Journal and Review.* See note 285, Nov. 30, 1860.

[72] See letter to Kennedy of April 11.

[73] The well-known, frequently reproduced engraving entitled "Washington
Irving and His Literary Friends at Sunnyside."

1157: To John Pendleton Kennedy [74]

Office of South Carolinian.
Charleston, 11th. April '66.

Hon. J. P. Kennedy.

My dear Kennedy.

I enclose you a brief paragraph which I published in the Carolinian the day after you left. You will take it as a proof of my continued regard. [75] You will recieve the expression of my hopes as to your future as being quite as sincere in print, as I could make them in MS. Should I come through Balto. in going North, in season to find you there, I shall certainly look you up. If not, I hope to encounter you in New York. Excuse brevity; but in truth, I have no better excuse than sheer weariness. I am sick of pen & paper, — MS. and the eternally recurring cry of the devil, for copy. God be with you in mercy, wherever you go.

Yours Ever as Ever.

W. Gilmore Simms.

1158: To William Hawkins Ferris

Charleston, 13th April [1866] [76]

My dear Ferris.

I enclose you a Ballad which you may read, & I hope with pleasure. I wish to tax your kindness in seeing that it is then sealed & delivered to Mess'rs Cauldwell & Whitney, Publishers of the Sunday Mercury, in Fulton Street, with the enclosure which you will find within. This I also request that you will read, as something further depends upon it. Briefly, I could wish you to say, according to the reference that I shall make to them, that you will recieve any money & forward which they may desire to send to me. I have a pressing need at present for

---

[74] See introductory sketch.

[75] Simms says in the *Daily South Carolinian* of April 6: "We had the pleasure, yesterday, of a long and grateful interview with our old friend, the Hon. John P. Kennedy, and were delighted to find, not only that his mind was in its fullest vigor, but that his health, which had been much impaired, had been greatly restored by his trip to Cuba, from which the approaching Summer finds him returning towards the cooler regions of Maryland. He probably left our city last night by the Northeastern Railway."

[76] Dated by Simms' remarks about the *Daily South Carolinian*.

all the money that I can command, as my son having engaged
the services of a dozen negroes, and having mules also to feed,
and as they made no corn last season, I am required to buy Corn
as well as Bacon, besides keeping up my little establishment
here.[77] The anxieties on these subjects naturally lessen my
capacity for composition; but you will say to Mess'rs C & W.
that I am busily engaged on "The Brothers of the Coast," making
all the headway that I can — that I have some 200 pp. of MS.
written, and hope to be in New York, in *pro. per.* by the 1st.
June, prepared to begin the serial publication in their paper.
I have been embarrassed also in my progress by my failure to
procure certain books, for which I have been waiting & looking
in vain. Say to them that they will please put their valuation on
"Isadore" — that is, if it shall suit them at all, and beg them
to let me have the money for it immediately. You will see from
the weird character of the production that it is no commonplace,
and that it is susceptible of happy illustration by the artist,
and C & W. have an artist who is evidently quite capable of
good things in the way of illustrating such topics. Should they
pay you any money, be pleased to send it (as you may think)
through the safest medium.[78] My children are all well. Say to
Mrs. F. that Mrs. Roach has heard from her, & has, I believe,
written in reply. In a day or two, I propose to make my escape
from the city, on a hurried visit to the plantation — the last
visit I shall probably make before flitting to your city. De Fontaine
has just got back. He proposes to change the South Carolinian
from a morning to an afternoon paper, and he is about to re-
establish also, his paper once more in Columbia, while keeping
up the publication in Charleston. He will have his hands full.
Whether I shall continue to write for him after the 1st. of
June is a question not decided in my own mind. My pecuniary
necessity has alone prompted me to do so, hitherto; and I find
that the daily duty of the paper very materially interferes with
the regular progress of my profession.[79] — The boys [80] are catch-

---

[77] Gilmore was managing Woodlands.

[78] "The Ballad of Isadore" was published in the *New York Mercury,* XXVIII
(June 16, 1866), 4. We do not know who illustrated the poem. "The Brothers of
the Coast" was probably never finished (see note 60, March 24, 1866).

[79] We do not know the exact date on which the *Daily South Carolinian* was
removed from Charleston to Columbia, but it was before May 25, 1866 (see
letter to Lawson of that date).

[80] Gilmore and Donald Rowe. Govan and Carroll were with Simms in
Charleston (see letters to Duyckinck of Feb. 10 and to Ferris of March 24).

ing fish famously at the plantation — Shad, Trout, Perch, &c. are all to be found on their tables. Best regards to Mrs. F. Tell Josey dont use [*one word illegible*].

Good bye & God bless you.

Yours Ever

W. Gilmore Simms

W. H. Ferris, Esq.

1159: To James Lawson

Charleston, 14 April 1866

My dear Lawson.

I write in a hurry as I am just about to set forth for Woodlands where I hope to spend a week not unprofitably. I have been looking to hear from you for some weeks but in vain. Yet I must be your Creditor for at least three Letters. *N'importe.* You are all well I trust, & take for granted that you all love me as well as ever. But to business. I enclose you a list of coins, copper & silver, which belong to a reduced widow.[81] Her husband made the collection, having a passion for such things like your own. The poor woman is of the faith that these things will bring her money. Pray give me some definite idea of their value, & say whether you want them yourself. I write to Duyckinck, at the same time, on the same subject. Love to Lyde & Mary, Mr. S.[82] Jimmy and the Girls. In haste, but God bless you

Ever yours

W. Gilmore Simms

1160: To Evert Augustus Duyckinck

Charleston 14 April 1866

My dear Duyckinck.

I have only time for a few words, as I am preparing to make a rush in the morning to Woodlands, where I hope to enjoy a week of spring freshness, among opening buds & bursting blossoms. I write simply with the view to do, if possible, a service

---

[81] Mrs. Mathews. See letter to Gilmore of June 24.
[82] Thomas Sarjeant Sandford.

to the reduced widow of an old friend. Her husband, like Lawson, affected virtu, and made a considerable collection of coins supposed to be valuable among collectors. I enclose you a List of them. The poor woman is in great need, and is persuaded that from these coins a goodly sum may be derived. It is this fact which I desire to arrive at. Will you see Mr. Dexter,[83] or any party of whom you know who is making a collection. I have written to Lawson to the same effect, enclosing him a List of the Coins also.[84] Pray, obtain the necessary information and let me know promptly if any offer should be made for them. Please see Lawson also & get from him for the examination of Mr. Dexter — if that has not already been made — the collection which I left with L. of Continental money. — I will write you on my return to the City. No time at this moment. All well with me physically. Pecuniarily, I am still in a strait. Times here very hard. Have recieved none of the books, save Cooke's Stonewall Jackson, and his Surry of Eagle Nest. — Nothing from Widdleton, or Ticknor or Harper. Neither Freneau nor Francis.[85] If sent to my address through the Captains either of the Moneka or Emily Souder,[86] I shall get them promptly within 5 days. — Just got a letter from Cooke. Hope to be in New York by June 1. and will bring on with me my whole collection of Rev. Doc. Best love.

Yours Ever

W. Gilmore Simms

1161: To John Esten Cooke

Office South Carolinian.

Charleston 14th. April '66.

My dear Cooke.

God bless you. Yours just recieved, & I am just about to leave the city for my plantation to be gone a week. I have too much to say to say any thing. I hope to be in N. Y. about the 1st June. Have just read your Jackson & your Surry. Am de-

---

[83] Probably Henry Dexter (1813-1910), New York City businessman, who contributed $225,000 towards building the present home of the New-York Historical Society and who was a liberal contributor to the Metropolitan Museum of Art.

[84] This list is missing from Simms' letter to Lawson of April 14.

[85] See letter to Duyckinck of April 5.

[86] C. P. Marshman and R. W. Lockwood.

lighted with them both & shall say so.[87] Do not bother your self-esteem about Boston.[88] Time will do its work. To wait upon time is to wait upon God — to be feverish with the one is to be impatient with the other. And there is no wisdom in that. Send me copies of any poems about the War which you may have written. Pick up what you can for me, of the writings of other people. I wish to make a good book. Try & procure for me the several poems written by Thompson & Barron Hope.[89] I will write you when I return from Woodlands. Meanwhile, let me hear from you. You are working well and should be working profitably. Go ahead fearlessly. When we meet!

Àdios. Yours Ever truly

W. Gilmore Simms

1162: To ANDREW H. H. DAWSON [90]

Charleston, S. C.
April 27. 1866.

Andrew H. H. Dawson, Esq.

My dear Sir:

I find much pleasure in complying with your request, and if my humble autograph can impart any value to the collection which Mrs. T. J. Welby [91] is now making, and for so laudable a purpose, I shall be very much rejoiced. My answer has been delayed in consequence of my temporary absence from the city. I trust that it will reach you in season.

Very respectfully
Your Obt. Servt &c.

W. Gilmore Simms.

---

[87] Simms reviewed Cooke's *Stonewall Jackson* and *Surry of Eagle's Nest* in issues of the *Daily South Carolinian* which we have not seen. See letter to Cooke of May 4, 1866.

[88] Evidently Cooke's books had been unfavorably received in Boston.

[89] James Barron Hope (1829-1887), a Virginian, was the author of *Leoni di Monota: And Other Poems* (Philadelphia: J. B. Lippincott & Co., 1857) and *A Collection of Poems* (Richmond, Va.: A. Morris, 1859).

Hope's "The Oath of Freedom" and " 'Libera Nos, O Domine!' "; Cooke's "The Band in the Pines" and "The Broken Mug"; and Thompson's "Coercion: A Poem for Then and Now," "Joe Johnston," "A Farewell to Pope," "England's Neutrality. A Parliamentary Debate," "On to Richmond," "Turner Ashby," "Captain Latane," and "The Battle Rainbow" are included in *War Poetry of the South*, pp. 35-37, 445-448, 209-210, 269-274, 46-48, 123-126, 149-151, 181-187, 378-387, 430-432.

[90] Not identified.

[91] Not identified.

1163: To James Lawson

Charleston, April 27. 1866.

Your letter, my poor, dear, old friend, of the 23d., fills me with quite as much surprise as anxiety. When I left New York I should have said, as I thought, that Christina was a perfect picture of not only good, but robust health. And at that time none of you expressed the slightest apprehensions on her account. That so recently a chronic form of disease should exhibit itself, without any premonition, is to me astonishing. Had she never complained to any of you — did she not know herself — that there was something wrong? I really & sincerely hope and believe that in your anxiety, you exaggerate the evidence of danger. I trust that your Surgeon does the same, & that a closer examination, watchfulness & painstaking, with simpler remedies, will avert the supposed necessity of a surgical operation. Let me counsel you, as I have so repeatedly done before, to give some heed to Hydropathy, — the Cold Water Cure, — and if there be any establishment, under good hands — as there was in Jersey some years ago, — Bockee can tell you all about it — try it & take her there for the summer. My impression is that there is one contiguous to Newark. Greatly do I sympathise with you and poor Lyde under this new dispensation of Providence. That your afflictions should thus rapidly crowd upon you, is terrible, and serves to illustrate the well known proverb, that afflictions seldom come singly, or, if they do, it is as the swallow comes, only as the Pioneer of a swarm. I can well concieve the solitude of your household, and pray that the raven which screams above it may be hushed before many days.[92] Be of hope, as you have faith; for Hope is properly the child of Faith, and builds in wisdom upon the grand prophecies of God. Submission is the first step to faith, resignation the next.— Housekeeping will not injure, but probably benefit & strengthen the health of Mary. An active, bustling life, in the daily duties of the household, should be beneficial & need not be oppressive. — I know not what Augusta & Mary Lawson have written to you. I have no idea of bringing her on with me this summer. I am too poor even to pay her passage to & fro. I am overworked — working night & day, for the bread of life for me and my children. I earn very little — not enough even for the most simple needs. Gilmore is

---

[92] Christina Lawson lived until 1928.

at the plantation, with Chevillette & her Husband. The latter plants in Orangeburg, & rides to his plantation twice a week — a distance of 10 miles. He plants somewhat largely & has fair hopes of making a crop. Gilmore employs some 10 hands, but they do as little as they can, since they are no longer stimulated by the "Must!" He has too little capital to supply the horse power for a larger force, & is scantly supplied for the uses of the few negroes whom he does employ. He himself is quite energetic, and works in the field with his hoe, proposing to himself, meanwhile, the study of law, and applying himself to his books during certain hours of the day. He is cheerful, but thinner than usual — feeling the loss of all those hopes which warmed his heart but a few years ago. I am sometimes dreadfully depressed with reflections upon his fortunes & my own. Mary L.[,] Govan & Carroll are here with me in town, but I shall not keep them here much longer. It is too expensive. I propose, before going north, to take them up to the plantation, where I shall be able, with God's favour, to supply them with corn & bacon for the rest of the summer. The country is in great distress from want of food. White as well as black are threatened with famine. There is not a bushel of corn to be bought in the interior. It is all supplied in Charleston, brought from Maryland & the North, and now commands 1.35 per bushel. My former slaves are now applying to me, whom they have deserted, to advance them money for the purchase of corn! What I live on now is the fruit of my daily labour as an Associate Editor of the South-Carolinian. I have some 170 pages of MS. on a new romance,[93] but I am so distressed in spirit, so worked in brain,[94] so fevered with anxiety & trouble, that I make slow progress. At this moment I have not a dollar that I can call my own. Today, Saturday, I expect to draw from the office which is two weeks in my debt. Advise me of Bockee's proper address.[95] I have written to him in vain, without an answer. Love to all & God's blessing upon all.

W. Gilmore Simms.

---

[93] "The Brothers of the Coast."

[94] Simms wrote *brained*.

[95] Bockee lived at 95 3rd Place, Brooklyn. See the Brooklyn directories for 1865-1869.

1164: To John Esten Cooke

Charleston, May 4. [1866][96]

My dear Cooke.

I had just folded in an envelope for you two articles of the Carolinian, one on your Jackson, the other on your Surrey, and a third cut out of the Selma, Ala. Weekly.[97] Our space does not admit of any thing elaborate or in detail. But I think I have treated you fairly, and trust that you will be quite satisfied. I am obliged to you also for the one poem sent me. Let me have others, if you can lay hands on them, and as soon as possible. Procure me, also, as fast as you can, the several poems of Hope & Thompson. The former is, in person, available to you. The poems of Thompson, I take for granted, can also be procured in Richmond. I propose (D. V.) to be in New York, by the 1 June. Let me hear of, or see you there. Richardson will publish for me the Poems. I shall make a good collection. Do not fail to send me any, of merit, by any hands, upon which you can lay your hands. I could wish Virginia to be well represented in the collection.[98] I am under the weather, my head out of order, my mind troubled greatly, & write hurriedly, but Ever affectionately Yours

W. Gilmore Simms.

1165: To John Pendleton Kennedy

Charleston, S. C.
May 15. 1866.

Hon. J. P. Kennedy.

My dear Kennedy.

Bryan [99] reminds me that I promised to send you a copy of my "Areytos &c." a volume printed before the war, but never pub-

---

[96] Dated by Simms' references to the *Daily South Carolinian* and to *War Poetry of the South.*

[97] The last issue of the *Daily South Carolinian* which we have seen is that for April 17. Cooke's *Stonewall Jackson* and *Surry of Eagle's Nest* were probably reviewed after that date, though they may have been reviewed in earlier issues missing from the file of the newspaper to which we have had access. We have not had access to any one of the several Selma, Ala., weeklies published at this time.

[98] For Cooke's, Hope's, and Thompson's contributions to *War Poetry of the South,* see note 89, April 14, 1866. At this time Thompson was in England.

[99] George S. Bryan. See note 122, May 1, 1850.

lished.[100] He undertakes to have it committed to your hands before your departure for Europe, and with this letter, I confide it to his hands. It may beguile you of some tedious hours on the passage. The preface will account to you for the capricious character of the contents which represent so many phases of a most capricious life. Between the 1st. & 20th. of June, I expect to be in New York. You will hear of me at the publishing house of Richardson, 540 Broadway. Let me see you before you depart, and I presume you will need to pass through New York in order to do so. When you return in winter try Florida, should your health need a Southern climate. Âdios!

Yours ever truly

W. Gilmore Simms.

1166: To James Lawson

Charleston, May 25. '66.

My dear Lawson.

I have been waiting anxiously to hear from you in relation to the case of Christina. I wrote you instantly after the reciept of yours apprising me of her illness; not hearing from you since, I am induced to hope that your very natural anxiety & apprehensions had been dissipated, but my own anxiety still continues, & I now write to beg to hear from you in respect to her condition. — We are all tolerably well here, in Charleston as at Woodlands. Here, I have with me Augusta & *her* family, and my little boy, Govan, who is at school here, & whom I shall keep here, at school, until the Autumn vacation, unless the city shall become unhealthy.[101] In that event, I shall send him up to Woodlands. There, now residing, are Gilmore, Mary Lawson, little Carroll, and Chevillette & her Husband. Gilmore, with some 10 or a dozen of the virtuous freedmen, is planting Corn & Cotton, with a very bad prospect — which is general — in respect to the latter. Donald, my son in law, plants, in Orangeburg Dist. some 8 or 10 miles from Woodlands, & is working on a much larger scale. The want of means contracts the labors of Gilmore. He left the city this morning, having been under arrest, as well as Donald,

---

[100] John Russell did contract for 100 or 200 copies of *Simms's Poems Areytos* (see letter to Lawson of *c.* Nov. 22, 1860, and following letters to Lawson) and the title-page of the volume does carry his imprint; thus in a sense he was the publisher of the volume.

[101] We do not know what school Govan attended at this time.

by the Military, for threatening a Yankee preacher with a horse-whipping — the said preacher having been playing the incendiary, teaching sedition to the negroes, & — taking up — as usual — a *Collection*. These wretches will never let us or the negro be at peace. He told some 3000 of them, that, in a short time, all the lands in the neighbourhood would be divided among them, in tracts of 50 acres each; that they should not work as hirelings any longer, but should become the masters & proprietors of the soil; and that the white nabobs should ride behind their carriages, and be only too happy to lift their beavers when they met. Gilmore & Donald were discharged on pledging themselves to keep the peace towards the scoundrel. I have withdrawn from my connection with the Carolinian which has been removed from the city to Columbia, the original seat of publication.[102] I now write for the Ch. Courier, & shall correspond with that journal while I am at the North this summer.[103] The pay is small but certain, & with that & other things, I trust to be able to get along through the year. But my resources from all quarters have barely sufficed to keep up the family & give Gilmore a start with mules & implements at Woodlands. It is my hope to start for N. Y. somewhere towards the 10th. proxo. I have a most pressing invitation from my new friend, Mr. Ferris, who, with his family, spent his Christmas at Woodlands, to stay with him during my visit this summer, & I have pledged to him a portion of my time at least. He lives at Brooklyn.[104] I shall give our friend Bockee a week; and if the condition of your household will permit, I hope to give you a portion of my time. You must write & let me know. I have much work on my hands, which I trust to make compensative (Quien Sabe?) and fortunately can do this just as well at Brooklyn, or Yonkers,[105] as in the City of N. Y. — You should be at Woodlands this summer, & must certainly take a month or two there as soon as you can command the time. The fish are abundant. You can fling your Line or Bob, and take the finest perch, bream, pike, cat, & lake trout, at every flirt. The boys have constructed

---

[102] We have been unable to discover the exact date of the removal of the *Daily South Carolinian* from Charleston to Columbia.

[103] We do not know the extent of Simms' contributions to the *Courier* during 1866, but evidently he wrote all the book notices for the newspaper after Bruns went to Europe (see note 57, March 21, 1866). His "New York Correspondence," signed "St. Pol" (omitted from this edition of Simms' *Letters* because of lack of space), was published in the *Courier* during July–Sept., 1866.

[104] Ferris' address was 78 Dean Street. See the Brooklyn *Directory* for 1866-1867.

[105] Simms wrote *Yonkeers*.

a trap besides in which they sometimes find 50 of a day. Very soon the deer will be in season for the Hunters, & there are plenty in our swamps. During the winter & spring, Gilmore & Donald, lived almost entirely on game, partridges, doves, snipe, squirrels, rabbits &c. But for these resources, their supplies of *meats* would have been angelic visitations. So Forrest has gone to California.[106] Did he make out to see you before he went? And how comes on the Tragedy? Have you finished it? If so, do not print till I come on, & help you in its revision.[107] Bockee has responded to my letter in a well written reply. How does Jimmy get on, & the young couple, the Sandfords? Well, I am at the bottom of my sheet, which I trust you will find satisfactorily filled. My love to Lyde & the girls. Best regards to Mr. Sandford, Mr. Walker,[108] & Jamie, the Younger Lawson.

Yours Ever truly

W. Gilmore Simms.

Coins. I have picked up for you a Chihuahua Penny, which may be new to your collection — date 1855.

1167: To William Hawkins Ferris

Charleston, 25 May 1866.

My dear Ferris.

Your long & acceptable letter reached me yesterday & was taken off by Gilmore who left for Woodlands this morning. He & my son in law were arrested by the military a few days ago, for threatening a Yankee abolitionist with the horsewhip because of certain seditious preachings to the negroes. The boys got off by pledging themselves *not* to resort to the horsewhip, but to the Courts, in all such cases. These young fellows, by their rashness, frequently get me into hot water. The event compelled me to take another flying visit to Woodlands, to see to the comfort & security of the family during their absence. Well, Gilmore went off this morning, taking your Letter which, as it contained some reference to himself, I had handed him to read. It follows, accordingly, that,

---

[106] Forrest arrived in San Francisco on May 3, and on May 14 he made his bow in *Richelieu.* See Moses, *The Fabulous Forrest,* pp. 315-316.

[107] *Giordano. A Tragedy* (Yonkers: Printed, Not Published, 1867). *Giordano* was first published in 1832 (see note 3, July 4, 1832, and note 38, Feb. 26, 1860).

[108] William Augustus Walker, of the firm of Lawson and Walker. See note 213, Oct. 22, 1860.

as I have it not beside me, there may be some of its points which will escape my memory. Touching the coins, I will communicate with Mrs. Tefft, to whom Mrs. Roach recently paid a visit in Savannah. I took her along with me when I took my run to Florida. I fear the poor old Lady, if she had any collection of Coins, was more likely to expend them first, as more available in the market than any of her other property. I will write her, however.[109] The mocking birds are numerous. Hardly a tree in my grounds at Woodlands, but has its nest, and I can promise that Gilmore will do his best to procure you a pair or two. The male bird is the bird of musical power. The female has but small reputation as a singer. I shall try to obtain males for you. But the bird is a difficult one to raise. It is delicate, and frequently dies while yet young in the cage and before its singing robes are yet put on. The food with us consists of well boiled eggs & Irish potatoes, mixed together, worms, & grasshoppers especially, the wings & feet of the grasshoppers being carefully stript off. But if I procure you the birds, I shall endeavour to provide you with all the necessary information as to their treatment. Members of my family have had them, at various periods, but have been generally unfortunate with them; so much so that I have rather discouraged their capture of them. The negroes however, frequently take the young ones out of their nests, & sell them to passengers in the cars, or send them to the cities. They must be pretty well grown & out of danger, when they are sent to you, and I fear that your climate is much too cold to suffer them to live through one of your winters unless in a conservatory kept constantly at an even temperature. My son in law [110] goes in a few days to Woodlands when I will instruct him & Gilmore to use all possible efforts to secure you a pair or two. — I am now a contributor to the Ch. Courier, from which I draw a small weekly stipend, sufficient to satisfy the abdominal wolf, but nothing more. I shall probably contribute to that paper a series of letters from the North, while I am there, & you can probably help me to some of the material, while I sojourn with you.[111] I am busily engaged, closing rivets up, dismissing correspondents, & studying how far I can condense

---

[109] Tefft died in 1862. Mrs. Tefft later sold his collection of autographs (see letter to Leavitt, Strebeigh and Co. of Oct. 3, 1866). We do not know when Simms made this trip to Florida.

[110] Donald Rowe. See following letter.

[111] See note 103, May 25, 1866. A visit Simms made with Ferris to the United States Sub-Treasury in Wall Street is the subject of one of these letters (see note 199, Aug. 7, 1866).

into a decent compass the vast body of MS.S. which I propose
to carry or send. Did I understand you to say that you had the
freedom of the Adams' Express, & that whatever I should find
to send you would go without charge? And if so, would that
cover a box of MSS. of some size and no little weight. There are
some 6 or 8 folios, bound, of foolscap dimensions & much foolscap
contents.[112] Let me know. The collection of Poems during the war
will be also of considerable dimensions. You have hardly concieved the danger you incur, when you so boldly challenge me to
try if you have houseroom enough! — I have written to Lawson
to say that I shall give you a portion of my time, and I shall need
to say the same thing to my old friend, Mr Bockee. How, when
I reach the wharf in N. Y. shall I direct my Luggage so as to
reach your domain in safety. Do the Express Companies send
their wagons to these places. Repeat to me also in your next, the
number of your House in Dean Street. My object will be to make
as few transshipments as possible. It has become apparent to me
that I shall hardly be able to get away from the South before
the 10th. proxo. I shall need to pay another visit to Woodlands
& to give them three or four days there. Returning here, I shall
be required to linger for a few days. And in all these places, &
with all these changes, I am required to be busied with my poor
brain from morning to night, & I fear, sometimes, from night to
morning. But, what would you have, in this atrocious world,
where the parties seem pretty equally divided, between the Mill
Horse & the Miller, the one who does the grinding, & the other
who gets the meal. As for Miss Josie, be pleased to say to her
that she will find Grandpa, a monstrous tease. He will worry her
little life out, and take his reward in kisses. And she shall bring
his blessings. Oh! And Oh! to bring his slippers too, and when
he worries Josie, Oh. — What will little Josie do? Only a little
worrying, perhaps, on her own account. I brought you an orange
stick from Florida, not a very large or handsome one, but the
best that I could get, & I will bring you a pair of splendid deer
antlers from Woodlands, and you shall have them set, & they will
constitute together quite a classical support for your steps as you
walk the Halls of the National Mammon, where, like the poor
devil of antiquity — what was his name? — Tantalus — wherein
we get tantalize — you are up to your neck in gold, without being
allowed the privilege of helping yourself. Gilmore sends his regards, — so, Mrs. Ed. Roach, to your wife. You will of course

---

[112] Simms' collection of Revolutionary letters and documents.

convey mine as gratefully and gracefully as possible. To Josie I send sundry infinitesimal kisses, carefully adapted to her pretty little mouth. And so, with no more to say, I commend you to the mercies of God.

Àdios.

Yours Ever truly

W. Gilmore Simms

1168: To WILLIAM HAWKINS FERRIS

Charleston, May 28. 1866.

My dear Ferris.

As I wrote you but a day or two ago, I have very little now to say, and simply write to enclose you a list of the coins sent you, not remembering whether I sent you one before. I have written to Mrs. Tefft with the view to know whether her husband left any collection & whether she has disposed of it or not. Your last brief note, acknowledging the arrival of the collection reached me yesterday. Times are very stringent here. The cry is — No money! — All the business men, when you meet them, groan, with flat faces & cry — 'business flat!' Donald Rowe & wife are both with us, and will remain a few days more. A great freshet in our rivers, has so raised the waters that, for the present, we can get no fish at Woodlands, &, perforce, the order of the day is corned pork & bacon. I am apprehensive that we are about to have such a crash in the financial world every where, as will confound all parts of the world. War is the parent of all destructiveness. In destroying the South, the Yankees have destroyed their own golden goose. What a monstrous thing, on any pretence, to make war upon a people who were their own *best customers,* to the tune of hundreds of millions *per annum,* and whose grand staples, brought in annually 235 millions. The country will bring in no more. The Cotton crop is destined this year to be nearly as grand a failure as the last. It will be [liberal] in my poor opinion, to set the production down at even one million of bales, and had I the green backs now, I should buy up all the cotton I could command, at present prices, & store it away for the future. But, poor as Job's Turkey, I can only brood & not buy. Pray ask Mrs. F. why Job's Turkey should be more poor than that of any body else. It would seem to argue that Mrs. Job stinted the poor creature in corn. Put the problem to Josey when her mother fails to answer. Being very dull today, I write *à l'abandon.* — Had a whist table on Saturday night [113] & supper. You must certainly learn to play whist. I will teach you. Ah hah! — I am wandering. Best regards to Madame F. & a kiss for Josey. I should be her creditor to a great degree, unless the maiden kisses free.

> Àdios.
> Yours Ever.
> W. Gilmore Simms.

1169: To WILLIAM HAWKINS FERRIS

> [June 1, 1866][114]

My dear Ferris.

My present purpose is to sail the Emily P. Souder, on Thursday next the 7th. Inst. Leitch [115] is also to be a Passenger. Tomorrow (Saturday) I run up to the plantation (D. V.) until Tuesday. I shall then have 2 days for preparing & packing up. It is possible I may not get quite ready; but will try. Be on the look out at all events. I write simply to apprise you of this plan & its probabili-ties. It will try my mental & physical resources, to get in readiness, but where theres the will there's the way. Major Rowe goes up with me tomorrow. His wife remains here a week longer. Gilmore is in a worry as usual, and the river is too full for fish. Love to all — and Josey.

> Yours Ever
> W. G. S.

1170: To WILLIAM GILMORE SIMMS, JR.

> Charleston, Friday Night — 8th June. [1866][116]

My dear Gilmore.

I propose to depart tomorrow by the Quaker City. Edward will send you Twenty Dollars of Donald's money. Send down to

---

[113] May 26.

[114] 1866 is the only year after the Confederate War that Simms planned to sail for New York in any month on which Thursday fell on the 7th. His reference to "tomorrow (Saturday)" dates the letter as June 1.

[115] William Y. Leitch, of Charleston, was a broker, an auctioneer, and a real estate agent, in partnership with Robert S. Bruns (see note 15, Jan. 16, 1866). His wife was Harriet, sister of Dr. William Sims Reynolds.

[116] 1866 is the only year after the Confederate War that Simms sailed for New York City at the time indicated in this letter.

Edward the first of the *five* drafts I sent you, endorsed simply with your name. He will procure forty Dollars for it, will replace the $20 of Donald's money, & leave $20 to your credit. You must economize this money. Have no *wants* which are not *needs*. There will be from the 4 drafts remaining to you $180. This you will hoard to meet *emergencies,* whether of building or of whatever kind. Mr. Schubert [117] could only pay $50. Of this $10 went for sheriffs expenses. I have, accordingly, just $40. with which to go to New York! I shall probably need it all. As my fortunes there are very problematical, you will readily concieve the propriety of spending not a copper which is not imperatively called for. So far as I can see, you will have no need to expend any thing this summer. Your larder is amply supplied. Your corn will suffice till your own crop comes in. Of clothes, you have enough, & so have the girls. There is no wolf at your gate, and all you have need to do, is patiently to wait upon Providence, & earnestly to strive, according to your strength. Between Donald & yourself, there will be no need to strain a single muscle; and in the hot hours of the day, pore over your Blackstone; go to work doggedly; — it will be a tedious struggle for you, to subdue that demon of Unrest which the last five years has reared up in your bosom keeping you forever feverish. Your condition & the suffering which must follow from its cure, will be not unlike that of a man breaking off from the habit of strong drink or tobacco chewing or smoking. Persevere for 3 months, and you will triumph. You will suffer; but you will succeed. And remember, how much of all your future, must depend upon the fact that you do succeed. You have to make up for a great deal of lost time. You should prepare yourself for the law, and might do so, with proper diligence, by the May or Spring term next year. Blackstone — master him first. Yeadon, Aldrich, Whaley, Lord,[118] all will supply you with the necessary books. See that you comprehend what you read. Nay, you are not simply to read. You are to study. When doubtful or puzzled, ride over to Charles Carroll & let him explain. Let him

---

[117] Perhaps C. Schubert, a repairer of musical instruments at 22 George Street, Charleston. See the Charleston *Directory* for this year.

[118] Richard Yeadon, Alfred Proctor Aldrich, B. J. Whaley, and Samuel Lord, Jr. Prior to the Confederate War Whaley (admitted to the bar at Charleston in 1846) and Lord (admitted to the bar at Columbia in 1853) were partners in the firm of Whaley and Lord, 21 Broad Street, Charleston (see the Charleston *Directory* for 1860). Evidently the partnership was dissolved during or shortly after the Confederate War, since the Charleston *Directory* for 1867-1868 gives different addresses for each man.

drill you. Get the *nomenclature* of the Law as soon as possible. Then fathom the principles. Read the Statutes on certain subjects, such as C. Carroll will suggest. Read Froude's England which I have sent up to you. Address your mind earnestly to the mastery of this most noble study, and it will reward you in a twofold sense, as a mental acquisition, & as a means of fortune. You are not always to be a desultory, purposeless young man, dawdling over life, as if it were a perpetual *picnic,* or slavishly struggling for mere bread, in perpetual conflict with skulking, shuffling & worthless negroes. Rise to a sense of your high calling — your great & pressing responsibilities — the old father who will soon be unable to serve *you,* & whom it may be necessary that you shall serve — the dear brothers & sisters, who will look up to you as to a father, when I am only one in memory. God forever bless & keep you all, my son, in the hollow of his fraternal hand.

À Dios.

W. Gilmore Simms.

Return my Internal Revenue Tax & pay it. It is only on one watch, valued at $75.

1171: To Anna Augusta Singleton Simms Roach

Brooklyn, June 12, '66.

My dear Daughter.

We reached New York in safety at about 5 oclock this morning, having had a very pleasant passage. I was quite well during the voyage and continue so. I left the ship for Brooklyn, direct, & am now here comfortably domiciled with Mr. Ferris, who was expecting me. I have a comfortable & airy chamber, from which I now write. Passing only from the Dock near Wall Street, to the Fulton Ferry contiguous, I saw nothing of Lawson, or any of my N. Y. friends. It is possible that I shall see none of them till tomorrow, when I propose to go up to the city. As yet, my trunks, sent forward by Xpress, have not reached me; but I look for them every moment. As a matter of course, I have nothing of which to write or report. The weather for the last 20 hours of our voyage was so cool — nay, cold, — that I regretted that I left my overcoat behind me in the country. If Chevillette be still with you, beg her to say to Mary L. that she must see to it, have it occasionally brushed, as well as kept out of the dust. Such of the clothes that I left, for Chevy, to take up into the country, as will suit Gilmore to use, he will take possession of. Let the others be carefully kept, as I may possibly need them in the winter. In writing to Gilmore, I neglected to ask if he had recieved the 5 several drafts which I sent him drawn on Mr. Wagner, the first one of which I wished him to employ in returning to Donald the money which Edward furnished out of Donald's funds in his hands. I should like to be assured on this subject, as upon all others affecting the interests of the family. Mr. & Mrs. Ferris, speak most warmly & affectionately of yourself, husband, Gilmore & the Girls. She was particularly curious about your little baby, of whose personal appearance she speaks in terms which would gratify the most partial mother.[119] She begs her best remembrances to you, Edw. Gilmore & the Girls. I write this having nothing more to report than my own safe arrival & present good condition. My love to Edward, Chevy, Julia, Claudia, Clara, Mrs. Petigru,[120] Govan & the Baby. God bless & be with you all in mercy. Àdios.

Yours affecy.

W. Gilmore Simms.

1172: To William Gilmore Simms, Jr.

New York. 12 June 1866.

My dear Gilmore.

I reached New York this morning at 5 oclock, and at 7 was at the House of Mr. Ferris, whence I now write this letter. I write merely to apprise you that I arrived in safety, have been quite well throughout the passage, and continue so, at the present moment. There are two ships from Europe, quarantined with cholera on board, in the lower harbour; but, so far as I can learn there is no cholera in New York or Brooklyn. I came directly from the steamer to Brooklyn, and as yet have not seen Lawson, or any body in New York. It is possible that, as soon as my trunks shall arrive this morning, I will dress & proceed up to the

---

[119] The Ferrises had seen Augusta's baby, Esther Singleton Roach (Nov. 15, 1865—Feb. 8, 1868), when they visited Simms during Christmas, 1865.

[120] Jane Amelia Postell Petigru (1795-1868), widow of James Louis Petigru (see introductory sketch).

latter city. Our passage was a very pleasant one; but last night & this morning were so cold as almost to make me regret that I had left my cloak. The season seems to be as anomalous here as in the South; and it is held to be backward, as with us, among the Northern farmers. I left all well in Charleston. I trust that all keep so at Woodlands. I shall look to hear from some of you at least weekly; and pray God that you will always be able to report favorably. My anxieties are all with my children. Tell Donald that when Chevillette returns to the country, he must keep her from fatigue, long walks & much physical exertion. She should take as little medicine as possible, & if sick at any time, Donald must get his mother to come over & see her.[121] I fear that her walks in Charleston taken with Clara, are quite too long, and may prove injurious. She had better devolve as much of the house duties on M. L. as possible. M. L. is quite willing and the exercise will do *her* good. For yourself, let me beg that you will economize yourself, & take no idle risks, in the hot sun, whether for sports or labours. In the hotter parts of the day, grapple with Blackstone, keep a note book beside you, & put on record in your own hand, the leading ideas or principles, which that great oracle of the Common Law lays down. I surely need not repeat to you that your whole future of successful performance, to say nothing of dignity & respectability will depend upon your strenuous efforts now to make yourself a master of your profession & commence the practice. You will, at first, find the labour dreary enough, considering the very desultory life that you have led during the past five years; but this only makes it incumbent upon you to exert & assert the highest will, & the most dogged determination, to acquire, and still acquire, & never rest from acquisition, untill you are able to perform. Make yourself independent of the plantation, if you would ever be able to convert the plantation itself to pleasant & profitable uses. It is for your own sake, my dear son, & that of your dear brothers & sisters, that I entreat you to the exercise of this — as I esteem it — the most perfect manhood. My Love to Donald, Chevy, M. L. & all. Kisses for all, from, my dear Gilmore,

Your ever affec father

W. Gilmore Simms

---

[121] Chevillette's first child, born probably in Jan., 1867 (see letter to Ferris of Jan. 8, 1867), was named Chevillette Simms. She died probably in Sept., 1867 (see letter to Gilmore of Sept. 14, 1867).

1173: To William Gilmore Simms, Jr.

Brooklyn, June 24 '66.

My dear Son.

I wrote you but a day or two ago, & now write again, simply to acknowledge the reciept of yours of the 16th. & M. L's of the 17th. inst. I am sorry to hear that Chevy still looks badly; but tell Donald that he must not suffer her to tamper with medicine. Let her use the cold bath freely; give up tea & coffee for awhile, and, in place of these, if you can possibly arrange it, get up 100 lbs of ice per week. You can contrive some mode by which you can keep that quantity for a week. See Whetstone on this subject. But the free use of cool water from the well, drunk copiously, and free use of the bath, will do her more good than any medicines. Let her get back my hip-bath tub from Mrs. Fuller,[122] and use it morning, noon & night. So, too, should M. L. & Little Carroll, every morning, just as he pops out of bed. See to this. Tell M. L. that I thank her for her letter, but that I am too busy to write to all of you, & one Letter a week, no matter to whom addressed, must suffice for all. She should relieve Chevy of the cares & burdens of the house, while Chevy is an invalid. Let her take the morning bath also. And, let her congratulate Mary Rivers, on the providential escape of Tommy,[123] & on his good conduct. I congratulate you on your beef club. I have spent two nights at Yonkers with the Lawsons. Christina is better again, but still in the hands of the surgeon. She has had to undergo an operation. Her case seems to be not dissimilar to that of Washy[124] — a disease of the womb. I did not see *her*. I am still with Mr. Ferris, and find him & his family very genial. But to-morrow, I am to go for a few days to spend with Bockee. He & wife[125] were here last night, & as he is of a jealous temperament, I am solicitous to disarm his moods by a timely concession to his wishes. I have given out a considerable body of M.S.S. to the publishers, for the collection of the war poems of the South. We shall make a vol. of 500 pages. It keeps me busy. Besides this, I have done nothing with the publishers as yet. Will see some of them in a few days. I sate yesterday to Brady, for a full length

---

[122] Elizabeth Middleton Fuller, widow of Thomas Fuller and mother of Dr. William Fuller.
[123] Thomas Francis Rivers (d. 1904) was later a minister.
[124] Anna Washington Govan Steele Fuller.
[125] Isabella Smith Donaldson Bockee. See note 21, April 30, 1853.

photograph, designed for an engraving for a quarto volume —
sate, full bearded, — with all my weight of grey on head & cheek
& chin! So you may expect a very frightful presentment of your
papa.[126] I have just had occasion to write to Charlotte Percival
touching the collection of Mrs. Mathews'[127] coins. Nothing much
can be done with them. They are not estimated by the numisma-
tists as of any rarity or worth. Tell Chevillette to stay at home for
the present. Wandering will do her no good. Stay at home, read,
avoid excitements, & regularly try the cold bath — for a few
minutes only, say 5, at a time. — Your letter, my son, pleases
me more than usual. It is written more coherently & shows more
painstaking. Without painstaking, and laborious concentration of
the mind upon the task in hand, nothing can be done well. With
painstaking & you may do almost every thing. For example, you
have the power really to write not only a good & legible, but a
noble, bold & graceful [*Remainder of letter missing.*]

1174: To John Pendleton Kennedy

New York:
24 June 1866.

Hon. Jno. P. Kennedy.

My dear Kennedy.

Thanks for your kind Letter which was duly recieved, a few
days ago. Let me beg that you will apprise me, through "C. B.
Richardson, 540 Broadway," on your arrival in N. Y. and I will
instantly seek you out. I ask this, as I am dividing my time, temporarily, between Brooklyn & Yonkers, and only occasionally
visit the great city. I have in press, a volume of the Southern
poetry of the war, & shall make a creditable volume of it. Have
you any photographs of yourself to spare? If so, pray bring one
with you. I am making a collection of my friends heads — i. e.

---

[126] It is probable that the engraving of Simms in Duyckinck's *National
Portrait Gallery of Eminent Americans* is actually from this photograph by
Mathew B. Brady (*c.* 1823-1896), the well-known photographer, rather than
from a painting by Alonzo Chappel, as is said on the engraving. We are led
to this conclusion by Simms' remarks about the photograph in this letter and
about both the photograph and the engraving in later letters to Duyckinck.

[127] Charlotte Percival (1816-1899), daughter of Eleanor Marshall and Dr.
Samuel Percival (1781-1848), one of the founders of Trinity Church in Co-
lumbia, was born in or near Columbia. She later made her home with Dr.
William Percival, of Aiken. We are unable to identify Mrs. Mathews.

where they have any thing in them — for an album, which I
design to keep for my children; taking for granted that they will
learn to estimate & study the aspects of those whom I have known
equally in head & heart.[128] In haste (reserving much to say when
we meet) but

> Ever truly as Ever,
> Your friend &c.
>
> W. Gilmore Simms.

1175: To James Lawrence Orr [129]

Brooklyn, N. Y. June 24. 1866.

Excellency
J. L. Orr.

My dear Orr.

I enclose you a Letter recd. by me some time ago, which explains itself. Mr. Moore is the author of the recent publication
giving a good history, showing the Yankees up, of Negro Slavery, & their agency in it. I wrote you in regard to Mr. Moore's
application, & sent you some time ago, a sheet of his book.[130]
But to this I got no answer. I have written to Capt. Bachman, at
Columbia, to see Hunt, the Secy of State, and ascertain what
he can in respect to the condition of the State Archives, and
whether they are destroyed or not. I could wish that when you
next visit Columbia, you would set on foot a train of inquiry
into this subject, & especially compel the proper working of
those who are the custodians of the public archives.[131] — I have
not been here sufficiently long to arrive at any just conclusions
on any subject; but it strikes me that Radicalism is disgusting
the people very generally. In a recent conversation with a man
of the West, he told me very confidently that you would be

---

[128] We have been unable to locate this album.

[129] Orr was inaugurated governor of South Carolina in Nov., 1865.

[130] George Henry Moore (1823-1892), librarian of the New-York Historical
Society during 1849-1876, was the author of *Notes on the History of Slavery
in Massachusetts* (New-York: D. Appleton & Co., 1866).

[131] William K. Bachman (d. 1901), the son of the Rev. John Bachman (see
note 60, Feb. 26, 1852), was a lawyer in Columbia. During the Confederate
War he was captain of the German Artillery Volunteers, known as the Bachman Battery of the Hampton Legion. In 1866 he was a member from Richland
District of the South Carolina House of Representatives. William R. Huntt
was secretary of state of South Carolina during 1862-1866.

brought out by the Democratic Party for the Presidency! So lay in supplies for the White House, give me a sinecure, or "rob me the King's Exchequer." [132] Let me hear from you, & hold me truly Yours &c.

W. Gilmore Simms.

1176: To Evert Augustus Duyckinck

Brooklyn. 1 July 1866.

My dear Duyckinck.

I am still too much a sufferer from the inflamed condition of my tongue, to expose myself to contact with the friends who would nevertheless require me to talk. Briefly, I cannot talk without pain, and I am sucking lozenges, and alum, & Borax, and using mouth-washes, blending all of these, with sage & other weeds, which were never gathered on Hymettus. I hope, however, to be relieved next week, and as soon as I am relieved, you shall see me. Meanwhile, I will endeavour to have sent up to you five volumes of the Revolutionary papers. On Friday last, I prepared and sent you up three small pieces of verse, of religious character which I thought might suit the tone of Scribner's Magazine. In regard to these pieces, I said to you all that needed to be said.[133] I take leave still further to trespass upon your kindness as you will see by the enclosure which I have made, of what I concieve to be a very fanciful poem. It is suitable for the pages of the Argosy, and, as you suggested to me this new magazine, as one of good conduct & ability — which is also able to compensate its contributors — I could wish, if *quite* convenient & agreeable to you, that you would submit it to the Publisher, & contrive to put me *en rapport* with him. I have not attached my name to the poem, but he is at liberty to do so, — unless it be equally agreeable to him that I should adopt a *nom de plume,* which I should prefer. You are at liberty to state to him my situation, needing present & prompt compensation, and as liberal as circumstances will allow him to make it.

---

[132] Simms misquotes *I Henry IV,* III, iii, 205.

[133] "Friday last" was June 29. Simms published two signed poems in *Hours at Home*: "A Dream of the Beautiful" (see note 146, Dec. 19, 1865) and "At Greenwood Cemetery," IV (Nov., 1866), 47. Four of Simms' "St. Pol" letters (see note 103, May 25, 1866), published in the Charleston *Courier* of July 7, 9, 10, and 11, 1866, are also concerned with Greenwood Cemetery, in Long Island.

With a little more leisure, and with such an understanding with a Publisher, as would enable me to concentrate myself on one or more periodicals, I should be soon prepared to work in prose — the tale or essay, criticism or 'what not.' At all events, if the accompanying poem should please, I could furnish one, as good or better, & of more or less length, monthly; and shall be glad to do so. — It is possible that there may be some other periodicals, within your knowledge, to whom this, or other pieces would be profitably presentable. If so, and the Argosy is unwilling to have my consignments on friend to Port Public, I shall be glad if you will think of these *alternative* publications. But, from my readings of the Argosy, it strikes me that the poem will be acceptable in that quarter.[134] — While in Richardson's the other day, I happened upon a quarto weekly in which I found some literary notes which I suspected to come from your pen. It was *not* the 'Round Table,' but like it; and I know not why I should forget its name.[135] I am now writing to the Charleston Courier, & your memoranda will be grateful to me, and of great help, to my letters in that direction.[136] My address, — which you are at liberty to give to any friends seeking me — will be, from Monday next — at "78 Dean Street, Brooklyn." — I should not omit to add that, among the acquaintances met & made here, is Mr.   the Librarian of the Brooklyn Hist. Library.[137] I have shown him some of the vols. of the Hist. documents, & he betrays considerable anxiety to procure them for the Society & for publication. He suggests a like process for publication with that of yours & Richardson's; but — *nous verrons*. Mr.   professes to know you very well, and I have referred him to you for any future examination which he may desire to make into the contents of the volumes. You will of course, on no account, suffer

---

[134] The first issue of the *Argosy*, published by Strahan and Co., 148 Strand, London, and 178 Grand Street, New York, is dated Jan., 1866. We have examined a file of the periodical, but can find nothing which we can identify as Simms'.

[135] We do not know what weekly Simms here has in mind. The *Round Table* (New York) was a weekly which ran from Dec. 19, 1863, through July 3, 1869.

[136] See note 103, May 25, 1866.

[137] The "Brooklyn Hist. Library" is the Long Island Historical Society Library. George Hannah was librarian during 1865-1889. Simms evidently planned to fill in his name, but he failed to do so.

them to go out of your possession.[138] — I shall be grateful to you for any letter.

Yours Ever truly

W. Gilmore Simms.

Redfield has been to see me. He has no idea of again becoming a Publisher. He says that the proprietor of my two volumes, "Histy of S. C." & ["]Cassique of Kiawah," not in Widdleton's Collection will cheerfully yield himself to any plan which will be for my benefit, and will render the edition complete.[139] He looks well.

W. G. S.

1177: To Evert Augustus Duyckinck

7th. July. Brooklyn.
78 Dean St. 1866

My dear Duyckinck.

I got up to the city yesterday, but not early enough to hope to find you in; and in my efforts at walking, I completely broke down, especially as the terrible weather, in spite of my own efforts, was enough to send me half fainting to couch upon an iceberg. Today, I am too headachy & otherwise unwell, to keep tryst with Jamie Lawson with whom I was to go to Yonkers for a few days. My tongue troubles me also this morning, & denies free speech. I shall need to take more medicine tonight. — I am surprised that you did not recieve the poems for Scribner.[140] They were enclosed in another Envelope, and addressed, as I still believe, to you; but it is just possible that I may, in the hurry of writing, have erred in addressing them direct to Scribner. If so, the letter which accompanies them is certainly written to you.

---

[138] The Long Island Historical Society purchased Simms' collection of Laurens MSS. in 1867. See letters to Duyckinck of that year.

[139] Richardson and Co. (Charles Benjamin Richardson), New York, published an edition of *The History of South Carolina* dated 1866. This edition is printed from the plates of Redfield's edition dated 1860 (see note 191, July 26, 1859). *The Cassique of Kiawah* was not republished until after Simms' death. We are unable to identify "the proprietor" of the two works.

In a review of *The History of South Carolina* the Charleston *Courier* of Feb. 25, 1867, says: "Mr. Simms has done much for the literature of the South. In fact this State owes him a debt of gratitude which she can never repay for the zeal he has exhibited in placing upon record the deeds of her illustrious sons."

[140] See letter to Duyckinck of July 1.

But it is just as likely that there is only some tardiness in the
post & that you will yet recieve the packet, which was sent to
the P. O. at the very time with that which has reached you. — I
thank you for the interest you have taken in the communication
to the Publisher of the Galaxy. Fair compensation and a *regu-*
lar employment, monthly, would enable me (or any author) to
do far better things than can possibly be expected from one who
contributes only occasionally.[141] I trust that you have recieved
in safety, by Adams Express, the Box of Revolutionary papers.
Will you have it opened, & examine them at your leisure, so as
to possess yourself fully of their contents. When I see you, as I
shall as soon as I can, I will furnish any explanation. Meanwhile,
you are fully authorized to confer with any parties on the subject
of their publication. In a Courier which has just reached me,
there are two letters of mine one of which contains a report of
the Proceedings at the meeting of the Historical Society, when
we were present. In a day or two, I will cover them to you for
perusal, & perhaps, Mr. Moore will not be displeased to see what
I have said of him. Of his book I could only speak from the
opinions of another. I have not seen his volume, & can no longer
buy books.[142] — I saw Richardson yesterday. Have you seen the
page which he has chosen for the War Poems of the South? Look
at it. — Have you seen Mr. Miller lately, and will he do any thing
for Mother Goose? An occasional kindly mention from you might
help his motors.[143] I thank you & Mr. Buckingham Smith for the
copy of the Floridian Letter.[144] I have a poem descriptive of a

---

[141] Nothing by Simms appears to have been published in the *Galaxy* (New
York), edited by William Conant Church (1836-1917) and Francis Pharcellus
Church from the first issue of May 1, 1866, through the last issue of Jan.,
1878. The Churches were also the publishers of the magazine during 1866-1868.

[142] Simms discusses his visit to the New-York Historical Society in a letter
dated "New York, June 25, 1866," and signed "St. Pol," published in the
Charleston *Courier* of July 3, 1866. In it he says of George Henry Moore's
Notes on the History of Slavery in Massachusetts: "This gentleman . . . ,
who is . . . a man of fine talents and literary acquisition, has recently been
doing good yeoman service to the cause of truth and history, by his history of
negro slavery in the New England States; showing up the chronicle of Massachusetts, in such a character, as to make her much more eminent for her
cupidity than her virtues."

[143] James Miller was a publisher at 522 Broadway. He lived at 167 Adelphi
Street, Brooklyn. See the Brooklyn directories for this period.

[144] Buckingham Smith (1810-1871), lawyer, politician, and antiquarian, was
born on Cumberland Island, Ga. At an early age he removed to St. Augustine,
Fla., where he later practiced law. He held various diplomatic posts in Mexico
and Spain and was a Northern sympathizer during the Confederate War. "The
Floridian Letter" is doubtless Smith's translation *Letter of Hernando de Soto,*
and Memoir of Hernando de Escalante Fontaneda (Washington: [Privately

"Mid Summer forest Lunch, in Florida,["] which as soon as copied & revised shall be sent you, and which it might please Mr. Smith to peruse. It will no doubt be suggestive to him of reminiscences, in the past, which even the present may not always obscure, & certainly cannot wholly obliterate. Nay, there may be a revival of them. It is just possible, too, that Mr. S. may be able to detect Mine Host, of the Lunch, & indicate the Locality. — I will revise this Poem & send it you, in the hope that you may be able to find a market for it.[145] What I write here, & now, must needs be short & desultory. And while here, my object is to make such arrangements for permanent writing as will enable me to return to Woodlands, in the autumn, with full & regular employment on hand to exercise my pen all the winter. I propose, if possible, to concentrate myself this winter on a romance, and on "My Life and Times, an Autobiography, and a History." [146] I have personally known a large number of the chief men of the South, for the last forty years; have been ruined, as a Union Man, by Nullification, and more lately by Secession; & have to commence life *de novo,* but with youth gone, and with young children looking to me for the wherewithall of life. Of all that I had; slaves, stocks, furniture, books, pictures, horses, mules, carriages &c. — a property which was worth $150,000 in gold — I have nothing left me but my Lands, and these so long as we shall lack labour, must remain comparatively valueless. But, we must strive, not whine. Thanks, — & God be with you in mercy.

Yours Ever truly

W. Gilmore Simms

Printed,] 1854). In 1866 the Bradford Club, New York, published his translation of *Narratives of the Career of Hernando de Soto* . . . (see note 254, Sept. 28, 1866).

[145] "Midsummer Forest Lunch a Scene in Florida" is published in the *Old Guard,* IV (Oct., 1866), 603-608. We cannot identify Simms' "Host, of the Lunch."

[146] The "romance" is "Joscelyn." Simms did not write an autobiography.

1178: To Anna Augusta Singleton Simms Roach

Brooklyn, 78 Dean St.
7 July. [1866][147]

My dear Daughter.

I have been for the last two weeks suffering from soreness of tongue, the result, as I thought, of *nicotine* from some bad tobacco, & much smoking. But I have now reason to suspect that it was due in part, if not wholly, to a disordered stomach. I took Rhubarb a few nights ago, & improved, but shall need to take more tonight. Meanwhile, I have been unable to talk or eat, without pain, for more than 10 days. Today, I am again tongue tyed. The weather here is so excessively hot, that it is scarcely possible to breathe freely. Yesterday I went to N. Y. for the first time in ten days; and broke down in an attempt to visit sundry people & places. Your letter advising me of Mrs. Teffts wishes, & that of date 29 June, both came yesterday together. I will take an early chance as soon as I get well enough to visit the city again, to see Mr. Leavitt about her business.[148] I am glad that you can again report the recovery & health of the children. Gilmore writes me that he too has been sick. The rest seem to be doing well. If the weather be as hot with you as it is here, you should never budge a foot from the house, or use any great exertions. The letter of Miss Percival, came, together with another *direct,* both at the same time. My letters must needs be short. Before you recieve this, you will have got one covering draft for $25 upon the Courier,[149] which you will appropriate to the House, &c. according to previous instructions. A few days ago I put your brother's daguerreotype into the hands of a photographer, to be copied. It is to be done on Tuesday.[150] A *single* copy will cost $3.00. Framing it, will cost a like sum. Additional copies are to be had, after the first, at $2. or $2.50. But, where is this money to come from. We can hardly spare a dollar now. I shall procure two copies & frame them — but as for getting a copy for each member of the family, the thing is impossible. It is not more easy to get money here than in Charleston. I will do all I can, to please my children,

---

[147] Dated by Simms' remarks about his health. See letter to Duyckinck of the same date.

[148] Evidently Mrs. Tefft had asked Augusta to get her father to arrange for the sale of her late husband's collection of autographs (see letter to Leavitt, Strebeigh and Co. of Oct. 3, 1866).

[149] Payment for his contributions to the *Courier.* See note 103, May 25, 1866.

[150] We have been unable to locate a copy of this picture of Gilmore. Tuesday was July 10.

& they must be content if the all should prove little. I was to have gone up with Lawson today, but am too unwell for it. I shall be on the look out for Wm. Tell Govan & Chevy to make pictures as fast as they can; I will find the pencils. Love to the Girls, & all the family.

Yours Ever affectly. &c

W. Gilmore Simms.

1179: To Evert Augustus Duyckinck

78 Dean Street, Brooklyn.

[July 11, 1866][151]

My dear Duyckinck.

I had purposed coming over & seeing you today, but an excursion last evening on the water, & some too free potations of various beverages, finds me rather headachy this morning, and I feel it safer, & more in the line of duty this morning to remain at home, and attend to sundry Correspondents, whose letters lie before me. I enclose you one of my letters published in the Ch. Courier, reporting my experiences along with you, at the Historical Society.[152] It may please Mr. Moore if you show it to him. I have spoken of his History only from the reports of others; not having seen the work; but I am quite prepared to believe its value as reported. — After leaving you yesterday, I looked in at the office of the "Galaxy", and saw one of the Proprietors, Mr. Church.[153] But nothing came of the interview. He spoke vaguely of compensation; but I should much question the disposition to make it such as to fully deserve the name. We had some talk of things in general, as regards letters & periodicals; but it struck me that he had no very definite ideas, by which to render the work very materially different from old models, even while agreeing with me, in general terms, upon the necessity of salience, novelty & variety. The result was that I gave him my address. He did not even say whether he had decided to take the Poem [154] sent him, or not; but did say something as to its length; it being *longer* than the pieces usually published. Should you look in at

---

[151] This letter is dated "July 11/66," but the handwriting appears to be Duyckinck's. The date is probably correct (see preceding and following letters).
[152] See note 142, July 7, 1866.
[153] William Conant Church and Francis Pharcellus Church were editors and publishers of the *Galaxy.* See note 141, July 7, 1866.
[154] Not identified.

Scribner's, ask for the missing letter.[155] Mr. Church, by the way, spoke of *short* stories, not to be published as serials. I replied that such productions were the most difficult of all to write, as they depended upon incidents which did not depend on *character*, — while the development of character, was the chief source & secret for the discovery & development of incidents. Do you know any thing of the "Old Guard", & its resources? [156] Please do not forget that I asked you for photographs of yourself & brother, & say to Panton, I should like to have his & Darley's.

Yours Ever truly

W. Gilmore Simms

1180: To WILLIAM GILMORE SIMMS, JR.

Brooklyn, July 12, 1866.

My dear Son.

I have not heard from you or Augusta for a week, and trust that there is safety in your silence & that none of you are sick or suffering. Still, I should like to hear weekly from both. I have been quite unwell myself for more than two weeks. I have had a tongue so inflamed that I could neither eat nor speak without pain. Accordingly, I was confined to the house during all that time. At first, it was ascribed to the use of tobacco; — it was supposed that the *nicotine* or the badness of the tobacco, was the cause; but subsequently, I have had reason to believe that it was due to the heated & disordered state of the stomach. A few doses of rhubarb seems to have relieved it, but I still feel that I shall need more; though I am better now, & it is only occasionally that my tongue occasions me any trouble. I have had a correspondence with Mr. Sherwood at Great Barrington & propose shortly to pay him & the Kellogg's a visit. I have been spending my time

---

[155] See letters to Duyckinck of July 1 and 7.

[156] The *Old Guard* (New York), a monthly, was published from June, 1862, through Dec., 1870. Charles Chauncey Burr (1817-1883) was editor until 1870, when he was succeeded by Thomas Dunn English (1819-1902). Burr was publisher until 1863, when he was succeeded by Van Evrie, Horton and Co. (John H. Van Evrie and Rushmore G. Horton), followed, in 1870, by English. During the Confederate War the *Old Guard* was anti-Lincoln and defended slavery and the right of secession.

Simms became a frequent contributor to the *Old Guard,* and during 1866 the periodical published the following poems by him: "Midsummer Forest Lunch a Scene in Florida," IV (Oct.), 603-608; "Star-Smiling," IV (Oct.), 608; "Harmonies of Nature," IV (Nov.), 679-682; "Voices of Solitude," IV (Dec.), 723-726; and "The Belle of the Ball Room a Ballad," IV (Dec.), 752

alternately with Ferris, Bockee & Lawson, giving the most time
to the former. On Friday next,[157] I propose going up to Yonkers
with Lawson, for a few days; after that shall visit Bockee, if I
do not take that time to visit Barrington. — Thus far, there is
little to encourage me in the literary prospect. The hands of the
Publishers are full of Books, & the public demand for them seems
to be lessened, except in regard to books of a certain class, such
chiefly as have originated in the war. As a matter of course,
Southern books on this frightful subject, have a more limited
demand, and one written & published under such embarrasments,
that a truly Southern man who is patriotic & honest, cannot
readily write them. My volume of the War Poems, is now in the
hands of the printers, & I shall hurry it through in order to start
for home early in August, if possible. My calculation was to be
absent only for two months & I do not wish that my stay here
should be longer. I have as yet made no engagements for the
future, or for any other work; and I confess to some anxiety on
the subject. My engagement with the "Courier" affords me less
money than I had hoped for; and I have only drawn for $25 in
favour of E. R.[158] which I have assigned for the board of Govan.
You must economize your money in every possible way, & expend
nothing except for what you deem absolute necessaries. I still
hope to be able to do something here, & to bring some money
home with me, but as yet have only recieved $100 — that being
advanced by the Publisher, Richardson, on the strength of the
war poems, making the sum $300 which I have had from this
one source alone. You will see from what I have said, & from
my anxieties, the importance to you of rapid progress in your
studies. Neither you nor I can make any calculations on the
plantation this year. I suppose you have but little cotton growing,
and that, in all probability, is unpromising. I trust that Donald's
crop is more encouraging. My next letter will be addressed to
him. I hope Chevillette continues to improve. The more you are all
accustomed to the use of the cold bath, the more strength will you
gain and the more security will you have. Let me know how your
food holds out, and see that the housekeeping of the girls is not
improvident, or wasteful. Let me know when you write, how the
Jamison's, Carroll's &c all are, and report me the news in your
neighbourhood. There is nothing here of moment. I enclose you a

---

[157] July 13.
[158] Edward Roach.

letter from Dickson [159] which it may please you to read. Tell the girls to take care of all the photographs I left with them, as I shall bring with me an album for framing them all, & perhaps a good many other photographs of friends &c. I wish you also to be at some pains in gathering up the loose correspondence in your escritoir, & having it tied up & put away carefully. I have a number of books here, which, as they increase, I will box up & forward by vessel to the care of W. Roach. Do not you expose yourself too much in the sun, & in very severe physical exertions, and especially see to the security of Carroll from similar causes. Avoid & counsel the girls to avoid picknicking & all such sources of trouble & danger. My regards to Fuller, Carroll, Whetstone, Rivers the Jamison's, Patterson's [160] &c. To Washy & Mary Rivers especially, & tell the latter to keep John & Tom employed constantly, either in study or at work.[161] Kisses & love for the girls & Carroll. And affectionate remembrances of heart & head for yourself & Donald.

Your father as Ever

W. Gilmore Simms.

P. S. Tell Fuller, I have been using the Wine of Rhubarb as a gentle purgative and like it very much. I propose to bring a good sized bottle of it home with me. — I have just submitted to Brady, the great photographer of this city, who has made a large portrait of me, with all my weight of beard and hair & whisker, an awfully grim, griesly Bear picture, which is to be engraved for one of the quartos in the Press.[162] I shall bring home copies. Copies will also be made, one for Augusta & one for Woodlands, of your dear Mother's picture.[163] Once more, God bless & keep you all.

1181: To EDWARD ROACH

Brooklyn, 25 July 1866.

My dear Edward.

Yours of the 19th. inst. reached me with its enclosures this morning. I rejoice to hear that you are all well. Tell Augusta to

---

[159] John Dickson Bruns.
[160] The family of Angus Patterson, at Briarwood.
[161] Washy is Anna Washington Govan Steele Fuller. John and Tom are Mary Rivers' little boys.
[162] See note 126, June 24, 1866.
[163] See the picture of Chevillette Simms facing p. 134 of Volume III of *The Letters of William Gilmore Simms.*

keep Govan in town as long as the place is healthy, & while he keeps so; but if Cholera or Yellow fever appear there, to have him taken up to Woodlands immediately. I am sorry that Mr. Laidler [164] is so costive in money matters. He has greatly disappointed me on this score. But I shall try him a little longer, and before very long send you another draft upon him. You will have seen from the Courier that I have done quite work enough to entitle me to much more compensation than he seems willing to give. I hope you preserve all these papers. [165] I shall try & look out for the arrival of Wm., [166] but I rarely go to New York, being kept quite busy here. I am now the guest of Mr. & Mrs. Bockee, "95 *Third Place,* Brooklyn." Tell Wm. that, by crossing the Fulton Ferry, & taking the Court Street Car, at the Brooklyn side, he can ride up in 20 minutes, to the corner of Court Street & Third Place, which is only a hundred yards from 95, where I lodge. I enclose a brief note for Robt. Bruns, [167] which you will please deliver. I have nothing to say, & but little leisure to say it in. It must be enough for me to report that I am now very well, & quite relieved of the sore tongue. My love to Augusta, the girls & children, and kisses all round. The weather here has relaxed & become much pleasanter. God be with you.

Your affectionate father

W. Gilmore Simms.

1182: To EVERT AUGUSTUS DUYCKINCK

Brooklyn, 28 July 1866.

My dear Duyckinck.

It was fully my purpose to run up to N. Y. this morning, but feeling badly, and with sundry letters to write, I have concluded to defer my visit untill some early day next week. It is not improbable (D. V.) that you may see me at Clinton Place on Monday. [168] Meanwhile, I could wish, as soon as convenient to you, that you would see the members of the Bradford Club and ascertain what they decide upon touching the suggested publication of a portion of the Laurens papers. I am quite willing to

---

[164] William Laidler (1812-1892), the son of Capt. William Laidler, of Charleston, was one of the proprietors of the Charleston *Courier*.
[165] See note 103, May 25, 1866.
[166] William Roach.
[167] Robert Stewart Bruns. See note 15, Jan. 16, 1866.
[168] Duyckinck lived at 20 Clinton Place. Monday was July 30.

make the arrangement upon the plan proposed by you, and, if the work is to be done, I should like to address myself to it at the earliest moment, as it is my desire — indeed, almost my necessity — to return to Carolina, by the 1st. of September.[169] Of course, I need not repeat to you how important to me is the money consideration, however small. You know my condition, almost as well as I do myself. Miller was to give me answer today, touching the "Mother Goose," but his decision will keep till I see him. Should he decline, I should like to try Appleton. It appears to me, indeed, that the Appletons are the very parties to make a magnificent book of it, having permanent & long continued circulation, as the only work of its class that has ever been designed in this country, & one that should be specially acceptable, as being the only thing which contemplates what is peculiar to the country, dealing also with topics which are of especial interest to the young. Should it happen in your way to step into their office, I should be pleased if you would broach the subject, and, as you well can, indicate what are the characteristics of the book. I should make it a large book, have it well illustrated, so that, at the very outset, it should take rank, as *the* volume, *par excellence,* of its kind. I am inclined to think from our conversations with Miller, that he does not regard the *prospects* of such a book as we do, nor does he rise above the ordinary estimates of the juvenile publications which are so common, and — so little or only temporarily attractive. Your memoranda of topics, yet to be handled, could be taken up promptly & soon dismissed. There is another matter in which you can serve me, & presuming on your will to do so, & the kind attention which you have always given to my little commissions, I do not hesitate to trouble you again. Among the books lost in the destruction of my Library, were sundry of the Congressional publications. I should like to obtain some of these, of peculiar interest to the Historian, the student and the man of Letters. Such was the set comprising the survey &c. of the Mexican Boundary Line, & that devoted to a survey of Canal or R. Road Routes to the Pacific. The latter work which contained a great deal of suggestive matter for Art & Literature, was contained in 11 or 12 vols.[170] These I should like to repossess, together with

---

[169] The Bradford Club, named for the colonial printer William Bradford, was founded in 1859 by John B. Moreau (1812-1886). Moreau acted as secretary of the Club, which issued historical publications from time to time. For Simms' edition of *The Army Correspondence of Colonel John Laurens,* published by the Bradford Club, see note 65, April 5, 1866.

[170] William Hensley Emory's *Report on the United States and Mexican Boundary Survey . . . ,* 3 vols. (Washington, 1857-1859) ; and *Reports of*

such others as may be obtained, of like order; not forgetting Reports on General National topics, & such books as those of Mordecai & McClellan, the fruit of their observations on the Art of War in Europe.[171] I take for granted that you have friends in Congress, who would be able to procure these books or some of them, and who would cheerfully serve us both in procuring them. If you know of such parties, you might frankly tell them, for whom it is that you desire to procure them. I do not myself know any of them personally, and, as a rebel, should be reluctant to obtrude myself upon their attention, especially as a supplicant. Politicians, however, are to be found, whose veneration for literature & regard for literary men, are not to be *oversloughed* by party, or by the passing interests of politics, and I trust that you have some political friend to whom you can confidently make appeal in this behalf. I shall be glad of any volumes comprising matter of national, historical, art or Literary interest. I have long entertained views in respect to the Ancient Mexican, or Maya cities & states, & if life is spared me, hope still, through the medium of Romance, to make such a *restoration* of some of these ancient states or cities, as will be equally consistent with what we know, and with what Art & Imagination, may with propriety concieve.[172] — Next week (D V.) I hope to spend chiefly with our friend at Yonkers.[173] I shall venture to leave my name at Mr. Butler's portals, & shall be glad if he will welcome me into a resumption of our Ethnological speculations.[174] If you see Gayarré, tell him I would like to have a gripe of his hand before he returns South. Did I not understand you that he was a delegate to the Phila. Convention.[175] Don't forget to send the *printed Letter* to Mr. Moore; [176] and please remember to read & to preserve for me the printed poem which I handed you at Yonkers.[177] It is in a vein that I think will please you. At your leisure, too,

Explorations and Surveys, to Ascertain the Most Practicable and Economical Route for a Railroad from the Mississippi River to the Pacific Ocean . . . , 11 vols. (Washington, 1855-1859).

[171] *Military Commission to Europe in 1855-1856. Report of Major Alfred Mordecai . . .* (Washington, 1860) and *Report of George B. McClellan . . .* (Washington, 1857).

[172] Simms did not write a romance on this subject.

[173] Lawson.

[174] William Allen Butler. See letters to Duyckinck of Aug. 3 and to Ferris of Aug. 7 and 9.

[175] Charles Arthur Étienne Gayarré (see introductory sketch) was not a delegate to the National Union Convention, which met in Philadelphia during Aug. 14-16, 1866.

[176] See note 142, July 7, 1866.

[177] Not identified.

remember to gather me the photographs for which I begged you.[178] I propose to have an album of my own, which shall include all my friends, living or dead, whose "counterfeit present- ments"[179] may be had; men of letters, statesmen, soldiers &c. which I may contemplate while in my native woods, and thus stir up old memories which shall kindle fresh fancies. — I am, as poor Charles Lamb phrased it, "rather unwellish," and the hot sun afflicts me. I find it no easy thing to muster up my thoughts for action, and as for march or action, I am just now as incapable of it, as if legs and arms had wholly resigned their offices. A Letter just recieved from my young friend Bruns, in England, does not present a flattering portrait of that people. He says, among other things, "that we are not so far behind these Englishers in art and science, as one might think sitting at home. They are better *pathologists* than we" (he is a medical man) "but our *practice* is infinitely superior; and, as surgeons, they are not to be com- pared with out first class men."[180] — There! You have a full sheet. As I have not been able to see you today, I am resolved that you shall hear me. Heaven grant you the patience to get through the screed which I fear you will find too heavy for song, and much too light for sermon. God forgive you your sins.

Yours faithfully

W. Gilmore Simms

Evert A. Duyckinck, Esq.

1183: To FLETCHER HARPER?[181]

[*c.* August 1, 1866][182]

if (as I believe) you still have a desire to promote in some de- gree the fortunes of an old friend. I would see you in person, but

---

[178] In his letter of July 11 Simms asked Duyckinck for pictures of himself and George Long Duyckinck and requested him to ask Henry Panton for pictures of himself and Felix Octavius Carr Darley.

[179] *Hamlet,* III, iv, 54.

[180] Simms later gave William Hawkins Ferris the original of this letter from John Dickson Bruns, dated "London June 30 '66." It is now in the Ferris Collection, Columbia University Library.

[181] This fragment appears to have been written to a publisher whom Simms had known for many years, and his reference to "the Bretheren" indicates, we think, one of the Harpers. Since Simms in his letter to Duyckinck of March 5, 1866, says he has written Fletcher Harper for books, it is possible that this letter was also addressed to him.

[182] Dated by Simms' reference to his plan to visit Lawson. See preceding and following letters.

that I am on the eve of setting forth on an expedition to Yonkers, where I am to spend ten days or so, with my old gossip Jemmy Lawson. With best regards to the Bretheren, I am

Ever truly Yours

W. Gilmore Simms —

1184: To William Hawkins Ferris

Yonkers 2 Aug. '66.

My dear Ferris.

There is an Express from N. Y. to Yonkers, & Mr. Lawson says, if you will get my valise to *his* office, he will have it brought up by Express. The sooner the better. I was quite unwell this morning, but feel better this evening. A letter from Mrs. Roach reports all well & the City healthy. She begs her special regards to Mrs. F. & yourself. When you get the photographs[183] send a few, under envelope to Lawson. Some letters just recieved threaten me with hands full of work. God bless you all. Love to wife & children.

Ever truly Yours

W. Gilmore Simms

1185: To Evert Augustus Duyckinck

Yonkers 3 August 1866.

My dear Duyckinck.

I am very glad, & grateful, that you have succeeded in making the arrangement about the Letters of J. Laurens with the Bradford Club. It is quite satisfactory to me, and I will cheerfully dispose of the Letters of Washington at the designated price.[184] Surely, you may confide the volume to Mr. Moreau,[185] or any *Gentleman* you please. When the Letters are copied, I should like to run over them, in order, where the text seems to require it, to interpolate an occasional note or suggestion. If you will do me the favour to request of Mess'rs Appleton a Copy of the vol. of the Cyclopædia[186] which contains my biographical sketches

[183] Probably of Simms himself. See letter to Gilmore of July 12.
[184] We do not know to whom Simms sold this collection. The price was $250 (see letter to Duyckinck of Aug. 15).
[185] John B. Moreau. See note 169, July 28, 1866.
[186] *The New American Cyclopædia.*

of the Laurens's I shall at once devote myself to a preparation of
the Memoirs. I will write home at once with the hope to procure
a photograph of Laurens.[187] It may be that the family will be
unwilling to permit the original portrait to pass out of their possession. I trust, & believe, that it has been saved; I know that
they formerly possessed a good one. Could I get the vol. of
Bancroft's History which covers the period included within the
Laurens' camp letters, it is possible that some good use might be
made of them, by employing notes from him in illustration of
the text; which, by the way may sometimes be found in conflict
with the Historian.[188] *Nous verrons!* — Miller declines "Mother
Goose" — professes to like it very much, & avows his readiness
to publish it next year. At present he declares his funds to be too
much absorbed already by books which he yet cannot get out this
season — says, to prepare & put forth such a volume in becoming style, would require an outlay of at least $3000. He spoke
very kindly & seemingly with great frankness, and really seemed
quite sincere in his regrets — said he had read the matter, & was
satisfied of its merit & great superiority to every thing of the
kind. I beg'd him to put up the MS. in a packet to be delivered
to you or to myself when called for. And now, what remains?
Wait a year? While the grass grows the horse starves! It occurred to me that such a book might well be put forth by the
Appleton's. Their great resources would enable them to make a
grand *national* book of it, such as would render it perhaps the
best Christmas volume for the Young in all the market. With
numerous & fine wood cuts, in a style at once bolder & more
beautiful than any thing yet done,[189] & with its *nationality* prominent, as a work peculiarly American, it seems to me that a great
hit would be made with it, & that it would continue to grow in
ever permanent value for a hundred years. Think of it, and,
should you see the Mess'rs A. it would be easy to bring the subject before them, with all these suggestions, which no one can
better enforce than yourself. Once resolved upon, I should immediately address myself to the list of subjects which you gave
me, not omitting (though you did omit) the *Glorious Fourth!*

---

[187] See letter to Augusta of Aug. 3.
[188] There are no footnotes in Simms' edition of *The Army Correspondence
of Colonel John Laurens.*
[189] Simms wrote *donn.*

"When the rockets go so high
As to hit the man in the moon in the eye, &c.
And the wheels with a merry go round & round,
   Even more blazing, with colors amazing,
Brighten & burst with a thunder of sound, &c. ["]

I shall be at pains to see Mr. Butler,[190] who seems to me a pleasant as well as thoughtful companion. Meanwhile, I am at the bottom of my sheet, with room only to say how grateful I am for your kindness & the trouble you are so cheerfully taking in my affairs. God be with you & yours in mercy!

Your friend Ever:

W. Gilmore Simms.

1186: To Evert Augustus Duyckinck

3 August. 1866.

My dear Duyckinck.

A reperusal of your letter, after I had written & sealed my answer to it, tells me of Mr. Butler's Library, & the probability of my being able to procure from it, while here, all the books that I shall need. So do not trouble yourself to ask Mess'rs Appleton for the Cyclopædia. It is quite probable that Mr. Butler has Bancroft also. I shall pen a note to him this evening. Do you know any thing of the "Old Guard Magazine["] ? — or of Van Evrie & Horton.[191] From the latter I have recieved communications which cut out a good deal of future work for me, but the writer does not mention the *compensation* — which, as you know, is the important item to the Contributor. He desires sketches of the War & of Warriors. He would also like short stories &c. The obtaining of materials for the one, and the tasking invention for the other, makes these classes of writing more *costly,* to an author, than any other. The latter especially, since, in a short story where no room is allowed you for the development of character, you have to rely chiefly on incident and this tasks invention to the uttermost. What ought to be the compensation for a biographical sketch of half a dozen octavo pages? What the proper pay, for a tale running through eight or ten pages of the same size?

---

[190] William Allen Butler. See letters to Duyckinck of July 28 and to Ferris of Aug. 7 and 9.
[191] See note 156, July 11, 1866.

As a tale writer especially I have achieved a great many successes; and I do not believe that my right hand hath lost any of her cunning. But, to address myself to these things there should be a becoming motive, and I am now constrained to consider this motive as paramount, where I have to excite my imagination especially in the business of invention. A hint from you as to what should be a *decent* compensation would be desirable. The Mess'rs Church also desire the same kind of material. My poem would occupy too many pages of their work; and Poetry, unless made fashionable, is not in demand in magazines.[192] This is to be expected at a period when we are getting back to second childhood, and when a literary magazine is expected to be a Picture Book. Where is Gayarré? I have suggested to Richardson a plan for a Library of Southern Authors, one vol. to each.[193]

Yours hurriedly

W. Gilmore Simms

1187: To Anna Augusta Singleton Simms Roach

Yonkers, Augt. 3. 1866.

My dear daughter.

I have leisure only to say that yours of the 29th. ult. has been recieved. I rejoice to find that you all continue well. I am now anxious about all in the country, all of whom seem imprudently to expose themselves in this hot & unseemly weather. Do write & exhort them to stay at home, avoid exposure, and use quinine freely, as a prophylactic. Keep Govan with you untill I return, unless some epidemic shall break out in Charleston. I am here, very busied with composition & proofsheets.[194] I shall be here, (D V) some 10 days, when I expect to return to Brooklyn. I enclose you a note for Mrs. John Laurens, which I have left open that you may read & see what is to be done, and what I wish you to do. I wish two copies of the miniature to be made as *cartes de visites,* both sent me by mail, in envelope & as soon as convenient. You will pay the photographer for making the copies, &

---

[192] Nothing by Simms appears to have been published in the *Galaxy,* at this time edited and published by William Conant Church and Francis Pharcellus Church. See note 141, July 7, 1866.

[193] This plan was not carried out.

[194] Of *War Poetry of the South.*

I will repay you.[195] All are now well here, except Christina, who is better, but who, it is feared, has some affection of the lungs. I have been suffering a little, from heat & fatigue, but am better today; and should perhaps feel particularly well, but for my uneasiness about them at the plantation. Gilmore's imprudence is wholly inexcusable after my repeated exhortations & entreaties. The Cholera increases in New York & Brooklyn. It is supposed that it will reach its highest rate of mortality this week, & then gradually decline. Be cautious about food, especially vegetables, & let all parties beware how they eat too much of any thing. Avoid fatigue.[196] Address me always, to "The Care of Mess'rs Lawson & Walker 62 Wall Street, New York." I enclose a letter to Govan. It will hardly be possible for me to return home before the middle of Sept. Love to Edward & the girls, and God be with you all in mercy.

Your affecte. father

W. Gilmore Simms.

P. S. You will find some ruled paper in one of the drawers of my desk. Let Govan have some of it sparingly, to practise, but not to waste. Tell him I will try & bring him some thing. Young Bockee has a drum for Carroll. Did you recieve the photographs sent by Mrs. Ferris? [197] I have just sate for mine. You shall have the *cartes de visites* through letter as soon as they reach me.

1188: To William Hawkins Ferris

Yonkers 7th. Aug. 1866

My dear Ferris.

Last night I penned you a hasty scrawl in pencil, which I take for granted you recieved today, and trust that you found legible. I enclose with this two Letters, both from Poets, which will serve in your collection. One is from Wm. Allen Butler, author of

---

195 The Charleston *Directory* for this year lists Mrs. John Laurens' address as 12 Smith Street. Her miniature of Laurens was engraved and used as the frontispiece to *The Army Correspondence of Colonel John Laurens.*

196 In his letters to the Charleston *Courier* (see note 103, May 25, 1866) Simms frequently writes about the cholera. Simms' letters dated July 26 and Aug. 10 (published in the *Courier* of July 30 and Aug. 15) are wholly concerned with the dreaded disease.

197 Photographs of Gilmore and Mrs. Simms? See letters to Augusta of July 7 and to Gilmore of July 12.

"Nothing to Wear" & "Two Millions" very clever & sprightly *vers des societé*,[198] and the other by Timrod, whose vein, less flexible, is much deeper & higher. He is one of the best of the Southern Poets, refined & highly polished, with fine meditative tone, & a pure & graceful fancy. You will see from his letter what are the distresses & difficulties of these children of Song, who are helpless because of their endowment, in a world which knows not its uses, and again helpless, in his case, by reason of health & temperament. Unluckily, in answering his melancholy letter, I had nothing encouraging to write. My own experience with magazine publishers has long taught me their proper value as sources of revenue to the author, especially if he be simply a Poet. My own case is hardly better than Timrod, save that I have a hardier will, & perhaps a better constitution, to say nothing of the longer lessons supplied by the endurance of *sixty* years as against *thirty*. — I am really vexed that our temple of Mammon letter should be so mangled.[199] — It is possible that I may get down to you on Friday, [200] but it will depend upon a better condition of my head. I dreadfully need repose from all excitement, & were this only possible, from all anxiety. But! — there will come a time for sleep, — tomorrow — and tomorrow, & tomorrow. For the present, for the day, I trust that we shall both keep pleasantly wakeful. That you may do so, still let me counsel you to the constant employment of your prophylactic tonic. Note its effects, and learn what is the smallest quantity which will suffice to keep you in tone. This is all the secret. Best regards to the Priesthood of the Temple — to all the venerable fathers in Mam-

---

[198] William Allen Butler (1825-1902), lawyer and author, born in Albany, N. Y., wrote *Nothing to Wear: An Episode of City Life* (New York: Rudd & Carleton, 1857) and *Two Millions* (New York: D. Appleton & Co., 1858). In 1865 he moved to Yonkers and became a close friend of both Duyckinck and Lawson.

[199] In a letter dated July 26 and signed "St. Pol," published in the Charleston *Courier* of July 30 (see note 103, May 25, 1866), Simms writes of "A Visit [with Ferris] to the United States Sub-Treasury in Wall-Street—Mysteries of the Great Temple of Mammon—The Dignitaries of the Institution—Division of Labor—Tantalizing Sights, Etc., Etc." When Simms speaks of the letter as "mangled" he probably has in mind the following paragraph on Ferris: "Over the 'Disbursing Bureau' presides Mr. Wm. Hawkins Jervis [*sic*], the Assistant Cashier, or Priest; of whose powers for mischief, you may judge when I tell you that he *disbursed*—that is, paid out—for the corruption of mankind, in the single year, 1864, no less than six hundred millions of dollars; and his wicked practice so continues still, that he makes a daily average payment of moneys, no less than one thousand, to several parties. This is very terrible."

[200] Aug. 10.

mon, not forgetting him of archest cunning & diplomacy, the venerable who is of all the Birds, the Bird — Father Rose in Bloom.[201] Love at home

Yours Ever

W. G. S.

Mons. Ferris.

1189: To WILLIAM HAWKINS FERRIS

Yonkers, Thursday MG 9th. [August, 1866] [202]

My dear Ferris.

I will not forget your wish to procure from Mr. Butler a copy of his Uhland,[203] should any legitimate opportunity occur. He called to see me, on my arrival here, & invited me to dine with him the next day. He was cordial enough, & seems a pleasant man, & is described to me as a good fellow also. At present, the family does not see *company*—in any proper sense of the word, in consequence of the recent death of Mrs. B's father.[204] Mr. Lawson will tell me today, in respect to the specimens of fractional currency. I enclose with this a copy, in the MS. of James R. Randall, of his "Maryland," which may suit your collection. He was one of the most spirited of the Southern Lyrists during the war. I enclose also a letter from Professor Dickson, of Philadelphia, formerly of S. C. and the author of several volumes & pamphlets. Professor D. was one of the chief founders of the Medical College of S. C. and distinguished there, not only for his professional ability, but as a popular Lecturer, Orator and Essayist. He is the author of an elaborate work on Medical Practice, in 2 vols. 8 vo.; of a volume of Essays, on Life, Death, Sleep, Pain &c. & of a volume of Poems, printed for private circulation, but never published. Several of his public addresses & orations have appeared in pamphlet form, and he has written several able papers for the South. Quarterly Review. You will no doubt be pleased

---

[201] Edward H. Birdsall. See note 207, Aug. 9, 1866.

[202] Dated by Simms' references to his own and to Ferris' health. See letter to Ferris of Aug. 7.

[203] William Allen Butler's "Uhland, with Translations" is included in his *Poems* (Boston, 1871). It is a poem on Uhland, pp. 227-229, plus ten translations, pp. 230-256.

[204] Butler's wife was Mary Russell Marshall, the daughter of Capt. Charles E. Marshall, the agent and part owner of the Black Ball line of Liverpool packets.

with his letter. His style is easy, graceful & polished, that of a good Essayist of the Goldsmith school—his vigour by no means lessened in consequence of his polish.[205] A third letter, which you will find in the enclosure, is from Prof. J. Dickson Bruns, M D. of the Medical College of South Carolina. He is a young man of brilliant promise, with various endowments; a good writer of prose & verse; vigorous & thoughtful. For several years he edited a Monthly Medical Review, with great power & intelligence. Several of his war poems will be found in the Collection which I am now editing. He served alternately at our Batteries & Hospitals, and was one of those who accompanied Davis in his flight—was the last to leave him, & did so only at the urgent plea of Davis, who sought to divert from his own pursuit by scattering his party.[206]—I trust that you will find a value in these enclosures at some future day. I am still unwell & the weather is unfavorable. The prospect is that I shall not be with you tomorrow. Should you go to Mr. Tuckerman's, avoid fatigue, do not sit up late, & take a dose of your Quinine before you retire. My head is in bad condition and I begin to yearn for Home,—by which I do not mean Dean Street, though yours and your wife's kind solicitude, was of such a genial nature as, in some degree to reconcile me to absence from my own home, making yours so grateful as a substitute. I am glad to hear that the Priesthood take my revelations in good part; and pray say to Father Rose in Bloom that in hinting at his *seeming effeminancy,* I had no design to disparage any of his *parts,* whether of speech or action.[207] It pleases me to learn also that Mr. Seymour & the

---

[205] The original of Dr. Samuel Henry Dickson's letter to Simms, dated "Philada. June 27th 1866," is now in the Ferris Collection, Columbia University Library. For Dickson and his various publications, see introductory sketch and note 141, July 17, 1854.

[206] Bruns was editor of the *Charleston Medical Journal and Review* during 1858-1860 (see note 285, Nov. 30, 1860). Bruns' "Our Christmas Hymn," "O, Tempora! O, Mores!," and "The Foe at the Gates.—Charleston" are included in *War Poetry of the South,* pp. 196-199, 283-286, 454-456. The original of Bruns' letter to Simms, dated "London June 30 '66," is now in the Ferris Collection, Columbia University Library.

[207] In his letter to the Charleston *Courier* about his "Visit to the United States Sub-Treasury in Wall-Street" (see note 199, Aug. 7, 1866) Simms writes: "The 'Gold Note Bureau' is conducted very ably, it is said, by Mr. Edward H. Birdsall, who, under the guise of youth, and frank and even gay exterior, conceals the subtlest workings of a brain wholly delivered up to the worship and the tasks of this dreadful deity! His approaches to you are so graceful and gentle and good humored, so insidiously sweet, that no one would suspect the profound subtlety with which he works for this god of iniquity. With a benign smile upon his countenance, and a fresh *rose* ever in his buttonhole, he gives you his hand with a cordiality and ease which are admirably

Irving's were gratified.[208] My tongue begins again to trouble me, & between head & tongue, my brain will shortly lack all proper organ of utterance.

Yours Ever truly

W. Gilmore Simms

1190: To Evert Augustus Duyckinck

78 Dean Street, Brooklyn.

[August 15, 1866] [209]

You will see from this, my dear Duyckinck that I have got back from Yonkers, to my old lodging place in Brooklyn. It

---

calculated to deceive and beguile. He wears his hair short, *a la Brutus;* and, so youthful and even feminine in his appearance, that no one would suspect him to be what he is—next to the very oldest of all the priesthood of this temple! Of the magnitude of evil which lies within his power, you may judge from the single fact that the 'Gold Note Bureau' which he controls has received in the last eight months, counted and weighed, no less than $104,000,000 in gold, and gold notes issued for the same! . . . Of his capacity as an *expert,* I may mention that, at a glance of the eye or a touch of the hand, he can almost certainly detect the spurious coin or counterfeit. . . ."

[208] In two of his "St. Pol" letters (see note 103, May 25, 1866), published in the Charleston *Courier* of July 27 and 28, Simms writes of having seen at a dinner party in Bergen, New Jersey, John Beaufain Irving (1800-1881), author of *A Day on Cooper River* (Charleston: A. E. Miller, 1842) and other books, and his son John Beaufain Irving, Jr. (1825-1877), the genre, portrait, and historical painter. Both of the Irvings had removed from Charleston to New York City after the Confederate War. Perhaps Seymour, whom we have been unable to identify, was the host of the dinner.

Simms had known the Irvings for a number of years, and during 1843-1844 he had been a contributor to the *Rambler* (Charleston), published as a tri-weekly, then as a weekly, and edited by the elder Irving. The first issue of the *Rambler* is dated Oct. 2, 1843; the last which we have been able to locate is dated March 20, 1844. Each issue has separate pagination. Simms published in the *Rambler* a poem ("To the Insensible") and three epigrams, all signed "W. G. S." (see the issues for Oct. 4, Oct. 6, Oct. 11, and Oct. 16). His most important contribution to the *Rambler* is "Pelayo, a Dramatic Poem," published in the issues for Nov. 14, Nov. 21, Nov. 28, Dec. 12, Dec. 21, and Dec. 28. In his "Preface" to "Pelayo" Simms says: "The highly able and intellectual friend to whom 'Pelayo,' [the romance] was dedicated [William Hayne Simmons], in a private letter, is pleased to remark upon the susceptibility of the work for dramatic illustration. He did not know that the work, including the Sequel [*Count Julian*], was in fact, drawn from a dramatic poem—in which form the story, was originally written many years before it appeared in the form which it now assumes. . . . Portions of this drama . . . were permitted to remain in the original proof sheets of the Romance, and were only omitted from it when the stereotype plates were to be cast. A rapid rendering of these parts into prose of a corresponding sense, supplied the space. [See, in this connection, Simms' letter to Lawson of Sept. 10, 1837.] These fragments were preserved, and the suggestion of the esteemed friend of whom I have spoken, persuades me to think that their perusal would not be altogether uninteresting to our readers. . . ."

[209] Duyckinck dated this letter "Aug. 15/66," and the date appears to be correct (see preceding and following letters).

will be several days before I can get up to the city; and, meanwhile, I conclude, in reference to my needs, to dispose of the whole collection of the W. Letters, since $250 is more important to me than the half of it, & since it is perhaps best that the Letters should go together. So please, at your leisure, make the arrangement. I have not yet begun the memoir of Laurens, in the hope, by an examination of the previous letters, to find more material for the sketch, by which to enrich it, & render it more complete. I have written home, as you suggested, to procure, if possible, the original portrait. The book might still further be illustrated by an engraved copy of a portion of one of the letters, on a single page, with his signature.[210] The War Poems are going gradually through the press. Some 150 pages are in type. The volume will be quite 450, and yet more than half of the collection will be omitted. De Bow writes to me for the use of the engraved portrait accompanying my poems. He wishes it to illustrate his Review.[211] I have referred him to Widdleton, & counselled him to refer also to you as one who might favorably influence the Publisher. Not wholly well, & uneasy at not hearing from home. I have been so much a sufferer, through my children, that I am kept terribly uneasy while they remain silent. I will see you as soon as I reach the City

À Dios!

W. Gilmore Simms.

E. A. D

1191: To Edward Roach

Brooklyn, Sep. 1. 1866.

My dear Edward

Yesterday, I sent two boxes on board the Saragossa, addressed to the care of Wm. Roach. See to them, & perhaps you had better forward them at once to the plantation. They contain books & papers. It is probable that I shall visit Mr. Sherwood [212] next

---

[210] Simms' edition of *The Army Correspondence of Colonel John Laurens* has only one illustration, an engraving of John Laurens, published as the frontispiece to the volume (see note 195, Aug. 3, 1866).

[211] This engraving of Simms (see the frontispiece to Volume I of *The Letters of William Gilmore Simms*) was not published in *De Bow's Review*.

[212] At Great Barrington, Mass.

week. Very much hurried just now, but better. Love to Augusta & all.

Your aff. Father

W. Gilmore Simms.

E Roach Esq.

1192: To Anna Augusta Singleton Simms Roach

Brooklyn Sep. 2. 1866.

My dear Daughter.

Yours of the 28th. ult. just recieved. Glad that you are all well. I am grieved & anxious in regard to Edward & the money. He should offer to renew in full, & take his chance of safety through the intervention of Mr. Wagner.[213] It doubly grieves me that I can do nothing. As yet, I have little or no money, though I hope to realize enough to help us through the winter, if not the year. Times are hard, & money not to be borrowed by outsiders, except for a brief time, subject to call at any moment, & then at enormous interest. M. L. writes me that Mrs. Fishburne (Caroline) is at the point of death.[214] Chevillette had better be with you, in town, during her accouchement.[215] Still, Fuller will be on the spot, & is, I believe, skilful in this province. I could buy clothes here, for Govan, ready made, but for the doubt about the fit. I will see about the stuff. Write me how much will be needed, and what would be the amt. required for him, if things were to be bought in Charleston. I doubt if there is much difference in prices. W. R.[216] was looking well. I have not seen him since the first evening. Has Edw. collected the $25 from Laidler.[217] If so, apply a part of it to Govan's clothing, and appropriate what remains (if any) to household expenses. Mr. Bockee has sent a drum for Carroll, which Govan can help beat when he goes to Woodlands. On Friday next,[218] I expect to visit Gt. Barrington. Mr. & Mrs. Ferris have moved into their new house, which he has just bought, a very pleasant place

---

[213] Theodore D. Wagner.

[214] Caroline Fishburne (see note 147, Aug.? 1861) lived until 1885.

[215] Chevillette Simms Rowe was born probably in Jan., 1867. See note 121, June 12, 1866.

[216] William Roach.

[217] See letters to Augusta of July 7 and to Edward Roach of July 25.

[218] Sept. 7.

upon which you may congratulate them.[219] I am now at Bockee's.
Nothing new, & I am too weary of the pen to be discursive.
Love to the Girls—Kisses for all & the children, and God's
blessing upon you all.

> Your affec. father
>
> W. Gilmore Simms.

1193: To Anna Augusta Singleton Simms Roach

> Yonkers 15 Sep. '66.

My dear daughter.

I am now paying my last visit to the Lawsons. It was my hope
to turn my face homewards by the 22d. but this I think doubtful.
I still have something like a week's work here, and will probably
be delayed till about the 25th. or 28th. when it is probable that
I shall take the steamer. I still keep well. Has Wm.[220] got home.
We have only seen him once when he went East, & we have heard
nothing of his return. Did you recieve the picture sent by Mr.
Hummell [221] through Adams Express? If not have it enquired after.
Christina is improving.[222] I have just got back from Barrington
where I spent five days. Saw Mr. Sherwood & both Frances &
Lydia, who are now on a visit to Misses K.[223] All spoke of & enquired in regard to you very affectionately. The Misses K. offered
me money to buy something for Mary Lawson, but I told them to
send it to you, who knew better what to get for M. L. and could,
indeed, get her own instructions on the subject. Lydia sends
you a pincushion which I have for you. She regretted her inability in G. B. to find you any thing better. They were all very
kind & affectionate. I propose to remain here till next Wednesday,[224] then return to Brooklyn, & divide my remaining time
between Ferris & Bockee. I have nothing new to report to you

---

[219] Ferris moved to 9th Street near 3rd Avenue. See the Brooklyn *Directory*
for 1867-1868.

[220] William Roach.

[221] We are unable to identify this Hummell among the various men by that
name listed in the New York City and Brooklyn directories for this period.

[222] See letter to Augusta of Aug. 3.

[223] William K. Sherwood had married Frances Kellogg, sister of Sarah,
Mary, and Nancy Kellogg (see note 11, March 28, 1838). Sherwood's daughter
Mary Frances had married Mark Hopkins, the financier, in 1854 and was at
this time living in California. Her sister, Lydia, was married to Hiram Crittenden.

[224] Sept. 19.

which will not keep till my return. And you are not to expect long letters from one who has so much daily work with the pen. Tell Julia I have had some samples of southern school books sent her, through Mr. Russell. Let her enquire after them. I am glad to hear that her school still continues to flourish.[225] You & Edward say nothing of your Banknote difficulties. I sincerely trust that he has been enabled to meet & overcome them.[226] Most bitterly do I regret my own inability to render him any present succour. It will require me to strain every string to procure means for the children this winter, as it is evident that they have done & can do nothing for themselves. The plantation & freedman's labour appears to have ended in a miserable fizzle, as, indeed, I was very sure they would. We must economize as well as we can, & pray & hope for better things. At all events, it will be of no use to fret in anticipation. Be cheerful, and trust to God to extricate you when you can no longer do any thing for yourself. Love to all & God bless you all.

Your affec. father

W Gilmore Simms

P. S. Were the two boxes [227] recieved by the steamer?

1194: To ANNA AUGUSTA SINGLETON SIMMS ROACH

Yonkers, 18th. Sep. 1866.

My dear Daughter.

Yours of the 11th. reached me yesterday, while I was in N. Y. I had proposed leaving Yonkers tomorrow, making the present my last visit, but an unlucky accident has compelled for the present the abandonment of all my previous arrangements. Last night, stepping out of the rear porch of Lawson's House, I miss'd one of the steps, my right ancle turned under me, & I fell incontinently to the ground. The sprain is a serious one, but there is no dislocation or break of bone. The Dr. has just examined the limb, & prescribed cold embrocations. I am thus a prisoner here for several days. I suffer but little pain, and need not task the leg. Rest is the one essential necessity. But the occurrence

---

[225] Julia, Claudia, and Clara Roach conducted a school in their home at 13 Society Street, Charleston.

[226] See letter to Augusta of Sept. 2.

[227] Of books and papers. See letter to Edward Roach of Sept. 1.

will prevent my return certainly before the 29th. if then. I shall have a week's work in New York after I get down there, & shall try to do a week's work, during my imprisonment here. I communicated the contents of your letter, such as referred to Mrs. F. to Mr. F.[228] I am sorry that you could not procure some choice potatoes. Do not trouble yourself about the room at present. In a day after I arrive I shall need to run up to the plantation & see about things in that quarter. You had best persuade Chevillette to stay with you during her period of *accouchement.*[229] But I suppose this is not very near at hand. It will be far better that she should be with you, & convenient to Geddings, at that time. Mrs. F. will see to the sack & other samples for you. Tell Wm.[230] that Mr. Lawson was exceedingly mortified that he should not see him while in N. Y. I rejoice that his business prospects are improving, and sympathize with him in his catarrhal afflictions. Did Edw. get the $25 from Laidler?[231] If so, do not hesitate to use it. Does Mr. Wagner answer the dfts of Gilmore? And how has Edward satisfied the Banks. I have been very uneasy about him & them. Love to the girls, Edward & the children and God's blessing on you all. In haste & some suffering.

Your affe. father

W. Gilmore Simms

1195: To SIMMS' CHILDREN

Yonkers, 18 Sep. 1866.

My dear Children.

It was my hope to get off for home, by the steamer of the 22d. but an accident will keep me here some time longer. Last night, stepping from the rear porch at Lawson's, I missed one of the steps, my right ancle turned under me, & I fell heavily to the ground. Fortunately, there is no dislocation, or break of the bones. The Dr. has just examined the limb, & pronounces it a severe sprain. It is quite swollen, and we are using cold

---

[228] Ferris.

[229] Chevillette Simms Rowe's first child was named Chevillette Simms. See note 121, June 12, 1866.

[230] William Roach.

[231] See letters to Augusta of July 7 and Sept. 2 and to Edward Roach of July 26.

embrocations. The pain is not very great even when I move upon it, and with the aid of a cane I can slowly hobble in & out of the house. But I fear I shall need to nurse it & do nothing else, for the next week or ten days. I mention the occurrence solely to account for my delay in turning homewards. There is nothing to alarm you, however much there may be to inconvenience me. I wrote you only a day or two ago.[232] Yours & the letters of the girls were all recieved. I am afraid that Donald & yourself have begun to haul your lumber to the river at too early a period & while the weather is yet too warm for your oxen & horses. *Your* lumber must be sold to pay the money you get & have gotten from Wagner. I trust to have money enough to pay Burke and Hoffman.[233] I hope to realize $1000 from my labours this summer, & this, I hope, will suffice to feed & clothe us all, & leave something towards rebuilding the wing of the House. I hope also to make such contracts, as will enable me to earn a like sum during the winter. I need not say, my dear children — my son especially — that you are all to do what you can. Your father will divide himself among you, & so long as his poor brains can be turned to profit, he will use them for your good. Tell Donald that my fisherman friend [234] has taken his memorandum, & sent me a bundle of hooks, lines & flies, which he thinks suitable for our rivers. Jimmie Lawson will probably send to Gilmore a breech loading and six shooter rifle. There are others things. I got a pair of good boots in Brooklyn for $5. I propose to get a pair for Gilmore — my boots will fit him. Were I sure of Donald's measure, I would procure for him also. I have had a beautiful album given to me for Woodlands, stamped thus

W O O D L A N D S
Simms
South   Carolina

and in this, I have already a number of photographs. Tell M. L. that Misses Kellogg offered me money to buy something for her; G. B.[235] not affording any thing that might please. I refused the money, & on their persisting, told them to send it to Augusta, who could get M. L.'s instructions for what she wanted.

---

[232] We have not located this letter.

[233] James Burke and Jacob Alonzo Hoffman, merchants at Midway.

[234] George D. Coaney. See letters to Ferris of Sept. 18 and Dec. 21, 1866.

[235] Great Barrington.

It was a trifle only.[236] You should now, both Donald & yourself, be getting in *hay*. You will need provender. Get as much for forage as you can. Corn for the family may be bought. But I will not discuss with you now, of the future. It will do when we meet. I shall come home (D. V.) *via* Charleston, stay there but a night, & then come up to you. At present, it is impossible to say when I shall come. Be assured it shall be as soon as possible. Meanwhile, I can be doing good work here. I will try. I have a promise of the game of War Chess — a good set. Col. Richardson, the Inventor, was a Col. in the Confed. Service.[237] This will exercise Donald & yourself, in strategies. But do not forget your law. By this time, you have discovered the full worthlessness of the negro, when no longer under the govt. of a master. I had long ago been sickened of the race, & but for the will of your grandfather, would now probably, be able to render you all Independent.[238] We must work out our independence with our own hands. But this requires more brain than muscle. I fear that you & Donald will exhaust yourselves in your lumber hauling. God bless you all, my children, & enable us to meet again. Hope on & be cheerful. With proper will & energy, & concentrative purpose, hope, faith & work will achieve every thing. Love to all & blessing.

Your affe. father

W. Gilmore Simms

Have the boxes reached you?[239]

1196: To William Hawkins Ferris

Yonkers, 18 Sep. 1866.

My dear Ferris.

Enclosed you have the Poem of Mr. Butler.[240] You will also find within a budget of selections for your scrapbook. I had fully expected to be in the city this morning, when I should have presented these in Pro. Per. but for an unlucky little accident which had like to have been a very serious one to me. As it is,

---

[236] See letter to Augusta of Sept. 15.

[237] We have been unable to identify Col. Richardson.

[238] Nash Roach entailed Woodlands on Gilmore.

[239] Of books and papers. See letters to Edward of Sept. 1 and to Augusta of Sept. 15.

[240] "Uhland." See letter to Ferris of Aug. 9.

it incapacitates me at present from walking. Stepping down from Lawson's porch last evening, I missed one of the steps, lost my footing, & fell upon the stone pavement heavily. My right ancle is sprained or strained to such a degree that I can only limp about with a stick, and shall probably be unable to walk without pain & labour for several days. This event mars several of my arrangements. The ancle is a good deal swollen, & I expect a surgeon to examine it in the course of the morning. Nothing is broken, I think, as I can use the limb in every concievable mode. In reading to you portions of my daughter's [241] letter, there was one matter which I overlooked, to which you had best give immediate attention. She says — "Edward will write as soon as he ships the Potatoes — but I am sorry to add that they are very inferior this year." Now, it may be that he will ship them to me; or, it may be that, even shipping them to you, you may not seasonably recieve his letter, or the letter may be addressed to me. It will be well, accordingly, to look at the list of consignées in the newspapers, by the steamers arriving from Charleston twice a week. Usually, one line which leaves Charleston on Thursdays arrives in N. Y. on Sundays, & her reports will appear in Monday's papers. The other line sails on Saturday, & usually arrives by Tuesday night, or Wednesday morning.[242] *Verb. sap!* — I enclose a note from Mr. Bockee which I shall be glad if you can send him. You can send him, at the same time, the bundle of Lines & Hooks which my boys owe to the kindness of our fat friend The St. Peter (Fisherman) of the Temple of Mammon.[243] Say to Mrs. F. that Augusta begs that she will write her by me, and especially declare in what degree she likes her new dwelling. But my accident will compel me to defer my departure untill probably the close of next week. *Nous Verrons*! I shall have to linger here, untill my leg is sufficiently firm to enable me, without pain, to get about in New York. Ride as I will, there is much walking that is inevitable. Present me very gratefully at home, and to all admiring & enquiring friends.

                                        Yours Ever truly

W. Hawkins Ferris, Esqr.   W. Gilmore Simms.

---

[241] Augusta's.

[242] The Regular United States Mail Line of First Class Steam Ships and the New York and Charleston People's Steam Ship Company. See the advertisements in the Charleston newspapers during this period.

[243] George D. Coaney. See letter to Ferris of Dec. 21, 1866.

P. S. If Willie [244] has been able to complete the copy of the piece I left with him, please envelope it carefully to my address, & send it through Lawson.

1197: To Evert Augustus Duyckinck

Yonkers, 20th. Sept. '66.

My dear Duyckinck.

Whether I shall be able to see you on Saturday,[245] as I hoped to do, is a problem. I should have seen you on Tuesday last or Wednesday, as I purposed, but for an unlucky accident, which while putting me hors de combat, & subjecting me to some pain, had admonished me that I am no longer a young man. Leaving Lawson's villa by the rear porch, I miscounted my steps in the dark, lost my footing, sprained my ancle & fell incontinently to the ground. The limb was soon swollen and I have only to console myself with the fact that no dislocation or breakage of bone, followed. Embrocations have reduced the swelling, & tho there is still some pain, if I can get my boot on by Saturday next, or at farthest, Monday, I shall make a decided effort to see you. I take for granted that, had you known my helpless condition, you would have availed yourself of the proverbial hospitality, of my Scottish Laird, Lawson, to have run up to commiserate me. Sore, suffering, & somewhat depressed — as, we phrase it in the South, "Somewhat off my feed," — I have been able to do nothing. But in the week or ten days which are still left me in the North, I trust (D. V.) to do the Laurens' memoir.[246] I have not seen Mr. Butler; was to see him the night when, like Miss Jemima Jenkins, I made my misstep in the rear.[247] Let me hope that all is well with you.

Yours Ever truly

W. Gilmore Simms

P. S. I had the pleasure just before I went to Lawsons, of an interview with your friend Moreau, — whom I should be pleased to find my friend also. He seems one of these gentle moderate

---

[244] Ferris' son.
[245] Sept. 22.
[246] Simms' "Memoir of John Laurens," included in *The Army Correspondence of Colonel John Laurens,* pp. 9-54.
[247] We are unable to explain this allusion.

& unexacting men whom I like. He had, most industriously copied the Letters I had indicated to him, & I have them in possession. Do, should you see him before I do, report how very grateful I am to him for his kindness in this respect.

W. G. S.

1198: To EVERT AUGUSTUS DUYCKINCK

95 Third Place, Brooklyn
28 Sep. 1866.

My dear Duyckinck.

I succeeded in getting to N. York yesterday & finally to Brooklyn, got up as far as Richardson's, and had hope to see you at Clinton Place, but for painful expostulatory monitions from my poor leg, which gave way prematurely, & compelled me to make my way as well as I could & as fast as possible, to the Brooklyn Cars, in hope to rest the member & myself, in a spot where the wicked would cease from troubling, and the *sole* would be at rest. I cannot yet get on my boot, & have to wear my well worn old shoes, which are large & easy, but a little too thin for the season. But, if confined to the house — for I dare not attempt too much at present with the limb, — I have not been altogether idle. I have prepared in a rough pencilled draft, the memoir of Laurens, which I will begin to revise & copy off tomorrow. It will be somewhat longer perhaps, than you & I contemplated, & will probably require 40 or 50 pp. in print. I include Hamilton's Letter, Hayne's Speech, & one or two Letters of Laurens himself, & propose, at your suggestion, to wind up with Freneau's verses on his death. Will you oblige me by making a copy of them for the press? [248] — When I shall have finished this job, & put the MS. in your hands, I shall have finished all my labours, for the season, in New York. It is my hope to start for S. C. sometime next week, and I shall strive to close all rivets up [249] in this. With this hope, & with the belief that you are prepared

---

[248] Simms' "Memoir of John Laurens" ends "with a letter, never before published, of the Hon. John C. Hamilton, son of Alexander Hamilton, and a copy of the speech made by the Hon. Robert Y. Hayne, in the senate of the United States, on the bill for the relief of the grandson of Col. John Laurens . . . [and] the elegiac poem of Philip Freneau . . . on the death of Laurens ['Lines on the Death of Colonel Laurens']." See *The Army Correspondence of Colonel John Laurens,* pp. 40-56.

[249] *Henry V,* IV, Prologue, 13.

to second my desires even at some trouble to yourself, let me chronicle for you the extent of my expectations at your hands. And, 1. Do not forget to send me the photographs of your brother & yourself. If you have any extra copies of your brother's several vols. of biography, let me have them.[250] 2. Procure for me from Mr. Johnson copies of my own several photographs [251] by Brady, and remind Mr. J. of his gracious promise to send me copies of his publications, especially yours of the Eminent Men.[252] You may intimate to Mr. J. that I shall probably be always connected with the press of the South, & as the Mercury is shortly to be revived, I expect to exercise no small influence through that medium which will always be one of the most influential of the South.[253] 3. Let me remind you to look up for me all the duplicates you can find of the Literary World. Whatever packets may be furnished by Mr. Johnson, yourself or others, have sent me to the care of Richardson & Co. If I do not succeed in getting to see you on Saturday, I shall certainly (D. V.) do so on Monday next. I looked in upon Mr. Moreau, when I came down in the boat on Tuesday, & found that he had, most kindly, made all the copies for me, from the Laurens letters, that I had desired. I am much pleased with him. He too has kindly promised me copies of several of the Bradford publications, among them, the Portuguese narrative of De Soto, by Mr Smith.[254] These will prove great contributions to my poor book collection. — I have done with the War Poems, shall be able, I hope, on Monday, to bring you the Memoir of Laurens, & shall then close rivets up, & hasten my departure. It is probable that I shall leave on Wednesdays steamer for Charleston. What I hear from Carolina, tho' all remain well, is calculated to make me anxious to be there. No crops are made. Between the drouth, lack of means & appliances, & the *dolce far niente* of the virtuous freedmen, nothing has been done. I venture to think that the whole

---

[250] Among George Long Duyckinck's biographies are *The Life of Jeremy Taylor* (see note 117, May 28, 1860) and *The Life of George Herbert* (New York: General Protestant Episcopal Sunday School Union and Church Book Society, 1859).

[251] Simms wrote *autographs.*

[252] The firm of Johnson, Fry and Co. (Henry Johnson and William H. Fry) was the publisher of Duyckinck's *National Portrait Gallery of Eminent Americans* (see note 80, March 15, 1861).

[253] The Charleston *Mercury* was revived on Nov. 19.

[254] Buckingham Smith, tr., *Narratives of the Career of Hernando de Soto in the Conquest of Florida, as Told by a Knight of Elvas* . . . (New York: [Bradford Club], 1866).

upland Cotton Crop of the South will not exceed 800,000 bales, instead of 2½ millions. Now is the time to speculate. If you can command a million, use it up in buying Cotton at present prices. It will give you another million clear. But, I suspect that you are as poor a financier as myself, so God keep you, secure at least, in your present condition. À Dios!

Yours Ever

W. Gilmore Simms.

E. A. D.

1199: To Thomas Addis Emmet

Brooklyn Oct. 2. '66.

Dr Emmet

My dear Sir.

Will you please accept for your collection a set of the Bills of the Confederacy of the Southern States, and oblige

Your obt. Servt.

W. Gilmore Simms

1200: To Leavitt, Strebeigh and Company [255]

Brooklyn, October 3, 1866.

Messrs. Leavitt, Strebeigh & Co.

Gentlemen : —

I was just pulling on my boots, preparatory to my departure for the South, when your letter was recieved, and it is not easy at such a moment, while packing boxes and "closing rivets up," even to address myself to the task which you have set me. To do full justice to it, and make a becoming report to you, or to the public, in respect to the autographical collection of my late excellent and venerable friend, I. K. Tefft, would be on my part, at any time, simply an impossibility. I have never myself been

---

[255] We have not located the original of this letter. Our text is from *Catalogue of the Entire Collection of Autographs of the Late Mr. I. K. Tefft, of Savannah, Ga.* (New York: Leavitt, Strebeigh & Co., 1867), pp. 20-23. The sale of Tefft's collection occupied several days, beginning on March 4, 1867. The members of the firm of Leavitt, Strebeigh and Co. were George A. Leavitt and Robert M. Strebeigh, listed as auctioneers in the New York City *Directory* for 1866.

a collector of autographs, though frequently a dispenser of them, and possess and profess none of the qualities necessary to an expert. But, surely, in the case of Mr. Tefft and his collection, the American people can need no information now. He has been, proverbially, for the last thirty years, the best known and most notoriously active of all the collectors of such material in all the United States. He is the Upcott [256] of America, as we should be apt to style the English Upcott the Tefft of Great Britain. Both seem to have pursued a like plan in their collections, and both, in similar degree, have gone beyond all contemporaries.

I take for granted that no collection in this country can well compare with that of my late excellent and much lamented friend. What I know of autography was imbibed from him. Knowing him intimately — frequently his guest — always indeed, when, during the last thirty years, I have happened to visit Savannah, it was morally impossible that I should escape his specialty, or fail to imbibe something from his peculiar passion. With him, it was indeed a passion; his pleasant study through the day, his dream of pleasure through the night. His natural tastes — his own talents, which were excellent — his judgment, which was sound — and the indefatigable diligence which he brought to bear upon this one pursuit, must have led to very great success in its prosecution.

But he possessed other advantages. Hospitable without limit, my friend welcomed to his house the distinguished persons of all countries, and made them inmates of his home. There might you meet the Martineaus,[257] the Thackerays, the Bremers, the Halls,[258] the Hamiltons,[259] my Lord of Morpeth,[260] and the Prince Achille Murat. With an annual supply of such guests, foreign and native, my friend found it easy to increase that capital, in the accumulation of which alone might he be accused of avarice. Never was mortal more avid in the pursuit of gains in letters

---

[256] William Upcott (1779-1845), the English antiquary and autograph-collector.

[257] Harriet Martineau (1802-1876), the English writer, visited in the United States during 1834-1835 and was the author of *Society in America* (London, 1837).

[258] Basil Hall (1788-1844), a captain in the British navy, was the author of *Travels in North America in the Years 1827 and 1828* (London, 1829).

[259] Thomas Hamilton (1789-1842), a retired British army captain, was the author of *Men and Manners in America* (London, 1833).

[260] George William Frederick Howard, 7th Earl of Carlisle (1802-1864), visited in the United States during 1841-1842 and published an account of his travels in *Two Lectures, on the Poetry of Pope, and on His Own Travels in America* . . . (London, 1851).

and manuscripts. His gentleness, tender consideration, mild and grateful manners, and general though unobtrusive intelligence, made his way [261] easy to the affections of others, most of whom were at pains accordingly to yield *him* pleasure by ministering to his ruling passion. Day and night would he be found poring over his collection, with one or more friends, who sought to gratify mere curiosity or to obtain rare and valuable biographical and historical material.

His plan was such as to enable him to satisfy all classes of seekers. He was not content with the mere letter or the simple signature. He hunted up rare documents in every quarter: he traced their history, and the lives of their writers. He thus accumulated masses of fact in relation to the country as well as the individual; coupled the portrait of the individual; wherever this was possible, with the document, and referred, for illustration of the document, to contemporary history. It is in this mode of his proceeding, that his collection became singularly valuable, especially to the student; and to his own memory, which was of wonderful tenacity and grasp, and to his collection, have I had, scores of times, to resort, as to a joint record, for the materials which I could nowhere else discover, and for the matter illustrative of that which I already had in possession. My friend's capacity for discriminating between his documents, and deciding their respective values, had been sharpened to perfection by long practice and experience, which came to the aid of a native instinct. He was not to be imposed upon by any forgeries, however adroitly made. He brought to bear upon his papers all the tests of historical authenticity. Nor did he mistake in the relative value of his subjects, confounding the obscure with the eminent. On the contrary, while gratefully receiving, and, indeed, seeking, all manner of papers as well as correspondents, he knew well how to class them in the degree of their several merits. He knew well the rare from the common, and set a proper valuation upon the record which illustrated a life or an event; and his collection, accordingly, will, in my opinion, be found to rise in rank in comparison with most others because of the aids which it can furnish to the biographer, the philosopher, and the historian.

I confess I should be sorry to see it dismembered. I prefer that it should be kept intact, as the good old man fondly hoped and fancied that it would be; so as to constitute forever, to the

---

[261] The *Catalogue* has a comma between *his* and *way*.

student, a certain treasure-house of records and memorials, having its well-known locality and home, and made accessible by some noble and wealthy proprietor, to the researches of the citizen. Surely there are some lordly minds among you corresponding to the lordly wealth which so many of your people possess, to whom such a collection, with such an object, should be a source of noble pride and honest satisfaction.

Let me hope that you will find it so. Knowing the pride of heart of my good old friend in making this collection, the almost life-long interest which he had in his daily accumulations, and his natural wish that it should remain whole, and subject to no change except in continued accumulation by some industrious successor, I should feel much pain myself in its dispersion, and a corresponding sentiment of gratitude to that liberal gentleman who should make it his own, and find for it a befitting temple. I know it to be well worthy a fine one, in a great city like yours; and here, worthily enshrined, it would doubtless become a subject of like pride, attraction, and interest with your famous libraries and academies of literature, art and science.

Greatly regretting that I cannot be more full or specific on this subject, I am your obedient servant,

W. Gilmore Simms.

1201: To Evert Augustus Duyckinck [262]

New York, 6 Oct. 1866.

My dear Duyckinck.

I am very much mortified that I cannot get up to see you; but I am suffering too much with my ancle to do any walking that is not absolutely necessary. Some of it I must needs do, in limping from wharf to wharf. It is my hope that, as you know of my designed departure, you will come down & see me off. I sail in the Quaker City from Wharf 14 East river, next to Wall Street Ferry. Bruns is to go with me & comes on today. Come & see us both.

Ever faithfully Yours

W. Gilmore Simms

P. S. Remembrances to Mr. Moreau.

---

[262] This letter is written on stationery carrying Charles Benjamin Richardson's letter-head.

1202: To Evert Augustus Duyckinck

Charleston, Oct. 10, '66

My dear Duyckinck.

You see that I am once more safely at home.[263] We had smooth seas, a fine ship & pleasant company. My friend, Professor Bruns joined me on board ship, having come on from Phila. that morning for the purpose. I had hoped to see you then also, as he would have been greatly pleased to meet you; and hoping this, I penned you a note from Richardson's to beg that you would do so.[264] I could not come to see you as I had purposed. I had so exercised my game leg in walking that I was completely broken down before midday & found it a hobbling business to get down from Lawson's (Wall Street) to the steamer, though at the next wharf below. My leg & foot are both still too much swollen by the exercise I gave them, to permit me to leave the house on foot, so I devote this day at the desk, in the hope to square my letterary accounts with friends & Correspondents. You must excuse me to our excellent friend Mr. Moreau, for my failure to come & bid him farewell, as I had confidently hoped to do, up to the last moment. I trust we shall meet again, as the world finds rare volumes "after certain days." I found that portion of my little flock which dwells in this ancient ilk, in good health, and tolerable condition. Tomorrow, if my ancle be not too painful for the trip, I propose to run up to Woodlands, & see how they get on there. I shall return (D. V.) by Monday.[265] I shall have to prosecute my labours in this city, as I have not, at the plantation, a single room in which I can write. I hear that all are well in that quarter, tho' the crop is a failure. I find by the papers here that our public is rapidly coming to the conclusion which I expressed to you that the cotton crop, will scarcely exceed the estimate of 700,000 bales — certainly, not reach a million. This is the evidence from the entire Southwest. Congress has struck a serious, if not fatal blow, at the cotton culture, by its export duty of 3 cents per lb! Good! The sooner we reach the end the better. Radicalism is just now an epidemic & must be suffered to run its course. We have reached the full extent of our suffering, & can endure

---

[263] Simms arrived in Charleston on Oct. 9. See letter to Lawson of Oct. 10.
[264] See preceding letter.
[265] Oct. 15.

no further loss. Time will show upon whom the next bolt of ruin will fall! I write simply to report my safety, & to express my great regret at not being able to give you a farewell gripe of the fist. God be with you in mercy.

Yours ever affectionately

W. Gilmore Simms

1203: To WILLIAM HAWKINS FERRIS

Charleston, Oct. 10. [1866][266]

My dear Ferris.

You see that I have reached my destined port in safety. I find all well in Charleston & hear a like report from Woodlands. I proceed (D. V.) to the latter place tomorrow. They were all greatly anxious for my safety, having in their minds the two fatal wrecks of sea steamers during the preceeding week,[267] and my daughter here had just instructed her husband to telegraph you on the subject of my departure. I presume that by the time this reaches you, you will have returned from the Great Cascade. I trust you have had none of your own to the discomfiture of your bowels. Make my best regards to Mrs. F. and kisses for the children. Please, when you see any of the family of Mr. Hughes,[268] express my regrets that I could not come to see them *pour prendre congé*. I had fully purposed to do so, and that I have failed is so much of a pleasure lost to me. But the attempt was physically impossible. From much walking the two or three days before I left N. Y. I had become so lame, that I was barely able finally to hobble from Wall Street to the ship at the next wharf. My ancle remains swollen now to such a degree that I find it hard work to get up & down stairs, and I have had to resort to those pitiable swathings of the limb which I had hoped to forego entirely. You will also make the same excuse for me to the Birds — All of the Temple. I had fully purposed to see them, & was on my way to do so, when I literally broke down & found that my only recourse was to go aboardship full an hour before it was necessary. Say to Mr. Seymour that I called

---

[266] Dated by Simms' remark about his arrival in Charleston. See letter to Duyckinck of the same date.
[267] The names of these ships were the *Andrew Johnson* and the *Evening Star*. See the Charleston *Courier* for this time.
[268] Not identified.

at his office the day before my departure — waited fully an hour to see him, — but that he was, no doubt, on one of his land cruises, after the spirit of the flesh, which may vex his soul hereafter, as it vexed my sole to get to him. To that venerable father in Mammon, the fat Priest Birdsall, say that I shall take an early opportunity to put myself *rectus in curia,* with such of his friends of the tender gender, who, having experience of his prowess, are grievously exercised at any imputation of femininity against him.[269] Poor fellow! that he should be a subject of doubt on this subject. Let me hear from you soon, and report yourself, & all, if you please, in good, hopeful & already prosperous condition.

Yours Ever truly

W. Gilmore Simms

Mr. & Mrs. E. R.[270] send best regards.

1204: To James Lawson

Wednesday MG. Oct. 10 [1866][271]

Charleston S. C.

My dear Lawson.

I reached Charleston in safety yesterday morning; had a pleasant voyage, the sea being as smooth as a lake the whole route. Tell Jamie the Quaker City is one of the sturdiest seaboats on the route, the Captain a capable & good fellow, & the average run of the boat is 10 knots.[272] I find all well here, & at latest advices, all were well in the country. Thither I go (D. V.) tomorrow morning. They were all greatly anxious for my safety, having just got tidings of the disastrous wrecks of 2 sea steamers, which, I fear *for you,* are total losses. My best love to wife & children. I have nothing to report yet save that I am as Ever

truly Yours

W. Gilmore Simms

---

[269] See note 207, Aug. 9, 1866.

[270] Edward Roach.

[271] Dated by Simms' remarks about his arrival in Charleston. See preceding letters.

[272] The captain of the *Quaker City* was named West. See the Charleston *Courier* of Oct. 10, which also lists Simms as among the passengers who arrived "yesterday."

1205: To PAUL HAMILTON HAYNE [273]

Charleston, Oct. 22 1866

My dear Paul:

Got your note yesterday and glad to see that you are in some-what better spirits. I ran up to Woodlands some 10 days ago, and found the ruins as much a solitude as ever, and the crops a ruin. No crop! Everything burned up. I should despond, despair, if I had ever been in practise of doing such things. But it is not in my blood, which comes to the relief of my brain when overborne or overworked, — the one being the parent of the other. I am cudgelling my brains at a new romance, the first scene of which opens at the Sand Hills of Augusta.[274] I have done some 120 pages — and hope, by the close of the week to have done 150 more! *Nous verrons* as old Ritchie[275] was wont to say. As Burns says — "Perhaps it may turn out a song, perhaps turn out a sermon."[276]

I am more in the mood to sermonize than sing.

John Bruns proposes to leave for New Orleans on Wednesday next.[277] Think it likely he will get off. If you happen in Augusta that night you may chance to see him — or should the great S. W. R. R. pass your cottage, you may get a grip of his fist *en passant.* John is in fine health and fine spirits, and looks like one of the Bull family.

Poor Timrod is the very prince of Dolefuls, and swallowed up in distresses. He now contemplates separation from his wife, that she may go forth as a governess, and he as a tutor, in private families. He can earn nothing where he is — has not a dollar — goes to bed hungry every night —, and suffers from bad health. It is the mortifying thing to all of us, that *none of us* can help him. Bruns and myself are both living from hand to mouth, and infrequently the hand carries nothing to the cavernous receptacle.[278] But I write simply to reply, and to say

---

[273] We have not located the original of this letter. Our text is from a type-script formerly belonging to Hayne's son, William Hamilton Hayne, and now in the Duke University Library. Part of the letter is printed in Trent, pp. 295-296, and in Hubbell, *The Last Years of Henry Timrod,* pp. 57-58.

[274] "Joscelyn." See letter to Duyckinck of Nov. 4, 1866.

[275] Thomas Ritchie. See note 91, March 29, 1847.

[276] See "Epistle to a Young Friend," lines 7f.

[277] Bruns had been appointed professor of physiology and pathology in the New Orleans School of Medicine. Wednesday was Oct. 24.

[278] The typescript has *recipient,* but Trent (who saw the original) has *receptacle,* which seems the more likely reading.

to you that *I hope* to be able to seize a week at Christmas, to visit the Hammonds, Redmond [279] and yourself. I enclose a note for him which you will please hand to him. He is, I believe, your next door neighbor. In covering both supplements under one envelope I not only kill two birds with one envelope, but save myself a post stamp besides. You must learn to be economical Paul, so take this lesson to heart. A very important one I assure you, since you will one day find, as I do at this moment, that I have but a single stamp left in my box, and for more, "where are the pennies to come from." Present me gratefully to your wife and mother, and believe me,

Ever truly

W. Gilmore Simms.

P. H. H.

P. S. Verb. Sap!

1206: To CHARLES WARREN STODDARD. [280]

Charleston, S. C.
Oct. 24. 1866.

Mr. Charles Warren Stoddard.

My dear Sir:

It is a pleasant surprise to find that, in the very land dedicated to Mammon, there should be found one of a Priesthood who prefers to worship at the shrines of Apollo. It is a good sign, and I welcome it as a proof that the true God does not wholly abandon the beautiful world which he has made. Let me commend you to a continued worship at an altar where the service admits & demands the presence & active uses of a soul. "The *world* is too much with us," says Wordsworth, meaning by

---

[279] "The Hammonds" are M. C. M. Hammond and his family (see letter to Ferris of Jan. 8, 1867) and possibly the family of James H. Hammond. Dennis Redmond was the owner of a large nursery near Augusta, which Simms describes in "Highways and Byways. VII" in the Charleston *Courier* of Jan. 31, 1867 (for Simms' "Highways and Byways," see note 2, Jan. 8, 1867). Redmond's plantation is the present site of the Augusta National Golf Course of America.

[280] Stoddard (1843-1909), born in Rochester, N. Y., removed with his family to San Francisco in 1855. He was a contributor of prose and verse to various periodicals, and in 1867 Bret Harte edited his *Poems* (San Francisco: A. Roman and Company). He is today chiefly remembered for his books about the South Seas.

world, the lowly & ordinary objects, desires & performances of man. The fine arts, of which Poetry is the very foundation, were designed, as among the best agencies to procure for us that wing which alone can lift us above the world, in the aspirations of a wingèd soul. I have read your little Poems with much satisfaction. They indicate poetical talents of no common order. They show in you the possession of thought, fancy, good taste and considerable art. It is my chief objection that they exhibit, also, a too decidedly imitative tendency which is too much the characteristic of the American Muse. You must study Tennyson less, and the earlier masters more. You should get back to Milton, Shakspeare & Dryden; and above all avoid that effort at the vague & unsubstantial, which finds it easier to employ Fancy than to command Thought. The vague, it is true, is, in a certain degree the necessity of Poetry; but only as it shall enable the Poet to escape the merely literal. Directness of aim, and concentration of Thought do not necessarily imply the literal, and these, with Imagination and Fancy, as a decorative quality, are the whole source of power in poetry, & so of permanent reputation. Poetry is wingèd Thought. It must be *thought;* this, founded upon close observation of man & nature, the moral & physical world; delivered with adequate emphasis, from the lips of art, and supported by Imagination which constitutes its wing, affords us that sort of Poetry which is the only sort that ever is transmitted through the ages. Such, we find in Homer, Æschylus, Milton, Dante, Shakspeare, & other great masters of the Past. Our American poets are too easily satisfied with a little play of fancy as the substitute of Thought, and for the scream of the eagle, give us the chirpings of the sparrow; for the chaunt of the skylark, at the portals of the dawn, the twitterings of the robin or the faint whistle of the thrush. To *think* & *feel* in poetry is the true secret of the voice in poetry. Observe closely, think earnestly, & sing boldly, not wantonly or diffusely, but with resolute purpose, not so much to sing as to strike, impress, conquer, and reach a result. And that result is not to tickle a fancy, but to penetrate a soul. But I must not write an essay. Your frank & ingenuous letter compels me to answer you frankly, and with that sympathy which the Poet should always feel for a younger brother, not yet fully assured of the strength of his own wing. Let me counsel you to study the grand old masters who have survived through all the ages, and beware of that sensuous which, in recent periods, is dethroning Thought and Imagination to make way for Fancy; putting a Butterfly upon that Pedestal, which, among the true Priesthood, always sustained a God. May the good God make you wise to pursue your vocation with industry & courage & crown it with success.

Your obt Servt.

W. Gilmore Simms

1207: To James Lawson

Charleston, Oct. 25. [1866]²⁸¹

My dear Lawson.

Tell Jimmy, on arriving at Charleston, to take a carriage, and drive at once to No. 13 Society Street, where we have a room in waiting for him. His lodgings will be rude enough, but comfortable, & he will find a hearty welcome. Gilmore will also be prepared for him at Woodlands; not altogether in the fashion of the past, but he can rough it with the rest. — I wish you would prepare & send on by Jimmy, your anecdote of Gilfert. It is too good to be lost, & I wish to employ it with other matters. Be particular in giving all the details. We are all quite well. I shall (D. V.) run up to the plantation for a day or two, on Saturday next. Love to Lyde & the girls & respects to Mr. S. & Jimmy. Say to Mary that I have not yet recieved her or Kates photographs. Mr. Sandford's will also be acceptable.

Yours Ever

W. G. S.

1208: To Evert Augustus Duyckinck

Charleston, 4th. Nov. 1866.

My dear Duyckinck. —

Your letter came to me while I was on a visit to my plantation. I found every thing very miserable there; no crop; a terrible

---

²⁸¹ Dated by Simms' reference to Jimmy's proposed trip to Charleston (see letter to Lawson of Oct. 10) and by his request for Lawson's anecdote about Charles Gilfert (1787-1829), the theatrical manager (see letter to Lawson of Feb. 8, 1867, in which he again requests this anecdote for his article later entitled "The Humours of the Manager"). Further evidence for the date is Simms' remark that he plans to go to Woodlands on "Saturday next" (Oct. 27): he refers to this visit in his letter to Duyckinck of Nov. 4.

drouth, and no work to be got out of the negroes, when work
is essential to the safety of the crop. The efforts of my son, & all
my expenditure of money, for the last 9 months, in vain. I shall
probably continue to work here in Charleston where I am tolerably comfortable, untill you see me again in New York. I have
paid 2 visits to the plantation, of a few days each, yet have been
sufficiently laborious, while here, to write some 250 pp. MS.
on a new revolutionary romance called "Joscelyn." This is to
be put forth serially.[282] I have recieved a letter from Widdleton.
Please say to him that I will write him in a few days. In the
meantime request him to send me a copy of my "Yemassee"
which I find wanting to my collection; and should he be in a
liberal vein, tell him that I will be grateful to him for copies —
his old editions will answer — of Poe's works; of the Noctes
Ambrosianæ, and of the Maginn papers, for all which I am
prepared to say a good word in one or other of our Newspapers.[283]
I enclose you a notice of Freneau, which was printed in the
Courier during my absence in N. Y.[284] I had left it, when I went
North, & its publication was delayed till some weeks after. I
take for granted that you or Widdleton have recieved the several
notices which I printed of his & your several publications (as
I recieved them) either in the Courier or the Carolinian. Shall
I remind you here not to forget to send me the photographs
promised me of yourself & brother; as also copies of his several
little volumes.[285] May I beg also that you will procure the publications of Mr. Johnson [286] which he was so good as to promise me.
These, if sent to Richardson & Co. will reach me in safety.
They have now on hand sundry packages for me, & will soon be
forwarding. I enclose you an autograph — a pair of them — of
Brig. Gen. Isaac Huger, of the Continental army. They are very
scarce. These you will please deliver, with my regards, to *our*
friend, Mr. Moreau, with a request from me that he will accept
& place the sheet in his collection. Did you not, on the morning

[282] "Joscelyn: A Tale of the Revolution" was published in the *Old Guard,*
V (Jan.–Dec., 1867), 1-17, 91-103, 161-176, 241-260, 321-339, 401-421, 481-500,
561-567, 668-681, 731-745, 822-834, 897-935. This work has never been republished.

[283] Widdleton had published an edition of Poe's *Poems* in 1863; Redfield
had published an edition of *Noctes Ambrosianae* in 1854 and a five-volume
edition of the *Miscellaneous Writings of the Late Dr. [William] Maginn* (ed.
Robert Shelton Mackenzie) in 1855-1857.

[284] See note 35, Feb. 20, 1866.

[285] See letter to Duyckinck of Sept. 28.

[286] Henry Johnson. See note 251, Sept. 28, 1866.

of my departure, recieve at an early hour, a note from me, apprising you of my inability to come, and begging you to meet me at the boat. I sent the note by one of Richardson's Clerks somewhere between 10 & 11 am. & saw him depart with it.[287] Had you been able to meet me at the boat you would have encountered Professor Bruns, fresh from Europe, who became my compagnon du voyage home. He was quite anxious to see you again. He has gone to take his Professor's Chair at New Orleans, & should you need or desire any relationships in that section, aside from Gayarré, write to him. He will respond with whole heart, & a good head. I was doubly & trebly unfortunate in missing Halleck & Verplanck [288] on two occasions. I should have rejoiced at a shake of the hand, once more, with two of those men, who never sunk the Gentleman in the author — a thing quite rare, as you & I have so frequently found in our experience. Halleck was always a true man, & by nature, an aristocrat! But I must hope for better luck hereafter. Meanwhile, should you see him again, give him a goodly gripe of the fist on my account, & believe me

Ever truly Yours

W. Gilmore Simms

1209: To William Gilmore Simms, Jr.

Charleston, Nov. 1866.

My dear Son,

Tell Hoffman & Brabham to send their account against you down to their store in town, & I will settle it immediately. Keep what little money you have got. There is a small bill at Simmons which you can pay, & I do not know, but, if there be any bill at Bamberg's, & a small one, you can pay that also.[289] Ascertain what you owe at Bamberg & Midway, & if the amt. be considerable, leave it to me. Only ascertain what it is. Hereafter, all our credit accounts should cease, and if we lack means for our purchases, we must forbear to make them. I will send you up this

---

[287] See letter to Duyckinck of Oct. 6.

[288] Fitz-Greene Halleck (see introductory sketch) and Gulian Crommelin Verplanck (1786-1870), the author, editor, and congressman.

[289] Hoffman, Brabham, Simmons, and Bamberg were merchants in Midway and Bamberg. Hoffman and Brabham also had a store in Charleston, which the Charleston *Directory* for 1867-1868 lists as H. Brabham and Co. (H. Brabham and G. Hoffman), 59 Smith Street.

week, a barrel containing the odds and ends of harness, collars
&c. which Bockee sent you. The two saddles are here, but one
of them I propose to send up also. They will be sent by Xpress
and the freight will be paid on them here. It is possible that I
may come up next Saturday, the 24th. unless, in the meantime,
I learn that you will be coming down on or before that time.
Let me hear promptly. The newest of the saddles, I will keep
here according to your wish. [*Remainder of letter missing.*]

1210: To WILLIAM HAWKINS FERRIS

Charleston, Nov. 27. [1866][290]

My dear Ferris.

Just got back from the plantation — terribly tired, — find your
welcome letter awaiting me. I send you, with this, a bundle of
old letters. Have not leisure to look over them. Where there are
duplicates, or letters by the same hand, divide with Bockee. When
you examine, write a list of names & ask me about them. Many
of the names you will find in the Cyclopædias. Some of them
are valuable. All will contribute to enable you to form some
idea of an author's life & operations. I have many more. Will
forward them as occasion serves. Destroy, if you please; but, as
no one knows, who, of the living, is to become famous, better
wait & see.[291] I brought with me, from the plantation, Mary L.
& Carroll. Gilmore will be down in a week to pursue his law
studies. Donald will carry on the plantation. I am too busy to
be able to do any thing. I have written nearly 500 pp. since I
have been home, upon a single work, & Heaven knows how
much random matter besides. Drudgery at the desk is my doom
now to the end of the chapter. The 'Old Guard' will begin a
novel of mine — revolutionary — on the 1 January. It is called
"Joscelyn." But whether it will turn out "song or sermon"
— *quien sabe?* No news here — all dull, & monstrous scarcity
of money. The people generally begin to say — "D——n restoration! Who cares for it. We are out of the Union. We are willing
to stay out!" So much for your radicals. Nor will they stand
to be driven against the wall. They will not suffer the South to

---

[290] Dated by Simms' remarks about "Joscelyn." See preceding and following
letters.

[291] Part of Ferris' collection of autograph letters is in the Columbia University Library. We have not located Bockee's.

be made a Poland or an Ireland of! *Nous Verrons!* Commend me to your wife & the children, a kiss for Josey, and my blessings on the New House. Mary L. — Mrs. R. and all send love

Àdios.

W. Gilmore Simms

1211: To Paul Hamilton Hayne [292]

Charleston Nov. 29 [1866][293]

My dear Paul.

It is now so many weeks since I wrote you of my intention to visit the Hammonds, yourself and Mr. Redmond, without receiving any answer from either, that I begin to doubt whether the letters were received. My letter to Mr. Redmond was covered in the one to you. I now write to repeat the contents of both letters, which were written to say that I had hoped to be able to come up somewhere in the neighborhood of Christmas, and to divide a week among my several friends in your precinct. I still retain and cherish this purpose, but will need to hear from you all before I shall act upon it. If I do not hear from you and Mr. R I shall certainly not extend my travel beyond Augusta, where I hope to meet with Mr. Randall and some of the Hammond family. In writing, you will please be specific as to the route by which I shall reach you — the road to be taken, the mode of conveyance, and the depot or point at which to stop. Since writing you my previous letter, to which I have been specially referring, I sent you a brief note, covering the graceful sonnet to myself, which I had published, with a little preface in the *Courier*.[294] I trust that this was not ungraciously, ungratefully, or ungracefully done, in your eyes. I suppose that, by this time, you have seen my collections of the War Poems, in which you will find yourself making a frequent figure. I have reason to think that the notice of it, in the Round Table, was

---

[292] We have not located the original of this letter. Our text is from a typescript formerly belonging to Hayne's son, William Hamilton Hayne, and now in the Duke University Library.

[293] Dated by Simms' remarks about his plan to visit the Hammonds, Hayne, and Redmond. See letter to Hayne of Oct. 22.

[294] Hayne's sonnet ("Old Friend! come to me while the woods are decked . . ."), an invitation to Simms to visit him at Copse Hill, near Augusta, Ga., is published in the Charleston *Courier* of Nov. 3.

from the pen of Mr. Stoddard.[295] What I have to communicate touching letters at the North, may be kept for your personal hearing. I am busily at work on a new novel,[296] the opening scene of which is placed in Augusta. I shall have to write a great deal and make considerable headway, in order to secure a respite of a week at Christmas, which I propose to divide among my friends in your precinct. J. Bruns has made a great hit in New Orleans. Timrod has been on the verge of starvation. He is now acting as private secty. to Governor Orr. My best regards to Mary and your mother. What has become of Dick Michel? [297]

Yours very truly

W. Gilmore Simms.

---

[295] We have been unable to discover the exact date of issuance of *The War Poetry of the South* (New York: C. B. Richardson, 1866). The earliest review of the volume which we have located is that in the *Round Table,* IV (Nov. 10, 1866), 244, which Simms here ascribes to Richard Henry Stoddard. Since this reviewer remarks that "Messrs. Richardson & Co. are about to publish" the volume, evidently it was issued between Nov. 10 and Nov. 23, when it is reviewed in the Charleston *Courier.* In the collection Simms included a number of his own poems (the Charleston *Daily News* of May 8, 1866, had urged him not to exclude them "from an excess of modesty"), some signed, some signed with pseudonyms, and some unsigned; and the reviewer in the *Round Table* remarks that "Mr. Simms [is] rhetorical but nervous, particularly in his balladry."

In the Charleston newspapers *The War Poetry of the South* and Simms are highly praised (see the *Courier* of Nov. 23, the *Mercury* of Nov. 29, and the *Daily News* of Nov. 27 and Dec. 25). The volume and Simms are also lauded in the *Old Guard,* V (March, 1867), 202-206; in *De Bow's Review,* N. S., II (Dec., 1866), 662; and in the *Land We Love,* II (Feb., 1867), 309, and III (May, 1867), 71-74.

A reviewer in the *Crescent Monthly* (New Orleans), II (Jan., 1867), 77-78, however, remarks "that we feared from the first that in one respect this volume would be found wanting; we feared, though the field was ample, that its scope would be too narrow, for we have never thought that Dr. Simms possessed a catholic taste in poetry, and we augured from his own poetical performances that he would have too great a sympathy for mediocrity in verse. His readers will readily perceive how much of justness there was in our apprehension." Simms is then criticized for showing "too much Palmetto partiality," for using "ambiguous and inelegant" expressions in his preface, for publishing many poems which "might very well have remained unpublished," for inaccurately assigning the authorship of some poems, and for including some poems which are neither American nor about the Confederate War. This reviewer was perhaps James Wood Davidson, who was a contributor to the *Crescent Monthly* and who had earlier written a somewhat derogatory article on Simms for the *Illustrated Mercury* (see note 73, *c.* Aug. 1, 1864), edited and published by William B. Smith, who was at this time the editor of the *Crescent Monthly.*

[296] "Joscelyn."

[297] Richard Frazer Michel (1827-1907), Hayne's brother-in-law, was a prominent physician in Charleston. Prior to the Confederate War he was on the faculty of the Medical College of the State of South Carolina, at Charleston, and during the War he served as a surgeon in the Confederate States Army. In 1865 he resumed the practice of medicine in Charleston.

1212: To William Hawkins Ferris

Charleston, Decr. 4. [1866][298]

My dear Ferris.

By the Steamer Granada which is to sail tomorrow, you will recieve a Barrel of Carolina Potatoes, raised by my son at Woodlands, which he trusts will commend themselves gratefully to Mrs. F. & the young folks as well as yourself. In consequence of the great drought, they are not so good or so large this season as usual, but we hope that they will be recieved as the best that we could send, & they are sent with that loving consideration which, we trust, will make them grateful — supplying all their own defects of size & sweetness. Please let Bockee know, if convenient, that there is a Bbl also for him in the same vessel. I have been at the plantation lately, am very busy at work, & unfortunately am rather under the weather physically. Commend us all affectionately to wife children & friends.

Yours Ever truly

W Gilmore Simms

1213: To Evert Augustus Duyckinck

Charleston, S. C.
December 13. 1866.

My dear Duyckinck.

I have left your last kind letter unanswered a longer time than usual, but it reached Charleston just as I was leaving for the plantation, and my hands have been so full, since my return, that I have been compelled to neglect all my correspondents for a season. I contracted, when in New York, with the Proprietors of the "Old Guard" for a Revolutionary Romance, which they required that I should begin and report progress on immediately, so that the publication might commence with their January number. It was necessary, for this end, that my instalments should begin to reach them before December; and, very much against the grain, though working for the grub, I had to grapple with my tasks almost immediately upon my return. You may judge with what earnestness I must have worked (with what

---

[298] Dated by Simms' remarks about sending Ferris potatoes. See preceding and following letters to Ferris.

success, I can say nothing) when I tell you that I have despatched to the Publishers 24 chapters, making some 550 pp. *MS.* The story will be called "Joscelyn, a Tale of the Revolution." I have had other reasons, however, for my delay to answer you as well as our friend Moreau. I have been labouring, as yet to no purpose, to secure the photograph portrait of Col Laurens. There are two miniatures extant, one contained in a breastpin of a lady, I am in hopes to procure. The other is in the possession of a member of the family whose whereabouts is uncertain. She is supposed to be somewhere in Maryland. The miniature is in possession of a venerable lady here who is unwilling to suffer it to leave her own possession for a moment, even to be taken down to the photographer; and she has got the idea in her head, that the operation of taking it, will, in some degree, injure the painting. Of these notions we must disabuse her, and by watching our moment, when she is in right condition, procure her to attend the photographer herself. I have got the promise of one of her kinswomen, to see that this is done, and I shall so continue to urge the matter through this medium that I hope ere long to effect the object. Say this, if you please to Mr. Moreau, to whom I hope shortly to write, reporting our success, and probably sending on the photograph.[299] — The next matter upon which I had to deliberate is that touching the sale of my documentary collections.[300] The conclusion I have come to is that I am unwilling to sell at present. At all events I shall defer the further consideration of the subject until I visit New York. Meanwhile, I should be unwilling that Mr. Bancroft should have free range among the papers. I am quite willing that he should use what he may find, in respect to the battle of Monmouth, — briefly, in such papers of John Laurens as you are about to publish — but no further. In particular, I could wish that you would suffer no inspection, beyond your own, of the [301] loose papers in bundles. These, I had reserved for my own exclusive use, and Editorship, & I should be sorry to be anticipated in their use, especially when I believe that there are few persons in the country, who can so satisfactorily analyse & edit them as myself. You may exhibit the *four* volumes freely to men of letters whom you respect, but suffer no copies to be made beyond the Camp Letters already

---

[299] See note 195, Aug. 3, 1866.
[300] Simms' collection of Laurens MSS. was purchased by the Long Island Historical Society in 1867. See Simms' letters to Duyckinck of that year.
[301] Simms wrote *the the.*

copied. To prepare these volumes, as biography & History, has been with me a leading idea for many years. — I will write to Widdleton in a few days. Meanwhile, will you see him and ascertain if he has yet succeeded in doing any thing with Childs or Peterson. It is important that I should know, at an early period, whether any thing can be done with them, as I shall need to make an arrangement with some publisher, for the publication of "Joscelyn["] in book form. When complete, it will be of the ordinary novel size, say a volume of 400 to 450 pp. in the style of the former publications. Widdleton may also say to these Gent., making any arrangement with them, that it will be my hope, policy & expectation, to provide an original work of prose fiction at least once a year. I have on hand several chapters of a Pirate Story,[302] — and I have in my *head* the plan of another tale of the Revolution. Nothing but the anxious, desultory and comfortless life which I have been living since the war, could have kept me from the preparation of both of these stories.[303] — I shall be desperately busied here untill about the 20 when I shall take a run up to the plantation where my youngest daughter now resides with her husband, Major Rowe. All of my children, with this exception are with me here in the city, where my eldest son is now reading law, trying to make up for lost time. He left college at 18 to join the army, and has lost five years of his student life. Every thing is gloomy here. The prostration is complete. The crops are a general failure — there is no money in the country, and we anticipate a general famine. God be with you & yours in mercy.

Yours Ever truly

W. Gilmore Simms.

---

[302] "The Brothers of the Coast."

[303] Childs and Peterson (George William Childs and Robert Evans Peterson), of Philadelphia, did not publish any of Simms' novels. The only one of Simms' novels or novellettes which was republished this year is *Marie De Berniere,* issued by Chapman and Co., 116 Nassau Street, New York City, under the title of *The Ghost of My Husband; a Tale of the Crescent City.* We have not located a copy of this volume, but it is reviewed in the Charleston *Courier* of Dec. 19, 1866.

1214: To WILLIAM HAWKINS FERRIS

Charleston, Decr. 20. [1866][304]

My dear Ferris.

It has not been possible with me, for some time past, to do justice to the correspondence of my friends; certainly I have been unable to give them much time in very long letters. Absorbed, indeed, almost wholly in labours of the desk, writing, on the average, 20 to 40 pages of MS. per day, I have no *fingers* left, and in my seclusion lack in all those social ideas which constitute the best materials for letter writing. But I have tried, in brief scribbles, to remind you of my own existence, & to show you that I was interested in yours. I gather from the tone as well as the contents of your letters, that you are in good spirits and that all are well with you. Let me hope that you will still continue to be able to make such fair report. I infer, also, though you say nothing about it, that the new house proves satisfactory to the whole firm of Ferris, Wife & Co; that you breathe gratefully its atmosphere, and sometimes persuade yourself that you are in Arcadia. Your wife has her new carpets, and you are making conundrums, of a Sunday, in your new library, with Josey occasionally popping in if only to suggest some new ideas. During the week you are in your priestly robes before the altar of Mammon surrounded by that devout priesthood whom I shall always remember with a reverence akin to awe, albeit one of their number lies under the reproach of a femininity which seems to amount to a forfeiture of his proper standing in society.[305] To him I have to write, at some early opportunity, relieving him, if possible, from the horrors of such an imputation. Say to our "fat friend", the venerable young father in Mammon,[306] that the Powhatan pipes shall be sent him, through you & by Adams Express, if possible this very week. — On Saturday next, I proceed (D. V.) to the plantation, and from thence, on a flying trip into Georgia.[307] At Woodlands now Mrs. Rowe and her husband are the sole occupants. Mary Lawson & Carroll are with me here, as also is Gilmore who attends regularly

---

[304] Dated by Simms' references to "Joscelyn." See preceding and following letters.

[305] For Simms' comments in the Charleston *Courier* about Edward H. Birdsall, see note 207, Aug. 9, 1866.

[306] George D. Coaney. See letters to Ferris of Sept. 18 and Dec. 31, 1866.

[307] To visit the Hammonds, Hayne, and Redmond. See letters to Hayne of Oct. 22 and Nov. 4.

at his Law office & studies every day. I am drudging at the Romance for the Old Guard,[308] & have sent the Publishers, since reaching Charleston 550 pp. of MSS. I find this concentration of thought & eye upon the one subject, with so little chance for relief, a severe strain upon the mind, but the work must be done. My brain is occasionally very foggy under the pressure. Your conundrum is a very happy one. I trust that your potatoes turned out good, but fear that you lost but too many by the rot. When I can command the time, I will forward you another packet of old Letters, enough for Bockee & yourself. By giving me any names of parties, about whom you desire to know, I will answer. My best regards to Mrs. F. & the young ones — not forgetting the ancient priesthood.

Yours ever

W. Gilmore Simms.

1215: To HENRY BARTON DAWSON

Charleston, Decr. 21. [1866][309]

My dear Mr. Dawson.

Enclosed you will find an Editorial which I prepared for the Ch. Mercury, where it appeared this morning.[310] I write you now simply to acknowledge your letter, some time ago recieved, and to say that I hope shortly to respond fully to the contents of yours. At this moment, I am hurriedly preparing to run up to my plantation, & thence for a flight of a few days into Georgia. We are terribly worried here with our plantation troubles which seem to grow worse than ever. Please send me the Hist. Magazine.[311] I have not recieved a number during the

---

[308] "Joscelyn."

[309] Dated by Simms' reference to his proposed trip to Georgia to visit the Hammonds, Hayne, and Redmond. See letters to Hayne of Oct. 22 and Nov. 4 and to Ferris of Dec. 20.

[310] In this editorial, entitled "Dawson's Publications," Simms discusses Dawson's work as an author and as an editor.

[311] The *Historical Magazine,* a monthly founded in Boston in 1857 and moved to New York City in 1858, had the following editors: John Ward Dean (1857), George Folsom (1858), John Dawson Gilmary Shea (1859-1865), Henry Reed Stiles (1866), and Henry Barton Dawson (1866-1875). Charles Benjamin Richardson was publisher during 1857-1863, Shea during 1864-1866, and Dawson during 1866-1875. During Dawson's editorship the magazine was published at Morrisania, New York.

Prior to the Confederate War Simms was a frequent contributor to the *Historical Magazine* of various "Revolutionary Letters," all prefaced by letters or notes from Simms to the editor. We have omitted these from this edition

year. The Gods send you a Sunny Christmas. Very truly though in haste,

Yours &c

W. Gilmore Simms

1216: To WILLIAM HAWKINS FERRIS

Charleston, S. C. Decr. 21. 1866.

My dear Ferris.

Enquire on board of the Quaker City, which sails tomorrow from this Port, for a small packet containing half a dozen of the Powhatan Pipes for the young Priest Coaney of the Province of Money, Piscatorial Precinct.[312] I wrote you only a day ago, have no more to say, & am busy packing up for the country. All well. The Gods send you all Christmas blessings. Love to all.

Yours Ever truly

W. Gilmore Simms

---

of Simms' letters because they are actually prefatory remarks about the documents he submitted for publication rather than personal letters. See the *Historical Magazine*, I (July, Sept., and Oct., 1857), 206-207, 266-270, 289-292; II (Jan., Sept., and Nov., 1858), 6-11, 259-261, 321-324; and III (June, 1859), 169-171. His contributions during Dawson's editorship of the magazine are noted elsewhere in this edition of Simms' letters.

[312] George Davis Coaney (1840-1902), born in Troy, N. Y., was in 1866 a clerk in the United States Sub-Treasury in Wall Street. He eventually became assistant secretary of the Metropolitan Trust Co., New York City, from which position he was retired in 1894 because of poor health. On Oct. 22, 1868, he was married in Jersey City, N. J., to Kate Davis (1844-1914). For this information we are indebted to Miss Geraldine Beard, of the New-York Historical Society, and to Miss Louise B. Coaney (daughter of George D. Coaney), of East Kingston, N. H.

INDEX

Since the final volume of Simms' *Letters* will contain an index of all volumes, this index is designed for temporary use only. It consists merely of two types of entries: the titles of Simms' published volumes and the names of people and firms mentioned by Simms in his letters. All references to these, both in the letters and in footnotes, are listed. The titles of books by writers other than Simms are not given, though in each case an entry is made under the name of the author, editor, or translator. Women are indexed under their married names, with their maiden names given if possible. There are no analyses of entries, and there is no entry under William Gilmore Simms.

When the most complete identification of a person is not on the first page referred to after his name, that page which does contain it is given first parenthetically; frequently this reference is to the first, second, or third volume of the *Letters*.

[629]